SAINT GENET

JEAN-PAUL SARTRE

SAINT GENET

ACTOR & MARTYR

TRANSLATED FROM THE FRENCH
BY BERNARD FRECHTMAN

PANTHEON BOOKS, NEW YORK

Library of Congress Cataloging in Publication Data
Sartre, Jean-Paul, 1905–1980.
Saint Genet, actor and martyr.
Translation of: Saint Genêt, comédien et martyr.
Reprint. Originally published: New York:
G. Braziller, 1963.
1. Genêt, Jean, 1910–   . 2. Dramatists, French—
20th century—Biography. I. Title.
PQ2613.E53Z883 1983   842′.912 [B]   83-2460
ISBN 0-394-71583-7

Manufactured in the United States of America

First Pantheon Paperback Edition

CONTENTS

The original title of the present work, Saint Genet: Comédien et Martyr, *loses its allusiveness in English translation.* Saint Genet *evokes the memory of St. Genestus (known in French as Genest, or Genêt), the third-century Roman actor and martyr and the patron saint of actors. His career is the subject of* Le Véritable Saint Genest, *a tragedy by the seventeenth-century dramatist Jean de Rotrou. In addition, the word* comédien *(which means actor—not necessarily comic) is used familiarly to designate a person who shams or "puts on an act."*

•

The absence of reference to Genet's later plays is explained by the fact that Sartre's study was published in 1952, at which time Deathwatch *and* The Maids *were the only works Genet had written for the theater.*

I. THE METAMORPHOSIS

*Bandit, thief, hoodlum,
    scamp!
It's the pack of decent folk
A-hunting the child.*

——PRÉVERT

THE MELODIOUS CHILD DEAD IN ME
LONG BEFORE THE AX CHOPS OFF MY HEAD

Genet is related to that family of people who are nowadays referred to by the barbaric name of *passéistes.** An accident riveted him to a childhood memory, and this memory became sacred. In his early childhood, a liturgical drama was performed, a drama of which he was the officiant: he knew paradise and lost it, he was a child and was driven from his childhood. No doubt this "break" is not easy to localize. It shifts back and forth, at the dictate of his moods and myths, between the ages of ten and fifteen. But that is unimportant. What matters is that it exists and that he believes in it. His life is divided into two heterogeneous parts: before and after the sacred drama. Indeed, it is not unusual for the memory to condense into a single mythical moment the contingencies and perpetual rebeginnings of an individual history. What matters is that Genet lives

---

* *Passéiste:* one who is not adapted to the present age, who is not a man of his time, who "lives in the past."—Translator's note.

and continues to relive this period of his life as if it had lasted only an instant.

To say "instant" is to say *fatal instant*. The instant is the reciprocal and contradictory envelopment of the before by the after. One is still what one is going to cease to be and already what one is going to become. One lives one's death, one dies one's life. One feels oneself to be one's own self and another; the eternal is present in an atom of duration. In the midst of the fullest life, one has a foreboding that one will merely survive, one is afraid of the future. It is the time of anguish and of heroism, of pleasure and of destruction. An instant is sufficient to destroy, to enjoy, to kill, to be killed, to make one's fortune at the turn of a card. Genet carries in his heart a bygone instant which has lost none of its virulence, an infinitesimal and sacred void which concludes a death and begins a horrible metamorphosis. The argument of this liturgical drama is as follows: a child dies of shame; a hoodlum rises up in his place; the hoodlum will be haunted by the child. One would have to speak of resurrection, to evoke the old initiatory rites of shamanism and secret societies, were it not that Genet refuses categorically to be a man who has been resuscitated.* There was a death, that is all. And Genet is nothing other than a dead man. If he appears to be still alive, it is with the larval existence which certain peoples ascribe to their defunct in the grave. All his heroes have died at least once in their life.

"After his first murder, Querelle experienced the feeling of being dead. . . . His human form—what is called the envelope of flesh—continued nevertheless to move about on the surface of the earth."

His works are filled with meditations on death. The peculiarity of these spiritual exercises is that they almost never concern his future death, his being-to-die, but rather his being-dead, his death as past event.

This original crisis also appears to him as a metamorphosis. The well-behaved child is suddenly transformed into a hoodlum, as Gregor Samsa was changed into a bug. Genet's attitude toward this metamorphosis is ambivalent: he both loathes it and yearns for it.

He lives in terror lest the original crisis recur; he fears it as one fears an attack of epilepsy. "Querelle could not get used to the idea, an idea never formulated, of being a monster. He would consider,

---

* The candidate for shamanic functions is killed by the spirits. His body is cut to pieces. Then he comes to life again. Only then is he a shaman. Almost all "rites of passage" center about death and rebirth. The theme of death and resurrection similarly governs all initiations.

would regard his past with a smile that was ironic, frightened and tender at the same time, insofar as this past merged with himself. A young boy who has been metamorphosed into an alligator and whose soul appears in his eyes might in like manner—if he is not quite conscious of his maw, of his enormous jaw—consider his scaly body, his solemn tail that slaps the water or the beach or grazes other monsters. . . . He knew the horror of being alone, stricken by an immortal enchantment in the midst of the living world."

The initial event determined Genet's inner climate, which will be horror.

"Few are the moments when I escape from horror, few the moments when I do not have a vision, or some horrifying perception of human beings and events."

This horror is both fear of past metamorphoses and terrified expectation of their repetition:

"A young Italian . . . was laughing and relating some trivial experiences. . . . I took him for an animal that had been metamorphosed into a man. I felt that, in the presence of this privilege which I thought he possessed, he could, at any given moment, turn me, by his simple wish, even unexpressed, into a jackal, a fox, a guinea fowl."

At every instant Genet fears "the miracle, that catastrophe of horror, horrifying as an angel . . . though radiant as the solution of a problem in mathematics, frighteningly exact." But the aim of these passages is to give poetic expression to his fear: it is not literally *true* that Genet is afraid of being changed into a jackal. In the following passage, however, he expresses himself almost without transposition. Genet, who is in the presence of a handsome young man, is afraid of dying:

"Which is to say that either I would become aware of being suddenly naked in a crowd which sees my nakedness; or that my hands would become overgrown with leaves and I would have to live with them, tie my shoelaces with them, hold my cigarette, scratch myself, open the door with them; or that he himself would know spontaneously what I am at bottom and would laugh at seeing me thus . . . or that I would see and feel my penis being eternally devoured by fish; or that a sudden friendship would permit me to caress toads and corpses to the point of orgasm, for when I evoke these—and other—torments, my death is in danger of being the knowledge of my shame which has appeared in the play of the manifestations most feared in the presence of the beloved being."

Note the connection between death and metamorphosis: "My

death is in danger of being the knowledge of my shame." "The child who is transformed into an alligator fears lest some gleam from the interior of his body or from his own consciousness illuminate him, hook on to his scaly carapace the reflection of a form and make him visible to men." When unmasked, he changes into himself. The metamorphosis that threatens him unceasingly is the constituent revelation that occurred one day through the mediation of others and that can recur at any moment.

And no doubt this myth is fed by ordinary and quite real worries. Having reached manhood, Genet, who considers himself a coward, is afraid of revealing his cowardice to his young lovers: "In the presence of the person I adore and in whose eyes I seemed an angel, here am I being knocked down, biting the dust, turning inside out like a glove and showing exactly the opposite of what I was."

As a professional thief, he is quite simply afraid of being caught: "A little old woman said to him quietly, 'What have you stolen, young man?' . . . a new universe instantly presented itself to Darling: the universe of the irremediable. It is the same as the one we were in, with one peculiar difference: instead of acting and knowing we are acting, we know we are acted upon . . . the order of this world—seen inside out—appears so perfect in its inevitability that this world has only to disappear."

But the striking thing is that the erotic humiliations of a homosexual and the occupational risks of a thief are tinged with an aura of the sacred. Confronted with a trivial, everyday event, Genet is "turned inside out," "like a glove"; the whole world is involved, one touches the ineluctable. These erotic and occupational accidents have a meaning which transcends them, and, as has been said of love, "They are much more than what they are," because they manifest the "immortal enchantment" that begot a monster and killed a child.

These metamorphoses fascinate him. He fears them and lives only for them. Apart from these brusque changes of Being, nothing in the world interests him. Having died in boyhood, Genet contains within him the dizziness of the irremediable, he wants to die again. He abandons himself to the instant, to the cathartic crises that reproduce the first enchantment and carry it to the sublime: crime, capital punishment, poetry, orgasm, homosexuality. In each case we shall find the paradox of the before and after, a rise and fall, a life staked on a single card, the play of the eternal and the fleeting. The very images and the words that designate them are of the same nature: from the bright scaffold spring roses, "lovely effect of death"; from the "ebony prick" spring white flowers, death and flowering of pleasure; a decapitated head falls from the guillotine, a black member shrivels and droops. If metamorphosis is a death, death and pleasure are metamorphoses.

Thus, Genet lives outside history, in parentheses. He no more cares about his individual adventure—which he contemptuously calls "the anecdote"—than did an ancient Egyptian about his national history. He deigns to take notice of the circumstances of his life only insofar as they seem to repeat the original drama of the lost paradise. He is a man of repetition: the drab, slack time of his daily life—a *profane* life in which everything is permissible—is shot through with blazing hierophanies which restore to him his original passion, as Holy Week restores to us that of Christ. Just as Jesus does not cease to die, so Genet does not cease to be metamorphosed into a foul insect: the same archetypical event is reproduced in the same symbolic and ritual form through the same ceremonies of transfiguration. To Genet, as to the faithful of a religious community, sacred time is cyclical: it is the time of Eternal Recurrence. Genet *has been,* he *has lived.* As for the event that determined his fate, it has long since ceased to be a memory and has entered the category of myths, so that what has been written about the mentality of the primitive might be applied to Genet word for word: "What we might call [his] 'history' is reduced exclusively to the mythical events which occurred *in illo tempore* and which have not ceased to repeat themselves from that time until ours."* Genet has no *profane history.* He has only a sacred history, or, if one prefers, like so-called "archaic" societies he is continually transforming history into mythical categories.

If we wish to understand this man, the only way to do so is to reconstruct carefully, through the mythical representations he has given us of his universe, the original event to which he constantly refers and which he reproduces in his secret ceremonies. By analysis of the myths we shall proceed to re-establish the facts in their true significance.

Genet is seven years old. The National Foundling Society has placed him in the care of Morvan peasants. Adrift in nature, he lives "in sweet confusion with the world." He fondles himself in the grass, in the water; he plays; the whole countryside passes through his vacant transparency. In short, he is innocent.

---

* Cf. Eliade, Mircea, *The Myth of the Eternal Return.*

This innocence comes to him from others—everything comes to us from others, even innocence. Grownups never weary of taking stock of their belongings: this is called regarding. The child is part of the lot, between two stools or under the table. He comes to know himself through their regard, and his happiness lies in being part of the stock. To Be is to belong to someone. If property defines Being, the quiet, sober steadiness of earthly possessions defines the Good. Good as good soil, faithful as a spade, as a rake, pure as milk, Genet grows up piously. He is a good little boy, a respectful and gentle child, weaker and smaller than his playmates, but more intelligent. He is always at the head of his class. In addition, he is serious, thoughtful, not talkative, in short, as good as gold. This Good is simple: one has parents whom one worships, one does one's homework in their presence, and before going to bed one says one's prayers. Later, one likewise becomes an owner of things and one works hard and saves. Work, family, country, honesty, property: such is his conception of the Good. It is graven forever upon his heart. Later on, despite the fact that he steals, begs, lies, prostitutes himself, it will not change. The local priest says that his is a religious nature.

This child is the victim of a cruel hoax. If you say to adults that they *are* innocent, they get annoyed, but they like to have *been* innocent. It is an alibi, an occasion for sentiment, a pathway to resentment and all forms of *"passéiste"* thinking, a ready-made refuge for times of misfortune, a way of asserting or implying that one was better than one's life. The myth of childhood innocence is a bastardized, positive and convenient form of the myth of Paradise Lost. As saints, intercessors and vestals of this pocket religion, it is the function of children, from the age of one to ten, to represent for grownups the original state of grace. Many of them find it to their advantage to become these sacred vessels, in particular those who are very secure, for example, the eldest of large families. But there are some whose actual situation contradicts the mythical virtues with which they have been adorned. Genet is one of these. He was given to believe, as were all the other village youngsters, that his soul was white; he therefore sees himself as white. Or rather, he sees nothing at all, but takes the grownups' word for it: they are able to discern his secret snows. This modest pride is going to determine his destiny: it consecrates, without his suspecting it, the priority of the object over the subject, of what one is to others over what one is to oneself. Nevertheless, the fact is that he *lives* his innocence, that he enjoys it, that it makes him happy. It would be wrong to paint Genet's childhood in colors that are too dark since he has been careful to inform us himself that it was the most beautiful period of his life.

And yet, from this moment on he lives in a state of uneasiness. The pious and lawful vocables which he has been made to learn are not quite applicable to what he is and what he feels. But as he possesses no others, he can neither describe nor define his malaise. Unnamed, unnamable, marginal, unexpressed, this anxiety, which is faceless and without consistency, seems to him a negligible mood. Genet *does not perceive it.* Yet it expresses his deepest reality, which is contradictory, for his self-certainty contradicts the truth that he is for others. Innocent *in general,* he senses that he is suspect in particular. He is obliged, by error, to use a language which is not his own, which belongs only to legitimate children. Genet has neither mother nor heritage—how could he be innocent? By virtue of his mere existence he disturbs the natural order and the social order. A human institution with its birth register and its bureaucracy has come between the species and himself. He is a fake child. No doubt he was born of a woman, but this origin has not been noted by the social memory. As far as everyone and, consequently, he himself are concerned, he appeared one fine day without having been carried in any known womb: he is a synthetic product. He is obscurely aware that he belongs legally to administrative bodies and laboratories, and so there is nothing surprising in the fact that he will later feel elective affinities with reformatories and prisons. Being a fabricated creature, he will find his truth in sophism; being a child of miracle, he will be mineral or spirit; but he does not belong to the intermediate kingdom: to life. He will never care for sports or physical pleasures; he will never be gluttonous or sensual; he will never have confidence in his body. For want of having known the primordial relationship with naked flesh, with the swooning fertility of a woman, he will never have that tender familiarity with his own flesh, that abandon which makes it possible for others to reproduce within themselves and by themselves the indissoluble intimacy of mother and nursling. He is said to be "contrary to nature." But the reason is that, as far back as he can remember, nature has been against him. We others who issue from the species have a mandate to continue the species. Genet, who was born without parents, is preparing to die without descendants. His sexuality will be sterility and abstract tension.

How does the little boy foresee his destiny? I cannot say, but there is no doubt that he already lives it in advance. Since his earliest childhood, the unknown mother has been one of the chief figures of his mythology. He both worships and hates her, smothers her with kisses and seeks to debase her. He is still fairly young when he addresses the Mettray Reformatory as if it were his own mother; he imagines that it appears to him "with all that is peculiar to women": tenderness, slightly nauseating stale smell emanating from the open mouth, deep heaving bosom, in short everything that makes the mother a mother. In short, the Mother Goddess, fertile and bountiful; better still, nature personified. Later, in his books, woman will appear only as mother. Genet disregards girls, except to turn them over to his handsome murderers who casually slaughter them. In fact, he peoples his works with guilty women whose children are dead and who mourn triumphantly, and if at times we do encounter amorous females in their forties, they too are mothers, incestuous and sacrilegious mothers, for they are laid by young lovers who could be their sons. But the theme of the "guilty mother" seems to be of recent origin in Genet's work. When he referred to the Reformatory in the past, that big woman was simply severe. At the beginning, *he* was the guilty one. Whenever the child tries to reach beyond the bureaucracy of which he seems an emanation to his true origins, he finds that his birth coincides with a gesture of rejection. He was driven out the very moment he was brought into the world. Later, it is all of society that will cast him out, but this social rejection is latent in the maternal rejection. The child senses that a woman tore him from herself, alive, covered with blood, and sent him rolling outside the world, and he feels himself an outcast. Ever since his birth he has been the unloved one, the inopportune, the superfluous. Undesirable *in his very being,* he is not that woman's son but her excrement. And we shall see how insistently, with what masochistic pleasure, Genet will later compare himself to filth, to a waste product. Psychoanalysts have observed that children often feel a parent's death to be a condemnation; the mother goes away so as no longer to see her unnatural son. The abandoning of a child signifies an even more radical condemnation! Is it a mysterious sentence that is punishing him for having committed the crime of being born? Is it a prophetic verdict that is making him pay in advance for future crimes? In any case, the judge is unknown, the child is ignorant of the charges and of the law, but the condemnation attacks his existence itself and eats away at it. Beneath the supposed innocence that adults have conferred upon him is hidden a sense of elusive guilt. Being nobody's son, he is nothing. As a result of his fault, disorder has wormed its way into the beautiful order of the world, a crack has appeared in the fullness of being.

Being nothing, he possesses nothing. Whether judged from the viewpoint of Having or that of Being, he is equally at fault. He knows that he does not quite belong to his foster parents, that the public authorities have loaned him to them and can take him back, and that consequently nothing his parents own belongs to him. For others, things are warm, alive, elastic, but if he takes them in his hands, they die. He can name them, count them, even try to use them, but their dense opacity becomes an absence; it is to the others that they address their homey smile. If, later on, in the presence of the handsome young men who fascinate him, he re-experiences that strange impression of being *kept at a distance*, it is because it has never left him: "Whenever I was close to an object he had touched, my hand would stop three inches from it, with the result that things, outlined by my gestures, seemed extraordinarily inflated—bristling with invisible rays or augmented by their metaphysical double—to my now sensitized fingers." It is the material possession of things that is forbidden him, and his life will be a long effort to dematerialize them, to construct with air their metaphysical double, which is all he can possess.

Of course, he is neither cold nor hungry. He is given board and lodging. But there's the rub—he is *given* them. This child has had more than enough of gifts. Everything is a gift, including the air he breathes. He has to say "thank you" for everything. Every minute a gift is put into his hands at the whim of a generosity that leaves its mark on him forever. Every minute Genet moves a little further away from his foster parents. All this bounty *obliges* him to recognize that they *were not obliged* to adopt him, to feed him, to take care of him, that they "owed him nothing," that he is *obliged* to them, that they were quite free not to give him what he was not free not to accept, in short, that he is not their son. A true son does not have to display his gratitude. He draws from the family purse, and it is his father's duty to bring him up. Deprived of everything through the kindness of others, Genet will later express his hatred of all generosity toward inferiors:

"Madame is kind! Madame adores us. She loves us the way she loves her armchair . . . like her bidet, rather. Like her pink enamel toilet seat. And we, we can't love each other. . . . Filth doesn't love filth. It's easy to be kind, and smiling, and sweet . . . when you're beautiful and rich. . . . But what if you're only a maid?"

A lady once said to him, "My maid must be pleased. I give her my dresses." "That's nice," he replied, "does she give you hers?"

Castoff of a society that defines being by having, the child Genet wants to have in order to be. However, the normal modes of appropriation are denied him. He will obtain nothing by purchase, nothing by heritage. The gift accords him a relative and provisional being but enslaves him forever to his benefactors. There remains work. But his work at school is also a gift: he *receives* general education just as later he will *receive* technical education; they want "to make a man of him." He helps in the fields, he helps at home. But this unproductive help confers no rights upon him. It will never pay for the care he is given; it is merely the expression of his gratitude.

A vicious circle. One might say about the little Genet what Rougemont has said about Don Juan: that he *is* not enough in order to have—and also the opposite: that he *has* not enough in order to be. Different circumstances might have broken the circle, might have dissociated being from having: had he been placed in a working-class home, had he lived in an industrial suburb of a big city, had be been accustomed, at an early age, to hearing the very right of ownership challenged, or had his foster father worked in a nationalized branch of industry, he might perhaps have learned that one *is* also what one *does*. But—height of misfortune—he had to be sent into the fields. Those who provided him with the first image of man were landowners. To that stern, that mineral race, the farmer and his land form an indissoluble couple: one *has* the property because one *is* the legitimate heir, and, vice versa, one *is* shaped by what one *has*. The peasant acquires the silent immobility of his field. Our future burglar starts by learning absolute respect for property.

How will this abstract child react to his double exile? By a miming of being and having, in short, by playing games, like all children. He will have two favorite games, saintliness and pilfering. Insufficiency of being prompts him to play the former, and lack of having, the latter.

Saintliness first. He is already fascinated by this word, which he will later call the most beautiful in the French language. Though he does not yet dream clearly of becoming a saint, he feels that a man is not worth much if he does not live on grasshoppers, if he does not die at the stake with a smile on his lips. This exaltation betrays his secret disorder. It is not unusual for young boys to have extreme tastes, for them to want to be perfect, to be everything, to be first in everything, but if they want to become great captains or great doctors, it is in order to be great among men and of a greatness recognized by men. In Genet's mysticism, however, we discern a rejection of the human order. An abandoned child, he takes revenge by admiring the children who abandon father and mother to follow Christ. It pleases him that the saints are answerable only to God, that they long to wrest themselves from the species and that they go counter to their most legitimate desires in order to achieve within themselves an anti-nature. His contempt for his body makes asceticism easy for him. For the same reasons we shall later see him make of love a form of torture. But, above all, he asks God to give him the rightful existence that men deny him. He derives at least one advantage from his orphan's solitude: his inner life is not socialized. No gaze disturbs his original privacy. A mother claims to know everything, she makes her child feel that she can read his mind, he thinks he is never alone. One evening, at dinner, it suddenly occurred to a little girl that her mother was silly. The child blushed to her ears and left the table, convinced that her parents had *heard* her inner voice. For a long time, our wicked thoughts will seem to us to be public knowledge; for a long time, we shall lie to others to the very depths of our being. But no family ceremony has consecrated Genet's union with his social image. Alone, without words, without a secret witness, he lives with himself in a state of concubinage. This solitude will later be mated; he will talk to *himself,* will worship *himself,* reinventing for his own use the archaic myths of the double and of the twins. For the time being, he takes it into his head to elect God witness to his secret life. God compensates for the absent mother, for indifferent Society. In becoming an object of concern to an infinite being, Genet will acquire the being which he lacks. He will be a saint, since he is not a son.

Another and even more amusing game: from time to time God turns his head away; whereupon soft, silent, unperceived acts flow from the child. Thefts. The budding saint robs his foster parents and sometimes their neighbors. He robs them in all innocence, without remorse and without shame, and without ceasing to want to be a saint. In his eyes this petty pilfering does not count. He is hardly aware of what he is doing; his hands simply wander. Moreover, his foster mother wasn't shy about filching. She was an "honest woman," of course, and remained honest while stealing. Honesty is an eternal essence which is not dimmed by accidental lapses.

Besides, it is unimportant who suggested to him his first thefts; it is unimportant whether he first stole alone or with playmates.

The essential point is that he thinks less of stealing than of engaging in imaginary experiments in appropriation. He experiments, as scientists say, "just to see." He is feeling his way with the aim of establishing forthwith a possessive relationship with things. Since an owner is a man who can use a thing without having to say "thank you," Genet will lay hands, in secret, on personal effects, tools, trinkets—in secret, so as not to have to thank anyone. He will use them in solitude. But *using* is, in this situation, only a means of possessing. The aim is not merely to take the object but also to assume the familiar, expert, offhand attitude which will indicate, to invisible witnesses, that he is its real owner. The servant girls Solange and Claire* do not rob Madame. They put on her dresses when she is out, they adjust them, drape them, they primp and preen; they admire themselves in the mirror, they receive the real caresses of the silk and satin as an investiture. Their sensations and gestures designate them, in their own sight, as Madame. It is Madame's reflection that they see in the mirror, and each in turn becomes more servantlike so that the other may feel more mistresslike. It is only a game. But should the dress be spotted, should it be burned by an ash, the imaginary using of it will end in real consumption: they will roll it up, carry it away and destroy it—and thus become thieves. Genet moves from game to theft with the same fatality. It is highly significant that his first acts of larceny did not spring from hunger and covetousness. These are needs that care not a rap about mine and thine, that demand simply to be satisfied. Under their pressure the hungry man challenges, provisionally or definitively, the right of others to possess. In the case of Genet, however, his thefts, far from challenging property, affirm it. This child who has enough to eat but whom society keeps at a distance wants, by means of a solitary act, to integrate himself into the community. He is aiming at the impossible. His austere and feverish quest for Being involves an imaginary satisfaction only. Thus is born that most peculiar nature which carries out a real operation whose aim and meaning lie in unreality.

The act is performed in two stages. The first does not count for anyone, not even for the one who commits it. The mind clouds over, everyone dies then and there, even the little thief. "The culprit is your hand."† In the absence of human creatures, a hand moves in the desert. When the people come to life again, nothing

---

* In Genet's play *The Maids.*
† Cocteau, *Anna la Bonne.*

has changed, except that there is a hundred francs less in a purse
and a hundred francs more in a pocket. The second moment, on
the other hand, requires the most intense consciousness: Genet
begins his spiritual exercises. Outcast of a consuming society, the
rites which he celebrates in secret reproduce the cardinal act of the
society that excludes him: he sacrifices, he consumes, that is, he
destroys. An object goes up in smoke, a piece of fruit melts in his
mouth, his pleasure blossoms and fades, it is going to die. It is
this process of dissolution that constitutes the entire ceremony. By
a fictive communion he touches, on this stolen food, on this evanescent and stealthy pleasure, his imaginary being as fair-haired-boy-
rightfully-possessing-the-fruits-of-his-earth; he eats it. Like "the
youngster too vacillating to be included in the breed . . . who turned
in on himself in the form of a slice of bread smeared with soft
cheese, already the snow of peaks, the lily or other whiteness constitutive of inner wings,"* he turns in on himself, he rewards himself. The pleasure is real. Real, too, the chewing and swallowing.
But their reality is of no interest in itself; it is there only to lend a
body to the desperate efforts of appropriation. The important thing
is to use these real facts as symbols. The legitimate owner puts out
his hand, picks a piece of fruit and eats it peacefully. Genet transfers
to himself the owner's gestures and sensations so as to identify himself with the latter by an effort of mind. He takes in order to convince himself that he has the right to take; he eats as an actor eats
on the stage; he is playing at possession; he embodies the owner
as Barrault embodies Hamlet. However, he makes, at the same
time, a considerable effort to be his own audience so as to catch
himself in the act of possessing. Need I say that he is always about
to succeed but never does? It doesn't matter. He already finds within
himself what the Marquis de Sade called the "principle of delicacy," which makes him prefer nothingness to being, imagination
to reality, tension to enjoyment. In short, his operation clearly
falls into the category of poetic acts: it is the systematic pursuit of
the impossible. No wonder that he wrote later that "the land of the
Chimeras is the only one worth inhabiting" and that he quoted the
following line from Pope: "Nothing is beautiful, save that which
is not."† But what appears with the first thefts is not only that
straining of the soul toward something beyond the true which will
henceforth characterize Genet's inner tempo, but also the particu-

---

* Mallarmé: Poèmes en prose. Réminiscence. *Œuvres complètes* (Pléiade), Paris, p. 278.
† This is not Pope's line but a translation of Genet's misquotation, from memory, of a
French rendering.—Translator's note.

lar nature of his poetic procedure. He never dreams. He does not turn away from the world in order to invent better worlds, he does not abandon himself to images, to musings. His imagination is a corrosive operation that is practiced *on* the real, an operation aimed not at evading but at transcending reality, and, as we have seen, at dematerializing it. Other children would have played at ownership with imaginary belongings. A pebble would have been a gold piece. They would have made believe they were buying or eating. But our little thief wants to eat "for real," wants to have *real* pleasure in his mouth. Only, this real pleasure is neither wanted nor felt for its own sake; it is in the service of an impossible attempt to coincide, in the realm of the imaginary, with the essence of an owner of things. As a result, the whole system is derealized, the very enjoyment becomes imaginary. The true pleasure of a thief becomes a fictive pleasure of a fake owner. Reality is worn so thin that one can see the light through it. To imagine is to give the imaginary a bit of the real to chew at. For this reason, Genet will be able to say of the chimerical Ernestine: "She never left reality." No imaginary without reality. It is in the movement of the real to annihilate itself that the pale shadows of the imagination are embodied. And thereby, despite all the differences which we shall point out later, Genet's thefts are not so far removed from the object-poems produced by surrealism, the inner contradiction of which represents the pure instant of the falling away to nothingness, through which can be perceived the eternal absence of another world.

The thefts spread and multiply. Genet now robs neighbors. There is no more effective defense against the temptation to have *everything* than to own something. If you have only a crumb that has fallen from the table, your life will be spent in defending that crumb, in convincing others and yourself that it is the best of crumbs and that, in the last analysis, it contains the universe. Genet has nothing, which amounts to saying that he has an eminent right over everything. At this point there begins the systematic turning of the positive into the negative and the negative into the positive which later, carried to an extreme, will lead Genet to "saintliness." In the "land of the Chimeras," a conversion of signs is sufficient to change penury into wealth. This pariah whom the world rejects is secretly pursuing the eminent possession of everything.

We have all known the kind of bright, healthy child with "winning gaze" and "frank smile" whom everyone takes for a little angel. One day we realize that he steals things. At first we simply can't understand, he seemed so nice! And then we feel personally offended. He fooled us, he's a little hypocrite. We start regarding his virtues as crimes; he assumed the appearance of honesty the better to deceive us.

We do not perceive the air-tight partition that separates his virtues from his pilfering. We do not see that he lives on two levels at the same time. Of course Genet condemns theft! But in the furtive acts he commits when he is all alone he *does not recognize* the offense which he condemns. He, steal? When what he is trying to do is to win, in defiance of destiny, a regular status, parents, property, when he is attempting to diminish his secret guilt and draw nearer to those whom he admires? What is he really seeking? To *be like others*, nothing more, and precisely because others are good and just, because they are right to be what they are. The truth is that he is impelled by anxiety. At times he feels obscurely within himself a kind of budding anguish, he feels that he is about to see clearly, that a veil is about to be torn and that he will know his destitution, his abandonment, his original offense. So he steals. He steals in order to ease the anguish that is coming on. When he has stolen the cakes and fruit, when he has eaten them in secret, his anxiety will disappear, he will once again find himself in the lawful and sunlit world of honesty. His conduct is not to be regarded as sneaky. He is really and truly well-behaved and virtuous, and there is only one life that counts for him, the one he leads in the presence of adults. Outside that life there is only a bad dream, a kind of nameless nightmare in which he sometimes feels he is going to be unhappy and from which he awakes very quickly, an obscure menace against which he has invented two exorcisms, the game of saintliness and that of stealing. I would compare this childish magic, which operates at the frontiers of nothingness, of sleep, to the fantasies of onanism rather than to anything else. To the child who steals and the child who masturbates, to exist is *to be seen by adults*, and since these secret activities take place in solitude, they *do not exist*. The truth is that little Genet has been taught an ethics *that condemns him*. He believes in it with all his soul, but by the same token he destroys himself, for this ethics of ownership casts him doubly into nothingness, as ragamuffin and as bastard. This is the key to his conduct and state of disturbance. In broad daylight he is luminous, honest, happy, but the more he asserts his happiness in the light, the more he ruins and tortures himself in the darkness. He is going to reduce himself to despair. If he steals, if he dreams of saintliness, it is not in defiance of peasant ethics, but because of it. He has recourse to this double compensatory activity because he is unable to liquidate a system of values that denies him his place in the sun.

Shall I say he is unhappy? Not yet. In fact, one should emphasize the optimism and will to happiness that characterize this child in the depths of his heart. Not for a moment has he wanted to believe that there was no way out of the situation. Not for a moment does he imagine that he is condemned to poverty and bastardy—it would not be just, it would not be right. God will substitute for the absent mother, theft will substitute for property. A petty theft here, a slight ecstasy there, these are enough to maintain his inner balance. Quickly he returns to sweet, natural confusion. But while he is stealing in innocence, while he modestly covets the martyr's palm, he is unaware that he is forging his destiny.

A DIZZYING WORD

*Our sentence is not severe. What-
ever commandment the culprit has
violated is simply written upon his
skin by the harrow.*

—KAFKA,
In the Penal Settlement

The child was playing in the kitchen. Suddenly he became aware of
his solitude and was seized with anxiety, as usual. So he "absented"
himself. Once again, he plunged into a kind of ecstasy. There is
now no one in the room. An abandoned consciousness is reflecting
utensils. A drawer is opening; a little hand moves forward.

Caught in the act. Someone has entered and is watching him.
Beneath this gaze the child comes to himself. He who was not yet
anyone suddenly becomes Jean Genet. He feels that he is blinding,
deafening; he is a beacon, an alarm that keeps ringing. *Who* is Jean
Genet? In a moment the whole village will know. . . . The child
alone is in ignorance. In a state of fear and shame he continues his
signal of distress. Suddenly

> . . . a dizzying word
> From the depths of the world abolishes
> the beautiful order. . . .*

A voice declares publicly: "You're a thief." The child is ten
years old.

That was how it happened, in that or some other way. In all
probability, there were offenses and then punishment, solemn oaths
and relapses. It does not matter. The important thing is that Genet
lived and has not stopped reliving this period of his life as if it had
lasted only an instant.

It is the moment of awakening. The sleepwalking child opens his
eyes and realizes he is stealing. It is revealed to him that he *is* a
thief and he pleads guilty, crushed by a fallacy which he is unable
to refute; he stole, he is therefore a thief. Can anything be more

---

* Genet, *Poèmes*, p. 56.

evident? Genet, thunderstruck, considers his act, looks at it from every angle. No doubt about it, it is a theft. And theft is an offense, a crime. What he *wanted* was to steal; what he *did*, a theft; what he *was*, a thief. A timid voice is still protesting within him; he does not *recognize* his intentions. But soon the voice grows silent. The act is so luminous, so sharply defined, that there is no mistaking its nature. He tries to go back, to understand himself, but it is too late, he has lost his bearings. The dazzlingly evident present confers its meaning on the past; Genet now *recalls* that he cynically decided to steal. What happened? Actually, almost nothing: an action undertaken without reflection, conceived and carried out in the secret, silent inwardness in which he often takes refuge, has just *become objective*. Genet learns what he *is objectively*. It is this *transition* that is going to determine his entire life.

The metamorphosis occurs immediately. He is nothing more than what he was before, yet he is now unrecognizable. Driven from the lost paradise, exiled from childhood, from the immediate, condemned to see himself, suddenly provided with a monstrous and guilty "ego," isolated, separated, in short changed into a bug. An evil principle dwelt in him unperceived, and now it has been discovered. It is this principle which is the source of everything. It produces the slightest impulses of his soul. The child lived at peace with himself; his desires seemed to him limpid and simple. Their transparency now appears to have been deceptive. They had a double bottom. Little Genet's shame reveals eternity to him. He is a thief by birth, he will remain one until his death. Time is only a dream in which his evil nature is refracted into a thousand gleams, a thousand petty thefts, but does not belong to the temporal order. *Genet is a thief;* that is his truth, his eternal essence. And, if he *is* a thief, he must therefore always be one, everywhere, not only when he steals, but when he eats, when he sleeps, when he kisses his foster mother. Each of his gestures betrays him, reveals his vile nature in broad daylight. At any moment the teacher may interrupt the lesson, look Genet in the eyes and cry out: "There's a thief!" It would be vain for him to think he deserved leniency by admitting his errors, by mastering the perversity of his instincts. All the impulses of his heart are equally guilty because all alike express his essence.

If only the dizzying word had been uttered by his own father, the discovery would have taken place within the indestructible family unit, in other words within the unit of a single collective mind. The young culprit, isolated for a moment within that mind like an alien thought, would have been resorbed into it immediately. One doesn't rob one's family. But though his foster parents' tenderness might at times have given Genet the illusion of his being their son, it is dissipated the moment they become his judges. Because he is regarded as a thief Genet *becomes* a foundling. Father and mother unknown. Nobody wants to take responsibility for his birth. He seems to have produced himself, in defiance of everyone, in a burst of evil will: Evil is self-caused. At the same time, his faults are explained by dark forces whose origin antedate his birth: "That little thief, where does he come from? He surely takes after someone. Only a slut would abandon her son. A chip off the old block." In short, everything hangs together, everything becomes clear. Born of nothingness, the child has nothing, is nothing. His being has the substantiality of nonbeing. If it exists, it does so like a corrosive acid. Besides, does it exist? Is it not simply the foul beast that rushes through the troubled dream of an honest man?

Jouhandeau, another pariah, has aptly expressed what might be called the ontological curse: "The insult is perpetual. It is not only in the mouth of this person or that, explicit, but on all the lips that name me. It is in 'being' itself, in my being, and I find it in all the eyes that look at me. It is in all the hearts that have dealings with me. It is in my blood and is inscribed on my face in letters of fire. It accompanies me everywhere and always, in this world and in the other. It is myself, and it is God in person who proffers it in proffering me, who eternally gives me that execrable name, who sees me from that standpoint of wrath."

There is not even the possibility of shifting the blame to God by saying "since it's you who made me, *you're* the guilty one," for in this magical concept nature and freedom are one and the same: although the thief is enchained since he is unable to change, he is free since he is condemned. This is reminiscent of Calvinistic predestination which leaves the evildoer full responsibility for Evil while taking from him the possibility of doing Good. Being is here a subtle and radical perversion of freedom, a constant inclination to do evil, a kind of wrong-way grace, a specific gravity of free will which makes it always fall to the very bottom. In this futile maneuver, freedom is responsible for Being and Being petrifies freedom. Although Genet is free to be guilty, he is not free to change. The reason is that the wrath of the just wants to perpetuate itself; if Genet became honest, it would lose its object. This virtuous anger is relentless. It is not enough for it to murder a child; it must also contrive a hopeless future for the monster it has just fabricated. He is told that prison and the penal colony are in store for him. Every-thing is decided; from an eternal cause derive irremediable conse-quences in the temporal order: "You'll end on the gallows!" In a state of dazzlement Genet contemplates the ineluctable course of the universe and the interdependence of the circumstances that will lead him to capital punishment. Only yesterday everything was possible. He was perhaps the son of a prince; he would perhaps become a saint. He lived in an anarchy of desire, his heart was gladdened by chance graces, the future was still open. But now all is in order: he has been provided with a nature, a guilty freedom and a destiny. He is ten years old and he already knows to the last detail the life that he will have to sip drop by drop: "The order of this world—seen inside out—appears so perfect in its inevitability that this world has only to disappear."

Indeed, what is the point of living? Time is only a tedious illu-sion, everything is already there, his future is only an eternal present and, since his death is at the end of it—his death, his sole release—since he is *already dead,* in short, already guillotined, it's better to get it over with right away. To vanish, to slip between their fingers, to flow out of the present and down the drain, to be swallowed up by nothingness. Who of us has not, at least once in his life, been struck, seized, crippled with shame and has not wanted to die on the spot? In vain: Genet remains alive, solid, bulky, scan-dalous, before the indignant eyes of adults. But he will preserve in the depths of his heart that old, sad, aching dream of disappearing. In fact, he will go even further: like old Lapérouse in *The Counter-feiters* who, lacking the courage to kill himself, decides that he is dead, Genet will henceforth date subsequent events from the day of his suicide. And later, in the dismal ceremonies which will restore the original crisis, the primary rite will be that of death.

Two types of persecution maniacs are found in asylums. On the one hand are those who are victims of a conspiracy. The entire world is secretly engaged in trying to destroy them. The passer-by is a spy, a provocateur, a judge, people are trying to dishonor them, imprison them, perhaps kill them. At least they remain free and sovereign in their heart of hearts. They scorn their opponents and foil their schemes. They enjoy their solitude with mingled pride and anxiety. But there are others who can no longer take refuge even within themselves, for the enemy is already installed there. Their persecutors have placed spies and torturers in the innermost recesses of their consciousness, in the privacy of their inner life. Their thoughts are stolen from them, they are made to utter words

which they loathe, their enemies infuse them, by means of strange
instruments, with evil certainties, terrible convictions, frightful
desires, which they do not recognize. I cannot imagine any suffering
worse than theirs. Outside are horror, monstrous beasts, the hatred
of a whole people, sometimes even of the universe. If they withdraw
into themselves, they find the situation even more ghastly: those
whom they were fleeing are already there, laughing and waiting
for them.

It is these wretched creatures that the child Genet has suddenly
begun to resemble. The contempt and anger of decent people
would be bearable if he could return blame for blame and hatred
for hatred. And that is what he probably would have done if the
"accident" had occurred a little later. Had he been called a thief
at the age of seventeen, Genet would have laughed. That is the
age at which one liquidates paternal values. He would have had a
thousand ways and means at his disposal. He could have retorted
that his accusers were themselves scoundrels, could have pointed to
evil everywhere and have forced it, by means of its very excess, to
be resorbed, along with good, into a kind of indifference and
wretchedness, he could have challenged the principles of public
morality in the name of a Nietzschean or anarchistic ethic, could
have denied the existence of values and deigned to recognize only
the law of force.* But it is a child who has been caught, a very
young child, timid, respectful, right-thinking, one who has had a
religious upbringing, in accordance with the best principles, who
has been imbued with so passionate a love of God that he desires
saintliness rather than wealth. Nor can he resort to self-defense by
accusing adults, for adults are gods to this religious little soul. He
is trapped like a rat: he has been so thoroughly inculcated with the
morality in whose name he is condemned that it is part of his very
fiber. No, whatever he does, the honest folk have the initiative and
will not lose it. They have penetrated to the very bottom of his
heart and installed there a permanent delegate which is himself. It
is he himself who will be both the court and the accused, the policeman and the thief. It is he who will commit the offense and who
will deliver sentence and apply it. If he tries to withdraw into himself in order to escape the censure of those about him, he will find
an even more severe censure, his own. He will be a zealous self-
tormentor and will henceforth experience his states of mind, moods,
thoughts, even his perceptions, in the form of a conflict. The sim-

---

* Cf. Appendix II.

plest, most legitimate desire will appear to him as a thief's desire, hence as a guilty one. The adults triumph; they have found an accomplice who is none other than the accused. One isn't as lucky as that every day. In fact, the situation is even better: had the child developed normally, he would have gradually freed himself from this simple-minded morality, he would at least have made it more flexible, broader, would have perhaps replaced it by a religious ethic, by mysticism, by a liberal eclecticism or by anarchism, but he would have done so quietly, without turmoil, without inner catastrophe. But the terrible blow he has just received will forever prevent this amicable liquidation. Genet will not change. In his worst deviations he will remain faithful to the morality of his childhood. He will flout it, he will perhaps hate it, he will try to drag it with him through the mud, but "the original crisis" has burned it into him as with a red-hot iron. Whatever happens from now on, whatever he may do, whatever way out he may invent, one thing remains forbidden him: *self-acceptance.* The law of his consciousness is conflict. Until the "crisis," he lived in the "sweet confusion" of the immediate, he was unaware that he was a person. He has learned that he is and, by the same token, that this person is a monster.

"Guilt," he will write later, "gives rise, first, to individuality." Beneath the accusing finger, it is all one, for the little thief, to discover that he is himself and that he is other than all. And no doubt many people have testified to the fact that, around the age of ten, they discovered their individuality with amazement or anguish. The child Gide wept in his mother's arms and screamed that he "was not like other children." But this discovery is usually made without much damage. Adults have nothing to do with it. The child is playing alone, a slight change in the landscape, an event, a fleeting thought, is enough to give rise to the reflective awareness which reveals our Ego to us. And, as I have shown elsewhere, this ego is not yet anything to itself, except the empty and universal form of individuality. To be unlike the others is to be like everyone, since each is other than all and the same as itself. If the reflective operation takes place normally, it not only does not prevent reciprocal relationships, it produces them. I feel that I am other than Peter and I know that Peter resembles me because he feels he is other than I. However, the otherness that Genet discovers in himself excludes any reciprocity. It is not a case of an empty and universal form but of an individual difference that has to do with both form and content. There is Genet and there are all the others. And it is the height of irony that the child's dreadful loneliness occasions a finer understanding among those who condemn him: when honest people baptize an evildoer, they are in raptures; they huddle together, the better to block his way; they would even be willing to love each other. Genet quite realizes that he is an oblate and that his sacrifice serves as a bond among his sacrificers. *All the others,* whatever the differences separating them, recognize that they are fellow creatures in that they are not, thank God, thieves. *All the others,* whatever their conflicting interests, recognize their kinship because each reads in his neighbors' eyes the horror that Genet inspires in them; they constitute a single monstrous consciousness that judges and curses. It is horrible to "achieve" unanimity, to see suddenly that it is possible, that it is present, that one is touching it, that one has built it, and to know at the same time that one has done so against oneself. It would be pointless for him to round on the others and exclude them in turn, for there is not a square yard on earth from which he can chase them; he possesses nothing of his own. Thus, the loathing he inspires is a one-way affair; he fills honest folk with loathing but cannot loathe them. The only feeling he retains in his heart is love, a humiliated, forbidden love which shamefully, humbly, seeks opportunities to manifest itself. Our Lady of the Flowers, in the criminal court, looks for the first time at the presiding magistrate who is going to condemn him to death: "It is so sweet to love that he could not keep from dissolving into a feeling of sweet, trusting tenderness for the judge. 'Maybe he ain't a louse!' he thought."

The child loves his judges, he tries to draw near them, to melt, even to the point of losing consciousness, into the unanimity which he has created. He finds no other way than to share the disgust he inspires in them, than to despise himself with their contempt. The trap works well. Genet tears himself apart with his own hands. He has now become an absolute object of loathing.

Once upon a time, in Bohemia, there was a flourishing industry which seems to have fallen off. One would take children, slit their lips, compress their skulls and keep them in a box day and night to prevent them from growing. As a result of this and similar treatment, the children were turned into amusing monsters who brought in handsome profits. A more subtle process was used in the making of Genet, but the result is the same: they took a child and made a monster of him for reasons of social utility. If we want to find the real culprits in this affair, let us turn to the decent folk and ask them by what strange cruelty they made of a child their scapegoat.*

---

* Cf. Appendix I.

Action, whatever it be, modifies that which is in the name of that which is not yet. Since it cannot be carried out without breaking up the old order, it is a permanent revolution. It demolishes in order to build and disassembles in order to reassemble. From morning to night we heap up shavings, ashes, scraps. All construction entails an at least equal amount of destruction. Our unstable societies fear lest a false movement cause them to lose their balance. They therefore ignore the negative moment of our activities. We must love without hating the enemy of what we love, must affirm without denying the contrary of what we affirm, must elect without spurning those we have not elected, must produce without consuming. We rapidly cart away the dead, we stealthily recover waste, every day we mask, in the name of cleaning up, the destruction of the day before. We conceal the pillaging of the planet. The fear of knocking down the edifice is so great that we even take from ourselves our power of creating: we say that man does not invent, that he discovers. We reduce the new to the old. Upkeep, maintenance, preservation, restoration, renewal—these are the actions that are permitted. They all fall under the heading of repetition. Everything is full, everything hangs together, everything is in order, everything has always existed, the world is a museum of which we are the curators. Nevertheless, spirit, as Hegel says, is anxiety. But this anxiety horrifies us. We must eliminate it and arrest spirit by ejecting its springwork of negativity. Unable to get rid of this malignant postulation completely, the right-thinking man castrates himself; he cuts the negative moment away from his freedom and casts out the bloody mess. Freedom is thus cut in two; each of its halves wilts away separately. One of them remains within us. It identifies forever Good with Being, hence with what already is. As Being is the measure of perfection, an existing regime is always more perfect than one which does not exist. It is said to have demonstrated its worth. Anyone wishing to introduce the slightest improvement (and it is quite assumed that improvement is a pious notion which implies no destruction; it is a transition to a higher perfection which envelops and includes the prior perfection) is likewise required to demonstrate its worth and to give evidence, in all other respects, of an all the more profound attachment to Being, that is, to customs and traditions. To the right-thinking man, to be alone and to be wrong are one and the same; to isolate oneself is to withdraw deliberately into one's finiteness, therefore to will one's own nothingness. His dream is that history may end and that there may come at last the time of happy repetition within the great sleep.

No doubt he may fall short, but if he does it is as a result of omission, ignorance, weakness, in short, because of the patch of nothingness which remains in him and to which he submits, though detesting it. He will compensate for this particularity by strict obedience to the imperatives of the group. Moreover, to fall short is *nothing*, literally: our shortcomings are lacks of being and they are efficacious only through the Being which sustains them. The worst is not always certain.

The other half of his freedom, though cut away from him and cast far off, does not, however, leave him undisturbed. Poor right-thinking man: he wanted, in the beginning, to concern himself only with the positive and with Being, to obey unerringly, to realize on his own little plot of ground a small, local end of history. But the fact is that history does not stop; Being is paralyzed, surrounded by Nonbeing; and, in addition, man, man himself, be he respectful or scoffing, insolent or servile, cannot affirm without denying. If he poses a limit, he does so necessarily in order to transgress it, for he cannot pose it without at the same time posing the unlimited. Does he mean to respect a social prohibition? By the same impulse his freedom suggests that he violate it, for to give oneself laws and to create the possibility of disobeying them come to the same thing. The right-thinking man shuts himself up in a voluntary prison and locks the doors, but his stubborn freedom makes him leave by the window. "By the law," says St. Paul, "is the knowledge of sin." The decent man will make himself deaf, dumb and paralyzed. It is he who has eyes that see not and ears that hear not. He is, by virtue of himself, the most abstract negation: the negation of negation. He will define himself narrowly by traditions, by obedience, by the automatism of Good, and will give the name *temptation* to the live, vague swarming which is still himself, but a himself which is wild, free, outside the limits he has marked out for himself. His own negativity falls outside him, since he denies it with all his might. Substantified, separated from any positive intention, it becomes a pure negation that poses itself for its own sake, a pure rage to destroy that goes round in circles, namely Evil. Evil is the unity of all his impulses to criticize, to judge, to reject insofar as he refuses to *recognize* them and regard them as the normal exercise of his freedom and insofar as he relates them to an external cause. It is his dangerous inclination to develop his ideas to their ultimate limits when decency or discipline bids him stop midway. It is his anxiety, his fundamental disbelief or his individuality that comes to him from without, like Another himself, to tempt him. It is what he wants but does not want to want. It is the object of a constant and constantly rejected will which he regards as other than his "true" will. In short, it is the maxim, both in him and outside of him, of the Other's will. Not the will of some particular Other, nor even of all Others, but of that which in each individual is other than himself, other than self, other than all. Evil is the Other. And it is himself insofar as he is for himself Other than Self. It is the will to be other and that all be Other. It is that which is always Other than that which is.

This strange object is a pure contradiction, which will not be surprising if we simply recall its origin: being the destruction of all, it destroys *itself;* it is, at every moment, its own contrary. If one had to examine its ins and outs, one would get lost in the maze of aporias and antinomies. It both is and is not: as pure negation, it reduces itself to pure nonbeing; but since it subsists before our eyes as a temptation, since it has enough reality to inspire hatred, it must also *be,* to a certain extent. One may reply, like Christians, that it borrows its being from being. But in order to "borrow," it must also be. And, from a certain point of view, one must recognize that Being is first: since Evil is defined as Other than Being, it does seem that Being arises, at least logically, before its "Other." And since evil power is in essence a will to destruction, it must have a being to corrode, and it cannot at all manifest itself unless this being is given. But as, on the other hand, we have forged its concept by dividing that which was not divisible and by separating with a single stroke the two indivisible moments of human freedom, we are forced to recognize that Good and Evil are rigorously contemporary, that is, in religious language, that they are two equally immortal principles: the respectable man is Manichaean. By Evil one therefore means both the Being of Nonbeing and the Nonbeing of Being. The same reasons will give rise to the second antinomy, for Evil, being first *the other than Being,* is relative in its essence, but as it is other *absolutely* and not in this or that particular respect, it must be an absolute in its own way. Absolute and relative at the same time, it is both an abstract principle and a particular will. Insofar as all kinds of attrition and ruin are ascribed to it, including those which are the effects of natural agents, it is a pneumatic principle that circulates through the world. There is an evil which is peculiar to consciousness as there is to everything, a leprosy that eats away at it and that is called hebetude, imbecility, darkness. But, in another sense, just as there is Good only in a will that wills itself unconditionally good, so there is Evil only in an intention that wills itself expressly evil. Evil is then consciousness itself at the height of its lucidity, for an evil mind is all the more perverse in that it is more aware of its damnation and wills it more. It pursues both its triumph and its ruin; firstly, because it will be engulfed in its victory along with Good, secondly, because its passion for destruction must know no limits and because it must end by turning this passion against itself. It was for the purpose of planting despair in the very heart of the joy of hurting that "fiendish laughter" and "evil pleasure" were invented. The Evil of consciousness, which is opacity, and consciousness in evil, which is transparency, must meet at the limit. The fact is that in this free and radical undertaking of demolition which claims responsibility for all the consequences of its acts, including its own ruin, one takes pleasure in recognizing at the same time an absolute servitude. Right-thinking people have developed the myth of Evil by depriving human freedom of its positive power and reducing it to its negativity alone. Hence, the evil man, who is negative in essence, is a man possessed whose destiny, whatever he may say, will always be to harm. He is free to do evil; for him the worst is always certain. Indeed, it is not sufficient that his conduct have harmful consequences for others or that it seem blameworthy in the eyes of others. If Evil wants to become absolute, it must be an object of loathing to the one who commits it. If the evil man could be in harmony with himself, this harmony would have the appearance of Good, and if his behavior seemed tolerable to him, he would sin out of ignorance or precipitancy, but not out of malignancy. He must plunge into the worst and at the same time be dragged into it by a kind of inverted grace; he must plunge and resist simultaneously; he must want both to stop and to be pushed even further; he must adhere unreservedly to his aim to harm and must thrust it aside as the effect of an abominable inclination. The evil man approves and loathes himself; he loathes himself for approving himself, he approves himself for loathing himself. His entire consciousness is darkness at the core of his translucidity. This secret hebetude of consciousness is otherness: self and other than self in the absolute identity of self. Evil, which is Being and Nonbeing, Absolute and Relative, Principle and Person, Self-Respect and Self-Hatred, is, in the last analysis, both Order and Disorder. It is Disorder on principle since all its efforts are aimed at destroying order; as Claudel says: "It does not compromise." And yet, if it is to be effective, it must at least have power to destroy, that is, it must have a kind of order, a technique, traditions. It is thus a disorder of all orders, an order of all disorders. It is a corrosive acid, a torment, an explosive, it is radical dispersion. It changes the most indissoluble unity into multiplicity. But since it strews Discord everywhere, since it is the greatest common factor, it must be the secret and imperceptible unity of all multiplicity.

If that is what Evil is, a geometric locus of all contradictions, it stands to reason that no one would dream of indulging in it unreservedly: "No man does evil voluntarily." Of course. What would he gain by it? Evil is gratuitous. It is a luxury activity that requires leisure and yields no profit. We are told that "crime doesn't pay," and that is so. Evil, like Good, requires that it be its own reward. If you steal, or even kill, in order to live, living is a good, you have reduced plunder and murder to the role of means. Evil is fatiguing, it requires an unmaintainable vigilance. Schiller, who was haunted by Kantian ethics, used to ask himself uneasily regarding each of his acts: "Have I probed my mind? Has a self-seeking motive escaped me?" Similarly, the evildoer should ask himself anxiously: "Have I really done Evil for Evil's sake? Have I not acted out of self-interest?" Furthermore, the evil action, even if performed for its own sake, should contain within itself—and should resolve—so many contradictions that it would require invention, inspiration, in a word, genius. It would thus be akin, as Genet often states, to a work of art. Better still, to poetry. The folk mind is clearly aware that evil is beyond its means. It has invented the myth of the man who sold his soul to the Devil. This future victim has not enough strength of soul to do evil *for Evil's sake*. He seeks his own advantage, his pleasure, he wants gold, women, power. And it is Satan who, through him, engages in destroying souls out of pure and gratuitous malignity. At the end of a lecture in which I had attempted to expound the views of some contemporary moralists in all their complexity, a bright-eyed minister came up to me and said: "It's so much easier to do one's duty." I must add that he corrected himself almost immediately. "And harder, too," he added. But I had understood his first reaction. Yes, Good, as they understand it, is easier than Evil. It is easy and reassuring "to do one's duty." It is a matter of training, since everything is repetition. Who would deliberately withdraw from the flock and its comfortable precepts to take up with that mutilated freedom whose bleeding stumps are writhing in the dust?

The conclusion that seems to follow is that the evildoer does not exist. It is only the Good man who is constantly preoccupied with Evil, since Evil is first his own freedom, that is, an enemy who is constantly springing up and whom he must constantly down. But let us not jump to conclusions. The evildoer does exist; we encounter him everywhere, at all times. He exists because the Good man invented him.

When King Louis XVI was brought back from Varennes, the bourgeois deputies realized with terror that all they had to do to become republicans was to carry their principles a bit further. Everything—their interests, their conservatism, their contempt for the masses—contributed to inspiring them with horror of a republic, and yet the idea was present, silent, passive, vertiginous. Their own freedom presented it to them as the logical consequence of their earlier act. Were they going to loathe themselves? Fortunately other citizens called for a republic. The Club des Cordeliers circulated a petition demanding that the King be deposed. What a relief! The possibility which they feared now became quite foreign to them. It was still supported by a freedom, but this time it was a totally *other* freedom. It was as if this importunate part of their free will had actually withdrawn from them and gone off to lead an independent existence elsewhere. Supported by others, the idea of a republic ceased to be a temptation and became an object of horror. The petitioners were *evildoers,* and they were told as much. And whom does one strike in the person of the "dirty, greedy, sensual, negating" Jew? One's self, one's own greed, one's own lechery. Whom does one lynch in the American South for raping a white woman? A Negro? No. Again one's self. Evil is a projection. I would go as far as to say that it is both the basis and aim of all projective activity.* As for the evildoer, we all have our own: he is a man whose situation makes it possible for him to present to us in broad daylight and in objective form the obscure temptations of our freedom. If you want to know a decent man, look for the vices he hates most in others. You will have the lines of force of his fears and terrors, you will breathe the odor that befouls his beauteous soul. In the case of those who condemn Genet most severely, I would say that homosexuality is their constant and

---

* Everything that can be said about projection has been said. I wish merely to relate an anecdote. A very good friend of mine had lived abroad for a long time, and his speech had become studded with Anglicisms. When he returned to France after the Liberation, we were delighted to see each other again, but shortly thereafter disagreements of a personal and political nature arose between us. We met frequently, but our relations were strained. One day, the discussion grew heated. He objected, courteously but with a good deal of annoyance, to my opinions (which had been his own before the war) and my conduct. As he grew more excited, his French became less correct and on three occasions the same Anglicism crept into his speech. The third time, he looked at me irritably and asked brusquely: "Why do you keep making that exasperating mistake?"

constantly rejected temptation, the object of their innermost hatred, and that they are glad to hate it in another person because they thus have an opportunity to look away from themselves. And I do not mean, to be sure, that this constantly rejected homosexuality seems to them an inclination of their nature. Quite the contrary, it is diffuse, it is a shifty something about persons and things, it is a certain disturbing appearance of the world that might very well open up suddenly and become dizzying, it is an inner uneasiness, it is the dim and constant consciousness that there is no recourse within themselves against themselves. Genet is useful to them; they can hate in him the half of themselves which they reject.

Thus, the evildoer is the Other. Evil—fleeting, artful, marginal Evil—can be seen only out of the corner of one's eye and in others. Never is it more perceptible than in wartime. We know the enemy only by comparison with ourselves; we imagine his intentions according to ours; we set traps for him into which we know we would fall if we were in his place and we avoid those which we would have set. The enemy is our twin brother, our image in the mirror. Yet the same conduct which we consider good when it is ours seems to us detestable when it is his. He is the evildoer par excellence. It is therefore during a war that a Good man has the clearest conscience. It is in time of war that there are the fewest lunatics. Unfortunately, one cannot always be fighting. From time to time there must be peace. For peacetime, society has, in its wisdom, created what might be called professional evildoers. These evil men are as necessary to good men as whores are to decent women. They are fixation abscesses. For a single sadist there is any number of appeased, clarified, relaxed consciousnesses. They are therefore very carefully recruited. They must be bad by birth and without hope of change. That is why one chooses men with whom the decent members of the community have no reciprocal relationship: so that these bad people cannot take it into their heads to pay us back in kind and start thinking of us what we think of them. And as Evil is negation, separation, disintegration, its natural representatives will be sought among the separated and separatists, among the unassimilable, the undesirable, the repressed, the rejected. The candidates include the oppressed and exploited in every category, the foreign workers, the national and ethnic minorities. But these are still not the best recruits. These people sometimes organize among themselves, educate themselves and become conscious of their race or class. They then discover, through hatred, the meaning of reciprocity, and the oppressor comes to personify Evil for them just as they personify Evil for the oppressor. Fortunately there exist in our society products of disassimilation, castoffs: abandoned children, "the poor," bourgeois who have lost their status, "lumpenproletariat," déclassés of all kinds, in short, all the wretched. With these we are tranquil. They cannot unite with any group since nobody wants them. And as solitude is their lot, we do not have to worry about their associating among themselves. That is why, in general, we give them preference.

Genet fulfills all the required conditions. This abandoned child is an authentic castoff. He seems overwhelmed by a fabulous bad luck that guarantees us against any accidental return of reciprocity. Placed under observation for a time, he gave evidence of evil instincts and committed punishable offenses. This is all that was needed. By the gaze that surprised him, by the finger that pointed at him, by the voice that called him a thief, the collectivity doomed him to Evil. They were waiting for him. There was going to be a vacancy: some old convict lay dying on Devil's Island; there has to be new blood among the wicked too. Thus, all the rungs of the ladder which he has to descend have been prepared in advance. Even before he emerged from his mother's womb, they had already reserved beds for him in all the prisons of Europe and places for him in all shipments of criminals. He had only to go to the trouble of being born; the gentle, inexorable hands of the Law will conduct him from the National Foundling Society to the penal colony.

If we want to know ourselves, we have two sources of information: our inner sense furnishes us with certain facts ("I'm happy, unhappy, I'm attracted, repelled, by such-and-such a person. I have an urge to travel," etc.), and the people about us furnish us with others. These data sometimes overlap and complement each other. We can correct one body of data by means of the other. For example, I can observe that I am angry when my brother points out to me that I am losing my self-control. My family can even draw my attention to an irritation that I am trying to hide from myself: "You're white as a sheet, your hands are trembling," etc. And, vice versa, by revealing this anger to them I can enable them to interpret certain aspects of my behavior which would otherwise remain mysterious to them: "So that's why you didn't say good morning to so-and-so," etc. To hesitate as to which of two roads to take is often to turn one's head to the right, then to the left, to take a few steps in one direction, then a few in the other. If I hesitate, there is probably nothing more in me than the consciousness of these bodily movements. But, inversely, the witness who observes me and *sees* me hesitating perceives nothing more than these same move-ments. Hence, the external perception of the witness and my inner sense agree on this point, and in this case there is no privileged observer.

But in the majority of cases, and particularly if it is a matter of feelings, qualities, traits of character, or complex behavior, we are unable to bring our inner data into line with the information given by our external informants because the two are not of the same nature. I am not an object to myself—at least not *at first*—and if I become one, this object is of a very particular nature. It remains the "incomparable monster" of which Malraux speaks, whereas to others I am first an object. Thus, the *objective qualities* which they recognize in me express not so much what I am in myself as what I am with *respect to them.* The quality that is being considered therefore represents a complex body of two terms: I and my witness, and the relationship between these two terms. In addition, most of the time it has a *practical* truth, that is, it is an item of information concerning, in particular, the behavior to adopt toward me. I therefore cannot internalize this information and dissolve it in my subjectivity. It is not *soluble* in my consciousness. If I am told that I am intelligent and witty or dull-witted and coarse, this informa-tion refers to the effect I produce on others. To be witty, for example, is to entertain a well-defined social set in conformity with certain rules. I cannot therefore have the intuition that I *am* witty; this intuition is necessarily given *to another,* and it is re-vealed by the pleasure he takes in listening to me. Similarly, I can know that I am *thinking* but not that I am *intelligent.* The idea of *intelligence* presupposes not only a certain intellectual ease or swiftness *observed from without,* but, in addition, certain subjective dispositions in the witness who recognizes this quality in me, for example, admiration and a readiness to have more confidence in me than in himself when it comes to solving certain difficulties: "See whether you understand this, you who are intelligent." Hence, when all goes well we can distinguish our being-for-self from our being-for-the-other. We know that our consciousness is infallible in a certain very limited area and that its intuitions are obviously true. We also know that information which another furnishes us is only probable (A. considers me intelligent, but B. finds me stupid. Who will decide between them? And is it possible, in this domain, to decide by majority vote?) and that it does not concern our inner depths but rather our external relations with others. It is therefore quite true that these qualities which are recognized in us elude our consciousness, not because they are hidden in an unconscious which is situated behind it, but because they are in front of us, in the world, and are originally a relationship to the other. "Wittiness" is, of course, a certain gift that I have—if I have it—without realizing it. But it is evident that this is no more a structure of my unconscious than an immediate datum of my consciousness. It is a feature which characterizes me not insofar as I am I to myself, but insofar as I am Another to Others.

But this information is sometimes communicated to us in such a way that we ascribe more reality to what others teach us than to what we could learn by ourself. Out of submission or respect, we take information which, in any event, is only probable as being an unconditional certainty. On the other hand, we are tempted to regard the information of our consciousness as dubious and obscure. This means that we have given primacy to the object which we are to Others over the subject we are to ourself. A young woman, for example, is having marital difficulties. She is not accepted unreservedly by her in-laws; she feels that her husband is slipping away from her. Tact, patience and a great deal of experience are required in order to keep him, in order to overcome the family's bias. Since she lacks these qualities, she feels that she is drowning. She flounders about. The difficulties are too great. She lives in a state of anxiety. And, as is to be expected, she reacts with anger, for anger is merely a blind and magical attempt to simplify situations that are too complex. Her consciousness will teach her all this if she observes herself with sufficient perseverance. She will become aware that she is trying to discard all rules by plunging into violence. She will therefore realize that anger is not a hereditary curse or a destiny but simply an inept reaction to a too complicated problem. If the problem changes, the mood will also change. Her husband, however, tells her that she is *irascible*. In a sense, this is true. It is a correct indication of the behavior to be adopted toward her *by others*. This *practical* notion indicates simply that she has disconcerting and unpredictable outbursts of temper and that consequently she must be treated with a certain consideration.

But if, out of remorse, out of masochism, out of a deep feeling of inferiority, this young woman adopts the social and objective datum as if it were the absolute truth about her, if she accuses herself of having an *irascible nature,* if she projects behind her, into the darkness of the unconscious, a permanent predisposition to anger of which each particular outburst is an emanation, then she subordinates her reality as a conscious subject to the Other that she is for Others, and she grants to the Other a superiority to herself and confers upon what is probable a superiority to what is certain. She endows that which had no meaning other than social with a metaphysical meaning, a meaning prior to any relationship with society. In short, I would say that she alienates herself from the object which she is to others.

This type of alienation is widespread. Most of the time, however, it is a matter of partial or temporary alienation. But when children are subjected, from their earliest days, to great social pressure, when their Being-for-Others is the subject of a collective image accompanied by value judgments and social prohibitions, the alienation is sometimes total and definitive. This is the case of most pariahs in caste societies. They internalize the objective and external judgments which the collectivity passes on them, and they view themselves in their subjective individuality on the basis of an "ethnic character," a "nature," an "essence" which merely express the contempt in which *others* hold them. The Indian untouchable thinks that he *is actually* untouchable. He internalizes the prohibition of which he is the object, and makes of it an inner principle which justifies and explains the conduct of the other Hindus toward him.

The situation is exactly the same for the small caste of untouchables whom our societies have charged with personifying Evil and whom they overwhelm with prohibitions under the name of criminals. Yes, they are criminals. This means, in all good logic, that they *have committed* one or more crimes and that they are liable to punishments set down in the statute book. But by virtue of the ambiguity of the term, society convinces them—and they let themselves be convinced—that this objective definition actually applies to their hidden, subjective being. The criminal that they were to others is now ensconced deep within them, like a monster. They thus allow themselves to be governed by *another*, that is, by a being who has reality only in the eyes of others. Their failings and errors are transformed into a permanent predisposition, that is, into a destiny.

Such is the case of the child Genet. Society has charged him with personifying the Evildoer, that is, the Other. Now, as we have seen, Evil is a concept for external use only. Nobody will say voluntarily, before being recognized as guilty, "I want Evil." Evil, which springs from the right-thinking man's fear of his freedom, is originally a projection and a catharsis. It is therefore *always* an object. Moreover, as we have seen, if we attempted to establish it within ourself, the contradictory terms composing it would repel each other violently and would each collapse separately. But this matters little to us, since the fact is that we perceive it in Others. Yes, *for us* Evil is impossible. Therefore, we do not seek to actualize it. But since this Other desires Evil, it is for him to take over its contradictions. Let him manage as best he can. The proof, moreover, that one can make everything hang together, with the aid of an efficacious grace that probably comes from Hell, is precisely the fact *that there are* evildoers. There are evildoers, therefore Evil is possible. Such is our proof *a posteriori*.

But what happens, then, to the poor wretch on whom the decent man has projected all his evil desires, his sadism, his homicidal impulses and his lustful dreams? How does he manage to make a whole of all these contradictory postulations? Ah, that's *his* affair. The decent man doesn't give a damn.

The respectful consciousness of little Genet has begun its work. To all the others Evil is outside, in others. To him alone, poor hoodwinked child, Evil is *in him.*

For the others, his function is to take their forbidden desires upon himself and to reflect them like a mirror; *for himself,* he must incorporate these desires into himself, must internalize them, must make them *his* desires. Not that he is asked to *desire* the impure or to *will* Evil by deliberate intentions of his consciousness. He is required only to recognize this evil will as inspiring his daily desires, his ordinary wishes. The child tries to do this as best he can. His candor, his confidence, his respect make him the best auxiliary of adults. He has been told that he is bad, he therefore believes it. He conscientiously seeks the evil desires and evil thoughts of decent people at the very source of his subjectivity. He is a diligent evildoer.

But, as it happens, Evil is the Other. The Other than Being, the Other than Good, the Other than self. Here we have the key to Genet. This is what must be understood first: Genet is a child who has been convinced that he is, in his very depths, *Another than Self.* His life will henceforth be only the history of his attempts to perceive this Other in himself and to look it in the face—that is, to have an immediate and subjective intuition of his wickedness, to *feel* he is wicked—or to flee it. But this phantom—precisely because it is nothing—will not let itself be grasped. When the child turns to it, it disappears. When Genet tries to run away from it, suddenly it is there, like Carmen's rebellious bird.

The most immediate result is that the child is "doctored." He regards the existence of adults as more certain than his own and their testimonies as truer than that of his consciousness. He affirms the priority of the object which he is to them over the subject which he is to himself. Therefore, without being clearly aware of it, he judges that the appearance (which he is to others) is the reality and that the reality (which he is to himself) is only appearance. He sacrifices his inner certainty to the principle of authority. He refuses to hear the voice of the *cogito*. He decides against himself in the very depths of his consciousness. He wants to regard the evident facts which his inner sense reveals to him about his own mental state as being mere lies, as approximations at best. On the other hand, he considers the merely probable hypotheses that the others set up about his conduct to be certainties. He makes every effort to believe that he must be informed of his particular essence by others and that he cannot attain it alone because it evades him on principle. The most inward part of himself is that which is most obscure to his eyes and most manifest to the eyes of others. He is a wrong-way Descartes who applies his methodical doubt to the content of the "I think," and it is hearsay knowledge that will provide him with his certainties. Out of a reverse idealism it is to himself that he applies the famous *esse est percipi*, and he recognizes himself as being only insofar as he is perceived. Our certainty of ourself finds its truth in the Other when the latter recognizes us. To Genet, the truth, separated from certainty, will be the intimidating, ceremonial, official thought of adults, judges, cops, decent people. He receives it without being allowed to practice it; it is communicated to him like a sentence. Nevertheless, his lonely, challenged, disregarded certainty of self grows within him like a weed in an abandoned garden.

No doubt, one does not impose silence on the *cogito;* consciousness will lose none of its transparency; it will not cease to reveal to him things that are indubitably evident. But he will zealously blindfold the eyes of his soul, will cast doubt on what is self-evident, will doubt the indubitable. Shuttling back and forth between two contradictory systems of reference, he regards as true what he does not succeed in believing, and as doubtful what he knows for a certainty. The most manifest intentions thereby become the most obscure; his passing states of consciousness are pure, iridescent reflections, without consistency. As for his own existence, since he attains it only through the mediation of others and merges it with the substantial being of "the Evildoer" or "the Thief," he is no more assured of it than of the existence of Greenland or of the Iron Mask. In short, he learns to think the unthinkable, to maintain the unmaintainable, to pose as true what he very well knows to be false. We shall see later that he will build a whole system of sophistry on this procedure and that he will one day be able to turn it against the flabbergasted right-thinking man.

In his very depths, Genet is first an object—and an object to others. It is too early to speak of his homosexuality, but we can at least indicate its origin. Simone de Beauvoir has pointed out that feminine sexuality derives its chief characteristics from the fact that woman is an object to the other and to herself before being a subject. One can expect that Genet, who is the object par excellence, *will make himself an object* in sexual relations and that his eroticism will bear a resemblance to feminine eroticism.

It is possible to retrace with a certain accuracy the stages whereby Genet slowly transforms himself into a stranger to himself. And we shall see that it is simply a matter of progressively internalizing the sentence imposed by adults.

First of all, he wants to escape his destiny. He must awake from a nightmare. Caught, exposed, punished, he swears he will never do it again. Of course, in all sincerity. He does not recognize this act which has become objective and has suddenly revealed itself to be so terribly Other—simply because it is seen by the others; he hates it; he wishes it had never taken place. In hastily manifesting his will never to steal again, he tries to destroy symbolically his hardened, congealed act which encloses him in its carapace. Only a while ago he wanted to flee into the past, into the eternal, he wanted to die. Now he reverses the direction of his flight; his oath testifies to a wild impatience to escape into the future. Three or four years will go by during which he will not commit another theft; he has sworn not to. Already the years have gone by, he *is already* in the future, he turns upon this wretched present and confers upon it its true significance: it was only an accident. But at the same moment the Others' gaze again supervenes and cuts him off from himself. The others have not the same reasons as he to believe in his oath, because, in the first place, their indignation also mortgages the future. If—which is unlikely—it were demonstrated that the child would not steal again, their sense of outrage would have to simmer down. In order to perpetuate itself—for, like all passions, it tends to persevere in its being—it must change into a prophetic transport. It therefore postulates the eternity of its object. What it is already aiming at through the child thief is the adult, the hardened criminal, the habitual offender. Thus, in addition, this sacred emotion goes hand in hand with a legitimate mistrust. From a *practical* point of view, the owners must take precautions; they would be guilty in their own eyes if they did not lock the closets. But these precautions foretoken a future that challenges Genet's oath. They are directed to a future that is both foreseeable and unforeseeable. Foreseeable: Genet has erred, *therefore* he will err. Unforeseeable: no one knows the hour or day of the next offense. Since the adults are unable to know the date of it, their vigilance confers upon the future theft a perpetual presence. It is in the air, in the silence of the grownups, in the severity of their faces, in the glance they exchange, in the locking of the drawer. Genet would like to forget about it, he buries himself in his work, but his foster mother, who tiptoed off, suddenly comes back and takes him by surprise: "What are you doing?" This is all that is needed: the forgotten theft comes to life again; it is present, vertiginous. Distrust and prophetic anger systematically project the past into the future; Genet's future fills with misdemeanors which are repeated at irregular intervals and which are the effect of a constant predisposition to steal. Obviously this predisposition is simply the reverse of the adults' expectation. It is their vigilance, but turned around and projected into Genet, who in turn reflects it back to them. If they must be constantly on guard against his thefts, it is because he is constantly ready to commit them, and the greater their fear of being robbed, the greater seems to them his inclination to theft. Naturally, after that, how could he be expected not to succumb? It is the adults themselves who want him to relapse. He will fall into error again, as often as they want him to.

So he now adopts the point of view of honest people. He docilely establishes within himself the inclination attributed to him. But this inclination is, in its very form, *the Other's*. It is never within our own self that we discover the unforeseeable foreseeability of which I have spoken; we discover it in those who we are not. In our own eyes, we are neither foreseeable nor unforeseeable. I do not *foresee* that I shall take the train this evening—I decide to take it, and if there remains a wide margin of possibility in my plans, the reason is that they depend on others as much as on me.* To be sure, I can at any moment change my plans, and I do not think of my versatility without a certain anxiety, but this anxiety comes from my feeling free and from the fact that nothing, not even my

---

* I can amuse myself by *foreseeing* what I shall be doing in ten years, but actually this future seems so remote that it appears to be that of another. And it is also true that the gambler who swears he will never again touch a card has only a limited confidence in his oath, not because he considers himself unforeseeable (or too foreseeable) but because he has a real and present knowledge of the inefficacy of oaths in the presence of his freedom.

own oaths, can tie me down. It is not a *fear* of a monster that may inhabit me and have reduced me to slavery, but rather the very opposite of such a fear.

Genet the thief will await himself as the others await him, with *their* expectations. Foreseeable to others, he will attempt to foresee himself. He will be afraid of his future thefts. Unforeseeable to honest people, he will become unforeseeable to himself; he will wonder every morning whether the new day will be marked by a theft. He will take precautions against himself as if he were another, another whom he has been told to keep an eye on. He will be careful not to leave *himself* alone. He will voluntarily leave an empty room to join his parents in the next one. He will keep an eye on himself; he will watch for the crisis, ready to call the others to the rescue against himself. He fears himself as one fears a fire, a flood, an avalanche. His thefts become external events which he is powerless to oppose and for which he is nevertheless responsible. He observes himself, spies on himself, foils himself, as if he were an odd instrument that one must learn to use. He struggles against an angel within him, an angel of Evil. In this dubious combat everything is inverted. Being oneself becomes being-other-than-self. It is no longer even possible to believe in one's own oaths; one distrusts them as one distrusts those of another. A foreign future challenges and mocks the future one has given oneself. And this future is a Destiny, a Fatality, because it is the reverse of *another freedom.* A freedom which is mine and which I do not know has prepared it for me, like a trap. In the depths of his consciousness Genet, like the animal in Kafka in the depths of its burrow, hears dull blows, scratchings. Another animal, a monster, is digging tunnels, is going to get at him and devour him. This other animal is himself. Yet he has *never seen it.*

For he has never seen it. A thief cannot have an intuition of himself *as thief.* The notion of "thief" is on principle incommensurate with the realities of the inner sense. It is of social origin and presupposes a prior definition of society, of the property system, a legal code, a judiciary apparatus and an ethical system of relationships among people. There can therefore be no question of a mind's *encountering* theft within itself, and with immediacy. On the other hand, the *Others,* all the Others, have this intuition at will; a thief is a palpable reality, like a tree, like a Gothic church. Here is a man being dragged along by two cops: "What has he done?" I ask. "He's a crook," answer the cops. The word strikes against its object like a crystal falling into a supersaturated solution. The solution immediately crystallizes, enclosing the word inside itself. In prose, the word dies so that the object may be born. "He's a crook!" I forget the word then and there, I see, I touch, I breathe a crook; with all my senses I feel that secret substance: crime. I did not, of course, witness the theft, but that doesn't matter! The guilty man's torn, dusty clothes (he fell while trying to run away, he was beaten) contrast with the decent dress of the onlookers, with my own. They make me see that this man is beyond the pale. He is an untouchable *since* I cannot touch him without soiling my hands. The mud that stains his shirt and jacket is the mud of his soul *become visible*. He engages in a strange dance composed of false steps; he moves backward, forward, changes position by fits and starts; each of his movements is constrained. Quite simply because he is being taken to the police station by force and is resisting. But this constraint and force and vain violence manifest to my eyes that he is possessed. He is struggling against the Demon, and the incoherence of his gestures reveals his maladjustment: his foot stumbles on the sidewalk, he almost falls, and I know intuitively, by the simple contrast between his blundering haste and the slow, sure movements of the decent people about him, that he is a déclassé, an incompetent who has never been able, or never wanted, to submit to any discipline. I can read on this messy body that "Evil does not compromise." He has been struck and he is bleeding. His tormented face should tell me that he is weak, defenseless, that a pack has brought him to bay and bitten him. But I combine my loathing of Evil and my loathing of Blood. It is Evil that is bleeding, Crime is oozing from those wounds. And the look on his face expresses a state of daze (he has been half-killed), of fear ("What are they going to do to me?"), of anger ("They've hurt me!"), of shame ("All those people looking at me and yelling!"). But *to me* this state of daze is the sottishness of the alcoholic and the degenerate. Through his rage I touch Evil's inexpressible hatred of Good. His shame manifests consciousness in Evil. Five minutes before this fortunate encounter, Evil was still a merely abstract concept. A word was sufficient *to make me experience it*. A flesh-and-blood thief is crime accessible to all the senses.

Genet will never have this intuition. To be sure, he understands the meaning of the word. He has seen petty thieves being roughly handled by policemen. But he is condemned to read words in reverse. Honest folk give names to things, and the things bear these names. Genet is on the side of the objects named, not of those who name them. I am aware that honest people are also objects to each other. I am given names: I am this fair-haired man who wears glasses, this Frenchman, this teacher. But if I am named, I name in turn. Thus, naming and named, I lived in a state of reciprocity. Words are thrown at me, I catch them and throw them at others, I understand, *in* others, what I am to them. *Genet is alone in stealing.* Later, he will know other thieves, but he will remain alone. We shall see that there is no reciprocity in the world of theft. This is not surprising, since these monsters have been fabricated in such a way as to be unable to make common cause.* Thus, when he is given this staggering name, he cannot make out its meaning in the persons of those who name him. It is as if a page of a book suddenly became conscious and felt itself *being read aloud* without being able *to read itself.* He is read, deciphered, designated. The others feel his being, but he feels their feeling as if it were a hemorrhage. He flows into the eyes of others, he leaks, he is emptied of his substance. He has *vertigo,* in the strict sense of the word. When we stand on a precipice and suddenly feel dizzy, we feel that we are slipping away from ourself, that we are flowing, falling. Something is calling to us from the bottom of the gulf. That something is ourself, that is, our being which is escaping from us and which we shall join in death. The word is vertiginous because it opens out on an impossible and fascinating task. I have shown elsewhere that certain extreme situations are necessarily experienced as unrealizable. Well then, Genet is unrealizable to himself. He repeats the magic word: "Thief! I'm a thief!" He even looks at himself in the mirror, even talks to himself as to someone else: "You're a thief." Is he going to *see himself,* to feel a bitter, feverish taste, the taste for crime that he gives off for others, is he at last going to feel his being? Nothing changes: a child scowls at his own reflection, that is all. Later, his creatures, one after the other, will stand in front of mirrors and name themselves: "I'm Erik Seidler, the

---

* The same absence of reciprocity can be observed among homosexuals. Every one of them has been called "homo" at least once in his life, and the name has remained graven on his flesh. He meditates endlessly upon the word. Moreover, he frequently calls other men homosexuals and is amused by them. A homosexual at the critical age will quite readily say: "I met an old queen. . . ." But they do not allow reciprocity of naming. A coal dealer, a chemist, a judge have an intuition of what they are when another judge, another chemist, another coal dealer is named in their presence. But the homosexual never thinks of himself when someone is branded in his presence with the name *homosexual.* His relationship to homosexuals is univocal. He is *the one* who receives with horror the name homosexual. It is not one quality among others; it is a destiny, a peculiar flaw of his being. *Elsewhere* there is a category of comic, shady people whom he jokes about with "straights," namely, the queers. His sexual tastes will doubtless lead him to enter into relationships with this suspect category, but he would like to make use of them without being likened to them. Here, too, the ban that is cast on certain men by society has destroyed all possibility of reciprocity among them. Shame isolates. As does pride, which is the obverse of shame.

executioner's lover." "I'm a German." "I'm a soldier." "I'm the maid." They want the word, in striking their image, to cause a crystallization, to make them see what a German, what a maid *is*. But the word scoots away, the image remains dull and all too familiar. Erik ends by taking out his revolver and firing at his reflection. Yet the solution is there, in the word. Genet is relentless. "I'm a thief," he cries. *He listens* to his voice; whereupon the relationship to language is inverted: the word ceases to be an indicator, it becomes a *being*. It resounds, it bursts upon the silence, one feels it running over one's tongue, it is real, it is true. It is a casket, a box with a double bottom which contains within it what Genet often calls "the mystery." If one could crack this nut, one would find inside it the very being of the thief; the being and the word are one and the same. The states of consciousness are thus changed into signs. They are a flickering that try to light up the darkness of the name. The latter, which, on the other hand, is dark, massive, impenetrable, has become the being which is signified. "Such-and-such an idea occurs to me, such-and-such a mood, desire, comes over me. Is *that* what's called being a thief?" The word, which was a means, rises to the rank of supreme reality. Silence, on the other hand, is now only a means of designating language. The trick is done: we have made a poet of the doctored child. He is haunted by a word, a single word which he contemplates in reverse and which contains his soul. He tries to see himself in it as in plate glass; he will spend his life meditating on a word.

One may say: "A word, what's a word? He has thirty thousand others. They're his as much as ours. All right, as far as 'thief' is concerned. But if I say that Genet is blond or short or French, this re-establishes reciprocity, for, after all, he can say about me what I say about him." But that is not true. If you touch a single word, language disintegrates in a chain reaction; not a single vocable is spared. The word "thief" is everywhere, extends through everything. Whatever you may say about Genet, *thief* is the permanent predicate of your propositions, and this suffices for him to be unable to apply the epithet to you. Do you assert that he is *blond?* That means: A thief is blond. But a thief is not blond as a decent man is. He is blond *as a thief*. Introduce an imaginary quantity into your calculations and all the results become imaginary. And so for Genet: as the original intuition of his being is denied him, all other intuitions concerning him are also rejected. He is absolutely *other;* all words designate what is manifest to others and hidden from him a priori.

Our familiar relationship to language makes it invisible to us in ordinary daily life. "We are so steeped in words," says Blanchot, "that words become useless." Words do not even have to be uttered between father and son, husband and wife, between workers on the same job, because things themselves cry them out to us. At the dinner table, my grandfather used to point silently to the piece of meat he wanted served to him. The gesture in itself was ambiguous, but we understood it immediately because it had, in the past, accompanied a phrase which gradually was dropped. Furthermore, even when we do use words, we pay no more attention to them than to our clothes or our fork. We speak in shorthand, in broken sentences. To speak is to pass over words in silence. But this invisibility of the Word obviously implies a deep understanding between those who are communicating. "If you do not act toward the utterances of others in accordance with the social norms of your age and milieu," says Brice Parain, "you have already ceased to be able to understand and interpret them." Now, the fact is that Genet has no milieu; he is alone. The norms set by society do not concern him. No more is needed for him to be astounded by the strangeness of human speech.

To be sure, there is not a single child who has not experienced this astonishment. When the poet Michel Leiris was little, he used to say *"reusement."* One day he was corrected: "One doesn't say '. . . *reusement,*' but *'heureusement'* [happily]." "The word which until then I had used as a pure interjection, without any awareness of its real meaning, was linked up with *'heureux'* [happy] and, by the magical virtue of such an association, was suddenly inserted into the whole sequence of precise meanings. The sudden apprehending of the complete word, which until then I had always slurred, took on the quality of a discovery. . . . It was no longer a thing that belonged to me alone. It partook of the reality which was the language of my brothers and sister and also of my parents. What had been a thing peculiarly mine became a common and open thing. All at once, in a flash, it had become a shared, or rather a socialized thing."*

But generally this astonishment does not last long. Usually it is precisely the Word which achieves the unity of the particular and the universal. If I talk about myself, I must universalize myself in order to be understood. Is not the very word "I" which I have just written a designation of myself and also of anyone? Words belong

---

* *Biffures,* p. 12.

to everybody; they are man himself as universal subject. If I say that I am unhappy, anyone will understand me, for anyone could have said and will be able to say that he is unhappy, and consequently, insofar as I *am understood,* I am anyone.

To Genet, however, there is no connection between the particular character that language has for him and the universal, socialized content of words. It is not even possible for him to express unambiguously the most immediate manifestations of his consciousness. He must have exclaimed more than once that he was unhappy, and his primary intention was to communicate knowledge of his state to others. What exactly was he trying to say? That he was lost within himself, that he was unable to feel guilty and that nevertheless he was making an effort to judge himself severely, that he seemed to himself to be both a monster and an innocent victim, that he had no more confidence in his will to mend his ways and that nevertheless he was horribly afraid of his destiny, that he was ashamed, that he wished his error were wiped away, though he knew it was irremediable, that he was longing to love, to be loved, that he was suffering above all from that ghastly, incomprehensible exclusion, that he begged to be readmitted to the community and allowed to regain his innocence. Now, that is precisely what is not communicable. To understand Genet's unhappiness really and truly would be to renounce Manichaeism, the convenient idea of Evil, the pride of being honest, to revoke the community's sentence, to annul its decree. The honest people would have to be ashamed of themselves; they would have to recognize reciprocity. The misfortune of a widow, of an orphan, that's something one is glad to understand: tomorrow we ourselves may lose our father, our wife, our child. These are recognized misfortunes that entail a ceremonial known to all. But to understand the misfortune of a young thief would be to recognize that I too can steal. The honest people obviously refuse to do this: "You shouldn't have stolen! You deserve what you got!" The decent man goes away, the child remains alone. Nevertheless, the remark is present, valid. It correctly designates his state of feeling. The child takes up the remark, repeats it to himself under his breath. The normal man expresses his unhappiness to others so as to be understood by them, hence to be like everyone else, whereas Genet, abandoned by all, repeats his lament without a witness so as to be understood by himself alone, hence to be more himself. Instead of the particularity's being socialized, it is the universal that becomes a means of achieving the particular. Or, to put it otherwise, he is trying to substitute himself for the missing witness, to be, for himself, someone else whom he informs of his suffering, someone else who, guided by the words, will make the intuitive discovery of his unhappiness as a *being*, that is, as an object. But the meaning remains stuck to the statement, for the purpose is to inform the other of what he does not yet know, and Genet knows only too well that he is unhappy. Thereupon the statement loses its indicative value. Falsely universal, falsely objective, it now serves only as a pseudo-communication, a pseudo-teaching. The words no longer designate the misfortune, they do not make it appear, they do not present it to the intuition of the other. The intuition of the misfortune exists in Genet long before he expresses it; it is his suffering itself, his actual suffering which words cannot increase or reveal. What purpose is served by his saying "I am unhappy"? To make his suffering exist in the absolute for a fictive witness. Dedicated to this phantom, the remark is transformed as the word "thief" was transformed. It contains Genet's being, his meaning, it is his misfortune become thing. He tries to impregnate it with his sufferings. But as the witness is no one, as Genet cannot be his own witness, it remains there, uttered and understood, an arrested flight toward nothingness; it contains, as it were, the being of the misfortune, that is, its objective aspect *for others*. But this very being, rarefied and evanescent, is, for Genet, only an absence.

His adventure is his having been *named*. The result has been a radical metamorphosis of his person and language. The ceremonious naming which transformed him, in his own eyes, into a *sacred object* initiated the slow progression that will one day make of him a "Prince of Thieves" and a poet. But at the present time he has not the slightest suspicion that he will glory in doing Evil. Overcome and bewildered, he merely submits. Referring to this period of his life, he will one day say that he was the football which is kicked from one end of the field to the other. He understands nothing of what is happening to him; he seeks himself gropingly and does not find himself. A dead child is smiling at him sadly from the other side of a glass, the paths leading to the woods are cut off. He is crushed by a horrible curse and guilt. He is a monster, he feels the monster breathing down the back of his neck, he turns around and finds no one. Everybody can see the huge bug, he alone does not see it. Other than all the others, he is other than himself. Child martyr, foundling, the others have hemmed him in, penetrated him, wander leisurely through his soul, like the judge, the lawyer and the executioner who entered Harcamone by the ear, descended to the depths of his heart and left by his asshole. Genet is a crowd, which is nobody. It is the *reverse side of the setting,* the reverse of Good and of Good men's hatred of evil. Society is not more terribly present to anyone than to this child whom it aims to reject. He is not a man, he is a creature of man, entirely occupied by men. They have produced him, manufactured him out of whole cloth. Not a breath of air has been allowed to enter this soul.

Paralyzed by men's gaze, marked by man in his very depths and transformed by man in his perception and even his inner language, he encounters everywhere, between him and men, between him and nature, between him and himself, the blurred transparency of human meanings. Only one question confronts this *homunculus:* man. The child Genet is an inhuman product of which man is the sole problem. How to be accepted by men? How to become a man? How to become oneself? It is not freedom that he wants, any more than does Kafka's monkey which has been uprooted from its forest and locked up in a case. Oh no, not freedom! Freedom is a man's problem, a problem of a higher order; Genet is seeking *a way out.* But everything is so well contrived that he cannot find one anywhere. Whatever the behavior he adopts in an effort to reclaim the criminal that he *is,* his acts will emanate from this criminal and be able only to perpetuate him. Similarly, Stilitano tries to get to the exit of the Palace of Mirrors and collides with his own image everywhere. What is to be done? Reject the morality in the name of which he is condemned? We have seen that this was not possible. Turn in on himself and try to recapture his lost innocence? But since innocence comes to the child through others, since it is the others who have taken it away from him, only the others can give it back to him. Then should he submit? But to whom? And to what? Is he even asked to submit? Though the adults are prompt to condemn, they are in no hurry to absolve. If a man is a thief, he is theirs; if honest, he escapes them. What do they want of him? He is ready for anything. But the fact is, they expect nothing. They needed a culprit, they chose him, but they are quite unconcerned about what goes on in his mind. Let him be, if he likes, a good culprit, that is, not too hardened and not too ready to repent. Let him try to mend his ways, but without arrogance, and with relapses. Above all, let him realize that forgiveness is a matter of generosity; he will never be entitled to it, whatever he may do. It may be granted him one day out of charity. (Out of charity, in other words, out of caprice. The truth is that no one has the right to forgive.) Meanwhile, let him resign his freedom and put it into the hands of those who condemn him, let him become their despised slave, let him worship them and loathe himself. Furthermore, he will gain nothing thereby, and if he thought he would that would be an additional offense. The child's suffering is so great that he asks nothing better than to conclude this bad deal. To obey, even without hope, to obey even a pitiless master, is also a way of escaping solitude. But the attitude which is imposed upon him is untenable. He is ready to hate himself if only he can manage to see himself face to face. But he never sees himself. His hatred, unable to settle on a real object, remains empty, abstract, acted rather than felt. Even his remorse is fake. Logically, the one who should repent is the child who stole. But this child stole innocently, and besides he is dead. The one who repents is the culprit they have manufactured. It seems to him that he is repenting the fault of another. In short, the culprit is asking the good man: "What must I do *to make amends?*" The good man replies: "Be abject." But, most fortunately, abjection *is not* a solution. In fact, it is the very state into which Genet has fallen and which he would like to get out of. He likewise rejects madness; the child is too upright, too real, too "willful" to make shift with imaginary escapes. He will consent neither to transferring guilt to other objects, nor to compensating for the original conflict by ideas of grandeur, nor to fleeing into a dream world. Madness does not pay. He did think of suicide. A little boy recently wrote to his parents: "Dear Daddy and Mama, I'm going to give you a nice surprise. I'm going to kill myself." And he did. The investigation concluded that the child had been mentally deficient. That was the best solution, unless the parents were sent to jail. I would bet that Genet must have thought more than once of giving his foster parents that nice surprise. The child steals, he is caught, he kills himself, that is, he carries the sentence of exclusion which society has delivered against him to its ultimate consequences. In so doing he anticipates the adults' desires and at the same time revenges himself on the adults, like the punished child who chastises his mother by depriving himself of dessert. It was, I think, Genet's optimism that kept him from adopting this conclusion in reality. I mean thereby to designate the very orientation of his freedom. Beyond certain limits of horror, honest minds are no longer sensitive to anything but the absurdity of the world. Their deaths are exemplary. But there are others who cling like vermin. Even in concentration camps they won't die. They have a deep, inner conviction that life has a meaning, that it must have one. The more horrible their situation, the tighter their grip. The more absurd the world is today, the more necessary it is to hold out until tomorrow. Tomorrow, dawn will break. The present darkness is warrant of the fact. Genet is one of these. This austere and desolate soul has the will to survive his shame and is certain that he will win out. He will later say, in *Miracle of the Rose,* that in the most hopeless situations he always had an unreasoned conviction that they would offer a way out. But his original situation is the worst of all. And there is no way out of it. Since he does not kill himself, there *must* be one, despite the evidence.

I WILL BE THE THIEF

Pinned by a look, a butterfly fixed to a cork, he is naked, everyone can see him and spit on him. The gaze of the adults is a *constituent power* which has transformed him into a *constituted nature*. He now has to live. In the pillory, with his neck in an iron collar, he still has to live. We are not lumps of clay, and what is important is not what people make of us but what we ourselves make of what they have made of us. By virtue of the option which they have taken on his being, the decent folk have made it necessary for a child to decide about himself prematurely. We can surmise that this decision will be of capital importance. Yes, one *must* decide. To kill oneself is also to decide. He has chosen to live; he has said, in defiance of all, I will be the Thief. I deeply admire this child who grimly *willed* himself at an age when *we* were merely playing the servile buffoon. So fierce a will to survive, such pure courage, such mad confidence within despair will bear their fruit. Twenty years later, this absurd determination will produce the poet Jean Genet.

So he has chosen the worst. He had no other choice. His life is all laid out: it will be a journey to the end of misfortune. He will later write: "I decided to be what crime made of me." Since he cannot escape fatality, he will be his own fatality; since they have made life unlivable for him, he will live this impossibility of living as if he had created it expressly for himself, a particular ordeal reserved for him alone. He wills his destiny; he will try to love it. How did this solution occur to him? I do not know. It came from the heart, no doubt of that. Moreover, he had been preparing himself for it by the game of saintliness. As an abandoned child he wished to attain the inhuman out of resentment toward men. They are casting him into it. Perfect. It was certainly not *that kind of inhuman* that he desired. He wanted to transcend the human condition, and he was relegated to a level below humanity. But in any case he was ready for an exceptional destiny. He dreamt of ordeals surmounted, of asceticism, of endless torments. Here they are, the ordeals and the torments! Perhaps the road to the heights and the road to the depths are one and the same. Perhaps they meet somewhere outside the world. Surely misfortune is a cipher, surely it *indicates* something. But it is not a matter of understanding; Evil must be lived unto death.

This conversion can be situated between the ages of ten and fifteen. I imagine it kept beginning anew, over and over. Again and again the child pledged himself to Evil in a state of rage, and then one of his judges had only to smile at him and the decision melted in the fire of love. I imagine too that he was afraid, afraid of himself and of the future. Then, at times, he would writhe in his bonds, he wanted *to awaken.* "I wanted to back up. Stop! No go! . . . I wanted to turn back the clock, to undo what I'd done, to live my life over until before the crime. It looks easy to go backward— but my body couldn't do it."* And then, one day, he found himself converted, exactly as one finds oneself cured of a passion that has caused long suffering. Converted, illumined, confirmed. Impossible to turn back. The paradox of every conversion is that it spreads over years and gathers together in an instant. He decided to be what he was, or, to put it otherwise, the matter was decided within him. He seizes upon the curse which goes back to the depths of his past, of his mother's past, and which has continued to the very present, and he projects it before him: it will be his future. It was a constraint; he makes of it his mission. He saw it as the raw fact of a tainted heredity; it becomes a value, an imperative. I was a thief, *I will be the Thief.* That is my profession of faith, it will be my martyrdom. He needed rules, precepts, advice; he loved the constraint of Good. He will now establish a black ethic, with precepts and rules, pitiless constraints, a Jansenism of Evil. But he will

* Green Eyes, in *Deathwatch.*

not thereby reject the simple-minded, theological morality of property owners. His system of values will be grafted on this morality and will develop on it like a cancer.

Some may regard this attitude as the defiance of the sulking child who boasts of the misdeeds of which he is accused. And what if it were? Does anyone think that this ten-year-old was going to react like a man of forty? Certainly, if Genet chose this defense he did so because it was within his scope. But when a systematized, hardened sulking holds out for ten years, thirty years, when it is at the root of the most singular, the most beautiful of poetic achievements, when it changes into a world system, into an occult religion, then it must singularly transcend the level of a simple childish reaction, a man's freedom must be thoroughly involved in it. To many sensible persons who are quite aware of the relativity of mores and beliefs and who make an effort to practice tolerance, the old ideas of Good and Evil—of Evil, in particular, with its demoniacal flavor—will seem old-fashioned, antiquated, irritating in their puerility.* All the same, it is not Genet they should attack, but rather the peasants who brought him up. Genet retains these antique notions with which he was inculcated in his early years as if they were a carapace. But underneath he has matured, aged. He is not an old child, he is a man who expresses a man's ideas in the language of childhood. If we want to understand what he is today and what he writes, we must go back to this original choice and try to give a phenomenological description of it.

Let us first situate it, for it is historical, as is the slightest of our gestures. Little Genet cares not a rap about history. Later, he will substitute mythologies for it. Nevertheless, his conversion involves him in history, for it expresses both his particularity and that of our age, which are indissolubly linked.

One of the most manifest characteristics of contemporary societies is that they are composed of heterogeneous groups, some of which still display archaic structures and others of which foreshadow a future that we can barely imagine. In India, the most modern forms of industry coexist with the most ancient form of polytheism. The same individuals belong at the same time to the most diverse groups and refer simultaneously to symbolic systems of very different, often incommunicable, types. We know about the conflicts, the outlandish syntheses, the revolts to which these contradictory allegiances give rise in individual minds. In France, the

---

* I, for my part, do not go so far. Or rather I do not pose the question as they do.

contrasts are less pronounced.* Nevertheless, Genet's misfortune
and conversion can be explained only by a *tension* between incompatible groups and ethical systems.

First, let us recognize that the pitiless and absurd sentence which
is imposed upon the child can come only from a strongly knit group
with a system of strict and simple prohibitions. Only such a community can react with righteous indignation—that is, by imposing
diffuse, repressive sanctions—to the petty pilferings of a ten-year-
old thief. Genet's "original crisis" can be understood only within
a village framework. Later, he will feel disconcerted by the popu-
lations of cities. Intimidated by the urban proletariat, he will see
the bourgeois as his natural enemies since it is they who make the
laws and control the police, but it will be very difficult for him to
find in their features the terrible visage of the Judge who condemned him for life. He will—not without a certain insincerity—
accuse the liberal bourgeoisie, in particular, of not dealing with
crime severely enough. The reason is that he does not find in the
city the simplistic and puerile ethics of the countryside. He feels
obscurely that he is in danger there, he is afraid of undergoing
corrupting influences, of relaxing, of forgetting the hatred and
despair that have become his reasons for living. In the city, among
snobs or intellectuals, the moral and religious drama which he
lived in suffering may come to seem to him an old anachronistic
dream.

Yet it was the urban masses, bourgeois culture and, above all,
the bureaucracy that, from a distance, exercised an attraction upon
him and that facilitated his effort to liberate himself. In a purely
agricultural society, he would have been irremediably lost. His
conversion is not even conceivable if one does not imagine an
incipient disintegration in the small village community which
brought him up and then banished him. What saves the child is
his obscure awareness that he has been *loaned* to these farmers.
Not long before, he was grieved at not belonging to them completely, of not having been born amidst them, and it was this
feeling of being *different* that led him to theft. At present, it is this
same feeling that makes his condemnation less terrible. The child
knows that he was born in Paris, that he belongs to an administrative body whose center is in the capital and whose network extends
throughout France. He knows that his stay in the country is bound

---

* But one would find the strangest conflicts in the mind of an Italian "progressive" who
was brought up in a Calabrian village and works in a Milan factory.

to be provisional and that, in accordance with its policy, the National Foundling Society will later recall him and apprentice him. He knows that he is dual in his objective reality: to the decent folk who surround him, he is an individual, little Jean, but somewhere in an office, four or five hundred miles away from his village, he is a number, *any child whatever*. This objective duality facilitates the effecting of the inner dissociation that will save him. If he is able to adopt a reflective attitude toward the propensities which are attributed to him, it is because he can find in his administrative anonymity a recourse against the particular idea that the villagers have of him. The peasants oblige him to *internalize* their sentence: he is an *evil* nature. Very well, but by the same movement he will internalize the objective indications conferred upon him by the National Foundling Society; the pure abstract number—assimilated, converted—which he is in the files of the Main Office changes into an abstract form of subjectivity. The foundling in Genet becomes a universal subject. In the period of sweet, natural confusion the remote existence of this Office acted like a leaven of anxiety in the child's heart because it prevented his integration into the group, but at present this urban, bureaucratic background furnishes him with a vague alibi, a recourse. He thus relives within himself the age-old conflict between the French city and countryside, and we find even in his works a primitive, almost archaic mythology, the themes of which are taken up and worked upon by a refined logic, by a townsman's sophistry. The following lines of Lévi-Strauss* are peculiarly applicable to him: "Every culture can be regarded as a body of symbolic systems in the forefront of which are language, marriage rules, economic relationships, art, science, religion. . . . [These systems] always remain incommensurable. . . . History introduces alogeneous elements into them, determines the shiftings of one society toward another and the inequalities in the relative rate of evolution of each particular system. . . . Any society is thus comparable to a universe in which only discrete masses are highly structured. Thus, in any society it is inevitable that a percentage— a variable one, be it added—of individuals find themselves placed, as it were, outside of any system or between two or more irreducible systems. The group asks and even requires that these individuals represent certain forms of compromise which cannot be achieved on the collective level, that they simulate imaginary transitions and embody incompatible syntheses."

---

* Lévi-Strauss: *Introduction à l'œuvre de Marcel Mauss.* (From Marcel Mauss: *Sociologie et Anthropologie.*)

Born in the heart of the city—in the fifth district—he is transplanted to the country. Driven from the country, he takes refuge in the city. Later, he will go from one to the other in order to escape legal prosecution, to get away from the police. Without fixed residence, without family, without work, even more of a vagabond than a thief, Genet, even in the fields, retains in his eyes the hues of the urban landscape. Even in the city streets he maintains close bonds with nature and the fields. Between these two groups which have not the same morphology, the same techniques, the same historical evolution or the same values he "represents a compromise which cannot be achieved," he "embodies an imaginary synthesis." That is why he is one of us, that is why he has "something to say to us." For we are all torn, like him, between the exigencies of an ethic *inherited* from individual property and a collectivistic ethic in the process of formation.

These considerations aim only at showing the objective factors of his sensibility. But the act itself whereby he takes a stand against the grownups and outdoes their condemnation is historical in its deeper intention. It is the typical reaction of all groups of untouchables when they have reached a certain stage of culture, that is, when they have achieved sufficient self-awareness to oppose their oppressors without having the means of imposing a change in their status. Lacking the means of overthrowing the existing order, they conceive no other and think only of demanding that they be integrated into the society which rejects them. But when they have realized that it rejects them forever, they themselves assume the ostracism of which they are victims so as not to leave the initiative to their oppressors: "It's not that you refuse to admit us, it's that we don't deign to join you." Their rebellion, unable to express itself by a concrete action, remains within the framework of a "dependency complex" and takes the form of an inner break. They admire nothing so much as the values, culture and mores of the privileged castes. They continue to view themselves with the concepts and according to the pattern furnished by their persecutors. But instead of bearing their stigma shamefully, they display it proudly. "Dirty nigger!" says a Negro poet. "Very well, I *am* a dirty nigger and I like my blackness better than your whiteness." In short, they become separatists because separation is forced upon them. This inner revolution is *realistic* because it maintains itself deliberately within the framework of existing institutions; the oppressed reckon with the real situation. They aim, as Descartes advises, to change themselves rather than the universe. But it is, at the same time, *idealistic,* for it entails no real improvement in the condition of the pariahs. In limiting himself to willing proudly that which is, in transforming an actual situation ("I'm excluded from the group") into an ethical imperative ("Therefore, I must take the initiative of withdrawing"), the untouchable is playing the game of the privileged class. The original form of the proud, lonely and ineffectual demand, which might be called the ethical stage of revolt, is *dignity.* With dignity the oppressed contains himself, affectedly, within the bounds that have been set for him and that he cannot overstep even if he wanted to. He remains in his place conspicuously when nobody has requested him to leave it. Dignity makes passivity a challenge and presents inertia as active rebellion. It is liquidated whenever conditions exist for an actual struggle.

In the case of Genet as in that of untouchables, for example the Negroes of Virginia, we find the same injustice (the latter are grandsons of slaves, the former is an abandoned child), reinforced by the same magical concepts (the "inferior race," the "evil nature" of the Negro, of the thief), and the same angry powerlessness that obliges them to adopt these concepts and turn them against their oppressors, in short the same passive revolt, the same realism masking the same idealism. Genet's *dignity* is the demand for evil.

As a *realist,* he wants to win or lose in *this* world. Rimbaud wanted to change life, and Marx to change society. Genet does not want to change anything at all. Do not count on him to criticize institutions. He needs them, as Prometheus needs his vulture. At most, he regrets that there is no longer an aristocracy in France and that class justice is not more ruthless. If, thinking to please him, one transported him into some future society that gave him a place of honor, he would feel frustrated. His business is here; it is here that he is despised and vilified; it is here that he must carry out his undertaking. He loves French society as the Negroes love America, with a love that is full of hatred and, at the same time, desperate. As for the social order which excludes him, he will do everything to perpetuate it. Its rigor must be perfect so that Genet can attain perfection in Evil. In short, he is realistic because he wants what is, in fact because he wants to want it. To live is now to watch himself live. It is to acquire a deeper understanding of his condition every single instant, as a whole and in its details, in order to assume it unreservedly, whatever it may be. He takes his bearings every second. Duality is the permanent structure of his consciousness. He seeks *himself* and wills *himself.* His spontaneity dwindles. To feel and to watch himself feel are to him one and the same. He inspects his feelings and his behavior in order to discover in them that dark vein, the will to evil. He checks them or drives them to extremes. He works away at himself in order to correspond more and more closely, every day, to others' opinion of him. Never again will he coincide with himself. Imagine a terrified cabin boy who has taken refuge at the top of a mast and who, from on high, is fascinated by the inky sea below, always ready to let himself fall into it and never letting go of the mast to which he clings. Such, henceforth, is Genet's inner landscape, although we must add that if the sea whips up enormous waves it is because the cabin boy is blowing on it. A passage in *Funeral Rites* will help us understand. Pierrot has inadvertently put a maggot into his mouth: "He found himself caught between fainting with nausea and dominating his situation by willing it. He willed it. He made his tongue and palate artfully and patiently feel the loathsome contact. This act of willing was his first poetic attitude governed by pride. He was ten years old."

He has to be able to "take everything," to dominate the situation. One can imagine in what an arid, desertlike climate this fierce will is going to make the child live. Rage, tears, despair, anything would be better than this fixed obstinacy. But Pierrot refuses to faint. Genet thrusts aside the idea of suicide and such substitutes for it as bursting into tears or fleeing into madness. He contains himself. Life becomes a choice; it is death, known, experienced and rejected. But the fact is that life is impossible; the *only* possibility was death. Henceforth, the child will therefore live in defiance of death, that is, in defiance of fact. Every pulse-beat will be conquered against the desire to efface himself from the world. He will be like Clément, that other hero of Genet who has just killed his girl friend and who undertakes to wall her up: "He worked like a sleepwalker, preoccupied and determined; he refused to see the gulf in order to escape from dizzying madness. . . . He knew that if he flinched, that is, if he relaxed that attitude, an attitude as severe as a bar of steel, he would have sunk. Sunk, that is, run to the police station and melted into tears." To sink—that is what Genet fears. To sink—to recognize the impossibility of his attitude, of his being, to become human again, to recognize men's gentle exigencies, and their tenderness. If he is only a man, he has lost; he will be unable to bear life. The runner of Marathon died long before reaching Athens. Though dead, he kept going. And so with Genet: he keeps going; if he stops for a moment, he will remember that he is dead. He contains himself; his extreme politeness, his prelate-like unction (shot through with lightning) , his very violence, which is never a first impulse,

everything reveals that the will to live has everywhere been substituted for life. He does not know life's pleasures because in order to
know them one must let oneself go; he does not drink because in
drunkenness one abandons oneself. He dedicates himself to life;
he enters it as one enters orders. This will to live must be as abstract, as rigorous, as pure as Kantian good will: and it is precisely
evil will.

Idealism: all this leads only to verifying the grownups' judgment,
just as the proud demand for "negritude" merely confirms segrega-
tion. Genet's "evil nature" existed at first only as a result of universal consent. His judges thought that they knew his nature, and
Genet believed his judges. He now strives to create it. Each of his
individual actions is going to give body to this phantom. He steals
everywhere and against everybody; he is the despair of those who
are bringing him up; he spares nothing and nobody. But this aggressiveness should not mislead us. It is purely defensive, it is the
defiance of impotence. Genet steals because they think he is a thief.
"Poetic attitude governed by pride." Perhaps. But he has also written: "Pride means nothing. . . . No pride without guilt." Pride is
the reaction of a mind which has been beleaguered by others and
which transforms its absolute dependency into absolute self-sufficiency. Simone de Beauvoir has pointed out that, around the age
of fifteen, girls often force themselves to touch repulsive insects and
sometimes put them to their mouths. One of the girls to whom she
refers in *The Second Sex* resembles Pierrot rather closely. She had
unwittingly eaten half of a worm that happened to be on a lettuce
leaf; she made herself eat the other half. We know the reason for
these exercises. Out of a mixture of hatred, curiosity and defiance,
these adolescents are making an effort to perform symbolically and
through their own initiative the act of deflowering, the obscure
presentiment of which is sufficient to fill them with horror and
which they know will be imposed upon them. Genet and these
young girls have in common the fact that their only recourse is to
will what is. In any case, the die is cast. Genet is a thief, the girls
will be deflowered. Since they are unable to escape the future in
store for them, all they can do is refuse to *undergo* it. Sentenced to
death, they demand the right to give the order to fire that will kill
them. Since men's contempt is inevitable, it must be provoked. A
newcomer who does not know who I am is friendly to me. There is
no time to lose. Any minute now people are going to start nudging
him and putting him on guard against me. I've got to steal his
watch or his money right away in order to disappoint his friendly

feeling for me, so that he will learn *from me* that I'm a monster.

This eagerness to discourage reciprocity will be called sneakiness, treachery. *We* know that it is *dignity*. To the "generous" whites who do not draw the color line the Negro says: "Come, come, you see very well that I'm a Negro. Remain in your place as I remain in mine." And Genet, in like manner, says to the bourgeois liberal who wants to help him, perhaps to "re-educate" him: "You see for yourself that I'm bad. The proof is that I've taken your watch." The common characteristic of these reactions of defensive aggressiveness is that they come too late. It is too late when Pierrot discovers the maggot in his mouth. Whatever he does, he will not prevent its having defiled him. Too late when Genet adopts the resolution to steal—he has already lost the initiative. When he launches his counterattack, the others have already organized their stand, they have occupied the avenues and public buildings. Before even dreaming of rebelling, he has already granted them the essential: that he is a thief and that theft is disgraceful. After that, his revolt is doomed to impotence and his most heinous crimes will merely justify the prison cell which they are preparing for him. Let him pillage, let him kill, he will provoke only one comment from his judges. "I predicted as much." Does he steal more often than he would have done if he had not been converted? Even that is not certain. He was condemned to theft, he would have stolen out of fear, out of resentment, out of confusion, out of bewilderment, out of need. Only one thing has changed, the inner meaning of his pilfering. In a carousel, a troop of horsemen are pursuing a rider. By dint of a supreme effort, the latter gains a few yards. He is equidistant from the vanguard and rearguard of his pursuers. This is perhaps enough for him to imagine that he is giving chase to them, but this is a point of view which remains personal to him. The Others will notice nothing.

Nothing! He has done nothing, they have seen nothing. This hard, cynical realism remains totally ineffectual precisely because it is striving to will the totality of the real. The pariah's intentness, his untenable contention, are, in the last analysis, only a change of mood. We shall deal more fully with this strange metamorphosis of absolute realism into absolute idealism. It is this transformation that will enable us to understand why the life of this evildoer who wants to be active, lucid and effectual has little by little changed into a daydream.

I DECIDED TO BE WHAT CRIME MADE OF ME

We have situated Genet's decision in its objective bearings. We know what it is in *itself*. We must now see what it is for him, that is, as a subjective moment of his conscious life. What does this will to be evil mean to Genet himself, what is its intentional structure? As soon as we begin to approach the problem, we discover an insurmountable contradiction.

"I decided to be what crime made of me." In this seemingly very simple statement there is "to decide." But there is also "to be." Now, the purpose of a decision is to effect a change in the world; a decision goes beyond what already is toward that which is not yet. To decide to be a teacher is to prepare for the necessary examinations; to decide to be a soldier is to enlist. But if I already am a professional soldier, I cannot decide to be one, for this decision will not effect the slightest change in reality. And if I persist in willing that which is, my will, gliding over the real without finding anything to take hold of, unable even to begin to be implemented, changes into a pure verbal determination. How could Genet *will* to be evil since he believes that he is *already evil* by nature and that he has no means of preventing his essence from being or of making it be. Yet the word "be" assumes in his writing an active, transitive value. In the sentence which I have quoted, to be is to throw oneself into one's being in order to coincide with it. The word suggests a compromise between the calm coinciding of an object with its essence and the storm-tossed development whereby a man fulfills himself. And I am aware that I can yield to the urge of a calling and become a sailor or a poet. In that case, it can be said, not without a certain impropriety, that I have become what I was, that is, that my life has gradually realized certain gifts which existed in me in the virtual state. But what if I already am what I am? What if I am enclosed, locked up, in my being? What can I *decide?*

The fact is, nothing is so simple. Obviously, if men existed in the manner of tables or chairs, there would be no question for them of acquiring their being. They *would be,* that is all. The twofold nature of Genet's undertaking comes from the ambiguity of our condition, for we are beings whose being is perpetually in question. Or, to put it otherwise, our way of being is to be in question in our being. Nobody is cowardly or brave in the way that a wall is white or a blanket green. To the most cowardly man, cowardice always manifests itself as a *possibility;* he can consent to it, reject it, flee it, find it even in actions that others consider daring, experience it without participating in it, etc. Thus, the paradoxical expression "to want to be what one is" can be meaningful: it may refer to the efforts we make to coincide with our being. In the case of Genet it would imply that he plunges with all his weight and force into the evil of which the others accuse him. And, no doubt, there *is that* in his decision. However, the fact remains that every decision emanates from a pure and unqualified freedom which aims at giving itself a being, though without ever quite succeeding. But the *being* which Genet thinks he has received from grownups is *already made.* As he sees it, it is a complex of real qualities and tendencies all of which impel to Evil. It is a *substance,* in the Cartesian sense of the word, as in the expression "thinking substance." It is his soul, the governing principle of his behavior, his entelechy. It is a *person* in the Latin sense of *persona*—I mean a mask and a role whose behavior and speeches are already set down. It is the Other, it is a "zar," which possesses him, an unconscious which, like that of psychoanalysis, proposes, imposes, uses trickery and outwits the precautions one takes against it. This complex reality has at least one simple characteristic: its being *is not in question,* it is stable and fixed, like that of objects. In short, it is a being *in itself* and *for others,* but it is not a being-for-itself. In his decision to be what they have made of him, Genet thus forcibly couples a pure will which will define him *afterward* by the totality of his acts, and a substance which is pre-existent to his actions and which produces them out of a kind of inner necessity, as consequences follow from a theorem. These two terms conflict: can one imagine a Spinozistic mode having abstract freedom in order to will or reject itself? All his acts of will issue from his being, and he cannot perform a single such act which is not implied in his being as the consequence of a mathematical concept is implied in its definition. If Genet is a "nature," everything is comprised in that nature, including the movement he makes to turn to it and lay claim to it. If Genet has the power to claim his essence, then he also has the power to reject it, to change it. He is free, and his nature is only a myth or a decoy. In short, Genet wants both to make himself evil because he does Evil and to do Evil because he is evil. This contradictory attitude is obviously the effect of his pride. People heap abuse upon him because he has stolen and because he is bad. He replies, "Yes, I'm bad and proud of it," and at the same time, "Yes, I've stolen. And I'll steal again." Nevertheless, the fact remains that he wants *everything at the same time:* to generate Evil *ex nihilo* by a sovereign decision and to produce it by natural necessity. To be at one and the same time Satan and pestilence; to be endowed with free will and slave will at the same time and in the same connection. This is so because he desires the worst and because he does not know which is more abominable, a mind possessed, all of whose intentions turn, despite itself, to crime, or a free mind which does wrong knowingly. Unable to choose, he yokes two incompatible world systems: substance and will, soul and consciousness, magic and freedom, concept and judgment. If he is free, each of his acts contributes to the drawing of his figure, but one cannot say that he is evil before the moment of his death. If he is not free, he is totally evil at every moment of his life, but he is no longer guilty.

One can readily imagine the emotional drive that impelled the child to choose at the same time two attitudes which cannot coexist. He had to achieve self-mastery, autonomy of will, lest he go mad, and to find a sanctuary in which the Other had not already installed himself. To affirm his sovereignty was to save his mental integrity. Against the dark forces that were hemming him in and that he suddenly found within himself when he least expected, he had to cry out: But it's me, me Genet, me all by myself, who want what I want, who do what I do. But he had no intention of liberating from Evil the freedom of will he was discovering within himself. While affirming his autonomy in self-defense, he challengingly insists on his badness. *Yes,* he is free, they won't succeed in convincing him otherwise; *yes,* he is bad, and even more than they think.

Be this as it may, the two terms, united by the same psychic reaction, borne up by the same movement, are nonetheless irreducible. At times the substance will be dissolved in the will, and at others the will will be estranged from substance. The fact is that there are in Genet two irreducible systems of values, two tables of categories which he uses simultaneously in order to reflect upon the world.

1. Categories of *Being*	2. Categories of *Doing*
Object	Subject, consciousness
Oneself as Other	Self as oneself
Essential which proves inessential	Inessential which proves essential
Fatality	Freedom, will
Tragedy	Comedy
Death, disappearance	Life, will to live
Hero	Saint
Criminal	Traitor
Beloved one	Lover
Male principle	Female principle

How can one be surprised at this duality of principles? Is not Genet himself an aberrant synthesis of two attitudes? As a product of both the naïve substantialism of rural areas and the rationalism of cities, does he not belong to two groups at the same time? As an anonymous ward of the National Foundling Society, he adopts the point of view of the universal, autonomous subject in order to consider the particular figure of little Jean Genet, adopted child of Morvan peasants.

This contradiction puts us into a difficult position. We ought, in all logic, to pursue our study from two points of view at the same time, but if we did we would inevitably fall into confusion. We shall therefore examine separately the intention of being and that of doing. In the present chapter we shall take Genet's conversion at its source and give a cross section of the two divergent intentions in order to make a surface examination of them in the instantaneousness of their emergence. The result will be, so to speak, a *static* description. But as we must not lose sight of the fact that these intentions coexist in the false unity conferred upon them by consciousness, we shall indicate, in a third section, the immediate and confused relationship that unites them.

However, this double decision does not remain inert. It lives, it changes, it grows richer over the years, it is transformed by contact with experience and by the dialectic of each of the components. We shall have to follow it in its evolution. That is what we shall attempt to do in the following chapters. There, too, it would be more in accordance with reality to study this pseudo-totality in its syncretic wholeness. However, the overlapping of the dialectic of doing and that of being which, from without, influence and react upon each other would render our exposition unintelligible. We shall have to expound them separately, to follow them one after the other in their temporal development over the decade following the conversion and to determine the extent to which each of them contributes to *make the history* of Genet. In a later chapter of this section, we shall attempt to get our bearings and, having familiarized ourselves with Genet's double postulation, shall endeavor to bring these partial analyses together and, by a study of the reciprocal action of *doing* and *being,* reconstitute the concrete totality of this inner experience.

1. The Intention of Being

He wants to have an intuition of himself. This subject wants to make himself an absolute object to himself; this consciousness wants to become both being and consciousness of being. Being is his desire, his wish, above all, his fundamental possibility. His life will be only an ontological adventure, and it is in terms of being that he will launch the challenge which will determine it: he does not say that he will steal but that he *will be* the thief. This thief is a stealing substance as the mind is a thinking substance. Men do not act: what we call their acts are simple attributes of the substance they embody.

The thing for him to do, therefore, is to *encounter* this substance which defines him. At the origin of this quest is a kind of passive and contemplative state of mind: one must be open to Being as the mystic is open to his God. Genet, haunted by that Other who is himself, senses the sacred through his own consciousness. The revelation of his Being will have the characteristics of a hierophany; it will wrest him from the human, from everyday life. It will be a religious experience, a communion. Is not the religious moment par excellence that in which a subjectivity, ceasing to disperse itself indefinitely in everyday reality, regains its eternal being, becomes a calm totality in full possession of itself? Eternity invades the state of flux, the absolute manifests itself, something new happens beneath the sun. Genet will escape from the trivial world of morality and reach the world of religion through a mystical experience. He has already set the conditions of the experience: he must encounter himself as what he is and as a *de facto* necessity. His being will be delivered up to him in an intuition of the same kind as the Cartesian *cogito,* but broader, for he does not wish to discover himself as a simple thinking substance but as a sacred, demoniacal reality. The intuition will be not merely a fact of thought but also a fact of the heart, a sexual fact. It will be achieved only through the amorous resignation of the will, which must turn over and *open up,* for the eagerly awaited being is a person, the actual person of Genet, the active principle that makes use of him to commit his crimes. The garrulous and amorous consciousness will passively receive its visitation; it will enter the consciousness as a lover enters his mistress; consciousness will love this being as the woman loves the male, as the faithful love their God. Is not this love precisely the horror which has been overcome? It *will be his being* by virtue of a mystic marriage. The contempt and hatred of the Just will serve to cement the union. To love each other amidst hoots and jeers and to draw from that love the strength to feel invulnerable —that is the aim. We find here the postulation of the mystics which is often defined as the quest of a state in which subject and object, consciousness and being, the eternal and the particular, merge in an absolute undifferentiation. This little scrounger aspires to the sacred moment in which he will be penetrated, torn apart, by the great and terrible essence of the Evildoer and in which he will no longer know whether his consciousness is a simple phosphorescence of this eternal essence or whether the eternal essence is the object of his consciousness.

Nevertheless, his passivity has its limits. Like mystical quietism, like Bergsonian intuitionism, it must be accompanied by a systematic and discursive labor of *preparation.* The Miracle must be solicited, one must become a prey in order to tempt the angelic Visitor, or at least one must purify oneself so as to be worthy of his Visit. In the last analysis, it is on the world that one refuses to act. And not even that: one will launch upon undertakings if one foresees that they may have happy effects on one's inner life. In short, quietism is not so much total inaction as it is activity aimed at making us passive. Genet wants the swift stream of his consciousness to freeze and crystallize into being. By means of a rigorously observed etiquette he attempts to confer upon himself, in his own eyes, an objectivity that flees him. He works upon his feelings in order to endow them with the stubbornness, bareness, silence and plenitude of the object. While exalting his sensibility, he secretly withdraws from it and attempts to examine it with borrowed eyes. He publicly reveals his most secret purpose; his existence is a ceremony. Whatever he may do, whatever he may think, he dissociates himself from himself and quickly makes himself Another in order to *catch himself unaware* as Another or to *be caught unaware* by his Other-Being. Thus, this too-deliberate passivity changes into willfulness. As a result of his wanting his states of mind to be too strongly felt, they are never entirely felt. At the core, so to speak, of this unbearable tension there is always an absence of the heart, a kind of distractedness. The reason is that he is *in a state of waiting:* both hunter and prey, he sets himself out like bait and lies in wait for the voracious bird to swoop down on him and be caught in the trap. While observing himself, he makes an effort to feel. It is not enough to be moved; the mental state must be perfect, as depraved and execrable as possible. On the one hand, he takes precautions against his feelings by becoming the spectator of them; on the other, he forces them in order to make them exemplary. Never again will he yield to passion, to surprise. Never again will he simply *feel* emotion as the result of an external cause. At most, certain events will be an opportunity for him to set in motion a complex and carefully adjusted mechanism whose purpose is to trap being. Between the world and him there is henceforth himself. As Gide has said, one can never know to what extent one feels and to what extent one plays at feeling, and this ambiguity constitutes the sentiment. Never has this been so true as in the case of this circumspect, close-grained little man who is bent on receiving only what comes from his will. He gains from these ceremonies a classicism of mind. Everything about him is measured, temperate, carefully wrought. This wicked and desolate soul has the look of a formal French garden. The Devil is classical.

This whole effort ends in failure. The soul is prepared for the visitation, but the angel does not come. It never comes; it is only an absence. Genet suffers continuously from this absence which dims the universe and preys on his mind. What he calls his Ego is this absence itself, the irritating indication of an intention forever promised and never fulfilled. It is a certain way of making appointments with himself at every corner, at every bend of the road, on all objects, in all gazes, and of never turning up, of remaining a fleeting silhouette on which a door has just closed and regarding which he cannot be sure whether he has caught a glimpse of it or merely assumed its presence. Thus, the decision to *be,* to receive his being like manna, in a state of blessed passivity, becomes a state of tension in a vacuum, a brief quest, vain and fruitless, a pure and abstract act of will. Since *being* is only the ever-retreating horizon of these minute preparations, the decision to coincide with his own nature fades away, disclosing this unceasing activity of a lost soul or of an ant. Being gives way to doing.

2. The Intention of Doing

We suddenly move to the other extreme. What Genet now demands is the contrary of a Nature: the autonomy of his will. This ought not to surprise us. When he lays claim to the nature that is ascribed to him, he is defiantly defending himself against the presence of a tribunal which has wormed its way into his heart. But when he wants to change himself into a pure will, it is in order to retrieve his own life, which the others have taken away from him. Ever since he was caught stealing, he has been the plaything of external forces. He is hunted, locked up, released, locked up again, transported from one end of France to the other. It is as if a raging sea were tossing him from shore to shore. He lands nowhere. His life literally *has no direction*. What is it if not this absurd hustle and bustle, this useless hubbub, this roving, this superficial agitation? One might reply that at least he takes the initiative when he steals. Hardly so: the punishment is out of proportion to the offense. He *did not want* to be that parentless, degenerate child; he *did not want* to be condemned by the people of the village; he *did not want* the government officials to take him back, to put him into a reformatory, to take him out of it, to put him back again. As he later said, the thefts seemed to be born of circumstances themselves, of objects; things are sometimes laid out in such a way as to suggest a theft, to beget it in the thief's body. And as soon as the offense is committed, the social world reveals its true face: an "ineluctable" sequence leads him to prison. No, Genet does not have the feeling of being free. At times it seems to him that he is witnessing his own life as if it were someone else's.

That is precisely why he had no resort other than to determine to will it. Green Eyes struggled for a long time against the fatality that had made a murderer of him. In vain. But from the moment he "simply made the gestures that led him as quietly as can be to the guillotine," "everything was easy." Therefore, the only way for Genet to regain his life is to will it as it is. Not for this or that particular reason, not because it is beautiful or adventurous or tragic, but simply in order to manifest himself in it as a sovereign will. In ruining his hopes, in revealing existence to him as an irremediable succession of calamities, misfortune produced in him the same result as reflective analysis produces in a Kantian: he eliminated all the imaginable motives of his act. Whatever he may spontaneously desire—wealth, happiness or simply tranquillity—he knows that such good fortune is forbidden him. Everything is born of Evil, everything turns into misery. Hence, the material content of his acts becomes a matter of complete indifference to him. It is not a question of willing this or that but of laying claim to whatever does harm to him in the world. Thus, there gradually emerges the notion of a pure will which wills itself unconditionally evil. The imperatives of this will might be summarized in four maxims:

1. "View each event, even—and particularly—if it is harmful, as if it were a product of your unconditioned will and a gratuitous gift which you had decided to make yourself."

2. "Let your chief motive be, on every occasion, the horror that your future act inspires in others and in yourself."

3. "Act in such a way that society always treats you as an object, a means, and never as an end, as a person."

4. "Act as if the maxim governing each of your acts were to serve as a rule in the den of thieves."

Is this a matter of a mere mental exercise without objective bearing? No, not quite. If he cannot improve his condition, he has leisure to make it worse. He will find a semblance of activity on the basis of his misfortune. He will strive to carry it as far as he can in order to be sure at least that he alone is responsible for it. Pierrot cannot prevent the maggot's being in his mouth, but he can suck it, he can eat it. Genet will invent exquisite tortures for himself, will refuse himself all hope, will impose vile contacts on himself, will besot himself with misfortune. He will have no tastes other than the distastes which he has overcome, and if he feels more delicate desires, he will tolerate them only in order to turn them into instruments of torture. Although it is pure freedom which is at stake in both cases, it would be an error to confuse this eagerness to desire the worst with Stoic will. If the Stoic declares that he *wills* the world, it is because he believes the world is good. But Genet feeds on misfortune and remains convinced that the universe is, at least for him, intolerable. His zeal recalls rather that of another solitary who cried out at Sils Maria that "all suffering wants eternity."

Since the decent folk depicted his destiny to him in the form of a radical and inevitable failure, since he loses his life, drop by drop, since it leaks out of him, since death will be administered to him by others and at a time chosen by them, Genet, in order to regain possession of his own existence, is going to make of this failure the product of his will. "He will make the gestures that lead him" to prison, if not to the guillotine. This is a game in which the loser wins. As a result, this defeat, which has been prepared for, meditated, carried to an extreme, will change, in the esoteric religion of the Thief, into the finest of victories.

But why stop on such an evil path? Since he wills his own misfortune, he must also will Evil. It is not enough to accept his *evil nature,* for it might, if need be, serve as an excuse. Genet owes it to himself to reject every excuse. Thus, the resort to the unconditioned will suddenly damages the relationship to Being and Essence which Genet adopted earlier. It is no longer a matter of abandoning himself to his nature or of letting himself be carried along by it. What Genet requires is Premeditation and *Consciousness in Evil.* He does not, to be sure, deny this nature—moreover, he will *never* deny it—but he wants his will to precede it. In order to take the initiative again, Genet will anticipate the impulse which he feels coming on and will leap to the crime in order to get there first. It is a race. His accursed Ego follows on his heels, he beats it by a length. Formerly, the occasion made the thief; now, it is the thief who makes the occasion. He will choose to steal when he has no desire to, like the young girl who was exasperated at having natural needs and forced herself to drink when she was not thirsty. Thus, there develops within Genet, along with the theme of the "evil nature," that of the gratuitous crime and the unconditionally evil will. In making contact with himself in this pure will, Genet seems to be nearing deliverance: everything about him disappears, save freedom. He who chooses to be wrong and who knowingly persists in being so cannot rely on collective forces, on tradition, on truth or on any kind of being. For error is *nothing.* He exhausts himself in upholding a Nothingness in solitude. The unrecognized scientist or artist dreams of future approval. When he is dead, at least his memory will be revered. But the name of the man who wants to be wrong is writ on water. The memory of him will disappear from the world with his life. He falls out of history and out of the world. If he muses on the infinite succession of the human generations that will impugn him, each in turn, it is in order proudly to confer upon himself an infinite guilt. Nevertheless, this will, which is bent on denying the evidence and on rejecting being, burns alone in defiance of all, infinitely alone, and feeds on itself. Without it, a certain contradictory, nonviable thinking would not even have come into existence. Emerging from nothingness for the purpose of supporting nothingness, this freedom knows that it will return to nothingness and is glad that it will. It can thus set up against history, which rejects it, a kind of negative eternity which is its own lot. Though rejected by all the forces of the world, crushed and finally annihilated, it did exist, and there is nothing the universe can do about it. It directs its negation against the universe; it shelves the universe. Stranded in failure, error and impotence, it decides, all by itself, against the world. Genet has felt this, and that is his greatness: he has willed his solitude, his exile and his nothingness. One step further and he would deliver himself from evil itself.

3. Doing for the Sake of Being

To adopt a mental attitude is to place oneself in a prison without bars. One seems able to escape from it at any moment, and in point of fact no wall or bars can prevent thinking from going as far as it likes. But actually, at the very moment this thinking believes that it has *gone beyond* the chosen attitude and that it is entering the world by a new path, with a new point of view entailing new commitments, it becomes aware that it has returned to its starting point. The moment Genet is about to escape from Evil, his thinking deviates. Instead of remaining on the ground of pure will, he subordinates this will to his "nature." The shackle that seems to be opening closes again. The fact is that he wanted to go even further, but he did not realize that he was retracing his steps. He had been told that his nature preceded his will; he now intends to prove to himself that he willed this nature. Child without a mother, effect without a cause, the victim of misfortune carries out, proudly and rebelliously, the superb project of being self-caused. On the occasion of a particular offense, a gaze took him by surprise and established him as a perverse nature. Genet wants to wrest from this gaze its constituent power. He commits his thefts deliberately as challenges and constitutive acts. Each of them will be both a particular, utilitarian larceny and a ceremony that revives the original crisis in the absence of the witness. By virtue of this ceremony Genet symbolically gives himself his thief's nature. It is a repetition of the crisis and of the rite of passage, a death followed by resurrection. The child *kills himself* each time in order to *come to life again* as a thief in the presence of imaginary witnesses. He stole because he "was" a thief; he now steals in order *to be* a thief. From this point on, to steal means to him to *consecrate* his thief's nature through the sovereign approbation of his freedom. That is the reason why he will later call theft a *poetic act*. Indeed, the term

must be understood in its original sense of *poiein*. By means of
theft Genet re-creates his nature and at the same time consecrates
it. But in point of fact this signifies that he agrees to give others a
hold upon him, that he voluntarily exposes himself to their gaze,
in short that he utilizes his freedom as a pure universal subject to
lower his status to that of object. And as a matter of fact, if he admires criminals so greatly, if he regrets his not daring to kill, it is
because the act of murder changes the victim into a thing and, at
the same time, the murderer into an object:

"Querelle [who has just committed murder] was the object of a
world in which danger does not exist—since one is an object. A
handsome object, motionless and somber, in the hollows of which
—for the emptiness was resonant—Querelle heard it break into
a spray, escape from him, surround and protect him . . . that astonishing object, resonant and empty, with the dark, gaping mouth . . .
and whose knees were perhaps covered with an Assyrian fleece. . . ."

Querelle is alone with a dead body; the time is night; there is
no one present to stare at his sailor trousers and wonder whether
they conceal an Assyrian fleece. Querelle is an object *in the absolute*. Why? The rest of the passage tells us: to commit a crime is to
make his objectivity exist in advance for the detectives who will
conduct the investigation, for the judges who will deliver sentence,
for the policemen and prison guards who will apply it. But what is
this congealing of the subject into an object, this extinguishing of
the lights of consciousness, what is it if not death? And, indeed,
Querelle is a "joyous moral suicide." A dead person is a being who
no longer exists for himself but only in himself, that is, through
others' opinion of him. One kills in order to be able to speak of
oneself in the third person: "Eh? Who am I? The monstrous soul
of servantdom! . . . No, Inspector, I'll explain nothing in their presence. That's *our* business. It would be a fine thing if masters could
pierce the shadows where servants live . . . that, my child, is our
darkness, ours . . . neither you nor anyone else will be told anything. Just tell yourselves that this time Solange has gone through
with it . . . you see her dressed in red. She is going out."

Solange is alone: neither Monsieur nor Madame nor the Inspector is present. They serve her as imaginary mediators, and she
thinks that, through their phantom eyes, she can at last perceive
herself as an object: "She is going out . . . she is carrying a torch
. . . she will lead the procession . . ." Genet, stealing in solitude, is
going to be confirmed in his being by causing a silent scandal. And
all at once—a further degradation—he will employ his pure free-

dom in invoking, by a magical conspiracy, the depraved Ego into which he dreams of melting.

Erik, the executioner's lover, walks up and down the room. He is naked, he washes himself, he starts to dress:

"You're handsome! . . . Every instant he awaited the cry that would strike him sharply, proving that he had just attained a point of *striking* beauty . . . he fell into the habit of knowing he was very handsome, and little by little he came to regard himself as a being who could act only in accordance with a beautiful gesture. . . . There were times when he desired to be the executioner in order to contemplate himself and to enjoy from without the beauty which he emitted: to receive it."

It does not matter that the question here is one of Beauty and not of Evil. We shall see that they come to the same thing. Both beauty and evil are pure appearance posing as absolute being. What counts is the operation. Thereafter, Erik washes and dresses every morning as usual, he "strikes no poses," that is, he does not deign to take beauty as the conscious end of his acts. But subtly, peripherally, each of his gestures, without ceasing to have a precise, utilitarian and commonplace purpose, foretokens that it is going to elicit from a mouth a cry of astonishment. Thus, while absorbing himself in practical activities, he becomes in his own eyes, which are careful to take no notice, and through the intermediary of another, "a being who can act only in accordance with a beautiful gesture." Beautiful, that is: whose beauty is the source, the substance and the end. Similarly, Genet, who likewise does not deign to strike poses and who honestly aims to do Evil for Evil's sake, adopts, stealthily, the sophism by means of which the Others have hoodwinked him: "I am," he thinks, "a Being who can act only in accordance with Evil." And while he is absorbed in doing evil, he wants to take himself by surprise, to elicit from his own throat the cry of astonishment that overwhelmed Erik. His acts are traps for being; he gives his full attention to forcing a lock, but out of the corner of his eye he steals a glance at himself. With a bit of luck, being will shimmer in his gestures, will alight in his open hand, and Genet will catch it.

We are going round in circles: Genet called forth his "nature," he was on the watch for himself in order to take his being by surprise. The necessity of bearing adversity suddenly raises him to the point of pure will. He *wants to will,* he *wants to act.* But suddenly he relapses into his obsession: he wants to act in order to be, to steal in order to be the thief, to do Evil in order to be the evildoer.

Whereupon the moment of the act and of the sovereign will disappears. An act which one performs in order to *be* is no longer an act, it is a gesture. Let us go further: the evildoer wants Evil for Evil's sake, that is, as an unconditional end. But Genet does Evil in order to be evil. Evil is therefore not the unconditional end of his undertakings, it is the means which he has chosen of being presented to his "nature." But if he *does not do* Evil, he *is not* evil. He is acting evil.

Does that mean he never commits "evil" actions? No. We are simply beginning to understand the extreme complexity of his attitude. At times he changes himself into a pure and unconditionally evil will—he then does Evil for Evil's sake, in all sovereignty, in all gratuitousness—and at times the presence within him of his ontological obsession taints his will to Evil, degrades it, transforms it into pure play acting and changes his acts into gestures. Like the mad needle of a compass, he oscillates perpetually from act to gesture, from doing to being, from freedom to nature, without ever stopping.

These attitudes are going to live and be transformed: each will have its dialectic, its historical development, its symbols. The quest of Being is going to lead Genet to homosexuality and, beyond it, to a solitude bordering on madness in which he will be tempted, for some time, to make of his "nature" his own God. The will to will is going to doom him to betrayal and, beyond that, to an even worse solitude which he will call Saintliness. It is these two contradictory processes which we are now going to study. We shall, as I said earlier, have to examine them separately. But let us bear in mind that however far this double dialectic may lead us its only source lies in Genet's conversion, that is, in his decision to accept responsibility for and to assume, by all the means at his disposal, the double malediction that was laid upon him.

THE ETERNAL COUPLE OF THE CRIMINAL
AND THE SAINT . . .

Thus, Genet seeks his Being. He looks for it first within himself; he spies on his inner life. But nothing comes of it, for the spy and what he spies on are one and the same. The first failure helps us to understand the importance which mirrors assume for him. A mirror is a consciousness in reverse. To the right-thinking man, it reveals only the appearance he offers to others. Sure of possessing the truth, concerned only with being reflected in his undertaking, he gives the mirror only this carcass to gnaw at. But for the woman and for the criminal, for all relative beings, this carcass is what is essential. If Genet looks at himself in the mirror, it is not primarily out of homosexual coquetry; he wants to understand his secret. He will later define the soul as "that which escapes from the eyes, from the tousled hair, from the mouth, from the curls, from the torso, from the penis." Let us take this to mean the psychic meanings perceived objectively in the movements of a body. The soul is the *visible* body and, at the same time, it is the being in the back of consciousness. How, after this, can one be surprised at Erik's wanting to take his soul by surprise in the mirror? "Deep inside the dark mass of his somberly clad body he guarded the name Erik Seidler, followed by a magical expression." The magical expression is: "the executioner's lover." Erik rolls it about in his head without being able to apply it to himself: how can one give a name to a transparent and mobile consciousness which *is not* anything. But finally Erik sees himself, he is going to be able to name himself. He approaches, and his soul rises up to meet him. As soon as he perceives that "dark mass": "I'm the only one who's Erik Seidler!" This name has spoken from the depths of his being, as his soul spoke from the depths of the mirror; it adheres to the dark mass, envelops it and clothes it in a dark phosphorescence. Murmuring "Genet the Thief," Genet gobbles up his reflection with his eyes. He tries to enjoy it. If only he could flatten himself against the glass so that the image could enter him entirely and he the image, if only he could, as Goethe says, put the whole outside inside and the whole inside outside, if only he could imbue that wandering soul with consciousness, could drown in the eyes of the Others and at the same time wrest his being from them in order to be possessed by it.

Vain efforts. No doubt the image of Erik appears to him at first to take on a semblance of objectivity. The mirror is as personal as an eye: "the seven bulbs of the chandelier and the four lighted bracket lamps" impart to the reflection a pompous brilliance which metamorphoses it. It is "the sparkling image of a warrior lit up with wine." For a second, Erik thinks he "is another." He finds himself to be "so handsome that he doubts that the face is his. . . ." He makes a gesture to subjugate and possess the male, to merge with him in an amorous embrace, but the mirage immediately disappears. The image docilely reflects his gesture. It is servile, inconsistent, relative, neither quite himself nor quite another. It is the impossible objectivity. He "is within an ace of losing his reason in the presence of his own beauty." He takes out his revolver and fires, in a panic at being unable to be either one or two. Narcissism? No doubt, but narcissism is not primary, any more than is pride or homosexuality: "One must first be guilty." Narcissus is at first bewitched; his being has been stolen from him. The mirror is the eyes of Others, and the dream of Narcissus expresses his secret will to pluck out those eyes and graft them on himself.

The glass is shattered, and Genet's failures teach him a lesson: one does not coincide with oneself without mediation. The mirror was an illusory mediation, but it incites to a quest of the true mediations which would confront Genet with himself and be eliminated immediately thereafter: since the thief is forbidden to enjoy his being and since others enjoy it insolently, if only he could at least possess those who possess it. Unable to enjoy it himself, if only he could enjoy the Other who enjoys it!

There is the scene in which Erik is getting dressed in the presence of his lover: "There were times when he desired to be the executioner so as to be able to contemplate himself and to enjoy from without the beauty which he emitted, to receive it."

This passage and any number of others prove that Genet has dreamt *of being loved*. Cannot a loving consciousness achieve what the chandeliers and bracket lamps and the psyche were unable to? In such a consciousness and in the unity of a common act of love, the beloved becomes an opaque fact and a pencil of rays that sparkle with meanings, he becomes a soul and a magical naming. His soul is his body in the heart of the Other, a glorified body, without parts, whose substance is the love that has been vowed to it. It is for this submissive heart that the Thief will be terrible and adorable; the fleeting feelings which he does not quite succeed in feeling have, for this heart, the cruelty and density of a beautiful stone. And—height of happiness—this receptacle of his image is there for the taking. It yields itself up, it opens out. The evildoer can grasp and feel that body which is only a temple in which he is worshiped, he can search it with his eyes, penetrate it with his tongue or penis in the hope of thrusting far enough to join his being. If, on the other hand, he allows himself to be caressed, he enjoys himself through the other's excitement. The lover, however, flees himself and forgets himself until he is only an absence; he is not in the way; he is now only the love which the beloved feels for himself. The tough Darling Daintyfoot "plunges into Divine as into a mirror and the slightly flabby beauty of his sweetheart tells him, without his understanding it quite clearly, of the nostalgia for a dead Darling, buried in great state, and never mourned." Gabriel the handsome soldier "lets himself be worshiped without batting an eyelash. He doesn't mind." Divine says to him: " 'I love you as if you were in my belly,' " and also, " 'You're not my sweetheart, you're myself.' " And Gabriel, "thrilled, though smiling with pride, replies, 'Oh, you little hussy!' " The beloved feels only indifference toward the lover. Since he is seeking only himself, it matters little to him whether he gazes into those eyes or others. What is Divine to this handsome male who lies stretched out with his eyes closed, who pretends to be dozing while Divine strokes him? A hand, any hand, all hands. The particularity of his lover escapes him. In fact, he asks it to represent generality. Man or woman, all is grist to his mill. In public, he acts as if he were a seducer of women, but he often allows himself to be adored, in secret, by a man. Women, who, like him, are victims and, like him, are condemned to *be*, do not have enough prestige to symbolize for him the society that has excluded him. Since it is men who make the law and who arrogate to themselves the right to judge him, only the submission of a male can redeem him, by humiliating in his presence his entire sex. Hence, Darling's proud cry: "A male that fucks another male is a double male!" In like manner, Genet will later be able to define the love of which he dreams as "consciousness of the separation from one person."

Can it be that this love is salvation? No. We shall see later that the lover is falsely inessential, for it is he who controls the other's being. Fascinated by his own image, Narcissus drowns in the eyes that adore him. In any case, Genet will never have an opportunity to have this experience. He is not and never will be called upon to play the role of the beloved. As they say in the theater, "He's not right for the character."

He is fifteen years old.* He has become what they wanted him to be: a hardened thief. The authorities examine the case and decide that his apprenticeship is over and that it is high time to send him to his post. They take him and throw him into jail and from there into a reformatory. The matter is settled. It does not require much imagination to guess what he suffered. Thus far, his exile has been only a moral one. Now he is being confined. They are cloistering him, they are cutting him off from the universe. The doors have closed upon him. He contemplates with terror the new world in which it has been decided that he is to pass his life and that other society which will henceforth be his. Firmly resolved to be submissive to nothing, bent on willing the fate which he has been assigned, he is about to decide to adapt himself to his new existence. But before he has had time to catch his breath, "the miracle of horror" has already occurred: that other society of castoffs, of dregs, that excremental society, rejects him.

"I suffered cruelly, I experienced the shame of having my head cropped, of being garbed in an unspeakable outfit, of being assigned to that vile place. I knew the contempt of the other inmates, who were stronger or more evil than I."

Condemned by Good, scorned by Evil, he is driven to the confines of two enemy societies which shuttle him back and forth. His sense of shame increases. His bourgeois ways, which he has not quite lost, cause him to feel cruelly the humiliation of being shorn and being dressed in an unspeakable outfit. But if he wants to find comfort in the thought that he has willed Evil with all the consequences that it entails, then he must admit to himself that he has found something more evil than himself. He is too young, too soft, too weak, too cowardly. Which means, above all: too gentle and

---

* In *Miracle of the Rose,* Genet writes: "When I was taken to the Mettray Reformatory, I was fifteen years and seventeen days old. . . ."

too conscious. The truth of the matter is what Green Eyes will later say to Lefranc: "You're not our kind." They badger him, they insult him, they brutalize him. He becomes a butt.

"I was sixteen years old. . . . I kept no place in my heart where the feeling of my innocence could dwell. I recognized myself as being the coward, the traitor, the thief, the homo that they saw in me. . . . With a little patience and reflection, I discovered within myself sufficient reason for being called by those names. It appalled me to realize that I was composed of filth. I became abject."

How could he be loved? By whom? They spit in his face. He dares to gaze upon the meanest and handsomest hoodlums, but he has not the audacity to want them to love him. He knows only too well that he is not lovable. The passionate decision to will his destiny imparts a kind of cynical and brutal realism to all his thoughts, all his desires, even to his dreams. Even in his dreams he endeavors, as Descartes says, "to conquer himself rather than fortune." And besides, those glamorous boys are not meant for loving. Surrounded by a court of admirers, they are the handsome object of everyone's attention. They are absolute ends, and as such they gather and fix upon themselves all the scattered love that floats within the four walls. They are, by nature, the beloved. Genet immediately effects one of the extraordinary reversals at which he is an old hand. While deciding, in accordance with the discipline he elaborated a few years earlier, "to say yea from the bottom of his heart to every charge brought against him," he makes a zealous effort to love those who despise him. Precisely because he is alone and wretched, because he is dying to be succored, to be comforted, because he has a fabulous need to *receive* love, he decides to *give* it. He adores all those cruel, handsome children who plague him mercilessly, he adores them, he servilely submits to their desires, he becomes a doormat. Since he is unable to be the beloved, he will become the lover. A strange operation, in which the most abject humility disguises the most stiff-necked pride, in which the most utter love masks the most corrosive hatred. If we succeed in grasping the meaning of this, we shall be very close to deciphering Genet's secret: his passive homosexuality.

Not that it is to be dated from this new choice. He himself has informed us that, as far as he remembers, he felt his first homosexual desire—a quite innocent desire aroused by a handsome child on a bicycle—at the age of ten. He has even written that his homosexuality preceded his stealing and that the latter was merely a consequence of the former. But we cannot follow him in this. I can very well imagine that it flatters his self-esteem to trace his pilferings, which are more external and vulgar, and which might, after all, have sprung from the occasion, to a deeper, more singular, more autonomous taste. But since, by his own confession, he stole before having relations with boys, even before desiring their caresses, we cannot help but regard his claim as merely the effect of a pious wish: if he wanted to support it, he would have to project his homosexuality, without proof, as some kind of metaphysical virtue beyond his memories. I quite recognize that at the present time he is more essentially a homosexual than a thief. But what does that prove? One of the constant characteristics of the psychic life is the fact that later determinations act upon earlier ones, envelop them and endow them with a new meaning. At present, Genet is perhaps a thief because he is a homosexual. But he became a homosexual because he was a thief. A person is not born homosexual or normal. He becomes one or the other, according to the accidents of his history and to his own reaction to these accidents. I maintain that inversion is the effect of neither a prenatal choice nor an endocrinian malformation nor even the passive and determined result of complexes. It is an outlet that a child discovers when he is suffocating.

Genet's early states of sexual agitation—those he experienced before entering the reformatory—must be regarded as rehearsals, experiences and experiments, not as manifestations of a bent. Can any man maintain that he never dreamed, in childhood, of caressing a playmate? And what of it! And even if there were an actual exchange of caresses, would that be a reason to speak of homosexuality? It is only afterward that these tentative efforts take on meaning. When the individual definitively takes one path rather than another, "the retrospective illusion" then detects in them the premonitory signs of disorder or decides to regard them only as inconsequential deviations. Inversely, our inventions are mainly decisions and clarifications. What we think we discover in a moment of special insight is what we have been inventing for years, bit by bit, absent-mindedly as it were, without being completely involved. Following close upon his early thefts and his original crisis, Genet's homosexual desires were at first merely "experiments just to see," attempts to discover, on the periphery of his fundamental decision, a safety exit. But if he desired boys, he did so with a kind of innocence. The passage which we quoted above makes this quite clear: applying to his new state the severe discipline which he had elaborated five years earlier, "I recognized myself," he says,

". . . as being the *homo* that they saw in me. . . . With a little patience and reflection, I discovered within myself sufficient reason
for being called by that name." This means that he had never
previously considered himself an invert. The illumination which
establishes himself in his own eyes as a "homo" cannot be distinguished from the will to become one, that is, to give his past a
meaning and a name and to consider it the preformation of his
future. Deciding both to be the lover and to claim the insulting
name of homo, Genet *learns,* by this very decision, that he has
always been an invert. By the same token he realizes that the safety
exit merges with the main exit: to want to be *the* thief and to decide
that he will be a homosexual are one and the same thing. If his first
sexual experiments had not been games, even if shared, and dreams,
he would have realized this earlier. In any case, the will to Evil is
primary, and, even though he may claim the contrary, Genet is
well aware of this. Let us bear in mind, rather, Querelle, his hero:
if he decides to be caught by Norbert, he does so after having killed
and because he has killed.

As a result of his original crisis and of the ensuing decision,
Genet finds himself immersed in a situation that might be called
prehomosexual. Even if he had never subsequently slept with a man
or dreamed of doing so, he was marked, set off. He would have
remained, like so many others, a Vestal of homosexuality. Like the
trim, smart, nimble, graceful banker whom everyone took for a fairy
and who was always getting involved in long-drawn-out affairs with
women without even suspecting the existence of forbidden love,
until a chance debauch revealed it to him at the age of forty and
thereupon changed him retrospectively into *what he was.* Sexually,
Genet is first of all a raped child. This first rape was the gaze of the
other, who took him by surprise, penetrated him, transformed him
forever into an object. Let there be no misunderstanding: I am not
saying that his original crisis *resembles* a rape, I say that it *is* one.
The events which strike us take place at the same time on all levels
of our mental life and express themselves, on each level, in a different language. An actual rape can become, in our conscience, an
iniquitous and yet ineluctable condemnation and, vice versa, a
condemnation can be felt as a rape. Both acts transform the guilty
person into an object, and if, in his heart, he feels his objectification
as a shameful thing, he feels it in his sex as an act of coitus to which
he has been subjected. Genet has now been deflowered; an iron
embrace has made him a woman. All that is left for him is to put
up with *being.* He is the village whore; everyone can have him at

will. Undressed by the eyes of the decent folk as women are by those of males, he carries his fault as they do their breasts and behind. Many women loathe their backside, that blind and public mass which belongs to everyone before belonging to them. When they are grazed from behind, their excitement and their shame will mount together. The same holds for Genet. Having been caught stealing *from behind*, his back opens when he steals; it is with his back that he awaits human gazes and catastrophe. Why be surprised if, after that, he feels more like an object by virtue of his back and behind and if he has a kind of sexual reverence for them? The guilty child has been unmasked, possessed, and it is as a culprit that he will experience excitement and desire. And since he wills to become what they have made him, that is, an object, this willing will have repercussions even in the way he feels his body and the erection of his penis. To the man who makes himself a hunter, his penis is a knife, but to the one who becomes an object, it is a still life, a *thing*, which hardens only so as to give a better grip and to become easier to handle. It is typical that Proust, who was a homosexual, never called the penis a sword or a scythe, as do our village Lotharios, but a "clamp."* The turgescence that the male feels as the aggressive stiffening of a muscle will be felt by Genet as the blossoming of a flower. Whether it be the swelling up of an inert air chamber or the unsheathing of a sword, nothing is decided in advance: the entire choice which one makes of oneself gives its meaning to this inner perception. One man feels his transcendence in his penis; another, his passivity. And, in point of fact, it is quite true that an erection is a hardening, a spurt, but it is also true that this induration is undergone. The raw fact is ambiguous; the meaning depends on the individual. But the male swoops down on the female, carries her off, subjects her and feeds her. The very way in which he makes love reflects his economic situation and his pride in earning his living. Where do you expect Genet to get his pride? He does not earn his living, he loses it. Parasite of a society that denies him salvation through action, excluded from all undertakings, where would he find that mixture of oppressive imperialism and generosity which at present characterizes manly sexuality? The male rarely wishes to seduce by his physical qualities. He has received them, not made them. He makes his woman love him for his power, his courage, his pride, his aggressiveness, in short he makes her desire him as a faceless force, a pure power to do and

---

* Another homosexual has called it "a slug" in an excellent but unpublishable short story.

take, not as an object agreeable to the touch. He seeks in submissive eyes the reflection of his infinite freedom. But the acts of Genet, who does nothing, who undoes, who acts only in order to be, are effectual only in appearance. They reveal not his force but his essence. They are *gestures*. He says about Divine: "She tried for male gestures . . . whistled, put her hands into her pockets, and this whole performance was carried out so unskillfully that in the course of a single evening she seemed to be four or five characters at the same time." Divine is himself. He displays himself, he makes himself an object. That being so, how could he take? And what need has he of a woman, that other object which competes with him? All they could do would be to dance in front of each other, each wanting to be taken, not to take, to be seen, not to look.

This priority, in the subject itself, of the object over the subject leads, as we see, to amorous passivity, which, when it affects a male, inclines him to homosexuality.

In short, Genet decides to *realize* his being and knows that he cannot achieve this result unaided. He therefore resorts to the mediation of others. This means that he makes of his objectivity for others the *essential* and of his reality-for-himself the inessential. What he desires is to be manipulated passively by the Other so as to become an object in his own eyes. Any man who places his truth in his Being-for-the-Other finds himself in a situation which I have called prehomosexual. And this is the case, for example, of many actors, even if they enjoy sleeping only with women.

But in the case of Genet there is something else; he is inclined to homosexuality by other factors. Before there was any sexual determination, Genet reacted to his condemnation by effecting an ethical and generalized inversion. He was, as he has said, turned inside-out like a glove. Since he has been cast into nothingness, it is from nothingness alone that he wishes to derive. He is a monster, the exception to the rule, the improbable, in fact the impossible. He is an undesirable, born not of man but of some incubus. He cannot found a family. Thus, he has not only been exiled from the fields, woods and springs, he has been excluded *from his own nature*. We bathe in our life, in our blood, in our sperm. Our body is a dense water that carries us along; we have only to let ourselves go. A lowly Venus who is hardly to be distinguished from digestion, from respiration, from the beating of our heart, gently inclines us toward woman. We have only to trust her. The servant goddess will attend to everything, to our pleasure and to the species. But Genet *is dead*. His life is no more *natural* than his birth, it haunts a corpse. He hangs on only by power of will. If he pays any attention to the muted sensations which come to him from his organs, he feels impossible and falls into astonishment. He does not find within himself any of those powerful instincts that support the desires of the decent man. He knows only the death instinct. His sexual desires will be phantoms, as his life itself is a phantom. Whatever their object, they are condemned in advance. He is *forbidden from the beginning* to desire. All societies castrate the maladjusted. This castration can be actually physical or can be achieved by persuasion. The result is the same. The desire of Genet, who is condemned, outside of nature, impossible, becomes a desire for the impossible and for what is against nature. And since this outcast child is only an appearance, his sexuality itself must be a sham, a trick of nothingness. None of the ordinary sources can determine it; it does not emanate from universal nature; it does not have its roots there. The fact is, it is up in the air, a pure, diabolical imitation of the legitimate movements of our senses. In assuming his situation, Genet takes his stand on absolute particularity; he will derive only from himself. This upheaval affects even his sexuality. His contorted desire, sharp and nervous, derives only from itself. It can have no natural relationship with its object. And since Genet's sincerity is the demand for artifice, his excitement will be all the more sincere insofar as he feels more artificial, more free. He does not know abandon, swooning. If he lets himself go, he falls into a pit. Thus, *he does not abandon himself* to sexuality. On the contrary, it appears at the maximum of tension. At the height of passion it retains a taste of ashes and freedom. And since negative freedom and Evil are one and the same, his sexual life is a new field which opens out to his perversity. Desire of nothingness, nothingness of desire, exhausting effort of the entire being, sterile, rootless and aimless, Genet's sexual desire contains within itself a fierce demand for its autonomy and singularity, in defiance of the rules, in defiance of nature, in defiance of life, in defiance of the species and in defiance of society. It will reflect him completely in the realm of the flesh.

Such is the situation that has been created for him. And though it inclines him strongly to homosexuality, it does not yet determine whether Genet will be a boy queen or a girl queen. It is here that the aforementioned upheaval occurs. Genet, who is the butt of the young big shots of the reformatory, is metamorphosed into a lover, that is, into a woman. But why? We have seen what the beloved gains in playing his role: he is magnified in the lover's heart. He is

sheltered, saved. But what of the lover? Why does he demand disgust and rebuffs, the other's indifference, the tortures of jealousy
and, in the end, the despair that comes from the certainty of not
being loved? And yet he must have something to gain by this. What
is behind it all? For Genet, the answer is clear: love is a magical
ceremonial whereby the lover steals the beloved's being in order to
incorporate it into himself:

"The earliest form of love that I remember is my desire *to be* a
pretty boy . . . whom I saw going by."*

The earliest, perhaps. But Genet adopted it later. Divine says to
Gabriel: "You're myself," and Gabriel, decent chap that he is,
smiles fatuously without realizing that his blood is being sucked
from him. And the lieutenant's passionate, fierce love of Querelle
is the desire to take away his penis and testicles and graft them on
himself.

To those who have a sense of belonging, to the just, to the
honorable, this identification may seem a vain and absurd endeavor.
But I would like to ask them whether they are quite sure of being
themselves. How do I know that they have not obtained that inner
peace of theirs by surrendering to a foreign protector who reigns
in their stead? I know that the man whom I hear utter the words
"We doctors . . ." is in bondage. This *we doctors* is his ego, a para-
sitical creature that sucks his blood. And even if he were only himself, there are a thousand ways of being delivered to oneself as to
beasts, of feeding with one's own flesh an invisible and insatiable
idol. For nobody may say the simple words: I am I. The best and
freest of men may say: I exist. Which is already too much. For the
others, I suggest that they use such formulae as: "I am Himself" or
"I am so-and-so *in person*." If they do not aim at changing their
skin, it is because the force that governs them does not allow them
the leisure to do so; above all, it is because society has long since
recognized and consecrated this symbiosis by according glory or
simply honorability to the couple formed by the sick man and his
parasite: it is a legitimate hell. As for me, I keep away from them if
I can: I don't like inhabited souls. But as for the children of Cain,
who are the horses of a zar that society reproves, I understand their
longing to change masters. And it is no more vain to long to become
"that gentleman going by," as Fantasio desired, than to want to be
the doctor when one practices medicine. The two operations are of
the same nature, and failure is certain in both cases. If, for your-

---

* Cf. Cocteau, *Le Grand Écart* (*Œuvres complètes*, I, 15): "Ever since childhood he had
felt the desire to be those whom he found beautiful, not to be loved by them."

self, you are already the Other, if you suffer a perpetual absence at your very core, then you can live this absence as if it were that of any other. That other will never be more absent than you are, for the way in which he is not himself (that is, in which he himself is, for himself, Another) , the way in which you are not you and the way in which you are not he do not differ appreciably.

Genet, too, suffers at never keeping the appointment. He, too, is haunted by an unrealizable intuition, as by a sneeze that neither comes off nor fades away. He is an empty palace. The tables are set, the torches lit, the beds made, footsteps resound in the corridors, doors open and shut, the glasses and plates are found empty, orders are left on the table, but no one ever appears. He has lain in wait, set traps and placed mirrors: all in vain.

But that invisible Other who prowls behind him and who cannot be taken by surprise, why may it not be *that hoodlum?* That charming young hoodlum passing by is no doubt a stranger to him, but not more of a stranger than Genet is to himself. He is an external object, an animated body. But what is the Other, the one absent from the deserted palace, what is he if not an object? Is it not the dark, terrible bulk that Erik saw in the mirror and *that was called Erik Seidler?* The little "tough" is insensitive, rebellious to Genet's will, to his voice, even unpredictable. But do you think that Genet's "Nature" obeys him? Quite the contrary, it governs him. So let the hoodlum govern him, let him impose his will upon Genet. He has a manifest superiority to the invisible Lord: although he *is not* Genet, at least he is present to him. Let him be as much of an object as one likes, but at least he is given to Genet, precisely for that reason, in an intuition that satisfies all the senses. Genet is *full of him.* In short, he has brusquely passed *in front of* the Other whom Genet wished to get at from behind himself. Is he not indeed a hoodlum, a thief, desolate, wicked? Does he not come to Genet from the dark, formless depths of the universe as the reflection came to Erik from the depths of the mirror? Or rather as Erik came to his reflection from the depths of the room? For in order that the hoodlum become for Genet his being, Genet must become the reflection of the hoodlum. His consciousness turned like an eye toward the darkness within. If it had been able to *manifest* that Other at the back of his head, to surround it, to illuminate it with its rays, and if the latter had had manifest reality only because of the brightness thus shed upon it, the trick would have come off. The reversal will thus consist in directing the eye of consciousness toward the appearance *from in front* and in emptying consciousness of all concerns other than that of *manifesting* the handsome youngster. The reflective consciousness must fall back into the immediate consciousness and fade out there. For the reflective consciousness was a flashlight that searched the immediate consciousness with the aim of discovering the Other there. But it failed in its task and could only produce a paltry Ego. Let it drown and let Genet's Ego go down with it. His Ego no longer dwells in his consciousness. It strolls about on the legs of a handsome hoodlum. But that is not enough. Empty and anonymous, the immediate consciousness is still a consciousness of the entire universe. If it reduces the diaphragm, if it sees nothing but the beloved, if it is fascinated by him, as is a bird by a reptile, as was Rousseau, at certain times, by the entire world, if it falls endlessly toward him and feels itself falling, if it is convinced that it has no other reason for being than to make his charms glitter, if it regards itself as a property of the Other, a phosphorescence that *radiates* from that handsome body, the heat that *emanates* from it, the brilliance of its youth, the invisible sheath that shelters it, if it, with absolute oblivion of self, is only the considerable presence of beauty, then, in recompense, it will alienate itself within him, it will be his essence, his goal and his Ego. To belong to it unreservedly, and even unto death, is the cunningest and surest way of possessing it. Fascination, self-oblivion, dizziness, absolute submission in the service of a masterly act of inveigling: that is what defines more than one religious ecstasy, and love according to Genet.

Actually, this love is not addressed to the young hoodlum in his particularity. It is not at all concerned with the plans of the beloved and their success, that is, with his transcendence; it does not reflect him as a woman's love reflects the man she loves. It is addressed to a being who definitely has the appearance of a man and who is nevertheless an object, as is a woman, to a being who is utterly absorbed in criminal plans but whose undertakings, though not ceasing thereby to be efficacious, are essentially and primarily gestures, in short, to a *fake male,* to one of those supposed "double males" who "fuck men" because they themselves are women. Genet wants to be him whom he loves precisely insofar as the latter is already Genet. As soon as he meets a handsome hoodlum, the boy's beauty strikes and staggers him, knocks him down. But the angel who makes him bite the dust is himself. What loomed before him was objective Evil coming to him *in person.* Evil in the eyes, cowardice in the twist of the mouth, violence contained in the muscles, everything that he could *not discern sufficiently* in the image reflected to him by the mirror, all the pitiless guises of Evil, perceived pell-mell in an illumination—these are what it takes to subject him. For a moment he had the impression of seeing *himself*, with the same astonishment we feel when we unexpectedly meet a friend who we thought had left for Texas, that uncertainty which shifts to certainty, that bewilderment which contracts into recognition, that doubt which vanishes when one would like to continue doubting, that plenitude which entails our surrendering to reality because it is the highest tribunal. It is not so much the skin, the hardness of the muscles, the hair, the odor which stagger him and flood him with desire. It is, of course, all that, but all that as an embodiment of being, of *his* being. In that other who resembles him—or rather resembles what he would like to be—he at last sees himself as others see him. Hence, each of the men to whom Genet gives himself becomes the variable and imperfect representative of that identical Other whom Genet wants to be for himself. In loving that indifferent charmer with his body and soul, the abandoned child fulfills his impossible dream of being loved. For since he *is* the Other, it is he, he alone, who *is loved in the Other*. Genet, who is cleverer than Erik Seidler, has realized that in order to *be* the adorable Erik he has had *to make himself* the executioner, his worshiper. Through a thousand individual figures it is he himself that Genet is going to pursue, but himself as Other, himself untrammeled by his scruples, his cowardice, his wretchedness, his muscular weakness, a kind of titan of Evil, greater than his temporary incarnation and greater than Genet. Thus are born spontaneously the myth of the criminal, that is, the projection upon others of the qualities which the others have attributed to him, and the dichotomic conception of an outcast humanity which will be the major theme of his poetry: "the eternal couple of the criminal and the saint."

Later, we shall see these complementary themes little by little develop, enter into conflict and then unite. For the time being, we shall consider only the criminal, that is, the pure object of Genet's desire, or, if one prefers, the instrument of his new attempts to retrieve the Other. The phrase from *The Maids*, "the eternal couple of the criminal and the saint," makes the matter quite clear. This couple may seem ill-matched. If so, it is because Genet has deliberately upset the balance by linking a term of black ethics with a term of white ethics. "Criminal" conceals "hero." This hero who kills and gets killed gloriously, to the exalted admiration of a whole collectivity, becomes, after changing sign, the criminal of black ethics who kills in order to get killed and whose death may become as legendary as that of a great captain. The term "saint" is retained as its correlative, firstly because "it is the most beautiful word in the French language," the pole which magnetized the daydreams of the child Genet, and secondly because saintliness is by nature antisocial. It is a direct relationship of the soul to God. In a word, Genet himself will decide about it. There is thus no need for him to challenge it, whereas heroism, which society consecrates, cannot appear under its "white" name in black ethics. But the description of the criminal which we shall be given will very often recall that of the warrior contained in the epic poems of military societies. As for the saint, a slight deflection will be enough for the word to appear suspect to us. Genet will say *"la sainte"** and this unexpected feminine form of the word should warn us that we have unwittingly entered the world upside-down. Hero, saint, in any case, we have understood: they are *examples,* models. Of the three ideals of ethics, Genet retains only two. The sage does not interest him at all. The reason is clear enough: it is wisdom which accepts the universe. And there is no reason for Genet to accept what is not offered him, what is denied him on principle. On the other hand, the root of heroism and saintliness is, in one way or another, challenge. No doubt the "white" hero defends a social order, but he defends it by destroying and by destroying himself. As for the saint, he challenges the human condition in its totality. Thus, the criminal is an archetype of the Ethics of Evil. And, in point of fact, the great murderers whose photos Genet pins on the walls of his prison cell play for him the role of intercessors. He prays, he meditates, while contemplating them. These sacred images facilitate his elevations. Nevertheless, he does not make use of them the way right-thinking people generally make use of their heroes. For the latter, as for Genet, there is identification. The bourgeois of 1789 actually wanted to *be* the heroes of Plutarch. But they proceeded by imitation. This means that they wanted to *act* like their great men in order to *become similar* to them. Genet does not dream of imitating. On the contrary, he is convinced that an imitation, even if one goes all the way, is a truthless aping. One must incorporate the heroic substance into oneself, and there are only two ways of doing so: cannibalism and the rites of possession. We shall later see a long, quiet dream of anthropophagy germinating within Genet. He is the praying mantis that eats her males. Throughout *Funeral*

---

* "The female saint."—Translator's note.

Rites he develops in magnificent images the desire to eat Jean Decarnin, his dead lover. But what we shall first examine is the resort to possession. Let us ask ourselves *by whom* Genet wants to be possessed and *how* this possession is going to operate.

By whom? The answer appears simple. By *the* criminal. There is a "participationist" belief underlying the whole operation. Genet has no illusions. He is quite aware that the hoodlums who subjugate him are never *the* criminal nor even criminals at all. But in order for him to accept servitude it suffices that they participate in some way in the ideal essence of crime. Thus, it is not so much to them that he gives himself as to the criminal of whom they are the momentary and imperfect embodiment, that is, to Genet himself as he is and as he ought to be. Part of his worship of those he loves consists of a systematic and continuous interpretation of signs. Without respite, his eyes register, manifest and glorify the touch of black heroism which is expressed in features and gestures.

But what exactly is *the* criminal?

In the first place, of course, a man who has committed a crime or who most certainly will commit one. Not that Genet has ever committed a murder or even, if we are to believe *Our Lady of the Flowers,* really dreamed of committing one, except, perhaps, some sadistic and passionate murder that would transform a handsome youngster into his pure earthly appearance so as to deliver him more fully to his lover. Indeed, I think that the fundamental conflict on the basis of which he shaped himself is not of the kind that finds its outlet in murder. One resorts to murder in order to cut the Gordian knot of an intolerable situation. But this situation must be felt as a direct relationship with one or more other persons. Genet, however, who is a victim of *all* others, is not oppressed or wronged by anyone in particular, and, in the last analysis, it is with himself that he has to deal. One kills when one thinks one is in the right or when one does not care a rap about rights and duties, but very rarely—although it can happen—when one knows one is in the wrong and in order to be more so. Although, in the latter case, one may want to get rid of *a* judge, like the honorable Spaniard who strangled a taxi driver so as not to have to admit to him that he was unable to pay the fare. But who would dream of annihilating a hundred thousand judges? What makes Genet's case singular is that he has to deal with himself or with everybody, never with a few, or, if one prefers, that his relations with individuals are never anything but a symbolic specification of those he maintains with all of society. Finally, if he wants to survive, he will have to bring his enemies to their knees. But as they are legion and he is alone, he will have to invent some brilliant action that has a universal bearing. For the time being, this hounded adolescent, this inmate of a reformatory, this little Barcelona beggar, has not yet thought about the matter. Nevertheless, the fact remains that the mythical Other must reflect to him the image of the greatest objective Evil and that this evil is crime. There is, as we shall see, a greater Evil, namely betrayal. But Genet reserves this one for himself. It is a subjective evil, without pomp, without display, a constant exercise of the mental restriction which necessitates consciousness in Evil. Crime is the greatest Object-Evil. It is showy: blood, cries, death, night endow it with tragic pomp. And this is essential, since it is the Act of the Other and since it is committed so that it can be contemplated from without. In its essence, it is the suppression of Good by Evil, of Being by Nonbeing, of the Absolute by the Relative, and it is at the same time the swallowing up of the Relative, of the Reflection and of Evil, which are drawn into the shipwreck into which they have caused Good to be engulfed. For a moment, pure Appearance exists in the absolute, since the consciousness of the respectable man is abolished. For a moment, Appearance assumes the functions of the Being which no longer is, and then it itself is annihilated in turn. It is this ephemeral and complete being of Nonbeing—Querelle, pure object—that gives its value to the criminal act. The murder is the instant. Moreover, of the common-law offenses condemned by society, murder is the one with which it deals most severely. It is therefore murder which most surely establishes its author as the evildoer in men's eyes. Now, as we already know, Genet must always return to this tribunal. However, it is not sufficient to commit a crime in order *to be* a criminal. For this solipsist, murder is defined by its origin even more than by its results. The suffering of the victim, his frightful anguish at the sight of the arm raised to strike him, the grief of his family and friends, all this matters little to Genet. He doesn't think about it. I cannot repeat often enough that Genet is far too unconcerned with the consciousness of others to be sadistic. It is not the death which is *felt* that he appreciates in murder; it is the *objective* death and the objective act which causes it. Although these interest him only insofar as they confer *criminal being* upon the murderer. Lefranc, who kills in order to be admitted to the feudal brotherhood of murderers, derives no benefit from his forced, imitated crime, a crime which was not implied by his nature. The death of Maurice does not reflect glory upon him, does not metamorphose him; it remains separate, authorless, an accident, an error. In *The Maids,* Genet is even more categorical: in vain do Solange and Claire dream of, premeditate, cunningly prepare and finally attempt the murder of Madame; they fail because they were bound to fail. Through all these fables, Genet is admonishing himself: "There's no point in dreaming of committing a crime. You won't carry it off. And even if, by chance, you finally did kill, you wouldn't be a criminal. That's not the way to *absorb* murder." For crime is an election; it requires the help of grace. Phineus, Andromeda's fiancé, apologizes, in Corneille's play, for not having fought to deliver her from the monster. He wasn't sure of the place, Perseus had the luck to happen to be there. He is severely answered that this kind of luck is called grace and that it is by such good fortune that one recognizes merit and predestination. Genet might, like this unfortunate lover, be told by one of his criminals:

> Heaven, which knows better than we what we are,
> Measures its favors by men's merit.
> And you would have had the benefit of such aid
> Had it been able to find in you the virtues it found in him.
> These are graces from on high, rare and singular,
> Which do not descend for vulgar souls.

Thus, by a vicious circle characteristic of all ethics of being, one kills in order to *be* a criminal, but it would be vain merely to try to become a criminal if one *were* not a criminal in advance. "You would not seek me if you had not found me."

This simplifies matters for Genet: since being comes to the murderer by grace from on high, the actual murder is no longer necessary. What he will love in hoodlums is the visible sign of election. And he surrounds himself, in his prison cells, with pictures of great and famous murderers, but does not disdain to pin on the wall photos of unknowns which he has culled here and there when the anonymous faces, which may be those of athletes or merchants, seem to him to bear the mark of crime. And insofar as we can know about his sexual adventures from his books, he seems to have dreamed a great deal of giving himself to criminals like Weidmann, Pilorge and Harcamone, but to have yielded particularly to the Darlings and Stilitanos, that is, to fake toughs whose muscles and gait gave him, for a moment, the illusion that they would one day kill or that they could kill in certain favorable circumstances. For in this inverted world which takes Being as a goal and doing as a means, it is all the better if one can economize on the means. In short, the beloved must manifest by indubitable signs that he belongs to a military aristocracy. After that, it matters little whether or not he has an opportunity to demonstrate his worth. One trusts him.

There is something that counts far more: it is not enough that the beloved be a beautiful appearance; he must *be only that*. If Genet is to be able to identify himself with the one he loves, if his consciousness, though remaining inessential, is to be the indispensable brilliance which draws that great and terrible figure from the shadow, it is not permissible for another consciousness to assume the same task. He does not fear the consciousness of the just, of decent people. Their consciousness, which is outraged and full of hatred, serves only to stress the urgency of his mission, which is to surround the most decried of men with religious respect. The screams of the mob confirm him in the feeling of his perfect solitude. He is alone in loving the one whom all others detest. His very love is a crime. To love murder in defiance of all is his way of committing it. As for the other queers, who perhaps dream of stealing his man from him, he is not afraid of them either. He will fight them, and the stronger will prevail. The only consciousness that would reduce his amorous endeavor to nothingness would be the consciousness of the criminal himself. If the latter could make contact with himself and love himself, what need would he have for Genet to love him? If the unity of being and knowing were achieved within a pure diamond, Genet would be only the superfluous ray that glided over that phosphorescence without being able to add light to it. A consciousness that knew its appearance would be self-sufficient. In order for Genet to be an absolute consciousness of this appearance, it must remain, without him, in the shadow, all by itself. Thus, his mission as *revealer* leads him to deny passionately the consciousness of the beloved: "When the train, while going at top speed, lets me see a youngster amidst wet leaves, dead branches, fog . . . I envy his beauty, his ragamuffin grace and his luck to serve a happy minute. I console myself with the thought that he cannot enjoy this instant of whose charm he is unaware."

Can he quite deny the consciousness of Harcamone and of Our Lady? That would be a lack of verisimilitude. But he can convince himself that it is only a dead light or a bit of turbid water in the hollow of a rock, tepid, vain, superfluous. In real life this means that a certain air of glum stupidity and conceit sets him all aflutter: that head is unoccupied, he is going to be able to install himself in it, like a hermit crab in an empty shell:

"Our Lady thought about nothing, and that is what gave him the air of knowing everything straight off."

"Those handsome, vacant-eyed heads. . . . Men with such faces terrify me when I have to cross their paths warily, but what a dazzling surprise when, in their landscape, at the turn of a deserted lane, I approach, with my heart racing like mad, and discover nothing, nothing but looming emptiness, sensitive and proud like a tall foxglove."

"Armand . . . subjected me to his pleasure. . . . Crushed by that mass of flesh, which was devoid of the slightest spirituality, I experienced the giddiness of finally meeting the perfect brute."

Thus, the Other is, once again, totally Other, Other than self. He escapes. We are back at the play of reflections which we described at the beginning of the present work. The right-thinking man had freed himself from his negative powers by projecting them upon Genet, whom he charged with embodying them. Genet gets rid of them in turn and projects this absolute otherness upon the beloved. Foreign to himself, he can love only Another-than-self, for it is himself in his absolute otherness that he loves in the guise of the other.

This exigency contains another exigency, one which is perhaps less essential but more immediate and which creeps into his very perception. Since he cannot be quite one with the beloved, nor quite two, the latter's body must not be offered to him, by movements, gestures and words, as quite his own body or quite that of another. He does not learn the movements of his own body, he does not witness them. To will them, execute them and feel them are one and the same. This transparent intimacy kills desire. But if the other's gestures are unpredictable to him or if, after a period of apprenticeship, he predicts them with a certain margin of uncertainty, a certain percentage of error, if he has to observe them in order to know them, if he has to interpret them patiently, if he is likely at any moment to be surprised or upset by some unexpected reaction, then the beloved will be only one among others and Genet will lose all hope of identifying himself with him. This behavior must not be completely transparent lest it lose its magic, though it must not be completely opaque either. It must be other and yet his, must come to him from the depths of the Other, more rebellious than a simple reflection, and yet must, each time, fulfill a desire, an anticipation, an expectation, so that he no longer knows whether he is learning of his desire through the Other's gestures, whether it is his desire that has provoked these gestures or whether an ineluctable necessity has at the same time produced desire in him and, in the other, the movements which satisfy it. We are all familiar with the illusion of false recognition: on certain days when we are tired we have the feeling that we have already seen the objects which are about us, have already witnessed the events which are taking place, so that the new, without losing its novelty, seems to us a restoration of the old and we are unable to decide whether each incident is confirming an earlier anticipation or is provoking, subsequently, the feeling of having anticipated. Such is the impression Genet must constantly have in the presence of the beautiful spectacle offered him by the beloved. In each of the other's movements, in each word, Genet must perceive both the necessity of his own nature which does not cease to be the worst and the strangeness which will enable him to enjoy it. Amorous bliss will spring from a gesture which is so *evident* and yet so *new* that it becomes as perfect as a poem. This obviously implies that the beloved's consciousness has little to do with his acts, and yet it need hardly be said that he must not be a pure mechanism. Genet can love in the other only his own freedom in reverse. But the reverse of freedom is called Destiny. All the preceding exigencies lead to this crossroad. If a murder which is due to chance or is an act of defiance is not sufficient to confer the title of criminal, it is because Destiny alone is qualified to call for a crime. And it is one and the same to call the criminal a member of the elect, an aristocrat or a man of Destiny.

Genet, Lefranc, the girl queens and Solange the maid fail to go through with their murders because their nimble, loquacious minds envisage too many possibilities. And when they finally do decide on one, it never quite belongs to them since there exist an infinite number of others which are likewise their possibilities. We may find this surprising: the influence of the world of labor and of conditions of production leads us increasingly to consider things from the point of view of praxis. From this point of view we say that a possibility is ours when we have chosen it and when we have at least begun to implement it. But with regard to the ethics of being, which, whether white or black, emanate from the parasitic classes, *my* possibility lies in my nature a priori, and it is not even necessary that I think at once of conforming to it. I will even be allowed to try to escape from it, for I have not chosen it. The possibility has elected me, and it will always find me. It should not be thought that Destiny assumes only the form of the Ananke that weighs upon Oedipus and Laius. The adventure of this father, who is assured of being killed by his son and who decides to do away with him and thus takes the path which will lead him most surely to death, is certainly a fine example of Fatality. But every conscious member of the aristocratic classes is a Laius and an Oedipus. There are any number of novels and stories in which young sons of distinguished family do the most outlandish things or throw themselves into reckless undertakings in an effort to elude the sole possibility which is *their* possibility, only to find themselves ultimately led back, by unexpected ways, to their starting point, that is, to the Destiny which has been awaiting them. We have recently been told of how the sons of Bordeaux wine merchants attempted to escape their destiny as wine merchants through debauchery and literature. All in vain. These businessmen are the object of a special grace. The son will sell wine as did his father, and, like him, will pay his harvesters less than the union wage. The same holds for the criminal: he is a man with a single possibility, what the Americans call a "one-track mind." In each circumstance of his life, there exists for him only one possible line of action, the one that will lead him most surely to crime or that will most perfectly express his criminal nature. He will stick to this line, even if his intelligence makes him aware that there is another, even if he *believes* he is following another. Our Lady of the Flowers, who is tired of always relating his crime in the same terms, attempts, on the day of the trial, to give a different account of it. In vain. The same words group themselves in the same order to shape the same sentences: "For to Our Lady, a gesture is a poem and can be expressed only with the help of a symbol which is always, always the same." What the murderer wants to think, or believes he thinks, about the murder is unimportant. What counts is the way in which the crime is thought within him. "We do not think," said the poet Francis Ponge, "we are thought." For Genet, who is also a poet, murder and poetry are of the same nature because the poet and the criminal are thought when they believe that they are thinking. Crime is thought-as-Other.

It is also an act. The act of the Other. That is precisely what Genet makes one of his murderers say: "We are acted upon." He thus transfers to the beloved his old anxieties of the time when his powerless consciousness was in rebellion against his nature. The "chosen one" rebels in vain against the crime which is awaiting him; he attempts in vain to elude his destiny. He will go the limit. What happens on the day of the murder? Simply this: the Other who he was potentially becomes Another actually. "The murderer forces my respect . . . [he is] at the bottom of a pit into which, with his feet together, he has—curious prospector—hurled himself with a ludicrously bold leap." He lets himself fall into his image, like Narcissus. Green Eyes, too, speaks of his crime in similar terms: he

says that he has *fallen*. And, after the murder, he "was scared . . .
of finding himself in someone else's boots." He explains: "I wanted
to back up. Stop! No go! I tried hard. I ran in all directions. . . . I
wanted to turn back the clock, to undo what I'd done, to live my
life over until before the crime. It looks easy to go backward—but
my body couldn't do it." All that is left for him is to will his coinciding with his destiny: "Things happened by themselves. I simply
made the gestures that led me as quietly as can be to the guillotine."

"Falling," "fall," these words indicate that at certain moments
the earth opens beneath our feet. The entire universe becomes an
occasion, suddenly becomes dizzying, because the circumstances
have, all by themselves, begun to act in concert with the sole possibility of the future murderer. The perception itself has changed:
"Moments like that are awful. They're awful because they're sweet
. . . they're too sweet . . . it's by its sweetness that you recognize
catastrophe." It's sweet because one glides sweetly, gently, things
mime the act to be performed, they outline it. Our Lady is asked
"who gave him the idea of this method of committing murder."
He replies that it was the murdered man himself. "Monsieur
Ragon was wearing a tie that was too tight. He was all red. So he
took it off . . . so I thought that if I tightened it, it'd be worse . . .
because I got good arms." In short, the act is there, ready-made,
suggested by the tie which chokes, by the gesture the old man
makes to loosen it, by the purpleness of his cheeks. It is the world
that offers the act, exactly as the steep line of the cliffs offers me, if
I lean forward, my fall and death. The strange sexual impression
felt by Genet in the presence of these handsome, obstinate males
is prophetic, for it interprets the sign which they bear on their
forehead, discloses upon them the dark radiance of the future crime
and their will to bring down upon themselves the destiny of which
they are perhaps unaware, which they still refuse. While the young
hoodlum, who is as noble and stupid as a bull, feels his way, becomes confused, loses his bearings, Genet's consciousness, the only
vigilant element in this forsaken carcass, sees from afar the dawn-
ing catastrophe. Every gesture of his idol surprises, enriches and
satisfies him to the full. Not that he quite foresaw it. He knew only
that this gesture, whatever it might be, would perfectly express this
criminal nature and would bring its author closer to crime. He
knew it and willed it. And when the act looms up, it always surpasses his hopes. It is more beautiful than any he could have invented, and at the same time it is obviously what was to be expected.
No other was possible. No sooner does it begin than it entails the

certainty that it has always been expected to be exactly what it is. And its lightning-like consequences pierce the future with their flashes. The murderer is going to fall: his fall is contained in his empty eyes, in his ill-omened face. He is already dizzy but does not realize it. Genet feels this dizziness in the Other's place. His legs sag, he falls to his knees, but *with the Other's fall.* Minute by minute he lives this fall, which the murderer does not yet experience, for it is a rehearsal, on a larger stage, of his own fall. For him, too, a day came when everything was too easy; he too, "curious prospector," hurled himself to the bottom of a pit. The criminal, carrying Evil to the point of murder and catastrophe to the point of his own death, transforms Genet's original adventure into a sacred mystery. Thus, by a kind of osmosis, the murderer reproduces Genet's fall and Genet becomes a consciousness of the murderer's fall. Clutching each other, the two men sink to the bottom of the well. This, then, is the key to the impression of *déjà vu* which governs Genet's love. It is not enough to say that he foresees the other's gestures, that he awaits them, that he wills them; he *recognizes* them. And he himself does not know whether he is prostrating himself before the pompous and sinister future of the beloved, like the Starets before the future sufferings of Dmitri Karamazov, or before his own past.

And, of course, the act must not be gratuitous, for the murderer is not the demoniacal Prince of Evil; he is its tragic hero. Therefore, the murder must be rigorously determined by external circumstances and empirical motives: hunger, poverty, fury. When Our Lady is questioned about the motives of his crime, Genet is careful not to let him reply "I was forced by Fate" or "It's because I'm a murderer." Quite the contrary, he gives the simplest, most trivial answer: "Because I was fabulously broke." And this answer is true. In fact, Genet establishes a hierarchy of crime according to the degree of necessity of the motives. At the bottom, there is the gratuitous crime, that of Lefranc. But Green Eyes himself admits: "Maybe I'm not as strong as Snowball because his crime was a little more necessary than mine. Because he killed in order to rob and loot, but, like him, I killed in order to live, and now I'm smiling." However, we have understood that, for the born criminal, need, gain, fear and anger are only seeming motives. Or rather they are those which he knows, those which he gives to himself. But for Genet, who contemplates him, they are the ways whereby Providence manifests his election. Thus, for Bossuet, God utilizes the greed of kings or of their ministers, the vainglory of a captain or the cowardice of his soldiers in order to attain his ends. And the cowardice, greed and vainglory are true, as is the fact that Our Lady was fabulously broke. But, after all, there have been other cowards whose downfall has not destroyed an empire; others have been equally broke without committing murder. It is the Other who dictates to Our Lady the poetic and ridiculous word "fabulous," which rises from the depths with the purpose of suggesting that this impecuniousness was not quite natural, that it resembled grace. The lover knows the beloved better than the beloved knows himself. Where the criminal sees only a consequence of hunger, of cold, of hatred, Genet immediately discerns the hand of destiny. He himself discloses the mechanism of his faking in the following passage from one of his poems: "I must make the situation as obscure as possible (and strained to the breaking-point) so that the drama is inevitable and can be ascribed to fatality."

Although the vertiginous attraction of Evil is primary, the inversion of time appears as patently as in the *Discourse on Universal History:* it is the future which prepares the present. Since being is subordinated to doing, since one kills in order to be a criminal and because one already is, the criminal that I shall be, that I have been since the beginning of time, stirs up within me a murder which chooses its own pretexts. Henceforth the act becomes aesthetic: it is a finality without an end. The murderer kills in order to manifest the crime which is already more than half inside things but which appears only to his murderer's eyes: "And for me everything became simpler. The girl was already under me. All I had to do was put one hand delicately on her mouth and the other delicately on her neck." In like manner, the artist paints his canvas in order to disengage and bring into focus a meaning in the landscape which is visible only to him. The criminal dances his crime as the ballerina dances the dagger step. The author of the ballet conceived his work for this dance precisely because the ballerina excelled in it. This fact determines the plot: the daughter of a Cossack has been seduced and avenges herself by murdering her seducer. For the spectator, she killed because she had been raped. The truth is that she was raped because she had to kill. The murderer, like Erik, is "a being who can exist only in accordance with a beautiful gesture": he is hungry because he must stab. The murder becomes an *aesthetic gesture.* The objection may be raised, however, that he took money. Hence, his act had a practical result, an end. Yes, but the money is of little use to him; he is inevitably arrested and sentenced. Yet he has at least killed his victim. But Genet doesn't give a damn about the victim. Who is Monsieur Ragon? And Vic, who is he? Who is the Armenian whom Querelle killed? Who is the child who was murdered by Divine, the one shot by Erik? Who is the woman who was killed by Gorgui? And the one Green Eyes strangled? The victim is a pure pretext for a gesture whose beauty suffices unto itself. "But *I'm* a fine phrase," says Green Eyes. Let there be no misunderstanding: Genet is very far from regarding "murder as one of the fine arts." The criminal does *not make* beauty —he *is* himself raw beauty. By virtue of each of his acts he changes into what he is, and indeed one of the chief aspects of the beautiful is the perfect appropriateness of act to essence, the subordination of becoming to being; Destiny is thus perceptible and temporality is subdued to expressing only the eternal.

"The Eternal passed by in the form of a pimp," says Genet. And what actually is this pimp who is so constantly invariable, so foreseeable, so fatal, whose every swagger, every word, whose gesture in rolling a cigarette or slipping his hands into his pockets seems less the effect of a particular act of will than the perfect and necessary fulfillment of his essence? What is he if not the idea accessible to the senses, the reflection of eternity in the moving world of becoming? Genet lives in deep sympathy with all these movements because they all manifest, though to different degrees, the same crime. Stilitano constantly rolls a white blob of spit from one corner of his open mouth to the other, and Genet is in raptures because this nasty little habit, by virtue of its ceremonious repetition, of the insolence, abandon and narcissism which it manifests, of the blithe perfection with which it is executed, reveals Stilitano in his entirety each and every instant. We now recognize this impression of having willed what the other does while one is learning it, and of foreseeing what one does not know as if one were recalling it. As Bergson has shown in a famous analysis, it is the effect of *grace*. Destiny is, in both meanings of the term, the grace of criminals.

Grace, beauty: expressions which are disconcerting here because we usually give them a content which is voluptuously sensual. One says "grace" and we see a pretty girl, more rarely a very young man. But Genet has a severe conception of beauty. He cares little about the substance of the beautiful; only its form matters. "Beauty," he says, "is the perfection of organization." But the purpose of organization may be to terrify. The beauty of the criminal is the perfect organization of Evil, its plenitude, its perfect visibility, its purity, its power, its staggering evidence. Beauty can be perfection *in ugliness*. Does not Genet say that ugliness is beauty at rest and, about one of his friends who is pale with cowardice, that his face was radiant with beauty? "Armand's face was false, cunning, mean, sneaky, brutal. No doubt it is easy for me to discover these things after knowing the man, but I know that the impression I had at the time could have been the result only of the miraculous union of these qualities on a single face. . . . He exhibited no regular beauty, but the presence on his face of what I have mentioned— and which was pure because so unmarred by its opposite—gave him a somber though sparkling appearance. His physical strength was prodigious." The reader may regard this as a kind of taste for paradox or merely for systematizing. To do so would be to simplify: Genet *really* has an impression of beauty in the presence of this brute. The proof is that he immediately submits to Armand's pleasure: he has come to the Beautiful through Evil.

If one carries matters to their ultimate conclusion—and Genet always does—the fact is that the criminal is already dead. This big, grim, mindless piece of window dressing is a dead man; Genet submits to a dead man. We have already seen the child Genet die. And since, as a result of the vanishing of consciousness, death shifts the existent to being and, in particular, to being for others, we already knew that the will to become the Other, to become absolute appearance, entails death for all the embodiments of Evil. Genet says admirably of the Carolinas, who are Barcelona fairies:

"Covered with ridicule, the Carolinas were sheltered. . . . They were all dead. What we saw walking in the street were shades cut off from the world. Fairies are a pale and motley race that flower in the minds of decent folk."

But there are various ways of dying. The loftiest is probably that of the criminal, because he hurls himself with all his freedom— that strange freedom which merges with fatality—against the rock of his destiny. "To state only that the criminal thinks, while committing his crime, that he will never be caught is false. No doubt he refuses to distinguish precisely the frightful sequel which his act has for himself. Nevertheless, he knows that this act condemns him to death. We shall call Querelle a joyous moral suicide." And further on: "When the crime had been committed, Querelle felt upon his shoulder the hand of an ideal detective, and he continued walking with heavy steps from the edge of the corpse to that isolated spot, crushed by the astonishing destiny which will be his."

The reason is that, in this world of appearance, to be a murderer is not only to kill, nor even to kill because that is one's destiny, but also to be recognized and consecrated, hence pursued, hounded, ar-

rested, imprisoned, condemned, executed ingloriously. To will to
be a thief is to will that others have an advantage over me, to will
that each of my acts be henceforth only the seamy side of theirs.
After the commission of a crime (in this case, a theft, but it would
be even truer of a murder) : "A new universe instantaneously presented itself to Darling: the universe of the irremediable. It is the
same as the one we were in, with one peculiar difference: instead of
acting and knowing we are acting, we know we are acted upon."
Obliging wills substitute for his: instead of his going toward objects, instead of his putting out his hand to seize them, they fly into
his hand; things have lost their "coefficient of adversity." As if he
were a prince, others will mount his stairs and will help him to
descend them, a car will wait for him outside, doors will open by
themselves, hands will give him his food, judges will inconvenience
themselves for him, desiring only to hear him tell about his life,
and, as a finishing touch, in the early hours of the morning a throne
will be set up for him. He knows that this frightful kindness is
pushing him toward death. Let him consent to die, let him demand
his fate with pride. All wills will harmonize with his, he will become the center of the world. As soon as Green Eyes assumed his
crime, "everything became easy. He simply made the gestures that
led him as quietly as can be to the guillotine." The unity of minds,
which the Good and the True have such difficulty in achieving, will
be produced easily but in reverse, with resentment and hatred. And
for that very reason the criminal's death is his revenge and his
apotheosis.
Let us imagine this corpse which has already been turned over
to others, which is swarming with insects: its act, committed in
silence and darkness, has suddenly placed it before us, naked, in a
glaring light. An object of contempt and hatred because it caused
a death, it is also the object of universal respect because death inhabits it. It will know the joy of making right-thinking people
revere Evil in its person. In a certain sense, the criminal is still being
duped, for if the members of the social body bare their heads, it is
not for him, but for the decease which society has in store for him.
But he does not think of this, and, moreover, what he thinks hardly
matters: it is Genet who matters, Genet, lost in the crowd, who sees
him going by and who is enjoying the religious horror he inspires.
This great pompous and tragic appearance will have the destiny it
deserves. It is escorted to the throne in a chariot; it mounts the
steps of the throne, towers above and contemplates a sea of upturned
faces. Finally, it confronts them all and rises above them all. In the
muttering of the frightened voices it hears a hymn to its solitude

and silence. The child Genet is avenged by another. The abjection into which he had been cast by the condemnation of all men is assumed by another and changed into glory. In a moment he will be quite dead, with his head on one side and his body on the other. Genet's revenge will then be complete, for these pure appearances have a strange power beyond their life. As long as they are alive, the decent man rids himself of his negativity by discharging it upon them, then forgets them. The police serves as *censor:* "The police is to society what the dream is to daily life. That which society forbids itself it authorizes the police to evoke as soon as it wants it." The police filters the decent man's consciousness and protects it from the dark phantoms which, in the last analysis, are only the objective manifestations of his propensity for doing wrong. And besides, whether dead or alive, the small fry—fairies and thieves— "will never be entitled to broad daylight." But if one of the powers of darkness should commit an exemplary crime, his act overrides the censor, charges forward, and the right-thinking man cannot help but see it. If one thinks that one is getting rid of the criminal by executing him, the world of darkness triumphs, for the guillotine becomes legendary. Landru, Jack the Ripper and Weidmann have long since ceased to exist, *except in good consciences.* The latter are obliged to maintain them in being by a will contrary to good will. The police are powerless. What can cops do against a memory? So the decent man's loathing of the culprit becomes the decent man's self-loathing. He blamed the criminal for existing, he blames himself for evoking him. He is fascinated for a moment by that image which now derives its being only from him, and he suddenly realizes that it is his reflection. By virtue of his death the criminal gives back to the just what the just have given him. For want of a scapegoat, Evil reinstates the good consciences and poisons them in turn. Immortality itself is inverted. It is the great, stately shades of benefactors of mankind which seem lifeless appearances, since the decent man evokes them with pleasure and is very conscious of drawing them up from nothingness when it suits him to do so. On the other hand, the unholy shades, which he fears, seem to him to evoke themselves independently and against his will: Soleilland has more mana than St. Vincent de Paul. What Genet desires in a roughneck whom he happens to encounter is not only his fall, but his glory as well. If he later dreamed of literary glory, it was as a substitute for the criminal glory he was unable to acquire, somewhat as a symbolic sacrifice has, in certain religions, been substituted for human sacrifice.

For the time being, the criminal, standing on the scaffold with his hands tied, is not yet defunct; he has a moment left, a moment of that life which so relentlessly willed death, as Pierrot willed the presence in his mouth of the worm that froze him with horror. Faithful to himself, he strains his evil will to the breaking point in willing, as ultimate conclusion, his own Evil. He is pushed, he swings: at the instant when his life is exalted to its highest pitch, he is metamorphosed for others into the absolute Other who no longer exists except in terms of others. There is no doubt that Genet projects into this myth of the fatal instant that other instant which separated him from his childhood as the blade of the guillotine separates the head from the trunk. The crime, that vertiginous fall which transforms the innocent man into a guilty one, and the public execution, which changes life into death, are only the double repetition of this crisis. The criminal's entire life is summed up in two instants. And these two instants are ultimately one and the same, for the first opens up to allow a glimpse of the second. And both are only the objective representation of a third, that which Genet actually lived himself when the dizzying word rang in his ears. In this sense, the dual personality of Erik and his reflection, the dichotomy of the lover and the beloved, merely reproduce in space the myth of beheading. Erik crushing himself against the mirror and wanting to enter entirely into his reflection is the still living criminal pressing himself completely against his death and trying to go over alive to the other side of life. And just as, at the "fatal instant," the criminal contemplates himself as an absolute Other, that is, as a future dead man, so the lover, who alone is alive, devotes his life to contemplating, in the beloved, his own death.

The role of the beloved is to fulfill publicly, in heroic fashion, the destiny of Genet, even unto dying. His function is to give it the mystical and supernatural dimensions of a religious sacrifice and to confer upon it, in the eyes of Genet himself, the aspect of a Mystery. At the supreme instant, the greatest Evil and the greatest Good loom up together, separated by the infinitely thin gleam of the blade:

> . . . his apotheosis
> Will be the bright scaffold
> Lovely effect from which roses spring.

The reader will, I imagine, realize the advantages of the role Genet has chosen for himself: God immolating himself despite himself. It is for the salvation of the lover that the beloved dies.

But, after all, this Passion is only in prospect. As a matter of fact, it is dreamt. The males to whom Genet gives himself have never committed a murder, and actually they never will. But since the murderer is only an appearance, all that Genet asks of them is to have the stamp of the murderer. He won't be difficult: all he will require is that they be counterfeit murderers, just formidable enough for him to be able to dream up a magnificent destiny for them. Let them look mean and cruel; that will be in lieu of beauty. Let them be foolish, pigheaded, grim; that is enough for him to regard them as men "with a single possibility." Let their anger, their nervousness, their cowardice always get them into trouble; they will thus always have at least the trappings of fatality. Above all, let them be haughty; let their fierce pride make them burn with a desire to be terrible, that is, to be dreaded by others and to be unpredictable to themselves; let them dream only of appearing, of displaying themselves, of acting tough. They will then spontaneously establish themselves as pure appearances. Genet will do the rest and will convince himself that they are dead men. He will wrap the poor image that they want to give of themselves in the shroud of his love. Stupid and vile, often cowardly, conceited, blundering: there you have the picture of the males to whom Genet is going to submit. He will require of them only one virtue: indifference.

Indeed, in these living corpses life can be only a phantom life. They look, they talk, they command, but for Genet who contemplates them their looks, words and commands are only evil spells that escape from bewitched carcasses. Sacred because he is dead, the criminal is magical because he is alive. Magical indeed is the inanimate thing that produces human effects without ceasing to be a thing, and this is precisely what is done by that big male carcass which is haunted by a semblance of consciousness. Whatever human features it has are only a mirage that shimmers at the surface of matter. Thus, its beauty becomes a magical power which is nothing other than consciousness in reverse. The handsome, impenetrable Pimp has the powers of the negative. He can touch, push, enter, pound if he wants to, but one cannot touch him in return. He is a taboo object, like primitive kings who cast a blight on those who jostle them inadvertently. Beauty keeps one at a distance: "At times I would bring my hand very close to the edges without ever venturing to touch him, for I feared that he might dissolve, might drop dead or that I might die." A good definition of the satanic mirage. The pistoles in the Devil's purse change into dead leaves if one lays one's hand on it. Impelled by its inner logic, the notion of appearance spontaneously runs its course. Genet loves only appearance, submits only to appearance, which is simultaneously Evil, the Other and Beauty. But absolute appearance, like the big lakes of the Sahara, vanishes when one approaches it. If Genet stands too close to the handsome pimp whom he adores, the very appearance of the criminal will be dissipated. The handsome, spellbound corpse will become a live little brute. And it is Genet himself who begs beauty to keep away: "My hair shuddered, but at that instant the following prayer welled up in me: 'Do not let me touch you. Never address me.' " And he concludes: "Thus, I kept him at a distance." I cannot help but see a certain caution in this conjuration. Genet wants to keep his myth; he does not want to look at it too closely. But there is something else: he does not want to *take*. In order to achieve his ends, there is no need for him to feel a body, to possess it. If he wants to capture the appearance, he can make it descend into him only by a magical operation of submission. It is the appearance *as appearance* that he cherishes, with its borrowed and evanescent being. Not that he necessarily *resigns* himself to the mirage: he *loves* it as the thin film which separates being from nothingness. And one can maintain without fear of paradox that this beautiful image belongs to him more truly when it denies itself than when it gives itself. It is there, within reach, but if he takes another step, it is dissipated. Thus, it still depends on him since he forbids himself to take this step. It is born of his refusal to enjoy it, of the tension which mingles abstention with desire. If he bows to it and worships it, it grows stronger, it becomes hallucinatory. He believes in it without ceasing to know, in a corner of his mind, that he himself is the author of his belief. He says somewhere that "love is despair." It would be more correct to say that it is, in him, the proud will to solitude and despair in the presence of the other, for his pride is safe within the servitude: he submits to an absence.

We can understand why he regards indifference as the cardinal virtue of the beloved. But the object of worship must not think of reciprocating; he would lose his prestige, would cease at once to be the Other and become a lover, a burden. To serve him is perfect; but Genet refuses to be of service to him. If the beloved proved to be a consciousness, if he sought in Genet his other self, Genet would lose his solitude, would cease to be the purely relative, the inessential which he has striven to become, at the very moment when the beloved, descending from heaven to earth, lost his baleful and sublime virtue as a transfigured corpse. Once, however, during his adolescence, Genet desired a certain youngster. "You don't mean it," replied the other in surprise. "We're the same age." When

Genet realized what he had been doing, he approved the reply with all his heart. The episode is revealing: since the particularity which he has made of himself is the result of the fact that the others refuse to maintain reciprocal relations with him, Genet, who is nothing other than the demand for the particular, would think he was destroying himself if he accepted reciprocal love. Such a statement as Divine's saying to Gabriel "You're myself" might be misleading. And, in fact, Gabriel smiles with pride: he is thrilled, the idiot. But the words mean: I am your truth and you are not mine. We shall come back to this.

The indifference of the handsome males is not even cruelty, nor is it hardness of heart or coldness of temperament or any other inner, contingent trait of character. It is their very essence, their profound nature as things, as objects. For Genet, the couple is conceived as the union of the soul and the body, but inverted. It is composed of a consciousness and of a body, but the consciousness has turned to the body and made of it its sole object. Their relations cannot therefore be reciprocal, since the consciousness is a consciousness of the body and the body is quite simply a body. Or, if one prefers, the former is in itself and for itself a relationship, and the latter is an autonomous substance. It is this externality, this autonomy of the substance, that Genet calls indifference. "The queens . . . fancied they were enlacing this handsome man. . . . Indifferent and bright as a slaughterhouse knife, he passed by, cleaving them all in two slices which came together again noiselessly, though emitting a slight scent of hopelessness which no one betrayed." The words designating the loved ones are all disguised negations: "motionless and silent," "inflexible," "impenetrable," "the angel of death and death itself, as unyielding as a rock," "You did not move, you were not sleeping, you were not dreaming, you were in flight, motionless and pale, frozen, straight, stretched out stiff." This tough is absent. His purest virtues are destructive forces or deficiencies. He is first and foremost the *non:* nonlife, nonlove, nonpresence, nongood.

No doubt it is essential that the pimps have muscles. In the presence of a powerful build, Genet swoons and melts with love, excited by the simple display of virile strength, but these muscles serve no purpose. Too aristocratic to work, the beloved are too lazy to want to achieve the kind of athletic distinction of which the lover might be proud; and too serious as well, too absorbed in their austere and egotistical dances; and as for fighting, they are too cowardly. In fact, if we are to believe Genet's accounts, the stronger they are the more cowardly they are. Darling is a coward, Green Eyes is a coward, Bulkaen, Paulo and Stilitano are cowards. Far from reproaching them with this cowardice, Genet delights in it. If he is threatened, it does not even occur to him to take refuge under their wing. Those powerful arms are not meant for protecting him. Quite the contrary, Darling and Green Eyes snicker when the girl queens tear each other to pieces for love of them. The Germans rape Riton in front of Erik's eyes without the latter's making a move to defend him. No, the muscles are for display. They impart a quiet and terrible power to movements, they are the signs of transcendence. But only the signs, for the pimp never does anything. They are the epaulettes and gold braid which manifest his right to command. Above all, their compact solidity is the symbol of the criminal's absolute density, his impenetrability: muscles and frame represent the being of this appearance, the opacity of the in-itself. Impenetrable and tough, bulky, tense, rocky, the pimp will be defined by his rigidity. His body, drawn upward by the muscles, seems a penis taut with the desire to pierce, to bore, to split, rising toward the sky "with the cruel and sudden sharpness of a steeple puncturing a cloud of ink." *Rigidity,* word dear to Genet, both moral and sexual, designating the tension of his soul, his hatred of all abandon, and the fatal force that drives the criminal to his destruction. Rigidity: Destiny is a giant penis, the man is utterly a sex organ and the organ becomes a man. "The big, inflexible, strict pimps, their cocks in full bloom—I no longer know whether they are lilies or whether lilies and cocks are not totally they." Genet's pansexualism is going to find this muscular and sexual stiffness everywhere. The child Querelle, at the foot of one of the two massive towers that defend the port of La Rochelle, experienced "a feeling both of power and impotence. First of pride, pride at knowing that so high a tower is the symbol of his virility . . . and, at the same time, he had a feeling of quiet humility in the presence of the serious and incomparable potency of some indefinable male." When Genet describes the relationship of a girl queen to a male, he uses a comparison which recurs constantly, that of a spiral rolling about an upright rigidity. And this image evolves to the point of becoming a sexual motif which is reproduced by Nature everywhere. First, there is the *spectacle:*

"The girl queens are huddled together and chattering and cheeping around the boy queens who are straight, motionless and vertiginous, as motionless and silent as branches."

Then, the *gesture:*

"All the queens imparted to their bodies a tendril-like movement and fancied they were enlacing this handsome man, that they were twining around him."

Then, the *metaphor:*

"Round some, more upright, more solid than the others, twined clematis, convolvulus, nasturtium, little pimps too, tortuous."

Finally, the sexual pattern creeps into the perception: the sky in the middle of palaces becomes "the column of azure round which twines the marble."

But, inversely, this pansexualism is panmoralistic. Not a touch of sensuality in this universe. The penis is made of *metal;* Paulo's is a cannon. What excites Genet about a prick is never the flesh of which it is composed but its power of penetration, its mineral hardness. It is a drill, a pile driver, it will be a dagger, "a torture machine." The sex organ and the muscles are of the same nature: rods, iron bars, steel claws whose function is to subdue him in spite of himself, to support, by means of a foreign constraint, his will to be enslaved. Genet, as we have seen, loathes gratuitousness. To submit voluntarily would be pointless. That is what "normal" lovers do when they yield to the will of their mistresses. And they always retain the feeling that this submission is an act, that they are the masters. Genet's excitement requires that the servitude be effective, imposed. In order for him to feel that he belongs to the Other and that through this surrender he becomes the Other in his own eyes, the strength of the beloved must force him to the floor. Let the male violate him, bully him, beat him. Above all, he himself must not be able to break his chains on pain of death. Gorgui kills his mistress who wanted to leave him, Divine fears that Gorgui may kill "her." Erik despises the executioner because the latter has not killed him. Armand excites Genet more than anyone else because "his muscular power, visible in the shape of the skull and the base of the neck, further proclaimed, and imposed, these detestable qualities. It made them sparkle." Genet reads his fate in this muscularity, a horrible destiny of docility. Desire immediately reduces him to submission. But what is his desire if not dizziness? And what is dizziness if not a fall that is felt in advance and mimed in his flesh, the fall into the Other's heart from the top of the cliff that stands against the sky? The movement is relative. This penis rises up with the speed of Genet's fall, and the deeper the abyss into which Genet falls, the more dizzying is its height. At the bottom of the precipice the lover finds the corpse of the beloved who has fallen there before him: the fist that makes Genet grovel before the

pimp is one and the same as the Fatality that drives the latter to
death. Thus, this universe of strongholds, minarets and bell towers,
this phallic bristling of nature, is the vision of a man who is falling
and who sees high walls rising above him and hiding the sun.
Genet's sexuality is the dynamism of the fall, the gravity of Evil
felt in the flesh. Bachelard would say that he has an "Icarus complex." In this sense, the sexual act proper represents the religious
ceremony, which makes it possible to gather into an instant the
infiniteness of daily submission. Genet undergoes Armand's brutality, his exigencies; he begs, steals and prostitutes himself for
him; he laces his shoes, lights his cigarettes. All these jobs take time
and patience. Servitude is a long-term undertaking; it is broken up
into a thousand particular dislikes which conceal the whole. In
order for him to enjoy them, there must be a violent contraction, a
spasm which sums up everything in a moment, in short a *festival*,
which is a kind of *sacred time* that emerges cyclically amidst profane
time and endows the latter with new force. The sexual act is the
festival of submission;* it is also the ritual renewal of the feudal
contract whereby the vassal becomes his lord's liegeman.

But the posture of the officiants confers a new meaning upon
this Black Mass. The beloved goes behind Genet and casually subjects him to his pleasure. Now, the Other, in Genet, the Thief, was
also behind his consciousness. He maneuvered it, watched it, and
it was unable to turn around to see. That was why Genet ended by
projecting his nature upon another. But now that this other, who
is lying on his back, crushes him, digs into him and penetrates him,
Genet at last enjoys his Nature. He enjoys it with all his muscles,
which grow taut so as to bear the enormous weight, enjoys it with
his whole body, which stifles beneath this iron bulk. For him, the
sexual act always resembles a rape. His submission does not exclude
the frightful resistance of his pride, which is represented in his
flesh by the vanquished resistance of his sphincter. But he enjoys
this resistance and is glad that he is vanquished, for the struggle
and the defeat lead him back to the original conflict between his
will and itself, to the inner contradiction of the will-to-Evil. The
agonizing thing about this conflict is not so much the fact that it
was lived as that it was willed and acted, that he had to maintain,
knowingly, a contradiction that asked only to vanish. But now an
evil—and absolutely other—will is being substituted for the phan-

---

* At least such is its manifest aspect. We shall see later that it also represents the passion
and ritual murder of the beloved.

tom will which he has been vainly trying to raise to the level of being. He thrashes about, but in vain. Each of his efforts to shake off the embrace makes him feel, through his impotence, the triumph of his Nature. He experiences the pleasure of *being acted upon* which he envied the murderer. The other is crushing his conscious will, his desire to preserve a semblance of dignity in abjection, to remain at the source of his actions. Another is penetrating him, furrowing him with suffering, and this other, who has been transformed into a torture machine, is the handsome lad whose venomous splendor he has been admiring. Beauty is painful, beauty is frightful. Behind its appearance is revealed the unbearable horror of the universe. The catastrophe is complete, the failure irremediable, but Genet's victory is thereby assured, since he wanted to play the game of loser wins. What is manifested through his humiliation, rage and pain is *at last* the presence of Evil. This visitation is effected, as is fitting, not by way of the noble parts, as in the mystics, who value intellectual intuition above all else, but by that of the ignoble parts, those meant for excretion. Are not Evil, the criminal and Genet himself the excrement of society? Even the burning sensation which he feels is ambiguous, contradictory in its essence. The homosexual does not know, in the griping ache of his pain, whether he is expelling excrement or opening himself to a foreign body. Rejection and acceptance are intimately mingled in the most immediate impression.

And yet, in this abject and ridiculous posture, amidst his suffering and his muck, it is nevertheless his God that he is receiving. This is apparent in the following reflection of Paulo, whom the Other pretends to be taking but finally does not take:

"He suffered when confronted with his newly acquired integrity, when confronted with his free and lonely personality, the solitude of which was revealed to him by the detachment of God himself. The blow made him feel a sorrow which might be expressed by the following reflection which I am making in his place: 'What can you do now without him?' "

Does this not have the ring of the mystic's laments in moments of aridity? But this dreadful God, this God in reverse, remains, to the very end, the opposite of God. The ecstasy of the passive homosexual is a torture. The inflexible male homosexual seeks in the girl queen only himself. He wants to coincide with the image he has glimpsed in submissive eyes. And when he thinks he has succeeded, the image dies as a result of being attained, and the desire with it: this is the orgasm. What becomes of Genet in all this? He

no longer counts; he is the instrument and the place; and this in-
toxicates him. When his consciousness was empty, it was still in the
way; insofar as it remained conscious of being empty, it was present
to itself, it still prevented him from being absorbed through all the
pores of the beloved. But now it is a cask that has been broached.
A hidden being has broken through it in order to join the appearance which it carries in front of it. Genet's evil Nature rips this
spider's web in order to melt into the Being that he is in the eyes
of others. The erect penis of the beloved is a sudden concretion of
pure Being. Impaled by Being! Another, in pursuing only his
pleasure, achieves for Genet the identification of Genet with himself. Crushed, compressed, perforated, consciousness dies so that
the In-itself may be born.

This is a murder: submissive to a corpse, neglected, unnoticed,
gazed at unmindfully and manipulated from behind, the girl queen
is metamorphosed into a contemptible female object. She does not
even have for the pimp the importance that the sadist attributes
to his victim. The latter, though tortured and humiliated, at least
remains the focal point of her tormentor's concern. It is indeed she
whom he wishes to reach, in her particularity, in the depths of her
consciousness. But the fairy is only a receptacle, a vase, a spittoon
which one uses and thinks no more of and which one discards by
the very use one makes of it. The pimp masturbates in her. At the
very instant when an irresistible force knocks her down, turns her
over and punctures her, a dizzying word swoops down upon her, a
power hammer that strikes her as if she were a medal: *"Enculé!"**
This is the word that Querelle keeps turning over in his mind
after giving himself to a man. It is striking that Genet regards the
metamorphosis of an adolescent into a passive homosexual as an
irremediable change, strictly comparable to the effect that the crime
has upon the criminal. In order to cancel the murder which he has
just committed by a countermurder of himself, Querelle lets himself be taken by Norbert. The murder of Vic had transformed him
into that absolute and solitary object, the criminal. In order to
escape his "amazing destiny," Querelle, like Green Eyes dancing
in an effort to elude his crime, imagines himself being changed
into *another object:* the girl queen. Thus, the sexual act which
confers upon Genet a fairy's destiny renews the crisis that transforms him into a thief. In both cases, a child is pinned to the floor
by the gazes of strong, cruel men. But this time the crisis is pro-

---

* *Enculé:* Literally, "one who gets buggered." As a term of abuse, it is the French equivalent of the English "cocksucker."—Translator's note.

voked, accepted, and, as in psychoanalytic treatment, acquires a cathartic value. As a rigorous identification of himself with the other and the other with himself, as a willed and ceremonial repetition of the original crisis, the intercourse is doubly sacred: it is the fatal instant; it gathers within itself all the evil elements of theft, crime and beheading. It is not surprising that all of Genet's rivers converge toward it, that all his propensities lead to it. It is his whole life condensed into a spasm, his whole past, his whole destiny. It is the accident which affected him with passivity forever, and it is the brave decision which transformed the catastrophe into a choice. It is the Kierkegaardian paradox. The opposites which coexist without merging are the sacred time of the mystic visitation and that of destruction. As opposed to the time of construction which extends to the far reaches of the future, it is the time of passive intuition and of being. It is eternity. In an instant Genet risks himself, transforms himself and damns himself forever. He loses his soul in an instant.

Sensual pleasure is rigorously excluded from this ceremony. The beauty which Genet serves is inflexibly severe. The male never caresses the girl queen. If he touches her, it is only to place her roughly in a position that will heighten his pleasure. What rightfully reverts to Genet is the suffering which is flight, which is self-hatred. He boldly demands it as his share. He says of an adolescent who is possessed by a pimp: "He desired only an increase of pain so as to lose himself in it." And another of his characters cries out, while being taken: "Kill me!" Even the orgasm is denied the lover, at least during intercourse. Or rather it is the lover himself who denies himself the right to ejaculate. If, out of kindness (which, be it added, is very rare), the beloved makes an effort to give him pleasure, he declines. Riton gently pushes Erik's hand away because "It was normal that Erik get pleasure from Riton, who was younger than he, and normal that Riton serve Erik." The lover, who is the beloved's slave, takes his pleasure alone, afterward, and hides himself to do so. Divine goes to finish off in the toilet—and quite likely he does not choose this unclean place at random—or else quickly and ashamedly masturbates behind Our Lady's back. The lover's pleasure is the upbeat. It is glossed over. It is already the moment of separation, of solitude. The downbeat is the pleasure of the beloved. They both exhaust themselves, amidst violence and pain, in serving it; they both sacrifice themselves so that the absolute, namely, the male's orgasm, may come into being. Thus, it is both true and false that Genet gets no pleasure during intercourse. *There is* pleasure within him, deep in his martyrized flesh; only, it is the other who gets it. But the Other is his own Nature, himself as he is changed into himself. Little by little, as the thrusts which are tearing him apart become increasingly brutal, Genet begins to feel, deep inside him, the gradual birth of a phantom of pleasure, an urgent absence, *his* gratification insofar as he is the Other, his pleasure as *other pleasure,* an absolute begotten by his body, a pleasure which the movements of his loins cause the beloved to bring forth and which finally emerges beneath the sky, an autonomous and self-sufficient reality. Thus, the supreme moment of coitus is not that of abandon to natural plenitude, of letting go, of release of tension, of satisfied expectation. Quite the contrary, it is at the maximum of tension; his whole body grows taut and offers itself as a receptacle for the pleasure which grazes him, which inhabits him, which blossoms in the darkness of his bowels and of which he will never experience anything but the *reverse,* that is, suffering. Suffering is the necessary complement of the other's pleasure; he enjoys it as pleasure insofar as he is other. We are thus back at the generalized inversion that characterizes Evil, the will that is eager—since he is denied everything—to seize upon privation as the mark of plenitude, to be filled by emptiness. His pain is imaginary pleasure. He grows tense, gives himself, pants, swoons, in short makes all the movements and moans of a woman who is coming. In the case of the latter, however, this behavior accompanies the orgasm, it is its expression and effect, whereas in Genet it is a magical attitude that aims at *treating suffering as pleasure.* He imitates abandon at the price of extreme tension, he cries aloud and tosses about so that the pleasure he receives may become, in the eyes of invisible witnesses, the meaning of his attitudes. No one is more active than this homosexual who is called a passive homosexual. I would compare him to the frigid woman who strains against herself in an effort to feel an absent ecstasy. But there is a fundamental difference between them. The latter is actually rebelling against her frigidity. The phantom of pleasure which she finally attains seems to her only a makeshift. Genet, lord of Evil, deliberately substitutes appearance for being. He *could* give himself the orgasm, and refuses it. If he pursues this imaginary gratification, it is not in defiance of its unreality but because of it. The frigid wife looks forward to a stroke of luck, to a late awakening of her senses. Genet looks forward *to nothing.* At the core of the sexual act we find a mad desire for the impossible. The two stages of the sexual act both involve a structure of make-believe. The downbeat is a real presence of the Other, a felt visitation and a virtual presence of pleasure; the upbeat of masturbation is a real presence of pleasure, but accompanied by fantasy: Divine masturbates while thinking of Our Lady, but Our Lady has come out of Divine and forgotten him. In the last analysis, it is this creative tension which is the goal. At the moment when he charges the Other with crushing his consciousness and shattering it, Genet, emperor of sham, remains a free and exasperated consciousness which supports, all by itself, an imaginary world. The highest moment of this consciousness is that in which it becomes a consciousness which forgets itself, a consciousness aware of forgetting itself, just as the highest moment of the criminal's life is that of his death. The summit of pride is the abyss of humility. It is when his God visits him that Genet, inverted mystic, is at the height of solitude.

This savage and contorted life, this exalted affirmation of the impossible, is followed by death, like the instant of beheading. Are not the "white flowers" which come out of the beloved's penis sisters of the red flowers which sprang from the decapitated body of Pilorge? The orgasm is the paradoxical instant of the most intense pleasure and of the end of pleasure. Within Genet the beloved dies. Genet senses this death and accompanies it. He suddenly relaxes, expands, "sinks into darkness," dies with the other's death: he swoons. Thus, beneath the constructions of his will, we find the foundation of his basic anxieties and his humble desire for suicide, a desire which is forever being rejected, repressed, forever being reborn. Indeed, it frequently happens that our most constantly repudiated primary desires give consistency and flesh to the acts of will that contradict them most, and there is thus a double determination of the most important acts of our life, which thus admit of two opposite interpretations. The dizziness that overcomes Genet in the presence of a handsome male certainly expresses this extraordinarily complex construction which causes Genet to choose to be the other and to find his destiny in the stately tragedy of capital punishment. But at the same time, this infinite fall is, in an obscure, in a muted way, a kind of leave which he grants himself: leave to die.

He does not die. Consciousness flows back, Genet is reborn from his ashes. The girl queen, who has been cut in two by the slaughterhouse knife, is glued together, emitting a slight fragrance of desolation. She survives herself, just as the child survived the malediction that killed him. The Other has withdrawn from her. She is empty. Nothing remains of the madness that convulsed her, nothing but a bit of pain and blood. To the very end the Other has remained the Other; this pursuit of the impossible will have to be resumed over and over, indefinitely. Genet knows this, and that is what he wants. He knows that the identification of which he dreams can be effected only at the limit, that it is one and the same as the infinite movement of sexuality which is forever resumed. He wants it to be so. His day-to-day life as a slave drives him to the brief, tragic condensation of coupling, and the latter, in vanishing, drives him back to his entire life as a slave, to, as it were, his guarantee and his development. The instant sends him back to temporality in its entirety, and vice versa. Exhausted but not appeased, Genet gazes at the beautiful, tranquil appearance which has taken shape again beyond his reach, and he concludes: "Love is despair." But we now know that this despair is willed and that he first rejected the only chance of salvation through love: reciprocity.

He has refused it so utterly that he completes the sexual myth of the criminal by building a feudal system which he arranges with the express purpose of reserving the lowest place in it for himself. Imagine a small military or quasi-military community which evolves on the fringes of real society. One enters it by virtue of an initiation, the three major ceremonies of which are crime, theft and anal intercourse. This parasitic minority, which is composed of a noble caste and its mob of vassals, is not permitted to engage in any work. It lives on the work of the others, it is an association of consumers. Its members likewise have nothing to do with the system of large-scale industrial production and that of private property. It is not that they possess their property in common, for they possess nothing at all. They are nomadic or seminomadic and, by force of trickery, seize the belongings of the sedentary population and consume their booty on the spot. Cut off from contact with the forces of nature and knowing matter only in the state of manufactured products, they have not yet raised themselves to the plane of positive thought. They have not the slightest idea of determinism and of the laws of nature, and, though they usually live in the slums of big cities, nothing is more remote from them than the mentality of the proletariat. In fact, they bear a resemblance to the middle class in that they consider the course of the world to be governed by human wills. Their mind, which has remained fetishistic, is a compound of ceremonious politeness and aggressiveness. And as they cannot be bound among themselves by a hierarchy of functions based on division of labor, they justify social distinctions by differences of nature or essence and divide the members of their society into two major categories: the tough and the soft. And the tough are tough by nature and for all eternity. Toughness is not identical with strength; it is rather the union of strength and meanness. In a duel between toughs, victory is not to the huskier or the better armed, but to the tougher, that is, to the one who is superior by nature. Similarly, the soft is soft by nature, and there is nothing he can do about it: "Divine is soft. . . . She is she-who-is-soft. That is, whose character is soft, whose cheeks are soft, whose tongue is soft. . . . With Gorgui, all is hard." The tough is a criminal, the soft a thief or beggar. They both destroy. But the criminal destroys man, whereas the thief destroys only the human significations which are *on* things, that is, he attempts, by the use he makes of the objects he steals, to efface the mark which their legitimate owner has left upon them.

Between toughs and softs the natural relationship is vassalage. The bond between man and object—the relationship based on production or appropriation—which characterizes our societies is replaced by the feudal person-to-person bond. The toughs do not possess things. Crime and theft procure for them the fleeting and hidden enjoyment of an object which remains duly possessed by its legal owner. But they possess men. The soft *pays homage* to the tough with his body; he becomes his liegeman.* The tough can allow himself to be as unfaithful as he likes; the soft must remain faithful to him or die. Thus, in *Raoul de Cambrai,* Bernier le Vavasseur keeps his faith in his lord who betrays him publicly. What does the tough give in return? His person, his protection. But let there be no misunderstanding: we have already seen that he never defended his vassals, that he let them be raped and massacred without lifting a finger. Singular kind of protection: without bothering about them, in fact seeming often to ignore their existence, he protects them against the great metaphysical fear inspired by contingency and freedom. As far as he is concerned, he does not act on anyone's behalf and derives his justification only from himself: "He is his own heaven." This is what constitutes his greatness and his weakness. He decides alone, he is his own witness, legislator and judge. No mission, no mandate, ever relieves him of his aloneness. That is why he allows himself to be cowardly, at times even, like Green Eyes, to betray. Law does not exist for him. It is he who defines law for the others. By virtue of this fact, he *gives,* he is *generous.* Thanks to him, there is law for the soft, an ethic, a supreme

---

* "Homage" derives from *homme,* the French word for "man."—Translator's note.

end. The vassal derives from his absolute obedience the actual justification of his existence. No doubt about it, he is born to serve. If he obeys, he becomes sacred, for he bears within him, like a relic, the chief's mandate. Genet says of Stilitano, for whom he smuggles dope, "Thanks to him, I was no longer going to cross a border for my own paltry needs but rather out of obedience, out of submission to a sovereign Power." And "realizing that it was through me that he had to act, I attached myself to him, sure of drawing strength from the elementary and disorganized power that shaped him." We find again in the sphere of action what we noted in connection with sexual possession: another crosses the border in the guise of Genet; the sovereign power is Genet's Nature or, if one prefers, inverted duty; it is Evil as supreme legislator of the universe. For all his vassals the Tough is the Roof, he is the Mandate. We are reminded of the strange perplexity of Kafka: "I am mandated," he said, "but mandated by *no one.*" Thanks to Stilitano, to Armand, Genet can at times avoid this anxiety. The general mandate to do evil which he discovered within himself and which no one gave him is converted into particular mandates to steal, to prostitute himself, to smuggle dope. And these are given him by a person who is quite alive. The Tough is, to speak like Hegel, Evil transformed into absolute subject. That is why Genet can talk about the *kindness* of that inhuman brute Armand without surprising us. Armand is kind because he is a source of Being and justification. A hierarchy will be established among the toughs, and their place in it will depend on the height and breadth of the sky they shoulder and on the number of persons they shelter in their shade. "Here in the cell," says Green Eyes, a local squireen, "I'm the one who bears the brunt. . . . I need a strong back. Like Snowball. He bears the same weight. But for the whole prison. Maybe there's someone else, a Number One Big Shot, who bears it for the whole world." Thus, by an inversion dear to Genet, the virtue of the chiefs is cowardice, because it expresses the great and bitter anguish of solitude and freedom. Courage, on the other hand, is the vulgar quality of the vassals, who are no more a prey to anguish than are children to the moral problems which torment their parents. They receive a ready-made ethic, and it does not occur to them to question it. If they distinguish themselves, it is by doing more than is required of them and by risking everything, even death, in order to enhance themselves in their master's eyes. Thus, the greatest tenderness, the greatest kindness, which the lord can manifest toward his men is extreme severity. He need not fear to ask the impossible of them. Since it is from him that they derive their Being and the particle of the Sacred which justifies their existing, it follows that the more redoubtable his demands the higher will they rise above themselves. If he tempts them by the Worst, by what is most difficult, by a mortal whim, he deserves to be worshiped. That is what Claudel does: his priests and judges practice temptation by Good upon Sygne, upon Prouhèze. In both cases, the master fascinates the creatures by values which they have not found themselves. In both cases, one decides without them as to their Evil or their Good. And in Claudel the Good is meant first to inspire terror whereas in Genet the terror practiced by the Big Shot is called kindness. This is quite to be expected: it is the same feudal dream. The only difference is that Genet is at the bottom of his hierarchy and Claudel at the top of his. In any case, in Genet the man-to-man relationship rigorously excludes reciprocity. It is neither a fellowship-in-work nor a brotherhood-in-arms. It is hardly a complicity. At times a word rises to his lips; he says: "It's *almost* a friendship." He would no doubt subscribe to the definition recorded by Gide in the *Journal of the Counterfeiters:* "A friend is a person with whom one would be glad to do a dirty job."

This vertical relationship is the axis of feodality about which are established horizontal relationships of juxtaposition. The Lords behave to each other as one power to another and give each other gifts. Snowball, who is at the top of the hierarchy, sends Green Eyes smiles, advice and cigarettes. And Green Eyes thinks: "Snowball is at my side." These ceremonies, however, cloak the true nature of their relations: they keep each other at a respectful distance. One might regard this as a kind of thieves' *justice,* taking the word in the sense used by Nietzsche in *Human, All Too Human:* "Justice (equity) originates among men who are more or less equally powerful. . . . The idea of reaching an understanding arises where there is no clearly recognized predominant power and where a struggle would entail only mutual damage without result." It is rather clear that this justice is negative: if you don't touch me, I'll let you alone. Fundamentally, the toughs are united—except in the case of a job to be undertaken jointly—by bonds of "mechanical solidarity." They encounter each other, exchange greetings and avoid each other. Between the tough and the soft there is a transitory category: that of the young toughs, adolescents who have not yet assumed the toga virilis. Like the soft, they serve the Big Shots' pleasure, but the latter recognize them as being of their kind. These future criminals are hated and envied by the soft, to whom they are superior in both virility and femininity. But, at the same time, the girl queens swoon in the presence of the masculine inflexibility which they sense in those youthful bodies. These contradictory feelings provoke diverse reactions: Lefranc, a girl queen, strangles Maurice, a future hero of crime. Divine, who is older than Our Lady, wants to subjugate him and treat him as a woman. He lets her have her way, just for the fun of it. But at the moment of possessing him, Divine swoons and, submissive despite herself, slides under him to be taken.

As for the soft, justice cannot reign among them since they derive their strength from that of the Master. And if they live in peace, it is a shadow of peace which falls from above. The Lord's caprice establishes amongst them a hierarchy which is always provisional and which he modifies as he sees fit. They therefore challenge the prevailing order by invoking yesterday's or tomorrow's favor. They loathe each other and spend their time fighting and playing dirty tricks on each other. At times they kill one another before the amused eyes of the master. Even when they are under iron discipline and resign themselves to tolerating one another, not the slightest suspicion of fellowship exists among them. In order to communicate among themselves, they must do so through the lord, even when he is away. And as they are not coordinated by division of labor, they live *juxtaposed*. Unlike harem women, they do not even make love among themselves because each is, for the other, the image of his abjection and his "bad smell." "We can't love each other in slavery," say Solange and Claire, the maids, whom Genet explicitly charges with representing passive homosexuals on the stage. And since, as we shall see, they are traitors by nature, they never think of betraying together. Genet writes of one of them: "He is loath to have me as a companion in abjection because I am less glamorous in his eyes than some other thief, less sparkling." In betrayal, as in love, the girl queen remains alone.

Such, then, is the society of criminals and thieves. Obviously it has no real existence, as Genet himself is careful to inform us; it is he who puts us on guard against the fables of cheap fiction: there is no solidarity in evil, no "band," no "gang"; at most, there are short-lived associations which come into being when a "job" is to be done, and then immediately break up. When choosing scapegoats, the society of the just was careful to remove their means of uniting. When it convinced them that they wanted to do evil, it intimated to them that they ought to make it a point of honor to remain alone. If they formed a group, they would discover a Good:

theirs. But what possible demand could unite them? Theft, crime and falsehood do not warrant being raised to the Universal. Moreover, the mythical society which Genet has built collapses as soon as you look at it. It is not even a "solitude in common," it is a juxtaposition of individual solitudes. Among tough and soft alike, the only bonds are hatred, mistrust and indifference. And the vertical relationship, which serves as a backbone to this pseudo-community, the passive homosexual's sexual and feudal relationship with the criminal, protects neither one nor the other against loneliness. Homeless, with no rule other than the one he has given himself, the tough, upright as a penis, pierces the sky and drifts into the void. And the soft, that fidgety zealot, rushes into slavery and abjection to find solitude. Even in copulation they are alone.

Nevertheless, the fact is that Genet dreamed of this society for a long time and thought for a moment he had found a perfect image of it in Darnand's militia, which was both criminal and military.* The reason for this is clear. Rejected by the inmates of Mettray, having become, for the second time, a scapegoat and butt, he again resorted to the method which had worked for him once before: he began earnestly to will the situation in which he had been placed so as to have at least the satisfaction of transcending fortune by heightening its rigors. He could not be satisfied with accepting abjection as a contingent and provisional effect of circumstances; that would have been resignation. Since others were the makers of his misfortune, his only resort, if he meant to keep the initiative, was to raise it to the absolute and regard it as a condemnation by the universe. In like manner, Nietzsche, at Sils Maria, demanded the eternal recurrence of his sufferings. The invention of the "breed of the soft" is Genet's eternal recurrence. He would have been ashamed to attribute others' contempt for him to his extreme youth, to a lack of force which could have been only temporary. He wanted to merit this contempt on the grounds of his deeper nature and he wanted it to be beyond appeal. The Mettray Reformatory, which was an artificial society, in a vacuum, a society of youngsters, a secret society, certainly offered an embryonic form of initiatory rites. Sporadic adumbrations of feodality must have occasionally exposed the weaker boys to the persecution of a few bullies. Genet carried these indications to extremes, developed them, linked them up and constructed the myth of criminal feodality. Let us not forget

---

* At least, so he says in *Funeral Rites*. This quite platonic admiration was not, of course, followed by any actual enlistment.

that his first calamity was of social origin. He constructed his new misfortunes in the image of the old and willed them social because the relationship to the social is the constituent element of his person. He conceived a criminal society in which he had the lowest rank so that condemnation by that black community would be in the image of the one which had been issued against him by the community of the just. He can now be satisfied: banned by a criminal feodality, itself banned by real society, he has sunk straight down to the lowest depths of abjection and despair, into the inhuman.

But this relentlessness should arouse our suspicion. On the flyleaf of a copy of *Funeral Rites* which I once had in my hands Genet had scrawled: "Jean Genet, the weakest of all and the strongest." What if he cried up his weakness only to prepare a reversal? The truth is that Genet's undertaking constantly shifts from essentialism to existentialism. His aim is to regain his being so as to ensure his salvation. But when he has established himself in the core of his essence, he realizes that he has derived it only from himself, and the reversal, analogous to that effected by Auguste Comte, is achieved under the name of subjective synthesis: the objective system in its entirety and the very place occupied in it by Genet suddenly appear in the lighting which Genet gives to them. It is consciousness that draws them from the darkness and maintains them in being. Just as the impossibility of Evil will presently refer us to the subjective will to achieve the impossible, so the dark society refers us to the creative consciousness which has isolated it from experience and which manifests it. The same movement which makes of Genet a martyr who has been crushed by the world launches an inverse movement at the end of which Genet will find himself as a constituent consciousness. Whereupon the beloved, with all his self-importance, moves to the rank of the inessential, and it is the aching consciousness of the lover which becomes essential. Genet himself relates an experience which enables us to grasp this reversal in a scene taken from life:

"Regarding revelation, there is not much I can say, for all I know of it is what was granted me to know, thanks to God, in a Yugoslav prison."

A score of prisoners are practicing the art of picking pockets to while away the time. One of the prisoners has fallen asleep. Their aim is to remove the objects in his pockets and then put them back without waking him. When Genet's turn comes, he faints. He is carried to the other end of the cell, near the window: "In the other corner, standing in a bunch, were the other men. They looked at me and burst out laughing. As I did not know their language, one of them pointed at me and made the following gesture: he scratched his hair, and, as if he had pulled out a louse, made a show of eating it . . . it was at that moment that I understood the room. I realized —for a fraction of a second—its essence. It remained a room, though a prison of the world. I was, through my monstrous horror, exiled to the confines of the obscene (which is outside the scene of the world), facing the graceful pupils of the school of light-fingered theft. I saw clearly . . . what that room and those men were, what role they were *playing:* it was a major role in the march of the world . . . it seemed to me suddenly, thanks to a kind of extraordinary lucidity, that I understood the system. The world dwindled, and its mystery too, as soon as I was cut off from it. It was a supernatural moment."

Let us try to understand, that is, to sympathize. Let us imagine Genet excluded from the social world, imprisoned, thrown among a group of men who do not speak his language. As soon as he enters the cell, the others unite against him solely because of this mutual lack of understanding. Thus, by virtue of its essential structure the situation reproduces symbolically that of Mettray and the double exile from which he suffered. The other prisoners invite him by gestures to simulate a theft. The best way of assimilating himself would be to obey and, above all, to succeed, to pass the test. The difficulty of communicating would no doubt remain an obstacle; he must give up all hope of occupying a choice place in this little group. But at least he would be left in peace. However, he seems to refuse this integration. Rather than pass unnoticed, he actually courts mockery, he chooses the role of buffoon. A strange fainting fit. The theft involved no danger. Had he awakened the sleeper, he would have incurred a less serious condemnation than he did for the sudden swoon. His cellmates would perhaps have made allowances for his inexperience, for his clumsiness. In refusing to submit to the ordeal, he revealed to them a far graver, an inexpiable flaw: that he was not of their kind. Underlying this negative behavior we discern a secret will to be rejected, to demand the lowest rank for want of being able to have the highest, in short, an attitude of failure. But this is not the only nor perhaps the chief cause of his conduct. I allow, of course, for physical fatigue, fear, disgust. Yet there is something else: Genet fainted *because the theft was fictive.* Impelled by hunger, by necessity, he had already stolen a thousand times. In fact, it was for a theft that he had been imprisoned. But then the urgency of his needs and their necessity had not left him the leisure to consider his act; the things themselves had suggested it to him. It had appeared as a spontaneous reaction to the demands of the situation. On the other hand, the theft which they propose to him is a game, a piece of play acting. Since it is a foreign society which calls upon him to perform, the act becomes a challenge, a test, a comparison, in short a public ceremony which should conclude with his being granted the sacred title of *thief*. As he approaches his sleeping cellmate, Genet feels the gazes of initiates converging on his back. His attempted theft is a re-enactment, in the same sense in which an accused person and the district attorney's staff are taken to the scene of the crime for the purpose of re-enacting the crime. In this tomb, the factitious and public offense becomes a pure repetition of the original crisis. Genet, who is requested to *enact* his first theft, finds himself in the exact situation of a patient who is asked by a modern psychiatrist to enact his obsessions on a stage. He is *possessed,* in the realm of the imaginary, by his fundamental behavior. He responds to this possession by adopting a form of conduct which he has always rejected *in reality* but which remains his most constant temptation: to let go, to slip away into nothingness, to kill himself. In everyday life he survives each theft because to steal is to will to survive. But since he is being offered an opportunity to recommit his first theft fictively, he will treat himself to the luxury of giving it the solution which it entailed logically and which he dismissed. He satisfies himself in the realm of the imaginary by a symbolic suicide, just as, in a brothel, certain depraved customers poetically satisfy their desire to reign by putting a cardboard crown on their head and surrounding themselves with naked slaves who are paid at a fixed rate per hour. Thus, Genet's fainting fit has a threefold meaning: this proud, deliberate failure, this anarchistic refusal to be integrated into the community of crime, is the symbolic death of the child who was caught by adults and the imaginary actualization of a solution which Genet rejected in order "to live out the impossibility of living." This "loss of his wits," like the terminal swoon of the sexual rape, is the sudden, spasmodic abandon of a mind that rejects abandon.

So he dies. And when he regains consciousness he is dead, as he gathers from his reclining, corpselike position, off to the side, and from the sight of the huddled group of men who are insulting him in a foreign language. He has been exiled, and it was he himself who arranged matters so as to provoke the exile. Everything concurs in making him see the situation from the viewpoint of the radical rejection of all human signification, that is, from the viewpoint of death. For man's actions appear normal only to those who, to speak like the Germans, base the *mit-Sein* on the *mit-Machen*. The strangest mores of the most out-of-the-way societies will, in spite of everything, be relatively comprehensible to the person who has a flesh-and-blood knowledge of man's needs, anxieties and hopes. If, on the other hand, this experience is lacking, he will not even be able to understand the customs of those about him. As for Genet, he wants nothing, does nothing, rejects all fellowship with men and obliges them to reject all fellowship with him. Like Querelle, that corpse who left his grave to go prowling about among the living, he is separated from the compact little group of Yugoslav thieves by a transparent and unpassable nothingness. This experience is possible only in a society which carries parasitism to an extreme and whose members are, as it were, spoon-fed. But what society can be more parasitic than that of prisoners whose food is served at fixed times by a guard? The live dead-man is dead as a producer and alive insofar as he consumes. In any case, Genet, who has withdrawn from the cycle of praxis, who has "fallen outside the human," is here a pure gaze. And the only feeling that accompanies his passive contemplation, his astonishment at the strangeness of the world, is that which invades certain mental patients when they have what is called "attacks of depersonalization." They think they are dead, or else it is other people who seem to them to be corpses. The slightest gesture seems to them comic and terrible at the same time. In general, "depersonalized" individuals are dissatisfied with themselves and their lives; they are frequently imbued with a crushing sense of guilt. The following passage from Dr. Hesnard's *Univers morbide de la faute* seems to apply rather exactly to Genet's fainting and to the amazement which followed it:

". . . he abandons all systematic adaptation to this changed situation since it has less and less meaning for him, like existence itself. [He] actualizes what Merleau-Ponty calls 'the disease of the *Cogito*.' . . . Should this lowering of moral existence which crudely abolishes all conflict be regarded as a kind of deeper defense, an organic or biological defense which, in order to avoid living the Prohibition, consists in living henceforth only in a singular but still living world which has no name in any language and which means nothing to others if not to oneself? A romantic and mystical conception of this kind is to be found in the Freudian notion of integral narcissism."* And further on: "The schizophrenic no longer has the ethical sense of existence insofar as he no longer has an existence."

---

* Hesnard adds that he does not subscribe to Freud's "integral narcissism."

But Genet is a touchstone that enables us to determine the limits of psychoanalytical interpretation. We have already seen that the concepts of "stereotyped revival of the original crisis," "narcissism" and "sado-masochism" cannot, as such, apply to his case because an uncritical use of them may lead one to regard as rough data of a psychosis what is actually the labor of a freedom relentlessly working out its salvation. The same holds for the case with which we are concerned at the moment. To be sure, when Genet regains consciousness, he finds himself *in the situation* of a depersonalized individual, but he transcends this situation by using his depersonalization as an instrument of knowledge. The word *revelation* characterizes it sufficiently, for it means both that the aspect of the world is imposed and that Genet has the power to transform this vision into a teaching. Indeed, he takes advantage of the fact that he is no longer immersed in the universe or constrained to assume human ends, and considers them, for once, *from without*. To his critical and unbiased eyes, they appear as simple facts. *It is a fact* that the human species pursues one or another end, as does the species of bees or ants. Having dropped to the rank of pure empirical data, values also lose their urgency and seriousness. Men *play* at being thieves. Play is at the origin of the world. There is *world* (that is, a close connection between human society and nature) when collective conventions establish the rules of the game. The only effect of these conventions, which are absurd and gratuitous, is to transform human activity, in all domains, into a ballet. Let us bear in mind here that prison and play have always been the favorite symbols of thinkers who have attempted to describe human activity by placing themselves outside the human. I am thinking particularly of Pascal, Nietzsche and Kafka. If only Genet had extended his experience to the ethical activities of respectable men he would have been delivered from Evil forever; Good and Evil would have collapsed together, would have become outworn conventions. But Genet is dead set against such an extension. Good is the vulture that gnaws at his liver, and he values his vulture. He wants to save himself *with* Good and *against* it. It is Evil which is a ballet. We now see the matter more clearly: if the world of Evil is only a play of appearances and conventions, it depends on the consciousness of the spectator who contemplates it. Genet's gaze is necessary to transform all those men—who insult him and then tiptoe across the cell to remove a filthy handkerchief from an open pocket—into ballerinas, into *"graceful* pupils of the school of light-fingered theft." *Graceful:* this is the word that enlightens us. Mystified by conventions which are established through them and almost in spite of them, the prisoners pursue absurd enterprises with the utmost seriousness. Their only justification will be the gracefulness of their gestures, that is, *the appearance*. We have already seen that the criminal is only a graceful and terrible appearance. But an appearance requires a consciousness to grasp and fix it; without a spectator it disappears. Thus, the world's secret all at once passes into Genet's consciousness: it is his consciousness which becomes essential. But in order for this to have happened, he first had to be dismissed from the corps de ballet. Were it not for this exclusion, which he provoked, he would still be dancing with the others, doing his utmost to describe the figures of a masked ball for an invisible audience. To roll out of the world through a mudhole is, like breaking through its ceiling with a flap of the wings, a way of emerging from it and of becoming its incorruptible witness. *Abjection* is a methodical conversion, like Cartesian doubt and Husserlian *epoche:* it establishes the world as a closed system which consciousness regards from without, in the manner of the divine understanding. The superiority of this method to the other two lies in its being lived in pain and pride. It therefore does not lead to the transcendental and universal consciousness of Husserl, the formal and abstract thinking of the Stoics or the substantial *cogito* of Descartes, but to an individual existence at its highest degree of tension and lucidity; it is master of itself and of all others since it accepts them only insofar as it manifests them. At the very moment when Genet submits to their force, he reduces them to being only shadows and to existing only through him. This is the chief source of what he will later call his *betrayals*. A work of Genet's, like Hegel's phenomenology, is a consciousness which sinks into appearances, discovers itself in the depths of alienation, saves itself and relegates things to the rank of *its objects*. Consciousness is treacherous because it obeys only in order the better to dominate. At the end of *Deathwatch*, Genet brings out in strong relief the contrast between the fatal criminal and the faker, who is a criminal by imposture but a free spirit:

GREEN EYES: You don't know the first thing about misfortune if you think you can choose it. I didn't want mine. It chose me.

LEFRANC: I'm stronger than you. My misfortune comes from something deeper. It comes from myself.

GREEN EYES: I'm calling the guards. You'll know by the look on their mugs whether you can be with us or not.

LEFRANC: Green Eyes!
GREEN EYES: You bastard!
LEFRANC: I really am all alone!

It is the contradiction between these two misfortunes, one unconscious and noble, the other conscious and abject, the first despising the second, the second dissolving the first, that accounts for the
peculiar tension of Genet's works. Because he wants to do and to
be, to be in order to do and to do in order to be, he is, at one and
the same time, the master, the slave and their merciless struggle.
For the master does nothing; he is. And the slave is not; he does.
Genet gives himself servilely to various masters who are only passing images of himself. Wishing *to be,* he makes himself a thing and
submits to the reign of things; everything fades into pure subjectivity. But the inner contradiction of willing-being breaks forth
and manifests itself in an unexpected dialectic: those pure objects
which crush him, those handsome, unconscious masters, resolve in
turn into pure appearances, and this world of appearances refers
to the true subject *for whom* the appearances exist. The horrible
universe surrounding him changes into a graceful ballet. At the
limit of the quest for being, just after the engulfment of consciousness, being reveals its secret weakness: it *was* only insofar as it
appeared, and consciousness rises up again from its own ashes in
the absolute solitude of an aesthetic solipsism. Carried to its ultimate consequence, the quest turns against itself, corrodes the real
and allows only the seeker-of-self as pure consciousness to subsist.
What, then, remains of the feodality of crime and of the glamorous
murderous-looking pimps? Nothing. Ballet figures that are directed
by Genet himself. The notorious "maliciousness" of homosexuals is
due in part to their having at their disposal, simultaneously, two
systems of reference: sexual rapture transports them to a platonic
climate; each of the men they seek is the passing embodiment of an
Idea; it is *the* Sailor, *the* Parachute Trooper that they want to embrace through the husky who lends himself to their desire. But as
soon as their desire is satisfied, they re-enter themselves and consider their wonderful lovers from the angle of a cynical nominalism.
Good-by to essences, farewell archetypes, there remain only commonplace and interchangeable individuals. "But I didn't know,"
a homosexual once said to me, pointing to a little Montparnasse
hoodlum, "that that young man was a MURDERER!" And the following day: "Adrien? A dull little faggot."

These remarks enable us to consider Genet's sexuality in its other aspect, that of hatred.

For he no doubt loves these tough, handsome pimps. But we know what this love is. He gets knocked down, with humiliation and horror, by their brutal force. What he seeks in them is himself, and this quest ends in failure. Penetration by the male leaves him *other*, filled *emptily* with a nothingness of pleasure. The disappointment is foreseen and repeated a hundred times. What can this vainly accepted abjection engender if not hatred? He cries out in *Our Lady of the Flowers:* "Oh those males, I hate them lovingly!"

And in *Funeral Rites:*

"I loved him out of hatred . . ."

And again:

"My hatred of the militiaman was so strong and so beautiful that it was equivalent to the most sturdy love."

He writes about Paulo:

"Abandoned on my bed, he will be, naked, polished, an instrument of torture, a vise, a dagger ready to function, functioning by its mere presence, which was evil, and springing, pale and with clenched teeth, from my despair. It is my despair become flesh."

His love is a desperate attempt to *become* them; it is therefore accompanied by hatred. He hates them for *not already being* him. He loves them because he needs them in order to submit to the worst, but he hates them precisely because he asks them to subjugate him. This should not surprise us. I would even say that the hatred is born first, and, since he has made it a personal rule to have no tastes other than distastes which have been overcome, it is the most hateful that he will love most. Is not this the necessary consequence of his original choice to do evil, that is, to will what he does not want?

"Culafroy and Divine, with their delicate tastes, will always be forced to love what they loathe, and this constitutes something of their saintliness, for that is renunciation."

And, finally, the sexual act itself is a distaste which has been overcome. When Genet plunges into his long excremental descriptions of anal intercourse, he irresistibly brings to mind Marie Alacoque gathering up the dejecta of sick persons with her tongue. He frequently boasts of loving in a state of queasiness, but there are times when he also complains of it: "To hate is nothing, but to love what one hates causes loathing. To kiss him or let oneself be kissed by him was little, but it was a great deal to be aroused and to come as a result of the kisses given and received." This hatred, which is

willed and sought at the core of love, is already a betrayal; the first
time he submits to Armand's pleasure, he writes: "Crushed by that
mass of flesh, which was devoid of the slightest spirituality, I experienced the giddiness of finally meeting the perfect brute, indifferent to my happiness." Hence all the unconscious brutes are
interchangeable "masses of flesh." It is no longer the beloved in his
particularity that Genet desires, but rather pure generality. Earlier,
it was the lover who represented the interchangeable universal;
but now the universal moves into the beloved. In taking his pleasure, Armand, who is dominated by instinctive forces, becomes an
instrument that Genet maneuvers at the dictate of his tortuous
ends. A woman receives pleasure insofar as she gives it, and whatever the violence, in other respects, of the sexual conflict between
her and her lover, she has not leisure to betray him at the moment
he satisfies her. But Genet, precisely because he rejects pleasure,
has full latitude, at the height of the other's pleasure, to practice
mental restriction: "My imagination invents for them the following humiliations. I let one of them [subdue me]. He enters me until
he becomes myself, to the point of taking up, by the presence of his
prick alone, all the place which I occupy, and then, at the extreme
moment of leaving my personality, I attract to myself the memory
of another male to whom I offer myself."

But there is a worse kind of treason, and it is the male himself
who provides the occasion for it. It should first be noted that in
Genet's world fellatio is regarded as the function of the passive
homosexual; it is a part of the service that the latter renders to his
lord. The symbol of the worm that comes to life again in Pierrot's
mouth and that he makes himself suck would suffice to prove that
fellatio is particularly ignominious,* that it is more repulsive than
anal intercourse. But I shall now quote a strange passage, which
will set us on a quite other path. This time it is Genet himself
who makes a try at playing the male role, who takes a stand with
rigidity as Divine once did and as did Lieutenant Seblon another
time. But the thief to whom he addresses himself looks at him with
contemptuous surprise: "I knew his contempt. He came very near
to dissolving me like a sugar candy. I had to preserve my rigidity,
though not too fixedly."

A rigidity that melts beneath contempt like barley sugar on the
tongue: the image has deep roots. We now know the secret weakness of the handsome pimp's rigidity: it melts on the tongue. Thus,

---

* Not in itself, but because it is in this case without reciprocity.

at the heart of his submission Genet takes his revenge: the aim of his caresses is the softening of the male. And when the latter, exhausted, finally collapses and becomes limp, a sentiment which his false slave thought had died in his childhood rises from the depths and comes to life again: *tenderness*. Tenderness, immediate reaction of the lover to the devirilization of the beloved. Emptied, drooping, a piece of wet rag, the virile member is no longer formidable. It was a cannon, a tower, a torture machine; it becomes flesh, it can be stroked lightly without springing up. As we saw earlier, the hardness of the pimp's erect penis and his compact, terrible force were one and the same. The drooping of the one symbolizes the vanishing of the other. In giving himself to the tough pimps, Genet becomes a trap; they are caught in his pestilential swamps and their virility abandons them. In the last analysis, fellatio is castration. Coitus is the systematically pursued death of the beloved. Caught, possessed *in appearance,* Genet, at the moment of his false pleasure, feels the false possession take a sharp turn and then collapse. In the presence of the castrated male who rolls over on his back and releases him from his weight, Genet's consciousness remains alone and pure and, by a premeditated reversal, the penis of the passive homosexual, still erect because he has refused pleasure, bears witness to his vigilance. Genet will later find an epic symbol for this omnipotence of the weakest: Hitler. Hitler declares in *Funeral Rites*—and it is Genet who speaks through his mouth: "I, puny and ridiculous little man, unloosed upon the world a power extracted from the pure and clear beauty of athletes and hoodlums. For nothing but beauty could have elicited such a burst of love as that which every day, for seven years, caused the death of strong and fierce young creatures." Every day Genet, too, causes the death of fierce young men. And their death imparts to him "a power extracted from their beauty." Coitus is a grafting. Genet, the praying mantis, devours his male. Tenderness is then born, a quiet, triumphant, maternal superiority. It is a deliverance and a joy, a feeling of security in the face of the evident fact that the most rigid hardness conceals a deep softness. Tenderness and pity go hand and hand when tenderness wells up in an inferior and is addressed to a waning superior. Genet will write about Pilorge, a formidable murderer who was guillotined: "It was when I could say 'poor kid' that I loved him." But did he not claim earlier that execution was an apotheosis, that the beheaded criminal became even more terrible? Yes, of course, but it was a trap, a booby trap. Those fierce fellows will run into it with their heads down, and then they will become children who die prematurely, like Vergil's Marcellus or the child Septentrio.

For, let us not forget, the male also represents the adult who condemned Genet to do evil. He is the terrifying archangel whose flaming sword defends the entrance to Paradise. The fire goes out and the sword bends: it was tin, coated with phosphorus. A judge's eyes close. In reducing the big chief to this sprawling mildness, Genet has *killed the law*. The sacrifice of the Male puts an end to the Old Testament. His great passion on the scaffold is only the heroic symbol of the little bedroom passion which he renews each day. With the law dead and the archangel disarmed, the murdered child comes to life again in Genet. Delivered from adults, he can love like a child, he can love the child in the young tough who has been reduced to impotence. That little penis is a childhood figure, a rag doll. Genet's tenderness goes from childhood to childhood, and it is his own childhood that he finds in the beloved.

> *The child dead in me*
> *Long before the ax chops off my head,*

says Pilorge, and we do not know whether he is speaking for himself or for Genet. The defeat of the archangel reopens the gates of the lost paradise. After the purifying repetition of the crisis, a human sacrifice restores to Genet the sweet confusion with the world, restores innocence. Not for long: the male will soon come to life again, will rise up with renewed indifference. Genet's tenderness is shot through with despair. It is going to wane into desolation. It is only a respite from hell, for it was born of a failure: Genet has been unable to become the other. However, we shall encounter it again, for it is, with poetry, one of the paths which will lead him to salvation.

For the time being, he must take precautions against the awakening of the male. First, he must carefully conceal this melting mood. It doesn't mean a thing to the beloved. If he sensed that he was the object of a gentle affection, half childish, half maternal, he would feel obscurely that the sources of his virility were being attacked. He would respond with anger. "What's eating you?" asked Armand with annoyed astonishment when, after lovemaking, Genet once went so far as to kiss the bend of his arm, the only spot on the body where the flesh remains as soft as a child's. The girl queen will therefore carry on the systematic labor of devirilization in secret. Genet will make a relentless effort to discover a secret femininity in all the toughs who subdue him. In his books, he produces these great criminal figures, who at first delude us, only to amuse himself slyly by putting them into female situations: Querelle, the most male of them all, forces himself to become a passive homosexual, then acquires a taste for such pleasures; Armand, the toughest of them, earns his living by doing lacework; Erik is raped by the executioner; Stilitano is a coward, Green Eyes a squealer. But Darling Daintyfoot should be given particular attention, for it is in his case that Genet has shown most clearly the stages of a concerted labor of feminization.

Darling at first pays no attention to Divine; he lets himself be worshiped. For him "Divine is barely a pretext, an occasion." Little by little, very discreetly, without even admitting it to himself, he grows attached to her and thereby becomes feminized: "It took [him] some time to get used to talking about her and to her in the feminine. He finally succeeded, but did not tolerate her talking to him as to a girl friend. Then, little by little, he let her do it. Divine dared say to him, 'You're pretty.' "

Little by little Divine's very gestures settle into him and the metamorphosis is complete:

"Inadvertently certain gestures, though very restrained, certain mannerisms of Divine escaped him. At first, he had dared a few just for the fun of it, but slyly, little by little, they were conquering the stronghold, and Darling did not even notice that he was shedding his skin. It was at a later time . . . that he realized the falsity of what he had blurted out one evening: 'A male that fucks another male is a double male.' "

A male that fucks another male is not a double male: he is a female without realizing it. In the end, by settling into Darling, Divine's feminine gestures lead him to his downfall: he will steal, as she does, and will be caught. In like manner, Divine's odd, mad, poetic inventions will gradually corrupt Our Lady, the young male "with a single possibility." If he adopts any one of them, the gesture will be incongruous, like surrealist feathers on a statue; it will arouse the attention of the detectives and will lead to the discovery of his crime.

"Here we must perhaps recognize Divine's influence. She is present wherever the inexplicable arises. She, the Giddy One, strewed in her wake traps, artful pitfalls, deep dungeon cells . . . and because of her the minds of Darling, Our Lady and their cronies bristle with incredible gestures. With their heads high, they take falls that doom them to the worst of fates."

The girl queens are soft and poisonous. They cause the slightest seed of femininity in their males to sprout and flower. And this diligent labor is only the sublimation of the sexual activity of *deflation* that we described above.

The *same reality* is the object of a simultaneous double operation: Genet elevates it with one hand while lowering it with the other. On the one hand, he claims to have a little of Armand's "severe kindness" which consists "in his transforming into a revel, into a solemn and ridiculous display, what is only a contemptible desertion of duty," and to share his concern, "which was rehabilitation. Not of others or of himself, but of moral wretchedness." But, on the other hand, he himself dissolves the flamboyant appearances which he has just painted into "wretchedness," "vileness," "a contemptible desertion of duty." With a spontaneous movement he heads for the myth, he adorns the little tramps of the criminal world with a tragic brilliance, but only to arrange them, to scatter them in unknotted sheaves of weaknesses, of loosely bound gestures, of chance. He has revealed to us the secret of this method at the end of a splendid poem in which he applies to prisons the terms usually reserved for palaces: "Their gravity makes me consider them without pity. I recognize that they have their foundations within myself; they are the signs of the most violent of my extreme tendencies and my corrosive spirit is already working at their destruction." Genet commands two powers: one, which is mythological, comes to him from gestures, from ceremonies, from language; the other, which is "corrosive," comes from his analytical mind. One does not exist without the other; they condition each other; one subdues him, without force, to the cruel beauty of the universe, and the other delivers him by obliging this beauty to depend on his consciousness. By means of the first he makes manifest the Other, the shimmering world of essences into which he wants to melt, and suddenly, just as he is about to lose himself in it, he re-establishes himself in his pure existence, his cold breath extinguishes the phantasmagoria. It is in order to make the castration more magnificent that he models the males as granite-like erections. And that is what gives his works their so profoundly, so paradoxically human character. For at a first reading we do not detect the unceasing ravages caused by these two conflicting activities which work at *digesting* a too coriaceous reality. At first, we do not discern in Genet the insect eager to sting its victim's nerve centers in order to paralyze it, drag it into its cave and devour the corpse alive; it is to something quite other that we are sensitive, to a wearied but tenacious effort to transcend everyday reality and attain beauty without in any way renouncing a ruthless lucidity. This effort is manifest in spite of Genet himself; it is he who expresses himself in the sentence I quoted earlier: "Transforming into a revel *what is only* a contemptible desertion of duty." And this maintaining of values (aesthetic ones, it is true) within the most utter despair is something which I do not fear to call grandeur.

This grandeur, which is still only embryonic and which will attain its full development later, springs, nevertheless, from a humiliated adolescent's amorous hatred of the handsome big shots of Mettray. Its origin lies in a premeditated betrayal. Note, rather, how the virtues with which he adorns the beloved are at the same time the instruments which will make it possible to dissolve him. Riton's beauty is even more beautiful for his being unaware of it. Were he conscious of it, it would become artifice, dressing. And Genet swoons before this mute, quite mindless flower. But let us beware: this ecstasy is already a betrayal, for what he actually loves in Riton is something quite different from what Riton thinks he is and wants to be. Ignoring the beloved's deeper intentions, efforts and activities, inverted love is the opposite of Pascalian esteem-love. For in esteem-love I espouse the will of the person I love, I adopt her values, and I am willing to judge her acts—severely—be it only in the name of her own principles. Quite the contrary, the girl queen, at the height of bliss, despises her males and commits the affront of regarding what they undertake as worthless. In short, her love is nothing other than a hostile decision to treat certain lords of the earth as objects. Far from adhering to their principles, Genet snuffs out their freedom, for he claims to appreciate in them only the qualities of which they are unaware and which they cannot want to acquire without spoiling everything. He adopts the same attitude toward the aristocracy of crime that Proust does toward the nobility. Proust, too, loves the Guermantes for reasons of which they are unaware, and when they think they are interesting him by what they say or by their merits, he delights in the fact that he is fooling them. All he asks of them is that they be myths, heraldic animals, figures in a tapestry, so that he can admire them in his solitude. His hero, a commoner who is made much of by princes, is as profoundly treacherous in a Faubourg St. Germain drawing room as Genet in the Mettray Reformatory. They both have wicked souls, that is, souls which are solitary and tender, fabulous and corrosive. This is not surprising, for analysis and myth are, in the passive homosexual, the double revenge of passivity.

The magnificent words which celebrate the criminal are two-edged. The tragic unconsciousness of Our Lady is also the most profound stupidity. His impenetrability is not a massiveness of mind, but rather so total a void that nothing can fill it. The Tough is *hollow*. There is nothing in him but the vague and foolish dream of appearing tough. To be tragic, handsome, noble, frightening is to depend completely on the opinion of others. It is not without reason that the heroes of our tragedies are kings and emperors; it is not without reason that Genet compares his heroes to emperors and kings. And if he often presents them as military leaders, it is because, as Gide has said, "The leader is a man who has need of others"—and, indeed, is nothing other than the opinion which others have of him.

"I . . . knew that Stilitano was my own creation and that it depended upon me to destroy it."

It was *by submission* that he learned it. We saw him leave on an expedition, happy to find his justification in the will of a sovereign power. But by the same token he frees himself: the mission was easy, Stilitano could have carried it out himself and had no need to send him "to expose himself to the danger of being caught in his stead." Whereupon Genet "dimly suspects him of being incapable of an act involving his whole person." Like the Hegelian slave, he frees himself through obedience, fear and work; he realizes that he is his master's truth and that the latter without his servant is merely a shadow. But in the case of the slave, liberation is achieved by revolt because submission was a constraint. In the case of Genet, it will be achieved by betrayal because submission is voluntary. Inessential to Stilitano, treated as a thrall, as a pure pretext, he suddenly discovers that it is through him that Stilitano exists. This discovery should shatter his bonds: quite the contrary, it attaches him. He submits to Stilitano all the more in that he sees clearly that Stilitano can do nothing without him. He keeps his balance on the infinitely narrow ridge that separates submission from revolt. That is what makes him write the following astonishing sentence: "Had he revealed himself to me by a rather considerable number of bold deeds in which I had been forbidden to take part, thus becoming both cause and end, Stilitano would have lost all power over me." It is at the very antipodes of esteem-love that he situates his love. If Stilitano were really courageous, really strong, really able, he would no longer be lovable, he would be self-sufficient, he would therefore no longer need Genet, and thereupon Genet would no longer need him, for, in the last analysis, he needs only the need which his master has of him. Cowardly, empty, feminine, Stilitano is only an incomplete creature. The virility and courage which he cannot acquire alone are loaned to him by Genet's submission and respect. On the basis of this, the fake tough will become the sovereign power who must justify his slave.

A strange respect that envelops its own negation, since it knows that it is the creator of the respectable object. In submitting, Genet is not unaware that he becomes an accomplice of an imposture. In fact, it is in order to be its accomplice that he submits. Is he putting on an act? Yes and no. His obedience is *real* since he really and truly fulfills his mission, since he runs real risks in order to carry out the beloved's orders. But, on the other hand, it is *imaginary* because he submits only to a creature of his mind. We find here the equivalent of Pascal's advice: "Kneel and you will believe." Stilitano's sovereign power is the only valid explanation of Genet's acts. And he performs these acts only for the explanation which they require. But at the same time he cannot prevent himself from knowing that he is acting freely and that his thralldom is a deliberate resignation. In fact, his pride requires that in every circumstance he retain consciousness of his freedom. We are back at the paradox which, as we saw above, was the original and deep-seated structure of Genet's sensibility: one cannot distinguish what he feels from what he plays at feeling. In this *true* submission to a sham, is it the submission which communicates its truth to the appearance or the appearance which infects the submission with its falseness? Both, for Genet wants both. He wants his crushed, emptied, inessential consciousness to be only a lamp whose one function is to light up the beauty alone, the glory alone, of the beloved. But in depriving the latter of his soul, he also wants this beautiful image to be the pure means which he is using to make contact with himself, in short, an inessential mediation between Genet and Genet. And since, as we have seen, abjection is an ascesis, an *epoche,* the consciousness that wants to alienate itself finds itself one and alone, confronting the appearance as a consciousness of wanting to alienate itself. The willed, actual contradiction is expressed in two sentences from *Our Lady of the Flowers:* "The Eternal passed by in the form of a Pimp" and "God was hollow." In the first, the pimp represents the heartbreaking and eternal Beauty of a pitiless God. In the second, God collapses. Beauty, Impenetrability and Toughness collapse with him: they were hollow. Genet's essentialism brings him back to his pure power of existing. He paralyzed his Masters in order to relieve them of their con-

sciousness. In bewitching himself with their beauty, he has gently
seduced them, he leads them to cease to exist except in terms of
their *gestures,* to bewitch themselves with their own appearance. If
Darling and Our Lady are ruined by Divine, it is because they live
with her in the worship of the image of them which she has created.
And when the handsome, bamboozled pimps are reduced to the
state of aesthetic fantasies, then, brusquely, Genet the traitor pulls
himself together, disenchants himself and asserts himself as a poetic
consciousness in the presence of these emptied carcasses. We have
already seen, before the broken mirror, Being, by its very impossibility, reflect to Doing: Genet's hostile eroticism reproduces this
conjuring trick; but this time it is the Other which is shattered.

Is Genet satisfied? Certainly not. His hatred triumphs, but in him
hatred is a subordinate feeling. At bottom, this dissolution of the
beloved represents a further failure. The whole dialectic which referred us from the self-executioner to the mirror, from the mirror
to the beloved, from the beloved to the lover, was, fundamentally,
only the succession of the figures assumed by his fierce will to become *for himself* the Other that he was for others. Lastly, if he
bewitched himself with the Beloved, if he wanted to live in symbiosis with him, it was in order to annihilate himself as *himself* for
the benefit of an Other-Self. And so now his corrosive pride has
restored to him his integrity as a *person* by reducing the Other to
being merely a fantasy, a creation of the mind. But it was precisely
the opposite that he was seeking. So Genet has to recognize his
series of reverses: I cannot grasp myself as an object; I cannot enjoy
the object which I am for the Other; I cannot identify myself with
the object that the Other is for me. Is he going to give up? Not yet.
How could he do so before delivering himself from the malediction
that weighs on him? He must meet *his* Being-Other face to face,
either to claim it proudly or to dissolve it and free himself from it.
When all is said and done, this long circumnavigation has brought
us back to our starting point.

Not quite, however, for the homosexual attempt can be regarded, despite everything, as an effort to enter into communication with other men. Until then, he was alone before a gaze which
he was unable to return. A dazzling spotlight transpierced him with
its beams and he was too busy struggling in that shaft of light to
bother about others. However proud his solitude might have been,
it could have passed for ignorance. But it finally occurs to him to
turn to the vague shadows surrounding him and ask them for help.
He makes an effort to love, to get out of himself, to say You and

We. He makes an actual attempt, he has companions, accomplices, tyrants. To be sure, in order for the experience of love to have been valid, he should not have begun by eliminating the consciousness of those he loved. He was unable to keep from doing so, because the consciousness of others horrified him. If there is a consciousness, before long there will be a judge. He refuses to understand what goes on in people's hearts. Not that he does not have a very fine sense of the workings of the soul, but that these workings fill him with terror. Even at the present time, now that he is a triumphant hero and is made much of by middle-class society, he hastens to please in order to disarm, and if he suspects that his charm has not worked, if he senses that there is a spot of freedom in the other person's eyes, he gets worried and irritated. He dislikes anyone's criticizing his works, not so much out of pride as out of confusion in the presence of an intelligence which he thought submissive and which suddenly reveals its independence. Whatever mistakes I may make about him, I am sure that I know him better than he knows me, because I have a passion for understanding men and he a passion for not knowing them. Ever since our first meeting, I have no recollection of our having spoken of anything other than him. That suits both of us. Of course, the result of his first contact with others was his being cast into solitude. He found everywhere only empty shells, corpses, abandoned houses.

But this new solitude is deliberate, it has been pondered, it is based on experience of the world and on the failure of love. He has got out of himself, he has gone toward his fellow man and encountered only appearances. He now returns to himself. He is alone beneath the fixed light which has not ceased to traverse him.

I IS ANOTHER

Twice dead the Toughs, the Murderers, the handsome, criminal Pimps. Dead the appearances, dissolved in his acid lucidity. He finds himself free. What then? Free *to do what?* Is he any less wretched? When he discovers this freedom, he is in prison, or begging in Barcelona, crushed by contempt. He has nothing to do with this inner autonomy which can change nothing and which casts him into the most frightful solitude. Until then, he fought against all, he could say: "I alone, and that's enough." But he no longer has the strength to continue the struggle. He must receive encouragement, regardless of whence it comes. Suddenly he glimpses salvation: since the alternating voices of the just and of the criminal constantly repeat to him his condemnation, what if he set another judge against them? Since he is, in the depths of his soul, a man who is being watched, what if he called another gaze to his rescue? Since he is an outcast, what if he transformed himself into one of the elect?

Thus, at a certain stage of the "delirium of influence," when for years the sick man has been hearing furious voices whispering threats in his ears, suddenly a new voice arises amidst the tumult to comfort him: "Don't believe them. You're a Saint, a martyr. Don't be afraid of them. I'm here." He relaxes, abandons himself. At last a bit of love and pity! But the guardian angel is only an envoy of the devil. His appearance marks a new and more advanced phase of mental disintegration: madness is approaching.

So Genet changes witnesses. This is a new reversal. Thus far, he has been trying to see himself through the gaze of Others. His consciousness was an eye which peered into the semidarkness in an

attempt to perceive Genet *as an object*. He now resigns himself to
never being an object for himself, provided that he be an object
in the eyes of an absolute and benevolent witness. This means that
he wants to be Genet in the eyes of a God of love. In a highly
structured group, God is, for each member, the Other, the absolute
and infinite Other who legitimates tradition, customs and law. He
is the foundation and guarantee of order and social imperatives;
he completes the integration of the individual into the community;
he acts as a factor of *normalization*. But if, as a result of the operation of centrifugal forces, an individual is expelled from the group,
the idea of God runs amok within him. In some cases, it is resorbed
slowly, in the course of a lifetime, as with Gide, leaving a sacred
residue, the word God, which alters all of language. But, in most
cases, the idea, cut off from its living roots, becomes abstract; it
remains a kind of resort for the lonely man against the society
which has exiled him: it is an abstract Society which the Pariah
uses as a Countersociety. But it suffers from this new use, it wilts,
grows pale, is transformed in accordance with situations and needs.
God was the Judge; he becomes the Justification. When this factor
of normalization is used against the community's customs and imperatives, it completes, rather, the perversion of the elect.

Driven from his village, Genet thinks he is carrying away with
him the Christian God to whom he prayed with the other boys and
girls. But his religious notions are already tainted. He had decided
to be wrong and to counterbalance universal contempt by the
weight of his will alone. He now places on his side a supreme power
which all at once tips the balance. But actually this power does not
exist: God's power is, for the integrated faithful, the collective
power. Genet, who has been disintegrated and expelled, attempts
to turn against Society the mythical image of this society itself.
Evil has ceased to be the impossible goal of a freedom strained to
the breaking point: it is an absolute value which comes from on
high. It resembles Good in every respect. Conceived as an *imperative*, it becomes the commandment of the Person who embodies the
collectivity and who gathers unto himself all the collective powers.
And the child, more exigent than Abraham, asks for a sign, a mark
of favor. Earlier, it sufficed for him to will Evil. He now asks to be
him who has the right to will it. In short, he demands, against society, a kind of *social investiture:* if he is to continue his undertaking, let a notice from on high manifest to him that he is a *sacred
object* to celestial eyes. He will not thereby escape the paradox that
characterizes him, for in order to encounter a sign one must first

decide that one will encounter it, and when one discovers it, one finds only what one has put into it. Once again, Genet is obliged to *will* what he would like to *receive*. But there is a particular aspect of his condition which is going to enable him to convince himself without too much difficulty that he has *encountered* the mark of his election.

He is eighteen years old, perhaps twenty. He roams all over Europe, he begs, he prostitutes himself, he comes to know the prisons of Poland, of Czechoslovakia, the low quarters of Amsterdam and Barcelona, the Courts of Miracles of all countries. Poverty, filth, vermin, blows, hunger, cold, contempt, nothing is spared him. But he has already decided to be proud. No doubt he first had to be guilty: "Pride comes afterward." But when it comes, everything gives pain. Pride is thorough, it goes into detail, it infects wounds; the universe thereby acquires a deplorable richness. "It is to be noted further that Culafroy and Divine, with their delicate tastes . . . have *always* found themselves in situations repulsive to them." I think, rather, that the delicate tastes were not given at first and that Genet gained in refinement as a result of inspecting his sensations with the aim of finding concrete proofs of his abjection. Pride is a forward-looking vigilance: in order to retain a semblance of initiative in a situation where everything is imposed, this sentiment foresees affronts long in advance, applies itself to discovering the germs of them before they have developed, anticipates abuse, provokes it and puts itself in a state of grace to receive it, tears off dressings, enlarges the wounds so that it itself is the cause of the increase in unhappiness. It descends into the sense of smell in order to sniff the scents of shame; it is an anxiety of the nostrils and the tongue; it tingles at the fingertips; it contrives ever more exquisite, ever more penetrating humiliations. It is Genet's distastes that have formed his taste.

Genet, who is already in a state of almost unbearable unhappiness, is so afraid of being caught napping, of being turned around and invaded, that he is bent on foreseeing the worst. To foresee here is to beget: attention develops and is thoroughgoing. Every pinprick becomes a stab. Consequently, everything takes on meaning, intentions are revealed everywhere: the lice in his hair have been put there by someone; the cold that nips him is not the contingent and immediate relationship of the universe to his body but the calculated effect of a death sentence, the reverse of warm clothing, of the stove that is denied him. While Nature was being humanized for the others, an inhuman Nature was being manufactured for his use. He was excluded by the same decree from both Society and the Universe, and the moral rigor of the one finds its permanent symbol in the physical rigor of the other. If he suffered only in his flesh, it would not matter; the horror lies in the fact that his judges have re-created winter for him alone, and out of special consideration. Thus, the sequence of physical phenomena manifests the sustained plan to persecute him. The order of things expresses the order of ends, the anonymous indifference of the elements whispers the name Genet. Astonishing ecstasy: everything points to him, the world is a torture machine designed for him alone, the storm which is gathering over the Atlantic has no other aim than to produce clouds which will drench him to the bone. Winter becomes the seasonal sign of his vocation. But since he has decided to live the impossibility of living, every misfortune is an opportunity which lays this impossibility before his eyes and obliges him to decide, once again, not to die. He is tested, he is tempted, he is forbidden any abandon, any hope, he is made to maintain, without a moment's respite, an inhuman tension. Whatever the misfortune it may forecast, his expectation is never disappointed. He can count on the fact that the most unbearable suffering is only a message, a friendly sign for him to be patient, the promise of an even more unbearable suffering. He feels he is being cajoled by a reverse providence. He prophesies infallibly: the first time that little Culafroy is put into prison, he discerns in his fright the presentiment of a worse horror. He is gratified: his cellmate "pulled back the covers daintily . . . he had a wooden leg." Culafroy has always been terrified by cripples. This apparition exceeds his hope; he recognizes in it the hand of God. And yet, nothing can be more necessary: the prison contains monsters; since he has been thrown into it, it is inevitable that he live in a state of promiscuity with the underground race. But it is precisely the double determination of this meeting—by the freedom of the ends and by the necessity of the causes—that plunges Culafroy into an extraordinary rapture: "And the miracle, that catastrophe of horror, horrifying as an angel, blazed forth, though radiant as the solution of a mathematical problem, frighteningly exact."

The miracle is that there is no miracle. It is not the momentary suspension of the course of the world. Quite the contrary, it is that "the order of the world appears perfect in its inevitability" and that it is, for Genet and for Genet alone, without a single exception, without a lapse, utterly unbearable. Genet's theodicy is the opposite of that of Leibniz: he believes in God (we shall see in what God) because *for him alone* the world is the worst of possible worlds. That is why he cannot be accused of contradicting himself when, after almost praying for the resurrection of a dead friend, he rejects this temptation: "I don't want miracles!" No, indeed, he has nothing to do with those white miracles which suspend the course of nature in order to fulfill a wish and to calm suffering. He wants no exception in his favor, for the good reason that he himself is the exception. By a further paradox, the miracle would merely send him back to share in the common lot: the most miserable creatures have known, if only for an instant, the smile of fortune. Tormented unremittingly by a providence that merges with the necessity of the universe, Genet is the object of the only miracle he tolerates: the black miracle which designates him in his own eyes as one of the elect: "Envisaging the external world, its indefiniteness, its confusion, which is even more perfect at night, I set it up as a divinity of which I was not only the cherished pretext, an object of great care and caution, chosen and led in masterly fashion, though through painful and exhausting ordeals, to the verge of despair, but also the sole object of all this labor."

Thus, Genet is of the elect. He wants only one proof of this, only one sign: the universe. He is elected to suffer, to hate himself and to do evil. In a certain sense, this is not untrue. However, his election comes from the society of decent people. The error is to attribute it to a metaphysical being. A passage in *Our Lady of the Flowers* will enable us to grasp concretely this substitution of elector. In a moment of proud gaiety, little Culafroy, who is in a public park, "about-faces smartly. He was about to begin a dance. . . ." In short, for once he forgets himself, he yields to the temptation of gracefulness, to the appeal of elegance. The torn sole of his shoe stops his pirouette and brings him down to earth again:

"He sauntered back slowly. The strollers in the park watched him go by. Culafroy saw that they noticed his paleness, his thinness, his lowered eyelids. . . . He bowed his head more deeply . . . and whispered aloud a cry, 'Lord, I am among thy elect.' For a few steps, God carried him off to his throne."

An accident of his wretchedness prevents him from performing the luxurious little movement which would have made of him, for a moment, a lord in high heels. Immediately he reverts to humility. He recognizes the immutable severity of the world and the fact that he is not meant for fine whims. At the same moment, he feels upon him the contempt of the Others, their pity. For us, the circle closes: the Others have put him into this intolerable situation, he recognizes his abjection in their gaze, and they, satisfied, contemplate their work. But, for Genet, there is a resort: he escapes. Gazed upon by the crowd, he frees himself by invoking another gaze. Nothing has changed: the torn sole, the ragged clothes, the sickly pallor, the thinness, everything is there; it is *the object Genet*. But, by an imperceptible displacement, Genet makes himself an object for an invisible gaze which touches him like a magic wand and endows his wretchedness with a sacred dimension.

In short, the mechanism is simple: Genet has had a religious upbringing, society has left its mark on him, that is, it has impressed upon him, like a seal, the idea of God, who is the mythical basis of the collective imperatives. And in point of fact it is indeed God who legitimates, *for the Just,* that is, for those who are "integrated," the sentence of exile which they impose on the thief: God forbids theft. Genet, in flight, carries off with him the idea of God. This means that two notions are available to him for pondering the collective, that of Society and that of Divine Person. But the two concepts have a single object. Genet will therefore give two simultaneous interpretations of the same fact: his exile is the consequence of merciless social justice and, at the same time, of divine kindness. And the secret of Providence is none other than the secret of the Group, but *in reverse.* Genet and M. Mauriac are in agreement: God was aiming at Genet through social condemnation. Let us go further: for both of them, this condemnation must have moral consequences. It must *purify.* And when they say God, both of them are actually naming Society as a concrete totality of the Others. But M. Mauriac says condemnation where Genet says election; he recognizes that Genet has defied God when Genet thinks that God has provoked him. He regards purification as a progressive return to the Good, and Genet believes that the torments will make of him an utterly pure evildoer. In short, Genet steals the name that the sacred society gives itself and turns it against the secular society.

It remains to be seen in what form this God, whose gaze transfigures him, appears to him. If he is the Almighty, Genet is done for. For God can opt only for the Good. If Genet is elected by God the Father, he becomes an innocent victim whose sufferings and pitifulness deserve heaven. He departs forever from the evil path which he has chosen and which, if followed to the very end, should lead him to salvation. He does not stop stealing, since he has to steal in order to live. But he sinks into sanctimoniousness with his faking, his insincerity, his false justifications. He acquires a good conscience in a roundabout way, since the order of Evil on earth seems to him only the reverse side of the heavenly order of Good. And if it appears that the Eternal can order a crime, it is because the religious life is situated above the moral life. So Genet becomes Abraham: Abraham, too, was asked by an Angel to commit a murder.

Fortunately, he no longer quite believes in God. By the time Culafroy is carried off to a heavenly throne, an unpunished sacrilege has long since revealed to him that "the Eternal was hollow." Genet plays at belief as he does at other feelings: it is constantly oscillating between different levels, from a veiled atheism to Black Mass and sacrilege. It is not so much that he *doubts* or that he has lost his faith as a result of clear thinking. No, but what has happened to him is what happens in all cases of ostracism: for a true believer, who is an obedient member of the group and of the Church, divine *transcendence* is guaranteed by that of institutions and customs; the Other is outside; for those who are excluded, God falls into immanence. This transcendent God remains in the group, and the God they take away with them is diluted in their inner life for want of being supported by a church.

The God of Genet is Genet himself. By a stroke of genius he inverts his project radically. The others had convinced him that he harbored within himself a pernicious nature, an evil will. He sought for years to perceive it, he even tried, though in vain, to put his conscious freedom at the source of this nature. In short, he wanted to make an object of it. He now changes his line of attack: he makes himself an object for it. He resigns himself to never seeing it, provided he is conscious of being seen by it. This demoniacal postulation toward Evil expresses his will, his absolute freedom which has flung itself into an irremediable commitment. But it is his will as Other. It is still a nature, but a nature-making nature, and it is Genet's clear consciousness which becomes a nature-made nature. He makes of the propensity for evil which the decent people discern in him a nontemporal choice of doing evil. Beyond heredity, instincts, all forms of passivity, a Kantian noumenal freedom has decided, in an intelligible world, in favor of radical evil. Does this mean that there are two Genets? No, not quite. The "empirical" little thief is closely united to this pure will by the gaze it directs upon him. He feels himself to be a reflected consciousness with respect to a reflective consciousness, with one difference, to wit, that the reflective consciousness is in heaven, out of reach. But it sees him, it guides and approves him. The decisions he makes from day to day are only the coin of the great fixed and eternal choice which constitutes him to the depths of his being. Thus, by a sudden reversal, consciousness becomes an object, and the imperceptible object of consciousness assumes the rank of an absolute subject which watches him. Of course, this is achieved at the cost of a further effort: it involves becoming a *consciousness watched from behind*. Before the transpiercing gazes of the just, he must feel himself fleeing toward himself from behind himself; he must play, must mime, until he feels a kind of inner flowing.

"Much solitude had forced me to become my own companion . . . and little by little, through a kind of operation which I cannot quite describe, without modifying the dimensions of my body, and perhaps because it was easier to contain so precious a reason for such glory, it was within me that I established this divinity—origin and disposition of myself. I swallowed it. I dedicated to it songs of my own invention. At night I would whistle. The melody was a religious one. It was slow. Its rhythm was somewhat heavy. I thought that I was thereby entering into communication with God: which is what happened, God being only the hope and fervor contained in my song."

Is this change so surprising? For right-thinking people, Genet embodies the Other. And as he has fallen into their trap, he embodies the Other in his own eyes too. But this Other, who has been installed within him by a decree of society, is first *a collective representation*, of which it has all the characteristics. Fixed and intangible, it cannot be reduced to the contingent movements of an individual consciousness. It is Genet himself, but *with another nature*. It is *sacred* Genet haunting the everyday soul of profane Genet. It is actually like the zars which "possess" certain natives of Ethiopia and which are none other than the possessed themselves, but objectified and rendered sacred. And Genet does what the Ethiopians do: he worships his zar. But since this Sacred Ego is the product of the gazes of all, how could it not reflect these gazes upon its worshiper? Thus, without his suspecting it, once again the gazes of all converge upon Genet through this Dark Power which he reveres. Only, those thousands of eyes are internalized. They have gone behind him. The hatred they express has changed into a terrible love, and the punishments to which they have condemned him now become providential ordeals. A close correspondence is established between the course of the world and this intelligible character. The particular categorical imperative that Genet is for himself is expressed both by the impulses which flash through his consciousness and by the tests, the temptations, offered him by the outer world. Or, if one prefers, the entire world, in its indissoluble unity as a torture machine, is the material image of the sacred subject. Both of them, like Spinozistic thought and extension, are only the two attributes of one and the same substance. In making a choice of his intelligible character Genet *has elected himself* in his empirical reality, and the martyrdom to which the world subjects him is the evident sign, the chief effect, of this election. That is what I call Genet's solipsistic temptation, for a consciousness which contented itself with being a consciousness of self could not fall into solipsism precisely because the world is immediately given as *that which is not made for us.* In order for a consciousness to adopt this attitude, it must already be possessed by the Other and must have endowed this Other with substantiality to the detriment of the world and of itself. A solipsist is a man who denies his empirical existence for the benefit of his noumenal and sacred existence. For the solipsist and for Genet, *I is Another* and this Other is God.

This curious companion whom Genet has given himself has inherited from God his sacred powers (he *is* the Sacred "in person") and from Genet his finiteness. He is, of course, an interlocutor: Genet is constantly talking to him and calling him to witness. This kind of dissociation of the personality is not rare among solitaries.* But the essential function of this Power is to transform Genet's individual history, as it unfolds, into sacred history, that is, as we shall see, to destroy its historicity.

We have accompanied Genet to the ultimate stage of his attempt to find his being through the mediation of others. We can now indicate its dialectical movement.

At the outset, it is a strict intention of achieving as quickly as possible and by every available means the total alienation of his person. In the will to *do,* which we shall examine presently, the structure of the act itself imposes a moment of autonomy: action wants to change the world, to impose upon it a status which does not yet exist; it frees itself from being by nonbeing, since it envisages that which is in the light of that which is not yet. Freedom must therefore be posed for its own sake, even if only to be denied immediately thereafter. But the cruder, more magical project of requesting his being of Others severely proscribes this moment of freedom. In a movement of despair, in a narcissism of horror, Genet

---

* Although it generally takes place in the opposite direction, where consciousness takes *for object* the object that one is for others: "I said to myself, 'My boy, you're going to get into trouble.' "

seeks to deny himself in servitude: he submits to a sacred object which represents his own nature visible in the guise of Another. He worships, he melts into ecstasy. The first moment of the dialectical progression is thus alienation. Genet is himself *in Another;* his consciousness poses the being of the Other as essential and regards itself as inessential: this is Love. Strictly speaking, in order to be able to decide as to what will be the essential and what the inessential, consciousness must already be conscious of being sovereign, therefore essential. In other words, Genet must *decide* upon his servitude. But this sovereign consciousness is not an object to itself; it is aware of its sovereignty only through a kind of secret knowledge.* Genet is in a good position to ignore it: he bewitches himself in the Other and flees his own consciousness of self. In this first moment, consciousness flees itself and throws itself upon the Other; it tries to be external to itself. It is pure consciousness *of* the Other.

But in order for consciousness to be able to be absorbed completely in its servile function, which is to reflect the merits of the Other, it must deny all consciousness of itself in the Other. If the pure object is actually conscious of itself, it becomes an object for itself and has no need to receive lighting from without; it decides, as subject, on its own truth, and Genet becomes an object in turn. He therefore resolves not to allow the Other to have being-for-itself so that the latter may have being only through the light which is shed upon it. In fact, he disqualifies the other consciousnesses, which might aspire, like his, to reflect the object. He chooses the most feared, most hated man in order to worship him as a god, feeling sure that he is alone in perceiving the god's secret virtues. Thus, the beauty and kindness of Armand, a repulsive brute, exist only in and through Genet's idolatry. Thereupon, the classical reversal takes place: the inessential becomes the essential and the essential the inessential. Armand's being no longer exists except in itself, that is, for that single, privileged Other who is Genet. The Other was to have served as mediator between Genet and his being; it is now Genet who is a mediator between the criminal and the criminal's being. The pimps, the toughs, the murderers, are reduced to simple appearances; they have existence only insofar as Genet's consciousness gives it to them. Consciousness, now liberated, re-enters itself; it can no longer conceal from itself, even if it performs acrobatics of dishonesty, the fact that it itself creates these phan-

---

* The words "aware of" and "know" are inappropriate. It is a matter of what I have elsewhere called "nonthetic consciousness of self."

tasmagoria. Thus, the second moment of the process vigorously
contradicts Genet's primary intention. He wanted to become an
object and finds himself a subject despite himself. Despite himself?
Not quite. Indeed, insofar as his love of the Male included hatred,
Genet always had a foreboding of this reversal and even desired it.
He would never have accepted servitude if he had not secretly felt
sure that he could break free.

Can it be that he has finally freed himself of his chains? No. No
doubt he is a free will that makes contact with itself while the appearance sinks. But this will connects with itself as a free will to
subject itself. It has freed itself of its fascination in the presence of
the Other, but it returns to itself to find its basic choice, which is to
sacrifice itself to being. Having looked back on itself, it apprehends
itself by a reflective act which is already vitiated by the intention
of going over to being. This reflection grows anxious when confronted with the emptiness of consciousness, when confronted with
its freedom. Genet is afraid of suddenly discovering that he is master
of Good and Evil. Subjected in childhood to the ethics of Good,
submissive, thereafter, to the orders of the Big Shots, he is suddenly
scared of "becoming his own heaven." In order to avoid this shocking possibility, he is going to rush once again into fatality. In
short, he cannot free himself so long as he will not make liberation
his goal, but in order to do this he would have to be already
liberated; otherwise, the encountering of freedom can only be accidental. This is the classic pattern of all types of discursive madness:
the patient is constantly on the brink of lucidity only to start raving
again immediately. "I have a chronic hallucinatory psychosis," said
a psychiatrist. And he diagnosed his case quite pertinently, only
to add immediately thereafter: "It's my confrere So-and-So who
gave it to me." Thus, Genet's frightened consciousness once again
desires to be inessential, but this time it is going to estrange itself
from itself. It is going to lure the Big Shot who gives orders, and
incorporate him into itself. Thus far, Genet's wicked Nature was
little more than a kind of opacity, a jumbled heap of fatality. It was
situated at the back of Genet's consciousness like a naïve image of
the unconscious, a pure object which had not found its subject. The
terms are now reversed. This constituted "essence" or "nature"
becomes a constituting subject. He hands over to it his own freedom, his lucidity; it becomes the Demon at the back of his head; it
sees him, and this omnipotent gaze impastes his consciousness with
a secret objectivity. This consciousness, now chilled by a foreign
gaze, loses its freedom, its autonomy: it retains a modicum of reality

only insofar as it is the object of this new gaze. To think, to speak, to feel, are henceforth to worship this Demon, which is oneself, or to offer words as sacrifice in propitiatory ceremonies; all is a religious gift, all is worship. Thus, the liberation was only a moment in the dialectical process, only the transition from one alienation to another. Is it possible to will oneself, at the same time and in the same connection, as a pure object and as an absolute subject? But the moment of alienation proves insufficient in turn: this invisible God is too abstract; Genet's subjection is too deliberate, it has not the violence of the desires that stagger him and throw him at the feet of good-looking roughnecks. Thus, the dialectical progression which I have just indicated deviates into a circular movement: subjection to the Other, return to self, subjection to self as other, return to amorous subjection, etc. Genet looks at himself, despairs of making contact with himself, goes to give himself to a tough, secretly debunks him, leaves him, magnifies his adventures without ceasing to take them for what they are worth, is disgusted by the poetic failure and comes back to look at himself and to make love. He goes round in circles, he can keep his balance only by moving faster and faster, going from one pimp to another pimp, from one embrace to another embrace, from essence to existence and from existence to essence, from poetic glorification to corrosive lucidity. If he stops, he is dead. Is he fleeing his original malediction or is he pursuing his being? Both at the same time.

Yet there is another way: during all this time, he steals, lies, betrays. Will he make contact with himself at least by what he *does?* Or is this new path only a new circuit which he will have to travel without respite? We must go back to evil will and follow Genet on the paths of Evil.

A DAILY LABOR, LONG AND DISAPPOINTING...

Let us go back to the moment of the conversion. The child has decided both to *be* evil and *do* Evil. We have followed him in the labyrinth where he is misled by his will to be. Will he have better luck when he aims only at acting? One would think so at first: does he not discard the contradictions of ontological and theological morals in order to grapple with an ethic of action?

Yes, he does: in deciding to act, Genet connects with himself at the source of his freedom, in his pure and formal possibility of willing. For this unconditioned will, all particular and material ends are equivalent. Wealth can help or corrupt, depending on the case; thus, it is neither good nor evil in itself; all depends on the use to which it is put. An unconditionally evil will will deign to procure it only if it is the best *means* of doing evil. Genet recognizes only one end: Evil, consciousness in Evil. The quest for being began with a will to total subservience to the Other, that is, to the world, to Being itself, and although Genet raised himself from that state to one of passing autonomy, he did so in spite of himself. He had no rest until he hurried back into servitude again. On the other hand, evil will starts by willing itself as a primary and inexcusable cause: thus, the first moment of this new dialectic is that of freedom; we shall see Genet rising from being to *existence*. Let us say that the quest for being reveals the magical and religious aspect of this consciousness: it goes round in circles, it eats and is eaten, it exhausts itself in a cannibal ritual. The pure will to Evil, on the other hand, represents spirituality. The mind, which has been freed, here makes contact with itself, gives itself rules, confers upon the world its status.

And yet we have left the aporias of Being only to fall into those of Nonbeing. Let us not think that it is easy to do evil or even to know what Evil is. It was a lotion for external use: Genet swallows it; the result is a generalized poisoning. We have, in fact, seen that the Society of decent folk has manufactured this shaky concept for the express purpose of projecting it on others. Evil is what my enemy does; it is *never* what I do myself. We have recognized in it the negative part of our freedom which we pluck from ourselves in order to throw it, like the robe of Nessus, on an ethnic or religious minority. Thus, evil is, in its principle, evil-object. If any right-thinking man tried to introduce it into himself, this unstable mixture would be diluted in his subjectivity. But when one of the scapegoats whom Society has chosen and whose only task is to commit a few crimes in a state of debasement and to let himself be carted from prison to prison amidst the jeers of the mob, when one of these helots happens to be intelligent, willful, sensitive and pious, when he takes his role seriously and tries to live within himself in accordance with the principles that are imposed upon him from without, in short, when he endeavors to fulfill, in and by his subjectivity, a notion which has meaning only in the objective, he then finds himself confronted with endless contradictions and becomes himself contradictory, for he must install in his consciousness —and must assume—all the divergent characteristics which the respectable man has thrown pell-mell into this catchall concept. Because the evildoer is the *absolute Other*, we have seen Genet attempt to fulfill his Ego as the Other-than-self and drift into narcissism and then into homosexuality. But when he wants to *do* evil, he is no better off: order and disorder, relative and absolute, Being of Nonbeing and Nonbeing of Being, principle and person, such is the end he must achieve in the World. Can he even *conceive* it? Can he focus on the various characteristics of Evil at the same time?

If one wants, on every occasion, to do the worst, one must have a special sensibility in order to discern it: one must be "sensitized" to evil, must have, in general and in each particular case, a clear and distinct idea of it. There are people who say of themselves that they "never see Evil," and that is true. Not that they are better than others. Quite the contrary. But as they have a sweeping view of Good, they see Evil sweepingly, without going into detail. In order to be evil, one needs experience, shrewdness, a subtle knowledge of the heart; one must be able to sense unfailingly the word that will hurt most, to invent the act that wounds irreparably. But the heart knows itself through the heart: a person to whom I am indifferent cannot wound me. It is not enough even to know what our victim wants most; we must want it with him, we must sympathize with his desires, we must espouse them. In fact, we must love him; one must love in order to cause suffering. The reader may observe that hatred, too, knows its object. To which I reply: because of the portion of attentive love that it contains. Let us bear in mind the universal tenderness of the child Genet: it is not dead but only disguised, and it is this tenderness that will inspire him to do evil. In short, since Evil is a negation, one cannot discover it unless one first, or at least at the same time, perceives what it denies. Genet's tact, his "sensitization," includes a positive content: sensitization to Good. Thus, knowledge of Evil presupposes that of Good, but the previous intuition of Good cannot be a cold, languid contemplation. Such contemplation would offer us facts, not values. In order to know Good, one must want it. Let the evildoer therefore know, love and want Good, let him not cease for an instant to want it and love it, even in the depths of vice. The more distinct the knowledge and the stronger the will, the more criminal will be his intention of doing evil. Evil will is more complex than good will, just as a second-degree equation is more complex than a first. For good will wants Good without any other presupposition, and though it too may sometimes have to overcome resistance, such resistance is external to it and does not spring from its original intention but from another region of the soul, whereas in order to deny Good the will to Evil must first pose Good and will it. Inversely, evil will must not cease to hate the crime which it plans. The only immediate and universal sign available for recognizing Evil is that it is detestable. Not detestable to this one or that one, but to everyone, hence to the evildoer himself. I shall know unmistakably that an action is evil when the very idea that I might commit it horrifies me. Though it may appear that this horror ought to prevent me from doing evil, such is not the case; it is the horror itself that ought to be my most powerful motive. It may well be that the crime seems to me momentarily to be desirable *in spite* of the horror with which it fills me: for example, if it is the only means of regaining my freedom. A prisoner who escapes may find himself forced to kill a guard. But in that case the aim is not murder but escape. Evil is not the end, it is only the means, and, in the last analysis, one has chosen not the worse but the *lesser evil*. The prisoner deemed that it was better to kill the guard than go back to jail. To be sure, *for the others* this act is a crime. If he is caught, he may be shot. But *for him* it is an unavoidable accident: he judges that he is in a state of legitimate defense. No: the ideal thing would be that the evil act be gratuitous; Evil is the action that we have no reason to perform and every reason to avoid. And that is just how Genet, in his books, presents the crimes of his heroes. Erik, alone in the countryside, suddenly notices a child playing. The child is charming, confident, he enjoys being alive, he is happy. The sight of him immediately arouses in Erik a feeling of sympathy, in fact a feeling of love. But love immediately awakens the idea of murder in this soul which is involved in evil. The idea first manifests itself in the form of anguish: it would be *awful* to kill the child. Or, if one prefers, if only I'm not seized with a desire to kill him! That is all. No hatred, no sadism, no resentment. The idea takes shape, it is exacerbated, it becomes Erik's greatest terror. With all his heart he wants the child to live, he would like to talk to it, caress it, make it happy; he knows that nothing is more loathsome, nothing more cowardly, than the murder of a child; he already imagines how the little victim would look at him if he aimed his revolver; beads of sweat stand out on his forehead; he rebels completely against this abominable possibility, which is nevertheless *his* possibility. *Precisely because of that,* he will kill. He takes his revolver, slowly; he looks the child in the eyes in order to see his last expression. At that moment there is no telling which of the two is more afraid, which of the two is suffering more. He fires and causes two deaths: one kills in order to kill oneself.

There, at least, we have the *ideal* evil action. I am not inventing anything; neither is Genet. Everything is already contained in the notion of radical Evil concocted by right-thinking people. The Evildoer must will Evil for Evil's sake, and since Good is prior to Evil, as Being is to Nothingness, it is *from his original love of Good* that he must draw the motives for doing evil and *in his loathing of Evil* that he must discover the attraction of Sin. The Evildoer's will must be dual, since it wills Evil in direct relation to its fundamental will to Good, while rigorously preserving its inner unity. This duality is not inconceivable. Indeed, we see in the act of reflection the simultaneous emerging of two consciousnesses which have distinct objects, since the first relates to the world and the second relates to the first: I perceive and I know that I perceive; I act and I watch myself acting; I talk and I listen to myself talking. Is it not precisely on this reflective ground that Genet has condemned himself to dwell forever? Is he not the man who is always spying on himself, judging himself and comparing himself? It would be convenient to say that the will to Good, which is immediate and unthinking, applies itself to external objects, to the sick person who *must* be taken care of, to the penniless man who *must* be helped, and that the will to Evil, being a knowledge of our first will, operates on the plane of reflectiveness: I would perceive in my heart a desire to aid the afflicted, and my reflective consciousness would immediately check it. Yet reflective scissiparity furnishes only a very rough image of the duality of evil will. It is not enough to will Good and deny it at one and the same time: this might be weakness, surrender. And even if I refuse, *precisely because it is a good deed,* to perform the action suggested to me by my immediate will, that would still be insufficient: I may be yielding to a burst of temper, to a passing fit of misanthropy: "What's the good of helping him? He's just as bad as the others," etc. But that would be merely an abstention. The sight of the Good must arouse the will to harm. Far from helping the poor fellow, I will crush him, and all the more in that he deserves greater sympathy or pity. And that is still not enough: even if I pitilessly violated all prohibitions, even if I thwarted all my spontaneous good intentions, I would not be utterly lost since they exist, since there is still a kind of original goodness in me. The ideal thing would be for me to be good with the express purpose of being evil: not only should reflection contradict the spontaneous intention, but, in addition, a deeper will should produce this first intention with the express purpose of its being contradictory. In short, the impulse to Good should be produced only in a consciousness already polarized toward Evil and as a means of doing the greatest Evil, that is, of also thwarting Good in me.

We have just encountered the first aporia of Evil, a simple internalization of an objective contradiction which was pointed out above. For the Being of Evil is both the Being of Nonbeing and the Nonbeing of Being. It is at one and the same time relative to Good and absolute. Thus, in a sense, the greatest evil is to have an intimate knowledge of Good, to be *born good* like every human creature, and to reject that blinding light, to plunge deliberately into darkness. That is why the fully responsible adult who has acted with premeditation is judged to be necessarily more guilty. From this point of view, Evil arises after Good and relatively to it. But, once again, if Evil is perfect, it must be absolute; therefore, the evildoer must be totally evil; it is still too much that he be good at the beginning. This time, Being appears in order to be destroyed. Goodness is awakened in the evildoer only as an indispensable moment of evildoing, *in order* to be thwarted and trampled on.

How is one to choose? And, in the second case, how is one to ask nothingness to produce being, to ask negation to beget affirmation while remaining negative? Moreover, if the evildoer becomes good in order to make himself worse, how will he be able to be really good, how will he be able *really* to feel that horror of doing evil which is one of the necessary conditions of the evil deed? But if he does not abhor Evil, if he does it out of passion, then, as Genet himself says, Evil becomes a Good. In actual fact, the person who *loves* blood and rape, like the butcher of Hamburg, is a criminal lunatic but not a true evildoer.

We shall see that Genet chooses the first solution. This child who wishes to purify himself through crime will make of Evil the instrument of his own punishment. Moreover, the best way of attaining pure will is to make of crime an ascesis: we know very well that Genet was good. With each of his crimes he will free himself a little more from his past, from his tastes, from his gentleness. His freedom will assert itself *against his sensibility*. But the second solution cannot be dismissed so easily. In a sense, one solution cannot be chosen without the other. Its invisible presence will blight all of Genet's fine reasoning.

But here we have a further aporia: since Genet's sensibility is entirely at variance with his undertakings, where will he find a *motive* for doing evil? We have deduced from the nature of Evil that the evildoer derives his reasons for killing from the horror with which the crime inspires him and from his original love of Good. The deduction is correct, but it leads to absurdities, for it amounts to saying that our chief motive in performing a certain category of actions is both our desire not to perform them and our will to perform the contrary action. How is one to find in Good a reason for doing Evil? And in the rejection of Evil? The conversion of Evil to Good is conceivable: evil is disorder and nonbeing; it is possible to find in it reasons for willing being and order. This relative refers us from the self to the absolute. Or, as Catholics say, Sin is the gaping void of God. But what about conversion of Good to Evil? How could one even consider it? Good is Being, Positivity, Order, absolute Plenitude. Where can one find the slightest flaw in it? And Evil, being nothingness, can exist only if it is willed. How could it possess the slightest force of attraction? It does not even pay, since it must horrify us to the very end. Let us imagine a torturer gently questioning his future victim: "What is the torture you dread most, the one that you pray to God every day to spare you?" The victim naïvely replies: "The strappado." The torturer:

"That's the very one I'm going to inflict on you." The same holds for the evildoer in relation to himself. Since the subjective criterion of Evil is the horror it inspires, the evildoer knows that the greatest Evil is also that which will pain him most. After deliberately betraying a friend, Genet declares: "My betrayal causes me unspeakable suffering." The very excess of the contradiction gives the statement a slightly comic overtone that should arouse our mistrust. Be that as it may, is it an appetite for suffering that inclines him to Evil? But Genet's attitude remains quite ambiguous: let us bear in mind that he wants to go to crime *despite* this suffering and not *because* of it. Indeed, it resists him, it prevents him from establishing himself at once in the depths of Evil. He has to train himself, has to use the latest misdeeds he has committed as a springboard for even more detestable inventions. "Evil," he writes, "is achieved little by little, through a discovery of genius which makes you drift far away from men. But most often by a daily labor, long and disappointing." He even apologizes: "I had to rely on a bit of physical beauty to attain Evil." As if the horror were such that he could not attain it without help, somewhat as Dante needs Vergil's arm to descend to Hell. There is progress in Evil, and it is by constant training that the resistances are, one by one, broken down and that one achieves the progressive racking of the will. But here is the immediate counterpart: one must not, under any circumstance, eliminate, or even reduce, suffering. The ideal thing would be even to increase it: one should train oneself and not harden oneself. Genet writes: "That inhuman life might too quickly have led Erik to detachment." During a scene of sadism, the torturers scowl, and he says: "I knew that they had to indulge in scowls because their contempt was in danger of becoming an indifference to Evil to the point of pity for those who commit it." He thus wants to install himself at the very heart of the contradiction. The subjective aspect of Evil is a suffering to the very marrow, a contempt for oneself and one's accomplices which under no circumstances must change to pity. Genet deliberately wants the downfall within consciousness, in short what Bataille would call *torment*.

> I am the wound and the knife . . .
> The victim and the hangman.*

Is this, then, his goal?
The fact remains that if Genet wants to be self-caused he must

---

* Baudelaire, *Les Fleurs du Mal*, "L'Héautontimorouménos."—Translator's note.

either get rid of his sufferings or become their perpetrator. And as his original crisis plunged him, despite himself, into a horror of which he cannot be cured, his only way of deriving this horror from himself is to intensify it and carry it to the extreme. What is more, it is only in a state of suffering that he can *feel* free, for suffering is the only feeling that can come from him. Unless one is a god, one cannot make oneself happy without the help of the universe; to make oneself unhappy, one needs only oneself.

But we immediately encounter further difficulties: as a free man, Genet must want to acquire the autonomy of his *sensibility,* but insofar as he wants to be evil, that is, to acquire the autonomy of his *will,* he cannot will Evil merely because of the horror it inspires in him. If torment were the supreme end, it would not differ greatly from the self-inflicted ordeals of the Saint. Or else, quite the contrary, it would become the expression of a deep resentment: tortured and becoming his own torturer, Genet would want to shame respectable people just as Baudelaire becomes the Heautontimoroumenos in order to shame Madame Aupick. And, most certainly, Genet shifts from one attitude to the other: he has not lost the ambition to be a saint and, on the other hand, his rancor is so manifest that Scheler would certainly have included him among the "men of resentment." But the suffering which is caused us by the Evil we do is equidistant from the tortures one inflicts upon oneself out of asceticism and those one imposes upon oneself out of sulkiness. And besides, Genet's pride tries to squelch his rancor: he is not allowed to complain, since one complains *to others* and of the wrongs they do one. Although Genet often strays from his path, he always comes back to it. It is indeed Evil that he wills and that he must will in order to retain the initiative. An exclusively psychoanalytical interpretation of his attitude would beg the question: to be sure, the intelligent solicitude of decent people did its utmost to burden the child with every possible complex. Rancor, feeling of inferiority, overcompensation, Genet has known them all. But we will understand nothing about his case if we are unwilling to recognize that he undertook, with exceptional intelligence and vigor, to carry out his own psychoanalysis. It would be absurd to explain him by impulses when the fact is that it is against these impulses that he wants to regain his autonomy. No doubt at the root of his decision there is what I shall call a psychoanalytical situation. And it is true that Genet does Evil because men and circumstances impel him to. But if that were all, he would be one of the countless victims of our despicable society, he would not be

Jean Genet. Jean Genet is a thief who wanted *to change his motives for stealing* and who thereby transcended his original situation. His astounding effort to regain freedom in Evil deserves therefore to be explained by his object and not by a *vis a tergo,* which, in point of fact, he escapes. Although he may occasionally relapse into resentment, in the manner of very young children who momentarily regress to an earlier stage of their development, nevertheless the fact remains that he invented the willing of Evil for Evil's sake. And not only Evil for its own sake, but Evil in itself. It will not suffice for him to attain the absolute of suffering; he wants to make new and absolutely evil events appear in the universe. And when he is in full possession of himself, at the highest pitch of his inner tension, it is not of the appetite for suffering that he will ask the motive for his evil deeds; he wants them to be the effects of an absolute willing which derives its motivation from itself and not from the world. We return to our starting point and again ask the question: What is the motive for doing evil that can be derived from consideration of the Good? There is only one: the absence of motives. All the others, whatever they may be, have a positive content, and the Good, as an absolute positivity, is the geometric locus of the positive contents of all motives. Thus, every wish, every desire, every passion, contributes to impelling me to Good exactly insofar as it contains a thin vein of the positive and of being. The Good has no need of me. It exists by itself, it is God, it is the social machine. And I, on the other hand, have need of *it.* An irresistible force inclines me to do Good just as the quiet power of the evident obliges me to affirm clear and distinct ideas. This Good is the universal objective which appears to all human beings in the same way. It is what anyone would do in my place, and, consequently, it is that with respect to which I am inessential and undistinguished. In doing Good, I lose myself in Being, I abandon my particularity, I become a universal subject. With respect to the Good, men of good will are interchangeable. They *are,* it is *good* that they are, being is a good, Good is Being. Through them, being goes to Good as the cow goes to the bull. A husband who was on his deathbed thanked the persons about him in the most heartfelt terms; to his wife, who had nursed him unsparingly, he said only: "As for you, I'm not thanking you. You simply did your duty." She did not reply. What could she have answered? The most natural, the easiest thing was to spend her nights at the sick man's bedside. Since she loved him, since she was his wife, she could find within herself no reason for letting him die. She had therefore done what any wife would have done in her place. She did not reply, but she must, I imagine, have thought to herself what Kafka writes in his journal: "Good is sometimes disheartening." On the other hand, Evil needs me in order to exist. It is all weakness. In fact, it is dizzying only because of its nothingness. It will begin to be only if I think it, it will gain force only if I undertake to achieve it. In short, it is never anything but the exact correlative of my attitude toward it. If I turn away from it, it vanishes. I must constantly support it in its wavering being by a continuous creation. As it is always the exception to the rule, the unique, the instantaneous—just try to make universals of theft, crime and lying!—it reflects, at the same time, my particularity. Hence, there is in the Good which attracts me a motive for my turning away from it, to wit, the fact that it already is, that it is everywhere, that it is as plain as a pikestaff, that it is irresistible and foreseen and that I lose myself in it, forget myself and swoon in a kind of pantheistic ecstasy. And in the Evil which horrifies me there is a motive for attracting me, the fact that it comes from myself and will cease whenever I like and that consequently I cannot lose myself in it. Indeed, I find myself in it, I am never more present to myself than in that grating consciousness of wanting what I do not want. Gide is right in saying that the Devil has won if he convinces me that he does not exist. If he did exist, what would it matter to me? To abandon God in order to follow Satan would be to exchange one mode of being for another. But if nothing is only Being, if being is everywhere, if error is *nothing,* if evil is *nothing,* if everything one may want or conceive or love is also being and, hence, an aspect of Good, then the temptation of Evil begins, that is, freedom tempts itself. The universal subject looks down into the well and sees at the bottom his own image as a negativity, a particularity, a freedom. And furthermore, nonbeing attracts me, or, if one prefers, I attract myself from the depths of nonbeing: as a being, I am encircled and hemmed in by being, God's eye sees me. But since God, the infinite Being, cannot even conceive nothingness, in nothingness I escape him and derive only from myself. Not that I annihilate myself, but in absorbing myself in conceiving nonbeing I am still a consciousness or, if one prefers, a presence of nothingness to itself. This trinity of represented nothingness, or pure appearance, whose *esse* is only a *percipi,* of the reflected-reflecting nothingness and of the reflecting-reflected nothingness (which pair constitutes the nonthetic consciousness of self) has no being other than the consciousness of being, hence no basis, no support outside of self. And, on the other hand, the existence of this consciousness, which has no outside by which it can be taken, destroyed or modi-fied, confers upon the complete system of nonbeing an absolute *presence.* Who could then dislodge me from my darkness, who could join me there? As a being who thinks about being, I am a creature of God; as a nothingness thinking nothingness, I am my own cause. And no doubt I then produce only appearances. But nothing is more dizzying than appearance, for if I discovered a truth, it would immediately belong to everyone and no longer to me. And if, to suppose the impossible, I created being, this being would continue in its being without me, through inertia or with the help of God. But appearance *is not I;* it steals from being its transcendency, and yet it sticks to the skin of my consciousness as does a cataract to an eye; it depends on me alone. Appearance is satanic, because it caricatures being and because it is all that man can produce by his own means. Hence, evil is the absence of motives suggesting to me that I invent my motives; it is the destruction of being conceived as the creation of appearance. We shall see that this last formula can be rigorously applied to Genet's aesthetic for the reason that Evil is also called, quite simply, the Imaginary. But, it may be argued, is not the *real* Evil the *act* whereby Erik kills the child? No: the criminal is already calling for the aid of Being; he composes, combines and chooses. The moment of absolute Evil is that in which he dreams of killing a child and in which suddenly, without ceasing to be a dream, the imaginary terminates in a decision. Genet's acts are both poems and crimes, because they are dreamt for a long time before being committed and because he still dreams them while committing them. There we have the motive: the hounded child lets himself sink into the absolute solitude of a long, evil dream where no one can follow him.

But let us be cautious: no sooner have we found this motive than we must, in turn, abandon it, in the first place because Genet does not want to remain in the dream, even if, as is the case, it is tougher and sharper than the most realistic calculation. His pride refuses evasion. The entire world will have to *become* his dream, will have to dream for him and with him, will have to reveal its shadowy face. Crime is a means of forcing the world to dream nothingness. In addition, and above all, if we must do Evil *in order to attain* this singular freedom, then once again Evil becomes a means and it is freedom which becomes an end. It is freedom, it is particularity, it is solitude that we are aiming at, and not Evil for its own sake. Genet is not always able to avoid this substitution of ends, as appears from such passages as the following: "His sufferings are of metaphysical origin. . . . Of his solitude had been born anxiety about the problem of Evil, and he had postulated Evil out of despair." And: "[I thought] that the domains of Evil were less frequented than those of Good and that I would be alone there. . . . My taste for solitude incited me to seek out the most virgin lands." The relationship of Evil to Solitude remains uncertain. In the first quotation, the former is the effect of the latter, and in the second, the means of obtaining it. Both formulas are true: solitude, which at first is undergone, chooses itself and, in so doing, becomes Evil. Nevertheless, the fact remains that Genet goes round in circles: in order to avoid evil-out-of-resentment, which is only sulkiness, he plunges into evil-as-torment, which very soon changes into pure asceticism. In order to escape both, he finally invents the notion of doing Evil gratuitously, but, as a result, it is gratuitousness which becomes his final end because it manifests the solitude of his freedom. Perhaps evil is impossible? Perhaps those who say that "nobody is willfully evil" are right?

And yet, what if that were the solution to the problem? Since the synthesis of the Nonbeing of Being and the Being of Nonbeing is appearance, and since appearance manifests to the evildoer his horrible freedom, what if Genet, by an extraordinary effort, transformed acts into gestures, being into the imaginary, the world into phantasmagoria and himself into an appearance? What if he replaced the impossible destruction of the universe by its *derealization*? What if this boy transformed himself—like Divine—into an imaginary woman? And what if, by means of this make-believe, he drew everything—trees, plants, utensils, animals, women and men —into a derealizing whirl? We shall see later that this mad attempt to replace the entire world by a world of appearance is called the aesthetic and that the aesthete is an evildoer. For ten years of his life Genet was an aesthete, and beauty was at first, for him, only a hate-ridden dream of universal conflagration.

But the child has not yet reached this point. He is stumbling over difficulties of a new order. We have just seen that he has decided to attain Evil by means of a conscious and painful exercise. And, to be sure, this continually increasing torture is the greatest Evil per se. But, if Evil must exist, it must also be *in se*. Can these purely subjective tortures be regarded as the greatest Evil per se? If Genet hurt only himself, he would cut a paltry figure indeed compared to the criminal who, without making such a to-do, slaughtered a whole family. Is there a correspondence between subjective Evil—the thankless efforts, the self-disgust, the suffering—

and objective evil, that which is condemned by Religion and Morality? Is it possible to find a crime that is the worst *in both systems at the same time?*

As a matter of fact, there exist, for a single kind of being, several kinds of nonbeing: several errors for a single truth. And, in a given case, for a single way of being just there are several ways of being unjust. How is one to decide? Genet, who betrays in despair and renounces friendship out of fidelity to Evil, is the exact counterpart of Philoctetes, who renounces hatred and gives away his bow. This means that extreme Evil is modeled on Sovereign Good. It will be defined, like Good, by the austere purity of the intention; it is a will that wills itself unconditionally evil. But there is another way of betraying, to wit, handing over one's friend out of cowardice, out of baseness, out of low envy or quite simply for money. This is obviously another kind of Evil. Which is worse? The first is "Consciousness in Evil," which Baudelaire considered the supreme Evil. But this exquisite consciousness, which, as we have seen, envelops even that of Good, is, in a certain way, itself a Good. Genet recognizes this explicitly when he declares that to kill oneself is the greatest crime because one does away with the mind, by which the entire world, Good and Evil alike, is lit up. Thus, like consciousness *of* Evil, consciousness will be evil; it will be good like consciousness in general. And what about evil will? It is a will to Evil, no doubt, but it is pure, and purity must be considered a good, wherever it lodges.* Similarly, the severe training to which Genet subjects himself in order to attain "little by little" the worst is blameworthy with respect to its object but praiseworthy with respect to its principle: it requires will power, courage, a sense of method, all of which are virtues. A keen sensibility, exceptional intelligence, incomparable firmness of mind, unwearying patience, a deep sense of the human, these are what are required of a prince of Evil. Thereupon he becomes admirable: he is Maldoror or Fantomas. The other Evil is quite simply vile. It is out of ignorance and barbarism that the brute breaks rare objects while looting; it is out of insensitivity and not out of sadism that he lets his victim scream without finishing him off; it is out of coldheartedness that he informs on his friend and his brother for thirty pieces of silver. This evil lacks the elegance and style of the great satanic Evil, but it is truer. One does not meet Fra Diavolo or Mandrin every day, but one is always meeting cowards. Less pure, less systematic and, above all, much more conscious than the other, it barely exists *for*

---

* "The devil is pure because he wants only Evil" (Maritain).

itself. In itself, it is perhaps worse. The first Evil necessitates the human order and, in a certain sense, preserves it. The second destroys it mercilessly: it crushes man and is unaware of him. The brute who tortures out of cowardice, out of insensitivity, is perhaps less guilty, since he does not know what he is doing. He is more terrible. His heart and mind are consumed by darkness. He is stricken with the *Evil of Consciousness* which we contrasted above with *Consciousness in Evil.* Genet is so clearly aware of this opposition that he envies the brute his vileness; he would like to win on both boards, to incur truly the Evil of Consciousness in order then to suffer it as if it were a kind of gangrene. This dream assumes a delicately comic form in *Funeral Rites.* In connection with the betrayal of which we have spoken, he writes: "Refusing to let my gesture be heightened by disinterestedness, to let it be a purely gratuitous act, performed, as it were, for the fun of it, I completed my ignominy. I required that my betrayal be paid for. . . ."

It is glaringly obvious that he is the Prince who asks to be paid, who pretends that he is led by the lure of gain. If Genet can believe for a moment that he has lowered himself to the level of a brute, it is because he has a mystique of the gesture. In putting out his hand to receive the wages of his betrayal, he confers a low and imaginary motive on an act which is thoroughly perverse, but not vile. In fact, each Evil challenges the other: the princely Evil is only a deceptive game, it will never have the dense seriousness of abjection. Inversely, the darkness in which the brute lives can serve as an excuse for Genet: he destroys the human within and around himself, but he thereby situates himself in an actual world on which no value judgment has a hold. He does not *do* Evil, he is a carrier of it as a fly is a carrier of germs. Thus, each refers to the other, and the two would complete each other if only they could correspond to each other. But they are quite distinct, and Genet must go from one to the other with a rapid and constant movement, for each appears to him to be the true Evil when it is the other which he is pursuing—without, be it added, ever attaining one or the other, since he cannot find motives for doing the first and since the second has motives which are foreign to him. Evil, being Other than Being, is always *elsewhere,* always elusive. It is a "marginal hallucination"; it is never in the direct line of vision, it can be seen only out of the corner of the eye. In order to will it, however, he would have to look it in the face. Genet moves his eyes in order to bring it into focus. In vain: at every moment, Evil jumps aside; it always remains at the trembling edge of the eye.

Furthermore, we have not reached the end of our difficulties, for we have set forth only purely formal determinations of Evil. We still have to define it materially. What is the most criminal Act? Is it that which society will condemn most severely? We are again confronted, in another area, with a question we left unanswered. Besides, no agreement on what is the greatest Good has ever been possible. Is it life? No, since one can risk it for freedom. Then is it freedom? But is freedom above love? And isn't love blind? Must it not be guided by reason? What about happiness? And pleasure? If there is such uncertainty as to the Sovereign Good, then what will there be with respect to the Sovereign Evil? And, in fact, at times Genet decrees that it is crime and at times betrayal; and at times it is no longer either, as in the following curious passage where crime itself engenders life and Good:

"By evil I mean here the sin against social laws or religious laws (of the State religion) , whereas Evil really exists only in the fact of causing death or preventing life. Do not try to use this rapid definition as a basis for condemning murder. To kill is often to give life. Killing can be good. This can be recognized by the joyous exaltation of the murderer. It is the joy of the savage who kills for his tribe. Riton is not here to kill, but it doesn't matter. The sin isn't here. He kills in order to live, since these murders are the pretext for and means of a higher life. The only crime would be to destroy oneself, for one thereby kills the only life that matters, that of one's mind."

Here Genet's thinking, which is usually so nimble, bogs down. Or rather it tires itself in playing puss-in-the-corner with Evil. The fact is that, despite himself, a liquidation of his childish beliefs is taking place here and there as he approaches the age at which the adolescent begins to question family values. He sometimes looks at the society about him and does not recognize in the paltry morality of right-thinking people the terrible God of wrath whom he saw gleaming for an instant in the eyes of the villagers who condemned him. Social good, which is compounded of mystification and oppression, and which, in the most favorable cases, does not rise above a rather crude utilitarianism, cannot create, as a by-product, an absolute and metaphysical Evil: the pair would not be homo-geneous. The mores define an evil which is on a par with them-selves: relative, mediocre, crude. It would not take much for the liquidation which has begun to continue and be completed: then, perhaps, for Genet as for the Greek thief, there would no longer be right or wrong. But no, the shock he received at the age of ten has fixed within him forever the idea of absolute Good, and, though the social content of this Good tends to lose all importance, Genet will always bear the ineradicable mark of a condemnation issued in the name of a divine morality; he will rebelliously maintain the necessity of willing Evil. Thus, the balance is destroyed, and this time it is the Good which is elusive. Beyond the empirical and utilitarian couple, good-evil, about which he is unconcerned, Genet pursues absolute Evil. But if Evil is in itself and for itself the stubborn, solitary and desperate rejection of Good, where then is he to find a Good up to the mark? At certain times it will quite simply be God himself. Unable to find, in the dupes he despises, the frightful gravity of grownups, Genet will lodge it in an absolute consciousness. "Pride is the boldest freedom: Lucifer lashing out against God." But God himself has lost some of his power; the child now only half-believes in him. *Our Lady of the Flowers* relates how little Culafroy (who is Genet himself) stole up to the altar and secretly committed a sacrilege, a profanation of the host. He thereby tried willfully to reconstitute the original crisis which obsessed him by giving it the dimensions of a religious tragedy. Everything was set up: the church was empty, the child was alone, or pretended to think he was alone, and he committed the inexpiable sin. God was going to appear, His face blazing with wrath, was going to catch him in the act and to manifest by a sign that He condemned him forever. The child was yielding to the double giddiness of carrying his offense to the absolute in order to assure himself that the sentence was beyond appeal and of mastering the event which crucified him by reproducing it on his own initiative and with infinite dimensions. But the miracle did not occur. God proved to be far inferior to men: he remained silent. Whereupon faith collapses: if God is not a God of wrath, if He does not keep the appointment, if He does not reduce the evildoer to dust, it is because He does not exist. "The miracle," Genet tells us, "was that there was no miracle: God was hollow." He lost faith, but not religiosity: the world must remain sacred so that his acts all retain an aspect of the sacrilegious. God becomes in his mind a dishonest notion, as it was for Gide for a long time, a half-poetic, half-metaphysical catchall, at times the unknown object of a passing fervor, at times the warrant for Morality and the Sacred. And sometimes He even becomes, as we have seen, the source and basis of Evil. Indeed, at times Evil no longer has a positive correspondence, since Good, which is unobtrusive, bourgeois, terrestrial, is no longer commensurate with it: so God joins its side. A priest in *Funeral Rites* is upset about being caught in the act of sinning, "whereas it was precisely sin which had put him in a state of grace." At times the child, overwhelmed with disgust and loneliness, abandons himself for a moment: he is about to pray. But the prayer immediately stops on his lips: if God *wills* Evil, even as a test, then Evil is Good. At the moment of his death, Pilorge cries out:

> Forgive me, my God, because I have sinned.

But in the following stanza this God is already

> The Lord of dark places,

that is, a Demiurge who greatly resembles Satan. And, as a finishing touch, Genet transforms him into a pagan and symbolic divinity in whom he does not believe:

> Soft-footed Hermes,

god of shopkeepers and thieves.

But if neither God nor society any longer guarantees the Good, where is one to find a guarantee? Genet's cardinal notions are already wavering: "*Killing* can be good." Indeed, if the sign of Evil is *torment*, the sign of Good should be joy. "This can be recognized by the joyous exaltation of the murderer." One step further and we arrive at the conclusion we were *bound* to reach: Genet himself will be a warrant of Good and Evil alike. The only crime would be *self-destruction*. For Mind is life, light. But *who* can define suicide as the Absolute of Evil if not the very person who is *himself* for himself, if not Genet in person? Indeed, we have seen the child *poetically* become, by deliberate compensation, his own god. Thus, Genet becomes the source of Good and Evil; it is he who produces, for himself, Good and Evil in themselves and for themselves. Starting from an objective morality and an objective relationship with men, he attains moral solipsism. Can he stick to it? Hardly. For, after all, if he decides as a sovereign legislator, what reason can he find for performing forbidden acts *against* himself? Why continue to will Evil? And against whom? He has to assume otherness, and the one who legislates must be other than the one who obeys. Not long ago, it was the Other who willed Evil in Genet, and his powerless consciousness that willed Good. At present, it is his consciousness that wills Evil, and it is the Other who wills Good. But if, once again, a powerful outsider with whom he is battling has installed himself within him, then it is the entire mob which has re-entered him, and God as well: solipsism is untenable.[*]

---

[*] The dialectic of doing has a solipsistic *moment* (and *only* a moment), like the dialectic of being.

Even if we did, for a moment, accept it, we would not thereby get out of the circle of contradictions: if suicide is the greatest crime, it is also the only one which it is impossible to commit. As we have seen, evil will and the will to live are one and the same in the child. To kill oneself is to commit the worst, but at the same time it is to renounce Evil, not only because, with the bursting of this desperate little soul, good and evil, judge and culprit, torturer and victim, would disappear together, but above all because suicide is also abandon, slackening, because the choice of living in order to do evil was a revolt against the impossibility of life. Nevertheless, he must kill himself or rather must convince himself that it is as if he had killed himself. Unable to do away with himself all at once, the child will kill himself piecemeal: he will internalize his suicide and spread it over his entire existence. Moreover, the choice of living was already a choice of surviving himself. Everything jibes: there is an intelligible choice of death, and life is its temporal development. On the imaginary level where Genet made himself the cause of himself, he becomes the cause of his death: to create oneself and to kill oneself come to the same thing. Existence is no longer anything but an interminable death-agony which has been willed. And each crime will have value not so much for the Evil it brings to the universe as for its being a willed repetition of the original death. One kills in order to kill oneself. Querelle, the murderer, is a "joyous suicide." And in *Funeral Rites* Genet wonders "what one kills in oneself" when one commits a crime. He concludes that "[to kill] is to fire at God, to wound God and to make a mortal enemy of him." We have already encountered this theme: death is the condemnation by society, which kills a child and creates a culprit. But in this case murder is no longer "a gift of life." "Riton," writes Genet, "kills so that he may live, since these murders are the pretext for and means of a higher life." No doubt, but this higher life is precisely the achieving of one's symbolic death. In that case, the joyous exaltation of living is the exaltation of dying. We relapse into the stereotyped repetition of the original crisis: the child dies because he has stolen, then he steals in order to die. But at the same time the paradox recurs: if the moment of self-willed death is the *absolute* moment, does it result in our attaining Sovereign Good—since Good is Being and is Life—or Sovereign Evil? Unable to decide, Genet abandons immanence: there is a transcendent Good, a God whose orders one cannot transgress and who damns, an all-powerful Society. Whereupon the cycle starts again; we shall not escape from it. Evil is always elsewhere.

If I look for it in the Subject, it jumps into the Object; if I rush to the Object, it returns to the Subject. Hidden, lateral, evanescent, it derives all its force from Good. In fact, its favorite food is the fat souls of the respectable. He who wants Evil for Evil's sake is staggered, blinded, paralyzed by Good. But he who claims, with peace in his heart, to conform to good principles is he who is rotted from beneath by the unclean, velvety existence of a satanic postulation. "The Worst is not always sure," says Claudel. Indeed, for Genet it is not sure. But for him who proclaims that it is not sure, who is chock-full of Being and turns everything to the glory of Good, the worst is always sure: the Evil that Genet seeks in agony is quietly installed in Claudel's heart.

Genet would no doubt grant all this. He is far too clear-minded to be unaware of his contradictions. And he states outright in *Funeral Rites:* "If Evil arouses such passion, the reason is that it is itself a Good, since one can love only what is good, that is, alive."

What then? If the will to Evil was, at the very moment of its birth, already transformed into a will to *some good,* one must recognize that this will *is impossible.* Genet's endeavor ends in failure.

But what if this failure were a victory? What if he realized, at the very moment of renouncing Evil, that this radical impossibility is what he always *wanted?* Have we not said that he is playing *loser wins?* The intention of doing evil is riddled with contradictions. Agreed. But there is in Genet an even more radical intention which he does not have to prove possible since it already exists, to wit, *the intention of willing Evil.* This intention is purely and simply himself. At the moment of sinking and being sucked into the swamp, the child decided to will what was imposed upon him, and by means of that perfectly pure and categorical decision he achieved the *disconnection;* he wrested himself from the toils of being; he *defined* and *created* himself, for he is that and that alone: the sudden movement of the back that transforms the fall into a plunge. From then on, there is no longer either fall or plunge, but simply the eternal transformation of one into the other, and *that* is Jean Genet: the indefinitely prolonged moment of the break. Evil offers itself and Genet throws himself into it. And no doubt he will never encounter it. He will steal and betray and lie, but in vain; absolute evil cannot be captured by these gestures. The will to will can never become an effective and conscious will. At times a "verbal idea" occurs to us, not only a thought, but a thought which already secretes the sentence that will express it. The music of the sentence, its rhythm, its cut, the arrangement of the words, everything is given simultaneously as a presentiment and a desire in the indistinction of the original project; the meaning and the expression are one and the same. We seem to be already touching the words which will render the thought explicit. And then the words never come. We try several, one after the other, and each of them coarsens the thought, falsifies and deflects it. In the end, we do not know whether our vocabulary is inadequate or whether the idea is, by its nature, inexpressible. Similarly with Genet: each concrete achievement falsifies the original intention. It doesn't matter; he rids himself of it and attempts to achieve something else. No sooner does he will a particular evil or a pure motive for willing Evil than he falls into the infernal circle. But he doesn't care: the essential thing is never to abandon the original melody, the precise, yet unformulated idea of the sentence to be shaped. Since he is in the circle, he goes round and round. He is constantly jumping from one Evil to another, from one motive to another, from others to self, from the Evil of Consciousness to Consciousness in Evil, from torment to joyous exaltation, from death to life, from life to death, without ever stopping anywhere, clearly aware that he will never catch up with the Worst but that at least, by this infinite movement, he makes it exist beyond its very impossibility, like the shadow of an ideal, and that he confronts being, life and men as an infinite dissatisfaction, as an unrealizable exigency. Genet wants not only to will Evil, he wants to be the martyr of the impossibility of willing it. Not only does he decide to attempt the best and the worst, but he demands the radical failure of his attempt. He might, like certain great demoniacs—and like Baudelaire himself or Lautréamont—have placed himself under the protection of Satan. But he is too aware of his situation to fall into Manichaeism. The evildoer is not Manichaeist; Manichaeism defines the thinking of the honest man. "God always wins the game," says Genet. Lucifer crosses swords with God. Well and good. But God eternally knocks the sword from Lucifer's hand. When Genet decides to will the Worst, he knows that the Worst has lost, that it had lost before his birth, even before the birth of the world, and that there would have been no Evil, from the very beginning, if there did not appear in every generation a few headstrong men who relentlessly go on playing a game, trickily, which has *already been won* by the opponent. And his defeat takes place not only in the noble theater of metaphysics; he lives it from day to day in the vulgar world of daily existence. In this world Genet is vanquished in advance, not only by the crushing machinery of the police, but above all because society has anticipated the existence of thieves and regards them calmly as normal products of nonassimilation. Somewhere in his books he compares Evil to excrement, and if shit flows freely in his works, it does so because it represents brute evil, for Evil and Shit both imply the insolent health of a stomach that digests well. Genet *is* excrement, and it is as such that he asserts himself. What is more, he is a negligible quantity. What do a few lice in his hair matter to society? An evildoer who elects to become an evildoer succeeds only in enhancing social morality, since he is acknowledging that Evil is loathsome. He would be far more feared if he were willing to say that he was a revolutionary. If Genet were a Communist, he would be worthy of the hatred of middle-class people; he is only evil: his sufferings, his spasms and the terrible work that he is doing on himself will fail to disturb the composure of these good consciences; he tortures himself in vain.

But that is what he must want; that is what he does want. All his heroes, the toughest, the most criminal, the handsomest, are arrested, imprisoned, humiliated. It is to the vanquished that his love goes out. Marchetti and Darling languish in prison; Harcamone, Pilorge, Our Lady of the Flowers will be guillotined, and the moment of their supreme glory coincides with that of their ignominious death. Shortly after the liberation of Paris a newsreel was shown on a Paris screen: it showed a young militiaman* who had been caught on a roof by members of the Resistance; his companions were dead; the triumphant enemy was surrounding him and sneering, crushing him with its contempt. He was not even given the honors of war; letting himself be caught was probably his last act of cowardice; no doubt he was brooding on the shame of surviving. In the theater, the audience is laughing with hatred and disgust. In the midst of this crowd which is drunk with triumph, Genet is thrilled: to the young coward wallowing in abjection he delivers a silent and passionate declaration of love, elated at being the only one who loves him. I can testify to the fact that during the occupation he had no particular liking for the Germans. No doubt he admired, on principle, Nazi malevolence. But then what? They were victors, their triumphant Evil was likely to become institutional, it would be a new order, a new Good. And this order, like the other, would condemn theft and common-law crime. When they were defeated, routed, humiliated, he began to love them, and I heard him defend them publicly when it was highly dangerous

---

* The *Milice* (Militia) was a Nazi military organization composed of Frenchmen.—Translator's note.

to do so. We have seen Genet playing at baseness; we can guess that he will dream of playing at failure: in *The Thief's Journal* a band of counterfeiters surrenders to the police without putting up a fight. When someone becomes indignant, Armand, a hero of Evil, so evil that Genet finally says he is good, declares: "They wanted to give themselves a treat that they never in their lives had time for: getting cold feet." In the very depths of the Evil to which they had had the courage to penetrate, they were asked to make a further effort: to give up even their courage and finally to act like cowards. This theme has so fascinated Genet that only recently he thought of making it the subject of a play. But deliberate cowardice is courage. And furthermore, in order to be able to carry on his evil activity, it is advisable, despite everything, that Genet not be caught. His thefts, though successfully carried out, must be failures *in the imaginary*. Nevertheless, his whole life is a deliberate defeat, and this defeat *designates* him, reveals him in his absolute existence.

Indeed, at this point is revealed a monstrous and providential concording of the misfortune of his own life with the basic structure of Evil. For Genet's life is an accepted failure, and evil, which is a destruction of *everything*, must, as a consequence, aim at the destruction of itself. Evil wishes for the failure of the evildoer, Evil *wishes* Evil *evil*.* Thus, at the heart of evil is a sanctuary wherein dwells the deepest Evil, the final and lamentable failure of every evil undertaking, the betrayal of Evil by Evil. That is how we must interpret Claudel's formula: "Evil does not compromise." Radical Evil is the misfortune of the evildoer who is reduced to impotence. The failure of his life, of his will to do evil and of Evil itself— Genet must will this trinity all together. Since he wills Evil to the limit, he must will it until it is totally impotent, until the bad is crushed by the good, until the final triumph of Good.

All at once, Genet has just discovered the greatest Evil: to betray. For betrayal is not a return to Good. It is the Evil which does evil to itself. Two negations are not equivalent to an affirmation: they get lost, tangled up in each other, in the mad darkness of the nay. Genet had discovered an immediate and tragic Evil: crime. He will never be a criminal, but he can be the canker of crime, the gnawing parasite of Evil. Betrayal is, in effect, a parasitic crime since it has to be grafted on another crime. It is, so to speak, a second-degree crime, a reflexive crime. That suits Genet to a T. His mind is made up: he will be a traitor.

---

* As in the expression "to wish someone well."—Translator's note.

We thus come to the famous decision to betray which has earned him so many enemies. As a criminal, he would, if necessary, be accepted; as a traitor, he horrifies. Our loathing of betrayal must be very strong for us to prefer even murder. I would like to offer proof of this, an amusing proof. Everyone knows that the surrealists took it upon themselves to destroy the values of Christian civilization. They invited the Mongol horsemen to take their horses to pasture on the hills of the Sacred Heart, to water them in the Seine. They declared that the simplest surrealist act was to fire a revolver into a crowd. Yet, in the concert of outcries provoked by the apology for betrayal that Genet published in *Les Temps Modernes* it was the surrealists who yelled loudest. They had already condemned his homosexuality, and now they were outraged by his delations. One would think that in their undertaking of demolition they have systematically spared heterosexuality and respect for plighted faith. These values can, in certain moral frameworks and, in particular, in Christian ethics, be perfectly justified, but I do not see how surrealism as such can stand up for them. In fact, the great sexual orgies in the works of the Marquis de Sade almost always include homosexual coupling, with anal intercourse and fellatio. The surrealists ought first to read *Philosophy in the Boudoir*. And one could cite a number of characters in *Juliette* who gained the confidence of their future victims only to ruin them more surely. Is not this betrayal? And what about Maldoror, what is he doing when he lavishes tenderness on the child he means to slaughter? Furthermore, in the Spanish-fly affair, it is certain that Sade was buggered by his valet. How can the surrealists reconcile their admiration for Lautréamont and Sade with the contempt they profess for Genet? But, after all, that's their affair. I wished merely to show that Genet has made a good choice: the loathing of traitors must be very primitive and deeply rooted in our hearts for it to impose limits on so radical and sincere an undertaking of liberation.

Did Genet choose betrayal or did betrayal choose him? Both. He reached a decision at the end of a dialectical process which took a long time to mature in him, but when he took the plunge, he had long since been driven to betray. Before he even dreamed of an act of delation, everyone knew he was a traitor. At Mettray, that was the first insult hurled at him. Once again, events have outstripped him. Once again, all he can do is internalize the judgment which constitutes him from without. When he wants to do Evil, Society has already ordained him an evildoer, and when he wants to betray, he is already an *objective traitor*.

Objectively, betrayal is a social fact. Initiate of a sacred community to which he owes his rebirth, the traitor takes advantage of
this new existence to turn against the society that begot him and to
betray its secrets. The criminal is less hated: if one of the initiates
commits a murder, he becomes Another, but it suffices to exclude
him in order to preserve the group's integrity. If he betrays, it is
the entire society which becomes Another. To be sure, the society
originally established itself against an enemy, against Another (another religious persuasion, another country, another class) , and it
knows that to that Other it is the Enemy, it is Evil, but it does not
care about this, for it is outside. The judgment of this external
adversary is, in fact, useful to it, cements it, supports its internal
unity by an external cohesion. What it is for the Other is its body;
what it is for itself is its soul. But if it should suspect that there is
a traitor in its midst, everything changes: the Other's gaze, suddenly
conveyed within its soul, petrifies it; the soul becomes a body, the
outside moves inside, what was most private becomes public, subjectivity changes into an object. Above all, what makes the situation
intolerable is that it itself has, through the initiation ceremonies,
produced the traitor who looks at it with the Other's eyes. Its deepest inwardness has secreted the externality which is going to wreck
it. "There's a traitor among us!" That is all that is needed; we feel
the metamorphosis to our very depths; each of us becomes, for all
the others, a potential traitor; each of us feels the petrifying gaze
of the Other upon him. The original unity explodes; there remains
only a large number of solitudes. And yet the traitor's gaze is still
our gaze; it is a perversion of our own eyes. For to betray is not
to spy. The spy is only dangerous; he has had himself initiated only
with the intention of spying on us. Consequently, his initiation is
not valid; owing to the very fact of his evil intentions, it was only
make-believe. But the traitor (when he was not thinking of betraying) was the object of a veritable consecration. He really emanates
from the community; he is a thought which a mind conceives only
to discover suddenly that it is Another's thought. The consciousness of being betrayed is to the collective consciousness of a scared
group what a certain form of schizophrenia is to the individual.
Like the latter, society could cry out: "I've been robbed of my
thought." In short, it is a form of madness.

Is it possible to believe, after this, that betrayal is a matter of
chance? As social integration grows stronger, there are fewer traitors. When a certain point has been reached, they are not even
conceivable. Their existence reveals a certain slackening of the
collective bond, and the degree to which an army has grown weaker

is usually measured by the number of turncoats. But even in a disintegrating society they are recruited according to certain rules: not all who would be are traitors. The man who aspires to deliver his brothers is the first victim of the group's dissolution; it was in himself that the dissolution first occurred. Before he stole the thought of others he felt with terror that his own was being stolen. While considering the society about him with enemy eyes, he still feels that he belongs to it. He knows that he owes his existence to it, and even the possibility of harming it. I would go so far as to say that he is all the more aware of it in that he is closer to selling himself. "And then madness was very near," says T. E. Lawrence, "as I believe it would be near the man who could see things through the veils at once of two customs, two educations, two environments." Such is the case of the traitor. Within the group he is the Other and the man through whom the group will know itself as Another. But this is so because he is first, within himself, another than himself. This traitor is a madman, it is *himself* whom he betrays. A disintegrating society, an individual who is an enemy to himself and who experiences this disintegration as a disease of his personality: such are the necessary and sufficient conditions for betrayal to occur.

Both conditions are fulfilled in the case of Genet. What can he actually betray? Nothing other than the society of thieves. Honest people are not involved, since they have excluded him; in fact, it is *for their benefit* that he will commit his act of betrayal. No doubt the social nature of delation is not immediately apparent: in the facts which are reported it is always a matter of "squealing" on a companion. One would think that a crime had been committed against friendship, against love, that is, against the couple and not against the group. But this is an illusion which is quickly dissipated. One has only to read *The Thief's Journal:* Guy and Genet are thinking of robbing a friend who himself seems to be a thief or swindler. In order to enter his home without running a risk, they decide to get rid of him. Guy thinks of killing him; Genet suggests that they squeal on him. This is a blunder. Guy looks at him in amazement which quickly changes to outrage. In order to appease him, Genet assures him that the suggestion was meant only to test him.

Now, Guy has just serenely agreed to rob a fellow thief. Therefore his scruples cannot be attributed to respect for friendship. Nor has he any intention of handling the victim with kid gloves, since he declares himself ready to "bump him off." Quite the contrary, the lesser evil for the victim would be to inform against him; he would get off with a few months in prison. But what Guy hates about betrayal is not that it causes needless suffering, but that it is a taboo. To bump off a pal when he is off guard or by stabbing him in the back is perfectly all right. But one mustn't turn him over to the cops: that kind of thing isn't done. Guy's indignation is of social origin; through it the whole Underworld defends itself against an act of sacrilege.

However, the fact is that this collectivity is in a state of chronic disintegration. There is no true bond among thieves. All that they have in common is the cult of Evil. This cult unites them only in appearance; Evil isolates, it excludes reciprocity. The piquancy of the story lies in the fact that Guy is himself a squealer, that Genet knows it and that Guy suspects he knows it. This is unimportant: they are both traitors, but Genet should not have said so. Thus, the society of crime, with its rites and prohibitions, becomes a sham, a kind of dream that hoodlums harbor so as not to have to face their solitude. The permanent and constantly unmentioned fact of this society is delation, and the fundamental human relationship is not that of thief to thief but of thief to police. It is the criminal who creates the police, and it is the police who create the criminal. They fascinate him, they present him with his image in reverse. Narcissus gazes at himself in the eyes of the cops. The Cop is the Other, he who harbors in his depths the secret essence of the thief. "The opposite of his friend," says the guard in *Deathwatch*, "which doesn't mean his enemy." The bond which unites them is as close as that between the executioner and his victim. In Genet's books they track each other down, fight, kill each other and finally make love. The fascination that the police have for the thief is manifested by the thief's temptation to confess when he is arrested. In the presence of the examining magistrate who questions him, he is seized with giddiness: the magistrate speaks gently to him, perhaps with kindness, explaining what is expected of him; practically nothing: an assent. If only once, just once, he did what was asked of him, if he uttered the "yes" that is requested, harmony of minds would be achieved. He would be told, "That's fine," perhaps he would be congratulated. It would be the end of hatred. The desire to confess is the mad dream of universal love; it is, as Genet himself says, the temptation of the human. But complete confession does not differ from betrayal. Even if he confessed without naming his accomplices, he would already be betraying them:* the mere desire to "cross

---

* Moreover, how could he give details about his crime without furnishing information that would lead to their arrest?

the line," to be among the honest people, is a traitor's desire. If he opens his mouth, all is consummated: nothing can stop him, since there is no sharp dividing line between confession and delation. Furthermore, the criminal, possessed by Evil, is constrained to live in appearance to the very end: no sooner has he confessed to his crime than he sheds his illusion. The judge's tone will change at once, the appearance of harmony and love will vanish. By wanting to deserve gentleness the criminal has earned reprobation. When he has signed his confession, he is tossed back into the world of Evil, but this world itself rejects him since he returns to it as a traitor. The criminal knows all this before breathing a word. Nevertheless, he will confess. A shipwrecked man on a raft cannot keep from drinking sea water, although he knows perfectly well that it will intensify his thirst.

It is this double fascination, by the Police and the Society of Theft, which explains the nervousness of Genet's heroes and their sudden changes of mood which he describes so often. They practice, as it were, double-entry bookkeeping; that is, they are always ready to betray in order to achieve, be it only for a moment, a semblance of harmony with honest people, and they are always ready to return amongst their fellows, to conceal their delation, to pursue an appearance of brotherhood-in-crime. At times, all these squealers tearfully throw themselves into each other's arms, they cherish and cajole each other, lull each other with a great initiatic dream of sacred union. And then, the very next moment, the queen, drying her tears, goes to the local police station and denounces her lover. One need only recall the extraordinary versatility of "The Maids," screaming, laughing, weeping, spitting in each other's face and kissing each other on the lips; one would think one were witnessing a tragic version of *Gros chagrins.* After all these demonstrations of tenderness, one says to the other, without anger: "If I had killed Madame, you'd have been the first to denounce me." This instability of mood is due to an instability of situation; it gives evidence of the fact that the sacred unity of the couple, which is always about to be achieved, always fails to come off at the last moment.

Furthermore, the conflicts of interest which, for want of arbitration, set thieves against each other lead to betrayal. Plato points out, in *The Republic,* that a society of unjust men cannot be effectual unless it observes, at least within itself, the rules of justice: "These unjust men are in no way capable of acting in cohesion with each other. . . . If, however, one speaks of men who, though unjust, have practiced, in cohesion with each other, a solid community of action, one is not, in saying this, expressing the full truth, for they would not have spared each other if they had been entirely unjust. Indeed, it is manifest that they had within them a certain justice, the simultaneous effect of which was that, at least with respect to each other, they firmly abstained from injustice, whereas they practiced it against their adversaries."

From which he concludes, of course, that radical injustice is radical impotence: "Those who are complete evildoers and thoroughly unjust are, ultimately, incapable of acting." But he does not convince us because his argumentation remains too abstract, too purely logical. If he had gone to the trouble of considering the underworld of his time, he would have seen that societies of unjust men can maintain a certain efficacy in destructive undertakings, provided only that they be inhabited by an *appearance* of justice. But this deceptive justice is itself the worst of injustices. He is right in saying that the society of the unjust would be radically pulverized if injustice manifested itself openly and exposed itself as a universal practice, for it cannot suffer universalization. But avowed injustice is not, contrary to what he thinks, the supreme injustice. Since it declares itself, at least it contains a modicum of truth. The worst is the best concealed; it cares very little about being raised to the universal, because of the fact that it secretly longs to be the sole exception to the rule. The unjust man requires that the others observe this rule among themselves and in relation to him, for he needs a certain external order to be able to act, and though he may not really conform to it, he at least pretends to submit to it in order to incite the others to obey it and the better to deceive them, and also because he loves the criminal community and is glad to belong to it. And he no doubt is quite aware that his apparent submission to the common rites confers upon him only an apparent freedom of the city in that society, but this pretense is enough for him. In fact, that is what he is seeking, for it is the essential nature of the evildoer to prefer the reflection to being and the diabolical image to reality. A strange society, in which each individual retains the trappings of order both out of love and the better to attain final disorder. But precisely because of this hypocrisy, it presents an appearance of morals and regularity, of values, rites, prohibitions. And this apparent justice, which is a diabolical imitation of the real one and which issues entirely from the desire to do evil, is sufficient to ensure the efficacy of a common undertaking, provided that the latter aims at destruction. A leader who is only the ghost of a leader commands phantom soldiers who obey him only so as the better to destroy him. He is aware of this without saying so, and will pretend to be a leader in order to be able to get his hands on the cash and flee at the right moment. This is all that is needed to "do a job," to break into a house and carry out a burglary. For the betrayal is prepared long in advance, is thought about for a long time, and, while it is being organized, discipline is observed all the more strictly in that the participants are more urgently obliged to shift suspicion, whereas one needs only a few hours to plan a holdup. Plato, in a more inspired mood, has shown that the total negation of unity requires and produces a kind of nightmarish unity: "In groups of several . . . however many there be, they will be other with respect to each other; indeed, one by one it would be impossible, since there is not a one. But amongst them, as I have heard, the singularity of a mass is an infinite plurality and, even if one took what seems to be the smallest possible piece, as in a dream, it appears to be several all at once instead of one as it seemed to be." The smallest piece is several, but, inversely, the largest plurality seems to be one. For the multiple requires distinct individualities which frankly oppose each other. The world of plurality is the world of the atom or, in the social sphere, that of brutality. To make of individuals the seat of an indivisible unity is to restore with one hand what one destroys with the other and, in the case with which we are concerned, is to deny unity to the universe in order to discover it in the inwardness of the individual consciousness. But, in the absolute negation of unity, the individual himself, who is other than all the others, is other than himself in his own consciousness. Thus, he does not have enough force really to oppose all and to engender a true, anarchic plurality. Unity and multiplicity disappear together, their specters remain and shimmer at the surface of being: no unity means unity everywhere and of anything with anything; being presents itself in huge, massive aggregates; but this large appearance collapses as soon as one touches it, only to be reborn elsewhere, always elsewhere. Absence of unity is appearance playing at being; it is *unity become an evil*. Such is the society of thieves, such is the thief in himself. If he makes an effort to feel, to live his membership in the community, the illusion is dissipated, he is alone, but if he wishes to draw the inferences from his solitude and to pursue his own ends, he is haunted by his elusive unity with the sacred society.

In this nursery of informers, Genet, more than anyone else, is doomed to betrayal, and the young hoodlums of Mettray were right about him. To begin with, he is doomed despite himself and simply because he exists, and also because he is Another to himself and betrays himself, whatever he may do; in addition, he is doomed because he has taken refuge on the plane of reflective consciousness and is never quite *with* his fellow inmates, never quite involved in their passions and projects. He watches them and sees himself watching them, he talks to them and listens to himself talking to them. This already amounts to practicing mental restriction. Lastly, he is a traitor because he has made himself a lucid man, a homosexual, an aesthete and a poet. As a lucid man, he betrays thieves by his corrosive power; as a homosexual, by his fake submission; as an aesthete, by his admiration for the qualities which they possess unwittingly and which they despise in others; as a poet, by the songs he dedicates to them. He will claim later that he lends them a language, like Lefranc, who writes love letters for Green Eyes. But neither Green Eyes nor Maurice is taken in; when Lefranc wants to *manifest* their merits, he steals their brilliant deeds to adorn himself with them.

But that is not all. The moment the gates of Mettray closed behind Genet, he found himself in the position of a double agent, but in reverse. It is not that two societies fight to have him, but rather that they toss him back and forth like a ball. In the present case, it amounts to the same thing. Rigorously excluded from the society of the good, he is reluctantly tolerated at the lowest level in that of the bad. His integration into the latter is not complete enough to dispel his longing for the former, and the place he occupies in it is too low for him not to have the ambition to rise in it, that is, to be more integrated into it. Thus, he finds himself under the sway of two contrary and simultaneous forces. And of two resentments as well: in order to hurt the white society which has rejected him, he would devote himself with all his soul to the black society, but the latter persecutes and humiliates him. In fact, it brands him with the name of traitor even before he proves himself one. He tells us that when he was sixteen the inmates "regarded him as a coward, traitor . . . homo. . . ." Another "dizzying" word that brands him, another Destiny that is forged for him. The reason is that he is not their kind; because he is too intelligent, too glib, too educated, he disturbs them; because he is too weak, he cannot impose respect. Guilty in the eyes of honest people, he is *suspect* in the eyes of thieves. One can understand his being torn at first between the passionate desire to dispel these biases and the eagerness to justify them. And as they cannot be overcome, it is the eagerness that prevails. What else could he have done? Taken refuge in a haughty solitude? That, in fact, is what he tried to do, but the only way of access was precisely betrayal. Even had he retired to a desert, he could not have escaped from these two opposing societies, for he carried them within himself. He had only one way of ensuring his protection against them: to play each against the other. Once again the *unity* of his person lies in his double-dealing.

Be that as it may, delation is only a dizzying fate until the moment Genet sees it as the supreme Evil. The historical event then emerges at the meeting point of an objective process of disintegration and of a subjective dialectic of evil will: a freedom chooses betrayal as its supreme end. Thereupon, betrayal is integrated into Genet's universe and acquires the chief characteristics of that universe. *Lived by Genet,* it becomes sacrilege, poetry, paradoxical ambiguity of the instant, ascesis.

Sacrilege first, because it undertakes deliberately to violate a religious prohibition. Genet is too unconcerned about the consciousness of others to be interested in the sufferings he is likely to cause. On the other hand, he has an essentially religious mind, and the sacred is a permanent concern of his. Similar in this respect to the sociologists of the French School, he regards society as the source of the sacred. He once believed in God, and if he no longer does it is not as a result of having turned his corrosive power upon the truth of the church, but because his condemnation comes from men. He profaned a host without damage; God remained silent. The church which excommunicated him was secular society. Now, betrayal directly attacks the social bond, the essence of the collectivity. And no doubt it is the community of crime that he will betray, but through it he is aiming at the unity of the church. He knows perfectly well that he will not shatter it, that he will not even manage to endanger it. But he doesn't care: the aim of his act is to endow him with a certain being and not to change the order of the world; he betrays in order to become sacrilegious. Thus, despite the fact that the words "betrayal" and "saintliness" scream in protest when one tries to yoke them, we must recognize that the concepts which correspond to them are homogeneous in Genet's mind, though to us they are remote from each other. Both designate an immediate relationship of man to the sacred. The saint transcends all written law; he does more and other than what he is ordered to do. In like manner, betrayal—at least in the case of "squealing" on thieves—is not forbidden by the code; it entails no legal sanction. In fact, Good uses it to combat Evil. Betrayal thus appears to be a refinement upon vulgar offenses. It is the transcendence of the forbidden as saintliness is the transcendence of duty.

If poetry is very likely to become betrayal, betrayal, when practiced systematically, certainly becomes poetry. Betrayal is carried out by means of words and manifests the omnipotence of the Logos. It is Evil rid of its retinue of violent emotions—gunfire, bloodshed, pursuit—and reduced to the simple demoniacal utilization of speech. No doubt, in a certain sense, the statement of denunciation remains prose: "Yesterday, at such and such a time, X broke into Y's home." One seems to be limiting oneself to stating facts. But these few words, murmured in a judge's chamber, operate like a spell cast from a distance. This magic formula will necessarily cause a man's arrest and perhaps his death. To betray is to engender a destiny by means of words.

This whispered conversation has the diabolical aspect that appeals to Genet more than anything else: it is a game of appearances, a shimmering of nothingness and being. It has the appearance of a complicity with Good: in answering the kindly questions of the sacred representative of Society, Genet can retain for a moment the illusion of reciprocity. But as soon as the reply has been given, the illusion disappears along with the kindliness of the judge. The latter defends himself, against the Evil of which he has made use, by displaying his contempt. But the irritating disappearance of the mirage of reciprocity is just what Genet wanted and what he wished to cause. A strange situation: at one and the same moment, Good uses Evil to attain Good, and Evil uses Good to attain a worse Evil. But Evil emerges strengthened; it has compelled Good to serve it. To harm Evil with evil intention and to reduce it to impotence is the height of perversity. The undertaking remains in the usual order of things: Evil, which is absolute negation, must, as we have seen, be its own negation; it aspires to failure. Good, on the other hand, compromises with the worst; it has rewarded delation, the traitor remains unpunished, he has perhaps been paid. Thus, the just man admits that his Justice does not pursue *Evil* but a certain *particular* Evil and that, in order to demolish it, he does not hesitate to become an accomplice of a worse Evil. This entire metamorphosis takes place in an instant. The moment the judge's smile congeals, reciprocity becomes an exile and the temptation of the human causes Genet to sink and drown in the inhuman. Here, as everywhere, we find again the cathartic crisis and the paradox of the instant.

Above all, betrayal has the merit of being repulsive to the traitor.

The traitor is ugly, he is cowardly, he is weak. He hides himself in order to denounce. He will live in terror. Genet knows all this. For him these are reasons for betraying. There is an even deeper reason: one can betray only what one loves. The spy has a clear conscience. He helps to destroy the enemy. He lies, he fakes, but he has allegiances of which he is proud. The criminal kills unknown people in order to rob them: what is Monsieur Ragon to Our Lady? But it is *against* his allegiances, *against* his loves, that the traitor's zeal is directed. If he were not yet bound with all his fibers to the society he denounces, if he did not still love with all his soul the friend he is going to turn in, would he be a traitor? The man who wants to raise betrayal to the height of a principle will draw from his love a motive for betraying. If crime is suicide, the only valid delation is a brutal amputation. But one must go through with the operation, must cut into the flesh, must rip away, one by one, all the persons whom one loves, must deserve their contempt. Then, having reached the limit of this systematic deprivation, one will be able to say, like Lefranc: "I really am all alone." One will still be living in the world, but the world will then be only a flat painting, an optical illusion. One will know that sounds and lights, words, smiles, blows, are only glittering appearances at the surface of a dark emptiness. The criminal dies at the moment of the crime. That is why the second murder is superfluous: it will bring nothing more. Betrayal, on the other hand, is an ascesis which little by little dissipates the phantasmagoria and leads by degrees to a horrible nirvana of despair, darkness and self-hatred.

It seems that the pure Will, in liquidating all the materiality which still encumbered it, has finally taken itself as goal, for, as we have just seen, the impossibility of conceiving a coherent Evil incites the will to will itself as a pure intention—forever disappointed —of doing evil. In short, Genet then identifies himself with the *spiritual* project of a will willing itself evil, that is, a *will to will*, a reflective whole that quite naturally finds a place in the development of this consciousness which ponders itself. By means of treason Genet wrests himself from his body, from his life, even from his sensibility. He ruins his loves, destroys his self, confers upon himself a new dignity in infamy which enables him to despise himself more thoroughly. What remains? Not even a will that wills itself evil: a will that wills the failure of its project, that wants to will Evil and wants Evil to be impossible. The intention of doing Evil is torn by a contradiction as soon as it manifests itself, but at this point a deeper choice is revealed, one which supports this intention only because it desires this conflict. The evil intention is conceived only *in order* to contradict itself, because this contradiction reveals to us that Evil is an unattainable and inconceivable end of human freedom and because a fundamental act of will decrees that the impossibility of Evil *is* the greatest evil. An entire life dooms itself to failure; a hounded man, exiled from Good and from Being, learns to his cost that he cannot enter either Evil or Nonbeing; crimes are committed and yet they fail; murderers are denounced; Evil makes inroads into Good since there are corpses, victims, pain, but Good triumphs over Evil since the guilty person is reduced to impotence. But as a result of this Pyrrhic victory, Being and Good are soiled forever since they have prevailed over Evil only by coming to terms with it. As for Evil, it is resorbed into itself, without being able either to destroy itself completely or to destroy Being. It remains merely a rudderless negation which goes round in circles, maintains its demands hopelessly, a negation that can be neither named nor conceived: it is the "bastard dream" of which Plato speaks in the *Timaeus,* other than Good, other than Being, other than Consciousness and, finally, *other than itself.* But the profound will that we find in Genet assumes the impossibility of Evil and the annihilation of Being and (since evil is other than itself) it will will Evil to the point of that inner enmity which is none other than betrayal. The consciousness willing Evil for the World and for itself will pursue its own destruction in a universal conflagration. But this conflagration will never take place; the secret flaw of Evil, its destiny, is that it has always been conquered, it is conquered in advance. And consciousness assimilates the failure of its own life and the ontological failure of Evil. It betrays itself and others, it betrays its own acts of will by rejecting whatever positive elements they may still retain. Thus, it pursues its own nothingness. But since it is a consciousness of destroying itself and since it has rejected suicide once and for all, the quest for Nothingness is, for it, only the way in which it affirms its existence; and the more ruthless it is with itself, the more it exists. That is what Genet calls "the impossible nullity." Everything is impossible: the evildoer cannot *be,* but neither can he evaporate into nothingness. All the efforts he makes to be his being lead him back to that pure *conscious nonbeing:* consciousness. But if he returns to this nonbeing in order to vanish into it, he exists for himself in broad daylight, in a merciless transparency. The dazzling emergence of his subjectivity corresponds to the vanishing of his Ego. Thus, for Genet the general pattern of his projects must remain the generalized *loser wins*. The impossibility of living is precisely the mainspring of his life, the impossibility of Evil is the triumph of the evil principle. The willed failure which is pursued unceasingly in his particular undertakings as in his total destiny becomes his victory. He is the being who makes himself exist through his impossible will to be. The traitor is the winner: he makes Evil win by forcing it to lose. He thrusts aside the great classical malignities—violence, murder—and finds at the core of Evil an emptiness, a fissure, that ontological crack which comes from its being a nonbeing and which will forever prevent it from "coming to terms." The traitor's choice is to become that fissure at the core of Evil, to be the Being of that Nonbeing in the very depths of the Nonbeing of Being. It is in this ontological fistula that Failure and Victory, Being and Nonbeing, Life and Death, Crime and Betrayal, meet and join each other. For if Evil is the Nonbeing of Being and if the impotence of Evil is the reappearance of Being in the depths of Nonbeing, there emerges a new reality which is both the Nonbeing of Being and the Being of Nonbeing, to wit, *appearance*. To destroy Being is to reduce it to pure appearance; to make of Evil an impotence is to convert it into *appearance;* to live the impossibility of living is to pursue, throughout a lifetime, an appearance of suicide; to discover oneself as an "impossible nullity" is to recognize that in pursuing within oneself one's own liquidation one makes oneself *appear* to oneself as a liquidator; to take refuge in lofty reflective consciousness is to discover that consciousness has alienated itself in appearance and to make it return into oneself, where it discovers that it has no being other than appearing, in other words, that it exists only insofar as it *appears to itself*. And, indeed, pure appearance is a nonbeing with respect to being since it *is not* but only appears; being is its impossibility. But, with respect to Nothingness, it is a being, for, as Hegel says, appearance qua appearance must, at the very least, *be;* therefore, its other possibility is *not to be*. Thus, Evil as an impossibility is appearance itself; betrayal is the revelation of appearance as such; what is harmful is the challenging of being by appearance. We shall see that Genet will come close to madness —then will save himself by art—for having devoted his life to making appearance as such exist against Being and against Nonbeing. For the moment, let us limit ourselves to noting that he thereby attains the dreadful freedom of which we spoke above. Convinced of being impossible, he aims at giving existence, in the teeth of the evidence, to the impossibility which he is. He becomes, in this pure, desperate project, both the being who sustains in being his own impossibility of being and the being who makes himself exist by means of his own impossibility. One can find no better definition for a freedom which is both finite—hence tainted with nothingness —and absolute. Confronted with the divine *causa sui,* creator of itself and of the universe, Genet sets himself up as a demoniacal self-cause which enjoys its impotence and whose creative power is defined as an ascertained impossibility of giving itself being.

Here, for the first time, Genet makes contact with himself, but what he finds is not the *character* whom we have seen him seeking in mirrors, in the eyes of others, in the indifferent and terrible bodies of the handsome pimps. This unthinkable subjectivity which he touches beyond and within being, within and beyond the possible, is *existence.*

"There are few *good* thieves who do not reprobate theft. The following, noted in the cell during one of my incarcerations . . .

" 'If everybody stole, it would be a fine state of affairs.'

" 'That's not what I'm asking you. The question is, for me, whether *I* should steal.'

" 'Why you more than anyone else?'

"The person with whom I was conversing was a burglar. I willed myself a thief. But I claim to be a good thief. A philosophy, with its politics and ethics, cannot be derived from theft. Stealing is an activity I reserve for myself, hoping it will lead me to the possession of the maximum possible freedom."

We recognize the burglar's question: "Why *you* more than anyone else?"

It is the question that Abraham asks himself. When Genet says: "The question is, for me, whether *I* should steal," and the burglar replies: "Why *you?*" they are not speaking of the same Self. The burglar has been caught in the toils of the universal. The *self* of which he speaks is the universalizable particular, the one which shares with all others this state of being *self* and other than the others. It is the Hegelian particular, established, supported, transcended and absorbed by the universal. That of Genet is the individual I which has no common measure with the universal and the particular, which cannot be fixed in concepts but can only take risks and live its life. Genet does not resolve the contradiction; he lives it. If it transcended itself within him toward any synthesis, *Jean Genet* would disappear. The terms must be kept together *by means of speed.* If he stops, he is lost. In short, he *exists.* And when he declares that "a philosophy cannot be derived from theft," it is evident that he draws even nearer to Kierkegaard, since the latter declares that existence *is* simply and cannot furnish any philosophy.

Is he going to stop at that point? One step further and all the phantoms which hem him in will disappear. He will perhaps recognize that he was hoodwinked at the very beginning. He will perceive that the labyrinth of Good and Evil in which he lost his way was constructed by the respectable people the day when, out of sheer terror, they cut freedom in two. Being, Nonbeing, Nonbeing of Being and Being of Nonbeing, Sovereign Good, Sovereign Evil: he will now see these only as reflections which the two pieces shoot back and forth to each other. He has only to reweld these pieces for freedom to be re-established in its prime dignity. Then, perhaps, he will be tempted by real morality because it is beyond Being as it is beyond Evil, because it is as impossible as Evil and, like Evil, is doomed to failure, and because, in addition, it is one with Evil.*

But it should first be noted that Abraham is not so pure. There is a seed of alienation in Kierkegaardian ascesis itself. No doubt Abraham is seeking himself in anguish, no doubt he perceives no sign within himself or outside himself of his election, no doubt he refrains from acting *in order* to be Abraham. But this does not matter. Whatever his uncertainty, for God he either is Abraham or is not. God's gaze has constituted him from without: *Abraham is an object.*† In other words, the very form of the question "Am I Abraham?" subordinates praxis to Being. And similarly the following: "Should *I* steal?" For despite the fact that this *I* lives in a state of the most unbearable existential tension, the interrogation *relates* to it as if the latter were defined before the action. One can conceive

---

* And with Good. Either morality is stuff-and-nonsense or it is a concrete totality which achieves a synthesis of Good and Evil. For Good without Evil is Parmenidean Being, that is, Death, and Evil without Good is pure Nonbeing. To this objective synthesis there corresponds, as a subjective synthesis, the recovery of negative freedom and its integration into absolute freedom or freedom properly so-called. The reader will understand, I hope, that what is involved here is not a Nietzschean "beyond" Good and Evil, but rather a Hegelian "*Aufhebung*." The abstract separation of these two concepts expresses simply the alienation of man. The fact remains that, in the historical situation, this synthesis cannot be achieved. Thus, any Ethic which does not explicitly profess that it is *impossible today* contributes to the bamboozling and alienation of men. The ethical "problem" arises from the fact that Ethics is *for us* inevitable and at the same time impossible. Action must give itself ethical norms in this climate of nontranscendable impossibility. It is from this outlook that, for example, we must view the problem of violence or that of the relationship between ends and means. To a mind that experienced this agony and that was at the same time forced to will and to decide, all high-minded rebellion, all outcries of refusal, all virtuous indignation would seem a kind of outworn rhetoric.

† "No," says a certain believer: "God is *within* us." "How dishonest! God *within us* is the entire external in the internal." "Why not?" "Very well. But do you believe that you will remain 'internal'?"

of a starving man questioning himself to know whether hunger and destitution make theft legitimate, that is, whether there are well-defined situations which justify certain violent acts. But how could an *I* legitimize certain undertakings if this *I* were not given a priori and as a *Being?* In an ethic of praxis, the Ego is not distinguishable from its possibilities and projects. It is therefore defined by the complex body of its decisions, which are supported by an original choice, and is revealed only in and by acts. It can be the subject of investigation and evaluation only afterward. As soon as I wonder, *before* the theft, whether *I* should steal, I detach myself from my undertaking, I am no longer at one with it; I separate the maxim of my act from my intuition of myself as if they were two separate realities, and I decide as to their suitability or unsuitability as if it were a matter of a necktie and a shirt. This abstract attitude is called *nobility;* it is ruinous for both the act and the man. For if the *I* is no longer the inward quality which a freedom gives itself through the changes it effects in the world, it becomes, in one way or another, a reality which is without being made, that is, finally a substance. And, to be sure, Genet does not believe in the God of Abraham: nevertheless he cannot abstain from watching—through this free *existence for the impossible* which he has just attained and lived—for the revelation of a being that would be an object neither for himself nor for any other gaze and yet which would effect, in the mystery of its invisibility, the condensation of all objectivity. We are thus back at the starting point. The demand for freedom was only *a moment.* Genet did not desire it for its own sake. His other, older, more magical project still exists, nearby: he wants *to be,* he wants to derive his being from himself and to derive all his acts from his being. The presence of this ontological system influences, from a distance, his free project of existing and vitiates it at its source. Here again *doing* is subordinated to *being.* But Genet has become more profound, shrewder, he has acquired experience of himself. What he is going to aim at this time is not simply and crudely to *do* evil in order to be able to say to himself that he *is* wicked, but to make of being the invisible and subtle reverse of nothingness.

It suffices to *will* the failure for it to change into a success. There is nothing mysterious about this, except that we have launched, by means of words, one of those whirligigs of being and nonbeing, the sophistical character of which Jouhandeau neatly exposes when he writes: "If a man diverts himself by being bored, is he bored or is he diverting himself?" One says to a child who has been toying with a precious piece of china and who finally breaks it: "Well, are you satisfied? You finally got what you wanted." And of course he was looking for the slaps that rained down on him: he was looking for them out of terror of receiving them. At the origin, there is nothing more. And there is nothing more in the zeal that certain people expend in destroying their happiness. It is the vertigo of the negative or the proud defense of the fox whose tail was cut off. Or both. But let us suppose that thereupon I move to the absolute. My failure was this quite dubious victory only by virtue of the obstinacy with which I had willed it. But what if I forgot that my will was only a paltry ruse? What if I made of this Pyrrhic victory an a priori characteristic of *every* defeat? Shall I not then discover a secret positivity which would be a kind of reverse of the negative?* I shall carry off this feat if I view my own failures from *both* my personal standpoint and that of Others.

In the case of a combatant who preferred his cause to all else and who did everything possible to win, failure is experienced in a state of despair. Action, says Malraux, is Manichaean. It follows that the man of action identifies his cause with that of the human race. From his point of view, when he loses and dies it is mankind that loses the contest in his person; the Devil triumphs—or matter. In any case, man's impossibility is proven. As long as he could still fight, the unhappy soldier thought that the future was in his hands. He *was* his own possibilities, and the *human* remained his fundamental possibility. As Ponge has aptly put it, man is the future of man. Captive, condemned to life imprisonment, to death, the man who is vanquished depends on the good pleasure of the victor; his potentialities break away from him and scatter through the universe. The idea of a kingdom of man becomes the dream of an idea. The prisoner is now only a thing that dreams of man. And since all human transcendency is taken away from him, man is a botch, freedom a dupery, mankind a time bomb that was set at the end of the Tertiary period to explode at that very minute. Thus, failure is Evil.

But later, for posterity, the failure becomes, as Jaspers puts it, a "figure." The reason is that the lost cause no longer finds defenders. It has ceased to be a matter of present interest. We dismiss both opponents, Barnave and Brissot, Danton and Robespierre. And we no doubt see clearly that Barnave was wrong: he vainly tried to stop the machine which he had set in motion. But what does it matter to us? We simply observe that the man had a certain grandeur and

---

* "The only durable aesthetic is that of failure. He who does not understand failure is lost. . . . If one has not understood this secret, this aesthetic, this ethic, one has understood nothing and glory is vain." (Jean Cocteau, *Opium*.)

that he was able to give his life for a value. Obviously, in doing so we are inverting the terms of the problem: *for him* his finest virtues were only means which he placed in the service of his cause; *for us* the cause is the means which enabled him to display his finest virtues: clear-sightedness, strength of mind in adversity. But this is so because we are no longer involved: the aim does not concern us; for us it is the attitude that matters. And if we adopt this point of view, we must admit that the victor does not appear to advantage. For the success is incorporated into being and immediately partakes of its contingency and inertia: the achievements which surround us and which we want to change are old victories that have rotted. In the last analysis, every achievement is a victory, and every victory becomes an achievement; human successes, taken as a whole, can be identified with what Hegel called the course of the world and what Marxists call the historical process. Thus, being blurs our triumphs and we no longer recognize them. There is nothing more than being, there never was anything but being, and being is all that there can be, neither more nor less. For the victor, too, victory makes man impossible. Since he has put his essence into his work, his life reverts to contingency, becomes a languid survival. Success entails a secret failure. On the other hand, a man who dies vanquished and jealously guards within him his unachieved work is defined forever by the frightful clearness of his last moments. If he had resigned himself, if he had begged for mercy, if he had adopted the views of the enemy, then *there would be nothing but being* and the order of causes would determine the order of ideas. If, on the other hand, he dies in a state of horror, when everything is achieved and explained, when it is demonstrated that the sequence of causes entailed no other conclusion and that nothing could have happened other than what did happen, there remains before our eyes something which prevents the synthesis from being completed: the death of the vanquished. Society cannot salvage this subjective death struggle, it cannot even attempt to regard it as a minor evil necessary to the advent of a greater Good, for a comparison of Good and Evil must be made within a single system and this closed consciousness is a system in itself. Its scales of value and its norms were not ours, and it shaped itself in accordance with them. Nobody can take upon himself that dead suffering, nobody can convince the departed that, all things considered, it was better that he suffered. Thus, this death, which, in a sense, is only an event of the world, seems to be a fixed and reproachful gaze which contemplates us. Beyond being there persists the affirmation of right; beyond every object appears a nonobjectifiable subjectivity which illuminates the facts with its cold light. Haunted by the souls of those it has conquered, triumphant society will never close: it is shot through with holes. Death has saved the values by brilliantly manifesting their irreducibility. This irreducibility usually remains purely logical; it is boring. By virtue of failure, it is humanized and becomes tragedy. Inversely, the values redeem the death and even the birth of the vanquished through the well-known effect of retrospective illusion; the terminal defeat appears to us to be the meaning and supreme end of that lost life. One is born in order to lose; one is doomed, from childhood, to failure. Hence, death is a completion; delivered from its accidental aspect, it becomes the act of a subjectivity which is resorbed into the value that it posed. One of these two nothingnesses becomes embodied in the other. The historical, dated absence of the martyr, of the executed Communard, symbolizes the eternal absence of the values. The latter becomes the soul, the former the glorious body. By virtue of the failure, the value is historified without ceasing to be eternal; it is the subject's substance, and, through the final shipwreck, it surrenders to intuition its pure absence, in the sense that Simone Weil could say that the universal absence of God manifests His omnipresence. Thus, the vanquished wrests himself from the original contingency and becomes a *value-subject*. Society recovers this value-subject in an indirect way after a few years of purgatory and uses it to prove that *there is in being something other than being,* a residue that remains inexplicable when everything has been explained. In fact, the failure becomes the man's essence. A value, has, in fact, two contradictory exigencies: on the one hand, we must try to incorporate it into being, and, on the other, it requires that we situate it beyond any realization. The moral agent can satisfy this twofold exigency only, so it seems, by giving his life to realize the ethical imperative and by dying as a result of not having achieved his goal. Our social pantheon abounds in exemplary catastrophes. We pay homage to them and we bear adversity better because it seems to us that our own failures are magically involved in grandiose disasters.

But note: in order to find beauty in these historical failures, they must not, of necessity, be *our* failures. To be sure, all languages have a saying to the effect that there are defeats that are finer than victory. But who says that? The *others,* those who have no connection with the enterprise.* It is *the others* who prefer a dissatisfied Socrates to a contented pig. For if Socrates is dissatisfied with him-

---

* The vanquished sometimes say it, but they repeat, in order to conceal their anguish, out of vainglory, what they think the others will say of them.

self and with mankind, that means he is not so sure, in view of human folly and wickedness, that man is superior to the pig. Victims and vanquished are in agreement about preferring victory. Only a neutral, who is indifferent to the stake and perhaps to all stakes, can appreciate aesthetically the grandeur of a fine disaster. But in the case of Genet, it is the failure that is the real object of his undertaking. He can therefore set himself up as the combatant who suffers the blows and as the neutral who judges them. His defeat astonishes and overwhelms him, but he claims that he has doomed himself to it since childhood. He throws himself wholeheartedly into his cause, but at the same time he views it only as a means of assuming an attitude. Although he is alive, he wants to see himself as society sees Vercingetorix, that is, as dead, vanquished and triumphant. He wants to be both the hand that stones him and the pious fingers that lay flowers on his grave. Submerged in a ghastly present, he leaps, at the same time, far into the future, turns to look at his dead life and finds it exemplary. He is himself and the Other, as always; and, as always, the Other is imaginary. At times, this Other, calm and detached, *appreciates,* through Genet's sufferings, his intransigent attitude, and at times it is the Other who suffers and it is Genet who, in a state of detachment, watches him suffer. In the former case, it is the victory which is feigned, and in the latter, it is the despair. Has he not written the following disturbing remark: "Grief and despair are possible only if there is a way out, whether visible or secret"? In short, despair—or absence of all hope—implies that hope remains. Or, if one prefers, hopelessness is its own hope. He creates the way out by himself; he is even the way out; and he knows it. He knows that he is being observed by an invisible witness who will come and lay his hand on Genet's brow and whisper gentle things to him: "You would not seek me if you had not found me."

Genet is a man-failure: he wills the impossible in order to be sure of being unable to achieve it and in order to derive from the tragic grandeur of this defeat the assurance that there is something other than the possible. When everything has been explained, when it has been proved that his defeat was inevitable, that the course of the world could not tolerate his undertaking, when the fact has closed in on him and swallowed him up, there remains an inexplicable residue, because he knew it all in advance, because he knew about his future failure in detail, he knew it by heart, and because he nevertheless willed the impossible. This means then that the impossible *is,* that the impossible came to tempt him in the very depths of his heart, that man is impossible and is meant to will the impossible beyond the world of facts. At least that is what a fictive Genet whispers into the ear of the flesh-and-blood Genet. *We* know the truth: that he willed the impossible *so that* this phantom Genet would come and speak into his ear. We know it and we know that he knows it too. He is not dead; he is dreaming. He is dreaming that he is dead, lying in a coffin, and at the same time standing in the pulpit and delivering his own funeral oration. Everything is a mirage: his will to succeed, the cause he defends, his failure, his despair, his death and his victory. His deepest dream is not expressed by a parade of images or words. It is a certain nuance of his inner climate. He strives to live the present *in the past,* to perceive as one remembers. In his inner monologue he speaks of himself in the third person and in the past tense. Watching himself perform an act, he thinks: "He spun about." He relates to himself the events of his life, while they are unfolding, as if they were the episodes of a tragic story; he experiences them simultaneously in the *present,* in a state of despair, as victories of Nature, of Fact, of Matter, and in the *past* as the tragic triumph of the human.

Failure and betrayal are one and the same. As we have seen, betrayal is a will to failure. It means causing the joint enterprise of the criminal association to fail. But, reciprocally, the will to failure is a betrayal. To hurl oneself headlong into an action, into an attack, to involve others in the act and to keep hoping that it will all end in disaster, to undo every night, like Penelope, what one did during the day, to choose carefully the best devices and secretly to deprive them of their efficacy, to convert subtly all acts into gestures, is this not tantamount to betraying and to betraying *oneself?* Genet wants to do Evil, fails, decides to will his failure; whereupon he changes into a traitor, his acts change into gestures and being changes into appearance.* Now, the law of appearances and gestures is Beauty. We have got to the heart of this strange endeavor, in that secret place where Evil, engendering its own betrayal, is metamorphosed into Beauty. Evil, betrayal, failure, gestures, appearances, Beauty: this complex assemblage is the "tangle of snakes" which we have been seeking. Not quite: one snake is lacking. But here it is: it is Saintliness. It is born before our eyes.

Genet has willed Evil unto the failure of Evil, he has willed the impossibility of living unto the systematic destruction of his own life. He carries on relentlessly and, at the same time, watching him-

---

* At least he seeks a way out. I cannot say as much for Jaspers, whose intolerable chatter about failure is an act of studied humbug. Genet is a victim, Jaspers a charlatan.

self from the point of view of future generations, he sees in his shipwreck the proof that the Being of man is elsewhere, beyond his own nothingness. At an early stage, he threw himself into willing so that the action "might lead him to the possession of freedom," but he immediately pulled out of this action. He watches it and he meditates, with false detachment, on *the reverse of praxis*. To carry failure to the point of the destruction of everything, including Evil itself, is to betray. But from the point of view of the Other, of the absent and later witness, to betray to the point of despair, to the point of the self-denial that might be called abnegation, is *to be* a saint. When Evil was possible in his eyes, Genet did Evil in order to be wicked. Now that Evil proves impossible, Genet will do Evil in order to be a saint.

"TO SUCCEED IN BEING ALL, STRIVE TO BE
NOTHING IN ANYTHING"*

It did not occur to Genet all at once to become a saint or to give the name Saintliness to his longing to do harm. We have seen that as a child he dreamed of raising himself above men. Despite the frightful awakening, this dream has never left him. The source of the extraordinary paradoxes which we are going to discuss is to be found in the religious and archaic mentality that we have already described. Society defends itself against the tremendous powers latent in the universe, against the ambivalence of the "numinous," by means of custom, that is, by a body of observances. Inversely, infraction of the customary rules invests the offender with a sacred aura because it confers upon him the privilege of unloosing these powers. As a bastard and, later, a thief, Genet has been conscious since childhood of being sacred. If he dreams of asceticism in the time of his innocence, he does so, obscurely, in order to develop and exploit to his advantage the "numinous" power that emanates from him. Later, his will to do evil, the origin of which, as we have seen, is quite different, can easily be regarded by him as a form of asceticism. Since he wills his own misfortune and failure, since he relentlessly imposes upon himself distastes which his sensibility rejects, his attitude toward himself *resembles* that of the anchorite who makes a martyr of himself. Nietzsche has aptly said, in *Human, All Too Human:* "In every ascetic moral system, man addresses his prayer to a divinized part of himself, and it is consequently necessary that he diabolify the other part." Since the evildoer wills what horrifies him, he *sacrifices* himself to Evil, he realizes within himself the ascetic conflict. The mistreated child who claims to be the cause

---

* St. John of the Cross.

of his martyrdom will have no difficulty in regarding himself as an oblate.

Since we know that Genet believes in neither God nor the Devil, to whom, it may be asked, can he sacrifice himself? But, in its most primitive form, sacrifice is not addressed to any precise recipient. The sacrifice, says Gusdorf,* is "an action in accordance with the sacred." It is a "moment in the circulation of supernatural energy"; "in the operation of the sacrifice man can appropriate a part of the diffuse energy, but he can also attribute sacred force to beings external to himself." "This primitive sacrifice is carried out within a kind of concrete nebula, within a still undifferentiated religious bond." Nevertheless, the sacrifice is a gift. But it is a gift which is made to nobody. Genet makes a gift of himself to being, to the world, to destiny, to the sacred forces about him. And the purpose of this gift is to raise the donor to a higher potential of sacredness. Thus, without even thinking about it, Genet derives comfort from the obscure feeling that his misfortunes, his wounded self-esteem and even his misdeeds (since they cause him to suffer) increase his absolute value. This is certainly the deepest and most primitive view he has of his destiny. For him, the causality of suffering is sacred. It is on this foundation that he is going to build his theory of saintliness.

I am quite aware that his strange abuse of the "most beautiful word in the French language" has outraged more people than the accounts of his homosexual pleasures. Nevertheless, it must be admitted that his reasoning is specious. Viewed objectively, the thief and the saint resemble each other in that they consume without producing. To be sure, the effect of this unproductiveness is not to transform the saint into a crook, but it does, at times, enable the crook to pass for a saint. The saint deprives himself of everything, goes naked, eats roots; the most wretched slave is better fed, better clothed than he. I maintain, nevertheless, that the saint is a luxury flower that blossoms in the warmth of a particular sun, namely, the gold of the church. And if saintliness is defined objectively by the function it fulfills in a religious community, we shall see that Genet's betrayal performs a similar function in the society of crime.

1. Saintliness as a Social Fact

The phenomenon of saintliness appears chiefly in societies of consumers. A full description of such societies would be beyond

---

* *L'Expérience humaine du sacrifice,* p. 51.

the scope of the present work. I shall mention only a few of their features: they confuse the essence and the practical purpose of the manufactured object; work is not creative, it has no value in itself, it is the inessential mediation that the merchandise chooses in order to move from potentiality to the act; a simple-minded practicality stresses the final aspect of the product; the truth of its being appears when it is presented to the purchaser or user as a polished, varnished, sparkling object; it is then revealed as both a thing in the world and as an exigency; it demands, *in its being,* that it be consumed. The work is merely a *preparation:* servants dress the bride; consumption is a nuptial union; as a ritual destruction of the "commodity"—instantaneous in the case of food products, slow and progressive in that of clothing and tools—it eternalizes the destroyed object, joins it in its essence and changes it into itself, and, at the same time, incorporates it symbolically into its owner in the form of a *quality.* It will be noted at once that this creative and valorizing destruction furnishes the pattern of the moral systems we have just been imagining: in the case of food, fullness of being emerges at the moment it melts in a mouth and releases its flavor; moment of death and life, paradox of the instant: though still objective, the taste is at the same time a subjectivity. And in like manner with regard to the criminal at the moment of his beheading: an exquisite food which is consumed before our eyes; and with regard to the saint, who is sucked by God like a piece of candy and feels himself deliciously melting into an infinite mouth. Not all who would be are consumers: ritual destructions are carried out by an elite. The function of this class has been well defined by an American economist as "conspicuous consumption." The aristocrat consumes for the entire society. The mob is allowed to watch the king eat; the king eats with tireless generosity; the common people proclaim their gratitude through the gates, a Mass is being performed. In order to qualify as a consumer, one must satisfy two requirements. First, one must be *born.* This means—among other things —that a slow and agelong adaptation of your family to the most exquisite products has formed your tastes in such a way that the object will develop, in your mouth, its full flavor, will be more richly itself than in any other mouth. Then, one must be a soldier: one has the right to possess what one acquires or keeps at the peril of one's life. In short, destruction gives the right to destroy: the hero, an exemplary figure in societies of consumers, chooses to be consumed on the field. While waiting for the ceremony, he is given the finest products to waste. The destruction of the destroyer will complete the circle: his rich, spiced soul, tinted by wine, infused with the heaviest flavors, will delight the palate of the great Taster.

These strange communities pursue their own annihilation. The horrible bloodlettings practiced by the Aztecs and Toltecs in their own ranks led those people to their ruin, and it is known that the wasting of gold was one of the major causes of the fall of the Roman Empire. Thus, their chief virtue is the generosity of consumption which gives in order to destroy, and their great eschatological myth is universal conflagration, the "empyrosis" of the ancients. The members of the elite carry generosity to the point of absurdity. Each of them wants, like Nero, who burned Rome, to carry out his personal little empyrosis. "A chronicler," writes Marc Bloch, "has left us a report of the singular competition in waste that once took place at a great 'court' held in Limousin. One knight sowed a plowed field with silver coins; another burned tapers for the cooking of his food; a third, 'out of vainglory,' ordered that all his horses be burned alive."* The supreme refinement of consumption is to destroy the possession without enjoying it. Since the ultimate end of the commodity is to blossom at the moment of its death, the consumer lowers himself to the rank of an inessential means: the human species stands by and blissfully watches the goods which it has produced by the sweat of its brow or won at the risk of its life go up in smoke. But the aristocrat experiences at the same time the secret satisfaction of placing himself above the goods of this world. The crowd is not unaware that he is the source of this largesse, their applause is meant for him: he possesses eminently the goods which he destroys; to refuse enjoyment is the most exquisite enjoyment.

Christianity—which was born with the first emperors, triumphed over the Lower Empire and reigned over the feudal world— emanated from a society based on agriculture and war. The Church expressed, in its own way, the ideals of the Roman aristocracy and, later, of the feudal aristocracy. It proved its power by wasting human labor. Not that I wish to reproach the prelates for their display. I even recognize that most of the priests lived poorly. But behind this destitution can be discerned what Sorel has very aptly called an "idealistic economy."

"Authors of works of Christian archaeology inform us of the extraordinary luxury displayed in the Christian churches of the fourth century at a time when the Empire was so greatly in need of money. It was the stupid luxury of parvenus. The following are

---

* Marc Bloch, *La Société féodale*, Vol. II, Albin Michel.

a few examples: in the baptistery of the Lateran, a porphyry piscina, the inside of which was lined with silver; a gold lamb and seven silver starheads spurting water; two silver statues, five feet high, weighing 190 pounds."* The best of human production goes up in smoke, becomes a gratuitous gift to nothing.† And if the priest dies of hunger in the shadow of a solid gold basilica, we thereby see all the more clearly his kinship with the knight who scattered silver over the fields. The church has borrowed from the aristocracy its generosity in consumption, and part of the aristocracy starts, in turn, to imitate the Church. Paulinus, son of a former prefect of Gaul, left the world after giving his wealth to the poor; Pammachius, after the death of his second wife, gave up his fortune and became a monk, though not without first inviting all the beggars of Rome to a feast. These ostentatious acts perpetuate the secular tradition of the Roman government. For a long time, the plebs had been the passive object of the emperor's largesse. The avowed aim of this liberality was not, as can be imagined, to lead this "lumpen-proletariat" to participate in social and political life, but rather to divert it, to maintain it in its abjection. Similarly, individual acts of aristocratic generosity do not eliminate pauperism; they perpetuate it. It is the yawning chasm into which aristocrats throw their wealth, as the King of Thule threw his cup into the sea. The donor is quite aware that he will not enrich anyone; it is *for that reason* that he gives to beggars. He sells his land in order to ply the poor with drink, but it does not even occur to him to turn the land over to the peasants who farm it. Nor for a moment does he dream of helping small shopkeepers, of creating hospitals and free schools.‡ The acts of prodigality must *not profit*. One goes from the productive to the unproductive: land that yields a good return is converted into ready money. And from the highest potential to the lowest potential: a considerable amount is broken up into tiny quantities, each of which is barely sufficient to give a moment of physical joy to *one* poor person. Thus, charity is merely a pretext, and each of these acts of largesse, though it may overstimulate trade and impart to it an ephemeral appearance of health, concurs, by

---

* Sorel, *La Ruine du monde antique*, pp. 97-98.

† Even if the God of the Catholics existed, who can believe that He rejoiced when fierce priests made Mexican peasants sweat gold in order to coat the walls of churches? If He is omnipotent, this gift is ridiculously petty in comparison with what He can produce. "That's true," it may be answered, "but man gives what he can." In that case, it is the intention that counts. But then, if God is all love, how could He not be horrified by this gift which was extracted by force and cost such bitterness and suffering?

‡ It may be objected that initiative of this kind was hardly conceivable at the time. But that is exactly what I am saying.

virtue of its consequences, in dividing real property and increasing the drift of gold to the East, in short, in destroying civil society. The aristocratic ethic has taken on a religious aspect; it has been covered over with Christian myths and rites, but it has not changed in substance:* the consumer is God the Father; one gives, one destroys, "for the love of God," not for the love of the poor; the relinquishment is not to anyone's real benefit, it is accompanied by the public destruction of abandoned possessions, and as one takes credit for getting rid of them, this merit, which is recognized by everyone, is, as a consequence, the deep and manifest affirmation of the absolute right to property. As eminent owner of the goods which he spoils, the aristocrat raises himself above them as in the past. But the fact is that, from this new point of view, the elevation brings him closer to the Eternal Father: his act is confirmed by a heavenly judgment. Even the old myth of "empyrosis" enters the new religion unchanged under the name of "End of the World," "Reign of God," "Last Judgment." Later, when the Crusader, who is a sacred soldier, kills and gets killed for the Christian cause, when he offers up hecatombs of infidels to God, when he destroys, in huge potlatches, the possessions which they have amassed, the transformation is completed. At most, the merchandise becomes an idol: it *is produced* by workers from whom it is taken away in order to *be destroyed* ritually by idlers who do not enjoy it. To take an extreme situation, one can assume a secular society in its death throes: peasants working themselves to death so that aristocrats can die of hunger near burned crops. Of course, matters never reach such a point. Most of the rich will prefer to consume with enjoyment. Foreign wars will give the illusion of a constant renewal of possessions. Social movements, the infiltration of barbarians and then the appearance of a merchant class will modify the structure

---

* Christianity, which is a great syncretic current, has borne other ethics along with it. As a state religion, it has prescribed economy, temperance and wise administration of property for citizens of the middle classes. As a class religion, it preaches resignation to the lower classes. It addresses each individual in his own language. It convinces people that there is only one Christian ethic, which is the same for all. Its priests are shrewd enough to make the poor man believe that the resignation prescribed for him is basically of the same essence as the joyous renunciation of the aristocrats. In both cases, so he is told, one turns away from worldly goods. But it is easy to see that the abandoning of one's possessions is a princely act. It is to enjoy eminently. To renounce what one has not is to accept ignorance, hunger, servitude, in short, to accept being subhuman. If Genet can assert that the negative inhuman (being below man) joins the positive inhuman (rising above the human condition), it is because the Church brought about this confusion, and was the first to do so, by convincing the poor man that when he accepts his poverty he is performing *the same act* as the aristocrat who rejects his wealth. In this sense, *the Saint* has, in an aristocratic society, a mystifying function: his destitution is offered to the poor as an example and is falsely identified with theirs.

of the society. Finally, the aristocracy will ruin only itself; the progress of industry will transform consuming societies into producing societies. But the Saint, who is the fine flower of consuming societies, presents this aristocracy which is going to wrack and ruin with its most exact image. In him a whole community which is plunging into suicide finds what the Bishop of Nola proudly called his "folly," that is, his great funereal dream and his self-destructive generosity. His extreme destitution and lingering death are not even conceivable without the luxury and myths of a consuming society. In a society of the Soviet type, in which the supreme value is labor, other myths will operate, other rites, other hopes, and the members of the community will no longer be able to understand that blurred image of a bygone age: generosity of production, which *produces in order to give,* becomes the major virtue; the myth of the "end of the world" gives way to that of the creation of the world (death conquered, synthetic production of life, colonization of the stars) ; the Stakhanovite may very well work himself to death: it is not his death that will gain him credit, but his labor.

As for the hero and the saint, on the other hand, their only way of meriting social approval is to practice upon themselves the great, magnificent destruction which represents the ideal of their society. The hero comes first: no saint without a hero. The latter is not to be confused with the Chief; he does not win battles: he achieves by himself and at one fell swoop the glorious and sinister annihilation of a whole knighthood which is defeated by an enemy that is victorious but wonderstruck. The Saint internalizes this death and plays it in slow motion. In the beginning, he belongs to the military aristocracy: St. Martin, St. George, St. Ignatius, in our time Father de Foucauld, who is probably going to be canonized, are examples which show how easy it is to move from the military state to saintliness. In aristocratic societies, the professional soldier is an idler whom the community supports because he has sworn that he will die. He dies in every war. If he survives, it is a matter of chance or a miracle. As soon as he fights his first battle, he is, in effect, dead. The working classes produce implements of destruction for his use. He amasses them, he is the great master of destruction. It is he who ravages the enemy country and who decides, on occasion, to ravage his own, burning crops and towns before the victorious adversary. In consenting "to be no longer in the world," he places himself above all goods; they are all given to him, nothing is good enough for him. If some inner difficulty leads him away from war, he cannot come to life again; he must continue his death by some other means. Thus, he sometimes chooses Saintliness. The Saint, too, is a dead man; though he is in this world, he is no longer of it. He does not produce, he does not consume; he began by offering up his wealth to God, but that is not enough. It is the entire world that he wants to offer; to offer, that is, to destroy in a magnificent potlatch.

Aristocrats have made gold useless by applying it to the walls of churches. The Saint makes the world useless, symbolically and in his person, because he refuses to use it. He dies of hunger amidst riches. But it is necessary that these riches exist: divers must seek pearls in the ocean beds; miners must extract gold from the bowels of the earth; hunters must, at the risk of their lives, break down the defenses of the elephant; slaves must build palaces, cooks must invent the rarest dishes, so that the Saint, rejecting royal dignity, ivory, precious stones and the beauty of women, may lie at death's door, barren and disdainful, heaped with *everything* because he accepts *nothing*. Then the world, abandoned, empty, rises up like a useless cathedral. Man has withdrawn from it and offered it to God. Later, when the Church has been firmly established, recruiting its highest dignitaries among the secular aristocracy, saints will be born of commoners. They are clerks who are driven by wild ambition to the highest offices and who find them occupied by nobles. Unable to be the first among men, they will want to be above the first; they will turn their eagerness against themselves, and, by a long, conspicuous suicide, they will give the society which is rushing delightfully to its destruction the exemplary image of proud annihilation. These clerks are fakers. By going through the ecclesiastical mill they could have obtained *something:* some honors, some money, some power. In pursuing Saintliness, it is therefore *something* which they are refusing. But by means of the transport they display in refusing, by means of the self-torture which they practice, they convince themselves and others that they have refused *everything*. And as public destruction involves a public and conspicuous assertion of titles to property, these poor wretches are the richest of men. Their guile has given them the world. There is a whole society to bear witness to the fact that they possess it. With these men appeared the sophistry of the Nay which later achieved such brilliant success; in a destructive society which places the blossoming of being at the moment of its annihilation, the Saint, making use of divine mediation, claims that a Nay carried to the extreme is necessarily transformed into a Yea. Extreme poverty is wealth, refusal is acceptance, the absence of God is the dazzling manifestation of his presence, to live is to die, to die is to live, etc. One step further and we are back at the sophisms of Genet: sin is the yawning chasm of God. In going to the limit of nothingness one finds being, to love is to betray, etc. By a readily explicable paradox, this destructive logic is pleasing to conservatives because it is inoffensive. Abolishing *everything*, it touches *nothing*. Without efficacy, it is, at bottom, merely a kind of rhetoric. The course of the world will not be changed by a few faked states of soul, a few operations performed on language.*

Our society is ambiguous. Industrial development and the demands of an organized proletariat are transforming it, with horrible shocks, into a producing society. But the metamorphosis is far from complete. An oppressive class that is on the way out is mingling the old myths with the new. At times, it justifies its privileges by the excellence of its culture and taste, that is, by its aptitude for conserving. It claims to be the guardian of western values against the eastern democracies. At times, in order to meet the demands of the oppressed classes, it is willing to base property on labor, but it sets up a qualitative theory against the quantitative conception of the Marxists: it is entitled to possess more because of the superior quality of its labor. Meanwhile, the religion subsists, with its aging rites that it adapts to the new state of things as best it can. Everything is confused; the Church still canonizes, but listlessly; the faithful themselves have the vague feeling that the Saints belong to the past. In order to be sure that there will be a place for it in the forthcoming society, the Church has already begun to organize new groups and has launched the light cavalry of worker-priests in factories. I think, along with many others, that it is necessary to shorten the convulsions of a dying world, to help in the birth of a producing community and to try to draw up, with the workers and militants, the table of new values. That is why Saintliness, with its

---

* The mystics were highly skillful in the sophistry of the Nay. Here is St. John of the Cross:

"1. To succeed in tasting everything, strive to have no taste for anything.

"2. To succeed in knowing everything, strive to know nothing about anything.

"3. To succeed in possessing everything, strive to possess nothing of anything.

"4. To succeed in being all, strive to be nothing in anything. . . ."

Means of not preventing the whole:

"1. When you stop at something, you cease to abandon yourself.

"2. For in order to attain all, you must renounce all.

"3. And when you come to have all, you must have it without wanting anything."

And here is Meister Eckhart:

"As long as I am this or that or as I have this or that, I am not all things. Snatch yourself away so that you no longer are or have this or that, and you will be everywhere. Therefore, when you are neither this nor that, you are all things."

sophisms, rhetoric, and morose delectation repels me. It has only one use at the present time: to enable dishonest men to reason unsoundly.

But we have seen that a black aristocracy remains on the fringes of secular society. All the features of a feudal order are to be found in the knighthood of crime: parasitism, violence, potlatch, idleness and a taste for death, conspicuous destruction. All of them, even social conservatism, even religiosity, even anti-Semitism.* Amidst these soldiers Genet plays the role of a clerk: he is the only one who knows how to read, like the chaplain amidst the barons. Everyone who knows him is struck by the fact that he has the unction of a wicked priest. What can be more natural? He defends himself against violence by the traps of language. If he wants to convince guttersnipes, he has to utilize his unsoldierly qualities; he has to convince them that his preoccupations are of an order other than theirs; nor is it a bad thing that he is never quite present in their presence. If he is unobtrusive, he irritates them less; if he seems abstracted, he makes them feel uneasy; by an air of spirituality he shows that he has made himself the guardian of their values. Even his homosexuality is useful to him; he clothes himself in it as in a cassock. The rest comes automatically: as an ecclesiastical member of an outdated society, everything inclines him to indulge in the outdated game of Saintliness. And since his weakness and his intelligence make it impossible for him to be a tragic hero, he will internalize the destructive violence of the criminal. Living out the impossibility of living, he will be for these murderers the sacred image of their death. I know him as a beardless Landru, slightly formal in manner, always polite, frequently playful, in short a rather pleasant companion. But I readily imagine that he was a rather sinister figure in the feudal criminal world, often disliked and probably sacred: the hoodlums could read in his

---

* Genet is anti-Semitic. Or rather he plays at being so. As one can imagine, it is hard for him to support most of the theses of anti-Semitism. Deny the Jews political rights? But he doesn't give a rap about politics. Exclude them from the professions, forbid them to engage in business? That would amount to saying that is he unwilling to rob them, since businessmen are his victims. An anti-Semite who was defined by his unwillingness to rob Jews would be a curious anti-Semite indeed. Does he therefore want to kill them by the million? But massacres don't interest Genet; the murders of which he dreams are individual ones. What then? When cornered, he declares that he "couldn't go to bed with a Jew." Israel can sleep in peace.

I see only the following in his repugnance: as a victim of pogroms and age-old persecutions, the Jew appears as a martyr. His gentleness, humanism, endurance and sharp intelligence command our respect but cannot give him prestige in the eyes of Genet who, since he wants his lovers to be bullies, cannot be buggered by a victim. Genet is repelled by the Jews because he recognizes that he and they are both in the same situation.

eyes the dim reflection of their destiny; they felt, with indignation, that he was both a commoner and a churchman, the lowest amongst them, yet higher than the highest. The only way in which this little traitor, who might very well have been a soldier, can make a show of dignity is to become a black Saint, as Loyola, a cripple, became a white Saint. In a state of systematic transport, he will live, for all of them, their exile and their abasement; he will be, for all of them, the symbol of their idleness, of their wickedness, of their generosity. He will be a Saint because Saintliness is a function that awaits him; he will be the martyr of crime, in the double sense of victim and witness. For he differs from the criminal as the true Saint differs from the Hero: he transposes the military drama in terms of inner life.

2. Saintliness as a Subjective Determination

Although Saintliness, as an objective function, is a relatively simple fact, it becomes infinitely complicated when we consider it as a certain direction of the inner life. The hermit who endeavors to lead a godly existence is familiar with all the refinements of the dialectic of the Nay. In penetrating beneath this coarse envelope, we shall find in Genet the most exquisite religious culture.

The ascetic impulse is at the origin of an aristocratic ethic which has been expounded by Plato. We know the principle of *The Symposium:* the philosopher must die to his body in order to rise to the contemplation of the True and the Good. Let us interpret this to mean that we must renounce our particularity in order to attain the intuition of the Universal. The Christian consciousness will rediscover, through Gnosticism and Neo-Platonism, the tradition of this renunciation and will call it Saintliness in those who carry it to the limit. Hegel has shown its workings in his description of the unhappy consciousness. Consciousness is *both* the immutable and the universal by virtue of its being pure thought, an abstract subject and *at the same time* this particular contingency, this man who was born of flesh, who appeared in a particular situation, who is immersed in the flow of development; but it does not know that it is the universal; it thinks that this abstract and eternal universality transcends it and that this universality is God. It therefore attempts, since it is ashamed of its singularity, to destroy the particular in itself in order to raise itself to Him. But the movement whereby its element of particularity attempts to destroy itself does not depart from historical particularity. It is a given desire, at a given hour of a given day, that consciousness, in a given state of mind, will try, by a given means, to destroy; it will not escape unhappiness. It is this self-hatred that imparts to certain Christian mystical texts a tone which recalls the finest passages in Genet. We read, for example, in St. Theresa: "It is not sufficient to detach ourselves from those who are close to us if we do not detach ourselves from ourselves. . . . It is an arduous task to fight against our nature. We are so united with ourselves and we love ourselves very much . . . the first thing to do is to uproot the love of our body. . . . You came with the purpose of dying for Jesus Christ and not of treating yourself gently for Him. Let us strive to contradict our will in everything. . . . As soon as you are tempted, beg the Mother Superior to assign you to menial tasks, or do them voluntarily to the best of your ability. . . . Study ways and means of breaking your will in matters which are loathsome to it. . . . He who is truly humble must sincerely desire to be scorned, persecuted and condemned without reason, even in serious matters. Lord . . . give me the sincere desire to be scorned by all creatures." This wish to deserve universal scorn, this conflict of the will with the self, this firm intention not to live but to die one's life, evokes *The Thief's Journal;* and indeed the wily hoodlum counts on this resemblance to deserve the name of Saint. But let us not be misled by this family likeness; it conceals profound differences, not all of which are to the hoodlum's disadvantage.

Let us first note that a curious reversal has taken place since the advent of the bourgeoisie and that the ancient ethic of renunciation has been subdued to purposes which are the very opposite of the early ones. In a society based on agriculture and handicraft, it is the universal that must be conquered. But in our industrial and scientific world, we have it ready to hand: we find it in perception, in science, in technical and political action, in ethics. Indeed, the individual conquers himself as something beyond generality—and temporality as something beyond the eternal. A whole line of moralists and thinkers have used the ascetic method to attain the extreme particularity of the person. One must renounce the world and oneself, that is, the trivial, inauthentic, more than half universalized ego of daily practice, in order to make contact with oneself on the level of *pure exception*. This conception, which certainly colors present-day Christian mysticism and even the contemporary interpretation of ancient mysticism, leads philosophical minds to conceive the idea of existence in its early form, that is, as a reality which cannot be *pondered*—since all thought universalizes—but only lived in silence.* In the writings of men of letters it will be the subject of an aesthetic transcription: Gide teaches us not to prefer ourselves, shows us Philoctetes abandoning his bow and his hatred, the prodigal son drawn to the desert by a desire for thirst and not slaking it, but at the same time he requires of Nathanaël that he become the most irreplaceable of beings. Thus, contemporary ascesis, far from giving birth, as in the case of the "unhappy consciousness," to the formal and hypostasized pure abstraction of the *I think,* displays the most ineffable individuality.

Genet remains equidistant from both these types of asceticism. And I would like to set beside him another present-day writer who resembles him in more ways than one and whose work confirmed him in his choice, namely Jouhandeau, the author of the *Treatise on Abjection.* Jouhandeau, a Christian and a homosexual, and Genet, a homosexual and a thief, have, from the very start, such a particular position, one in Catholic society and the other in secular society, that there can be no question of their wresting themselves from the universal. They were excluded from it from the outset. From the very beginning they were denied the right to be like everyone else. And as they both know that society will blame them eternally (in the case of Jouhandeau it is, in addition, the Eternal himself who condemns him) , they are compressed in the historical moment. What they ask of the exercise of renunciation is therefore not that it lead them from the particular to the universal or from the universal to the particular, but that it enable them to achieve, by hostile destruction of the *suffered* and *given* particular, a *willed* particularity which is a law unto itself. Ascesis is here *re-creation.* One may find this surprising, for we are in the habit of conceiving creation as an affirmation, as a positive production, and it is difficult for us to understand how systematic self-destruction can result in the free production of self. But let us not forget that Jouhandeau's person and, particularly, Genet's are defined, at the outset, by privation. Exclusion, blame, condemnation, interdict, these are the great negative forces which constitute both of them from without. Jouhandeau writes the following, which could be signed by Genet:

"[I am] a victim of a lack of understanding, of a spontaneous aversion which in the end exiles me definitively. Certain people find my presence on earth suspect, and their hostile attitude thrusts me back into my secret. But nothing exalts me more surely than reprobation."

---

* I need hardly say that I am stating a case and not taking a stand. No ethic of the inhuman will have my approval.

In assuming, and with exaltation, the original factors of their situation, they will both be led to heighten the exile to which they have been condemned in order to be able to derive it from themselves. They will want to deserve the aversion of which they are the victims, and, since the movement which constitutes them from without aims at nothing less than to destroy them, they will have to espouse this movement, internalize it, direct it and continue it within themselves to the furthest limit. Thus, by an additional paradox, it is at the limit of annihilation that they will want to find the autonomous fullness of their being. Jouhandeau also says:

"Having reached the supreme degree beyond which one can no longer fall without ceasing at the same time to be, because there is no longer any possible access anywhere on that side for anyone or anything, because there is no lower place for being—I mean because being would cease to be there at the same time that it proceeded further; as it is impossible for me to cease to be, I necessarily stop."

From this point onward, it is the very movement of renunciation that is going to be reversed: St. Theresa, on the one hand, and Nietzsche and Gide, on the other, have something in common, despite the radical opposition of their ends, to wit, that the movement of their ascesis is upward: in Jouhandeau and Genet, this movement is downward. St. Theresa, Nietzsche and Gide, rising above the goods which they reject, preserve them eminently; whereas Jouhandeau and Genet sink *below* the possessions of which they strip themselves and actually lose them. The ascension of St. Theresa, Nietzsche and Gide is ideal. It takes place mentally, with the result that their operation is reversible. The descent of the others is real and is characterized by irreversibility.

Indeed, if we consider ascetic renunciation in St. Theresa or Plato, it is clear that the aim of the mystic and the philosopher is to renounce only nothingness, that is, the consequences of their finiteness. If one gets free of the shadows of the cave, it is in order to see things truly. In their perfection and universality, Platonic Ideas contain all Being and, insofar as the vain appearances of the physical world have any reality, they have received it from the intelligible world. Similarly, for St. Theresa the modicum of reality contained in love of creatures comes to her from the infinite love which we bear God through them; to renounce the former love is to reveal the latter in its radiant purity. Christian Saintliness is a negation of negation. It rejects only that part of ourself which comes only from us, that is, from our nothingness: error and passions. And for it, as for Hegel, the negation of negation bursts our limits and becomes an affirmation. At the end of the renunciation there remains only being, absolute positivity without any negative counterpart, that is, the creature insofar as he relates to God alone.

From a quite other point of view, it is also nothingness that Gide wishes to expel from himself. If he advises us not to linger over enjoyment, it is because protracted enjoyment diverts from everything; if he urges us to renounce our belongings, it is because the possessed object eventually possesses its possessor and shapes him in its image; if, in *Paludes,* he ridicules busy men who throw themselves into activities, it is because the latter, in sacrificing the present to the future and substance to shadow, make Nonbeing the supreme end of Being. God is all, He is everywhere, the totality of being should be perceived in each individual thing; the owner is defined, amidst his family and activities, by a *common* relationship (occupation, family ties, property) with *particular* objects. On the other hand, in order to become the most irreplaceable of beings, one must renounce the particular in order to become an *individual* relationship to the *totality* of the real. If he advises us to "separate the instants," it is in order to make each of them a "totality of isolated joy." Gide's instant is paradoxical in that it joins, in an intuition, the ineffable individuality of the subject to the pantheistic totality of the object.

In all these ascetics, the destruction of goods is carried out by a consciousness which retains them in their quintessential form in and by its destruction of them. I have explained elsewhere that the *gift* is actually the best way of fulfilling ourself as owner. In divesting ourselves of the object, we place ourselves above it, but by the act of giving we assert that it is ours, since we can give only what belongs to us. Consciousness renounces its connections with *this* article of furniture, *this* house, *this* family, but it consequently defines itself by means of these very acts of renunciation. Everything is restored to it inwardly and freely since it apprehends itself as the synthetic unity of these rejections. It will henceforth be free— depending on the point of view it adopts—to see within itself the challenging of the particular by the universal and of the finite by the infinite or the historical individuality of an ascesis. This presupposes, of course, indefinite progress, for, whatever the penury we have attained, we must free ourselves from it by a more rigorous penury. One "surmounts oneself"; the unity of absolute simplicity (we are nothing but the negation in act of everything) and of infinite wealth (since it is precisely the concrete all which is the

object of the rejection) is the ideal conclusion of this infinite movement. In short, it is Hegel who has revealed to us the secret of
ascetic ethics: transcendence preserves what it rejects.

However, there is in this destitution something which one does
not touch: the Other's esteem. No doubt one seeks contempt, one
arouses indignation, or, at least, one is not afraid of it. The fact
remains that St. Theresa is supported by divine approval. Her
fellow citizens may cast stones at her: it is in God's presence that she
fights against herself. As for the moralists, they are sure of winning
their trial on appeal. Nietzsche, unappreciated by his contemporaries, is convinced that posterity will erect statues to him. It is
striking that Gide has shown Ulysses, the man of action, the poli-
tician, admiring the gesture of Philoctetes. The reason is that the
divesting takes place in the direction of the metaphysical hierarchy.
Plato goes from shadows to images and from images to things; St.
Theresa, from the contingent to the necessary; Gide, from the particular to the totality. And the indubitable sign of this conformity,
the moral evidence, is the happiness or joy that accompanies renunciation. There is a happiness of the Sage who contemplates
the order of the world, a happiness of the Saint who is visited by
her god, a happiness of Abraham returning to the world, a
Nietzschean joy, an intoxication of Philoctetes whom Nature suddenly showers with her gifts. When one requires nothing more of
the world, it gives itself, because the positive is always attained in
the negation.

In Jouhandeau and Genet, on the other hand, the ascesis takes
place in the opposite direction of the metaphysical hierarchy, that
is, *in the direction of lesser being*. Being serves as a springboard for
leaping toward Nothingness. To renounce human love for the love
of God is to find all the being of the former in the latter. One does
not cease to love the creature: one loves him in God. Cured of its
deviation, purged of its nothingness, firmly applied to its sole real
object, love is an opening on the All, it is all loves in a single love,
the infinitude of my finiteness and the plenitude of my emptiness.
But if Jouhandeau renounces love of God for that of men, the result
for him is a dead loss; and if Genet renounces love of men for the
lure of gain, he hardens, desiccates, withers up his feelings, attempts
to incline them toward beings lower and lower in the metaphysical
hierarchy and consequently less and less lovable, attempts to increase the portion of nothingness and shadow within them. We
have already seen the example, comic in its abstractness, that Genet
gives of this downward ascesis: he denounces his best friend and is

paid off in his presence. I don't believe it: Genet's betrayals are more commonplace, less grave; the element of humor and weakness or of fear in them is greater than he cares to say. But, in any case, what he proposes to himself is the ideal, and that is enough for us to view him without laughing. *Therefore,* he destroys himself in a person's heart. That heart was his sole refuge; he dwelt within it, heedless of public rumor, truly pure. A gesture, three words: "There he is!" and he commits suicide in that bewildered heart. Truth, suddenly stirred within that foreign consciousness by an evil intention, becomes error, just as our certainty of having seen the seven of diamonds in the conjuror's left hand sometimes changes into a dream. Genet and the conjurors have in common the fact that their function is to produce the twilight moment in which our conviction, without losing its blinding evidence, already seems evidently false to us; in order to occasion this hesitation in people's minds, they trick them from a distance. Genet's art, in particular, is, as we shall see, a betrayal. But in the case with which we are concerned at present, to betray is to decide in favor of all against a single individual: Genet is jealous of the other's individuality and of his own individuality in the other's heart. What if the Button Molder of souls were right? What if the value of certain souls were due to the irreplaceable love which they have had the luck to inspire? What if Solveig, killing two birds with one stone, secured Peer Gynt's salvation and her own as well? What if Genet were going to be saved in spite of himself? What if the friend, that third knife, suddenly proved to be the true star of the melodrama? None of that! Rather than let himself be redeemed by another, Genet will ruin himself by his own devices; he will ensure his individuality all by himself. His misfortune and pride allow him to have no commerce other than with all: he is only the empty form of the particular in the presence of the universal, and he establishes himself permanently as a particular by rejection of the universal. What business has he with the mediation of someone else? Where does that friend think he gets the right to love him? Since he intends to distinguish himself by loving the monstrous object of public hatred, Genet will put him in his place by changing his love to hatred. As soon as he is back among the mob, he will again become what he should never have ceased to be: *one* among *all.* *"Who* are you to place your trust in me?" Genet asks him angrily. "What right have you, you noble soul, to tempt me with the Good?" He gets what was coming to him: systematically practiced trust is an educator's trap. To *trust* may be a fine thing. But to *place* one's trust—what outrageous mistrust! It's a cunning mortgage on the future. Against my future freedom, that undesirable, each defends himself as best he can, I by oaths, the other by protesting his trust. No sooner is it flaunted than it clings to me, it's a guardian angel, a cop, a chastity belt. But, it may be objected, Genet's friend *trusted*. Perhaps. But for the damned, trusting and placing one's trust are one and the same: wherever it comes from, that holy water burns them when they are sprinkled with it. Because it is a temptation by Good it is automatically transformed into a temptation by Evil. In short, it is ruined and the friend is locked up. That sweet and kind Genet was a fake Genet. But for Genet himself, the good Genet was a reality: he loved, he was glad to be helpful; through his contact with that affectionate soul he discovered in it the Other that he *also* was for a single Other: a faithful friend. He trusted *himself* through the other's trust, and it was nice indeed. He will destroy for himself that objective and secret Genet; he will renounce happiness, security. Fouché is said to have been a good husband and father; Himmler, to have loved birds. These hard, false men whose job was to harm allowed themselves occasionally to be relieved of their functions by a child, by a pet. Genet would have had his own wife and brats thrown into jail, he would have roasted and eaten the canary. No rest for the wicked. He must feel in his bones the staggering astonishment of his victim. Actually, Genet is even more mystified by the trick. The fact is that when the other thinks he has seen the light he is still mistaken: he imagines that Genet merely pretended to love him and turned him in for money. Genet, who is better informed, knows that he loved him, that he got paid in order to have a motive for betraying. Where is the appearance? Where is the sham? Was he pretending to love? Is he not rather pretending to betray? Not at all: the betrayal is real since the friend is in prison. But what is a *real* traitor: is he a false friend or a sincere friend who destroys his love—and who is all the more criminal in that he loved more sincerely? Here begin the self-tortures, and I do not mean only the privations that he inflicts upon himself. To be sure, he will never see his friend again, he will never hear him again. He deprives himself of the happiness of being loved, he makes himself unworthy of it. But that's not the worst: for he betrayed *in order to be unworthy of loving*. The future monk who separates from his family, the sad Dominique who sighingly renounces the melancholy object of his passion, can still love; in fact they do love. And when Kierkegaard takes leave of Regina, he takes pleasure in thinking that she is restored to him in her entirety. But Genet loses his faculty of loving: he no longer under-stands his love, his offense separates him from it, he sees it from the heart of his darkness as a light that dazzles him without illuminating him. Tender emotions rise up in him like bubbles, but only to burst immediately: when Genet the friend wants, despite himself, to see his friend again, Genet the traitor is frightened and thinks only of fleeing his victim's vengeance. The first impulse engenders the second, which cancels it. Moreover, hatred arouses hatred: from within his tenderness Genet sees emerging a hatred directly *induced* by that which he has deliberately provoked in the other. The stronger his impulse, the more bitter is his resentment in knowing that he is rejected and the more violent his hostility toward the other; love is constantly being reborn from its ashes and reviving the hatred that kills it. In the depths of certain loves there is a temptation to betray which issues from the love itself, a temptation which is a pure negativity, a dizziness in the presence of the void and the nay, a temptation which awakens and grows all the more restless in that the love is stronger. Love seeks, at one and the same time, to maintain itself, test itself, transcend itself and destroy itself.* Betrayal offers itself as a deliverance, but one delivers oneself from love only by falling below all love. A single betrayal, even if secret, makes *all* friendship impossible. For a friendship is born with a future of friendship. The friendships which Genet strikes up in the underworld† are nipped in the bud by a future of hatred; in the first smile of trust on the other's face he already reads the sneer of future contempt. Friendship, which is a pledge, a continu-ous line of conduct, breaks down into bitter little bursts of nervous sympathy because the pledge to love is canceled by the pledge to hate, and yet this spray of emotions calls for a unity which is re-jected. Loving *all* in God, St. Theresa feels less and less the desire to attach herself to *a* creature. On the other hand, as one descends lower and lower into hell, the need to love burns more intensely. All loves are there, past and future, but as *privation*. Genet con-tinues to be haunted by the inexhaustible richness of the world; he feels pain in the arm he has lost. He wants *All* to be for him an incurable wound. Saintliness thinks it will rise to the plane of

---

* Janet asked a patient who was obsessed by the temptation to murder her children, "Why your children? Why not your husband?" "Ah," she replied, "it's because I don't love him enough."

† For it is only in the underworld that he betrays. The friends he has recently made (bourgeois members of the French intelligentsia) he defends—at times even when it is dangerous to do so—with a warmth extremely rare in literary circles. I know some persons for whom he no longer cares but whom he continues to stand by.

supreme being, for the Saint has not cast off the illusion that fullness of being is contained in intelligible realities: the Gidian ethic
thinks that people receive in the instant the detailed and infinite
gift of all that exists. But Genet descends to the abstract. The love
he bears *a* creature may seem to saints and moralists a deviation
and limitation of true love: for him it is the only way of attaining
the concrete.* Betrayal, on the other hand, is a withdrawing into
oneself, a renunciation, and as he betrays in order *to conform in
every case* to his general will to do evil, treason is, for him, a return
to the order of Evil. In betraying he suppresses the actual exception
in order to remain the abstract will to be the pure, categorical exception to the rule. To betray is to apply in reverse the most abstract
of ethics, that of the Kantian imperative. The maxim which he has
laid down for himself, the rule which he observes in order to
escape the rule, might be expressed as follows: "Act in such a way
that you always treat mankind in your person and in the person of
others as a means and never as an end." As Camus has admirably
said in *The Plague,* pain is abstract. One will therefore readily
understand that Evil is the systematic substitution of the abstract
for the concrete.

The comparison with the author of the *Treatise on Abjection*
will enlighten us if we carry it far enough, for we find the same
impulse in Jouhandeau. He, however, has chosen the concrete of
the saints, God himself; and it is God whom he betrays. No doubt
he draws his accomplices into damnation. "I pursued X obstinately.
I found him, disturbed him, cast a spell on him. By dint of male-
fices, I made a monster of him. . . . It is to me that he owes his
downfall, his irreparable perversity. . . . Even if I save myself, I
shall have destroyed him." But he merely gives to the other the
purity in Evil which he is seeking for himself; he destroys him
without ceasing to love him or to want his love. He "loves beings
as God loves them"; he sacrifices everything to them: "What does
it matter to me that you are Nothingness and that I sacrifice everything to you?" He thereby reconstitutes a society of three: "Closed
Trinity: God, he and I." But God represents the victim in this
community, and betrayal results from the creature's using against
God the Being that comes to him from God alone. The freedom
which Jouhandeau has received for Good he will use for Evil: "If I
am freedom, the freedom to love Man more than God and more

---

* Although, as we have seen, he seeks the type, the imaginary essence, the general theme
of crime in the hoodlums he loves. Cut off from nature and from his own body, Genet
is abstract.

than myself, who can take it away from me, even if it dishonors me and ruins me eternally . . . ?"

It is a matter of wresting oneself from God, of settling into one's own finiteness and, since a servant of God is no longer anything but God himself, of engendering from nothingness a will to annihilation and becoming a twilight being, a movement toward Nothing. Since error and Evil, as Descartes has shown, come from the creature, he who becomes all error and all evil derives only from himself. Every undertaking is aimed only at denying increasingly the being which he is through the omnipotence of God: "Great progress has been made when one no longer has any consideration or pity for oneself." Since the Positive is God within him, since only the *limit* comes from him, he will become a limit: "It is my own limits, those which God imposes upon me, which deliver me." He delivers himself little by little from God; he systematically rids himself of "whatever was exigent and sublime in his desire," unlike St. Theresa who retains the quintessence of hers. He disappears into a darkness which the divine gaze cannot pierce: "Each soul's relations with itself are—from a certain point of view peculiar to the soul—not quite God's concern nor do they concern any other soul in any way. That is the great secret." These relationships are those of finiteness with itself, of the negative with the negative. God, who is all-positivity, an infinite being and infinitely being, is blinded by His omnipotence: He perceives the creature only insofar as it is a positivity. In order for the divine understanding to conceive the negative, it would, to a certain degree, have to be affected with negativity. Thus, the nothingness which is secreted by the creature is a veil that hides it from the sight of the Almighty, like the ink in which the cuttlefish envelops itself. It is into Nothingness that the creature draws those whom it loves because it wants to love them for their nothingness and for their finiteness. The hapless couple takes refuge at the confines of being, in error and evil: on this level, it exists through itself and without divine mediation. It creates the purely human in absolute immanence, in sacrilegious rejection of transcendence. It is "the infernal kiss that Nothingness gives Nothingness." But it is also: "Man end of man. . . . My obsession, my perpetual temptation, my sin, is man. . . . Man alone satisfies man. God transcends him." A strange humanism, the humanism of a Black Mass, which starts by posing the divine's infinite superiority to the human in order subsequently to affirm, in a state of terror, man alone against God. "The human is the human and the place of the human; the place of the Pure and

Absolute human is Hell." Hidden beneath his flaunting of vice, beneath his hatreds, almost imperceptible, we would find in Genet —and in many other homosexuals—an analogous humanism, a barren humanism of pure immanence. A hellish humanism. Jouhandeau loves man in defiance of divine transcendence, and Genet loves him in defiance of ethical and social transcendence. Heroically minded authors are fond of showing enemy soldiers who attain, over and above the conflict that sets them against each other, a kind of solidarity and mutual respect. In a moment they will resume the fight, but there is a truce: they rise above the causes which they are defending; within them transcendence goes beyond every possible end to be recognized as pure transcendence, as the agony and grandeur of man. Genet succeeds in giving an infernal image of this lofty reconciliation: far from outstripping values, he takes a resolute stand at a point short of the ethical world and of all loyalties. At the beginning of *Funeral Rites,* the reader is mystified: in the impulse of love that drives Genet, a Frenchman, toward Erik, a German soldier who has perhaps killed his lover ("Was it possible for me, without doing violence to my inner life, to accept one of those against whom Jean had fought to the death?") , he thinks that he will experience some of the grandeur ("Fortinbras has my dying voice") which prevails in literature at the reconciliation of soldiers. But this is an illusion. In actual fact, Genet refuses to judge according to *acts.* If he loves the man, he does so without regard to praxis, on the level of gesture, and he is as indifferent to the cause of Jean, who was a Communist and a member of the Resistance, as he is to that of Erik, who is a member of the occupying forces and a Nazi. Moreover, the optimistic generosity of the soldier which defines man by formal transcendency is akin to the pessimistic good will of the whore for whom all men and all causes add up to the same thing. Whether stated in the manner of the former ("We are alike. The ideal doesn't matter as long as you *have* an ideal. It's the will to sacrifice that counts.") or of the latter ("Men are all alike. They get drunk on big words and reach for the moon. Communists, Nazis, it's all the same hokum.") , the result is the same: a betrayal in the moment. We are not angels and we do not have the right to "understand" our enemies, we do not yet have the right to love *all* men. The fact remains that in Genet as in Jouhandeau the pessimism of immanence leads to a kind of humanism exactly as does formal transcendency. But the fact is, they cannot hold to that. Genet falls headlong and shoots like a meteor through that thin film of humanism; he is going to betray the friend whom he loves, despite transcendency. Jouhandeau sighs: "Image of man, how beautiful you would be if I could keep you. . . . I renounce you because you escape me on all sides. There is no possessing you. . . ." In other words, to use the language of Jean Wahl, rejection of trans-ascendence necessarily produces trans-descendence. For man holds his ground only by surpassing himself, in the same sense in which it is said that one ceases to love if one does not love increasingly every day. If he is pious, he surpasses himself toward his creator; if he is an atheist, toward the God he wants to be. Jouhandeau surpasses himself downward, toward the mineral. The kinship of the two traitors—the one who betrays God and the one who betrays men—is marked by the similarity of the images they invent: "To him alone," writes Genet, "was granted the fearful privilege of perceiving his monstrous participation in the kingdoms of the great muddy rivers and of the jungles." And Jouhandeau: "Having become an unclean animal and then a bog plant, adapted to the folds of a shameful sinuosity of Hell, you were for a moment less than that: protoplasm." In both cases they go back down the road that led from the protozoa to man. But the aim is not to achieve this simplification for its own sake. The protozoan interests our traitors only in that it is *below*, at the lowest degree of the scale. Furthermore, they are not interested in *being* at the bottom; they must *have arrived there*. The protoplasm to which they want to reduce themselves is not the explosive substance, pregnant with the whole future of living things, which was the starting point of creative evolution: it is the final end of an involution that remains haunted by the memory of the great complex forms—fish, bird, man—which it was and which it cannot become again or even quite understand. One suspects that simplicity in evil does not tempt these homosexuals and poets for its own sake, but only insofar as it is a conscious privation of complexity. Each of their transgressions effects a disintegration, breaks up a synthesis and replaces it by a vertical contradiction, one of whose terms, which is real, which is actually experienced, is given as a simplification, and the other of which is an absence. But it is the absence which is stressed in this fake simplicity. The sage wants to be simple in order to reconcile himself with himself, and our sinners, on the other hand, in order to kindle the conflicts with themselves.

It is then that Genet turns proudly to the recognized Saint to ask him: Which of us two experiences veritable privation? Jouhandeau had already drawn a parallel between the Saint and the sinner:

"Just as the Saint renounces, first, Evil, then the society of men and finally everything in himself that is not Virtue, in order to be attached only to God through contemplation and the practice of a perfect life until he himself is only Nothingness and until God alone is all to him, so the determined sinner renounces Good, Society and, in Society, esteem and honor, and finally himself and in himself everything that is not his sin in order to be attached, first through desire and then in act, only to his object, by turning everything to the triumph of his perversity until he is only Nothingness in himself and his evil the All Evil."

The canonized Saint used his negative freedom to destroy his limit; there remains in him only Being, that is, God. The sinner, on the other hand, uses being to intensify the existence of his limit as a bleeding wound; he wants to be nothing other than the limit of being; hence, all Being falls outside him. But we must conclude from this that the Saint's destitution exists only in the eyes of others: he has everything, God is with him, how could he suffer? And although the possessions and pleasures which he has abandoned may return at times to haunt him, he does not have great difficulty in resisting the temptation since all the positive powers are on his side. Whereas the privation of Jouhandeau and Genet, even if it is not always visible, is felt. A comparison of the following three texts is to the advantage of the sinner.

First, St. Theresa:

"He who is truly humble must sincerely desire to be scorned, persecuted and condemned without a reason, even in grave matters. . . . *What is very helpful is to consider . . . that we are never accused without a reason, for we are always full of faults.*"

Then Jouhandeau:

"Happiness of being an object of derision and contempt for the only man in whom I have placed my trust. . . . Happiness of having no more friends. . . . Happiness of having no more relatives. . . . Happiness of the impure. To be publicly insulted and scorned is a revelation. We make the acquaintance of certain words which hitherto were only appurtenances of tragedy and with which we suddenly find ourselves rigged out and weighed down. We are perhaps no longer the person we thought we were. We are no longer the person we knew, but the one whom others think they know, whom they think they recognize as such-and-such. *If anyone could have thought that of me, it means that there is a certain amount of truth in it. . . .*"*

Lastly, Genet:

---

* *Treatise on Abjection.*

"In order to weather my desolation . . . I worked out, without meaning to, a rigorous discipline: . . . to every accusation brought against me, unjust though it be, from the bottom of my heart I shall answer yes. . . . I owned to being the coward, traitor, thief and fairy they saw in me. An accusation may be brought without proof, but it will seem that in order to be found guilty I must have committed the acts which make traitors, thieves or cowards; but this was not at all the case: *within myself, with a little patience, I discovered, through reflection, adequate reasons for being named by these names.* And it staggered me to know that I was composed of impurities. I became abject."

The canonized Saint, the Sinner and the diabolical Saint all demand that they be arraigned and blamed for acts which they have not committed. And all three immediately declare that the inner essence of their hearts fully justifies this arraignment and blame. It will therefore seem that we are dealing, in the three cases, with the concerted practice of humility. But this is not so: it is the sinners who are running the entire risk; the Saint is shamming. And of the three it is Genet who risks most.

In the case of St. Theresa, the starting point is *general esteem.* No doubt she struggled, she was misunderstood, she sometimes shocked, but, after all, the leading theologians were always on her side. Her superiors almost always supported her, particularly between 1562 and 1567 when all Avila violently objected to her "reform." The text which we have quoted, far from being an extract from some confession, appears in *The Way of Perfection,* a work of moral instruction written at the request of her nuns and at the recommendation of her confessor. It is true that she wishes to be scorned, but the wish is quite Platonic since she is careful to write in the same paragraph: "I was unable to put myself to this test in important matters. When I did hear people speak ill of me, I always realized that they reproached me very little." Moreover, what is involved here is a rather particular humility, since she no doubt renounces men's esteem, but continues to deserve it. In point of fact, it is clearly specified that the accusations are *false,* as is attested by the continuation of the passage: "Even if embarrassment were the only advantage for the person who accused you falsely, if he sees that you let yourself be condemned unjustly, it would be enormous." Humility consists therefore in placing oneself *above* the judgment of men. One does not even deign to defend oneself; one accepts slander passively and already knows that this behavior is *exemplary,* that it even has an edifying value for others. The slanderer's embarrassment is a tribute to his victim and greatly resembles Ulysses' involuntary admiration for Philoctetes. One has risen above him, one draws him to God. St. Theresa is careful to tell us that this embarrassment "sometimes elevates the soul more than ten sermons." Thus, the slanderer is not at all an equal or superior whose scorn crushes us because it reveals to us the truth of our being-for-others; on the contrary, he is below us, and his scorn is a sin that falls on him without affecting us. At bottom, this would-be quest of scorn is rather a certain way of placing oneself above all esteem, because a contingent and finite creature cannot rightly evaluate another creature: "What can it profit us to satisfy creatures?" All that counts is valorization by the Almighty: "Even if all [creatures] imputed a host of faults to us, what does it matter if we are exempt from them in the eyes of the Lord . . . ?" What a cry of pride! At bottom, one deliberately challenges the natural witness—our fellow man—in order to substitute for him the only witness worthy of us, the Almighty. No intermediary between the soul and the infinite. The creature rejects all solidarity with creatures. To be sure, she is humble before God, but this humility costs little. How could finiteness not grovel before the infinite? Especially if the groveling is to raise it above the judgment of men? True humility, the humility that is agonizing, is to recognize that one is inferior to another finite creature. St. Theresa does, of course, declare in the aforementioned passage that we must "consider that we are never accused without a reason, for we are always full of faults." But what does she mean by that? That she has really committed the sins imputed to her? That she might have committed them? No, but that, in a quite general way, she is a sinner because God shaped her of clay, because she is a limited, contingent creature, composed partly of nothingness. This amounts to saying that she is not God. Scorn and slander are an opportunity for her to relate to God as to the measure of all things and to feel again her infinite smallness. But she does not deign to relate to any human creature because she does not accept man's being the measure of man. Indeed, she adds: "The just man falls seven times a day, and it would be untrue to assert that we are without sin. That is why, although we may be wrongly accused, we are never exempt from faults as was good Jesus." Of course, but Jesus is God himself, and our fundamental guilt does not prevent us, if we are strong enough, from being the Just man or the Saint, that is, the best among men. Furthermore, in order to promote detachment, it is not enough for her to set the testimony of God himself against the human witness:

she adds that one must want to be scorned *with* the Lord. It is God himself whom she takes as companion in abjection: "Could I desire that one ever speak well of a creature as wicked as I when one speaks so ill of You, O Good above all goods?" Whereupon contempt is destroyed by itself. What importance are we to grant it, since it is so ridiculous as to address itself to God too? In fact, since it was the Lord's will to allow himself to be scorned, disdain and condemnation honor us by fashioning us in His likeness. They must be sought as merits. And it is not surprising that humility, conceived at first as a suffering to be borne, changes with practice into pure indifference: "[The practiced soul] is no longer concerned with one's speaking ill or well of it; it feels that such talk is of a matter which is foreign to it." But is not this indifference to other people's judgment one of the characteristics of pride? Human scorn concerns appearance; the judgment of God concerns Being. Thus, the saint's humility is quite simply a preference for Being. Behind the sincere effort of self-renunciation made by the unhappy consciousness is an ethical optimism: it suffices that an absolute gaze penetrates us for us ourself to be valorized absolutely. Thus, ascetic elevation is true, but humility and privation are false. It is always a matter of existing in the eyes of Another and, consequently, of being for oneself other than self. Humility consists in choosing the Other in whose eyes one exists and, as a consequence, the Other that one is for oneself.

In Jouhandeau, we find the same duality of witnesses: there is God and there are all men. However, it is impossible for him to use one of the two testimonies to challenge the validity of the other because the two witnesses make the same statement: "Insult is perpetual. It is not only explicit, in the mouth of this one or that one, but on the lips of all who name me; it is in 'being' itself, in my being ... and it is God in person who utters it ... who eternally gives me that execrable name. . . ." For St. Theresa, the human judge attained only appearance, God alone saw being: one could therefore withdraw into being. But for Jouhandeau, the human gaze also attains him in his being. There is no longer any refuge, and humility before God becomes abjection before men. St. Theresa annihilates herself before God, but this annihilation raises her above the creature. It is *before the creature* that Jouhandeau annihilates himself: he is, like St. Theresa, a pismire in the eyes of God, but he is also a miserable wretch in the eyes of his fellows. When he cries out: "Happiness of being an object of derision and contempt for the only man in whom I have placed my trust," he uses the same or almost the same words as St. Theresa, but in his mouth they have a different ring: "I am always more pleased," admits the Saint, "that supposed faults are imputed to me rather than real faults." But it is *real* faults that are imputed to Jouhandeau. We are thus confronted with a strange paradox: the Saint must want to sin as little as possible, but he must also have, in the words of St. Theresa, "the sincere desire to be scorned by all creatures." Now, these two postulations are contradictory: if he scorns scorn, he cannot *desire* it, and if he desires it, he must want to deserve it. But he can deserve it only by *a fault,* and that is what he cannot will, for that would be to sin against God out of love of God. Jouhandeau, on the other hand, wants to play the dangerous game of betraying God out of love. It is because of his faults that he brings contempt upon himself, and he first recognizes that he deserves the slurs which are cast upon him. He thereby knows true humility. But he sins, and if he wants the scorn to continue, he must persevere in Evil: "Happiness of being disfigured by Evil, by one's own evil. One can no longer show oneself, or one shows one's evil, and that is a kind of emblem, a badge, a sign, the white robe of madness or the bell of the leper." There is no true destitution unless one regrets having given up one's possessions. In the case of the Saint who renounces the goods of this world in order to acquire those of heaven, this regret gradually diminishes and ends by giving way to beatitude. In order to regret having given something away, one must lose by the exchange, one must have less, be worth less, one must *go down.* In renouncing "what was exigent and sublime in his desire," Jouhandeau thinks he has acquired the right to say that "these sacrileges are perhaps a manner of sacrifice." The sinner has thus chosen the greatest sacrifice, since he lets himself sink into Hell, and the greatest risk, since he does not see, once he is there, how he can get out of it. However, let there be no misunderstanding: this will to self-destruction conceals a stratagem. The author is speculating on the ambiguity of Christian ethics, in which, as a matter of fact, a sacrifice is at times a means and at others an end.

The Church is first a spiritual community that wants to continue in its being. It cares little about states of soul, except insofar as they may endanger its existence. It has therefore instituted an *objective* ethic which defines the morality of its faithful by conformity to social laws, that is, to the Divine Word as contained in the sacred books and interpreted by authorized officials. It asks the faithful to help maintain the social bond by means of *faith,* that is, by unconditional adherence to the myths and by strict observance of the rites, to intensify the solidarity of the members of the religious body by the practice of *charity* or mutual assistance, to widen the influence of the community by their works and example, to identify, through *hope*, their individual ends with the collective ends and to expect their fulfillment not so much from their personal activity as from the transcendent triumph of the social body. As, owing to their collective character, these prescriptions quite naturally endanger our personal interests and our self-love, we are frequently led to sacrifice those interests and that love. But sacrifice is only a means; it has no value in itself. It may cause us great suffering, but that is our own affair. In fact, from this point of view it appears suspect if it is too painful. The soldier who enjoys the confidence of his leaders is not the one who has the greatest difficulty in overcoming his cowardice, but rather the one who displays a natural contempt for death. In order to show how praiseworthy he is, mention is sometimes made of the external difficulties he encountered and overcame: "They were outnumbered five to one, without food, cut off from the rear," etc. But nothing is said about the difficulties he encounters within himself. It is when the war is over that the soldier speaks of his fear to astonished women. And does anyone think that a dictatorial political party, which is also a church, will be grateful to the militant who had *the greatest difficulty* in giving up his "deviation" and going back to the "party line"? On the contrary, it will keep its eye on him and at the first purge will get rid of him. In militant communities, sacrifice has value only precisely insofar as it enables the group to preserve the integrity of the social body. This is the only way of guarding against human weakness. But it *would be better* not to have to make sacrifices, it would be better to abandon, without tears, family, wife and friends at the first call. We would sacrifice our intellectual pride *because* free examination may endanger the inner cohesion of the Church. But it would have been far better if our intelligence had stopped by itself at the threshold of the mystery, for we are now suspect despite the sacrifice, or rather because of it. We have already chafed at the bit. Who knows whether tomorrow we may not give ourselves free rein. We shall sacrifice our carnal desires *because* we may scandalize, that is, may disunite when we ought to be trying to create harmony by exemplary behavior. But let us not start boasting. There is something disturbing in a description of carnal temptations. Are you going to describe the charms of the Queen of Sheba whom you have spurned? You would cause others to hate your final victory and to dream of exquisite defeats. Precisely because a too-painful sacrifice seems disquieting, because our sobs lead others to think that the sacrificed object is of great value and may arouse guilty curiosity in them, objective morality requires that we *minimize* the value of the possessions that have been abandoned. This sacred utilitarianism stresses the fact that the individual interests of the faithful are nothing compared to those of the great body to which they have the good fortune to belong. As members of the religious community, they will find much more than what they lose as individuals. In exchanging their contingent, obscure and subjective individuality for a sacred, objective personality they have everything to gain. This point of view is, in a way, that of the Saint: mortification of the flesh and flagellation are not ends in themselves; they have value only because they weaken and chastise earthly instinct, selfish aspirations; the Saint renounces only nothingness and does so in order to raise himself to being.

But in this same Christianity, a more primitive ethic, and a more strictly religious one as well, emphasizes the intrinsic value of sacrifice, which it presents as a kind of mystical potlatch. In a society of consumers, that is, one which is governed by an aristocracy that sets itself up as the supreme end of human labor, the gods are the great consumers. The ruling class is entitled to the finest products; the finest of the finest are reserved for God, the King of Kings. The reasons for the sacrifice are inverted: if one renounces the goods of this world, it is no longer because they are false goods; rather, one offers them to God because they are true goods. The lord who has been touched by grace sells his beautiful palace. But not because he has contempt for the beauty of its architecture. He will use the money from the sale to build an even more beautiful church. Besides, most of the time God is not able to come and consume in person. The consumption is represented by a real destruction; for God, things are broken, burned, buried. The potlatches are an objective rite as long as the faithful are able to believe that God inhales with pleasure the smoke of the incense or that he loves to see the flow of victims' blood. Later, when divine omnipotence comes to be better understood, the values which God accords the object that is sacrificed to him will be measured by the importance it retains in the eyes of the sacrificer, hence in the resistance that the latter feels when he wants to dispossess himself of it. Stress is laid on subjectivity: to give to God—sorrowfully, rebelliously, despairingly—that which is most legitimately dear to us is an act of piety in the highest sense of the word. Abraham will kill his son. Ultimately—and since it seems that nothing is dearer to us than ourself—it is ourself that we shall give, by a kind of internalizing of the human sacrifice in which the sacrificer and the victim are one and the same. One lines the for-itself with a glorious in-itself; the reverse side of my grief is joy in heaven: to destroy the object is to create its celestial double.

These two ethics are not compatible. We are often mistaken about them since they both prescribe renunciation. But how can the Good of which we divest ourselves be *both* nothingness and the best? At the extreme limit of the objective ethic we abandon our possessions with indifference; this indifference is the mark of our love of God. At the extreme limit of the subjective ethic we dispossess ourselves in despair; despair is the measure of our love. One must therefore be *both* indifferent and despairing. I am not presenting these contradictions in order to condemn Christian ethics: I am far too convinced that *any* ethic is both impossible and necessary. I am describing. Although simultaneous practice of the two ethics is indeed impossible, it is at the same time indispensable, and if the Christian applies one without the other, he exposes himself to strange proceedings: if he remains purely objective, he will fall into the Catharist heresy by condemning all of creation, that is the divine work; if he is obstinately set on pure subjectivity, he will fall into Catharism backward, into the "leftish" religion of the author of the *Treatise on Abjection*.

In his view, the essential thing is the subjective movement of sacrifice. And in order to offer God the most magnificent gift, he presents him with his share of paradise and his right to do Good. In addition, as sacrifice is an act of formal destruction, it is he himself, a creature of God, that he destroys formally.* And since the greatest Evil is that which costs him most, it is the most heinous offense that will pass for the supreme sacrifice. Everything holds together if one recognizes that the greatest pain is the sign of the greatest gift, that is, if one eliminates the objective component of Christian ethics and makes of the self-inflicted torment the subjective criterion and the end of morality. One thus arrives at a religious "dolorism." Obviously a point remains to be discussed: even if one adopted this dolorism, is it true that there is more suffering and hence more merit in yielding to one's vice than in resisting it? I quite recognize the terror and disgust of the Christian who succumbs to the flesh, but I recognize equally the carnal and even emotional satisfactions, which are not to be disdained. Inversely,

---

* In the sense meant by Cocteau in a letter to Max Jacob which I quote from memory: "I love God to the point of being damned for love of Him."

I can readily conceive the pleasure one derives from a good conscience, but I am similarly aware of the bitter taste and painfulness
of renunciation. I would not dare to decide, and if Jouhandeau
decides, he does so by means of a further trick, by jumping artfully from the subjective to the objective: the superiority of vice
lies in its causing an objective lessening of our being. We are worth
less, even if we are not aware of it. Thus, even if carnal intercourse
fills him with pleasure, the voluntary outcast *supposedly* experiences the worst suffering since his soul shrivels up. As for pleasure,
he takes for granted that *objectively* it is only a dream. Consider his
misfortune: the pain is not felt but it is there, haunting him, it is
the objective truth of his situation; the pleasure, on the other hand,
is felt, but it is a false pleasure and its function is merely to abase.

I say it outright: this dialectic stinks to high heaven. In the first
place, it amounts to making a great to-do about a few acts of solitary
or mutual masturbation. It amounts to no more than that. Where's
the crime? Where's the enormity? Human relations are possible between homosexuals just as between a man and a woman. Homosexuals can love, give, elevate others and elevate themselves. It's
surely better to get into bed with a boy friend than to go traveling
in Nazi Germany when France has been defeated and strangled.
And besides, I have been observing the severe discipline of the
Cartesian *cogito* for too long to fall into these childish traps. A
suffering which is not felt is inexistent. And a pleasure which one
experiences is the very opposite of a dream. In what appeared to us
just before as true humility I now discern the shrill frenzy of pride.
It takes a lot of conceit to imagine that one has committed a damning sin. I would even say that Jouhandeau is playing a double game.
For he has, in the first place, the pride of having become a sinner:
he derives, in Evil, from himself alone; at one point he speaks of
the glory of Hell. But at the same time he counts on destitution and
voluntary abjection to save him: "Only passion or vice casts you
into the same destitution as Saintliness, and I am of the opinion
that it is only at the moment when man is so forsaken by everything
and by himself that he is closest to grace: I mean to being worthy
of it." We thought he was going to ruin himself, and that was what
he claimed to want. But when he is at the lowest point he starts
explaining that the highest and lowest merge: the essential thing
is to escape from the common herd by the greatness of one's virtue
or offenses: "There is a parallelism between the roads to Perfection and those to Perversion. The stages of these roads are the same,
but in opposite directions. They sometimes lead to the same light
through two kinds of contrary destitutions." "Going from defeat

to defeat, having completed all the stages, one ceases to want to understand, and it is in the heart of that Darkness that the Light reaches me. . . ." We discover that he was faking his humility in the depths of abjection. No doubt he wanted to *merit* the scorn that the Saint scorned, but it was only so that this will to sacrifice would confer upon him the highest merit. The Saint was close to God *despite* the scorn of others, our author *because* of this scorn. By dint of wanting to justify the horror he inspires, he ends, like the Saint, by placing himself above it. Destitution, remorse, grandeur, acute consciousness of his abjection and of the Supernatural: what is lacking for him to be elected? "He must not be saddened because of me who am only weariness and wretchedness on this side of the World, Triumph and Splendor on the side of the Eternal, but who can know this?" The Saint wants to annihilate his contingency, the Sinner wants to become his own nothingness, but that amounts to the same thing. When lived to the limit, contingency rejects itself, reveals itself as the *mere nothing* it was in the eyes of the Saint: "[When one is no longer anything] but . . . something eminently close to 'nothing' [one has] borne witness in the twinkling of an eye to the dizziness which is the other aspect of ourself: negation, absolute nothingness. . . ." But this nothingness which has been reduced to nothingness is self-annihilating; it is a transparency through which we perceive Being itself, that is, God: "God: the closest of the close, the most urgent, the only necessary fellow being . . . more essential to Myself than myself, since Myself can be only God and myself, since I cannot be completely Myself without God, but only nothingness."

And here is the final twist: "God alone knows the nature of man, which man himself is unaware of, and often perhaps when man shocks himself, God is edified." In *letter* this is conformable to dogma: it is true that God knows man better than man himself does. Yet the *spirit* has been altered. What does the Church actually mean? Two things: in the first place, that God can discern Evil, the offense, the guilty desire when man imagines he is practicing virtue; in addition, that God alone can judge and that such-and-such a man who shocks *us*, for example, Abraham, is perhaps a just man in the eyes of Him who knows his motives. Thus, He knows my evil will or the other person's good will better than I do.* But, in any case, He cannot know *my* good will better. This is

---

* This, be it added, is not so clear: how does God, who is all positivity, have knowledge of the negative? We have see Jouhandeau play on this ambiguity and slip into the darkness of Nonbeing in order to escape the divine gaze.

not a matter of limiting the might of the Almighty, but of defining the Christian conditions of virtue: in point of fact, for the Christian the good act is defined by the conscious intention of doing good. Since evil is darkness and nothingness, an evil intention may be hidden from me, but since Good is Being, light, self-mastery, mastery of my evil instincts, awareness—carried as far as my finiteness permits—of the consequences of my act, how could I do good unconsciously? To be sure, my acts, both good and bad, concur in maintaining the universal order. I cannot destroy the world that God has created, and, even if I am a criminal, I serve ends of which I am unaware: the ways of God are impenetrable. In a certain sense, therefore, even if the intention of my action is evil, the action is good since Christian theodicy makes Evil a condition of a greater Good. However, if God discerns in this action meanings of which I am unaware, if he foresees and approves their remote effects, he does not hold me accountable for these effects and meanings. I am responsible only for the consequences which I can know, but for these I am fully responsible; and this responsibility, which does not exceed my finiteness, is one and the same as my consciousness of it. Thus, my intention of serving God and Good exists only insofar as I am aware of it; however weak it may be, it cannot escape me. And, inversely, even if an evil action, deliberately committed, has the happiest consequences, God will take into account only my intention of doing harm. He thus knows the guilty background of my virtuous designs better than I do, but He cannot find in guilty designs a virtue of which I am unaware, for there is none.*

But our author fakes everything: he claims to be placing himself in front of his acts as in front of those of his fellow beings and to be *discovering* their meaning, which actually he *gives* them. He claims that his will to Evil is only probable, or rather, although his will knows itself in its spontaneity, that it is the effect of a deeper will to Good which is knowable only to God. At the same time, he deliberately confuses the objective conformity of the act (whatever it may be) to the designs of Providence with its subjective value, which only the intention defines. Once again he jumps from the subject to the object, from consciousness to being; and because the Sinner, despite himself, plays his part—even in his sin—in the concert of the world, he attributes to himself the full merit of cooper-

---

* No doubt we can judge our acts *too* severely, we can exaggerate their shadowy aspect, we can underrate ourselves. But this hypothetical reconstruction of our person takes place on another plane and from other points of view than the simple production of a good intention.

ating in this symphony, as if the sin had somewhere been expressly willed for that purpose. And as a matter of fact, if one has faith, it *was* willed somewhere and by someone: by God, who decides upon the means of maintaining the universal order. And as the Sinner is annihilated, all that remains is God himself, and everything vanishes into Good. Let us get away from this soul: it sounds phony.

But before taking leave of it, we should, nevertheless, note that it assumes greater risks than the smug soul of St. Theresa.

The tragedy of the bourgeois homosexual is that of nonconformism. How is he to preserve his guilty originality in a society into which he tends to be integrated, in other respects, by family, profession, fortune, culture and religion? Each invert solves this problem in his own way. Proust, an agnostic, bases his irresponsibility on a psychological determinism which he invents and perfects for the needs of the cause. The Proustian analyses are pleas in self-defense, even—and particularly—when they deal with behavior and feelings unrelated to his "vice." He adopts the attitude, with greater sublety, of the Greek thief whose answers to the questions of the Tzedek Test are reported in Appendix II. "There are no honest people," said the latter. And Proust: "There are no normal people. Charlus' homosexuality is a cancer that eats away at him, but the jealousy of Swann, a heterosexual, is just as destructive." Gide, a Protestant, a man trained to engage in free inquiry, accustomed from childhood to feel responsible, without intermediary, to an abstract God who is closer to a legislator than to a metaphysical and creative power, strives to wipe out social prohibitions on behalf of the impulses of his spontaneity. He shuts out the sacred, substitutes for the Supernatural a Nature which tolerates all sexual behavior with the same indifference. He transforms the concept of *inflicted* nonconformity into an ethico-aesthetic value: willed *irreplaceability*. Over the years, in the course of an uninterrupted dialogue with the Catholics, his idea of God changes into a foggy notion, half sacred, half secular, which unites the advantages of atheism with those of faith. Jouhandeau, a Catholic, is crushed by the Church. One does not "do away with" Catholicism. Although one sometime breaks with it, one is left half dead and marked forever. Jouhandeau temporizes, he tries to arrange a tolerable life for himself within the denominational community. If he resembles Genet so strongly, it is because he plays a losing game: Proust's homosexual imperialism does not hesitate to attack human nature; that of Gide attacks the reformed religion. Jouhandeau accepts the Church's dogmas, prohibitions, metaphysics, in fact everything,

including the traditional psychology of confessors. In this frame of
reference he is assured of damnation. There remains for him only
to try his hand at "loser wins." But in order to win, one must first
lose. The *only* salvation at which he can aim is something beyond
hell. But this something will be revealed only if he first conscientiously gets himself damned. We find in Jouhandeau the Gidian
idea of irreplaceability; he too starts from an inflicted nonconformity which has to be cultivated, deepened and transformed into a
work of art: "Every man is born evil and is entitled to his original
evilness, to the flaw in his makeup, and I am speaking not only of
the very particular flaw which affects the species in general, but
of the even more particular flaw with which each individual is
marked at birth." In Gide, however, the idea of the inherent flaw
disappears with that of the sacred: the systematic cultivation of
individual difference ends in breaking up the moral law of Prot-
estantism into an infinity of particular "categorical imperatives."
And this individualism opens out on a social optimism: in acquiring deeper knowledge of the individual, one will find the universal,
one will end perhaps in founding a new society. This is accounted
for by the fact that the Protestant's integration into the religious
community is not strong enough to restrain him. In Jouhandeau,
on the other hand, the cult of particularity, though revealing itself
as the *only* way out, remains a deadly sin because he has not even
attempted to liquidate the values of the denominational commu-
nity* and because it is a matter of keeping everything. And where

---

* The suicide rate is higher among Protestants than among Catholics. Durkheim concluded from this that the Protestant is less strongly integrated into his community than
the Catholic into his. Halbwachs, for reasons which it would take too long to go into and
not all of which seem to me convincing, has modified this conclusion: "Religious conceptions are not the central factor about which urban societies are organized and peasant
groups consolidate and perpetuate themselves. The principle of their cohesion lies not
in this but in a social structure made up of customs and institutions, some traditional and
others more recent. These include religious practices. But there is no reason to view complex groups from the religious standpoint alone. Thus, it is not the religious cohesion of
Catholic groups which explains the fact that their suicide rate is lower than that of less
conservative societies, but rather the traditional cohesion of groups which, though composed mainly of Catholics, are united by many other common features." (*Les Causes du
Suicide*, Alcan, p. 29.) However, even if we grant this modification, the differences of
social integration in the cases of Proust, Gide and Jouhandeau are glaringly evident. The
first, a rich Jewish intellectual, was a city man accustomed to scientific analysis (his father
and brother were doctors) ; his environment was that of "fashionable" society, that is, of
the sophisticated upper bourgeoisie and of the declining aristocracy which readily closed
its eyes to vices, provided they were not flaunted. The enemy did not dwell in its consciousness. The second belonged to the well-to-do Protestant bourgeoisie; he thought that
he summed up the characteristic features of several provinces; he lived successively in
social groups of different structures, in Paris, Uzès and Cuverville and, consequently, he
escaped from each of them. The habits of lucidity and critical analysis which he acquired
from an austere but universalist education could be turned against the religion that

Gide succeeds in developing a secular ethic of liberation through
a slow and patient sharpening of sacred concepts which end by
being convenient and harmless headings, Jouhandeau is forced to
invent a religious asceticism of damnation. The soul is entitled to
its individuality, but this individuality, which is its specific evil,
leads it straight to Hell. Both men seek a final justification because
both of them have tasted of the forbidden fruit. But Gide concludes: nothing that comes spontaneously from the deepest part of
oneself can be evil; it is oriented toward Good. And Jouhandeau:
one must go to the very limit of crime in order to find God. But, as
we saw above, the ethic of Evil is pitiless: a sin that has been committed with the certainty that it brings one closer to God, with the
will to draw closer to Him, is no longer a sin and consequently does
not bring one closer to the Almighty. If, as a result of the destructive suffering it causes in the sinner's soul, Evil can become a merit,
it must not be committed casually; the horror, the self-loathing, the
despair, must be true. One must keep going lower and lower without hope; one must will one's damnation and believe that one has
been damned forever. In a certain sense, Jouhandeau takes all the
risks, his abandonment is absolute; there will not be a word of
dogma, not a legend, not a confessor to encourage him. Sacred history does, to be sure, abound in edifying anecdotes about hardened
sinners who are saved at the brink of death. And, moreover, it is
forbidden to despair: hope is a theological virtue. But the purpose
of the stories to which I refer is to give us an indication of God's
immense kindness. The sinners in these stories have damned themselves beyond appeal, they have given God every reason for doom-
ing them, and if the Eternal saves them at the last moment, he does
so *despite* the reasons, despite simple justice, out of love. In short,
one must *hope* that God forgives. But our author's infernal pride
does not care about hoping, does not care about hypothetical forgiveness. No doubt he does not intend to force God to save him,
but at least he wants his behavior, though remaining perfectly
damnable, to provide Justice with reasons for absolving him. In
fact, if he gives up his place in Paradise, it is in order that it be

hampered him. Jouhandeau is a Catholic and a provincial, and comes from a poor and
pious family. As an underpaid employee, his situation in the secular society that crushes
him is in the image of that occupied by the sinner in a religious society. He is on the
lowest level of the bourgeoisie, and if he boasts of triumphing over those on the higher
levels, he does so by virtue of his secret spirituality and at the cost of an absolute reversal
of values. This provincial remains strongly attached to the small town from which he comes
and is aware of the repressive power of scandal, whereas Baron de Charlus, a rich, powerful, cultivated nobleman, has everything that is needed to place himself proudly above
public opinion.

restored to him at the right-hand side of the Lord. There is in this willful damnation the exigency found in all potlatch; it demands that its gift be paid for with another gift. But in that case, and if he wants to enter paradise with his head high, he has to hide this exigency from himself. Just as the pious man must do Good without hope of reward if he wants to be rewarded in the end, so Jouhandeau must do Evil for Evil's sake and without hope of salvation. He will find light only in the heart of darkness, he will know hope only beyond despair. He has, as we have seen, cleverly supposed that God discerns his good intentions better than he himself does. But he has to be unaware of them for that very reason. Although God may "often be edified when man is shocked," it is nevertheless necessary that man, here below, remain shocked. If he refuses to place his "hope of something beyond despair" in divine indulgence, he must then base it on ignorance. He has only a single weak reason for hoping, to wit, that he *does not know* how he appears in the eyes of the Creator. What he does *know* is that he is condemned by the Church and by Society. But he also knows that he does not know everything. The final light is the darkest Night, the great night of Unknowing. Beyond the blinding evidence of his damnation, this soul knows *nothing* more, and it is on this *nothing* that it founds its hope. It is *perhaps* elected, but if so, the human world is merely a farce, including revealed dogma and the entire Church. Perhaps. Perhaps it is necessary to go that far.*

He *thinks* that he is elected. He substantifies his ignorance and the "nothing" that protects him against *all*. He *thinks*, and this probabilism suddenly reveals, in a flash, his frightful resentment against those who scorn him. *Yes*, if he is saved, it is because there will be surprises on the Day of Judgment: they'll all be damned, all of them, the bourgeois, the priests, the cops, all except a few homosexuals—and perhaps the saints. The farce ends with this tremendous damnation.

Resentment, pride, Black Mass, dangerous games of evil and good, *merit* of the evildoer: at the point to which these descriptions have led us, we have only to take one step further to join Genet. After the canonized Saint, after the Sinner, what a relief to be with him again.

What rectitude he has, what frankness! The reckless daring with which he runs his risks! The acrobatics we have just described were all performed above a net. The net has now been removed:

---

* Cocteau goes that far in *Bacchus:* "If God's designs are impenetrable, it is possible that he punishes what you call good and rewards what you call evil" (Act II, Scene 4).

the acrobat is risking his life. We are, of course, going to meet again with the old battered concepts of destitution, humility, all the terms of hagiographic literature. Yet everything is new: the reason is that God has disappeared; God was the net.

To begin with, Genet breaks all the records in the big crime race. St. Theresa let herself be condemned for crimes she had not committed. The author of the *Treatise on Abjection* committed the crimes that are imputed to him, but he makes a devil of a fuss about a few venial, sensual pleasures. In the gallery of portraits of homosexuals, we find a great marshal, a member of Pétain's cabinet, very highly regarded by the clergy before the defeat of Germany, some very Catholic kings, popes, a famous agent of the Intelligence Service. Does anyone believe that these eminent personages are in hell? And if all the heterosexual Communists in the Eastern democracies were changed into anti-Soviet homosexuals, the Church would certainly proclaim it a miracle. The greatest Evil, for Genet, is to betray. That is sufficient: it is *true* that betrayal is inexpiable, it is *true* that it is the only offense for which history has no pity. Ivan the Terrible has been rehabilitated; before long Hitler may be rehabilitated; but the Duke of Bourbon, commander-in-chief of the French armies, is condemned without appeal. Genet has had the courage to choose the worst.

The offenses which are most cruelly punished are committed against men. To offend God, if he exists, is dreadful. But, after all, God loves us: if we repent when necessary, he will forgive us. "No sin but should find mercy." Men are not merciful; they never forgive grave offenses, they kill. Besides, even if there were a posthumous appeal for mercy, what would it matter to Genet since he does not believe that he is immortal? And, in addition, his semiatheism disarms him. He cannot, like Jouhandeau, divert himself by playing a double game: there is only one game. He cannot take advantage of the age-old conflict between God and men, he cannot go from the latter to the former the way a child utilizes marital discord to set his parents against each other in order to get from one what the other refuses him. There are only men. All the pious frauds of whom we have spoken thought they had their absolute excuse in God. The more Jouhandeau destroys himself here below, the more he re-creates himself in Heaven. Genet's *only truth* comes to him from men. Thereby the absolute drops back to earth. No angel will wipe away the spit with which he is covered, no eternity of glory will challenge his present wretchedness. This world has no underside; in this world, sufferings are inexpiable, ineffaceable. The pettiest of the disgusting experiences that he has put up with is an infinity that crushes him, since he knows that nothing will compensate for it. Jouhandeau, who is highly integrated into religious society, works himself into a good position and manages to live in it. I do not doubt that his anguish is unbearable, but the fact is that it all takes place in his head. Before 1942 I never met anyone who did not esteem him; he was a respectable person, just like the surrealists. Genet, who is excluded from secular society, suffers in his flesh. If he really commits acts of betrayal, he will be beaten up or stabbed. The destitution is therefore real: he deprives himself of *all* love. The humility is entire: men scorn him and he knows no judge to whom he can appeal.

No doubt about it, he is at the bottom of the ladder. From every point of view: deprived of love, thanks to himself, and burning with a desire to love, scorned by all, accepting their scorn, knowing that he deserves it and striving to deserve it even more, charged with the most serious offenses against others and against himself, simplified to the extreme and dragging his past complexity like a ball and chain; he has chosen finiteness, helplessness and hatred. For Faust to fool Satan, for Jouhandeau to betray Evil, is only to dissipate the darkness: God approves one's not keeping one's word when it has been given to the Demon. But for Genet to betray Evil is to corrode it by a worse evil: it is to achieve for himself discomfort in crime. In the case of Faust and Jouhandeau, the final betrayal is the trick that produces light; in that of Genet, it is the thickening of the darkness, it is the spinning of the compass needle. He literally "loses his bearings." Thinking in accordance with two systems and two languages, producing and destroying at the same time, hated by those who ought to love him, loved by those who are going to hate him, an abominable accomplice of Good which he rejects, a sworn enemy of Evil which he has adopted as an end, he attains such a degree of confusion that two simultaneous and opposed Evils cancel and strengthen each other at the same time. Urging his companions to steal, then denouncing them to the police who go after them and put them to flight, he prevents the theft from taking place. The final result is zero, but within himself this zero corresponds to the infinity of Evil. He has gone *mad*. And yet this madness is reason since it is the logical result of the lucid, rigorous, intense, austere quest of the greatest Evil. At the bottom of the ladder, he performs a feat: his reason, without ceasing to reason, becomes mad reasoning. We quoted earlier three strangely similar texts: one by the Saint, one by the Sinner and one by the

Thief. But a more searching study has shown us a kind of faking on the part of the first two. In the case of the third, the cloud is torn apart by a phrase, a princely phrase: "I became abject." Not that I like abjection. But there is something about the phrase that smacks of the swordsman: the decision is brusque and imperious, without whys and wherefores and without appeal. Jouhandeau does, of course, call his book *Treatise on Abjection,* but he is a man of law, a pettifogger. Abjection is always presented slantwise in his line of argument, in three-quarter face. Or else it is a toboggan, you shoot forward in one of his sentences, you slide down Evil, you finish in Good. His style—one of the finest of our time, with astonishing resources—displays at times a suspicious oiliness, a flabbiness, a glassy transparency, a hideous amiability. He writes: "It suffices that each man's Demon not have the last word." And, in fact, he so manages that a word, a supernumerary word, which represents Good, creeps into each of his sentences; sometimes it is simply the tense of the verb. He would not write "I became abject," but "I had become abject." Genet, a petty cavalier of crime, at times inserts, between two sentences, a short, hard word that stamps his will to the irremediable.

And yet, he no more escapes the fundamental question than do the others: why want to *be* a Saint? Earlier it was a question only of doing, in fact, of undoing, and now one has to act *in order to be.* Once again praxis is subordinated to ontology. Why? Genet wanted to resorb Being into consciousness and wanted consciousness to be dissipated while dissolving its object. We made a great effort to enter into his views despite our distaste, but now it appears that this will to nothingness concealed a recourse to Being, hence to optimism, hence to Good. Thus, ancient skepticism is secretly based on dogmatic reason: it poses the truth of skepticism. This time we refuse to go along with him. On the grounds of the effort we have made to understand him, we are unwilling to follow him in this strange whirligig wherein he seeks annihilation in order to attain fullness of being, wherein he will commit the most heinous act in order to achieve the greatest Good. As Camus would say, Genet has taken the plunge. Why did he not remain a pure existence, a pure evil will? This evil will declared that it was sovereign. Is sovereignty therefore no longer enough for it?

Yet this new reversal was almost necessary. It is explained by both the *structure* of criminal action and by Genet's *inner bent.*

First, by criminal action. As soon as Evil is achieved, it changes; Being deals with it in its own way and engulfs it. The evildoer betrays Evil, as we have seen. But that is not all: Evil also betrays the evildoer. Crime is the criminal's snare: he wanted to transform as much Being as possible into Nothingness. But as his act is an *achievement,* Nothingness is at the same time metamorphosed into Being and the sovereignty of the evildoer turns into slavery. The quest of Saintliness is, firstly, a defense of Genet against the betrayals of Evil.

As long as the experience of Evil remains at the stage of solitary rumination, it is a princely *cogito* which reveals to consciousness its particularity with respect to Being. I want to be a monster, a hurricane; everything human is alien to me, I transgress all man-made laws, I trample upon all values, nothing which *is* can define or limit me. Nevertheless, I exist, I will be the icy blast that will destroy all life. Therefore, I am *above essence:* I do whatever I like, I become whatever I like and I escape what I have just become because I decide to will the contrary of what I willed. I have no law other than my whim because whim, which is contradictory and fleeting, baffles all definition. I contemplate ironically, outside of myself and even within myself, where education has deposited them, the imperatives of the collectivity. They are there, but they no longer have any effect. I have shelved the world, Being is lit up by the dim light of nonbeing and the universal by that of the exception. The most clear-minded, most carefully premeditated decision to do evil remains a dream, it is a flickering of creation. How could I fail to want to eternalize by an act the wonderful instant in which Nothingness holds being suspended in brightness? The crime is a miracle; it will place legality in abeyance. One can kill only in lordly fashion. "And what if everyone did the same?" But the point is that *I* am not everyone. "And what proof have you?" Nothing other than the act itself. Wonderful, dizzying freedom of the Evildoer: Terror.

I commit the crime. All at once this whole phantasmagoria bursts like a bubble: I am again a being in the midst of other beings. In killing I have *given myself a nature. Before,* I dreamt of proving by my crime that I escaped all essence; *afterward,* my essence is my crime, it strangles me in its iron grip. It was meant to reveal to the universe the power of the exception, of particularity; and now it is incorporated into being and becomes an object among other objects; it enters statistics. What was it? An act of incest, a rape, an infanticide? There is a certain number of rapes, infanticides and acts of incest per year. The number will be no higher this year than last. Am I a monster? Probably: but monsters are categorized, compared. Sociologists, criminologists and psychiatrists are going to dissect this supposed miracle and reveal the rigorous laws that govern it. But, it may be argued, the same holds for all human actions. But the fact is, it doesn't: a technical invention, a work of art, have a positive content which remains irreducible. After you have explained Racine by his environment, by the age, by his childhood, there remains *Phèdre,* which is inexplicable. But as the evil action wills itself as pure destruction, when you have reduced its perpetrator to being only a *case,* only an illustration of contemporary society, there remains no residue; the crime is the criminal's failure. The culprit considers his act, that highly individual act which changes into a universal before his eyes, and he no longer recognizes it. The stupidest murderers will be content with muttering until the day of their execution: "I don't understand what I did." Others will yield, like the Marquis de Sade, to the ignoble intention of minimizing their offense: "All that fuss," he wrote from the Bastille, "because I whipped a whore."

Those who do not deign to repudiate themselves and who remain haunted by the obscure and glorious dream from which they have just awakened have only one expedient: they must *save their crime.* Not the great atrocity which they thought they had committed and which disdainfully rejected all justification, but the low, petty offense which they actually committed. And what does that mean? It means that since the evildoer, as a result of his crime, has fallen, has sunk into being, he will be able to save his crime by integrating it into being. Less well-tempered minds will dissolve Being into Good without intermediary; it was *right* to kill: the victim was a Jew, a Negro, a Communist. But if the criminal is tough-minded, he will want to remain an evildoer to the very end. This means that he will build a world system for the express purpose of justifying violence. But the latter will thereupon lose its sovereignty: it was a miracle against the grain, the lofty assertion of a right to exception, an extraordinary attempt to keep the universal suspended in the particular and being in nonbeing; it didn't give a damn about theories; it could will itself, live itself, *exist itself,* but not think itself, not deduce itself from principles. It was the unique and the ineffable. When the criminal has built, on the basis of being, an ethic of Evil which in *certain* cases legitimates *certain* acts of destruction, his crime will become a pure and simple application of the ethical law. Pure numerical individuality will substitute for his particularity. Whereupon Evil, in becoming the generating principle of *all* crimes, goes over to being. Though remaining nominally Evil, it subtly grounds itself, in secret, on an ineffable, invisible and dreadful good. The ethic of Evil is artfully completed by a religious mystery.

Such is the case of Genet. He steals in glory. Then, beaten and mocked, he is merely a petty scoundrel, the weakest of all burglars, the hoodlum, the pansy. The detectives search him and find in his pocket the tube of vaseline which he used in intercourse. They burst out laughing. Once again, the original crisis, the crisis which is forever repeated, overwhelms and metamorphoses him. The two moments of transformation correspond to two moments of self-defense: the "poetic" thief viewed himself as a *prince of evil;* the ridiculous tramp becomes the *female saint.* When he decides to steal, to betray, he does Evil for Evil's sake, without a reason, haughtily, by the simple, divine decree of His Will. When he serves his sentence, he *has done* Evil *in order* to attain abjection and the most utter destitution, in order to suffer. Before and during the crime, Genet wills suffering because it is the index of Evil; after it, he decides that he willed Evil for the suffering which he experiences in prison. In short, there is a time for wickedness: that of praxis, and a time for Saintliness: that of reflection on praxis, of retrospective interpretation of his activity. *Before:* "I, Genet, am doing Evil because such is my own sweet will. No ethic or philosophy can be derived from theft." *Afterward:* "Brethren, one must suffer." The retrospective illusion transforms the demoniacal project into a religion of suffering. Of course, once the principle of Saintliness has been established, the latter will remain as a permanent system of interpretation, and Genet will later refer to it *at the same time* as he refers to the explanation by the will to Evil. One can see the wiliness of this reversal: Genet claims to be saving Evil; in seeking suffering he does not cease, he says, to will the worst. Isn't suffering an Evil? Does it not horrify? And what about abjection? And self-hatred? May it not be that this bouquet of torments is the Supreme Evil? In willing Evil first, Genet wills, by the same token, the simplification and diminution of his moral person, and also destitution, failure, torments, the triumph of his enemies, the final punishment. All of this, as we have seen, is rigorously deduced from the concept of evil will. But if he should suddenly take it into his head to will this destitution, these torments, this failure, *for their own sake,* if he should take pleasure in doing so, we have an ethic of abjection, an ascesis which paves the way for itself to Saintliness. The motive of this sophism is that it preserves for suffering the *negative* value which it had in the system of Evil (when it was deduced from evil will), while integrating it into a positive ethic whose supreme end is purification. Since he is seeking suffering *for its own sake*, it thus becomes *a* good. But while asserting that it is his major end, he continues to maintain that it derives from Evil and that it is an Evil in itself and for itself. Whereupon Saintliness, the ideal of the one who is seeking suffering for the Evil that it does and, simultaneously, Evil for the suffering that it causes, is both good and bad, an appearance of Good which melts into Evil, an appearance of Evil which melts into Good. Genet therefore thinks that he has saved his offense in its very contingency while preserving the absolute right of Evil. If some invisible observer made the following comment: "So you see, you flaunter of vice, you wanted to blow up the world and what have you done? You committed a trivial little theft which was clumsily executed and which you didn't even carry off since you've landed in the jug," he would proudly reply: "You miss the point. I wanted the theft to be a botch. I willed its failure. I, Prince of Evil, wanted to be arrested as the clumsiest of hoodlums. In like manner, Christ chose to be incarnated in the most wretched of men. This ridiculous mess is my Passion." Let us imagine that the observer insists, that he asks Genet: "So it's for the beauty of sacrifice, for the love of Saintliness, that you made yourself abject? So you're pursuing Good in your own way, like everyone else?" Genet will answer: "Not at all. For the evildoer's failure is the necessary consequence of the will to do evil. The evildoer wants the action to be *conceived* as a terrifying sacrilege and *at the same time* wants it to be reduced, in the execution, to a mediocre, common-law offense. Insofar as he conceives it haughtily, he is a prince of Evil; insofar as he accepts it with suffering and humility, he is a Saint. But whichever his attitude, he remains the same evildoer."

Furthermore, the ambiguity of this asceticism, which is both good and evil, is itself an Evil, for it misleads. Later, when we examine Genet's work, we shall see him taking pleasure in constructing aberrant notions, the aim of which is to shake the tranquil assurance of honest folk. The name he has given to his present attitude is willfully blasphemous. He offers us a caricature of Saintliness, a diabolical and deceptive image which looks like the Saint but which burns with hell-fire whoever touches it. Thus, he takes every precaution: if he is driven into a corner, he will readily admit that he has been diverting himself at our expense, that he was only trying to shock us even more. If he has taken it into his head to give the name Saintliness to this demoniacal and spurious perversion of a sacred notion, it is because he felt like committing a sacrilege. Everything is set to rights again: Evil has been saved by being integrated into an ethic of Good; and when one tries to draw closer to this ethic, one realizes that it was only a mirage: it vanishes. But Genet is lying to us again: he wants to hide his defeat; he maintains that he is still a faithful partisan of Evil, but he has already sided with Good. He longs for Saintliness, he wants to acquire it. What is it that he wants? To be. To be a saint, to be an evildoer, it doesn't matter: to be his being. His fierce will to make contact with himself has not been dissipated. No doubt it was not involved at first. We have been examining in this chapter only his will to do, that is, the impulse to defy that made him, in each particular case, do what was expected of him; in short, the worst. But his passion for being influences from afar his practical will, just as a storm at sea influences the local sky. He acts, to be sure; he poses Evil as his supreme end; but at the same time he steals a glance at a fundamental and unformulated goal, which is to become what he is. Finally his acts change into gestures, his most heinous crimes are only incantatory dances which will make his sacred personality descend into him.

But the situation into which he has been put is such that he can affirm himself only by denying himself: his being is that of the evildoer, and the evildoer is relentless in destroying being. In order to touch his reflection, Narcissus plunges into abjection, into failure, into impotence, and when he makes contact with himself, he encounters only an abstraction, the empty shape of nothingness. This will to find himself, so clear in its principle, clouds over as soon as he starts to execute it. How is it conceivable that he must destroy himself systematically in order to endow himself with being? In a particular act, his position is tenable: self-destruction, when not carried out completely, can pass for the obverse of an act of self-creation. By informing on his friend for money, Genet loses love and gives himself greed. But if he is to carry the attempt to the limit, absolute self-destruction will have to coincide with absolute self-creation. Genet joins Jouhandeau, who finds all of being at the moment of sinking into nothingness. The latter, however, kept a card in reserve: God. Will Genet, who has done without that card, get out of the difficulty? His answer to our question is the Saintliness "trick." In order to grasp it, let us go back to the starting point.

He had chosen to contradict the general will in himself by a particular will. If he dreamt of killing a child, it was because he discovered within himself a respect for childhood which is common to all men. He now goes even further and chooses to contradict his particular will by another particular will: he betrays the person he loves. He is thus unable to discover his being in any of these wills: neither in the general will, which is immediately contradicted by a particular will, nor in the particular will, which will retain its sacrilegious character only if the general will is maintained against it, nor in the will to love, which presupposes the will to betray, nor in the will to betray, whose function is to contradict the will to love. *Who* is Genet? Nothing other than the contradiction itself, the pure instant when the Yea is in the Nay and the Nay in the Yea. Positive and negative should cancel each other, Yea and Nay should clear the board. He would thus attain pure nothingness. In that way, Genet *would be* nullity. But it is precisely consciousness which effects the opposition of the contradictions, and this consciousness is all the more acute in that the opposition is stronger: "I felt myself protected by the fabulous power of the Reich. Nevertheless, in my heart I was aware of the intense and incandescent presence of Jean Genet, who was mad with fear. But perhaps I had never been so aware of myself as in such moments. When I kept Jean clinging by the teeth to the muzzle of my revolver, the fear also shrank my center of consciousness by making it more intense. The fear of killing combating the fear of not killing." In short, this consciousness which wants to annihilate itself, this consciousness which is torn by contradiction, becomes, by the same token, the unity of the contradiction. Genet calls this paradox—which shifts from nothingness to existence and from conflict to unity and according to which one exists all the more in that one wants all the more to annihilate oneself—"the impossible Nullity."

Thus, the moment in which Genet's immediate consciousness borders on annihilation is precisely that in which his reflective consciousness *exists* most. It *exists*, but it *is not*. It is a supreme lucidity which watches its own destruction. No matter, he has the solution: since consciousness is all the more acute in that the contradiction is the more unbearable, since he exists all the more as a self-torturer in that he is closer to dying as a victim of himself, it is this consciousness that must be transformed into being. It must be given the somber density, the massive permanence, of fever. The being which he demands for it is thus the being of things. It must be able to be without having to act its being: *in itself*. But to be thus is to be in the manner of objects, and the object presupposes a subject for which it is an object. If Genet wants to discover the secret being of his consciousness, he must find out in *whose* eyes this consciousness is secretly an object.

Since childhood he has been living in a state of anxiety. The truth about himself escapes him, and yet others know it: they see him. First, it was the decent folk: when he lied, when he stole, innumerable eyes focused on his immediate consciousness, saw through his lies, were able to recognize him for the evildoer that he was. In order to combat them, to wrest his truth from them, he tried to watch himself, he spied on himself, but reflection did not disclose to him the *being* of his consciousness; it merely lit up more clearly his transparent moods. The Other's gaze did not disappear thereby. It, too, jumped to the higher level, and this time it focused on the reflective consciousness. While this consciousness is busy deciphering the immediate consciousness, it feels that it is being spied on. But this invisible witness has changed its nature and is no longer the stupid chorus of honest folk. It is Genet himself, but *Genet as Other.* The divine gaze, a stranger within the immanence, impassive, absent, divinized, perceives what underlies the poems, the language, the events, reads what is going on inside Genet as if he were an open book and deciphers his silent truth. The child grows up, leaves the theological age of childhood and enters the abstract, metaphysical age of youth. The personal God who contemplated him withers, becomes schematized; the idol changes into a metaphysical virtue. It is now merely a glassy, impersonal, absent gaze whose sole reason for being is to recover the *truth* which is eluding Genet's consciousness.

This is the moment for assigning it a new function. Since this shadow of a gaze changes everything upon which it touches into an object, it must petrify the reflective consciousness while the latter is at grips with itself. It is to this gaze that Genet's *being* will appear, and this being is merely the obverse of existence. "I think, therefore I am. I am a thinking substance." If Descartes has substantified thought, it is because he believes that God sees him: as an object for an absolute being who knows what is true and what is false, his truth is to be an absolute object. And Genet, in like manner: "I do Evil, therefore I am. I am an evildoing substance." This imaginary gaze of the God in whom he has ceased to believe is a crystal whose perpetual touch produces a perpetual crystallization. Genet is thus petrified at the moment when his existence is most intense. This absolute subject is *elsewhere,* for a certain gaze, an absolute object. And since this reflection which goes over to being is precisely the sparkling lucidity whose maximum intensity coincides with the radical dissolution of the human, since the extreme limit of annihilation marks the supreme intensity of the reflective consciousness, the maximum of *existence* becomes, for the gaze which *fixes* consciousness at this crucial moment, the maximum of being, but in reverse. The trick is done: destruction changes back into construction, the zero moment becomes identical with the moment of plenitude, the mystery of the impossible nullity discloses that of the ineluctable substance.

But then what is the difference, in the last analysis, between Jouhandeau and Genet? Simply this: in the former, God has remained a subject, He is a Person; in the latter, He has been transformed little by little into a simple power, He has become both the impersonal operation of objectification and the pure medium in which existence is refracted into essence. In short, He is now only the general and abstract condition for the transition to being. This God ends by being only a kind of bondsman; He becomes identified with Genet's unshakable optimism; He guarantees Genet that his wretched, suffering life has, somewhere in the absolute, a *meaning*. In short, there is henceforth a dimension of the sacred in which Genet's acts sculpt a statue for him.

But this mad hope is Genet's veritable treason. This time he is not betraying Evil for a worse Evil. He is simply going over to Good with bag and baggage. It is true that he wills himself an evildoing substance, but, however evildoing it may be, since it is a substance it is good, for its permanence and density come from being. And Being is Good.

Furthermore, Saintliness conceals a form of quietism, for he who does not believe himself to be a *substance* knows that he is only what he makes himself and that he cannot cease to make himself without ceasing to exist. As long as he is alive he must struggle, and everything must always start over again. Past successes cannot facilitate future victories. But, on the other hand, there is in Being a kind of inert perseverence: it can neither emerge from nothingness nor return to it without some external action. *To be* a Saint is therefore *to continue to be,* to take advantage of acquired momentum. Whatever the combats in which he engages on earth, Genet is relayed, in the abstract heaven where existence changes into essence, by the passivity of substance. Saintliness is eternal rest, it is that which has been attained, it is the reward. "In the midst of this suffering, it seemed to me that there remained—shame having burned me all over—in the midst of flames or rather the vapors of shame, an unattackable matter, of a shape formed by sharp, severe lines, a kind of diamond rightly called solitaire." Impossible to put it better: is not the diamond the quintessence of being? Of course

Genet has never claimed that he *was* a Saint, but only that he aspired to become one. In that case, to rest in being would be an ideal, the conclusion of a perhaps infinite progression. But to progress in Saintliness means to accumulate a little more being with each denial, with each betrayal. Genet may never finish his statue but he does not cease to shape it.

And, in addition, Being is, above all, *reconciliation*. One cannot imagine conflicts within it since it is, by definition, positivity. But Genet is photographed at the moment of the wrench, when his consciousness is torn by contradiction: loving and betraying, willing Good in order the better to do Evil, lowering himself in order to rise, annihilating himself in order to exist. For nothing in the world would this evildoer, who is relentlessly trying to live reality in all its conflicts, be willing to effect a synthesis of the contradictory elements. It is not unity that he wants, that gentle dream of Leibniz, of Aldous Huxley, of all naïve optimists, but laceration, division, despair. The following words of Jean Wahl are as applicable to him as they are to Kierkegaard, in fact more so:

"[He] wants to make things difficult, to do nothing that will blunt the terms of the problem. There is no possible meeting of these absolute oppositions. We no longer have mediations but paradox and the leap, the pathos of thought, the fever of thought. Here we are no longer in the world of homogeneity but in that of radical heterogeneities, of qualitative differences, of absolute novelties. And the absolute will no longer be that which unites, but, in conformity with the origin of the word, that which is separated and that which separates."

But the sly recourse to Being enables him, as it does Kierkegaard, to make the Leap. He rejects unification, but so manages matters as to have unity all the same. He will not synthesize opposites, but their reconciliation will take place by itself in being, or rather they will identify with each other without reconciling. Since he will *there* have all the more being in that he exists more and since the measure of his existence is the violence of his contradiction, the more he contradicts himself *for himself,* the more he *makes himself be in himself,* in a state of unalterable peace. The transition to being is not at all comparable to the Hegelian synthesis on which the thesis and the antithesis are based. It transports the conflicts to a ground of absolute positivity. There is no *solution* of the antinomies. But as there is no place for negation within being, the terms of the opposition lose their negative power. They are always contrary, but instead of repelling each other and of each being the other's nothingness, they interpenetrate. The willful and actual unity, whereby freedom made the contraries exist by virtue of and in opposition to each other, hardens into a substance, and the opposites are "stuck" in this mold, which hardens. In the calmness of being there is identity of discord and harmony. Breton wrote in 1930: "Everything leads us to believe that there is a certain point in the mind from which life and death, the real and the imaginary, past and future, the communicable and the incommunicable, the high and the low, cease to be perceived as contradictions. Surrealist activity has no motive other than the hope of determining this point. It is thus obviously absurd to ascribe to this activity a solely destructive, or constructive, tendency. The point in question is a fortiori that at which construction and destruction can no longer be set against each other. . . . [It will be] the annihilation of being within a blind, inner diamond which will no more be the soul of ice than that of fire." It is precisely this "point in the mind" that Genet is seeking. But Breton hopes, if not to "see" the superreal, at least to merge with it in a unity wherein vision and being are one and the same. Genet knows that enjoyment of it is denied him on principle. He can only set up his own superreality off to the side by a destructive movement which is a construction, in reverse, of being. In reverse, love and betrayal cease to "be set against each other"; in reverse, the high and the low cease to be perceived as contradictions and the greatest Evil is at the same time the greatest Good. In reverse, "the annihilation of being within a blind, inner diamond" becomes production of a diamond, that is, of pure being. Breton's superreal, perceived as the inaccessible and substantial reverse of existence, is Genet's Saintliness.

In short, what has he done? Examining his procedure from the point of view of logic, I would say that it resembles Descartes' in every way. There is in Genet a methodical doubt carried to the point of destruction of everything, a *cogito* of Evil and, in the end, an unforeseen return of substantialism. But as it is a matter not of knowledge but of praxis, we must realize that this logical reversal conceals a more or less obscure will to re-establish an order of Being and Good. It has been reported that he refused to make the acquaintance of Gide, because, he said, "his immorality is suspect." I would go further and would say that *all* systematic immorality is suspect and covers up a last recourse to Good. For Evil cannot be system: either it is an explosion or it is nothing at all.

However, it is not true that Genet is simply seeking to substitute one ethic for another, as Gide did, and as did Nietzsche and Stirner.

He has sincerely attempted to liquidate *all* ethics, that of anarchists as well as others, because every ethic implies humanism and humanism is the bugbear of this outcast who has been relegated to the inhuman. We would do better, once again, to compare Genet to Kierkegaard. They both wish to prove through action that the order of religious values is above and beyond the humanist ethic. For Genet, man's end is not man, not even the Superman who can appear only at the conclusion of a *social* evolution; it is, rather, to destroy, within himself, time, history and the human so that the reign of the eternal and the divine may be born *in the instant*. We come back to our starting point: the sacrifice. Abraham sacrificed only his son. Genet sacrifices the world and himself in order to have access to the universe of the sacred.

Should he be reproached for having *made the leap?* I haven't the heart to do that. One would first have to decide whether Genet wills evil *in order* to be a Saint or whether he is really eager to lose and whether his recourse to Saintliness is only a consolation that he accords himself, a hope that he allows himself in order to lighten his difficulties. But how is one to know? Does Genet himself know? At times it is one and at times the other, depending on the oscillations of his inner tension. I do not doubt that he sincerely seeks despair and failure when he is at his best. Saintliness is above all a great fever-dream that haunts him when he is a prisoner and cannot act. And even then there is something suspect about it, something that is indefinably disturbing. To reduce the Evil that he does to being only a means of attaining Being would be to impoverish his moral life. For it can be said with at least equal truth that Being is for him only a means of attaining the greatest Evil. I grant that Saintliness is the supreme goal of his efforts. But it is also an infernal caricature, the worst blasphemy. Moreover, I would like to know where one would find a more lucid spirit than his, for this outcast is the only one to have discovered the secret of humility, a secret about which the most loquacious Saints have succeeded in saying nothing. Attempting to define Saintliness, he writes tranquilly: "I think that it is called pride and also humility."

But even if I refuse to judge the ethic of Saintliness, I look at it through Genet's eyes, and I know that it is his only way out. Then, these quibbles and this procedure move me as does a cry of pain. They are a passionate casuistry. But if I stand away from it and, ceasing to regard it as the subtlest stratagem of this Ulysses, if I see it as an anonymous ethic that is offered up amongst many others, and without any recommendation, I immediately condemn it. And *in every shape and form*. Our decent folk are deeply moved by St. Labre, but they are slightly repelled by the befouled tongue of Marie Alacoque. But, after all, she nursed the sick. Besides, the French bourgeois doesn't dislike shit, provided it is served up to him at the right time;* he is "Rabelaisian," that is, he talks about purges and enemas while eating dessert and in his heart he merges the sexual organs with those of excretion. The gentleman from Poitiers who strolled through the corridors of his house wearing a bowler hat and sniffing at a full chamber pot is a saint of our bourgeoisie. As for myself, I am not as fond of shit as some people say I am. That is why I reject Saintliness wherever it manifests itself, among the canonized saints as well as in Genet;† and I smell it, even beneath their secular disguises, in Bataille, in Gide, in Jouhandeau. Always for the same reason, to wit, that it is, to my way of thinking, only the mystical bough of the generosity of consumption.

And besides, all this labor of the soul is, at least in the case of Genet, without any deep efficacy; it is all rhetoric. He lowers himself in order to elevate himself, but the elevation and the lowering remain symbolic. I am sure that he has betrayed very little, and mainly in thought. If he has betrayed more than I think he has, his treacherous acts would have ruined their victims without changing him. His whole system of Saintliness, as I have patiently expounded it, is based on the following principle: that betrayal effects a metamorphosis in the soul of the betrayer. If we are to believe Genet, he would destroy in order to destroy himself, would inform on his friend in order to make himself unworthy of loving, would descend, one by one, the rungs of the ladder of Evil. But the fact is that I don't believe him: he argues with himself, destroys himself sym-

---

* "The Frenchman . . . is an animal of Latin breed. He does not mind filth in his home, and in literature he is scatophagous. He is mad about excrement . . ." (Baudelaire, *My Heart Laid Bare*).

† The friendly feeling of the bourgeois for his excrement, of Mr. Bloom for "his own smell," pushes our civilization of solitude and individualism to its ultimate consequences. The individual, abandoned, lost in an indifferent or hostile society, coils about himself and attempts to find recourse in immanence against impossible transcendence. This abject intimacy, which is often that of the married couple itself and of the family, originates in the fear of the *outside*. These organic odors, waste products, stale smells symbolize the closed unit (which lives by itself and on itself) that each individual or family group wishes to become for want of a social valorization and a *recognition* of the *person*. Coprophagy is probably not a widespread sexual vice, but the conjugal climate disposes people to it more or less everywhere. Amongst us, coitus does not differ much from the digestive functions; it prolongs them; the couple really tries to become a single animal that smells itself, broods over itself, sniffs at itself, touches itself with its eight groping paws and pursues in the dampness of the bed the sad dream of absolute immanence.

bolically, suffers in the abstract, forgets his suffering, is reborn of his ashes and goes off to love elsewhere. All this intense destructive activity takes place on the spot and without his moving a muscle. One always forgets that the soul is elastic. I can readily imagine this rhetorical whirlwind in Genet; I can also imagine these vain and irritating efforts to mimic remorse, suffering and destitution, these efforts to transform a nothingness of suffering into a suffering before nothingness. He does not suffer and suffers at not suffering, he therefore suffers and is delighted that he suffers, therefore he no longer suffers, then he is delighted at no longer suffering. He suffers: this is the feeling of his downfall; he was won. He does not even suffer: the reason is that he has fallen too low to suffer; again he has won. It all takes place in the monkish cell in which he has been locked up, and one must keep busy in a cell. These abasements are the exact counterpart of the spiritual elevations of monks. States of soul. Meanwhile, the world runs its course.

Dialectic of being and dialectic of doing, quietism and activism: the contradictions of this divided soul can best be compared to the latent conflict in any religious collectivity between salvation by works and salvation by faith.

For faith is not simple belief in the Supreme Being. It becomes a humble and passive awaiting of His coming. Moreover, would it seek Him if it had not already found Him? Could it await Him if He were not already there? It is God who awaits himself through the believer. It is God who will attain himself in the mystical ecstasy, which is a fusion of the Subject and the Object. There is thus nothing to do but to await the sudden fulguration that will fill us with *being*, that will make of our fleeting consciousness the sheath of God. Genet, who has a mystic sense of himself, beseeches himself and awaits himself. He is the swooning female worshiper who asks to be pierced by the divine sword. The language of the female saints has amazing erotic overtones. Mystical possession is, in their case, a sublimated dream of amorous possession. In Genet, who gives his body to the Pimps, those handsome embodiments of Evil and Eternity, it is amorous possession which is dreamt as mystical possession. Thus, his faith impels him toward a fundamental quietism. He hates action, which is so vain, so limited. When God becomes incarnate in the beloved, Genet mimes with his body radical passivity and the return to nothingness: his breath is taken away, his legs melt beneath him. Sacrificial lamb, victim of "the cruel bird," he collapses, he dies. The ceremony is completed in the luminous darkness where the All and the Nothing coincide. Genet's amorous trances bring to mind irresistibly the swoons of Madame Guyon.

But all religions aim at governing our conduct. It is by action that we acquire merit, provided our intentions are pure and spring from the heart. It would be vain to seek God, to await Him; we are not in the world to enjoy Him but to serve Him. In order to acquire merit, we must try to forget that it is conferred by good deeds; we must act only for the love of God. Action, which is prescribed by a severe religion and which is prompt to show us our original downfall, calls for a certain hypocrisy: we must be unaware of what we know, must do Good for God alone when it is our Salvation that is our sole concern. If faith leads to quietism, the tense voluntarism of works leads to formal dryness, to Pharisaism. In any case, militant action, which is prescribed by sacred books, cannot be reconciled with passive waiting for God. Sadism or masochism, willful tension or abandon, dryness or effusion, discursive or intuitive reason, respect or love, militant or contemplative life, categorical imperative or passive beatitude: a choice must be made. One of these attitudes aims at the alienation, the disappearance, of the Ego, of freedom, of consciousness; the other, grounded in a kind of agnosticism, affirms with stubborn austerity the dignity of man, that finite creature, fallen but free. Yet they coexist in every religious syncretism; both are to be found in the most simple prayer, and the same words, "Lord, I will do thy bidding, I will be thy servant," are used for expressing them both. The same holds for Genet, who wants to find salvation by faith, by the abandoning of the I-subject to the I-object, and by works, by the militant achieving of Evil on earth. But he has taken the contradiction upon himself and has wished neither to underestimate it nor to resolve it. A spontaneous choice of taking himself in hand, of mastering his life, of espousing his destiny has been refracted in an impossible situation; he has had to express himself in two divergent directions. A second choice, a reflective choice, which is brought to bear on the first, has made this divergence more manifest: he has chosen to be this fundamental conflict, to exist simultaneously in two dimensions which are mutually exclusive, to explain himself at every moment by two frames of reference and to justify himself by two scales of value. And since he is playing the game of loser wins, let us say that he has decided to destroy himself at the same time by works and by faith. Genet's originality lies in his wanting to be and in his being the nonsynthetic unity of his contradictions.

We have assumed the existence of order in the chaotic richness of this mind and have attempted to examine separately the two dialectics which are fighting for it. We must now return to the disorder: since the characteristic of a "religious nature" is syncretism, it is in its syncretism that Genet's mind has to be studied. We must focus our attention on the nondifferentiation of what has actually been experienced, the interaction of the contradictory systems. Genet is eighteen years old, a thief, beggar, tramp, homosexual, traitor, evildoer, female saint, hidden divinity. He leaves prison to fall into the Court of Miracles and the Court of Miracles to return to prison. I have just made a chemical analysis of this divided soul: it must now be recomposed. I shall undertake to draw a portrait of Genet the adolescent.

CAIN

The eye was in the grave . . .

I shall not dwell on his voluntarism. We know that this soul is utter will, even in the passive waiting for Good. It is no longer a matter of explaining Genet by his history or of deriving his attitudes and behavior from an original choice. I wish to describe him from within, as he appeared to himself at about the age of eighteen.

1. The Emotional Climate

What can this child, who is not very fun-loving, and who is also deprived, find to love in life? Nothing, unless it be life itself. But he does not take it on the organic level. He refuses to abandon himself to the viscous chemistry of his body; he *does not love* his body. What he prizes above all is the self-awareness of consciousness. This frame of reference to which everything refers and which refers only to itself, this twofold aspect of thought which makes self-contact with certainty, is an absolute value. It is absolutely good that there are consciousnesses, in particular, that of Genet. Seeing, knowing, thinking are good. It is better to see than to be blind, to be blind than to be dead. The worst of misfortunes is still a stroke of luck, since one feels oneself living when one experiences it. Worries may cloud his optimism but no experience will challenge it, for it is prior to experience. It is one and the same as the passion for living, for being present and being aware of it, in the midst of all. This admirable and childish passion will save him. If life has not broken him, it is because he has always thought that nothing could hold a candle to life.

Life is made impossible for him. He was rushing toward the future with a spontaneous drive; the future, unalterably evil, breaks his drive. Genet gets into the habit, despite himself, of anticipating the worst; he continues to live only by sheer will, out of defiance, by fighting against the desire to die; he even asserts that he is dead. Has he lost his passion for living? Not at all. It has been put entirely into the austere undertaking to survive. The vital impulse which sustained a child's immediate desires has been blocked; it shifts its course and inflates the reflective consciousness. Genet directs to himself his feverish expectation, his curiosity, his confidence. His naïve, immediate consciousness, disappointed, thwarted, lacerated, groans with suffering. But there is a kind of enthusiasm and joy in the way he broods over it and listens to its groaning. He observes himself, spies on himself, works on himself with fiendish interest. When he feels hopeless, he becomes impassioned again; he is impassioned about his hopelessness. This child martyr knows every affliction except boredom. He has placed himself on the level of reflection in order to guide and, no doubt, understand himself and certainly also to place himself as high as he can above the rising tide of horror, but his chief concern is to hound himself.

Is it possible that he no longer ever has spontaneous desires, that he no longer ever dreams of a mitigation of his lot? Does this taut will never relax? And does this austere heart never feel the mad, youthful wish to exchange the martyr's palm for less difficult joys, for happiness? That would be too much to expect. Nobody achieves perfection, and, besides, this monstrous child is, after all, only a child. His childhood dreams are still close to him, and his optimism is so virulent that he sometimes has to defend himself against hope. Deep in his heart, the little hoodlum "with delicate tastes" has never ceased, will never cease, to long for all that life denies him: he is poor, and is filled with wonder by luxury; he is despised, and wants to assert himself by ostentatious generosity; he is an illegitimate child, and likes to imagine that he is the descendant of a great family: "Without thinking myself magnificently born, the uncertainty of my origin allowed me to interpret it. . . . My childhood imagination . . . invented for me (so that I might there squire about the slight and haughty person of an abandoned little boy) castles, parks peopled with guards rather than statues, wedding gowns, bereavements and nuptials." If he is willing to follow the natural course of his daydreams, they will help him to escape the dreadful reality of his life and to enter a vanished world: chivalry, heroic and lavish aristocracy, traditions, festivals. He learns to love this feudal, monarchic society through cloak-and-dagger novels. His first idea of luxury is inspired by popular songs: "The severe, naked world of factory workers is entwined with marvels, the popular songs . . . and these songs have phrases which I cannot think of without shame if I know they are sung by the grave mouths of factory workers which utter such words as: succumb . . . tenderness . . . ravishing . . . garden of roses . . . villa . . . marble steps . . . sweethearts . . . dear love . . . jewels . . . crown . . . oh my queen . . . dear stranger . . . gilded room . . . lovely lady . . . flowered basket . . . treasure of flesh . . . golden waning . . . my heart adores you . . . maiden with flowers . . . color of the evening . . . exquisite and pink . . . in short, those fiercely luxurious words, words which must slash their flesh like a ruby-crested dagger." For all his persistent will to become a monster, Genet's sensibility remains fresh and naïve, with a certain folk quality. He is thrilled by a facile kind of poetry: "Diamonds, purple, blood, flowers, oriflammes, gold, crowns, necklaces, arms, garlands, palaces, the icy, gleaming poles of the revery of the people." He himself says of his imagination that it is "in love with royal pomp" and that it embellishes the world with "ideal gilt." Later, in prison, he will take delight in shopgirl dreams: "It was the period of sober luxury. Divine cruised the Mediterranean, then went even farther, to the Sunda Isles, in a white yacht. She was always forging ahead of herself and her lover, a young American, modestly proud of his gold. When she returned, the yacht touched at Venice, where a film director was taken with her. They lived for a few months through the huge rooms . . . of a dilapidated palace. Then it was Vienna, a gilded hotel, nestling beneath the wings of a black eagle. Sleeping there in the arms of an English lord, deep in a canopied and curtained bed. Then there were rides in a heavy limousine . . . and off again to an elegant Renaissance castle, in the company of Guy de Roburant. She was thus a noble chatelaine . . . then back to Paris, and off again, and all in a warm, gilded luxury, all in such comfort that I need merely evoke it from time to time in its snug details for the vexations of my poor life as a prisoner to disappear, for me to console myself, console myself with the idea that such luxury exists. . . . I invent for Divine the coziest apartments where I myself wallow."

Then come the ordeal, the reformatory, the hardening, the will to assume his abject situation. If he still indulges in his childish daydreams, it is because he now assigns them a precise function in his ceremonies of sacrifice. These naïve desires help him to suffer. He cajoles them because he knows that they must remain unsatisfied. He abandons himself to dreams because the more gilded they are the more painful is the awakening. Their value for him lies in their making the horror of his condition more real. Were it not for these violent and spontaneous demands, he would perhaps put up with his wretchedness, he would wallow in it, he would resign himself. But the expiatory victim must be panting and horrified when it is led to the sacrifice. In order for his abnegation to have greater value, he must reject suffering with all his might. He now has other wishes: "The atmosphere of the planet Uranus is said to be so heavy that the ferns there are creepers; the animals drag along, crushed by the weight of the gases. I want to mingle with these humiliated creatures which are always on their bellies. If metempsychosis should grant me a new dwelling place, I choose that forlorn planet. I inhabit it with the convicts of my race." The *man* Genet has chosen himself. He therefore fears lest an unforeseen stroke of luck, an inopportune wave of happiness, weaken the inflexible severity of his choice. After relating how a little stolen money gave him for a moment the right to live like everyone else, he adds: "However, I was held back by my ingrained habit of living with my head bowed and in accordance with an ethic contrary to the one which governs the world. In short, I was afraid of losing the benefit of my laborious and painful efforts in the direction opposite to yours." He does not want his childhood wishes to be fulfilled; he retains them as wounds. The desires that well up in his immediate consciousness aim at being satisfied, but his *reflection* is delighted that this satisfaction is always denied them.

All his feelings are thus of a reflective nature. In each of them we find the curious symbiosis of a spontaneous desire which impels itself toward the world with naïve confidence and of a parasitic mental state whose only support and only food is the primary state which it directs, contradicts, adulterates and maneuvers. These twinned feelings are rare among simple souls, more frequent among the sophisticated. Thus, one can love and be ashamed of loving—and be all the more ashamed the more one loves. For Genet, reflective states of mind are the rule. And although they are of an unstable nature in everyone, in him they have even less equilibrium because the reflection is always contrary to the reflected feeling. He suffers and delights in suffering because he wants to defy his tormentors and because he sees in his sufferings the proof of his election. He is ashamed and he is proud of his shame. Is it joy that prevails or grief? Shame or pride? We find in him for the first time —but not the last—the ambiguous structures, the false unities, in which the two terms of a contradiction relate back and forth to each other in an infernal dance. I shall refer to these hereafter as whirligigs. He oscillates from a suffering in which the joy is only verbal to a joy in which the suffering is only an emotional abstraction. His consciousness is filled with empty assertions: I am joyful, I want to be joyful, I must be joyful. But frequently, too, equilibrium is achieved. Stress is spontaneously placed in the reflective consciousness, and, as we have seen, it is in this consciousness that all Genet's optimism has taken refuge. Consequently, since the best of himself and the maximum intensity of lighting are to be found in the reflective consciousness, the reflected consciousness wilts slightly, loses some of its brilliancy. It becomes merely a buffer between reflection and the world, a gelatinous transparency which makes external dangers less threatening. Genet sees the world through a window-pane. He may suffer dreadfully, but there will always be something cozy about his suffering because his consciousness caresses itself. He witnesses his misfortunes; he is present at them. Often, in fact, he relates them to himself, magnifying them in the telling. The interior of his mind is a consciousness stuffed with itself, like the prunes of Tours.

The basic component of these ambiguous states of mind is amazement, a fixed perplexity in the face of the misfortunes which tirelessly exceed his hope. Try as he may to look reality squarely in the face, he sometimes wonders whether he is dreaming: the real has an aftertaste of nightmare. But his amazement is mainly reflexive: Genet and the sphinx in a single person. Can one imagine the strange flavor that this consciousness has for itself? "Who am I? Why do I alone suffer so much? What have I done to be here? Who has destined these ordeals for me?" There is an answer to all these questions, there cannot fail to be an answer: that is what arouses his optimism. In fact, he himself is the answer; he will find it in finding himself. At every moment he perceives his own Ego as a vocation, as a call, as an expectation that will be fulfilled, as a promise that will be kept, as a suffering that will obtain for him eminent merits. But *who* calls him? *Who* will count his merits for him? *What* promise has been made? To whom? He sometimes falls into so deep a state of wonder that he thinks he is going to lose consciousness. In the Mettray mess hall he remains with his fork in the air, looking into space, forgetting to eat. To such a degree that the director of the reformatory, who has received a report from the supervisors, thinks it advisable to have him examined by a psychiatrist.

Nevertheless, his states of amazement are proof of his mental health. Contemporary writers think they have discovered the absurdity of the world and of man in the world. Genet is at the opposite pole of their conception. A man who considers life absurd does not dream of being surprised at his individual misfortunes; he regards them as confirmation of his theoretical views. But if Genet is astounded by the course of the world, it is precisely because events seem to him to have a meaning. In *The Myth of Sisyphus* Camus mentions some of the trivial experiences which sometimes reveal to us the fundamental absurdity of our condition: there are days when my best friend appears to me a stranger; what seems to me absurd, in this case, is that this stranger knows me intimately, that I have obligations to him. This is precisely the kind of experience that Genet does not have: his lovers and tormentors do not disconcert him because of their absurdity, but because of their *strangeness.*

As Camus sees it, the thin crust of meaning sometimes melts, disclosing the raw reality which signifies nothing. In the eyes of Genet, it is reality which tends to be effaced in favor of meaning. A given Pimp is an angel, a given guard is another. The word "angel"—which we encounter frequently in Genet's early works, and increasingly less thereafter—must be given its original meaning. An angel, an *angelos:* someone has sent him to Genet. Unfortunately, things and people are words of a foreign language. It always seems to him that they are assembled into sentences which speak about him, but he understands nothing of what he is told. In short, metaphysical intuition of the absurd leads to nominalism; that of Genet orients him toward a vague, Platonic realism.

Genet, a strange phenomenon in the universe, sees the universe as strange. Experience reveals to him in every object, in every event, the presence of *something else;* he senses the *supernatural.* And is it not precisely the sacred which thus manifests itself through the profane without ever letting itself be touched? The world is sacred because it gives an inkling of a meaning that escapes us. And Genet, an enigma that requires a solution, is himself sacred in a sacred world. The life of this adolescent is an uninterrupted experience—accompanied by horror, by amazement, by hope—of the Sacred within him and outside of him. That is probably what we shall have the greatest difficulty in understanding, for our consciousness has been secularized. Piece by piece, our life has been torn away from religion. For the more zealously devout, there are religious sectors and profane sectors. Genet constantly experiences the sacred in its ambivalence.* Since his optimism passionately rejects the absurdity of the universe, Genet's apparition, like his history, must present a meaning. He was born in order to manifest. By the manner in which he becomes aware of his being-in-the-world, he distinguishes himself from both the young bourgeois who knows that he is a *man by divine right* and the young worker who feels in his very bones that he has the contingency of a weed. Like the former, Genet feels his being as a *being-born-for*. . . . The dreadful and ceremonious circumstances of his birth are sufficient to dismiss any idea of contingency. He has been born *in order* to be abandoned, rejected, placed in the hands of strangers. Nevertheless, like the worker, he knows that he is exiled from that formidable culture center which is bourgeois society. But this very exile must have a meaning. All his misfortunes prove to him that he is *doomed*. He is called to account for all his gestures, all his feelings; he is responsible for himself and for the world; but he does not know in whose eyes this responsibility is manifested. He is the *oblate*. If you want to sense his inner tension, the urgent, racing rhythm of its duration, imagine him as an expiatory victim who is being led to the place of sacrifice and whose heart is torn between horror and enthusiasm.

2. The External World

Even a life which has been dedicated unreservedly to the sacred has its profane moments. But Genet is silent about those moments. He barely experiences them and absent-mindedly lets them go by. Although he has to dress and walk and eat and work, he absents himself and plunges into his meditations. Unless objects or events speak to him expressly of his martyrdom, he feels only indifference for what is around him. He *does not see* landscapes, even the most beautiful in the world. He *does not enjoy himself* amidst others who are having a gay time. He does not know sensual pleasure, for it presupposes an abandon of which he is no longer capable. Cold, courteous, secret, ceremonious, he makes himself suspect to all and takes as much pleasure in displeasing people as in charming them: his priestliness isolates him.

One may think that he is unaware of reality. But not at all, for

---

* "In commenting upon Vergil's phrase *auri sacra fames*, Servius (*Ad Aen.*, III, 75) points out . . . that *sacer* can mean both 'accursed' and 'holy.' Eustathius (*Ad Iliadem*, XXIII, 429) observes the same double meaning of *haghios*, which can express at the same time the notion of 'pure' and 'soiled.' And this same ambivalence of the sacred appears in the Paleosemitic . . . and Egyptian world." Mircéa Eliade, *Histoire des religions*, Payot, p. 27.

nothing can prevent its being present for all of us in its entirety and our being steeped in it. Genet perceives *all* of it, like everyone else. Does anyone think that Genet sees this chair, this sky, otherwise than we, that he goes up a flight of stairs any differently than we do? His perception *must indeed* be as full as ours; even his remoteness derives its particularity from the situation in which he finds himself: one turns one's mind away *from* this or *from* that: it is the prison that gives the escape its form. No, the difference lies elsewhere. On the level of signification. For us, most of the objects around us manifest an organization which refers to precise ends and finally to man himself: a city is only a collection of tools arranged in fitting order, it reflects to us the image of human reality; to Genet it signifies his exclusion from the human race; things *do not speak* to him.

1. *Tools.*—We are surrounded by utensils which have been manufactured by and for men and whose final end is any man. The industrial products that make up the urban landscape are the social will bottled and canned; they speak to us of our integration in society; men address us through the silence of these products: they are injunctions, recommendations, sometimes questionings or explanations; a new tool is the reverse of a new gesture. The gesture is described in a leaflet of instructions that we are given with the tool; when we perform it for the first time, we are engaging in a ceremony: the just man who uses a new corkscrew or the latest type of can opener plunges into the fine heart of society, perceives, through the object, the manufacturer, the merchant, the jurist, who advise, suggest, command delightfully. It is out of love of man that Americans buy gadgets, for the pleasure of hearing the sermonizing voice of the specialist ring out in the solitude of their apartments, of their lives; tools veil from us our forlornness.

Tools have nothing to command or forbid the disintegrated, vagabond element, the wandering individual who is Jean Genet. Of course, he is not unaware of them. He has read the notice tacked on the wall, he knows that the mat at the foot of the steps is a request that he wipe his feet. In fact, he will obey the injunction. But his act is only a feint: what does he care about leaving muddy footprints on the stairs when he has come to break into an apartment on the fourth floor? The mat was put there by a just man for other just men, by an owner for other owners: "Please leave this place as clean as you expect to find it when you enter." Genet will rub the soles of his shoes on the horsehair of the mat, but he does so in order to pretend to be one of the just, so as not to attract the janitor's attention. The low wall that encloses a field or an orchard cannot *prevent* one's entering: it *forbids* one to enter. But the prohibition is all right for the others, for the strollers who have never been in trouble with the police; for the hounded thief it loses all meaning. Nevertheless, it is there; he sees it; he cannot fail to see it, just as he sees on the sign which suddenly looms up in the woods where he is hiding the injunction not to smoke. Strange demands which confirm him in his generality as a human being and which are neutralized at the same time by the ban cast on his particularity as a thief. The wooden fence, the dead tree that may catch fire, the field through which a borderline runs, are rigid, upright thoughts, thoughts which are still human but which have no living bond with men, which have been frozen by a taboo; they speak to Genet of the lost paradise, of the Eden where even prohibitions bring men closer together. They perhaps evoke in him a desire to obey, to *do* as others do, to be *like everyone else*. But obedience would be vain and harmful. A burglar who was being chased by a fireman entered a public park. He saw a big lawn with a sign forbidding access to it: "Keep off the grass." The burglar had a longing for order: he went around the lawn. The fireman took the shortcut and caught him. Genet will not be so stupid: he ignores the reminders that are set all along the way, that gleam for a moment and then fade out. Yet, in a certain sense, they do not concern him: each of them is a reminder of his exile, each of them seeks in him the social man, the just man, and does not find him. All these frozen indexes show him in his abjection, in his guilt. Through them the society of the just *looks at* the guilty man; things have become the inert support of men's gazes. I am quite familiar with that sullen gaze: at a time when I was overworking, it pursued me everywhere, I was being hounded. Windows were eyes; I was entering a field of absolute visibility in which the magical identity of the gaze and the light was achieved. A dead gaze, a dead light. I looked for the source of the gaze and saw only windows. Windows with something added: the cold, livid brilliance of a petrified transcendency. Genet is the chosen victim of these mineral gazes. In short, the finality of utensils arraigns him.

What will he do? Will he flee those scornful looks? Not by a long shot. He is going to react. But how? Three ways lie open to the exile, three only. Genet takes all three simultaneously.

The first—the simplest—is to take upon himself the exile that is imposed upon him. Rejected by things, the outcast rejects them in turn, that is, he lies beside them like a thing, like a corpse. He replaces practical and technical connections with things by relationships of simple contiguity. I shall call this his attempt at quietism. We already know that Genet simulates death and aspires to contemplate the activities of decent people from his grave. He thereby deliberately deprives himself of all means of understanding the human enterprise. Of course he continues to be aware of practical ends: he knows that such-and-such a manufacturer aims at producing in greater quantity and at lower cost, that certain workmen are striking for higher pay, that certain consumers are uniting against retailers in order to buy goods at wholesale, that certain groups are fomenting an insurrection so as to seize power. But since he contemplates the world "from the realm of the obscene (which is outside the scene of this world)," since he refuses to be integrated into the human undertaking, the end that men pursue and the values that they pose appear to him as simple *facts*. It is a fact that certain men want to command, that others want to found a family. What of it? Human ends are dead, they float with their bellies up. Petrified ends, ends corroded from below, invaded by materiality, seen from without by an angel or a beast, ends *for others*, for a zoological species to which the quietist does not belong. Thereupon, the instruments rebel: each goes its own way. If it is no longer entirely obvious that one must get up every morning, must dress, must be neat, then a pin appears as an implement which is both too familiar and inscrutable: "I had the revelation of an absolute perception as I considered, in the state of luxurious detachment of which I have been speaking, a clothespin left on a line. The elegance and oddness of this familiar little object *appeared before me without astonishing me*." For a man who observes with indifference that the children of others go to school, a bus becomes a huge, absurd hornet whose idiotic task is to ingurgitate and pour out an interrupted stream of travelers. It becomes strange and comical that "the bus, which was full of serious and hurried people, would courteously stop at the diminutive sign of a child's fingers." Since Genet refuses to participate in men's effort to create an *antiphysis*, the bus reverts to nature, it is a voluminous assemblage of metal and dead wood. Not quite, however: since a man who has left his class and cannot return to it is called a déclassé, I would say that there are, for the quietist, declassed minerals. They have been exiled from the mineral kingdom by a kind of malediction: the stamp of man. When Genet considers the "rolling stock" which is going downhill, he places himself first only at the viewpoint of *physis:* from this point of view, that moving body should obey the law of gravity. If it stops

because a young, hairless animal has lifted a finger, that is an absurd little miracle, a laughable suspension of natural laws. The
stop would, indeed, have meaning only from a human outlook. But
quietism is a symbolic destruction of the human. "I felt I was perceiving things with blinding lucidity. Even the most trivial of them
had lost their usual meaning, and I reached the point of wondering
whether it was true that one drank from a glass or put on a shoe."
Tools float between Nature, which cannot produce them by herself, and the realm of man, which the quietist does not want to see.
We have noted that Genet used language in reverse; this inversion
now extends to the universe.

One can assume this sulking attitude for a moment; one cannot
maintain it permanently. Even at Mettray one has to eat, to dress,
to undress. If quietism were carried to an extreme, it would mean
death. Besides, in effacing the signification of tools, Genet runs the
risk of effacing the reality of the world. His abstentionism with respect to action changes into absenteeism in relation to being. Motionless, quiet, hardly breathing, I no longer have any way of
distinguishing being from appearing. One starts by wondering
"whether it is true that one drinks from a glass" and one ends by
no longer knowing whether the glass exists. As a result of not testing the real by action, one does not know its consistency; the world
becomes merely a flat, kaleidoscopic multiplicity. Genet has at
times a wild desire to do violence to the indifference of being, to
act, and, since he is forbidden to do so along common lines, then
let it be by havoc. He will know the density of being through the
effort required to destroy it. He will steal, will smash, will waste
in order to gouge all those eyes that are watching him. Theft is not
only a means of livelihood, it is a sacred destruction. In a burglary,
one must rip fences, break open doors, elude traps, kill dogs, allay
the suspicion of watchmen. If all goes well, one *enters a man,* for
the gaping, defenseless apartment, naked and paralyzed, is a man.
It reflects a person, his tastes, his ways, his vices: "I do not think
specifically of the proprietor of the place, but all my gestures evoke
him. . . . I am steeped in an idea of property while I loot property.
I re-create the absent proprietor. He lives, not facing me, but about
me. He is a fluid element which I breathe, which enters me, which
inflates my lungs." It is not enough to says that one rapes this live,
fluid person: one mutilates him. Gloved hands ransack that open
belly, pluck out the liver, grab a knickknack, a family heirloom.
This rape which is followed by murder is symbolic: thieves are so
aware of this that they want to achieve it in their flesh. Turn the

pages of Genet's works at random: such-and-such a burglar gets an erection when he steals,* another vomits on the banknotes that he takes from a drawer. "Guy almost always sits down and eats in the kitchen or the looted drawing room. Some burglars go to the can after ransacking the place." They are miming destruction in a kind of cathartic crisis. Then, a new destruction begins: the stolen object was, before the larceny, at its maximum power, unique, priceless; it was defined by its consumer value, by its integration into the objective person that an apartment is, by the family's devotion to it. The thief practices upon it an operation which is the inverse of appropriation: he converts the consumer value into exchange value: "I tore his watch from the buttonhole of his vest where it was held by a chain. 'It's a souvenir,' he murmured. 'That's just it. I like souvenirs.' I smashed him in the face." At that point there begins a series of drops in potential: disguised, the object becomes anonymous; it loses its inner substance, its inner life; transformed into money, it becomes for the thief a pure and impersonal purchasing power. In addition, the "fence" pays less for it than it is worth; if the sum must then be shared by accomplices, the degradation is complete: there is no longer any relationship, not even a quantitative one, between the jade Buddha that was once brought back to the head of the family by his naval officer grandfather, and the four or five banknotes in the thief's pocket. It should also be added that the money which has been acquired is unproductive: no investment is possible, no capitalization that is the source of new creations. It is squandered, it goes up in smoke. Thus, theft is a destructive operation that ends in the radical liquidation of the stolen object, in the disorganization of a whole, in an impoverishment of the human world. Now, our acts draw our portrait in being; the *created* object presents to the creator his own person in the realm of the objective. But to destroy is to create nothingness. In constructing, I externalize myself really among beings; destruction represents the resorption of the universe into myself. The Louis XVI drawing room which Genet has just entered signifies "French bourgeoisie"; it is *the* French bourgeoisie which piratically took over the furniture of a ruined aristocracy; our bourgeois society, with its values, myths and ceremonies, is present in its entirety in the driftwood of this memorable wreck. Genet, forcing drawers and breaking the panes of consoles, wants to attain the being of the bourgeoisie. In like manner, Caligula required that

---

* Bulkaen declared: "When I break into an apartment, I get a hard-on, I lubricate" (*Miracle of the Rose*).

the Senate have only one head so as to be able to cut it off with a single stroke. The bourgeoisie has only one drawing room, *is* only one drawing room. Genet will be the gravedigger of the European bourgeoisie. Since the others, the just, define themselves by their operation, since they are called masons, carpenters, architects, why should he not be defined by his? The truth of the constructor is the constructed object: Genet aspires to find his truth in the object he destroys; he thinks he is transformed into a proprietor by the negation of all property: "The decision [to leave the place of the theft] is born when the apartment contains no more secret corners, when I have taken the proprietor's place." And he writes as follows about Bulkaen, a petty burglar who likes to be called Kid Jewel: "It may well be that Bulkaen was in his own eyes only a constellation, or, if one prefers, the constellation of the jewels he had stolen. And that heightened the beauty of his icy flame." The honest woman owns jewels, she adorns herself with them. Bulkaen, who is excluded from the society of the just, cannot have them: he becomes a jewel himself. But this is a delusion: he imagines that the objects he destroys or disperses *change into his own substance* as food changes into the substance of the one who consumes it. The fact is that they do not, for there is no assimilation here. The image is misleading. It is true that the stolen objects reflect to him his being, but as they glide off into nothingness, the being which they reflect to him is in the process of *gradually disappearing*. The acts of destruction which he performs define him in his own eyes as a faceless force, an increasingly naked power, an increasingly abstract terror. The degree of degradation of his activity is exactly the same as that to which the object on which it operates is demolished. It moves, at the same time as the object, from the complex to the simple and from the living to the inanimate. It is a warlike fury when it is directed against a man, a senile and mechanical violence when the man is dead and it keeps hacking at his corpse. In the end, exhaustion lays the murderer out beside his victim: the murder is a suicide.

These ways are dead ends. In vain does Genet turn away from the world of instruments: he transforms being into appearances, everything escapes him, he drifts toward death. In vain does he then turn upon tools in order to force their inner resistance: he succeeds only in breaking them and in being changed into formless violence; society reorganizes itself elsewhere with its prohibitions and its utensils.

There remains the third way. A utensil, as we have seen, is the crystallization of a collective imperative which addresses itself within us to the average man, to the *uomo qualunque,* to the ordinary member of the community, and which requires conventional acts whose main characteristic is generality: *one* detaches the paper by cutting along the dotted line. Now, it so happens that, by a curious perversion of the course of the world, the *general* exigency of the tool relates to the solitary and the outlaw in their individuality. In being refracted through certain rigorously particular situations, the universal "instructions for use" present themselves to Genet as a queer, hybrid, half-individual, half-collective imperative, as an order which is no longer given to anyone or by anyone and which nevertheless remains an objective solicitation, which is not reducible to the simple reflection of an individual desire: "It was the sisters' clothes that gave Culafroy the idea of running away. All he had to do was to put into action a plan that the clothes conceived by themselves." To the nuns, these garments propose traditional acts which were long ago determined by the Church. Through them and through the intermediary of the dressmakers who made them, all of Christian society addresses itself to the sisters. Every morning they find in their robes the image of their sacrifice and of their dignity; the garments reflect to them their integration into the community of Christ and their rejected, neglected, yet ever-present femininity. Culafroy, as a prisoner, as a young boy, has nothing to do with a skirt and a coif. Nevertheless, he lights up these objects with his guilty desires: as a prisoner, he wishes to escape; as a boy, he dreams of a secret femininity. Society responds to his wishes with a twofold prohibition: thus, it is not society that addresses itself to him through the intermediary of these garments. And yet social exigencies, animated by his desires, begin, all by themselves, to concern him. The buttons are there to be buttoned, the skirt to be slipped on. Buttoned *by him,* slipped on *by him.* At the very moment when these imperatives address themselves to Culafroy, they cease to be social by becoming objective. They are secret solicitations—valid for him alone—that are born spontaneously of the garments. The gown and the headdress outline the image of a false femininity and of an escape without danger. The gesture is in the thing; it waits; it is a magical power. If Culafroy dresses up as a nun, he will be possessed by outlandish behavior; an outcast and homosexual nun will establish herself within him to govern his movements. But he will know the perverse joy of turning against men their own instruments. In order to escape from the just, the most decried of children uses the sacred garments that the just respect. The ideal thing would be to kill a blacksmith with his own hammer.

At times one almost does that: a complex system of gestures and tools takes shape before the outlaw's eyes and suggests to him an act of destruction. An old man suffocates in Our Lady's presence, a pair of hands try to loosen a necktie. The just will see in this spectacle only an occasion for helping, for affirming human solidarity. In a highly integrated society, the major ends are common to all, and the goal that others have set up becomes an exigency for each individual. The tie *must* be loosened, the tool must be repaired, readapted to its function. For the entire society, an instrument that has deteriorated is a disgrace that must be eliminated instantly; the fate of mankind, of *homo faber,* is at stake symbolically in every automobile that has broken down, in every airplane accident, in every watch that is out of order. But Our Lady, a pariah, a fairy, doubly excluded from the collectivity, perceives the act in reverse. His mad, obscure desire to destroy society becomes embodied in the rebellious object. He is in sympathy with the constricting necktie, not with the hands that loosen it. If a child drowns, Our Lady is the water that engulfs him; if a woman cries "Fire," Our Lady is the flame that licks and bares her. For the outlaw, an object becomes a tool the very moment an accident makes it unusable and harmful to others. The broken instrument is outside the law; among all the airplanes of a standard model, the one that goes down in flames is a black sheep; the outlaw becomes embodied in cars whose steering gear breaks, in horses that bolt, in masts that come crashing down on the decks of ships, in all utensils that turn against their creators and are all the more dangerous in that they have been granted more power. Our Lady lends the tie a hand, he helps it strangle the old man.

The exceptional gestures, which are acts in reverse, envelop the universal and that which challenges it. The social imperative inhabits them but in reverse, having become the magical exigency of things. They turn to account the work of others in order to destroy, and the useful in order to engender the gratuitous. Absurd even in the eyes of the one who makes them, they are, like the evil impulses of which Baudelaire speaks in *The Glazier,* the manifestation of the other, of the Devil in person. Genet calls them poetical: "Harcamone's crimes—the murder of the little girl, in the past, and, more recently, the murder of the guard—will appear to be idiotic acts. Certain slips of the tongue enlighten us about ourselves, replacing one word by the other, and this untoward word is a word whereby poetry escapes and perfumes the phrase. The words are a danger to the practical understanding of the statement. Similarly, certain acts in life."

Perhaps this poetic and demoniacal utilization is the only true relationship that the exile can maintain with the instruments and property of the society that exiles him. But it should be observed that these occasions are very rare. They can thus define only a quite exceptional relationship of man with things. And, in addition, the evildoer abdicates to the advantage of things; it is the things which indicate the gesture to be performed and it is the man who becomes their tool: Our Lady strangles on behalf of the tie. The gesture he performs is nobody's, above all not his: the destructive power of a tight slipknot has installed itself in his fingers, knots them around a throat and tightens them. He will be able to say, like Green Eyes: "It was fatality that took the form of my hands."

In short, the tools surrounding him are congealed, crystallized values that continually manifest to him his exile: they are human ethics graven in the inertness of matter; if he tries to break down their resistance, he succeeds only in destroying them; he can, at times, believe that he has used them, but it is actually they which have used him. A choice must be made: Genet will destroy the object if he takes hold of it; he will let himself be destroyed if the object takes hold of him.

2. *Nature.*—Will he at least have commerce with the great natural forces? Is not Nature precisely the region of being which man has not yet been able or never will be able to reduce to the state of tool? Since men have driven him out, it is for the inhuman solitudes to welcome him.

No. Nature is a utensil too. And it is social: "He [Feuerbach] does not see how the sensuous world around him is, not a thing given direct from all eternity, ever the same, but the product of industry and of the state of society. . . . Even the objects of the simplest 'sensuous certainty' are only given him through social development, industry and commercial intercourse. The cherry tree, like almost all fruit trees, was, as is well known, only a few centuries ago transplanted by commerce into our zone, and therefore only by the action of a definite society in a definite age provided for the evidence of Feuerbach's 'senses.' "*

That is exactly how the just man usually sees nature, that is, when he is a city dweller and reads statistics in his newspaper.

---

* Karl Marx, *The German Ideology*. Translated by W. Lough. Revised and edited by Roy Pascal. London: Lawrence and Wishart, 1942, p. 35.

"Landscape" is viewed as "land." Land is defined by its resources; its configuration is accounted for by the property system and agricultural techniques; the animals that live on it are transformed into cattle; the famous solitude of the country is merely a lesser density, a deplorable effect of the exodus to the cities, a situation which can be remedied by appropriate means.

But several times a year the urban communities of honest folk decide in common—taking into account the necessities of economic life—to change their attitude toward the big farming areas. On a given date, town society expands, plays at disintegration; its members betake themselves to the country where, under the ironic eyes of the workers, they are metamorphosed for a while into pure consumers. It is then that Nature appears. What is she? Nothing other than the external world when we cease to have technical relations with things. The producer and the distributor of merchandise have changed into consumers, and the consumers change into meditators. Correlatively, reality changes into a setting; the just man on vacation *is there,* simply there, in the fields, amidst the cattle; reciprocally, the fields and the cattle reveal to him only their simple *being-there.* That is what he calls perceiving life and matter in their absolute reality. A country road between two potato patches is enough to manifest Nature to the city dweller. The road was laid out by engineers, the patches are tilled by peasants. But the city dweller does not see the tilling, which is a kind of work that remains foreign to him. He thinks that he is seeing vegetables in the wild state and mineral matter in a state of freedom. If a farmer goes across the field, he will make a vegetable of him too. Thus, Nature appears at the horizon of the seasonal or weekly variations of our society; it reflects to the just their fictive disintegration, their temporary idleness, in short their paid vacations. They wander through the undergrowth as through the damp, tender soul of the children they once were; they consider the poplars and plane trees planted on the roadside; they find nothing to say about them since they do nothing about them, and they are astonished at the wonderful quality of this silence. If they seek Nature on the outside, they do so, in reality, in order to touch their own depths. The quiet growth of the forest reflects to them the image of a blind and sure finality; it makes them feel that social life is a surface disturbance. There is an order of the instincts that does not differ basically from the order of the world and that can be found in oneself when one abandons oneself to a sweet, silent swoon in the presence of plant life. But childhood itself is social; the powerful natural instincts which they seek in the depths of their heart are only the symbol of the legitimacy of their birth. The natural order which they perceive outside of and within themselves is quite simply the social order. Nature is a social myth; solitary self-enjoyment in the bosom of Nature is a ritual moment of life in society; the sky, the water, and the plants merely reflect to the just the image of their good conscience and of their prejudices.

Driven from Society, Genet is also driven from Nature. This homunculus who is a by-product of social chemistry, who spends his life all alone in the presence of all, has never felt natural. He dwells, of course, in the midst of the world: he has to, since he lives. He sometimes walks on the roads, wanders through the fields. But even if he is in the open country, he remains in exile. The site refuses to contain him, he is nowhere. He sees nature in reverse, and it appears to him bristling with human meanings. There would be no point in his seeking in it a refuge against man, for it is a big domesticated animal, a servant of the just. It is man whom he touches in the moss, whom he perceives in the vague movement of the foliage. This movement flees him; it will reflect to others the vacancy of their souls; it will represent for others leisure and abandon. Nature is the property of the others. In this road which, for the city dweller on vacation, is only a quiet flow, a solidified stream, Genet sees first the labor of the workers who condemn him; in the plants which grow in the fields, he sees that of the country folk who have driven him out. Everything is possessed, worked, occupied, from the sky to the subsoil. That which nobody owns belongs to the Nation, that community of decent people who reject him. It is not only the urban landscape but the entire universe that decomposes before his eyes into a collection of manufactured objects. Exile gives this child a mode of perceiving Nature which renders things artificial. This signifies that the "sensuous certainty"—which is at the same time a quiet self-certainty—remains foreign to him. In the flora of suburbs—he rarely gets far away from cities—he sees the product of human labor; the cherry tree is a social *act;* the very forest speaks of man: it is the property of a great lord, it is a reserve of firewood, it is a "national park" that the State takes under its protection. This tract of land is cut in two by an ideal line: the *frontier.* For Genet, this line is the essential thing, the tract is only a prop: on the other side of the line he will cease to be guilty; another society is going to welcome him. He deciphers meanings that are encrusted in bark or stone. In the very air there are meanings that float about, midway between the condensation of human thoughts and the scattered evanescence of natural events. Customs officers are hiding at the approaches to these frontiers, the wheat fields conceal policemen: no more is needed, all nature smacks of man. These meanings become sense organs: flowers are ears of policemen, trees have a gaze. Later, the words "await," "attentive," "attention," will characterize for him the mute, motionless kingdoms of the vegetable and the mineral: "The trees were caught, motionless, *attentive,* deathly pale and naked, captured by a net of hair or the singing of a harp." Thorns are "studded with black eyeballs." The water of a river "rolls with such solemnity that one would have thought it was delegated by the gods to render perceptible the slow course of the drama." Here is "the motionless foliage of the plane trees . . . animated by the very spirit of tragic waiting." Here is a day of mourning: "Perhaps the sun set and rose several times, but a kind of fixity—which was mainly in the gaze—made people, animals, plants and objects remain awake with flawless lucidity. Each object preserved within itself a motionless time from which sleep was banished. It is not in exceeding twenty-four hours that this day is lengthened: it draws out the moments, and each thing observes them with such attention that one feels nothing can get by. The trees in particular want to surprise: their immobility infuriates me. . . . The toothbrush glass of the colonel's wife makes its crystal observe a deeper self-communion. It listens. It registers. The trees can toss about, shake their feathers in the wind, they can growl, fight, sing, this agitation is deceptive: they are on the watch." As for night, it is at times a black light that dissolves him in the nothingness of things uncreate, an elementary consciousness which thinks him not as a finite mode but in the primitive lack of differentiation of infinite substance: he takes shelter in it as in a heart, no other can see him. Not that he is invisible; he is visible only to the calm, nocturnal gaze that spreads him like an ink spot on a great dark curtain and plunges him into his native "sweet confusion." At other times, Night denudes him: he alone is phosphorescent and scintillates against a black background, visible to the infinite and for the infinite. In any case, whatever the moods he ascribes to Nature, he is never alone there: he pursues his dialogue with the Just by means of new symbols.

There are times, however, when this strange gaze, which is both natural and social, petrifies or "vegetablizes" him. One can recognize in Genet the "Medusa complex" of which Bachelard speaks in connection with Huysmans and which he defines as "the way of sharing in the contemptuous hardness of stone by living, sympathetically as it were, the antipathy of hard matter, by making oneself a hard and indifferent matter." This "petrifying reverie," the origin of which is anger and resentment, can assume two distinct forms, one "extrovert," the other "introvert." It is, of course, introversion that characterizes Genet's reveries. To be sure, he retains "the desire to impose the immobility of stone upon the hostile world," but the stress is laid on the petrification that has been undergone. "Inland, I went through landscapes of sharp rocks that gnawed the sky and ripped the azure. This rigid, dry, malicious indigence flouted my own and my human tenderness. Yet it incited me to hardness. I was less alone upon discovering in nature one of my essential qualities: pride. I wanted to be a rock among rocks. I was happy to be one, and proud. Thus did I hold to the soil. I had my companions. I knew what the mineral kingdom was."

The "introverted reverie of petrification" leads us back, says Bachelard, "to the time when a father's gaze immobilized us." In the case of Genet, no father is involved. It leads us back to the moment of the original crisis. He was first petrified by the gaze of the Just. Genet might subscribe to the following verses of Pierre Emmanuel:

> . . . our limbs
> Are petrified in postures of sin
> Our gaze is a radiating of prayer.

At other times, beneath the gaze of plants, he has a sweet, passive dream of vegetablization. "I stopped shaving the down that Salvador found disagreeable, and began to look more and more like a mossy stalk." This is a homosexual dream. Soft, juicy, drooping stalk, defenseless against the fingers that break it in order to pick its flower. Genet, white and gentle, is lost in the undergrowth like a penis in pubic hair. The stiffness of the stalk, which is passive and slightly arched, is that of his prick in erection.

But, one may ask, in what way does he differ from the good citizen who devotes his vacation to changing himself into water, pebbles, sky and flowers? The difference is that the good citizen thinks that he effects his metamorphoses because he lives in sympathy with Nature; he modifies his inner rhythm; he falls into unison with the grass, the birds. But in the case of Genet, the universal gaze transforms him into a stone or a plant, which is a new way of signifying his exile. In the countryside, he is the Other for the rye and the wheat, for the stream, for the rocks "which flout him," just as he is, in cities, the Other for the passers-by. He plays the role of a rock

for an audience of rocks, that of a tuberose for a council of tuber-
oses, but always in Otherness, a stone in exile amidst stones, a bewitched plant in the heart of a forest, a tragedian who plays the
role of a king before an audience of kings. Even if he becomes
conscious of being a man amidst things, he does not do so directly,
by testing his power to change the order of the world, but because
their impenetrability, their stubborn muteness and the permanence
of their gaze exclude him from their assembly and inform him of
his humanness as a sentence of banishment. Man is the rock that is
other than all rocks, the plant that is other than all plants, the rose
"absent from any bouquet."

In its essence, Nature is a *gaze*. But it is also a *thing gazed at*.
This watchful gaze has always been the object of a gaze. Not of
Genet's gaze. Of a fundamental, objectifying, petrifying, absolute
gaze, that of the Just.

Genet is hidden in a Czech forest; his eyes are on Poland; he is
going to sneak across the border. The Poland which he is going to
enter illegally is an empty apartment, out-of-doors; he breaks into
it as if he were committing a burglary. But this golden plane is
seen; customs officers are perhaps hiding in the rye fields. In any
case, it is known, carefully watched by the police; it has been a
subject of negotiations; the line which divides it was established by
a treaty; and, lastly, it is implicitly present in the minds of all the
Just: it is mentioned in geography books, it contributes to shaping
the *physiognomy* of the Poland whose history, myths and culture
have fixed its traits. Genet is going to plunge into this country
which has already been seen, into this big reclining woman who has
already been studied, already been judged, who is a subject of a
hundred collective images, a subject that is going to contaminate
him with its visibility. Hidden behind a tree, still invisible, he contemplates it with the gaze that the child turns on things already lit
up by the gaze of its parents. He sees it in the process of being seen
by French eyes: "The borderline ran through a field of ripe rye,
the blondness of which was as blond as the hair of young Poles; it
had the somewhat buttery sweetness of Poland, about which I knew
that in the course of history it was always being hurt and sinned
against." He finally makes up his mind, he stands up, he abandons
his hiding place and enters a bath of visibility: he is making his
way *into a myth*. In like manner, the actor who is smoking his pipe
in the gray, dismal "greenroom" suddenly stands up: he is "on."
He is going to plunge into Elsinore. That means he is entering the
déjà vu, entering a phantasmagoria which is awaiting him and

which is *nothing* if not the vision of others. Genet enters Poland as Barrault enters Denmark every evening at twenty after nine. He is not entering a complex of real activities, a society of men who welcome him, but rather, as he admirably puts it, an image, the image that France has of Poland. "The crossing of the border and the excitement it aroused in me were to enable me to apprehend directly the essence of the nation I was entering. I was penetrating less into a country than to the interior of an image." Thereupon he becomes an image himself, for one cannot enter an image unless one makes oneself imaginary. An imaginary character of a Poland-as-martyr for an audience of just men (doubly symbolized by the customs officers who are perhaps hidden in the rye and by "the white eagle that soars invisible in the noonday sky"), he moves forward, highly visible on this eternally seen land, "with the certainty of being the heraldic character for whom a natural blazon has been shaped: azure, field of gold, sun, forest." He plunges—a future spy—into a handsome, blond, inanimate child and martyr, into the third fictive dimension of a tapestry. As he approaches the painted or woven trees, he feels himself dwindling and disappearing in the eyes of a motionless witness who sees him vanishing into the great natural appearance.

Whether it be a gaze or a setting, Nature escapes him. In any case, things are hollow; they flower in an incomprehensible medium which is called *sight*. They have lost their density, and the only characteristic which they have left, their objectivity, comes simply from the fact that they succeed each other *in the dream of another*. The natural gaze exiles him, metamorphoses him into water, into a tree, into a water that is always other, into a tree other than all trees. But a great major gaze envelops both Genet and nature, transforming the little thief into a figure in a stock image. Rejected *in truth* by the landscape, Genet can melt into it at times, but he does so in the realm of the imaginary.

3. *Miracles.*—Things do not speak to him: they look at him. He flees from the gaze of houses, shop windows, water, flowers; he has no access to the ordinary world. But there are spectacles and events which have no meaning and function for us other than to make us feel our exile or forlornness, in short, the limits of our powers. Genet feels himself designated by those spectacles and events. He discovers in them a finality which escapes us and which is intended only for him. We can understand his calling them *miracles:* they are the procession of sacred phenomena which accompany the pre-destined one and constantly remind him of his predestination. If

the reader has not forgotten what I have said about the ambivalence of the sacred, he will have realized that there are "miracles of horror" and "poetic miracles."

In the miracle of horror, the Sacred is revealed in its terrifying aspect. Miracles of horror: his visit to the French Consulate in Barcelona, his arrest in Spain and the joking of the cops who passed the tube of vaseline from hand to hand; miracles of horror: the pantomime of theft in the Yugoslav prison, the spitting game at Mettray. These are brief, lightning contacts with the world which draw him out of his absence and reveal to him his destiny. He was made to believe that his offenses would lead him to a penal colony or to death. He thus knows the future and there is nothing left for him but to live it; his life is closed, it is a somber, religious melody whose unfolding he foresees to the final chord. But there are certain events which enable him to live his entire life in an instant: profane duration opens up and discloses the sacred time of repetition and fatality. Of repetition: for the miracles reproduce symbolically the original crisis. Of fatality: if he is caught stealing, if he is arrested, the vague, lazy web of daily life rips apart, revealing the irremediable sequence and quasi-mechanical fatality of sacred time. The interrogations, the sentencing, prison, everything is already there, years are present in a single instant and these years themselves link up with other years, other arrests, other imprisonments and ultimately imprisonment for life.

But Genet also knows joys, a far greater number than one might think: only, they are not ours. From time to time, a whispered word, a suddenly discovered spectacle reminds him that the reverse of these disgusts is eternal glory, that his failures *are also* triumphs: the poetic miracle* is a hierophantic event, like the miracle of horror. But what it manifests is the stately and positive aspect of predestination.

We saw above that Genet relentlessly willed his failures in order to transform them into victories, and we have observed him trying to adopt the viewpoint of others on his own adventures: he becomes his own historiographer; he *relates his life to himself* as it unfolds. "He spun round": he speaks of himself in the third person, he expresses the present in the past, he mentally drafts his own golden legend, he is already beyond his death and it is *another* who lovingly broods over his lamentable disaster in order to discover in it a secret success. As if the expiatory victim who is being led to the

---

* One of these miracles gave Genet's second work its title: *Miracle of the Rose.*

place of sacrifice were attempting to borrow the dazzled memory of the crowd that will survive him *in order to remember his future death*. This constant effort of transfiguration does not pay: it remains verbal and abstract. But from time to time it is "relieved." External objects substitute for it, reflect to it its inner concept as if it were an objective structure of being, and bear witness at the same time to the human failure and to a victorious beyond.

Tulle, gauze, lace, veils "unkey his vision"; perception, veiled, blurred, clouded, appears as a recollection, invites to reminiscence; Culafroy has a revelation of the poetic world one day when he sees on the village road "a bride wearing a black dress, though wrapped in a veil of white tulle, lovely and sparkling, like a young shepherd beneath the hoarfrost, like a powdered young miller." These powdered objects manifest their present reality through a transparent layer of pastness; panes of glass insert themselves between the world and consciousness, as does the reflective consciousness between things and the reflexive consciousness. The urgency of being grows dim; nature seems to be remembering herself.

Other and even more poetic objects have a structure of pastness in their very being. It was on seeing red velvet chairs and gilt-framed mirrors in a green field that Genet felt one of his strongest poetic emotions. In the spectacle offered by these profoundly human objects that have been abandoned to nature we recognize Rimbaud's drawing room at the bottom of a lake and Mallarmé's play of being and nonbeing, in short an untenable contradiction. And yet Genet tells us, to the contrary, that poetry eliminates contradiction: "For a long time I thought that the poetic work offered conflicts: it cancels them." It does so because it actually presents them *realized*. Existence exhausts itself in *maintaining* a conflict without a solution; the poem, whether it be a written poem or an object-poem, is this same conflict, but at rest, contained in the calmness of being. The contradiction between the chair and the fields, between the drawing room and the lake, reflects to our eyes the ambiguity of the human condition: man is entirely nature and entirely contranature: he transcends the world and the world crushes him. But this ambiguity which we have to live is here presented to us as a thing; we are given it "to look at." To be sure, the presence of chairs in the meadow entails a positive explanation: they are put outside during house cleaning. There is a reason for everything: tradition, the taste of an age, of a class, of a family, human labor, explain the nature of chairs, their style, their color; the historical circumstances of peasant property explain the configuration of the meadow; climate, hydrography, the nature of the soil, economic necessities, explain the nature of the plants with which it is covered. But when all has been explained, when being is cut and dried, when reason has dissipated legend and dream, then the inexplicable manifests itself like a poetic residue; it is a residue that does not exist, for its nonexistence alone enables it to escape from the cycle of objective explanation, and yet it beckons to Genet, it manifests to his eyes the obscure meaning which remains when being has crushed the vanquished of history, that nonexistent victory of the vanquished which unceasingly haunts the victors. The chair is lost in the field; relationships are immediately established between its colors and those of the meadow; the red of the cloth and the green of the grass manifest their affinities. But contradiction blazes up in the heart of these affinities: the color of the cloth, invented by man and also by time, clashes with the crude green of the young shoots; it speaks of another world. The horizon surrounds the chairs and mirrors; they are lost in nature; but the sharp edges of these articles of furniture are in rigorous opposition to the soft natural curves. Moreover, the human and the non-human change places, move from tool to nature and from nature to tool: geometry is an invention of man, and yet there is nothing that is more inhuman; the sighs of nature are far closer to our contingency. In this sleight-of-hand no synthesis is possible, no pause. The chair evokes a society, an etiquette, ceremonies; but nature hems it in on all sides and strips it of man. It is a ruin; it is haunted by the absence of a house, of a town. It looks like the vestige of a vanished civilization. Yet, dead though it be, it is still at variance with the soft grass whose waves humbly lick its haunted feet. Man no longer is; human significations are seen in the wrong way by the eyes of cows or monkeys; Nature is victorious. But the failure of the human species, which has disappeared from the face of the earth, is a meaningless triumph. Its absence is legible within the nature that has choked it: a supernatural order shows through the *inexplicable* colors and forms which the plants are attacking and are going to cover. For a moment, the child Genet thought that man was dead; the chairs and mirrors spoke to him in the past tense as he speaks to himself about his own life. It seemed to him that a divine hand had placed them in the field as a friendly gesture to him. Divine hand, absolute transcendence: precisely because he saw his foster mother carry out the pieces of furniture and put them on the grass, he knows that an intervention of the Other is impossible; precisely because reason accounts for everything except the strange warning which prophesies the death of the human race, the impossible *must* be supposed in order to explain the superdetermination of the event.

What makes our contradictions unbearable is the fact that they *are* not; we cannot rely on them; in order for them to exist we are constantly obliged to make them; and we, we who maintain them in being, are not either: we make ourselves in making them. Nothing *obliges* Genet to live under pressure, in that unendurable state of tension; and yet he lives thus because nothing *prevents* him from doing so either. But when he discovers a poetic object in the world, it suddenly seems to him that things assume the contradictions which he exhausts himself in maintaining. One would think that they come up very gently, from behind, to help him bear his burden. This conflict of failure and victory, of the possible and the impossible, now suddenly appears as a structure of being. Objects proclaim that there is something beyond life; whereupon the outlaw falls into line; he is freed from his crushing responsibility. And, while discovering a hidden meaning in the arrangement of phenomena, he senses a pitiless and brotherly freedom which disposes things like the words of a sentence in order to speak to him about himself. Being reflects to him, with winning kindness, his own secret. For this reason a vulgar song, when it reaches him through the walls of the prison, moves him more than lofty music. The walls become a song, and the song becomes a wall; the song does not emerge from a man's throat: it is an emanation of the stone; the singer died hopeless, and his voice reaches Genet long afterward, like the light of a dead star. But the fact is that the song is a victory: a human life is resorbed into it as the subjectivity of the vanquished is resorbed into his ideal. Wall and song, chair and meadow: optimism without hope, love without tenderness, a stern brotherhood. His failure, perceived in him by another, perceived by him in objects arranged by another, manifests the triumph of the particular over the universal, of the subjective over the objective community, of the eternal over the historical, of value over fact. The object which offers him this ambiguous signification, which indicates to Genet alone the supernatural, remaining for all other eyes within the framework of nature, is an object-poem. The triumphant loser is doubly elect: firstly, because he alone is designated by the object-poem; secondly, because he alone is able to perceive, through nature, the supernatural.

At first sight, these sacred phenomena seem distinguishable from the miracles of horror in that they are *solicited*. "Poetry," says

Genet, "is a vision of the world achieved by a sometimes exhausting effort of the taut, buttressed will; poetry is willful. It is neither an abandonment nor a free and gratuitous entrance through the senses; it must not be confused with sensuality." The poet goes off to conquer the world; he does not receive poetic impressions—he takes them. The brotherly freedom which comforts Genet by its gentle exigencies is that of Genet himself. He hides behind the mirrors, the chairs, the voice that sings; he lives in a haunted universe, the ghost of which is none other than Genet himself; he engages in a dialogue with himself through the intermediary of things.

But do not the miracles of horror flow into the imaginary? Must not Genet make an effort, to a certain extent, to force them? Astounded as he is by the rigorous precision of catastrophes, horror takes away his feeling for reality; the obviousness of the frightful miracles that overwhelm him gives to the course of the world the necessity of a ballet. It is in nightmares that it suffices to fear the worst for the worst to occur immediately. In Genet, the highest pitch of lucidity coincides with the fright of the dream, and the most acute consciousness of misfortune with the quietism of aesthetic contemplation.

3. Language

Language is *nature* when I discover it within myself and outside of myself with its resistances and its laws which escape me: words have affinities and customs which I must *observe,* must *learn;* language is a *tool* as soon as I speak or listen to someone else; and words sometimes display surprising independence, marrying in defiance of all laws and thus producing puns and oracles within language; thus, the word is *miraculous.* With regard to language, which is both his most inward reality and the most rigorous expression of his exile, Genet adopts very early, long before dreaming of writing, a complex attitude which sums up, in a new unity, his attitudes toward Nature, the miracle and the tool.

Our society, which has been in a state of crisis since the First World War, uses a language that is too old for it. Many words, detached from objects, are adrift; many men who are out of their element in the bourgeois class, isolated by their history and their complexes, have a feeling that language does not quite belong to them. Brice Parain, a peasant boy who became a city dweller, a fighter who returned from the front, a Communist who was excluded from the party, has fallen into a chronic state of amazement in relation to words. Leiris, a bourgeois, son and grandson of bourgeois, feels ill at ease in bourgeois language and his uneasiness gives his writings a stilted quality. Bataille roars with laughter when he contemplates the absurdity of the world, of his body and of the word.

But this strangeness of language is, for all of them, an intermittent phenomenon. Bataille tortures himself "upon occasion"; the rest of the time he is a librarian. Leiris is an ethnographer. Ponge was an insurance agent. Parain works in a publishing house. In order to draw up an insurance policy, to catalogue a library, to communicate precise knowledge about Ethiopian zars or about Dogons one must use language as an exact and plain instrument, in short one must write prose. The fact is that these poets are also members of the bourgeoisie: as valued employees or officials of bourgeois society, their astonishment about language results from a slight and discontinuous maladjustment. The "socialization" of which Leiris spoke in the passage quoted earlier was effected somehow or other. Let us assume, however, that the maladjustment is constant and radical: the moment the child Genet realizes that the word is a "shared thing," that it is "socialized," he becomes aware that this socialization is effected against him; the terms, which belonged only to him, now "open out," but, it so happens, they open out on the language of his foster parents who condemn him and of the villagers who insult him. One can imagine the jolt: all his words are snatched from him! He will remain fixated in this childish amazement.

Genet was condemned to silence: a culprit does not speak. I still remember the indignant astonishment feigned by the adults when, having been punished, at the age of ten, for some misdeed or other, I dared address them. In the case of Genet, the astonishment continues: last year M. Mauriac advised him to remain silent forever. In the old days, they simply cut off a delinquent's tongue; our society, which is more humane, lets him keep his organs of phonation on condition that he not use them. Why should Genet speak? He can only lie or deceive, *since* he is a thief. The truth is that what they fear most is that he may defile words: in like manner, the women of certain tribes must express themselves by gestures; only the men have the right to use speech. If he violates the prohibition, one must neither listen to him nor, above all, answer him: one would be taken in or compromised. What is worse, in agreeing to carry on a dialogue, one would be maintaining, if only for an instant, a reciprocal relationship with him. When he is caught, the cops will require that he keep his mouth shut until he is questioned; during the questioning, he will have to answer briefly. *To answer:* not allowed to ask questions. As if they were lending him language the better to confound him. If he uses it in order to deny, they beat him: actually, he is not allowed to talk except to confess. In prison, silence. Five years, ten years of silence; if he is sent to a penal colony, he is silenced for life. Obviously they cannot prevent him from speaking soundlessly, in his throat, they cannot prevent him from writing on the walls of his cell, from exchanging signs, behind the guard's back, with the other prisoners: but these furtive, stolen communications confirm him in the feeling that he is stealing language *too.*

Moreover, let him use *words* as much as he likes: Society has put *things* in safekeeping. The vocables which he learns refer to forbidden realities. Those for commodities, realty, gardens designate the property of others: the designated objects remain forever inaccessible to him, turn to others their true faces, in short, are in themselves and on principle other than what they appear to him to be. Technical terms reflect an understanding among honest workers within an occupational group; but he will never share in this understanding, which was reached against him and his kind. The names that apply to the State, to national sovereignty, to the rights and duties of the citizens, concern realities which are thoroughly foreign to him. Political and social problems are second-degree matters in that the integrated citizen decides which influences he will undergo, combat and exercise in the collectivity. Those of Genet will never go beyond the first degree, since his very integration is in question. Our words turn their backs to him, designate absences, denote distances, name invisible things, refer to what is manifest to others and remains hidden from his eyes: they are repositories of unrealizable intuitions. No doubt he understands the "socialized" meaning of the vocables he uses, but this meaning remains abstract. No doubt he can assemble them to make sentences, but he does so like a blind man. *Blind Man's Works:* this is the title that Henri Thomas has given to his volume of poems; it is one that Genet could apply to everything he says. He speaks: this means that words pop up out there in society and assemble and take on all by themselves a meaning that escapes him. Somewhere in human eyes a light starts shining. *Therefore* he has struck home; someone within the collectivity has understood his statement as it was meant to be understood. But Genet does not know what has been understood: in like manner Aminadab's message has a quite different meaning for those who receive it than for the one who issues it.* Genet says: "Prison awaits me." For him, prison is his lot, his giddiness and his destiny, a threat, a bodily constraint and at the same time a refuge against men, a monastery. But the right-thinking man to whom these words are spoken does not take it in that sense: prison is a social institution, very comparable to the sewers of big cities and intended, like them, for disposing of waste products. The prison belongs to him; he shares the ownership of it with other right-thinking men, and, though he no more cares to think about it than about slaughterhouses, he is not unaware that part of the taxes he pays goes to make up the budget of the penitentiaries. How is one to make oneself understood if one uses haunted words?

Because this child is, for himself, another, language decomposes and alters within him, becomes the language of the others. To speak is to steal words, and the latter retain, even in the depths of his throat, the indelible traits of their true owners: cheated even in his inner monologue, Genet is a robbed thief; he steals language, and in return he is robbed of his thought. In our rapid, condensed, scraggy, hacked soliloquies, words pass unnoticed, they serve as points of reference for our thoughts and gestures; in the case of Genet, the constant displacement which separates them from what they name fixes his attention on them. He listens to himself speaking within himself, he does not have sufficient familiarity with language to dare cut into it, to abbreviate, to take shortcuts; it is not exactly that he composes sentences: substantives march by in his head, pompously, a bit stiff, jerkily, like pictures projected by a magic lantern. These substantives indicate to an imaginary witness the action that the child is performing, without ever being quite able to express it. Little Culafroy turns on himself; there immediately appear in his head the noble and graceful words: "spun round." But the torn, shabby soles of his shoes slacken his pirouette: the words evoke an exemplary reality that Genet does not succeed in imitating in his behavior. Whence the permanence of his astonishment: words, in him, are like foreign bodies; he observes them, examines them, runs them in neutral, just to see. As the designated objects are all equally taboo, myth and reality are equivalent: since they have bereft him of the world, since every-

---

* The reference here is to *Aminadab* by Maurice Blanchot.—Translator's note.

thing is more remote from and more fabulous to him than faraway
Asia, it matters little whether Genet calls his prison a clink or a
palace: it is equally impossible for him to live in a palace and to see
a prison with the eyes of a judge or a taxpayer. What counts is the
word's material presence, which symbolizes the signifying content
that, for Genet, is none other than the being of the thing signified.
To change words is to change being. His original crisis corresponded exactly to the intuitive crystallization that the word
effected for other eyes: the word "thief" was an astringent. Haunted
by this crisis, Genet aspires to provoke it, in turn, in other objects:
he wants to name, not in order to *designate* but to *transform*. He
looks at the walls of his cell, launches the word "palace" and waits:
nothing happens, nothing ever happens. But why should this disturb him? In any case, he knows that he is denied the experience of
intuitive crystallization: it will not take place if he says *palace;* nor
will it if he says *prison.* As for the inner metamorphosis of the
thing, since it is inner it will obviously escape him. The important
thing is that the word be in his mouth: things—forbidden, remote,
flowing—are the appearances of which words are the reality. There
is no doubt but that the child makes himself an accomplice and a
victim of a new mystification: the starving person is refused meat
and bread but is given, instead, the word "steak"; let him amuse
himself with it as much as he likes. In point of fact, if he merely
repeats it in a low voice this act will certainly be followed by movements of his jaws, an abundant flow of saliva, contractions of the
stomach accompanied by an emission of gastric juices, in short
digestion on no load. Now, it is precisely this empty digestion and
enjoyment, this exhausting delight of absence and nothingness,
that Genet will later decide to prefer to all else.

But he now "makes himself" a thief: immediately the fissure
spreads, multiplies in all directions. Language cracks from below;
the virus attacks other verbal strata. That was to be expected: the
decision to take upon himself what is imposed upon him and to
launch out voluntarily on the only path that lies open to him can
only hasten the course of his inner disturbances. It is he who becomes the agent of the disintegration of language: that is, without
yet giving a name to his undertaking, without making it the object
of a special act of will, he changes into a poet because he wills
himself a thief. Since his adolescence he has had no "normal"
relationship—that is, no prose relationship—with language. Two
phases are to be distinguished: in the first, which goes as far as the
solipsistic endeavor, the disturbances are not willed for their own

sake; they are the consequence of the decision to steal. But in the second, that is, as soon as Genet undertakes to become his own companion, he takes the initiative and deliberately sinks into verbal disease.

Let us begin with the first phase. Genet the thief decides to lie. I do not quite know what he stole or how he went about things, but no matter. We can take the liberty of choosing as an example one of the thefts he committed when he was about thirty: the relationship to language does not change. Well then, he enters a bookshop with a rigged briefcase and pretends that he wants to buy a rare book. While the bookseller goes to get the volume, Genet notices another on a table or a shelf and rapidly slips it into his briefcase. When he addressed the bookseller, it was for the purpose of informing him of an intention which did not exist: he was not concerned with *buying* and probably did not have enough money on him to pay for anything; he wished only to get a troublesome witness out of the way. Yet he *communicated* with the other person. But it was a pseudo-communication which destroyed all possibilities of real communication. In short, like the surrealists who painted with the aim of destroying painting, but more effectively than they, he uses language to destroy language. The bookseller actually thinks that he is performing once again the act which he constantly repeats in the course of the day; it seems to him that his movements express his sustained will to do his job and to serve the interests of his employer. But the fact is that he is not acting, he is dancing: he goes to get *for nothing* a book that nobody wants to buy; his eagerness, his smile, which ordinarily aim at charming customers, are mere pantomime since there are no customers in the shop but only a thief who cannot be charmed. And the result of this pantomime is a denial of the real world to the advantage of a universe of pure appearance. He thinks he is going to the back of the shop to get a valuable article: he is actually going off to leave Genet a clear field. He has become a fake bookseller, a true accomplice of a thief. He thinks he has understood Genet's request, and, in point of fact, his senses have transmitted to him correct indications which his mind has correctly interpreted. Nevertheless, to understand was, in this case, not to understand, for thorough understanding would have implied that he had discerned the intention to deceive in the physiognomy or intonation of his fake client. The statement made him deaf, blind, ignorant: in short, it made of him a thing that one pushes out of the way. Let us note in passing the resemblance of the universe of theft to that of homosexuality: in both cases, inner reality becomes pure appearance without efficacy, and it is appearance, on the other hand, that becomes reality. In this fake world, language is used in the wrong way: although its function is to unite, to reveal and to harmonize, it separates, conceals and estranges; although it is a body of signs which are meant to be offered to the intelligence of persons, it makes one of the speakers an unconscious instrument of the other.

Genet is aware that he is lying and knows that the object which is signified does not exist. He wants his statement, which for him is void of meaning, to offer the other an illusory plenitude. Signification exists *only for the other:* for the other, it transcends the words and aims at a certain object located in the back of the shop. Genet utters a sentence which he knows has meaning only for others. *For him* it is only a magical formula, the effect of which is to cast a spell on those who hear it and to make them do what they do not want to do by leading them to believe that they are doing what they want to do. In a sense, it is a cabalistic formula that is recited mechanically. And yet it is haunted by a signification that denies itself since Genet knows that the other understands it. The bookseller, who guides himself by means of the words, perceives Genet intuitively as a purchaser: proper clothing, relaxed attitude, these things tally with the statement and serve as a visible content. Thus, for Genet himself an intuitive meaning is present in the proposition, but *as another and for the other;* this meaning escapes him on principle, for he can no doubt know it in the abstract and by its effects on the person he addresses (he sees that the other smiles, walks away, etc.), but cannot enjoy it. From this point of view, it is a duplication of the original situation: the signification of the word "purchaser" is not given to Genet intuitively any more than was the word "thief." Here, however, the deformation is more serious, for this intuitive meaning is false while it is being lived by the other. The other just about manages, by his behavior, to impart to it an appearance of reality. There is thus, at the core of words, a concrete plenitude which refuses to give itself to Genet because it is lived by the other, and which is annihilated in the other, for it is only an illusion. When one tells a lie, language is isolated, stands out, imbibes its significations and constitutes an order apart: the order of the trap and the sham. But was it not actually that even before Genet dreamed of lying? Did not significations flee the child who wanted to grasp them? Was not speech already a breaking off of communication? Here as elsewhere Genet has merely adopted the given: cast out of language and out of the social world of tools, he uses instru-

ments and words *in reverse;* the separative power of the Word became a power to lie when he decided to accept it and turn it to
advantage.

When he pretended that he wanted to buy a book, he was affirming the existence of a nonexistent object. Here is the reverse
situation: he leaves the shop, an inspector who knows him challenges him: "What have you got in your briefcase?" "Nothing."
In this case, the negation becomes a pure, abstract refusal that plays
on the surface of being; it is objective, but dwells solely in the universe of words; it is only the materiality of the sound that sustains
it in its nothingness. And if the detective does not believe it, if
nevertheless Genet maintains it in despair, then it no longer exists
for anyone, it persists in the teeth of the glaring truth, of the tacit
agreement between cops and thieves: language functions idly and
in the void:

" 'You're the one who did the job on the Rue de Flandres.'
" 'No, it wasn't me.'
" 'It was you. The concierge recognized you.'
" 'It's someone who looks like me.'
" 'She says his name is Guy.'
" 'It's someone who looks like me and has the same name.'
" 'She recognizes your clothes.'
" 'He looks like me, has the same name and the same clothes.'
" 'He's got the same hair.'
" 'He looks like me, has the same name, the same clothes and the
same hair.'
" 'They found your fingerprints.'
" 'He looks like me, has the same name, the same clothes, the
same hair and the same fingerprints.'
" 'That can keep on.'
" 'To the very end.'
" 'It was you who did the job.'
" 'No, it wasn't me.' "*

That is what is called "denying the evidence." But evidence cannot be denied. In order for this taut, abstract will to nothingness to
be maintained in its absurdity, in its contradictions, it must be
based on being: otherwise it would be corroded by the void. Language imparts to it its materiality. And as it is always possible to
unite words when thoughts repel each other, it is pure language

---

* *The Thief's Journal.*

that sustains Genet in his will to the impossible. These words which clash, which burn each other, become for him a kind of index of the strictly impracticable operations to which he has dedicated his life. Thanks to language, Genet can impart a being to nothingness and remain resolutely in the domain of shadows, that is, of Evil. Thanks to language, Genet can realize his ambitious design of being wrong.

However, Genet does not steal all the time: he comes and goes, he talks. Given hospitality by middle-class people, he serves them, he exchanges comments with them. And, what is even better, he buys and sells, exactly as do consumers and merchants. Is there not, in these moments of respite, a normal use of speech, is there not prose and communication? Must not language lower itself to the rank of instruments, must not words efface themselves in the presence of the operations they govern or the objects they designate? No doubt. But let us not forget that Genet thinks he is a monster and that awareness of his abjection never leaves him. Amidst the honest folk who speak to him without knowing his true nature, he feels hounded: he can be unmasked at any moment. "He feared lest some gleam from the interior of his body or from his own consciousness illuminate him . . . and make him visible to men who would have forced him to the hunt." Like certain American Negroes who, by virtue of having an almost white skin, have "crossed the color line" and live among the whites at the cost of constant tension and in such a state of anxiety that many of them finally return to their black brothers, he constantly plays a role, and he must avoid, above all, being unmasked. Everything is faked, he is double and even triple: there is, firstly, the one he is for himself, "that incomparable monster, preferable to everything,"* and then there is the thief that he is for certain people and that he must hide, and finally the honest chap he pretends to be. The true and the false mingle: no doubt at times he buys clothing, food. But he does so with stolen money and because it would be too dangerous to take them without paying. Everything is make-believe: only language is true. If he says to the salesman, this time: "I'd like to buy a pair of shoes," he is not lying. Only, it is not Genet who is speaking: it is the actor playing the honest man. He coldly listens to himself reciting his role of honest man as the actor in Diderot's *Paradox* calmly listens to Hamlet or Britannicus thundering through his mouth. Language again eludes him. At times he is a

---

* Malraux, *Man's Fate.*

real thief lying and at others a fake bourgeois speaking the truth, but speech always remains foreign to him: he borrows it or steals it. The Word is the Other.

It may, however, be pointed out that there exists a community which has forged a language of its own against the bourgeois tongue, to wit, the community of tramps and gangsters to which Genet belongs. With them, at least, communication is possible. In the reformatory, in prison, in the Court of Miracles, Genet can talk in prose: he has only to use argot.

But, to begin with, argot itself is a poetic language. And I am not, of course, asserting that its terms are noble or charming; I mean that this fabricated language represents the attempt of a parasitic society, which feels itself cut off from reality, to make good a huge verbal deficit by means of lyricism and by inventing words. Thieves and criminals are all more or less in the same situation as Genet: they have to use common words and these words are forbidden them. They must, of course, have a noun to designate a door or a train. But if they use the words "door" and "train," they are communicating among themselves by means of the language of the enemy; they are installing within themselves the words of the bourgeois, hence his thoughts, values and *Weltanschauung;* they are almost at the point of judging their crimes by his principles; a spy, a witness, a court of law are established in their hearts. Thus, their crimes and their will to form a unity of Evil create an immense gap in their verbal universe. For them the social act par excellence will be the invention of new conventions. They can, of course, distort customary words in accordance with certain rules, as in pig Latin. But this is still to concede too much to honest people: it is tantamount to admitting that the basic language remains the *white* language of the society of the just. Fake languages can serve them on occasion, when they want to talk without being understood by others. But they want *words of their own* in order to *remain among themselves,* in order to designate objects without resorting to the mediation of the society that hounds them. And as they have neither the leisure nor the means to invent a language, and as, in addition, the objects which they have to designate are not new realities which, in the manner of industrial inventions or scientific discoveries, require new denominations, they will be unable to avoid using the words of the dictionary. It is then that they hit upon what will become one of the fundamental procedures of argot. In order to name an object, they choose the terms of the common language which apply to lateral, secondary or implicit properties of the object in question: most often these will be adjectives (*le dur* [the tough], *la lourde* [the door], *le grimpant* [the trousers]*) which they will transform into substantives.

In a certain sense, argot resembles the substitute language which is painfully reinvented by persons suffering from aphasia. For the aphasic, as for thieves, the *situation* is characterized by a heavy deficit, and he *reacts* by resorting to paraphrases. Argot is the aphasic language of gangsters. The word of the common language designates the object by its essence: "infant," for example, goes straight to the essential characteristic of a child, to wit, that it does not speak. If man is defined as a reasonable or a political animal, it is a fact of prime importance that he is unable, at the beginning, to use reason, because he does not possess speech, or to communicate with his fellow men. And even if its etymology has been lost, at least the word corresponds to the entire thing and consequently caps the hierarchized ensemble of its properties. In rejecting the proper word, argot is thus compelled to use improprieties; it is a deviating language. In order not to give the name *infans* to the newborn child, it is reduced to calling it a *crapper,* that is, to referring to it by its intestinal incontinence; the slang word will be understood only with reference to the common language, that is, to a whole labor of definition, grouping, classification and convention which allows the normal play of thought. The object of the slang word is not the naked thing but the thing with its name. A crapper is not simply a human offspring: it is *a human being already called an infant.* It is with things that have already been thought, classified and named in a forbidden and sacred language that argot establishes its relations, just as those who speak it have contact only with matter that has already been worked upon. It feeds on the common language as tramps feed on the work of others. And the slang expression is poetic because it always refers to an absent reality (the essence named by the proper word) about which there is an unspoken agreement between interlocutors. We find in an unexpected area the allusive words of Mallarmé. Argot is a half-mute, half-prolix language which replaces the straight line by oblique paths and through which the real—fleeting, imperfectly known, always veiled by a coarseness that resembles modesty—can be surmised. Comparisons in argot are materialistic, but as they pride themselves on not saying everything the true definition haunts them like a soul that is careful not to let itself be seen. *Repousser du*

---

* *Dur* = hard, *lourde* = heavy, *grimpant* = *climbing.*—Translator's note.

goulot, tuer la mouche, cocoter, cogner,* ignoble expressions for
not saying "to stink." But the dropping of all explanation makes
them poetic: a man goes by, children flee, flies drop dead at his feet,
there we have the picture. The only thing absent is the *odor*. It
thereby gains a kind of refinement, of spirituality, it vanishes; yet
it is there, all-powerful, despite its "vibratory disappearance." The
consequences are given without the premises, the part is taken for
the whole, the whole is given by the part, the appearance is substituted for the reality; thus, everything contributes to making argot
a restless, seeking soul that vainly sets traps to capture an elusive
reality. To talk argot is to choose Evil, that is, to know being and
truth but to reject them in favor of a nontruth which offers itself
for what it is; it is to choose the relative, parasitism, failure. For
that very reason argot is, in spite of itself, a poetic language.

Those who commonly use argot are probably not sensitive to this
poetry. Perhaps the need to communicate reduces it for them to
being only a kind of minor prose. But, as it happens, Genet *does
not have the right* to use it for purposes of communication. As a
passive homosexual, he is required to understand it but is forbidden to speak it: the language of the toughs, of the pimps, of the big
shots is not meant for a girl queen:

"The queens had their language apart. Argot was for men. It
was the male tongue. Like the men's language among the Caribbees,
it became a secondary sex attribute . . . everyone could understand
it, but the only ones who could speak it were the men, who, at birth,
received as a gift the gestures, the carriage of the hips, legs and
arms, the eyes, the chest, with which one could speak it. One day,
at one of our bars, when Mimosa ventured the following words in
the course of a sentence: '. . . his screwy stories . . .' the men
frowned. Someone said, with a threat in his voice, 'Broad acting
tough.' "

Excluded from the society of the just and then from the society
of the tough, Genet finds himself, with respect to the language of
the latter, in the strictly contemplative attitude which he was
forced to adopt toward the language of the former. And precisely
because he can *understand* the language but is forbidden to use it
as an instrument of communication, words lose for him their instru-
mental value: they thereby become all the more *present*. When one

---

* Literally: *repousser du goulot,* to push away with the spout or the mouth, the proper
meaning of *goulot* being the former and the slang meaning the latter; *tuer la mouche,* to
kill the fly; *cocoter* (of a hen), to cackle, when laying an egg; *cogner,* to whack.—Translator's note.

speaks, one picks up vocables anywhere, very quickly, and tosses them to the other person; one does not even notice the tool one is using; in short, one does not hear oneself. But if any permanent prohibition confines us to the role of passive listener, the speakers seem to be conducting a service; language is isolated, in the manner of the Latin of the Mass; it is the object of an aesthetic intuition: the play of these sonant volutes seems to obey a finality without end. *Visible* language has become a thing: "It was like the colored plumage of male birds, like the multicolored silk garments which are the prerogatives of the warriors of the tribe." Absorbed in understanding in order to reply, we rarely perceive the *voice,* we go directly to the meaning. Genet, who is kept in the background, does not distinguish the sacred words of the forbidden language from the rough and quiet voices which utter them. The male voice, which is a column of air, an upright penis, and the vocable, which is the sign of the virile member, are one and the same. For the girl queen, the primary function of argot, which is language in erection, is not signification; argot overwhelms and subjugates; it recalls the horrible and delightful servitude of lovemaking: "Argot in the mouths of their men disturbed the queens, though they were less disturbed by the invented words peculiar to that language than by expressions from the ordinary world that were violated by the pimps, adapted by them to their mysterious needs, perverted, deformed and tossed into the gutter and their beds."

Of course, we are sometimes delighted by a woman's voice, we are thrilled by its timbre or rhythm. But, in general, the quality of this voice remains unrelated to the meanings expressed.* That soft and low contralto voice wastes its rich sonority in saying to us: "How are you?" or "That's exactly what my husband thinks."

Genet, however, reveals an inner connection between argot, which is a language of men, and the male vocal organs that use it: each of these organs, by its timbre, its haughty slowness, its ruggedness, establishes and fortifies its privilege. The word is not carried by the voice as is a tool by a hand: it is the embodiment of the voice, the concrete, individual figure in which the voice has chosen to manifest itself. But the symbolic correspondence is even more complex: the mere presence of the Pimp is experienced by Genet as a rape; his sacred and powerful voice is a rape for the ear. We have seen that the rape is the original structure of Genet's sexuality. Now, argot is, in its words and syntax and by virtue of its whole

---

* Unless—and such a case is more complex and far more rare—the woman has created for herself a language that corresponds to her voice.

semantic content, the permanent practice of rape. We showed above how argot, by its refusal or inability to use the proper word, condemned itself to impropriety. This condemnation has a reverse side: argot is a physical constraint; it forces words which have a definite use to designate, despite themselves, objects that do not suit them. Thus, the sacred ceremony of speech, of which Genet makes himself the simple witness, represents in his eyes the permanent and overwhelming drama of his sexuality. Muscles, voice, use of words, everything is fused into an indissoluble unity. In addition, argot, which is a symbolic rape, does not simply excite Genet physically; it also satisfies his resentment. For the victim of its acts of violence is the language of the just, the language which Genet is denied. It is a revenge, quite like the capital punishment of criminals. Parasitic and destructive, argot is the very image of the Evil which borrows the Being of Good only to corrode it with its acids. This language, which designates the world only by its appearances, is an appearance in itself, and those who speak it are the great gruesome appearances of crime. It is all this that Genet will first perceive through his excitement and evil joy: a column of air rises and becomes a word; the word is a sacred drama, the affirmation of virility in Evil; it attacks the thing in a roundabout way and casts a spell on it instead of expressing it; in the end, raped and triumphant, there remains, like an overtone, the proper name, the unformulated foundation of the whole system. Argot is, for the girl queen, language in reverse. The just man sees in the words the souls of things. For Genet, argotic words are things which have a soul: it is through the voice, which is verbal flesh, and then through the sacred drama that he will grasp, very far off, in silhouette, their meaning.

And this meaning itself is not fixed and simple like that of ordinary words—"bread," "chair," "hammer"—which relates to a single object: it opens out on the infinite. Indeed, let us not forget that Genet, excluded from the society of crime, is an objective traitor. He will not limit himself to repeating in solitude the words of the slang tongue—such repetition is tantamount not to speaking but merely to playing at being a tough, to assuming, in the realm of the imaginary, the sacred personality of the initiate—he will betray argot; he will amuse himself by giving a bourgeois meaning to expressions which he has not the right to utter. The Pimp rapes the proper word, and Genet will challenge this act, in thought, by raping the slang term in turn.

"Just a while ago, in my cell, the two pimps said, 'We're making the pages.' They meant they were going to make the bed, but a kind of luminous idea transformed me there, with my legs spread apart, into a husky guard or a palace groom who 'makes' a palace page just as a young man 'makes a chick.' "

The procedure consisted in inverting the use of argot. The pimps took the verb "to make" in a familiar but common sense: all housewives, on all levels of society, speak of "making the beds." However, when the expression "page" is employed to designate a bed, it is specifically argotic. Genet performs the contrary operation: he takes the word "page" in the noble sense of "young aristocrat living in a king's palace" and the word "make" in the erotic and vulgar sense. He no doubt replied to the two hoodlums: "Yes, let's make the pages." And thereby the traitor gave, as it were, a real, an adapted reply; he achieved communication. But he did so in order the better to mislead, since, at the same time, he escaped into a strictly personal universe of imaginary meanings. Blanchot describes Mallarmé's poetic activity in the same way:

"This single word is only the beginning of the shift since, by means of the signification, it again renders present the object signified, the material reality of which it has set aside. It is therefore necessary, if the absence is to continue, that the word be replaced by another word which removes it further and the latter by another which flees it and this last by the very movement of the flight. It is thus that we gain entrance into the realm of images, and not into stable and solid images but into an order where every figure is a passage, a disquiet, a transition, an illusion, an act that has an infinite trajectory. . . ." But Mallarmé uses only one language, the lawful language, and Blanchot characterizes here the relations that the words of this language maintain among themselves. We shall find similar shifts in Genet the writer. But he has not yet begun to write; he is the young beggar who betrays pimps in secret, and as he has at his disposal, *for a single word,* significations borrowed from a double system of reference (the lawful language and the unlawful language) , it is within the same vocable that he plays this game of challenging. For Genet does not see the image of the guard pawing the pages, not even with the mind's eye. The image is, at the outermost point of the words "page" and "make," the indication of an absence, of a flight; it is an internal hemorrhage of the signification.

There remains, however, as might be pointed out, a group to which Genet rightfully belongs: that of the "soft," of the girl queens. Can he not use their language, can he not use prose; in short, can he not communicate? But the fact is that this group is only a conglomerate; it has none of the characteristics of a veritable society. Although each of its members wills himself a woman, he nevertheless detests the image of his femininity in all the others. Each of the girl queens is the others' "bad smell." Divine and Mimosa, each twining about a big Pimp, hate each other; they can only try to hurt or lie to each other. They are rivals, reflections of each other, never friends; they cannot *recognize* each other. Simone de Beauvoir has shown that there is no feminine society.

Nevertheless, it is true that they have developed a language to designate themselves to each other and to speak about their life. But it is a *fake* language, it fails to name accurately the objects for which it is intended. The girl queens are of the male sex, but in their tastes they are women, and they cannot speak of themselves entirely in the masculine nor entirely in the feminine. And if, despite everything, they choose the feminine, this verbal violence accelerates the disintegration of language within them:

"Though she felt as a 'woman,' [Divine] thought as a 'man.' . . . In order to think with precision it was necessary that Divine never formulate her thoughts aloud, for herself. Doubtless there had been times when she had said to herself aloud, 'I'm just a foolish girl,' but having felt this, she felt it no longer, and, in saying it, she no longer thought it. In Mimosa's presence, for example, she managed to think 'woman' with regard to serious but never essential things. Her femininity was not *only* a masquerade. But as for thinking 'woman' completely, her organs hindered her. To think is to perform an act. In order to act, you have to discard frivolity and set your idea on a solid basis. So she was aided by the idea of solidity, which she associated with the idea of virility, and it was in grammar that she found it near at hand. For if, to define a state of mind that she felt, Divine dared use the feminine, she was unable to do so in defining an action which she performed. And all the 'woman' judgments she made were, in reality, poetical conclusions. Hence, only then was Divine true."

In speaking of herself in the feminine, Divine makes herself understood by the other girl queens, but the agreement is made with respect to a signification that challenges the visible reality. It is "poetically" true that Divine is a woman, but it is not plainly and simply true. She herself does not wish to become a woman completely since she loathes women. She wants to be a man-woman: a woman when she is passive, a man when she acts. Thus, this language relates here to an absence; Genet's femininity is an evanescent being, the pure challenging of virility. Gestures, modulations of the voice, idiosyncrasies of language indicate and mime it in its absence. Speaking about herself, Divine *dares* use the feminine, that is, in stilted fashion she makes a sustained but vain effort to achieve the impossible, to attain a being that is barely outlined and that sums up in itself everything that she is not. It is beyond being that she is a woman, in the nothingness which, for poets alone, transcends being in dignity. She is a woman in her failure to be one. She therefore never succeeds in actualizing from within the mystery of her femininity. As soon as the word "she" or the expression "poor woman" is uttered, its being escapes her; it lies outside of her, in the word: similarly, all the pus which infects Genet lies outside of him in the name "thief," and this impossibility of being a woman is only one of the aspects of the radical impossibility of being the Other. Thus, to speak of oneself in the feminine is to trust to words, to leave to them the job of indicating a universe of essences beyond one's grasp.

No doubt the other girl queens understand Divine, but this understanding is likewise poetic. Only a queen can listen without laughing to Divine referring to herself in the feminine; she can do so only because she herself makes a similar effort. Thus, there is communication, but only by virtue of poetic nothingness and not by the designation of being; the girl queens are all accomplices in a huge hoax which must be kept going. If, however, Divine takes it into her head to refer to herself in the masculine, the queens listlessly or spitefully refuse communication: for them, Divine is *playing* the man. And, as a matter of fact, these queens have the misfortune of being obliged to play everything that they are: it is quite true that their femininity is only a game, but it is also true that they cannot be males, except in play. Since for them the man is the tough who subdues them, Divine will never be other than a "broad acting tough."* Her physical organism does not allow her to be a woman, and the social prohibition that weighs on her does not allow her to be a man. Caught between these two impossibilities, Divine, that is, Genet, will once again demand the worst. Instead of challenging the social taboo that exiles him from masculinity, he prefers to assume it: it is always *social* misfortune that he insists on; it is always against the Other and the Other's inten-

---

* A similar necessity is found in the case of the music-hall actor who disguises himself as a woman: "In order to become the man again it is not sufficient to run the film backward. It is also necessary that the truth be translated and that it have a relief which can be maintained along the same lines as the lie. That is why Barbette, as soon as his wig is torn off, performs a man's role. . . ." Jean Cocteau, *Le Numéro Barbette.*

tions that he has chosen to fight in becoming willfully and defiantly what the Other obliges him to be. Since he is denied the right to be a man, he will become a woman. But the metamorphosis is impossible: neither his body nor his sex can change; thus, he cannot become feminine *for himself,* inwardly. But it is not for himself that he wishes to effect this resentful metamorphosis: it is against the Other and in the presence of the Other. Thus, his gestures and language aim at obliging the society of men to see him only as a "broad." She utters *in public* such remarks as "I'm the Quite Mad" ("*Je suis la Toute Folle*") because she will thus become *the (la)* giddy one, capricious one, divine one for others.* But as soon as she is alone, the remark becomes pointless, for there is no witness to hear it: Divine cannot name herself to *herself* in the feminine. Thus, words flee her, their meaning will be lost in other ears and will never return to her to enlighten her. Her woman's personality and the extraordinary language that expresses it exist only for the other and in the other; Divine eludes herself. At the cost of constant strain she manages to feel herself grazed by the "broad" that she is for the pimp: that is all. And yet it is sufficient that she use the words which designate this imaginary personality for the whole verbal universe to be infected.

"I shall speak to you about Divine, mixing masculine and feminine as my mood dictates, and if, in the course of the tale, I shall have to refer to a woman, I shall manage, I shall find an expedient, a good device, so that there may be no confusion."

A "good device," that means another word or a substitute expression. It is a matter of filling in a crack or at least hiding it. The word "woman" designates *in prose* a biologically and socially defined individual: Genet wrests it by force from its natural object and obliges it to connote a class of individuals who possess *poetically* certain feminine qualities. Deprived of the word that names it, the reality remains naked, crude. If, however, it has to be referred to, he will find a poetic dodge, exactly as does the aphasic or the gangster who speaks argot. Poetry cannot be circumscribed: if you introduce it somewhere into speech, all speech becomes poetic. Genet is not yet a poet, but he is no longer able to express himself in prose. He knows three languages: the common language, argot, the dialect of the queens; and he cannot speak any of them. What is worse, each of them interferes with the other two, challenges them and finally destroys them. Whenever he speaks, he steals words, he

---

* The author's point is not clear in translation. He is stressing the fact that Divine uses "*la*," the feminine form of the definite article, rather than "*le*," the masculine.— Translator's note.

violates them. He is a real thief and the signification of the statements he utters is imaginary, he lies; he is a fake bourgeois, a fake
tough, a fake woman, he plays roles; the words are perhaps true,
but the speaker is imaginary. The willed and actual absence of all
reciprocity murders language; the words telescope, interfere, they
burn and corrode each other; as a result of the injury they do each
other, their meaning flees and is lost in the infinite. Genet literally
does not *know* what he says.

But is it not quite simply because he applies to language the
treatment he reserved for utensils? To both the common language
and argot he reacts as, in the passage quoted earlier, he reacted to the
bus, the toothbrush, the glass. Since words are taboo as tools, he
takes refuge, when confronted with them, in quietism. He continues
to know what they mean, but he no longer understands the utility
of speech. He said earlier: "I reached the point of wondering
whether it was true that one drank from a glass." He is now astounded that one can give the name *glass* to that fragile, transparent
thing resting on the table. The "luxurious detachment" which
reveals to him "the elegance and oddness" of a clothespin can disclose to him, in like manner, the strange beauty of a vocable. These
words hover between the material realm of sounds and the spiritual
realm of meanings, as do tools between the realm of man and that
of nature: they are declassed. Voluminous and fascinating, they
begin to exist all by themselves, outside of the denominative act;
they become gestures, appearances.

Genet cannot persist in holding aloof from language. He returns
to speech, but with the aim of destroying it or perverting its meaning. At times his discourse is a lie, that is, the equivalent of a burglary, and at times it is a subtle inversion of speech: commonplace
words give him, by their appearing, an opportunity to create, quite
deliberately, *misconceptions,* as the nun's gown and headdress gave
Culafroy the idea of disguising himself as a Sister: through the
universal he expresses, to himself and for himself alone, his particularity; he uses the crude but common expression "to make the
pages" to reveal aloud to everyone, without anyone's being able to
understand, the shameful secret of his homosexuality.

The effect of this particular attention to language and of this
illicit use of speech is to multiply the miracles. Often, in that long
daily discourse which is spoken everywhere at the same time by all
mouths, in that "prose of the world," he reveals strange encounters
similar to those of a lake and a drawing room, of an armchair and
a meadow.

When speaking, Genet *keeps an eye on himself*. He is the object of a double verdict: the Just have said to him: "You're a thief," the thieves: "You're a fairy." He has to be careful: what if he betrayed himself in speaking? As a thief, he has to go masked: the police are on the lookout for him. As a fairy, he runs the risk of being laughed at, despite himself: like all childish and secret societies, the society of gangsters is very fastidious about language, very quick to discover unspoken allusions in it. Genet is quite willing to speak like a girl, but he wants it to be known that he does so on purpose. He plays the simpleton: he makes a spectacle of himself in order to avoid playing the fool. Words can have secret meanings; a sentence which is uttered seriously can unloose gales of laughter and, without his realizing it, set the laughers against him. There is only one way of avoiding these pitfalls: to review rapidly, before the others do, all possible meanings, if necessary to shatter words, to link up the syllables among themselves in all kinds of ways, as do schoolboys who try to discover pornographic verses in *Polyeucte,* in short, to adopt toward language the attitude of the paranoiac toward the world, to seek in it all symbols, all signs, all allusions, all plays on words, so as to be able, if need be, to take them over and pass them off as the effect of his will. So there he is, talking and listening to himself at the same time: he wants to disclose the diabolical element in his own words. It is as if words, though seeming to obey his intentions, assemble in accordance with an objective finality that escapes him, as if, through his mouth, Another were speaking to Another. All the decompositions and recompositions to which he subjects his speech end by giving rise within him to the kind of illumination which suddenly transfigures the word "page." Imaginary illuminations, to be sure, since this remark is addressed to nobody and since nobody uttered it in that sense. But illuminations, all the same: for the words are there and it is quite true that they have a double signification. In order for their latent meaning to be realized, it would suffice that Another perceive it, with the result that, over and above the clear and intentional meaning which he confers upon the statement, Genet fears and requires a listener who would discover its secret face; over and above the impossible communication with human beings of flesh and blood, he postulates a poetic communication with an imaginary witness. Whether or not he gives this witness a face and name, whether or not he addresses him over the heads of the real persons to whom he is speaking, he will assume his verbal situation and will become a poet.

Now, this ideal interlocutor exists: it is Genet himself, Genet as

Other. We left him, a while ago, "swallowing" the divinity, establishing it within himself, identifying it with an intelligible and untemporal choice of Evil. He has made of sacred Genet the witness of profane Genet and, whatever the workings of his mind, he now knows that a gaze is contemplating them. Better still, he knows that this witness is considering, in kindly fashion, all the misfortunes with which his way has been strewn and, far from regarding them as the sordid effects of his punishment, that he is able to recognize them as tests, as stages of a magnificent series of stations of the Cross. Henceforth, each of Genet's thoughts, each moment of his inner monologue, is defined by two frames of reference: on the one hand, the simple daily and empirical manifestation of his presence to himself, the absolute inwardness of consciousness; and, on the other, a perpetual language, an endless discourse addressed to the other. But he does not speak to this Divinity at the back of his mind as he would to a flesh-and-blood person standing in front of him. We must indeed assume that he understands everything that the latter wishes to say and only what he says. But just as the Divinity discerns the secret face of the world and sees a test in what appears to men the sequence of causes and effects, it will, in like manner, hear the hidden spirit of language; what is *meaningless* in the expression—play on words, involuntary nonsense—is precisely what will be meaningful to the Divinity, and it is the intentional meaning that will be meaningless. When Genet addresses the Divinity, he places his trust in words; he knows that they have an absolute meaning which escapes him, and it is this mysterious meaning which he offers up as a sacrifice. And since he knows that in the eyes of the Divinity the accidents of his wretched life are the splendid signs of his election, he will name them for it in terms of splendor. Not that he himself perceives in them the magnificence with which he adorns them: he counts on the Divinity to find it there; unlike what happens in ordinary discourse, his words designate not so much what he sees as what he cannot see. By means of language one shows to the interlocutor what he is unaware of; Genet uses it to show the Divinity what it alone knows and what he cannot see. When he makes of his prison a palace, of a pimp a great lord and of himself a prince, the sumptuous words which he utters float above the sordid realities without shedding light on them or merging with them: nothing happens, just as nothing happened in the past when he uttered the word "thief" as he looked at himself in the mirror. But he counts on his supreme witness to effect the intuitive fusion of meaning and thing. He enjoins it to have the intuition in his place. We have already noted that he opposes other dizzying words to *the* "dizzying word," just as he opposes a sovereign judge to the society that has condemned him. When he kept repeating, uncomprehendingly, the name "thief," the meaning eluded him, flowed out of the word and into the minds that *saw him* as a thief and were bent on destroying him. Thus, he used a word which made it possible for the others to attain an intuition which for him was unattainable. Now he has understood: he picks up the leaking words, he utters them and feels the silky discharge of their meaning. But this discharge takes place in the opposite direction: not in front of him and toward others, but behind him and toward the Other who contemplates him. Furthermore, it is not a matter of Genet's informing the inner Divinity: he points out to it what it already sees; he teaches it nothing. The denominative operation here resembles the *montre,* a very old feudal ceremony, one which had fallen into disuse long before the end of the Middle Ages: after the homage, the vassal invited his lord to the estate with which the latter had invested him and, leading him to some high spot, showed [*montrait*] it to him. This gesture taught nothing to the donor, who was thoroughly familiar with the estate: it was rather a thanksgiving, a *recognition* on the part of the beneficiary. Similarly with Genet: the words which he utters in secret are not designation words but homage words. He began by whistling melodies which he dedicated to his divinity; he now sings even when he speaks to it: "The words which I use, even if they are meant to explain, will sing." He tells us: "I had gone across Europe by my own means, which are the opposite of glorious means. Yet I was writing for myself a secret history, in details as precious as the histories of the great conquerors." But he quite realizes that he is neither *relating* his story to himself nor *explaining* it: he marks it out "with glamorous words, *charged, I mean, in my mind, with more glamour than meaning.*"

It remains to be seen how one finds these beautiful painted shells which one dedicates to the divinity: by what does one recognize a glamorous word? Answer: by the poetic emotion it arouses. And what is poetic emotion? Nothing other than the exorcising repetitions of the original crisis. One day, when he was caught pilfering, the word "thief" struck him like lightning, and the earth opened beneath his feet: he felt himself escaping and becoming a thief elsewhere, in the minds of others; a social and inaccessible order of language manifested itself. The poetic emotion surges up when he hears certain words uttered unexpectedly, and this too is a dizziness. In the corridors of the prison Genet hears the word "yarded" [*envergué*] mentioned.

"The magnificence of such an achievement—impalement by a yard [*vergue*]—made me tremble from head to foot."* The same voice then utters some comic and obscene words. "[This expression] destroyed the charm of the other one, and I regained my footing on the solid basis of joking, whereas poetry always pulls the ground away from under your feet and sucks you into the bosom of a wonderful night."

Fall, void, night of unknowing: it is not a matter of an Apollonian poetry sparkling with brilliant, visible images. It is the vertigo, the want, the nothingness, and the negation which mark the poetic emotion. A word strikes him, the ground opens up: the poem is born (there exist, for Genet, poems composed of a single word). What has happened? The term or the phrase that suddenly loomed up bore witness to the existence of God, that is, of sacred Genet. It suddenly allowed a glimpse of something unrealizable over and above its prose signification, something which, beyond the place and the moment, above Genet's head, required a supreme consciousness that alone was capable, intuitively, of bringing this signification into being. The glamorous word repeats, while effacing it, the original crisis: it, too, hits him in the face and reveals the existence of Another, of a Gaze directed at Genet; but this Other is kindly, for it is the I-who-is-Another, it is Genet himself. Poetry is the antidote of the original condemnation; it appears when the word leads him to suspect a secret order of language and a secret conformity of language with the hidden aspect of things; the word is therefore manifestly addressed to an absence; it gives proof of God by the necessity of a consciousness that deciphers its esoteric meaning. The glamorous word is the one which creates in Genet the sudden impression that we are *spoken* rather than that we speak and that, through the words which we think we are assembling in order to communicate with our fellows, the World is addressing messages to God. And the emotion is a *happy* one; Genet has been allowed to discover the trace of this message, to have a foretaste of this secret language within our language. This is proof that he is of the elect, that he is on the side of God. He goes even further: his certainty of being *the only one* to catch a glimpse of the other face of speech manifests to him that he is the sole elect or, if one prefers,

---

* This passage involves a play on words which it is difficult to render fully in English. The word "yard" is to be taken in both the nautical sense and the obsolete sexual sense of penis.—Translator's note.

that he is his *own elect.* He has only to repeat the glamorous word to assure himself of the existence of an intelligible order in which he occupies first place:

"At times, during my most harrowing moments . . . I sing within me that poem, 'The Yard-On,' which I do not apply to anyone but which comforts me and dries unwelled tears as I sail across becalmed seas, a sailor of the crew which sailed around 1700 on the frigate *Culafroy.*"

Genet assigns himself his task: he will be a huntsman of glamorous words, he will repeat them inwardly in order to designate the situation in which he finds himself: they will be God-traps, for they require a witness who transfigures the world and Genet. At times they will be words without precise meaning but charged with a magical power of evocation:

"No episode from history or a novel organized the dream mass; only the murmur of a few magic words thickened the darkness, from which there loomed a page or horseman . . . *Natura fastuosa, Natura stramonium, Belladonna. . . .*"

"She described the blazon: 'It's argent and azure of ten pieces, over all a lion gules membered and langued. On the crest, Melusina.' It was the arms of the Lusignans. Culafroy listened to this splendid poem."

At times he will utilize the feeling of strangeness aroused in him by language and by the long mistrust that makes him review all the possible meanings of the most innocent phrases: he will hollow out a word with the aim of extracting its various meanings and will unite these meanings in a new, sumptuous and fanciful signification: the word Brazil—which evokes in him the idea of an "island beyond suns and seas, where men with rugged faces and the build of athletes squatted in the evening around huge fires . . . peeling . . . enormous oranges, with the fruit in one hand and a broadbladed knife in the other, as, in old pictures, emperors held the scepter and the golden globe . . ."—is suddenly transformed into a "one-word poem" that "falls from this vision": the word "suns." Brazil opens its blazing plumage, lays an egg, the one-word poem, which mingles oranges and the sun within him; suns-oranges whirl in the cell. Added to this is the idea of an "acrobat in light blue tights executing the grand circle* on the horizontal bar." *The* oranges have been transformed into *several* suns; the word "sun" emits an acrobat whose body describes a circle and who has been

---

* Grand circle: in French, *le grand soleil* (the big sun) .—Translator's note.

saturated with the sky in the form of light blue tights. The sky turns in the sun, the sun turns in the sky, the sun is man, the orange is sun, the sun is azure-colored, the sky is sun-colored, the man turns, the man turns in his hand oranges similar to terrestrial globes, to suns. Everything is given in the words, but *as an absence:* what human eye could see these contradictory splendors simultaneously in the unity of a single image? But the image *is to be seen,* and it is its flagrant absence that reveals the Other in his solitude. It is the Other who will see it, who *sees* it.

At other times, words will be used to effect symbolic transmutations:

"Each of us so eagerly desired a God that this God had to be born and manifest himself every time we needed him to justify our maddest acts. An eighteen-year-old St. John was writing his gospel. It also happens that, when speaking about an abstract thing, we have to use images in order to define it, to make it visible. The thing is thus given an increasingly concrete life. It is quickened by the sap transfused by the images. Before long, it detaches itself from them and, defined by concrete qualifiers, lives with its own life. That was what happened to the Reformatory. I would sometimes refer to it as 'the old lady,' and then as 'the strict lady.' These two expressions would probably not have been enough for me to make her merge with a woman, but, in addition to the fact that they usually qualify mothers, they occurred to me in connection with the Reformatory at a time when I was weary of my solitude as a lost child and my soul yearned for a mother, and for everything that is peculiar to women: tenderness, slightly nauseating whiffs from the half-open mouth . . . I endowed the Reformatory with all these ridiculous and touching attributes until it assumed, in my mind, the physical image of a woman and there was established between us a union of soul to soul which exists only between mother and son . . . I reached the point of addressing invocations to it. . . . It was the mystical period. . . ."

The "images" of which he speaks are not tangible figures but metaphors. In Genet, the image is rarely visual; it remains a secret cleft in words. The procedure which will make a mother of the Reformatory is similar to that which we described in connection with argot. Genet refuses to name his object by the proper term, which is ignominious; the gap which is thus created is filled by substantified adjectives that designate marginal and metaphoric qualities of the object considered: *la vieille* (the old lady), *la sévère* (the strict lady). He proceeds exactly as would an aphasic in his desperate effort to express himself. But, at the same time, he transfigures reality by virtue of the real content of the words he uses. He changes the punitive resentment of society into tender and maternal solicitude and transforms the careless gesture with which it thrusts him aside into the act of love of a divinity that is testing him. *Son* of the old lady, he is the *elect* of the Reformatory. And this absent mother becomes a divinity, that is, she merges with one of the multiple forms adopted by the Other, a divine Proteus, that Genet wants to be for himself.

At times, words which he utters in his throat without moving his lips beget gestures which are themselves ballets that are danced before the inner divinity:

"He saw that he would have to turn about so as not to walk on the lawn. As he watched himself moving, he thought: 'He spun about,' and the word 'spun,' immediately caught on the wing, made him about-face smartly."

The reader will note that Culafroy refers to himself in the third person. "He spun about." He does not exactly assume the viewpoint of the Other; rather, he speaks of himself to the Other as the Other would speak of him. The statement is a trap; it opens out on an absence. And its magnificence comes not from its signification but from the obscure import of the syllables *"volte"** which evoke for him a luxurious little movement, such as might be made by a great lord.

The glamorous, sacred, dizzying words will little by little become adornments; he puts them around the necks of thieves, of convicts, he bedecks their hair with them. But they have ceased to designate. He counts on the Other to make them meaningful.

"The words 'beautiful' and 'beauty' . . . have a power that lies in their very matter. They no longer signify anything intelligible. I use them as one puts a diamond on a gown, and not for it to serve as a button."

So Genet has become a poet. But let there be no misunderstanding: his poetry is not a literary art, it is a means of salvation. He does not write or recite his poems, which, moreover, are often reduced to a single word. Poetry does not issue forth from him, it is not intended for a public: it is a way of life. He magnifies his abjection so as to be able to bear it and he dedicates his poems to a divine absence. Is he aware that he is a poet? Not at all. He knows that he is defending himself against death. An abandoned child, disheartened by his solitude, is trying to be two in one: that is the

---

* *Virevolter:* to spin about.—Translator's note.

origin of this extraordinary endeavor. The appearance oı the word-poem is still only one of the secondary aspects of his effort to become the Other that he is in the eyes of others. It will enable us, however, to penetrate more deeply into his consciousness and to overhear his inner monologue. When Joyce reports to us the soliloquies of Mr. Bloom, they seem to be our own; we recognize the unconstraint, the complicity with oneself in abandon, the damp tenderness, the crushed, broken words, which roll off almost unnoticed because we are too sluggish to pronounce them entirely. Genet's inner monologue, on the other hand, unrolls in the presence of a divine witness. That mind does not know abandonment: it is rigged, it is taut, even in its most secret places; it becomes incantation, a prayer, a thanksgiving, whereas ours is frittered away in vague reveries. It does not let itself be guided by the external world, but interprets it. No doubt the inner monologue of the little tramp displays the same discontinuity as that of Mr. Bloom, but it does so in a quite different sense: from the confusion of subjective impressions spring whole words, word-poems: yard-on, spun about, the strict lady. They are rockets that set the darkness on fire, then fall and burn out. And it is not an inner sweetness of words already understood that imparts to them their poetic value: quite the contrary, they are glazed, varnished, stately, they are addressed to another and flee Genet in the night of unknowing: "Allusive words reduced to equal silence," like those of Mallarmé. One of Genet's most constant traits, which is evident even in his conversation, is his contempt for anecdote. His life appeared to him very early as a succession of negligible sketches from which he had simply, before letting them sink into oblivion, to extract the poetic essence, not by making them epical, in the manner of certain mythomaniacs who reconstruct their lives as they go along, but by culling the word that polarized, interpreted and transfigured them and that condensed their poetic substance in order to offer it to a divine absence. This raw poetry is a prodigious endeavor to save the sacred amidst the shipwreck of profane man.

But the *locale* of the poems shifts: it is now *within Genet* that chance produces them. The lonely adolescent's attention to words and the waxy flexibility of inner language finally result in the welling up of fragments of poems, of isolated lines.

Driven away everywhere, the young Cain roves about, in Spain, in Poland, in Czechoslovakia. He is twenty years old, twenty-two. He walks in silence. Yet at every breath words fill his mouth. They come all by themselves, as in dreams. The rhythm of his pace and breath gives rise to vague phrases which break beneath their own weight. To whom is he speaking? To nobody. No intention of designating, of communicating, of teaching. And who is speaking? Nobody. Or rather, language itself. And what is language when it speaks to itself if not the world with its suns, its breezes, its marble steps and its flower gardens, *the world producing itself in the verbal attribute*? The Word is an attribute of the divine substance, and the infinite succession of its particular modes expresses the substance by the same token as does the succession of extensive modes. These phrases which assemble by themselves have the inertia of material figures. Genet listens to them, he observes without intervening. This passivity is partly feigned: it is he who utters the words. It is true that the rhythm of his pace determines his breathing, that he feels the beat even in his throat, that it creates verbal patterns, selects words; it is true that Genet does not think, that he is thought; it is true that by dint of repeating the words with which he enraptures himself he engenders, by virtue of assonance, alliteration and external similitude, units of sound composed of agglutinative words; it is true that he is sometimes surprised by these conglomerates. But this policy of nonintervention is calculated: its aim is to capture the world; the more independence he allows words, the more they will resemble things; the less the verbal automatism is directed, the better it will represent the Necessity of Nature; if language plays freely, little by little Being will be caught up in it and reflected in it: Genet will contain the universe. If, on the other hand, he wanted to regain control of words, to associate them first in accordance with their meaning, to speak, things would jump back, he would relapse into prose. In short, Genet observes with respect to words, which are *tools*, the quietistic attitude he adopted toward all utensils: he waits for them to offer him, by themselves, inhuman dreams, as the garments of the nun offered him sacrilegious gestures. And the result is not slow in showing itself: one day, when he is roaming through the countryside, frightened in the presence of the "diurnal mystery" of Nature, a clot of words emerges from his mouth; this conglomerate turns out to be more solid than the others, it is an octosyllable: "The first line of verse which to my amazement I found myself composing was the following: *Moissoneur des souffles coupés.*"*

This cluster is not even a sentence: it contains neither negation

---

* *Moissoneur des souffles coupés:* harvester of cut breaths.—Translator's note.

nor affirmation. A verbal entity owes its unity to a negative or affirmative movement. The sentence *is* because my activity synthetically unites each word to the preceding word and the following one; it "hangs together" because I involve myself in it entirely and intend, by means of it, to express a will. Nothing of the kind happens here: we are not stating that anyone *is* a "harvester of cut breaths," we do not even say that such a harvester exists. The verse would vanish were it not for the extreme cohesion that comes from its material organization: it stands up because the elements composing it have gathered according to certain affinities of sound and certain rhythms; its shape retains the memory of a respiratory rhythm; inertia substitutes in it for freedom. If it *designated* a harvester, an intention would have bracketed the words, but the fact is that it designates nothing; it quite simply *is:* there is nothing to conclude from it and one cannot conclude it from anything. What can one conclude from the sun, from the crowing of the cock? They are. A body does not affirm, one cannot even say that it affirms itself; it is a being which perseveres in its being. No sooner does this monolithic block emerge from Genet than it stands before him like a thing.

Things signify nothing. Yet each of them has a meaning. By *signification* I mean a certain conventional relationship which makes a present object the substitute of an absent object; by *meaning* I denote the participation of the being of a present reality in the being of other realities, whether present or absent, visible or invisible, and, eventually, in the universe. Signification is conferred upon the object from without by a signifying intention; meaning is a natural quality of things. The former is a transcendent relationship between one object and another; the latter, a transcendence that has fallen into immanence. The first can prepare for an intuition, can orient it, but cannot furnish it since the object signified is, in essence, external to the sign; the second is by nature intuitive; it is the odor that permeates a handkerchief, the perfume that issues from an empty open bottle. The siglum "XVII" *signifies* a certain century, but in museums that entire period clings like a veil, like a spider's web, to the curls of a wig, escapes in whiffs from a sedan chair. In producing his first poem as an object, Genet transforms the *signification* of the words into a *meaning.* When we first encounter it, it is inert and voluminous, like a carriage or a wig; it indicates nothing; it refers only to itself; it is at first only a sounded rhythm that imposes itself on our breathing; and it is only after repeating it as a refrain that we discover in it a vague and, as it were, natural savor. It would be a waste of time to look for logical organization in it: it expresses, without differentiating, the countryside and fear, the diurnal mystery of Nature: all things interpenetrate. *Harvester,* which is still redolent of ripe wheat, falls into line with *cutting,* which vaguely suggests the sickle's biting at plant stems; at the same time, "breathing" and "cutting" are coupled and awake in us the locution *"couper le souffle,"** which colors the verse with its unpleasant shade of meaning. In Genet, the ceremony is always corrected by cynicism; in this very pompous verse is concealed, like a trapdoor, a very familiar expression. To cut stems, to cut breath: if the verse actually signified, we would have to choose. But the fact is that we do not choose; the two meanings spread blindly through each other and coexist without merging or conflicting. In addition, "harvester" evokes the vague idea of a person; I am even fairly certain that it derives from a reminiscence: "What God, what harvester of the eternal summer . . ."; in any case, it is difficult for the reader not to recall vaguely, like a harmonic, this line from Hugo's "Booz endormi." We shall see, moreover, that Genet's poems draw their substance from famous poems whose blood they suck. Isn't that logical? These demoniacal, baneful poems are the parasites of official poetry as Evil is the parasite of Good. "Harvester" is thus haunted by the invisible idea of "rustic God": these words are surrounded by a vague atmosphere of countryside and divinity. However, as we do not know whether the countryside is God or whether God traverses it, the absence of subject preserves the concrete meaning of the word and its vague, pastoral overtones (summer, work in the fields, etc.) . I can imagine Ponge amusing himself by singing the praises of a trapezist and calling him *"moissoneur des souffles coupés."* The verse would thereby gain in logical signification. The triumph that the acrobat harvests every evening is the thrill provoked by his boldness. And I can also imagine Genet himself magnifying a criminal who mounts the scaffold and whose proud attitude imposes respect: no one dares to breathe. But in both cases the word "harvester" would exchange its meaning for an abstract signification. Thus, we say: "a rich harvest of this or that" without for a single moment thinking of farm work; the circus lights or the gleam of the blade would extinguish the weak country sun. But this word is here neither entirely substantive (since it is neither subject, predicate nor complement) nor entirely an adjective (since *nobody* is a harvester) ; it is even, to some extent, a verb: someone

---

* Literally, "to cut (someone's) breath"; the French expression is the equivalent of the English "to take (someone's) breath away."—Translator's note.

harvests, the act is suggested without being shown. In this indefinite vocable, quality, event, accident and substance interpenetrate, and that is precisely what happens when we consider a *thing*, water, for example, which we envisage, at the same time, as a certain quality of the world, a calm substance and the effect of an incessant movement of atoms. Since the words *are* without *being affirmed,* since no consciousness effects a selection among their different acceptations, the latter are all present simultaneously.

Although "harvester" vaguely personalizes the countryside, "cut breaths" depersonalizes the men who move about in it. In certain circumstances, a human being's breath *is* taken away. In substantializing breath and in not mentioning the being who possesses it, Genet makes the human vanish from the face of the earth; he peoples the countryside with invisible plants whose stems are columns of air. Yet an *allusion* is made to man by the word "cut," not because of its signification, but because it evokes a proverbial locution which is ordinarily applied to persons. A vague allusion since the locution is not present in its entirety. Actually, *to cut* exercises upon "breath" a twofold and conflicting influence. On the one hand, it tends—because of the traditional association: to take one's breath away—to bring this vocable back to the original meaning: air exhaled by the lungs. But, on the other hand, it undergoes the attraction, from a distance, of the word "harvester," which forces it to evoke a particular operation in farm work (cutting stems with a sickle) , and in this new acceptation it tends to draw the word "breaths" along with it: if *cutting* is a concrete, technical operation, then *breath* becomes a stem, since it represents the matter which is acted upon. The contradiction which is determined in "cut" by the conflicting influence of the word *harvester* and of the locution *to take one's breath away* is thus transmitted to *breath,* which expresses, in the syncretic unity of a meaning, the idea of breathing and the idea of plant, of grain. And this indetermination is heightened by the fact that *breaths* precedes *cut:* it is read or heard (therefore understood) before being determined by this participle; the effect of the latter will be retroactive, hence weakened; *breaths* manifests a kind of independence which is due to its being plural (in the proverbial locution it is always in the singular) and limply orients us toward the idea of breeze, of zephyr: light breaths waft through the countryside. Three significations interpenetrate in this word: wind, plant, breathing, in a kind of whirligig. And as it is the vegetable idea that finally prevails, without succeeding in quite eliminating the other meanings, all these respirations arrange themselves in orderly fashion and gravitate about a circular stroke of a scythe. Thereupon, an inversion is effected in our vision of things: I usually regard nature as a collection of phenomena which my consciousness unifies synthetically by the "I think" and the act of perception. But Genet's verse prompts us to imagine Nature as a vaguely personified power whose movement reunites in a kind of roundelay the rural plants that we have become. In short, the verse bears witness to the amazement of the young hoodlum feeling himself become an object for the great petrifying gaze of things; it contains, in an indistinct state, the intuition that Genet has described in prose in *The Thief's Journal:* "I had just come to know, as a result of fear, an uneasiness in the presence of diurnal nature, at a time when the French countryside where I wandered about, chiefly at night, was peopled all over with the ghost of Vacher, the killer of shepherds. As I walked through it, I would listen within me to the accordion tunes he must have played there, and I would mentally invite the children to come and offer themselves to the cutthroat's hands. . . . Nature disturbed me, giving rise within me to the spontaneous creations of fabulous fauna, or of situations and accidents, whose fearful and enchanted prisoner I was." The reader will notice that the prose does not succeed in achieving the fusion of the mystery of Nature and the human mystery of Vacher. The countryside is "peopled all over with the ghost of Vacher": that is where the language of general communication stops. The verse expresses the countryside's *being* Vacher. Not that Vacher is purely and simply identified with the harvester: if he were, we would not leave the realm of prose; the verse must retain the ambiguity of natural things: it is great Nature which, by its terrifying mystery, takes Genet's breath away, and it is Vacher the killer who harvests beautiful children; dying of surprise, Genet is changed into a pebble, into a lump of earth in the deserted yet living countryside, just as a child is changed into a corpse in the hands of the murderer. But this statement is still too logical: it distinguishes, contrasts and compares. And it would be too prosaic to say that Genet engages, through Nature, in pagan worship of Vacher, a sinister god Pan. No, the verse is *entirely* the mystery of Nature and it is *entirely* Vacher. "What? Is it possible to say all that in eight syllables?" I reply: no, one cannot *say* it. Besides, a line *means* nothing at all: man and nature, murder and harvest, it *does not express* Genet's feeling: it *is* that feeling become thing, floating through the words, participating in the inertia of the sound unit and retaining, within its immanence, only a stale memory of its past transcendence. The words designated the world: Genet has put the world into the words; but in so doing he himself has crept into it. This sad, stunted verse achieves the unity of the subject and the object.

Our vagabond plays at capturing the universe. He does not create, but he makes himself the theater of Creation; he is not a poet, but he poetizes. Poems are born in him, like crimes; language turns away from its original destination. But we know him sufficiently to be aware that the game of creation must have a reverse side: if he captures the world, he certainly does so in order to destroy it.

Let us return to our octosyllable: it is understood that we cannot comprehend it. But the words are not only juxtaposed; they are united by logical connections over and above their sonant and rhythmic affinities: "breaths" is the "noun complement" of "harvester," "cut" is an adjective that modifies "breaths"; we are thus prompted by the grammatical structure of this sound unit to effect certain significations, as the mathematician effects the operations indicated in a polynomial although the quantities he manipulates are represented by symbols and he must always be unaware of the numerical results of his work. Now, if the mind, following the operative indications, beyond the trembling little soul of the verse, seeks to effect the formal and abstract significations that shimmer at the surface of this nonsignifying unit, everything sinks into nothingness, everything—even the poetic meaning—is canceled with a play on words. We expect the harvest of cut grain to be fine and rich; but these grains are breaths, and a cut breath is only the stopping of a breath, that is, nothing, not even a bit of air that one exhales: one will make sheaves of nothingness. The strange being who haunted the woods, whether woodland god or criminal, was defined only by his functions: having become a harvester of nothing, he vanishes with the breaths, everything is canceled; the rocky, compact density of this sound unit and the shimmering of the light around the stone concealed a cold, dark emptiness. A signification beyond the syncretic interpenetration of the meanings was suggested to us; and this signification is the destruction of all signification, the challenging of all prose; Genet put the whole countryside into this verse, but only to annihilate it. The capturing of the world, an act guided by resentment, ends in catastrophe. We find Genet in his entirety in this abrupt reversal, Genet with his loves and betrayals, his perpetual whirligigs of being and nonbeing. To be sure, he wanted to possess the universe; he abandoned himself to the Word; he played at quietistic contemplation; but he betrayed from below; his abstractedness was only a feint: underneath, this sly prestidigitator was composing without seeming to and let pass only the words that could serve him. If he applied himself with such passion to giving words a semblance of objective being, he did so in order the better to annihilate the being of the world. The verse was a trap; it appeared to be inert, abandoned; it was language without men; the universe let itself be caught in it. But no sooner did it descend into the words than everything vanished: one thought that the verse *meant* nothing; the fact is, it *meant to say nothing*.

The pages which Blanchot has written about Mallarmé apply admirably to Genet: "In the first place, language is characterized by a contradiction: in a general way, it is that which destroys the world in order to re-engender it in the realm of meaning, of significant 'values'; but in its creative form it settles only on the negative aspect of its task and becomes a pure power of contestation and transfiguration. . . . That is possible insofar as, taking on a tangible value, it becomes itself a thing, a body, an incarnate power. The real presence and material affirmation of language give it power to seize and dismiss the world. Density and thickness of sound are necessary for it to release the silence which it contains and which is the element of nothingness without which it would never give rise to a new meaning. Thus, it needs to be infinitely in order to produce the feeling of an absence—and to become similar to things in order to break up our natural relationships with them."*

Thus, the word is both a sonant object and a vehicle of signification. If you direct your attention to the signification, the word is effaced; you go beyond it and fuse the meaning with the thing signified. If, however, you are exiled from the universe and are attentive only to the verbal body, which is the only reality you can possess and hold between your tongue and lips, then it is the thing signified which disappears and the signification becomes a vanishing of being, a mist which, beyond the word, is in the process of being dissipated. Genet makes it his business to have eyes only for the word; the universe, captured and inserted into the statement, goes up in smoke. But this poetic procedure, far from liberating the poet, enslaves him further: Genet remains in Hell. He is not clearly aware of himself as a creative power: in aspiring to submit to the powers of language and to allow the vocables to arrange themselves within him according to their affinities in order to pro-

* *Faux-pas*, N.R.F., p. 44.

duce, as Mallarmé says, "the notion of an escaping object which is wanting," he absents himself from speech and lets it sound alone in the desert. Blanchot also says: "If language isolates itself from man as it isolates man from all things, if it is never the act of some-one who speaks with a view to being understood by someone, we shall realize that it offers to the one who considers it in this state of solitude the spectacle of a peculiar and quite magical power. It is a kind of consciousness without subject which, separated from being, is a detachment, a challenge, an infinite power of creating emptiness and of situating itself in a want."*

4. The Rejection of History

So Cain flees from the sight of God. The power of becoming an object, which has devolved upon all of us, has been exaggerated in him and been transformed into a permanent objectivity: *visibility* is his very substance; he is because he is perceived. For him, the world, even before it is divided into trees, rivers, houses, animals and people, is a gaze that draws him from nothingness, envelops him, condemns him. Things are eyes. They keep him at a distance. He glides on the surface of being, thrust back by the light that escapes from the leaves, from the corollas, from the windows and that exposes him to everyone. In order to defend himself he steps back and views himself in perspective; he looks at *himself* being looked at; a soft, transparent consciousness inserts itself between his reflective consciousness and the world. Being keeps him at a distance and he stands aside from being. He is the sole object of those millions of eyes and *his* sole object. From time to time, being rips apart like a piece of cloth, a *miracle* has taken place; for a fleeting moment Genet touches his life on things; he has the amaz-ing privilege of being able to total up his life, of gathering it up within that instant, he is a sacred totality for himself.

Whence an essential feature of this adolescence: Genet has no *history*. Or, if he does have one, it is behind him. In order for a man to have a history, he must evolve, the course of the world must change him in changing itself, and he must change in changing the world, his life must depend on everything and on himself alone, he must discover in it, at the moment of death, a vulgar product of the age and the singular achievement of his will. A historical life

---

* Blanchot adds (p. 48): "Perhaps this trickery is the truth of all written things." At this point I cease to follow him. He should, from this point of view, distinguish between poetry and prose and, in the case of prose, examine different types of writing.

is full of chance events, of encounters: one met one's future brother-in-law in a prison camp; a certain woman, for whom one thought one would die of love, in the course of a journey. The future is uncertain, we are our own risk, the world is our peril: we cannot exist in any time for ourself as a totality.

Genet is a totality for himself. He receives, at certain privileged moments, the power to see his entire life, from the "sweet natural confusion", to the penal colony and death. This is tantamount to saying that his undertaking is *done* and that nothing can act upon him from without. His only purpose, his only chance of salvation, is to act upon himself on the level of reflection, so as to accept unreservedly, with love, the horrible destiny in store for him.

It is quite true that he wanders about the world and that he has more adventures in a week than many men in a year. And yet nothing happens to him: in acting too strongly upon that soul when it was still young and tender, the world blocked it. Between the ages of fifteen, when he was at Mettray, and twenty-five, when he committed his first burglary, ten years go by without marking him. No doubt he sinks little by little to the depths of abjection, but he does so by his own weight; and besides, this abjection hardly affects him. Filthy, ragged, debased, hopeless, he prostitutes himself and begs. Is he more abject, more desolate than in the days when the little Mettray toughs made a butt of him? The original crisis raised horror to its highest pitch at the very beginning: it seems that nothing can increase it. The swift, brutal events that fill his daily life can *reveal* his destiny to him in an ecstasy of love or fright; none of them has the power to *make it*.

Theft, prison, what can they bring him? We have seen that his larcenies destroy both himself and objects. But the soul is elastic: after the ceremony of theft, Genet finds himself to be what he has always been, like the Christian after Mass. The *miracles of horror* make him enjoy his life but do not transform him, for he reacts to each of them in the same way. Compare the various episodes in *Our Lady of the Flowers, Miracle of the Rose* and *The Thief's Journal:* the event varies, but Genet's ritual conduct does not change a jot.* Little Culafroy notes that the sole of his shoe is torn. Immediately he abandons himself to the muscular arms of the angels, who carry him off to paradise. Youngsters amuse themselves

---

* Cf. a similar antihistoricism in Jean Cocteau: "The rhythm of our life develops in periods, all of them alike, except that they present themselves in a way that makes them unrecognizable. The event-trap or the person-trap is all the more dangerous in that it itself is governed by the same law and wears the mask sincerely" (*Opium*).

in covering the hero of *Miracle of the Rose* with gobs of spit: it is roses that they throw at him, a rain of flowers. Policemen amuse themselves with the tube of vaseline that they have found in his pocket: the tube, in its royal inertia, holds its own against them, disturbs them and radiates. As soon as the humiliation appears, it is effaced, "overcompensated for" by an invariable mechanism. The poetic miracles themselves are powerless to affect him, for it is he who produces them: "Poetry," he says, "is willful." As for his human relationships, they are all of the same type: his love is unrequited. But this secret will-to-be-unloved, this crafty refusal of reciprocity, is a way of keeping others at a distance: in one of Huxley's novels, the hero, who is shy and disdainful, gives big tips to waiters so as to avoid entering into contact with them. Genet, who is even more disdainful, imagines giving himself entirely so as to discourage friendship. The mad loves of Genet the Victim are rejected friendships. Moreover, he knows this very well, and we have only to let him talk in order to understand how the praying mantis kills its males and eats them in order to absorb them into its own substance.

Hearing him, one gets the impression that he always falls in love at first sight. The mere appearance one evening of Darling or Bulkaen or Stilitano overwhelms the victim. That is something *new,* the sudden intrusion of the unexpected; time staggers and destiny shifts. Later, Genet will take pleasure in magnifying by glittering words the memory of these amorous encounters. But he lies: one of the most singular characteristics of this overdetermined soul is that nothing ever *happens* to it. Or rather, it considers novelty to be negligible: novelty is the anecdote, the particular and fortuitous circumstance that he disregards in order to go straight to the essence, the contingency that conceals the ineluctable necessity, the profane matter through which he receives the sacred. The hosts are all new, they were blessed on a certain day, at a certain hour. But who cares about these sealing wafers? The faithful is mindful only of the eternal, eternally repeated union of the Christian soul with its God. The truth is that Genet never *encounters* anybody. He never sees a contingent, a particular creature moving toward him out of the night or from the back of a bar, a creature who would have to be observed, studied, comprehended: let a good-looking pimp or a sailor appear and he will *recognize* them right away, he will perceive the essence that they manifest: he sees *the* tough, *the* sailor; future and past become identical in a kind of prophetic, fatalistic and weary intuition. In like manner, the Platonic soul is awakened by the sight of tangible objects to a reminiscence of the archetypes which it formerly contemplated. *The* sailor, *the* criminal: Genet has known them from time immemorial; he knows that he has always been submissive to the Eternal who goes by in the form of a pimp. If he breaks down in the presence of the handsome murderer, it is because he *re-experiences* this submission as a hereditary bondage and as the terrible prefiguration of his future. Stilitano approaches him and "although it was he who made the first advance, I knew, as I answered, the *almost desperate nature of the gesture the invert dares when he approaches a young man."* What is Stilitano if not *the* tough? And Genet, if not *the* invert? And what is there between them if not *the* desperate gesture that the invert dares in the presence of a handsome young man? Genet lives in the midst of an Italian comedy in which Scapin, Pantaloon and Pulcinella are replaced by Chéri-bibi the convict, Rocambole the burglar, Javert the detective, Fantomas the prince of crime.* These are traditional fictions, of social origin. The criminal, the soldier, the traitor, the sailor, the jailor, the prisoner are born of the popular imagination; they haunt tales and legends; they are to be found even today in music-hall songs; for centuries their function has been to reflect to the multitude their nocturnal terrors and dreams of adventure, their fears and the grim ruminations of their resentment; ambivalent figures, baneful and tutelary, they will become—depending on one's mood—the fierce Cartouche or the magnanimous Lupin. Genet has fed on the serial stories which are the *chansons de geste* of these plebeian heroes. As a poor child, he participates in the collective reverie of the poor. This imagery, which is somewhat outdated, provides him with the great dignitaries of his black nobility. All his companions have been present for a long time, he knows their exploits and their roles by heart. But from time to time an actor lends them his gestures or voice. Through Stilitano, the one-armed Barcelona hoodlum, Genet discerns the Tough, his eternal love, just as Jean-Louis Barrault, when playing Hamlet, discerns Polonius, the old Danish pimp, through M. Brunot, ex-dean of the Comédie-Française. Only a few minutes ago Genet did not know Stilitano; now he is speaking to him and his legs tremble: yet nothing has happened, except that some gold dust has materialized a ray of light. Here is the description of another encounter; the mechanism is clearly apparent:

---

* Chéri-bibi, Rocambole, etc.: characters in well-known French serial stories.—Translator's note.

"Had he not spat in his hands to turn a crank, I would never have noticed a boy of my age. This gesture, which workmen make, made me so dizzy that I thought I was falling* straight down to a period—or region of myself—long since forgotten. My heart awoke, and at once my body thawed. With wild speed and precision the boy registered on me: his gestures, his hair, the jerk of his hips, the curve of his back, the merry-go-round on which he was working, the movements of the horses, the music, the fairground, the city of Antwerp containing them, the Earth cautiously turning, the Universe protecting so precious a burden, and I standing there, frightened at possessing the world and at knowing I possessed it.

"I did not see the spit on his hands: I recognized the puckering of the cheek, and the tip of the tongue between his teeth. I again saw the chap rubbing his tough, black palms. As he bent down to grab the handle, I noticed his crackled, but thick, leather belt. A belt of that kind could not be an ornament like the kind that holds up the trousers of a man of fashion. By its material and thickness it was penetrated with the following function: holding up the most obvious sign of masculinity which, without this strap, would be nothing, would no longer contain, would no longer guard its manly treasure but would tumble down on the heels of a shackled male. The boy was wearing a windbreaker. As the belt was not inserted into loops, at every movement it rose a bit as the pants slid down, revealing his skin. I stared at the belt, petrified. I saw it operating surely. At the sixth jerk of the hip, it girdled—except at the fly where the two ends were buckled—the chap's bare back and waist."

A passer-by who looks at a woman is sensitive only to personal details: a supple body, a triangular face, the sinuous faintness of a smile.† But it will be observed that in Genet's account the young boy remains undifferentiated. Had it not been for that chance gesture, Genet would not even have noticed him. Thus, it is *a gesture* that provokes his ecstasy: not even an act, a gesture. The workman's effort is in danger of making it ungraceful; in addition, it is too austere, it reminds the thief of the disconcerting existence of the proletariat. The gesture of spitting in his hands, which is a small rite, a ballet figure, evokes labor while remaining quite inefficacious

---

* It will be observed that the word *fall* designates in Genet, at one and the same time, the state of the criminal who consents to his crime, that of the poet who turns a felicitous phrase and that of the homosexual who recognizes his destiny in the features of a handsome man.

† I am simplifying in order to stress the differences. Masculine desire is not exempt from symbolic patterns; it has generalized structures. The fact remains that the male who "hunts" is seeking a new adventure; he wants to vary his life.

and gratuitous. It manifests virile transcendency, but without setting it at grips with objects: it is only *presented, acted;* in like manner, the useless muscles of Pimps display a power which is never of use to them. And the young man's movements no doubt have a certain beauty, but although this condition is necessary, it is not sufficient to awaken Genet's attention. What matters first is that the gesture is immediately perceived as typical. It is a "gesture which workmen make," not an ephemeral shudder on that particularly unique day. He employs a frequentative verb, half abstract, already generalized. The gesture is not even a copy of an attitude issued in millions of copies. The attitude itself, so pure in its beauty that it is no longer anyone's and that it is struck for its own sake, opens out like a fan and masks the child. Genet contemplates human labor, which is being danced before the eyes of a god; if he desires to be possessed, it is by all the young workmen of the world. But the gesture is thereby *recognized,* not perceived, it is prophesied and remembered at the same time: "I thought I was falling straight down to a period—or region of myself—long since forgotten." Starting from there, he "registers" the young boy, but only to fail once again to grasp his individual reality. A moment before, the boy was reduced to a symbolic gesture; now, he becomes diluted in the universe. Finally, he is only an unbalanced mediation between the totality of being and the choreographic figuration of human transcendency. Of course, no sooner is this totality given than Genet liberates himself from it and re-enters himself. In the movement of heterosexual ecstasy, desire is projected outward, the male forgets himself, he is only the delicate light which envelops the silk of a foreign flesh and makes it glow. Genet, on the other hand, returns to himself, he loses himself in order to find himself. The *recognized* gesture sends him back to the world and the world back to himself; he remains "frightened at possessing the world and at knowing I possessed it." That is, he shelves the world: if he does "possess" the universe, it is not in the manner of emperors or captains of industry who boast of leaving their mark on it, but in that of a contemplative who discovers that "the world is its representation." And in this great body of *things perceived,* a gesture stands out, object of an aesthetic intuition, which reflects to Genet only what Genet has put into it: it is the appearance to which the Thief has assigned the function of delivering to him the totality of appearances.

Nevertheless, this primary apprehension does not suffice. The amorous soul that swirls about a small earthly brilliance must swoop down on a concrete detail and carry it off in its talons. Now, it is noteworthy that the erotic object which Genet will choose remains a pure symbol: it is neither the young boy's face nor his hair nor even his legs or rump; it is a detail of his outfit, to wit, a badly attached belt. Genet is, in this case, like the "fetishist" who prefers a woman's shoes to the woman who wears them. The belt excites him *by its function:* it "is holding up the most obvious sign of masculinity." No doubt the flesh is present in his perception: he sees the young man's bare back. But it does not excite him directly: it is the passive background against which the movement of the belt appears, or, if one prefers, in sliding up and down the belt engenders by its caresses that soft, inert and polished matter as the mathematician, in laying out a circle, brings forth the surface of the circumference from an undifferentiated space. For this eroticism without sensuality, the privileged object is not the flesh but the gesture; the flesh subtends the pantomime as connective tissue unites vital organs.

After that, is the boy good-looking? The question is meaningless. An adorable gesture has alighted on a human being, like a pigeon on a statue: all that one asks of the flesh which carries this movement is that it not draw attention to itself. Stilitano, who represents for a time the gangster, is required only to have the right physique for the role, to "be the character," that is, to have a sufficiently terrible bearing to act out his role in the ritual ceremonies of love. Genet will then speak of his lover's *beauty*. But this beauty remains abstract; it does not live. A heterosexual experiences the beauty of his mistress, discovers it beneath the makeup, learns each day how fatigue decomposes it toward evening and how art composes it anew; it changes from minute to minute, depending on whether he moves away or draws nearer. Stilitano's beauty is stiff and fixed: the reason is that he does not possess it in his own right; it is that of the Tough of Toughs, eternal and impassive, which can neither increase nor decrease nor change. In like manner, Ophelia's face, on the stage, is given all at once, and at a fixed distance: if one approaches it, it grows blurred and disappears, revealing, like a mask that has been removed, the painted young face of the actress. Genet wants Stilitano's beauty to keep him at a distance; it is from afar that it holds up, that it fulfills its function, which is to *represent* the fatality of crime. Stilitano, Bulkaen, Darling, all of them together, have only a single beauty, that of the archetype which, each in turn, they embody for Genet.

The ice is broken: they speak to each other, Genet follows Stili-

tano, they are going to live together. Are real relationships going
to be established between them? Not at all. Genet suddenly discovers the nigger in the woodpile: Stilitano is playing the role of
Stilitano. What he wants is to *appear* to be the Tough whom Genet
wants to love in him. The two men secretly smell each other out
and, without even admitting it to himself, each is aware that the
other is an actor: "Stilitano was playing. He liked knowing that he
was outside the law; he liked feeling that he was in danger. An
aesthetic need placed him there. He was attempting to copy an
ideal hero, the Stilitano whose image was already inscribed in a
heaven of glory. . . . Blinded at first by his august solitude, by his
calmness and serenity, I believed him to be anarchically self-creat-
ing, guided by the sheer impudence, the nerviness, of his gestures.
The fact is, *he was seeking a type.* Could it have been the one represented by the conquering hero in the comic books?" As a matter
of fact, it is precisely with this comic-book hero that Genet wants
to have dealings. He doesn't care the least about the particular
features of the flesh-and-blood Stilitano, his weaknesses, his contingency, the slightly insipid flavor of this poisonous fruit, the
details of his history. These matters are only the anecdote. He pays
attention to them only in order to extract from them the elements
amenable to transfiguration: "For every behavior, however weird
in appearance, I knew at once, without thinking, a justification.
The strangest gesture or attitude seemed to me to correspond to
an inner necessity. . . . Every comment I heard, however preposterous, appeared to me to be made at exactly the right moment. I
would therefore have gone to penitentiaries, prisons, would have
known low dives, stations, roads, without being surprised. If I think
back, I do not find in my memory any of those characters which an
eye different from mine, a more amused eye, would have singled
out." Genet's world resembles that of the chronic paranoiac: he
interprets. He is, like Barrault, both actor and director: while
playing his own role, he helps Stilitano play his, he tries to find for
him situations and types of behavior which enable him to *appear:*
"The quality of my love for him required that he prove his manliness. If he was the splendid beast that sparkled with ferocity, let
him indulge in games worthy of it." One can surmise the patience,
craftiness and knowledge of the heart that the slave needs in order
to be able to "incite" the master to steal. Genet resembles the wife
who "knows how to handle" her husband: he puts in a word, at the
right moment, with humble and discreet insistency; he quietly
pulls the strings of vanity, of the love of lucre. But, it may be

argued, at least these are real relationships: Genet knows his Stilitano "like the fingers of his hand." So he does, but his tactic is only
half-conscious. He cannot make up his mind as to whether he is
trying to awaken the splendid beast by tempting him with the
highest danger* or whether he is trying to get a vain and stupid
animal to perform the gestures necessary to the show of Evil. At
bottom, he knows very well that Stilitano is a coward: "His cowardly acts themselves melt my rigor. I liked his taste for loafing."
But, after all, must one be a maiden to play the role of Joan of Arc?
Out of the corner of his eye Genet sees his partner's weakness, sees
through his paltry bragging and penetrates to the depths of his
heart. But he places this spiteful lucidity, this sharp sense of reality,
in the service of the lie. Barrault, director and actor, sees Ophelia,
Horatio and Polonius in like manner. If he is on the alert for real
incidents that can always happen, it is out of a marginal vigilance,
in order to preserve the illusion, to prevent tittering. If Ophelia
forgets her lines and starts spluttering, he will be able to invent
something on the spot so as to make the audience think that her
spluttering is deliberate, unless she herself regains her composure
and sets things straight. In that case, nobody on the stage will be
fooled, but they will be grateful to her for having prevented the
worst thing that could happen. Similarly, Genet the director is
grateful to Stilitano the actor for maintaining, in certain difficult
situations, the fiction that they are eagerly trying to impose on each
other. I shall cite only one example of this complicity in putting on
an act: Stilitano is in the habit of insulting fairies. He thereby
manifests his manly violence. This violence is, of course, a sham:
he knows very well that these timid little girls won't answer back.
But one day he is mistaken in his role: he calls out to some toughs
whom he has mistaken for girl queens. In like manner, Polonius,
who is going to move back into a chair, may one evening misjudge
the distance and fall flat on his back. "A fight seemed inevitable.
One of the young men provoked Stilitano outright: 'If you're not
fruit, come on and fight.' " Now Stilitano does not like to fight, and
Genet knows it; he is therefore not asked to perform an act of
courage but to find the gesture that will permit him to preserve an
appearance of gallantry: "Stilitano felt he was in danger. My presence no longer bothered him. He said: 'After all, fellows, you're
not going to fight with a cripple.' He held out his stump. But he
did it with such simplicity, such sobriety, that this vile hamming,

---

* Always the haunting parallelism with the ethics of Claudel.

instead of disgusting me with him, ennobled him. He withdrew, not to the sound of jeers, but to a murmur expressing the discomfort of decent men discovering the misery about them. Stilitano went off slowly, protected by his outstretched stump, which was placed simply in front of him. The absence of the hand was as real and effective as a royal attribute, as the hand of justice." Polonius has got to his feet again; he is inventing, while rubbing his back, a few well-chosen words about the woes of old age that stop the laughter or at least channelize it. Barrault and Genet look at their partners gratefully: they have saved the performance. To be sure, Genet is not fooled, but the contempt that he feels in his heart does not count: what matters is that the show can go on.

Meanwhile, Genet has persuaded Stilitano to steal. They now commit burglaries together. Are these shared experiences going to instill a bit of truth into their actions? After all, they have to smash a window, break a lock, help each other: one of them is on the lookout while the other ransacks the apartment. But theft is, for Genet, a religious ceremony; the accomplice participates in it as an officiant or as an actor. "The boldness of a thief's life—and its light —would have meant nothing if Stilitano at my side had not been proof of it. My life became magnificent by men's standards since I had a friend whose beauty derived from the idea of luxury. I was the valet whose job was to look after, to dust, polish and wax, an object of great value which, however, through the miracle of friendship, belonged to me." One would think he was talking about a fetishistic object or a theatrical mask or a religious prop.

Furthermore, with Stilitano, Genet does not experience the intoxication of burglary. Stilitano is a petty pimp, a phony, who lacks what it takes to play his role in so dangerous a game: "He was too unexcited by nocturnal adventures for me to experience any real intoxication with [him]." It is in this sense that an actor can say of his partner: "He believes in his role so little that I get no pleasure out of playing mine." What Genet requires of his accomplice at the ritual moment of the burglary is a transfiguration: the thief must rise to the plane of the sacred, his temporality must become a liturgical time, he must wear a mask and tragic rags, he must reflect to Genet the sudden brilliance which Genet feels that he himself is emitting. In short, Stilitano is unable to stir the feelings: as they say in the theater, he's not "right for the role." But let us assume for a moment that Genet meets a *real* burglar, one who believes in his role, who plays it with passion: will they achieve a solid and sincere comradeship based on the sense of danger, on mutual confidence? Genet will later do jobs with Guy, who loves burglary. Let us see what he says about him:

"It was with Guy, in France, that I was to have the profound revelation of what burglary is. When we were locked in the little lumber room waiting for night and the moment to enter the empty offices of the Municipal Pawnshop in B., Guy suddenly seemed to me inscrutable, secret. He was no longer the ordinary chap whom you happen to run into somewhere; he was a kind of destroying angel. He tried to smile. He even broke out into a silent laugh, but his eyebrows were knitted together. From within this little fairy where a hoodlum was confined there sprang forth a determined and terrifying fellow, ready for anything—and primarily for murder—if anyone made so bold as to hinder his action. He was laughing, and I thought I could read in his eyes a will to murder which might be practiced on me. The longer he stared at me, the more I had the feeling that he read in me the same determined will to be used against him."

The matter is now clear: once again we are witnessing a play of mirrors. Guy, transfigured, reflects to Genet his own transfiguration, and Genet, rigid, strained in a kind of hypnosis that provokes what psychiatrists call a "mirror imitation," in turn reflects to Guy his sacred image. Moreover, *it is death* that makes both burglars glow with a dark light. The burglary scheme—a very ordinary, mediocre project which in itself implies only the limited, mediocre risk of prison—is transformed into an inordinate project and is transcended toward the absolute of the human condition. The risk becomes total; one will kill if necessary, which means that one is ready to be killed. But this ritual celebration of death is, in actual fact, carried out in the realm of the imaginary. Would Guy have fired? I doubt it.* In any case, what is certain is that Genet is incapable of committing a murder: we know this since he has told us so in all kinds of ways; one of the favorite themes of his plays is that one cannot *become* a murderer. All this is only a dream. But this dismal and violent dream throws into relief the strange companionship of the two burglars. The enterprise—insofar as it is real—contains the elements of real friendship: even theft can serve as a bond. But hardly has the friendship dared come into being than Genet challenges it by this pompous and imaginary project of killing and being killed. He is probably distrustful of this fellow-

---

* For the reason Genet himself gives: that a burglar and a murderer are of two radically different species and that one does not move from the first to the second.

ship in work insofar as it may become a real relationship. Furthermore, there is a deep flaw in this complicity: since theft is destruction, the solidarity which it imposes on the accomplices slackens as the operation is carried out; no positive achievement will ever reflect to them the image of their collaboration. When a job is over, they divide a sum of money between them and their semblance of friendship is dissipated. There remains the simple coexistence of two solitudes. Similarly with all bonds between destroyers: the mechanical solidarity of adventurers and soldiers gives rise to the eternal dream of creating an indissoluble union through destruction: "The shortest path from one heart to the other is the sword," says the feudal Claudel. And Malraux expresses himself in much the same terms. Since the death which they deal unites brothers-in-arms with the enemy more closely than military comradeship unites them among themselves, each of them secretly harbors a desire to turn his arms against the others. Guy and Genet, adventurers, "soldiers of crime," are united because they play the same role at the same time: they are two embodiments of a single *"persona"* which they reflect back and forth to each other. But this *persona* is Solitude, solitude in death given and received. They look at each other, hate each other, and each is, for the other, the image of his own hatred: it is absolute separation which joins them. The great stiffened figure which each of them assumes and which he contemplates in the other is the symbol of both erection and corpselike rigidity. After that, Genet can therefore tell us that when their job is over thieves make love: homosexual love is a double murder; the Pimp stabs the girl queen and perishes in the quicksand. This double hit, this reciprocal murder which the two accomplices were meditating, was basically erotic; inversely, coitus will enact it symbolically.

But we must return to Stilitano, the fake tough. Genet is bound to him too by the identity of their *"persona."* What does this mean if not that Genet has reduced Stilitano to a pure appearance and the appearance itself to a collection of gestures? The *act* does not matter: the aim is to be. In order to be Stilitano, he must make the gestures that Stilitano makes. It would be all the easier to do so in that he has certainly borrowed them: a gesture is transmitted like a title, like a privilege: Darling—another replica of Stilitano— "keeps his shoulders hunched tight so as to resemble Sebastopol Pete, and Pete holds them like that so as to resemble Pauley the Rat, and Pauley so as to resemble Teewee, and so on." The essential characteristic of a gesture is that it has already been made. It is not an operation that we invent as we go along: it is a unit that is already constituted, a totality that governs its parts, something like a dance step. It must not be regarded as a unique, dated event, like, for example, "the ironic and fearful attitude which Stilitano assumed that September morning," but as an already pondered, half-abstract reality which exists only by virtue of its repetition and the origin of which is lost in the mists of time, in short a rite, a tradition: what matters is not the way in which Stilitano, *that evening*, brought a blob of white spittle to his lips, but the way in which he rolled it *tirelessly* in his open mouth. Frequentatives are midway between the abstract and the concrete: this smile is, despite everything, perceived this morning, at eight o'clock, in such-and-such a light; it is a particular event. But I immediately perceive it as the reappearance *of* Stilitano's smile; I identify it as soon as it appears; I see it as the dated manifestation of a nontemporal reality, a fixed, stable quality whose essential characteristic is permanence; it is a historical fact, a unique phenomenon which exists only in its happening. When Genet runs into Stilitano again in Antwerp, he immediately *recognizes* "his way of rolling a blob of spit from one corner of his mouth to the other" as he recognizes the color of his hair or his mutilated arm. Because the gesture presents itself as "having already been," it *possesses being*, it exists per se, it characterizes a person. But precisely for that reason, precisely because it has already been thought, already been acted, it remains radically *other,* other even than the one who makes it. Genet sees it unfolding from without, and Stilitano feels it settling upon him and marking him with its stamp: but it remains as external to the latter as to the former because it is, for Stilitano who has borrowed it, *the gesture of another*. By means of the gesture, Stilitano simultaneously plays, feels, recognizes and learns what he is. And what he is is precisely *another:* "Darling will never suffer, or will always be able to get out of a tight spot by his ease in taking on the gestures of some chap he admires who happens to be in the same situation . . . thus, his desires . . . were neither the desire to be a smuggler, king, juggler, explorer or slave trader, but the desire to be one of the smugglers, one of the kings, one of the jugglers, etc., that is, as if . . ."

For the gesture is *sacred:* it is the gesture of an emperor or of a hero; I borrow it from those terrifying beings; it settles on me, tightens my consciousness, which is always a bit slack, imposes an unaccustomed rhythm upon it: it is a sacrament. "In the most woeful of postures, Darling will be able to remember that it was also that of one of his gods . . . and his own posture will be sacred and thereby even better than merely tolerable." The gesture contains a *power*. And the greatness of this power is measured by the might of the one who first created it: "Acts have aesthetic and moral value only insofar as those who perform them are endowed with power. . . . This power is delegated to us sufficiently for us to feel it within us, and this is what enables us to bear our having to lower our head in order to step into a car, because at the moment that we lower it an imperceptible memory makes of us a movie star or a king or a vagrant (but he too is a king) who lowered his head in the same way (we saw him in the street or on the screen). . . . Priests who repeat symbolic gestures feel themselves imbued with the virtue not of the symbol but of the first executant." The gesture is thus a ritualistic and sacralizing communion with the ancestor of the clan or the eponymous hero. Its value is no longer due to its own content but to the rank and virtues of the first executant. Insofar as it is a repeated event, it is a religious ceremony; insofar as it is, in its synthetic unity, an organized being, it is a replica. In slipping into my muscles it retains the stamp of its origin; in fact it instills within me the person of its first executant which is transcendent in immanence; an imperceptible distance separates it from my consciousness, and this perspective enables me to revere within me the eminent presence of the emperor or of the king of the smugglers; but it is at the same time myself and it is I whom I respect in it.

Humble and lost in the crowd, Genet sees the star stepping into the auto, surrounded by universal respect. What the star *is* matters little; she is only her gestures. But what counts is that she *is really a star,* and this means, in any case, that the others recognize that she has the attributes of a star (rich clothing, fine car, money, royal beauty) and that they authenticate, by their reverence, the gestures which she performs. The original power of sacralization comes from the community and has its own law; if it settles upon objects, it does so by virtue of this law rather than with the aim of consecrating their value: "I wonder why Death, film stars, traveling virtuosos, queens in exile, banished kings, have a body, a face and hands. Their fascination lies in something other than a human charm, and without disappointing the enthusiasm of the peasants who wanted to catch a glimpse of her at the door of her train, Sarah Bernhardt could have appeared in the form of a little matchbox." The mirror is unimportant: its worshipers kneel before the reflection of their collective power. And since the embodiment of these powers can be anyone at all, any gesture whatever will, provided it emanates from this embodiment, partake of its sacred nature. "The sacred surrounds us and subdues us; it is the submission of flesh to flesh." Finally, the gesture is only the king's or the star's body *acting;* that "luminous" personality, which is a simple condensation of great social forces, slips into it. The gesture is the act *become object.* The consciousness which produced the action, which invented its successive moments and bound them together by the synthetic activity of the "I think," becomes a magical unit, an objective soul, an entelechy of that organism. And, in incorporating itself into this *act-object,* the respect of the crowd confers mana upon it. If we want to steal the star's or emperor's mana, we must steal his gestures. If Genet draws himself up in his cell and makes a royal sign with his hand, a diffused respect immediately surrounds him; the cell becomes a crowd, the walls have ears and eyes.

What, then, could prevent him from *becoming* Stilitano? Since we are merely playing at what we are, we are whatever we can play at, man, animal, plant, even mineral. Genet is very serious in making Green Eyes say: "I tried to be a dog, a cat, a horse, a tiger, a table, a stone! I even tried, me too, to be a rose! . . . I did what I could. I squirmed and twisted. People thought I had convulsions." This is not surprising: the being of the animal is its movement; if I make an animal movement, I too shall be an animal. Genet's poetic world is an indefinite exchange of forms and gestures, a crisscross of transmutations, because everything has been reduced to the gesture and because the inner substance of the gesture is the gaze of others. Genet *is* in all his characters, and they are by turns a rose, a dog, a cat, a clematis. He makes himself all of man and all of nature. Since all has been denied him, he tastes of everything by means of gesture: the abjection of the tramp and imperial pride alike. The gesture is a "spiritual exercise." Humiliated, undressed, inspected, Darling "could divine the soul of a bum." Naturally this unimaginative pimp "hardly paid any attention to these momentary exchanges of souls. He never knew why, after certain shocks, he was surprised to find himself back in his skin." Genet knows why. Genet systematically experiences all evil souls. He uses gestures as instruments of prospecting. He has informed us of his method: "I take gestures chosen from young men passing by. At times, it's a French soldier, an American, a hoodlum, a bartender. . . . They suddenly offer me a gesture which can be only Erik's. I shall take note of it. . . . *I sometimes try to imitate the discovered* gesture. *I note the state that it makes me know."* No doubt he is only momentarily a beggar, a fallen queen, a ship's ensign. But there are only momentary souls. The one that remains longest or that recurs most often we call *our* soul, and we are surprised to find it again after a long journey. Proust, too, experienced the surprise that Genet cultivates and that Darling tries to ignore, and he often wondered how, "after deep slumber . . . seeking one's mind, one's personality, as one seeks a lost object, one ends by finding one's own self rather than any other."

Genet can say: "I am Stilitano" as Emily Brontë's hero said: "I am Heathcliff." He is Stilitano as much as is Stilitano himself, since the one seeks to appropriate by amorous practices the ideal hero whom the other is attempting to copy in his bearing. They exchange gestures. Genet and Stilitano are two madmen who both think they are Stilitano. "Stilitano would subtly insinuate himself into me, he would fill out my muscles, loosen my gait, thicken my gestures, almost color me. He was in action. I felt, in my footsteps on the sidewalk, his crocodile leather shoes creaking with the weight of the ponderous body of that monarch of the slums."

Reduced to indefinite repetition of gestures already performed, this ceremonious love has no history. It was stereotyped at the first meeting. Which of the two could act on the other, since they are only *one* and since this *one,* this ideal Stilitano, is only a sum of traditions and rites that are to be copied without anything's being changed? The most formalistic of religions is not so finicky. These immutable gestures leave no trace: another gesture takes their place and the soul receives another stamp. The soul will remain, afterward, what it was before: a soft wax, able to receive all imprints. "During those years of softness," Genet will write later, "when my personality took on all kinds of forms, any male could press my flanks with his walls, could contain me. My moral substance (and my physical substance, too, which is its visible form, with my white skin, weak bones, flabby muscles, with the slowness of my gestures and their indecisiveness) was without sharpness, without contour. I aspired at the time to being embraced by the calm, splendid statue of a man of stone with sharp angles. And I felt that peace only if I could completely take over his qualities and virtues, when I imagined I was he, when I made his gestures, uttered his words, when I was he." We know the mechanism: being another for himself, he aspires to become Another in order to feel from within, as another and as himself, the Other that he is. But for that very reason his love is not *lived,* he *does not change.* When Genet is in

love, he is not transformed. Nothing marks him. His greatest passion is reduced to his contracting a few idiosyncrasies of which
another passion will rid him.

Stilitano wearies of his companion and drops him. This is an
event. Is Genet going to experience the kind of love pangs that
change a character, a destiny? No: there are no more ends in his
life than beginnings, no more breakups than encounters. It is true
that Stilitano has thrown him over. But that means for Genet that
he is now the sole holder of his role. He takes away with him the
"persona" of the Tough whom they both played. "It was no longer
even his memory that I carried away with me but rather the idea
of a fabulous creature, the origin and pretext of all my desires,
terrifying and gentle, remote and close to the point of containing
me, for, now being something dreamed, he had, though hard and
brutal, the gaseous insubstantiality of certain nebulae, their gigantic dimensions, their brilliance in the heavens and their name
as well. I trampled Stilitano beneath my feet as he lay battered by
sun and fatigue; the dust I raised was his impalpable substance,
while my burning eyes tried to make out the most precious details
of an image of him that was more human and equally inaccessible."
At times, it is a metaphysical virtue that can define, at Genet's will,
one or another region of the universe: the sun is Stilitano as the
plants and animals of the forest are bears for the clan of the bear.
"The coming of the sun excited me. I worshiped it. A kind of sly
intimacy developed between us . . . this star became my god. It was
within my body that it rose, that it continued its curve and completed it. If I saw it in the sky of the astronomers, it was because it
was the bold projection there of the one I preserved within myself.
Perhaps I even confused it in some obscure way with the vanished
Stilitano." If Poland is a wounded boy, why may not the dust of
Spain be a dismal Pimp? When the performer is absent, things
make his gestures: the sun rises, inevitably and ritually, as the Pimp
suddenly draws himself up in a bar. As times goes by, Stilitano's
essence is cleansed of its impurities and again becomes an Idea. It
still keeps his name, for a time: "My adventure with Stilitano re-
treated in my mind. He himself dwindled. All that remained of
him was a gleaming point, of marvelous purity. . . . The only thing
about him which retained any meaning for me was the manly qualities and gestures that I knew were his. Frozen, fixed forever in the
past, they composed a solid object, indestructible since it had been
achieved by those few unforgettable details." The details have
vanished; there remains a type; Stilitano, like "the sage" or "the

saint," enters the realm of the exemplary: "Within myself I pursued what I thought Stilitano had indicated to me." But what remains of the handsome hoodlum at this degree of schematization? Genet could just as well never have known him and have started musing over the linking of a name and a photograph as he mused over the naval officer and traitor Marc Aubert, of whose existence he learned from newspapers at about the same time. Stilitano, Marc Aubert: he met the one, he imagines the other, but both will serve him alike as guides and intercessors. The photo of the latter, cut out of a newspaper, and the abstract memory of the former will settle together on new "Big Shots," on Java, for example, the latest of Genet's friends, whose "muscle-bound, slightly swaying walk, as if he were cleaving the wind," evokes that of the Barcelona hoodlum, while "his face strangely resembles that of Marc Aubert." Rather than be of use to him in interpreting the real, these two patterns mask it from him, help him *not to see* the true Java. Finally, the Stilitano "idea," which is embodied for a moment by Stilitano himself and then by a series of good-looking boys, re-enters Genet: "Pretexts for my iridescence, then for my transparence, and finally for my absence, the lads I speak of evaporate. All that remains of them is what remains of me: I exist only through them, who are nothing, existing only through me. They shed light on me, but I am the zone of interference. These boys: my Twilight Guard."

And when Genet, with his usual lucidity, later reflects on his past, he will end by plunging the "boys" into a bath of sulfuric acid. They will no longer exist, they will be reduced to the absolute anonymity of "object X," a pure, abstract support of the "erotic situation": "Thus I realize that I have sought only situations charged with erotic intentions. That, among other things, is what directed my life. I know that there exist adventures the heroes and details of which are erotic. It is these that I have wanted to live."

The circle is completed: having taken leave of himself, Genet returns to himself. Meanwhile he has been through a whole love affair, and what remains of it? Not even a *real* memory. Has he even loved? Thrown into the company of ruffians who despise him, he seeks a friendly look and discovers their indifference: what he feels matters to no one; he is subdued by force and threats when he asks only to give himself. He can love if he wishes, but he will get nothing out of the experience, it will be a pure loss. He accepts the challenge and decides to love *for himself alone*. But it is the appeal of the Other that makes the reality of love. We are drawn, then held, by the promise of parted lips, by the expectation that we read in the other's eyes. In order to be able to love a voice, a face, we must feel that they are calling out for love; hence, the beauty that we ascribe to them is not likely to be a lie: it is a real gift, and the beloved, who feeds on it, draws new confidence from it, is beautified by joy. In order to be completely true, a love must be shared; it is a joint undertaking in which the feeling of each is the substance of that of the other. Each of the two freedoms addresses the other, captivates it, tempts it; each of the freedoms becomes the unfathomable depth of the other; it is the other's love of me that is the truth of my love: if my passion is solitary it becomes a cult or a phantasmagoria. Genet, who is doomed to solitude, wants to live in solitude the amorous passion which is an absolute relationship between persons. He assumes the only kind of love that has been left to him, which is masturbatory. He wants his tenderness to be impotent, contained, without reciprocity, without hope; he wants it not to be betrayed by any visible sign; and since the beloved has nothing to do with it, he wants it to be so light that the other does not even feel it touching him.* Since love finds its truth in the other's gaze, since the indifference of the beloved makes love imaginary, Genet, in his zealous will to realism, compels himself to will this indifference; he requires that the icy gaze of Stilitano or Armand abolish the feeling in which he is completely involved; the ardor that consumes him is, objectively, *nothing:* a painful emptiness; Genet's absolute realism derealizes his tenderness. His loves are figments of the imagination.

Between the ages of fifteen and twenty-five Genet's life is amazingly full: he is apprenticed, runs away, is caught; placed in a bourgeois family, he robs his foster parents, he is sent to Mettray, he escapes again, he begs, wanders all over France, joins the Foreign Legion, deserts, flees to Barcelona, lives by begging and prostitution in the Barrio Chino, steals again, leaves Spain and goes everywhere, to Italy, to Poland, Czechoslovakia, Germany, stealing as he goes and sneaking across borders; his adventures would furnish material for twenty picaresque novels; he loves, is jealous, is disdained or enslaved, is unhappy. Yet nothing marks him and nothing changes him; he finds himself at the age of twenty-five as he was at fifteen. Mircéa Eliade tells us that in archaic and traditionalist ontology *"reality* is acquired exclusively by *repetition* or *participation;* whatever does not have an exemplary model is 'devoid of sense,' that is,

* "If only I could cover those pale cheeks with kisses and you not feel it" *(The Red and the Black).*

lacks reality . . . the man of traditional cultures recognizes himself as being real only insofar as he ceases to be himself . . . and is content with *imitating* and *repeating* the gestures of another. In other words, he recognizes himself as being real, that is, as 'truly himself' only insofar as he ceases precisely to be so."* He shows us archaic humanity "defending itself as best it can against whatever is *new* and *irreversible* in history." And he adds, further on, that "in conferring a cyclical direction upon time the primitive annuls its irreversibility. . . . The past is only the prefiguration of the future. No event is irreversible and no transformation definitive. In a certain sense, one can even say that nothing new occurs in the world, for all is only repetition of the same primordial archetypes; in actualizing the mythical moment in which the archetypal gesture was revealed, this repetition continually maintains the world in the same auroral instant of the beginnings."

These remarks apply to Genet word for word: entirely taken up with reliving ceremoniously his original crisis, concerned solely with repeating and imitating the archetypal gestures of others, disdainful of profane time and deigning to know only the sacred time of eternal recurrence, this adolescent is not *historical.* He refuses irreversibility, change, the new: he has become a rigorously constructed and almost autonomous system that turns round and round and that is self-operating. There is nothing surprising in this: the monster was fabricated in the country, within a traditionalist and archaic culture, and his strange religion reflects the "primitive" mentality of property owners.

Does this mean that nothing takes place within him? Quite the contrary. But the sequence of his states, the succession of his feelings and acts of will, is *circular.* The two dialectics that control his inner life run counter to each other, they jam, and finally they get twisted and whirl about idly. We have set forth separately the two movements which lead Genet to homosexuality and Saintliness. The synthetic description which we have undertaken must now show them in their reciprocal action.

5. *The Whirligigs*

"Jean Genet, the weakest of all and the strongest." The kind of sentence that one reads casually and that the hasty reader imagines he has understood. What does it mean? That Jean Genet, in certain

---

* Mircéa Eliade: *The Myth of the Eternal Return.*

respects the weakest, is the strongest in other respects? But he has made no restriction: it is in all respects simultaneously that he claims to be both. Are we to believe that he is weak *in appearance* but strong *in reality*? That would be only a trivial truth, and we know Genet well enough to know that he is not concerned with stating—paradoxically or not—truths easily digested by a good citizen's stomach: he detests truth as he does all forms of Being; although he consents to using Reason for the purpose of engraving his fallacies, he has no intention of obeying it. No: it is *simultaneously and in all respects* that he claims to be the strongest and the weakest, in appearance and in reality. He refers to two opposing systems of values and refuses to choose one or the other. In the first, the Pimp is destiny, pure Evil in its glamorous appearance; Genet is nothing but a dissolute hoodlum, just about good enough to be the slave of a rigorous master. In the second, Jean Genet, a cold, lucid consciousness, chains the criminal by his words, by his charms, leads him to destruction by honeyed betrayals. But each system implies the other: if the criminal is only a robot, what pleasure will there be in maneuvering him? He must retain all of his superiority over the female Saint so that the latter, in duping him, acquires merits. Inversely, when the Pimp rides roughshod over her, the Saint must be conscious that she is of greater worth than that which crushes her: in order that Evil be perfect and justice entire, the best must be subjected to the worst. Thus, the Saint will be superior in her inferiority to the criminal who subjects her to his whims, as St. Blandine is superior to the torturers who kill her and as the criminal who is reduced to impotence will be superior to the saint who betrays him, as the blinded Samson is superior to Delilah. Each of the two, when he falls to the lowest depths, is raised above the other; each of the two turns against the other and thereby lowers himself below the other; each figures in the other's system and Genet upholds both systems at the same time. Jean Genet, the strongest and the weakest: the strongest of all when he is the weakest, the weakest when he is the strongest. He will enjoy the double pleasure of sadism and masochism, not in the alternating or composite form that psychoanalysts call sado-masochism, but simultaneously. His sadism is the secret dimension of his masochism and vice versa.

This sentence is typical of his way of thinking: he does not write it *in spite* of the contradiction it contains but *because* of it. Far from dreaming of concealing this contradiction, of transcending it toward some synthesis or other, he experiences keen satisfaction in making it sparkle in the false unity of the Word. Thus, he thinks falsely. Does that surprise anyone? Did anyone expect to find wisdom, justice and peace in that faked soul? Wanting to live the impossibility of living, he must want to think the impossibility of thinking. And since he discovers within himself the movement of two dialectics, he must at every moment take his bearings according to both at the same time. As an object among objects, he compares himself to other objects, in accordance with objective criteria: this vision of the world is a kind of neorealism; insofar as he is an absolute subject, objects exist only by virtue of his becoming conscious of them: this is a kind of idealism that is very likely to turn into solipsism. If he wants to survive, Genet must affirm simultaneously his neorealism and his solipsism, must pose at the same time the superiority of the object to the subject and that of the subject to the object. He is all and he is nothing, zero and infinity at the same time; the zero is in the depths of the infinite, the infinite is concealed in the zero. He has chosen to *will to be;* willing inclines him to activism, being to quietism. His undertaking will therefore be an activistic quietism or a quietistic activism or both at the same time. At the height of his willing-to-be he makes himself a receptive passivity; in the depths of his abandon to the other, we have seen him tighten and grow taut. The more he is made an object, the more he is a demanding subject; and the more completely he identifies himself with some archetype—Stilitano or Harcamone—the more he is himself. With the corrosive cynicism of homosexuals, he reduces reality to appearance and act to gesture: a man is nothing but a collection of gestures; the gestures alight where they will and transcend the agent who performs them as they do the witness who observes them. But, in the other system, these gestures must preserve their sacred value; otherwise, the Saint will cease to hope that God will descend into her. In Genet, as in all homosexuals, cynicism is accompanied by what he calls "enchantment"; the power of illusion and disenchantment coexist. The handsome Pimp is nothing but a gesture, but by virtue of the gesture an exemplary personality descends into each of us. Reality is only an appearance, but the appearance reveals the superreality.

Another would perhaps have resigned himself to being only the inert point of application of two divergent forces. But Genet wants to assume everything: it is not sufficient for him to want both dialectics; he must also want their simultaneity. And even that is not enough: one might imagine that he assumes his inner conflicts out of a kind of humanism, because human reality is dramatic, because mental suffering is the lot of every consciousness. But that would again be to submit; and besides, Genet's ethic is *inhumanism*. It matters little to him that others are at grips with such antinomies. He will live the conflict *as a unity;* his will will pose the incompatibility of the two theses and will decide in sovereign fashion that they constitute a fundamental unity. Do you say that that is impossible? But the fact is that Genet wants to think only the impossibility of thinking. To conceive by violence an idea one knows to be inconceivable—that is what defines radical Evil *in thinking*. There is, indeed, a parallelism of moral Evil and error. In the domain of knowledge, the impossibility of Evil finds an exact replica in the impossibility of deceiving oneself knowingly. As I have shown, the evildoer must know Good and must love it so that he can be more guilty; in like manner, if he reasons, he must know the True and must know that he knows it: only in that way will his error be inexcusable; far from being due to ignorance or haste, it will issue from lucid deliberation and from an enlightened will. The adolescent has devised for his personal use a logic of falsehood, that is, a technique for the nonsynthetic unification of contradictory propositions. Now, one has only to reflect for a moment to realize that this unification—since it is impossible—can be given only as a limit: it appears only at the end of a movement. And this movement cannot be a progression, for the only possible progress would necessarily be the synthesis of opposites: when two points of view are in opposition, discussion advances only if one sees a possibility of reconciling them. In Genet, the movement of thinking can be only *circular*. In Hegel, the thesis moves into the antithesis. But that in itself is already the synthesis. If the synthesis cannot be achieved—and in Genet it is a matter of uniting two dialectics rather than two terms—then the antithesis will move back into the thesis and so on ad infinitum. Genet arranges his oppositions in such a way that each term, without ceasing to exclude the other, remains in the background when the other is present. It suffices that he affirm one of the theses to discover suddenly that he is in the process of affirming the other. The *yea* is the sworn enemy of the *nay;* but in Genet's aporias no sooner has one said *yea* than the *yea* half-opens: we realize that we are saying *nay*. But we cannot adhere to this *nay* either, for it immediately tips us into the *yea;* and so on. Of course, there is never any progress, for the *yea* and the *nay* are always their own selves. The model of this circular sophistry is furnished by ancient skepticism. It is the argument of Epimenides: "Epimenides says that Cretans are liars.

But he is a Cretan. Therefore he lies. Therefore Cretans are not liars. Therefore he speaks the truth. Therefore Cretans are liars. Therefore he lies," etc. Truth leads to the lie and vice versa. Impossible to stop the round.*

The mind that enters one of these vicious circles goes round and round, unable to stop. With practice, Genet has managed to transmit to his thought an increasingly rapid circular movement. He has a vision of an infinitely rapid rotation which merges the two opposites, just as, when a multicolored disk is spun quickly enough, the colors of the rainbow interpenetrate and produce white. I have called these devices *whirligigs:* Genet constructs them by the hundred. They become his favorite mode of thinking. Ideas well up in him like small local whirlpools; the more rapid the movement, the more intense the thinking seems to be: the diabolical equivalent of a true idea is an error that one cannot shake off. He knows that the sudden flashes which dazzle him have only the momentary appearance of illumination, that they are pure impressions of speed, the effects of the purely aesthetic admiration into which we are plunged by a well-constructed sophism. But that is what he wants. His love of independence is such that he cannot even bear the gentle constraint of the evident: he tolerates only semblance-evidence, for it is he, he alone, who decrees by sovereign order that these semblances have convinced him. Genet applies himself to disordering reason as does Rimbaud to disordering the senses. He takes pleasure, out of resentment, in jeopardizing the thought of the Just; out of love of risk, in plunging into an adventure which in all probability will lead him astray; out of masochism, in settling into error; out of pride, in producing ideas that no one can share, in setting himself above logic in the royal solitude of the sophism;

---

* Don't shrug. For the argument of Epimenides could just as well be called the Kravchenko argument. In connection with the lawsuit that the latter brought against *Lettres Françaises,* his non-Communist opponents declared: "Kravchenko says that the methods of the Soviet government are abominable. But he was part of that government for a long time. Therefore he applied its methods. He is therefore abominable himself. And what faith can one have in the statements of an abominable man?" Kravchenko's supporters replied: "Let us admit that he is abominable for having applied Soviet methods for a long time, which means that they *are* abominable." Answer: "You admit that he is abominable. But perhaps he became so long before entering the government; perhaps he always was abominable. In that case, what is his testimony worth?" Answer: "If it was not his severity as an administrator that made him abominable, who can prove that he is?" Answer: "How, without being abominable, could he have been part of that iniquitous regime, if only for a single day?" etc. In other words: "Kravchenko says that Soviet methods are abominable. But he applied them. Therefore he is abominable. Therefore one cannot have faith in him. Therefore Soviet methods are perhaps not abominable. Therefore Kravchenko is not abominable. Therefore one can trust him. Therefore . . ." etc.

out of malignancy, in attempting to unite irreconcilables, to think *against nature,* in almost convincing himself that he succeeds in doing so—almost, not quite, for he wants to preserve, within his triumph, the irritating pleasure of failure. He knowingly engages in false reasoning so as to be able to ponder Evil and because error is an Evil. His true wickedness lies in this ineffectual zeal; it has a name: perversity.

It would be tedious to list these contraptions. But if we wish at least to know the patterns underlying their construction, we need only take the two tables of categories which we established above: as they correspond to each other, term for term, we have only to introduce each pair of opposites into a false circular unity.

GENERAL PRINCIPLE

If you affirm being, you find yourself in the process of affirming nothingness, but in this movement of affirmation you transcend nothingness and find yourself in the process of affirming being, etc.

It is understood that Genet is not concerned with reducing the objective essence of being to that of nothingness. Hegel, who studies objective structures, can show that pure being, that is, being without any determination, moves into nonbeing. But Genet cares nothing about the structures of the object. What interests him is the subject. He maintains the absolute heterogeneity of nothingness and of being qua *realities;* what he wants to show is that the will, as a subjective phenomenon, is forced to affirm the one when it wants to affirm the other.

What is the meaning of the sophism? That Genet wants *to be* his being. But his being is wickedness. He therefore wants *to be* wicked. But what does the wicked person want? The destruction of all and of himself. The being that he wants to be is a will to nonbeing which annihilates itself. Wanting being, he wants nothingness. But this nothingness, on the other hand, is a being, since the evildoer possesses an objective essence which is evident to everyone. Thus, it will want such-and-such destruction in the world or in itself in order *to be* the evildoer. And since it is in the most perverse acts that the evildoer will coincide most perfectly with his essence, it is at the moment when he will blow up the world and himself that Genet will attain, in absolute annihilation, fullness of being.

In accordance with this general pattern he will construct some whirligigs of lesser importance. Here are a few:

A.—Genet wills all reality (since he wills *"to be* what crime made of him" in the world as it *is*). He therefore wills *all being*. And since he wills his relationship to the world, he wills his exile: since the world rejects him, casts him into the nonworld, he wills this rejection, he wills his being *im-monde*,* which amounts to rejecting the world fiercely, to meditating on his destruction of it. Thus, the resolute decision to accept being as it is is immediately transformed into a decision to reject all being and to destroy it. But, at the same time, to reject the world which rejects him is to accept all, that is, to love and to will being, including the sentence of exile that being issues against him. Thus, the resolute will to *realism* is converted into a frenzied eagerness to destroy, but the eagerness to destroy is converted into an ecstatic acceptance of the miracle of horror. To will the world is to will to destroy it; to destroy the world is to accept destiny.

B.—Genet wants his life to be ruined, to be a failure, he wants "to drain the cup to the dregs." He therefore wills his failure. But if failure is achieved as failure, it is a success, since that is what Genet wanted. No, it is a failure; it was, after all, necessary that Genet first throw himself into an undertaking; otherwise there would be a failure of nothing. Wanting a certain result, Genet fails, and willing his failure, succeeds. He wills what he does not want and does not will what he wants.

To will his being is, for him, to will nothingness. Therefore, to attempt to coincide with the fullness of his being is to try to attain "the impossible nullity." But, inversely, the rigorous asceticism which he practices, the successive amputations which he inflicts on himself, cause him (in bringing him little by little closer to the animal, to protoplasm, and then to absolute nonbeing) progressively to attain saintliness, that is, pure being. But what is Genet's saintliness if not, by his own avowal, a word and gestures? And are not these gestures a caricature of true Saintliness? Replacing humility by abjection, and destitution by betrayal, does he not sink more deeply into Evil in presenting, by means of blasphemous mockery, a diabolical image of the supreme Morality? Have we attained absolute nonbeing? The absolute of Evil? No, for in flouting the Saintliness which he has not ceased to cherish since childhood, Genet effects a last renunciation: he becomes he who no longer

---

* *Immonde:* unclean, foul. In hyphenating the word, the author is playing on its etymology: *im* (not) *monde* (world), that is, not of the world.—Translator's note.

even believes in Saintliness, who has lost all hope. Thus, it is at the moment of this last sacrifice that this martyrized consciousness changes into a saintly consciousness for the absolute gaze which perceives it from on high. But no, that's just one more piece of humbug, a cheap trick, Saintliness does not exist, one does evil for evil's sake, etc. Although the whirligig is rather rapid, Genet can enjoy simultaneously—or almost—the bitter, desperate pleasure of flouting Saintliness itself and the mystical ecstasy of the Saint who feels he is being rewarded.

THE CATEGORIES: THE HERO AND THE SAINT*

We have seen them caught up in an eternal round, now at the top, now at the bottom of the wheel, both higher and lower than each other.

THE CRIMINAL AND THE TRAITOR

Thesis: The criminal does absolute Evil, objective evil. The traitor is his parasite. Hence, betrayal is only a secondary and derivative evil.

Antithesis: But as Evil is by nature parasitic, Betrayal, which is a parasite of a parasite, is the supreme Evil; it eats away the modicum of force and order, hence of being, that still remains in crime. The criminal is only the traitor's *means:* he is-in-order-to-be betrayed.

Return to the thesis: But in order for betrayal to be loathsome it must destroy effortlessly and in a cowardly manner what is superior to it; it must be "the grain of sand in Cromwell's bladder," the silly accident that trips up the hero. It will therefore be all the more dreadful in that the traitor is inferior to the criminal. Hence, it is the Crime which is the sacred outrage, which is Evil par excellence, etc.

THE ACTIVE HOMOSEXUAL and THE PASSIVE HOMOSEXUAL

(*essential which moves to the inessential*)	(*inessential which moves to the essential*)

Thesis: The active homosexual is the beloved, hence the essential. He subjugates the lover, he possesses him. *Transition to the*

---

* *La Sainte:* female saint.—Translator's note.

antithesis: But he derives his poignant beauty from the love that the girl queen bears him. Without her he would be merely a brute. The passive homosexual possesses him in turn: Genet possesses Stilitano because he installs him within himself; Divine possesses Darling because she infects him with her poetry. Thus, it is the passive homosexual who is the essential. *Return to the thesis:* But if the Pimp were not *really* glamorous, the beloved's consciousness, empty and liberated, would again be face to face with itself and its wretchedness. The beloved again becomes the inessential, the archetype that enables the lover to attain the sacred, etc.

THE EVIL OF CONSCIOUSNESS   and   CONSCIOUSNESS IN EVIL
        (being)   *(nothingness)*

Thesis: For Genet's optimism, Mind, Knowledge and Self-Awareness are the supreme good. Hence, the worst Evil is death and immediately afterward comes the Evil-that-eats-away-at-consciousness, that is, madness, stultification, fury, ignorance. The greatest of evils is the *degradation* of the human creature. But no—*Antithesis:* The madman is excused by reason of his madness, the ignorant and the idiot are only half responsible. The worst Evil is the lucid, perspicacious consciousness that does Evil with premeditation. *Return to the thesis:* Deliberate, contrived Evil calls for intelligence, tact, knowledge: and these are good. Indeed, it is the leprosy that eats away at consciousness, it is the hereditary taint, it is alcoholism that must be regarded as the supreme Evil. No, for . . . etc.

THE OBJECT AND THE SUBJECT
THE OTHER AND ONE'S SELF

Thesis: To be oneself is to be the Other. *Antithesis:* The Other vanishes, the self remains. *Return to the thesis:* This self is no longer anything *for itself,* for it was not aware of itself qua Other; it is again alienated in the other. In other words: Genet is first an object amidst objects that crush him. He frees himself and transforms the objects into appearances. He is a pure and empty subject. But this subject is seen by Another, a God who places himself at the back of his consciousness. It is thus Genet's very consciousness that changes into appearance. Perhaps it is only a nightmare of this evil God. Henceforth the objects of this consciousness have as much truth as the consciousness itself; they no longer depend on the light it sheds on them but on the God who sees them through it. They even have for the former a truth which they do not have for the latter. It is the consciousness which becomes relative, and objects regain their absolute density. Genet, an object among objects, becomes a consciousness surrounded by appearances; then, this consciousness changes into an appearance surrounded by real things. Of course, it does so in order to eat away at them again, and so on.

These whirligigs forcibly unite two dialectics which become entangled and draw each other into a circular movement: in each of them, the thesis represents being, the positive, death; the antithesis is the negative, freedom, consciousness and life. Freedom corrodes and dissolves pure being and is again alienated in all being; the thesis is the transcendent, the sacred; the antithesis is immanence. The thesis is mystical alienation and rejection of the human, the antithesis shadows forth a grim humanism. In short, thesis and antithesis represent the two moments of freedom. But these two segments, instead of merging in a harmonious synthesis (to deny the false *in order* to affirm the true, to destroy *in order* to build), remain mutilated and abstract and perpetuate their opposition. The *positive* moment remains what it is among the Just: conformism, blind submission; the *negative* moment remains the bloody half that the Just man tears from himself and projects upon the Other: pure negativity, negation of all. Submission to the "All-Evil," destruction of all: Genet moves continually from one to the other of these *absolute* attitudes. All or Nothing; he is not in a position to accept *something,* to refuse *something,* to invent *something.* Unable to station his individuality in the real by means of acts, he lets his Self roll away from him.

This adolescent has shut himself up in a veritably paranoiac system: he no longer sees himself or the universe except through little local maelstroms. Experience brings him nothing: at best it sets these automatisms going. His thinking becomes less and less communicable and he knows it: he is delighted to be the only one who has the key to it. Stilitano has already begun to look at him with surprise: "You nuts or something?" No, he is not nuts, at least not yet, but he now speaks only to himself, he makes conniving signs to himself above the head of the person he is talking to. He spins about more and more quickly: at times it seems to him that he has succeeded in embracing all contradictions in a single view. And then, no: he has to keep spinning: "Was it true that philosophers doubted the existence of things in back of them? How is one to detect the secret of the disappearance of things? By turning around very fast? No. But even faster? Faster than anything? I shot a look behind me. I spied, I turned my eyes and head, ready to . . . No, it was no use. Those things are never caught napping. You would have to wheel about with the speed of an airplane. You would then realize that the things have disappeared and yourself with them."* Meanwhile, he loses sight of his chief goal: he wanted to become an exemplary personality, the prophet of an inhuman religion. But his decision to become a saint prevents him from going on to crime, and his fondness for Evil-as-object prevents him from attaining Saintliness. Where are the great betrayals that he was to have committed? The great sufferings he was to have inflicted on himself? Without a history and without efficacy, he goes round in circles *in his life too:* he steals a little—very little—he begs, scrounges, prostitutes himself; he submits to some brute or other who subjects him to his pleasure; he gives way in the presence of force and takes revenge by petty betrayals that he never quite carries through, for fear of reprisals; kicked out or dropped, he starts stealing or begging again, comes under the thumb of another tyrant. He goes elsewhere and it is still the same place, he changes master and it is still the same master; his behavior starts to become stereotyped; he grows accustomed to Evil, to Misfortune; he repeats himself, imitates himself; he grows ossified. Nothing more can happen to him since everything is already decided, by others and by himself: at every instant he lives his destiny in its entirety, and each time his thinking covers the same monotonous circuit; the die is cast. Perhaps some day the adolescent will awaken: he will go to a mirror and see the image of an old, faded fairy. That is Genet's terror, the only human feeling he has left. Divine, that extraordinary character, will one day be born of this fear of aging. We are still far from that point: Genet does not even imagine that he may some day write. He has locked himself, beyond appeal, into that circular prison. At times he calls it a tomb.

THE LAST CONTRADICTION: DREAM AND REALITY

And yet, something is changing: that disk which is turning faster and faster is in the process of taking off from the real. Without a

---

* Compare, in the case of another writer who is "accused," namely Cocteau, the obsession with speed ("Everything is a question of speed"), circular speed (ventilator, etc.), and the image of the propeller whose speed makes it invisible and which can cut your arm off.

home, without friends, without real love, without a trade, cast out by men and their tools into a phantom Nature, condemned to think falsely, Genet, like a balloon whose moorings have been cut, leaves the earth and rises into the clouds. "For ten years," he once said to me, "I lived in a dream." What, indeed, is the glamour of Stilitano, of Armand, of Guy, what are the poetic miracle, the hostility of Nature, the gazes that hound this Cain even in solitude, what are they if not dreams? What are those spinning sophisms if not dreams of thought?

Nevertheless, he lives amidst dangers, enemies: he has to be alert, to calculate risks, to adapt himself to the unforeseen, to work out ingenious devices. This dreamer is essentially practical: could he have survived if he were not "the wiliest of hoodlums"?

Genet presents us with the strange figure of a man who dreams in the midst of action and without ceasing to act, maladjusted while fully adjusted, raving in a state of complete lucidity. He remains aware of both the true and the false, he is in control of both his acts and his reveries. But at the moment of action his reflection gives itself *false* motives; it deliberately deceives him as to the meaning of his acts, as to their purpose. In like manner, the primitive, so we are told, considers his arrows to be deadly because they have been smeared with a poisonous juice and because they were consecrated in a traditional ceremony. Genet, like the Maori, places himself simultaneously on the technical level and the magical level. And in order for the dream not to interfere with the practical outcome, reflection gives an interpretation of the act that tallies with reality: the false motives harmonize with the true, which they cover up; the false means are chosen in such a way as not to hamper the action of the true means and must even make it possible to invent practical solutions under cover of the imaginary. His reverie, instead of being *in action,* is a superaction—in the sense that one speaks of super-reality—whose complex structure presupposes both a spontaneous consciousness which interprets the real situation in the light of its real projects and a reflective consciousness which, while keeping an eye on the operations of the first, endeavors to look at reality from the viewpoint of the unreal. He splits his personality, he is torn between truth and fiction, he constructs his behavior according to two conflicting systems of interpretation and, while mobilizing his intelligence in order to attain his vital goals and to evade real dangers, he pretends to be in a state of absent-mindedness with regard to his petty preoccupations; he wants to be unaware of them and focuses his attention on the distorted image of them given by his reflective consciousness. He practices double vision: "They said I saw double whereas I saw the double of things." Pushed into a police wagon by a cop, he "makes of the Black Maria a carriage of exile, a coach wild with grandeur, slowly fleeing, when it carried me off, between the ranks of a people bowing in respect." At the same time, he knows very well that this princely chariot in which he sees "royal misfortune" is only a vulgar Black Maria. He knows it, he *needs* to know it and yet he strives to forget it. The climate of this inner experience is *exasperation:* "Overexcitement gives rise to the magical. It is when the soul is exasperated, for example by waiting, that one is open to the unreal, to the superreal."

Only constant overexcitement, instability of mood, can beget simultaneously this will to adjustment and this will to ignorance; he makes a relentless effort to doubt the indubitable, to believe in the unbelievable, to maintain transparent phantoms in the blinding light of the obvious; he does this in order to enjoy both his power and his impotence and out of resentment toward the God who created him. Thus, reverie appears, in this odd dreamer, at the maximum of tension and willing: "I was on horseback. Even though I am very calm, I feel myself being swept by a storm which is due, perhaps, to the rapid rhythm of my thinking which stumbles over every accident, to my desires which are violent because almost always curbed, and, when I live my inner scenes, I have the impression of always living them on horseback, on a galloping horse, one that rears. I am a horseman. . . . Not that it happens in quite that way, that is, that I know I am rearing or on horseback, but rather I make the gestures and have the soul of a man who is on horseback: my hands contract, my head is high, my voice is arrogant . . . and when this feeling of riding a noble, whinnying animal overflowed into my daily life, it gave me what is called a cavalier* look and the tone and bearing which I thought victorious."

Yet even if he does convince us that these enchantments are the effect of a lucid will, we cannot help but have misgivings: is that really what he wanted at the beginning? We are familiar with his aggressive imperialism, his rejection of evasion, his will to live the impossibility of living; we have not forgotten the zeal with which little Pierrot rolled his tongue over the repulsive insect that he put into his mouth unwittingly. We are therefore astounded to hear him declare that "the nothingness of human things is such that, save for the Being Who is by Himself, nothing is beautiful but

---

* The French word for "horseman" is *cavalier.*—Translator's note.

that which is not." How dare he—he who dripped with blood and passion when confronted with the universe—how dare he maintain that "the land of the Chimeras is the only one worth inhabiting"? Does it mean that the traitor he wanted to become was not a *true* traitor? Were those ten years of horrible asceticism to lead to hackneyed commonplaces worthy of a Marcel Schwob or a Heredia, to this trashy, imbecilic glorification of the Ideal?

However surprised we may be, Genet is even more so. At times he even gets panicky and tries to wake up: what he says about prisoners in *Miracle of the Rose* applies above all to himself: "Prisons are full of mouths that lie. Every inmate relates fake adventures in which he plays the role of hero. But these stories are never continued to the height of splendor. Sometimes the hero cuts himself short because he feels the need for sincerity when talking to himself, and we know that when the imagination is very strong it may make us lose sight of the dangers of real life. . . . It conceals reality from him, and *I do not know whether he is afraid of falling to the depths of the imagination and becoming an imaginary being himself or whether he is afraid of clashing with the real.** But when he feels the imagination besting him, invading him, he reviews the real dangers that he is running, and, to reassure himself, states them aloud."

Like these prisoners, Genet has terrible, cynical awakenings; he exercises his power of disenchantment against his own constructions. In vain: two negations do not equal an affirmation. If the persecuted lucidity takes its revenge, it is not in order to return to reality but to intensify the disintegration. The imagination reduced the world to a sum of miraculous gestures; analytical lucidity reduces the gesture to appearance. Nothing remains of external reality. Thereupon the dreams return: since all is appearance, one might as well choose the appearances which are most flattering. And Genet again falls into wonderment before himself: where do they come from, those tenacious, parasitic reveries which prevent him from performing on himself what he called "a daily labor, long and disappointing"? He senses a mystery in broad daylight, he feels himself the victim of an indefinable mystification. Not that he *does not want* to dream: what surprises him is that he wants to. If the schizophrenic still has leisure for questioning himself, he will be frightened by the *involuntary* proliferation of his images. As for Genet, it is his will that disturbs him, for it is in his will that

---

* My italics.

the metamorphosis has taken place. He amused himself earlier by constructing whirligigs: it pleased him to affirm the thesis and to find himself in the process of affirming the antithesis. But this is the most dizzying of all the whirligigs, and this one Genet has not constructed. How can a will that is bent on willing all the real possibly end—*without ceasing to be in harmony with itself*—by escaping from being toward nothingness? For, after all, he had chosen to live and watch over his situation, to inspect it minutely, to make the best of it whatever it might be, and it seems to him that he has kept his word. But the sole effect of this systematic and rigorous rejection of all dreams is to transform him into a visionary, an idle dreamer. Is he to believe that the oft-repeated vow to involve himself in a realistic, positive action must necessarily lead to dreaming his acts? Was the desperate eagerness to live life as it is, without appeal and without hedging, to make of him a Utopian leading, simultaneously, several imaginary lives in invented worlds? How can the austere resolution to confront the situation end by turning its back to him? Genet wants his prison, he inspects it without respite, he is proud of it, he sees the universe as a jail. And now this model prisoner finds that he has escaped despite himself. This strange King Midas puts out his hand to touch the walls of his jail, his straw mattress, the real attributes of his abjection; everything is transformed beneath his fingers into theatrical props: the mattress is a still-life deception painted on a cardboard floor.

When a realistic will applies itself unremittingly to its object and when it finds itself, without having been diverted by an external influence, in the process of willing the opposite of what it wills, there is a fundamental contradiction in its project. It is this contradiction that must be brought to light.

Genet wants to be what crime has made of him. We have shown the duality that manifests itself in this first act of willing: Genet wants *Being*. He is going to attempt to become the maker of the faked world which takes away his right to live; he is going to strive to produce the prefabricated destiny already awaiting him. But he also wants nonbeing: since this pitiless world is crushing him, he must will this crushing to the very end; since the just have made a destroyer of him, he will annihilate the universe. To want to be what he is is both to want the world and to reject it.

Now, these two conflicting acts of will have a common characteristic which he has not perceived: they are *imaginary*. One can neither reject the world nor accept it, save in dream.

One cannot reject the world unless one destroys it or kills oneself. Genet rejects suicide. Then what is the action which will blow up the universe? I know that certain lofty spirits make a name for themselves by illustrious refusals. They say *no*. What about it? These refusals are appearances which hide a shameful but utter submission. I hate the pretense that trammels people's minds and sells us cheap nobility. To refuse is not to say no, but to modify by work. It is a mistake to think that the revolutionary refuses capitalist society outright. How could he, since he is inside it? On the contrary, he accepts it as a fact which justifies his revolutionary action. "Change the world," says Marx. "Change life," says Rimbaud. Well and good: change them if you can. That means you will accept many things in order to modify a few. Refusal assumes its true nature within action: it is the abstract moment of negativity.

There are times, however, when the situation is unacceptable and we are unable to change it. The natural course of events sometimes throws us into these deadlocks: one has only to think of airplane or mountain-climbing accidents, the victims of which died in a state of horror; burned, slashed to pieces, they could no longer even attempt to live, they felt themselves dying. But why should they have *accepted* that irremediable death when all their life had been spent in fighting against it in an effort to establish a human order; to resign themselves *in extremis* would have been to deny themselves, to betray themselves. And how could they have rejected it? Their extreme weakness made it even impossible for them to hasten it by suicide. What remained for them? Mental lockjaw, vain physical agitation, or else, for the more clear-sighted, despair, the frightful, blindingly evident fact that man is impossible. But most of the time it is other men who throw us into the rat trap like rats: and the inhuman is even more unacceptable when it comes to man through men. In 1942, a sixteen-year-old Jew, who had been imprisoned before he had even heard of the Resistance, learned one morning that he was going to be shot as a hostage. The grownups had claimed that they had fashioned a world in which he could live; in return, they had asked for his confidence and he had given it to them: it was in order to murder him. In the name of that blind confidence, of the optimism which they had inculcated in him, in the name of his youth and of his infinite projects, he *had* to rebel. But against whom? *To whom* could he appeal? To God? He was an unbeliever. Besides, even if he had believed, that would not have changed anything: God was allowing him to be killed; He was on the side of the grownups. The boy's throttled rebellion grew all the more violent in that it felt it was ineffectual: his cries, which knew they were unheeded, enveloped a horrible silence. His refusal changed meaning. It was no longer a matter of rejecting an inevitable death, but of dying and saying no. As he was unable to bear the thought that this "no" was a mere puff of air, a breath that would be buried with him by the shovelfuls of earth that would fall on his mouth, he refused so as to compel the absolute to take over his refusal, so that the ether or some other incompressible fluid might become an eternal memory on which his revolt might be engraved forever; that "no" assured him immortality: his soul, separated from his body, would be only an immortal *no*. But the absolute is blind and deaf; we do not know the diamond that can scratch the ether; the refusal was transformed into a magical incantation, it was lived in reverse: since he had to, by virtue of his nature, address *someone*, the child refused *so that this someone might be born*, so as to give ears to the absolute. Thereby he *became imaginary*: his cries, his tears, the beating of his fists against the door, were stolen from him; he felt that an actor had been substituted for him. Then, his blood ran cold and he vaguely wondered what God of Wrath, not content with having condemned him to death, was making him die in a state of insincerity. We know that this God is man. The secret of these forced shammings lies in this: there are situations which one can only undergo, but to undergo is impossible because man is defined by his acts; when action is repressed by the world, it is internalized and derealized, it is play-acting; reduced to impotence, the agent becomes an actor. Such is precisely the case of Genet: his idle will moves into the realm of the imaginary; he becomes an actor despite himself, and his rejection of the world is only a gesture.

Will he have more luck when he attempts to assume it? But, as Alain has said: "The will has no hold outside of an action which it performs." And here there is no action to perform since there is nothing to change. Thus, one cannot will that which is. One can, of course, continue to will an act which one performed the day before because it is not finished, because it needs retouching; and besides, if one wants to survive, one must certainly adapt oneself to the inevitable, "to conquer oneself rather than fortune," to hasten at times the maturation of harmful events so as to make them occur at the least unfavorable moment. But Genet's situation was given to him as a whole and all at once: he finds in it nothing that he can delay or hasten; in short, he has nothing to will because there has never been anything that could be done about the situation: his future was stolen from him.

But what if he nevertheless persists in willing? What will happen?

At the end of the last century, history carried out a frightful and wonderfully readable experiment that is going to enlighten us: a man exhausted himself in the stupendous and vain endeavor *to will the totality of what is*. We know what happened to him.

Nietzsche *wanted to will* his moral solitude, his literary failure, the madness which he felt coming on, his partial blindness and, through his woes, the universe. Vain efforts: his will skidded over the glazed, slippery block of being without getting a hold. What could he do to will, *to have willed*, the clouds that passed over his eyes, the pounding in his head? He was on the lookout for his instinctive repulsions and as soon as he caught himself protesting, or begging for mercy, he clenched his fists, scowled and cried out: "I will it"; he was dancing the ballet of will. He also danced that of joy: since the completion of a work delights its creator's soul, he rejoiced at the history of the world in order to convince himself that it was his work, and as it ended in making him suffer every humiliation, he learned to call his tears of suffering tears of joy. If he writhed, *it could only be* with laughter; if he gasped, it was *necessarily* with pleasure. By means of the first dance he made himself, in the present, an imaginary legislator of a pre-established order; by the second, he transformed himself, in the past, into a mystical creator of increate reality. In short, he was like the fly on the wheel in La Fontaine's fable. Nevertheless, this play-acting had to be justified by a dogma: it was then that he had his famous vision at Surlej, a vision that had been anticipated, solicited, long cultivated. (He had written to Peter Gast, two years before: "I have reached the end of my thirty-fifth year. . . . It was at that age that Dante had his vision.") So at Surlej, "6,500 feet above sea level and much higher above all human things," was completed the metamorphosis of the most wildly, most bitterly realistic willing into pure poetry. There was an antinomy, since the Fiat of decision can be addressed only to what is not yet, to the possible, to being, to the real. At Surlej the antinomy was given an imaginary solution which enabled Zarathustra "to embody universal approbation, the yea, the limitless amen . . .":* "The knot of causes in which I am entwined will return—it will re-create me. I myself am one of the causes of eternal recurrence."† This taut and do-nothing will reverses the natural movement of praxis, for the act transforms the possible into reality, but Nietzsche—Nietzsche who says of himself: "My experi-

---

* *Ecce Homo.* Cf. also, *id.,* "There is no abyss to which I do not carry the benediction of my yea."

† *Zarathustra der Genesende.*

ence is completely unaware of what is meant by 'willing' something, 'working at it ambitiously,' aiming at a goal or at the realization of a desire. . . . I do not want a thing to become other than what it is . . . I do not want to change myself"*—dissolves the totality of being into possibility. The doctrine of Eternal Recurrence authorizes him to treat the real as a particular case of the possible (in the way the circle is said to be a particular case of the ellipse), the present as the infinitesimal instant in which the reminiscence of the past merges with the premonitory message of the future, and the present figure of Being as the finite image of infinite Nonbeing. I have explained elsewhere how the imagination seizes upon present objects in order to make contact, through them, with absent ones and how the imaginary act produces, by one and the same movement, a "presentification" of the absent and an "absentification" of the present; I have given the name *analogon* to a present object which is a prey to an absence. Thus, the Nietzschean will commits the world to phantoms, transforms the present state into an *analogon* of itself and causes it to be corroded by its own absence. We can say of someone who tends to be abstracted that "he has fits of absent-mindedness," "he is elsewhere"; inversely, Nietzsche puts *this* forest, *this* spring, *these* rocks into a state of abstractedness: they are no longer *here* and *now;* they become mirages which rise up from the future, the formal announcement of the infinite series of their reappearances. Is it the day before yesterday, today or the day after tomorrow? Since the future and the present are indiscernible, my perception prophesies, my will can fly ahead once again to that which is not yet and can *will the present as future.* The motive of all this machinery is as follows: in order to give oneself the right to will being, one must find a way of affecting it with nonbeing; the first step of absolute realism must be to derealize the real. But, it may be objected, Nietzsche has merely extended the problem, he has not eliminated it: even if present circumstances were to be repeated ad infinitum, he is forced to undergo their recurrence; the rigorous laws which govern development have nothing to do with our consent.

That is so, but you have not yet perceived the secret mechanism of the stratagem: as the real absents itself, the will's point of application is, at the same time, displaced. It is true that if this "recurrence" were to take place, it would be ineluctable, but it is also true that the present state of the system does not contain a single

---

* *Ecce Homo.*

sign, not the slightest beginning of a proof, not even an indication, of its later repetition. The myth of Eternal Recurrence is not in the least bit evident, and Nietzsche never bothered to furnish proof of it.* He vaguely thought, a year after his vision, of leaving for Paris or Vienna "to study the mathematical basis of Recurrence," but he very quickly dropped the plan. Moreover, as we have seen, this illumination had been in preparation for a long time, or rather he was preparing himself for it as for a sacred ceremony of initiation. In addition, the content of the vision presented no novelty for him, since, as Andler points out, he "describes in so many words the idea of Eternal Recurrence in *Vom Nutzen und Vorteil der Historie* (*W. C.,* 298) ." In this work, adds Andler, he "comes to no decision as to the truth of the idea."† What was new at Surlej was that he *did* come to a decision: he *decided* that the idea was true, without proof, in a burst of enthusiasm. The myth became an article of faith, hence of will. Thus, the act of will is not found where he claims to place it; he proclaims: "I know that my pains will come back and I want them to come back." But this is the public and mendacious expression of a strictly subjective fiat: "I do not know whether they will come back, but I want to *believe* it." If he displays no zeal in demonstrating his thesis, it is not because he thinks it undemonstrable, but because he has no wish to make a theorem of it and because he does not want his ideative will to be constrained by logical necessity as his practical will is by physical necessity. He wants "to think against himself" and to maintain his faith by a free act against the supplications of a body that would like to stop suffering. Freedom, work, effort, everything is transported to the plane of belief, for it is on this plane that one rediscovers the possible: it *would be possible* that Nietzsche not believe in Eternal Recurrence. Do you say that, on the basis of his doctrine, even that is not possible, that Nietzsche's very faith is conditioned by his nature and the latter by the universe? Yes, that is what one ought to think *if one already believes* in cyclical recurrence, but in one's deep inner solitude one has a quite other experience: one realizes rather that it is *almost impossible* to maintain an opinion that does violence to spontaneous inclinations and that

---

* Actually, one does find in his works *arguments* in favor of Recurrence. For example: "Whoever refuses to believe in a circular course of the universe is not far from believing in an absolute sovereign God" (*Werke*, XII, 57) . And the following: "If stability were *possible*, it would have come into being" (*id.*). But these puerile and abstract arguments do not convince anyone, above all not Nietzsche. They belong to what I shall call "the ballet of argumentation."

† Andler, *Nietzsche*, IV, 226, note 2.

is based neither on intuitive evidence nor on reasoning nor on the authority of a church. At the moment when the will seems sovereign, it is again derealized because it becomes gratuitous; one must again clench one's fists, beat the walls, scowl, cry out: "I believe it. I want to believe it." In short, one must dance the ballet of faith. Nietzsche *plays at* astonishment, exaltation, joy, anguish, he writes to his friends to inform them of his vision, he will celebrate its birthday, according to his custom, in order to integrate it into his sacred time. All in vain: behind the dance is only an absence of the soul. He does not believe; he wants to believe that he believes. The entire system founders in the imaginary. At night, during his spells of insomnia, he discovers the void: "The void: no more thought; the strong passions revolving about worthless subjects; being the spectator of these absurd movements pro or con; haughty, sardonic, judging oneself coldly." But he will carry through. While multiplying himself ad infinitum in the future, he projects himself into the past; an infinity of dead phoenixes have produced the living phoenix; he is the legendary ancestor of himself. This time, the trick comes off: torn between a future and a past which are equally imaginary, the present rips apart; the attention which Nietzsche gives to the real turns into abstractedness and the presence to the world into absence; unable to produce being, the will denies it. We can at last draw a conclusion from this astonishing defeat: if one does not succeed in changing an unacceptable situation, then it makes no difference whether one wills it or rejects it, for the one who publicly rejects it comes to terms with it in secret and the one who claims to will it hates it in his heart. In both cases, there is the same leap: from being to nothingness, from the evolving to the timeless. It is in order to "make the point" that one refuses or that one determines to will: in order to book one's place in the absolute. Both attitudes are condemned; they know this and they seek failure. Failure is the immediate object of the Nietzschean will: this man who is drowning demands that the instant of his choking last forever. As for the refusal, though it assumes at first a lofty attitude toward pain and misery, in short, though it is, in the immediate present, a revolt against failure, it wants to be, on another level, a failure of revolt. The reason is that for him man's grandeur lies in his being unsatisfied. In the first case, one relentlessly wills a disaster that one assumes to be inevitable so that the man's death may be identified with the triumph of his will; in the second, the aim of the refusal is to detach the soul from being in order to shape it into a likeness of values; the failure is experienced voluptuously as a condemnation of the world, as indirect proof that man is an angel; the man who refuses takes care not to desire a victory which, in fulfilling values, would destroy ethics; his refusal must be ineffectual, unheeded, inexpressible: the words themselves, insofar as they are involved in being, must betray him; to die refusing is to ensure one's triumph beyond defeat, it is to palm off on the absolute the order to say no. Both lines of conduct have the same principle: man is impossible. Mallarmé's old man who knows that "nothing will take place, that the excepted place may be a constellation," and who is swallowed up, bent "on not opening his clenched hand above his humble head," and Nietzsche's Zarathustra who wills his own decline and who sings: "Pain says, 'Pass,' but all joy wants eternity," are twin brothers, one a poet, the other, an actor, eager to light the same lamps in the sky.

We are now able to understand Genet's adventure. This energetic, active little man has dedicated himself to the mad undertaking of becoming what he already is and of destroying what he cannot prevent from being. Immediately his will volatilizes in the imaginary. Since it wills what cannot be willed, it is therefore dreaming that it wills it. Doomed by nature to remain ineffectual, his destruction and his approbation take place symbolically. The day he chose to will his destiny, Genet decided, unwittingly, to make himself a symbol, to express himself by symbols and to live amidst symbols.

It is true that, unlike Nietzsche, a man of independent income and free of financial worries, whose decisions were workings of the soul, Genet is constantly *active*. He has to steal in order to live. He plans a jewel theft, sets the day, the time, decides on the method, chooses his accomplices. Yes, to the very end this theft remains one of his possibilities, to the very end he can decide not to commit it. Within these narrow limits, he is free. But if he did not steal these jewels, he would steal others next week: he *is* a thief; each of his particular actions flows from the essence which it claims to constitute; he has been doomed to repetition. Since he wants to make himself what he is, all that remains for him is to dream that each burglary effects an irreparable leap into Evil, that his entire life is gathered up and determines itself in each of them. *In reality*, Genet steals because he is a thief and because he has no other means of existence; *in the imaginary*, he steals in order to become a thief. Consequently, he derealizes himself entirely, he rivets his attention on a fictive interpretation of his behavior, he becomes an actor. A performer who plays the role of Hamlet *really* sits down on a *real* chair because the director has so decided; his gesture is therefore incorporated into the *real* course of the world and contributes to the success of a commercial undertaking, which is what a theatrical performance is, but at the same time he expresses and constitutes in the imaginary the personality of the Prince of Denmark. The action of sitting down is therefore open to a twofold interpretation: it is a movement established by the staging and it is the effect of Hamlet's despondency in the presence of his mother. In like manner, Genet's theft is, according to his own terms, *poetic* because it unfolds both in the dimension of the real and in that of the dream.

What does our thief want? To derealize himself in a character who is none other than himself. He hopes thereby, as we have seen, to *encounter* himself. To steal is to re-enact willfully the original crisis. The gaze of others once rooted him to the spot and petrified him: the others *saw in him* a thief. To will to be a thief is to wrest from the others that original intuition and to live it for himself. Forcing doors and breaking locks, Genet enters an empty house in order to find himself there, that is, in order to be struck by the lightning of the evident: he will encounter "the exterminating angel locked up in a little pansy." But *we* know that this encounter is impossible; the image that the stolen objects reflect to him is in the process of gradually disappearing. Furthermore, the concrete being of the thief is accessible only to the consciousness of Others. Genet therefore finds himself compelled to have recourse to the Others at the very moment he thought he was freeing himself from them. It is through their eyes that he must make his being be reflected to him: they once caught him by surprise despite his precautions, he will force them to catch him by surprise; he was the terrified subject of a scandal, he will cause the scandal deliberately; he will read himself in those furious eyes, in those frowns, on those faces pale with fear. But it so happens that one steals in secret, that the burglar's first concern is not to be caught. That need not be an obstacle: instead of a real audience, Genet will content himself with a *supposed* audience. Thus, the unreal is multiplied by itself. First degree of derealization: Genet plays his being for himself alone; second degree: he transforms being into appearing and plays to the gallery; third degree: since *appearing* requires that one show oneself and crime that one hide oneself, Genet, who is alone in the apartment which he is burgling, plays at stealing for a fictive audience: "During the theft, my body is exposed. I know that it is sparkling with all my gestures. The world is attentive to all my

movements, though it may want me to trip up." His slightest movement is "as brilliant as the facet of a jewel." As for the audience, it
is ready to hand: it is the apartment itself. The setting and the
witnesses are one and the same: here again the negative becomes
the *analogon* of the imaginary positive: the real feeling that fills
the burglar is the fear of being seen. This fear gives the landscape
a soul. Everything is a trap. The floor is an infinity of possible creak-
ings; the Chinese vase is the threat of a crashing fall; the curio lying
innocently on a table will change into an alarm clock if it is
touched. "All of this light instant is under the threat of the single,
black and pitiless eye of a revolver. My precautions people the
empty rooms; thousands of ears sprout from the walls; the darkness
which envelops me is an infinite gaze; hands are crawling under
the tables." This "scintillation" of the body is quite simply his permanent possibility of becoming an object which he experiences in
the imaginary as a real presence of an audience that objectifies him.

So long as he succeeds, he keeps the spectators under the spell,
he obliges them to remain imaginary, they are the captive souls of
the tables, the closets, the consoles. If he botches the job, the enchantment ceases, real cops swoop down on him. But the performance will lose nothing thereby: the imaginary performer
becomes a real performer. So long as he operated in solitude, the
unreality of his acts was accessible only to him; it was their hidden
dimension: anyone observing him from a hiding place would have
seen only a diligent burglar whose precise movements conformed
to the requirements of the undertaking. If the cops and the raging
audience of the just should suddenly appear, the action loses its
efficacy, one commits it for display, it aims at becoming glamorous;
the imaginary corrodes praxis: "In order to flee from the store,
one of [the burglars] had tried to plunge through the glass. By
accumulating damage around his arrest, he no doubt thought he
was giving it an importance one would no longer grant the fact
preceding it: the burglary. He was already trying to surround his
person with a bloody, astounding, intimidating pomp. . . . The
criminal magnifies his exploit. He wants to disappear amid great
display, in an enormous setting brought on by destiny."

Cain is a dreamer. The dream takes everything, eats everything,
including the will to remain awake. A dreamer in spite of himself?
A willful dreamer? Both, and at the same time. He wanted to assume his entire condition, to carry the world on his shoulders and
to become, in defiance of all, what all have made of him: this proud

endeavor was bound to flow into the imaginary; the others had won in advance: they were maneuvering him while he was dreaming his acts. This marionette pretends not to feel the string that raises its little wooden arm; it imagines that it is making the movements it wants to make. Cain belongs to the irremediable, to that universe in which, as he himself says, "instead of acting and knowing we are acting, we know we are acted upon." He strikes out on paths already laid out which lead to the jail that has been prepared for him; meanwhile, his soul is a big poetic blank which widens at the edges: the more he strives to will the real, the more he fritters himself away in reveries. He must either disappear or transform himself.

It is precisely this new conflict which is going to save him. Without it, he went round in circles, unable to get out of the traps which he had set for himself. The liberating shock occurs when he realizes that he is dreaming, when he wonders perplexedly how his realism has changed into poetry, when he asks himself anxiously whether he is not going to be swallowed up, every bit of him, in the imaginary. For he immediately makes his second major decision: he will be *the* poet. Actually, this choice, which changes his life, involves nothing new: it is a reaffirmation of his original choice. He had decided to be what they had made of him; in striving to *be* a thief, he realized that he had become a *dreamer;* but his original will to assume himself entirely has not changed. Since dreamer there is, then dreamer he must will to be: he will be the thief become poet. Through this decision he escapes from the dream, since he transforms a dream of will into a will to dream; and above all, he finally acts upon himself: as a thief, he was lucky if he succeeded in verifying the forecasts of the good citizens; as a poet, he transcends them: this promotion will depend on him alone.

But let there be no misunderstanding: he is still far from being a writer. Evil remains his supreme end: he will first be a poet in his life, in his gestures, because this Poetry in act suddenly seems to him the best way of doing Evil and destroying being. He will be a poet because he is evil.

3. SECOND METAMORPHOSIS: THE AESTHETE

STRANGE HELL OF BEAUTY . . .

Genet drifts from the Ethics of Evil to a black aestheticism. The metamorphosis takes place at first without his realizing it: he thinks that he is still living beneath the sun of Satan when a new sun rises: Beauty. This future writer was obviously not spoiled at birth: no "artistic nature," no "poetic gift." At the age of fifteen, he dreamt only of doing harm. When he encountered beauty, it was a late revelation, a late-season fruit.

1. The Image

He *wants* and *does not want* to dream: with respect to his plan to assume the real, the dream is a betrayal. And that is the very reason why he is going to plunge into dreams: what one desires and refuses at the same time is Evil, is it not? The will that wills itself evil is a will that wants what it does not want. From these indubitable signs Genet knew that the imaginary was the worthy object of his evil will. So far, this is only formal; what actually decided him was the sudden realization that the dreamer is an evildoer. Indeed, what is a dream if not an appearance? Genet already knew that appearance belonged to the order of Evil: he is going to make of it Evil itself.

The Worst is in neither being, which is all good, nor in pure nonbeing, which is nothing and does nothing. It must manifest itself as a being, since being alone can allow for qualifications, but as a being which has eluded, a priori, the goodness of being and whose secret trend is a drifting to nothingness, in short, as a being whose only force lies in denying the reality that is in itself and in other beings. But that is precisely what appearance is: if, as Hegel says, there is a being of appearing as such, this being's reason for being and its destination are nothingness. If I think the moon is made of green cheese, this appearance has being only through what it denies: it is a negation of the moon by a nonbeing of cheese. No, Evil is not *done;* it is imagined; therein lies the solution to all its contradictions. Radical evil is not the choice of the sensibility but of the imaginary.

A king is about to go off to war; he orders a portrait of his favorite. He takes the picture with him, covers it with kisses, worships it, speaks to it as to his absent mistress: this king is a fine man. All decent people will approve of him. But when he returns from the campaign, he finds the beloved less beautiful than the portrait. He neglects her, locks himself up for hours on end with the picture, kisses the picture of a face more and more often and the flesh-and-blood face less and less often. A fire breaks out in the castle, the painting is burned to ashes. The king then goes back to the favorite, he visits her more frequently, he takes her in his arms, he contemplates her: but what he is seeking in her is not her real smile or the real color of her blue eyes; it is her resemblance to the painting. At this point, right-thinking people are astonished: "The king," they say "was quite mad." No, he was not mad, he had become evil.

Genet will be this fraudulent king. He has been dreaming that he is a prince, but reflection breaks in and shows him the vanity of his dream. Is he going to wake up? Quite the contrary, he sinks more deeply into his dreams. In spite of their inconsistency? No, because of it. If he preserves his childish reveries, it is because he regards them as falsehoods and because falsehood is an evil. In addition, he is going to subject them to a singular perversion: "I shall perhaps experience my greatest enjoyment when I play at imagining myself the heir of an old Italian family, but the impostor heir, for my true ancestor would be a handsome vagabond walking barefoot beneath the starry sky who, by his audacity, had taken the place of that Prince Aldini."

The child dreamed of being the real son of a real prince; the adult dreams of being a son of a fake prince, a fake son of a prince. The child, longing for tenderness, wanted to hope that he would one day know a mother's affection, the warmth of family life. Crushed and humiliated, he compensated for his present wretchedness by attributing to himself a noble origin: he is the king in his tent, beguiling his desire by rubbing his lips against a piece of painted canvas. The adult deigns, in addition, to imagine that a noble family is going to welcome him, but it must be by mistake. In short, he is effecting a derealization at one remove: he will play the role of a fake prince; the object of his dream is an appearance within appearance. "I adore imposture," he writes. What right would these nobles have to love him? Has he not decided to refuse reciprocity, to discourage love? Let them cherish him, if they wish to: it is to *another* that their affection must be directed through him. Genet will enjoy the advantages it procures for him, but will delight even more in the knowledge that he is fooling them. He wished earlier that he had been born a prince; now that he rejects being in all its forms, he wants to make princely gestures. Strange fiction: in a certain sense, the dream bears a resemblance to the real. He seems to be saying to himself: "I'm a hoodlum and I remain a hoodlum. At most, I may have the outward appearance of a grandee." The prince is the appearance and the hoodlum the truth. But in actual fact neither the supposed prince nor *this* hoodlum, the fake Aldini, exists. The only real hoodlum is the poor little wretch who begged in the Barrio Chino. Thus, the secret truth of the prince—his common extraction—is itself only a falsehood. Genet endeavors to live, via this false grandeur, his own present and real hoodlum's life as a pure appearance and relates real events to himself as if they were dreams: his fake family is waiting for him; if he is now in Barcelona, it is because he has run away; as a hoodlum and son of a hoodlum, he cares only for vagrancy, etc. The coins that *really* drop into his hands drop into a fake hand: the hoodlum is playing the role of a prince who is playing the role of a hoodlum. In short, Genet, at this very moment, *is not* a beggar: he is pretending to be one; therefore he does not feel humiliated by the alms that are tossed to him: it is all part of the staging. That is the aim: to put himself out of reach. I'm an actor, nothing can touch me. Thus, being appears to be corroding itself; it grows dim, and this flickering of the lights creates uncertainty as to whether the being of being is not actually appearance. When one dreams what one is, is it being which is the reality of the dream or the dream which is the reality of being? Being reveals the disturbing possibility of being only a dream, and appearance seems to be giving itself being through itself: what does the king who contemplates his favorite, the model of the destroyed painting, actually see? Being or appearance? Is the flesh-and-blood woman the truth of the painted image or is the image the truth of the actual creature? The king embraces her, caresses her, but all his gestures are derealized: he himself becomes an image; he is a painted king cajoling a painted favorite in the false world of kingly portraits. And that is the secret of homosexuality: it elects to be a crime. Not only because it is "against nature," but because it is *imaginary.* The homosexual is not an idle dreamer: he is an impostor, a faker. Genet elects to be a woman, but he does so as he elects to be a prince: falsely. "It would have mortified Divine to be mistaken for one of those awful titty females: 'Oh, those women, those bad, bad, nasty things. . . . Oh, those women, how I hate them!' she would say."

Yet Divine speaks of herself in the feminine. But the worst possible trick that a magician could play on her would be to transform her into an actual woman: as a woman, she would become a *nature,* a species, she would wallow in being, her desire to be taken by a man would become licit, would take on flesh, would be a true, substantial desire. Divine wants to be a woman because "she" is not one and will never be one. She plays at femininity in order to taste the radical impossibility of feminizing herself. Everything about her is false: the names she gives herself are false, her simpering gestures are false, her desire for the male is false, her love is false, her pleasures are false. She has not the slightest desire to *be* a woman; what she wants is to be *fake.**

We again find pride at the root of this perversion. Accustomed to finding its victory in the depths of failure, this perverted soul is going to seek its unique power in its profound impotence. As Jouhandeau has shown, even if God existed, there is a domain of man where man is alone. Being and the true, which are guaranteed by the Almighty, get on very well without man, but the false and the imaginary constantly require him. Appearance escapes pure Being, which can conceive only what is. God does not understand what those people who are playing the three-card trick are trying to do: he sees simultaneously the front and the back of the card which is moving from one pack to the other; he knows that it is the ace of spades. One of the players turns it over: well, yes, it was the ace of

* Cf. Appendix III.

spades; what about it? God is surprised at the audience's astonishment; he thinks that man will always elude him. Only a being which is not entirely can have the sense of nonbeing; in order to grasp a card trick and to see a Venus in a block of marble, one must suffer in one's very heart from a void which it is impossible to fill; in order to form an image, one must disconnect oneself from being and project oneself toward that which is not yet or that which no longer is. In short, one must *make oneself a nothingness.* What a galling amusement it is to find in our most authentic product the reflection of our finiteness: the same insufficiency enables man to form images and prevents him from creating being. Each time that he imagines, Genet experiences his nothingness; in each image he makes contact with himself at the heart of this "looming emptiness, sensitive and proud, like a tall foxglove," which is his alone. But by virtue of this nothingness he escapes from men, from the gaze of God himself, and the appearances which emanate from it are indestructible because of their inconsistency. The imagination is two-sided; if the just man wants to make good use of it, it is an admission of impotence: one imagines what one does not possess and what one cannot create; but if some lost, proud soul loves images for their own sake and aspires to create an order of shams, a parasitic universe that cynically feeds on ours, a diabolical caricature of Creation, then the imagination becomes a blasphemy and a challenge: since man as a being comes from God, he will choose himself resolutely imaginary so as to derive from himself alone. The dream manifests the realm of man because man alone can produce appearance, but it does so only to present this kingdom immediately as a nothingness. In dream, man can do all, but this absolute empire is only the absolute power of self-destruction. Genet's man, who is a creature of pride, breaks away from being in order to withdraw into pure *appearing.* Unable to create himself, he produces himself in appearance and as an appearance; he travels —in the opposite direction—the path of the great mystics. The latter, convinced that the image is nothing, attempted to tear it from themselves in order to attain a dazzling blindness; Genet, fleeing God, goes from light to darkness. But hell is not silence or darkness, it is a swarming of images, of flashes which one *thinks* one sees and which one does not *see,* of sounds one *thinks* one hears and which one *knows* that one does not hear; he plunges into it head first, he wants to become an illusion that maintains itself, an appearance that produces appearances; he has his being in his image, and it is he, he alone, who produces the image which contains his being: it is for this reason that he escapes; touch him with your finger and he crumbles into dust.

Nothing on earth belongs to this waking dreamer, except lies, fakes and counterfeits. He is the lord of hoaxes, booby traps and optical illusions. Wherever objects are presented as what they are not and are not presented as what they are, he is king. Sham king, king of sham. And what is sham if not the counterfeit of being? A fake diamond is a derealization of glass and a caricature of a real diamond. Genet was bound to affirm the absolute superiority of fake luxury to true luxury, of bad taste to good taste: "Her perfume is violent and vulgar. By means of it we can already tell that she is fond of vulgarity. Divine has sure taste, good taste, and it is very disturbing that life always puts her (she who is so delicate) into a vulgar position, into contact with all kinds of filth. She cherishes vulgarity because her greatest love was for a dark-skinned gypsy." And, in *The Thief's Journal:* "I was already refusing to have taste. I forbade myself to have it. Of course I would have displayed a great deal of it. I knew that the cultivation of it would have—not refined me but—softened me." He is readily moved by the bad taste of his characters: "To achieve harmony in bad taste is the height of elegance. Stilitano had resolutely chosen tan-and-green crocodile shoes, a brown suit, a white silk shirt, a pink tie, a multicolored scarf and a green hat. . . . Stilitano was elegant."

The true for God, the false for man. *True* luxury is homage rendered to creation; *false* luxury, which is a human hell, honors production. True luxury has never existed in the pure state except in aristocratic and agricultural societies. It was the ostentatious consumption of rare, natural objects by the elect of God. To be sure, legions of slaves were employed to discover, transport and refine these products of Nature. But human labor remained contemptible: upon contact with nature, it was reduced instantaneously to a natural activity. In the eyes of rajahs, the pearlfisher did not differ much from the pig that noses out truffles; the labor of the lacemaker never made of lace a human product; on the contrary, lace made a laceworm of the lacemaker. Truffles, diamonds, pearls, lace and gold naturally elicited the human instruments that would raise them to their highest degree of splendor. In the said societies, the worker is neither a man nor an animal; his traditional techniques, the origins of which are lost in the mists of time, have become natural and sacred; an intermediary between nature and man, he effaces himself when he has brought the two together. All that remains of his work is a drop of blood to brighten the sheen of the pearl, a bit of surface fever that enables fruits and meats the better to emit their odor. The Aristocrat eats Nature, and the product in whose form he consumes it should smell a little of entrails or urine; it is good that wool retain a musty smell of grease, that honey have a slight taste of wax, that the pearl be not quite round. Strong and vague odors, the taste of cooked blood, the exquisite imperfection of forms, the blurred discreetness of colors, are the best guarantees of authenticity. One is a man of taste if one is able, beneath the ostentatious appearance, to discern the carnal, clinging, humble, organic, milky *taste* of the creature. Supreme end of the Universe, king of Nature and natural product, the consumer of luxury sees the reflection of his sumptuous, blood-smeared birth in objects of consumption; through his commerce with the aristocracy of stones, plants and animals, the aristocrat effects the communion of his human "nature" and the great cosmic Nature. When he consumes his food, coarsely and magnificently, his fingers and beard dripping with sauce, the circle is completed; divine Creation enjoys itself in his person.

With industry appears *antiphysis;* as soon as the worker asserts his rights, the realm of man ceases to be natural. In producing, man forges his own essence; in consuming, the consumer recognizes himself and reappears *as producer* in the object consumed: he consumes what, in other circumstances, he could have produced, and what appeals to him in merchandise is the indubitable mark of human labor: a polish, a softness, a roundness, a sharpness of color that cannot be found in nature. With the advent of a manufacturing society, aristocracy, taste and naturalism disappear together, as is foretokened by what is happening in America. The aesthetic sensibility will preserve norms, but these will be very different. For the time being in our ambiguous society, at this strange moment in our history, significations interlace, naturalism and artificialism coexist; one starts a line of argument according to the rules of artificialism and ends according to naturalistic principles. There are still people who play the aristocrat and who have trained themselves to derive pleasure from lace; but ask them *why* they do. Well, it is because the machine—even when it imitates the lacemaker's actual mistakes—cannot replace her long patience, the humble taste, the eyes that are ruined by the work. In short, they are contaminated, without even realizing it, by present-day ideology; they base the value of the luxury article on human labor. Hand-made lace is more beautiful because the worker works more, more laboriously and at a lower salary. We caress this exhausting labor on the lace; fashionable people might even go so far as to say that it is *pure labor* (without machines) . Thus, *taste* remains, but it loses ground and takes on the name *good* taste in opposing pure artificialism, which becomes *bad* taste. Between the model and its imitation, between the natural product and its synthetic reconstitution, the man of bad taste, with inflexible rigor, immediately chooses the copy. But it would be a mistake to think that this is due to myopia, faulty vision, inability to distinguish the true from the false: if it were, he would make the right choice once out of twice. This admirable perseverance in error manifests rather that he likes falseness for its own sake. It is not that he necessarily *recognizes* it as falseness, but that he is attracted by its *visible* characteristics. The violence of a perfume, the gaudy exaggeration of a color, are symbols of *antiphysis*. To be sure, the more Nature recedes, the less we are tempted to admire the *imitative* character of industrial products. With the progress of dentistry, real and false teeth will disappear together: treated, worked on, transformed by the dentist, the tooth is no longer either real or false; there is no longer either good or bad taste. But, in this prehistory of industry, bad taste expresses the astonishment we feel at our own power: a synthetic pearl reminds us every moment, by its sheen, that man, who only yesterday was a natural creature, can produce in himself and outside of himself a false nature more sparkling and more rigorous than the true one.

Nevertheless, let there be no misunderstanding: Genet's bad taste is not that of the Oklahoma hardware dealer, but rather the reverse image of it. The latter finds in the electric corkscrew or the ball-point pen the *antiphysis* of which the gadget is the transitory expression, the other face of freedom of production, of the creative effort that transforms the world, in short, movement, progression, transcendence: this hardware dealer is a humanist. And, to be sure, what delights Genet in a gaudy assemblage of colors which nature could never have invented is *also antiphysis*. But for him, as for the Pimps, thieves, homosexuals and the whole parasitic brood, the labor which is condensed in the fake jewel is that of the Other; he cannot see in it the reflection of his own work since he does nothing. Since he steals or buys them with stolen money, his relationship to the glass diamond and synthetic pearl is that of the aristocrat to the real pearl: the mediation of labor is eliminated; just as nature was the very substance of the luxury product, so *antiphysis* becomes the pure, given essence of the manufactured product; it does not manifest to Genet human transcendency or the hard con-

quest of nature. Being a fabricated product of Society, it reflects to
the fabricated adolescent the simple fact that he is "against nature."
It is *first* his being-against-nature that Genet will find and valorize
in the sham jewel. This child who was not born of woman is mirrored in a pearl which was not born of an oyster. He will make use
of it to legitimize his perversion: if a cabochon is allowed to become a fake diamond, why is not Divine allowed to become a fake
woman? Violent perfumes justify the homosexual's artificialism:
they are as far removed from vague natural scents as the homosexual wants to remove himself from the species. But, above all, the
fake jewel is an *appearance:* for insofar as it is, it is not a jewel (it
is only a piece of cut glass) , and, insofar as it seems a jewel, it *is not*.
It reflects to Genet his nothingness, his inability to create being.
But, at the same time, it needs his gaze in order to exist. If Genet
lost interest in the jewel, the real diamond would remain a diamond, the fake would become a glass cabochon: there are fake
diamonds only for human freedom affirming its right to transcend
being and to emerge into illusory nothingness. In choosing to prefer *fake* luxury to everything else, Genet engages, without lifting
a finger, in the most highly human activity; he becomes the one
by whom and *for whom* there are specifically human objects which
escape the gaze of God, the one who takes it upon himself to see the
diamond where God sees only cut glass. *Antiphysis* reverses the
roles: a whole society is at work so that Genet's gaze can light up
an imaginary diamond.

In like manner, the girl queen, because she is fake, surrounds
herself with sham curios and, because she is bad, wants to have bad
taste. Immediately falseness increases and multiplies. In Stilitano,
bad taste is, in a way, natural; it is the spontaneous expression of
his condition. In Genet, taste for the false becomes false bad taste.
In order to caricature the true luxury of the true Prince Aldini,
Genet's aesthetic alternative bids this false son of a false prince to
utilize a false taste for false luxury which destroys itself. A pure
and secret taste will draw a subtle quintessence from colors that
clash, from vulgar perfumes, from glass trinkets; it will impose
upon these pure immaterial irisations the most severe, most classical unity. The reader has already gathered that this labor of distillation is bound to lead to the Word. We are drifting into the
universe of absences, into language. It is, indeed, one thing to write:
"I like vulgar perfumes," and another to spray oneself with them.
But we have not yet reached that point. For the time being, Genet
enjoys loving false jewels with false love—the same false love he

bears Stilitano, the false tough. Here, again, the game of imposture is played out to the end: he imagines that he loves an appearance of jewels. A false woman harboring an imaginary passion for an appearance of a man and adorning herself in order to please him with appearances of jewels: is not that the definition of the homosexual?

For one's feeling for appearances can be only an appearance of feeling: and that too is Evil. If I think I see a man in the darkness, I will perhaps be afraid, but if I realize that this man is an illusion of my senses, my fear will disappear. So will the illusion: as soon as I perceive the true, I can no longer *see* the man, I can no longer even understand how I could have seen him. If the phantom persists, it becomes flat, ineffectual: I know that it comes from me. One who, like Genet, delights in appearance qua appearance can therefore not receive his mental states from it. What fear, what disturbance, could be caused by the images which he is conscious of creating? And yet if he wants to love, to hate, to tremble because of them, he must affect himself with love, fear or hatred, and must, by means of a further lie, relate these feelings to the images as to their causes, while knowing very well that they come from him. Thus, the object is a nothingness, the feeling is shammed, and the relationship which unites them is imaginary: triumph of perversity. There we have something quite designed to enchant a man who, even in his passion, loathes passivity. Nothing disturbs him, nothing is too much for him: there is no more in the image than he wants and than he knows. To it and to it alone applies the famous definition: *esse est percipi*. A flesh-and-blood creature surprises, disappoints, thwarts plans, always gives more and less than one expects. But in the presence of these stereotyped, vapory appearances which are spotted with nothingness and of which only a few features, always the same, are emphasized, Genet delights in almost managing to excite himself. He imagines a handsome male and strokes his prick through his pocket: the prick hardens between his fingers, the excitement increases, the Pimp's image thereby acquires some consistency, but Genet takes pleasure in asserting that it is the image which gives him an erection. The reader will have some difficulty in conceiving this demoniacal labor: one must first retain the appearance of disappearing completely; beneath the cynical gaze which fixes the appearance and knows that it is producing it, the appearance grows pale, it is in the process of disappearing. Yet by a violent effort against himself, by a continued re-creation, Genet maintains for it a semblance of objectivity. In short, he is back again at willing the impossible. This conflicting tension delights him: his perversity loves to contract about emptiness; he knows that the image is nothingness, he is careful not to forget it. And since this knowledge is indestructible, since it is the very evidence of the "I think," his faith in the objectivity of the appearance becomes itself imaginary: Genet derealizes himself, he plays the role of a fake Genet who is a dupe of his phantasms. He *knows* that they are nothingness, he *pretends to believe* that they have being. At the same time, he hopes or pretends to hope that, in this strange place where the traitor changes into a Saint, where nothingness becomes being, where all contradictions attain unity, this new conflict between belief and knowledge will find a solution. Out there, elsewhere, belief changes into knowledge, the images become true, Genet finds himself the true hero of a royal adventure. He writes, in *Our Lady of the Flowers:* "At times . . . I really thought that a trifle, a slight, imperceptible displacement of the plane on which I live, would be sufficient for this world to surround me, to be real and really mine, that a slight effort of thought on my part would be sufficient for me to discover the magic formulas that open the floodgates." And in *Miracle of the Rose:* "Imagination surrounded me with a host of charming adventures, intended perhaps for easing my encounter with the bottom of that precipice—for I thought it had a bottom, though despair does not—and as I kept falling the speed accelerated my mental activity, my unflagging imagination was weaving. It was weaving other and new adventures, and with ever-increasing speed. At last, carried away, exalted by violence, it seemed to me several times to be no longer the imagination, but another, a higher faculty, a preservative faculty. All the splendid, invented adventures took on increasingly a kind of consistency in the physical world. They belonged to the world of matter, yet not here, but I sensed that they existed somewhere. It was not I who lived them: they lived elsewhere and without me. Exalted, as it were, this new faculty, which had sprung from and was higher than the imagination, showed them to me, prepared them for me, organized them, all ready to receive me. It would have taken little for me to give up the disastrous adventure which my body was living, for me to leave my body (I was therefore right in saying that despair makes one get away from oneself) and throw myself into those other comforting adventures which were unfolding parallel to my own poor ones. Was I, thanks to an immense fear, on the miraculous path to the secrets of India?"

To the secrets of India, no. And Genet knows it very well. If ever he came to believe *for good* that these phantasies were real, it would not mean that they had acquired being but that he had lost his. He cannot enter the world of dreams because he belongs to the real world. But if he could complete this incipient movement of derealization, if he could cling utterly to being and become utterly imaginary, the fictions which he imagines would then, without ceasing to be appearances, become truths *for this new fiction.* The phantasmagoria which I invent are falsehoods *for me,* but for the characters I install in them they represent the gauge of the real. For Stendhal, Fabrizio and the Farnese Tower are equally imaginary. But *in the imaginary* the tower in which Fabrizio is imprisoned is for him a real tower. What Genet would like is to be a Stendhal who, carrying his inventiveness to an extreme, transforms himself into a prisonmate of Fabrizio.* In a certain sense, this is quite impossible; in another, it is what happens to us every day when we sleep. Thus, we are back at the old dream of disappearing which Genet retains in the depths of himself. "To sleep . . . perchance to dream," says Hamlet. The annihilation of Genet, the impossible nullity which he is seeking, would not be a dreamless sleep: he would become one of the flat characters in his own nightmare.

But he stops in time: he *must not* disappear, he must recognize the failure of his attempt to derealize himself; he remains floating between true knowledge and sham belief, as the image he maintains floats between appearing and disappearing. And it is in this intermediary state that he produces phantom feelings within himself: phantom feelings, that is, gestures and words, the empty, abstract pattern of the emotion he wants to feel. Now, that is precisely the state he wished to attain: the image is now only a thin film separating his freedom from itself. Freedom is, as a rule, imperceptible: when it is inactive, we cannot touch it; when it is active, we lose sight of it, we are conscious only of the undertaking and of the tasks to be performed. But in the twilight moment when the image is about to dissolve, when the undertaking proposes no particular task because it is, by nature, impossible, then freedom, naked, inactive and yet contracted, makes contact with itself in its vain effort to endow nothingness with being, in its finiteness, in its failure, but also in its fundamental affirmation, in its defiance of

---

* "One day . . . he called a child who was playing. He had just painted a still-life deception; one saw a cloister bounded on the left by a wall and on the right by arcades. The child entered and looked about, surprised by the cloister, the existence of which he had not suspected. . . . He dashed into the wall, *purely and simply* penetrating the falsehood . . ." (Cocteau, *On the Fine Arts Considered as Murder*).

being and of God. We finally discover the secret of this imaginary life: the image is the inconsistent mediation which joins Narcissus with himself. The fabulous Opera ends in masturbation.

All prisoners engage in onanism. But usually it is for lack of something better. They would prefer the most lamentable whore to these solitary revels. In short, they put the imaginary to good use: they are honest onanists. "I," said a French journalist loftily, in Cincinnati, outraged by American puritanism, "I, thirty-five years of age, holder of the Military Cross, father of four children, masturbated this morning." There you have a just man. But Genet wants to make bad use of masturbation. To decide to prefer appearances to all else is to place onanism, out of principle, above all intercourse. Moreover, he was on the right track: flesh-and-blood hoodlums played the role of Pimp, loaned him their reality. But Genet was already saying: "Pretexts for my iridescence, then for my transparence, and finally for my absence, the lads I speak of evaporate. All that remains of them is what remains of me." Why not do away with them entirely? The *images* will amply suffice to manifest the great homosexual essences. The following sentence from Genet seems to me to define his masturbation: "I am only through them, who are nothing, being only through me."

Onanist by choice, Genet prefers his own caresses because the pleasure that is received coincides with the pleasure that is given, the moment of passivity with that of the greatest activity; he is both the consciousness that is curdling and the hand that is getting tired churning. Being, existence; faith, works; masochistic inertia and sadistic ferocity; petrification and freedom: at the moment of orgasm, Genet's two conflicting components coincide, he is the criminal who rapes and the Saint who lets herself be raped. On his body a hand is stroking Divine. Or else this hand which is stroking him is Darling's hand. The one who is being masturbated is derealized; he is at the point of discovering the magic formulas which open the floodgates. Genet has disappeared: Darling is making love to Divine. Nevertheless, be he victim or executioner, the caresser or the caressed, in the end these phantasies must be resorbed into Narcissus: Narcissus is afraid of men, of their judgments, of their real presence; he wishes only to experience a budding of love for himself, he asks only to have a bit of perspective in relation to his own body, only a slight glaze of otherness on his flesh and on his thoughts. His characters are candies that melt in the mouth; this inconsistency reassures him and serves his sacrilegious designs: it caricatures love. The one who is being masturbated is delighted at

never being able to feel himself sufficiently another and at producing all by himself the diabolical appearance of a couple which
withers as soon as it is touched. The failure of the pleasure is a
sour pleasure of failure. Onanism, which is a pure demoniacal act,
maintains an appearance of appearance in the heart of consciousness: masturbation is the derealization of the world and of the
person masturbated as well. But this man who is eaten by his own
dream is thoroughly aware that this dream holds up only by virtue
of his will; Divine is constantly absorbing Genet into herself and
Genet constantly resorbing Divine into himself. And yet, by a reversal which will bring the ecstasy to its climax, this limpid nothingness will cause real events in the real world: the erection, the
ejaculation, the damp spots on the covers, are caused by the imaginary. With one and the same movement the onanist gathers up the
world in order to dissolve it and introduces the order of the unreal
into the universe: the images are bound to *be,* since they act. No,
the onanism of Narcissus is not, as a vain people thinks, a little
favor that one bestows on oneself toward evening, a nice, saucy
recompense for a day of labor: it elects to be a crime. It is from his
nothingness that Genet has drawn his pleasure: solitude, impotence, the unreal, evil, have produced directly—and without recourse to being—an *event* in the world.

2. *The Gesture*

There can thus be a causality of the imaginary. Nothingness can,
without ceasing to be nothingness, produce real effects. In that
case, why not generalize the derealizing attitude? Will Genet be
able to derive from it rules for his entire behavior? We know that
he is never alone: even in prison, even in his "evil-smelling hole,
under the coarse wool of the covers," it is before the eyes of the just
that he masturbates; and then, despite everything, he does get out
of jail; and when he is free, he is forced to associate with toughs,
cops, judges, sometimes with middle-class people. The imaginary
would have to become an offensive weapon, a means of action
on others.

But we have just seen that the cult of appearance led to impotence, to utter solitude, to the limits of nothingness. If it remains
a *dream,* if it does not even begin to be actualized, how could the
dream be at the source of social events? What can a schizophrenic
do? Lie down, turn his face to the wall and deny the presence
of others.

But Genet does not care about engraving the imagination on the real in the manner of a white-collar worker who "realizes his dream of owning a house." He wants to draw the real into the imaginary and to drown it there. The dreamer must contaminate the others by his dream, he must make them fall into it: if he is to act upon Others, he must do so like a virus, like an agent of derealization.

He already is a virus by virtue of his very existence: since he lives without working, the others must feed him, either by giving him alms or by assuring him the vital necessities in one or another of those monasteries known as county jails; in any case, he is their parasite: a whole portion of human energy is spent in maintaining him so that he may employ his activity in chewing the cud of old dreams; thanks to him, a certain quantity of the world's goods goes up in smoke, men work *for nothing,* their hard labor is finally changed into dreams: "Board and lodging," as prisoners say, "at the taxpayer's expense." Genet jerks off at the taxpayer's expense; that increases his pleasure. If he so often compares prison to a palace, it is because he sees himself as a pensive and dreaded monarch, separated from his subjects, like so many archaic sovereigns, by impassable walls, by taboos, by the ambivalence of the sacred. He returns to it often: the repressive apparatus has been set up for him; the cops and judges are at his disposal; the Black Maria is a triumphal chariot; for whom, if not for this royal dreamer, do their tires wear out, is their gasoline consumed? A large staff of servants is concerned exclusively with him: the turnkeys are his guardians and his Guard; what would they be without him? Does he not tempt with his dream these severe men who are married and fathers of children? Do they not sometimes feel that their sole reason for being is that strange, invisible lacuna which expands like a spot of oil in the depths of his thought? At least, so he likes to think: in his privately shown film,* a jealous, obsessed turnkey spies on the prisoners through keyholes in an effort to catch a glimpse of their dreams; the prisoner's dream is the guard's spirituality.

But that is not enough: since he is forced, at times, to give up monastic life, he must contaminate all of the profane world. If a layman should mistake appearance for reality, all his behavior is derealized, becomes behavior *toward nothing,* manifests to everyone the absurdity of all human behavior. When a nearsighted visitor doffs his hat to the wax ladies of the Grévin Museum,† the gesture is suddenly engulfed in nothingness, dragging with it all

---

* *Un Chant d'amour (A Song of Love)*—Translator's note.
† A waxworks museum in Paris.—Translator's note.

politeness: it was a calculated act, an act of diplomacy, it becomes a gesture, a barbaric dance around an idol. A well-designed play of illusions turns the heads of the most sober of men: they will talk to empty space, will bow to gusts of air, will thrash shadows. One must therefore construct optical illusions, traps, which channelize human activity and make them empty directly into nothingness. Society manipulates Genet like a marionette: he *is acted upon,* despite himself; if he could invent a gigantic hoax, he would pay society back with its own coin: it would be dreamt, despite itself. For the time being, Genet hardly thinks about this; he will come to it later and will construct those admirable snares: *Our Lady of the Flowers, Miracle of the Rose, Funeral Rites.* He still lacks the matter of these make-believes: written words.

But there is another method: one can present derealization in broad daylight, as a *value,* one can propose it to human activity as a goal and compel the others to derealize themselves voluntarily. On his days off, the right-thinking man is not averse to spending a few hours in an inexpensive little spot of nothingness: he pays actors to perform for him. But he is always afraid that this entertainment may little by little undermine all his *serious* activities. The Greeks threw stones at Thespis and accused him of lying; the Church refused for a long time to bury actors in consecrated ground; our ant-societies sense an obscure danger in theatrical performance: "That *doesn't exist";* "What does that *prove?"* "Of what *use* is that?" Why should not the evildoer become a perpetual temptation? Let him become an actor in real life: through him the evil powers of the theater will destroy the seriousness of existence. Genet fled to the imaginary from the gazes of the just, like the mystics who escape from the human condition; let him now return to human beings, as did St. Theresa, and let him give them the benefit of his experience: let him derealize himself before them, in the light of day, in order to change the direction of the gaze that objectifies him and to direct it slyly to nonbeing. In short, let the dreamer transform himself into an aesthete. It is on this major occasion that his first encounter with Beauty will take place.

Evil and Beauty: one is surprised to find these two terms coupled so often. Are not statues and paintings *good* things? And, in addition, why does the evildoer, who is bent on destroying all values, make an exception for those of the Beautiful? Yet, it is a fact: the evildoer is very often an aesthete; the aesthete is always an evildoer. There must be certain affinities between the nature of Evil and that of the Beautiful which make it possible to bring them together.

The proper object of freedom is value. It matters little whether one consider it as an unattainable ideal or as the being of that which is beyond being: in any case, it is that which must be, it is never that which is. Thus, it is opposed to fact as nonbeing is to being: pure love, utter sincerity, "are not," as the expression goes, "of this world," and Kant maintained that nobody on earth has ever been able to act on the basis of morality. This is bound to upset the Just who, out of abhorrence of the negative, have assimilated Good to Being. Fortunately, it so happens that value requires acts, hence, achievements: it is not sufficient to love Good, one must also do it. The Just man therefore decides that being is the end and the beginning. Sprung from being, Man transcends being toward being, and the ethical defines the abstract moment of the transcending. It is being which tends, through human freedom, toward its own fullness, and freedom is eliminated when this fullness is attained. In the end, values seem to the good citizen to be only objective structures of reality. His projects, which are called for, supported and bounded on every side by the real, have only one aim: to bring forth being from itself; if they are successful, they disappear or become realities: progress is only the development of order. Ultimately, being again shuts itself up within itself, crushing within itself history, time and freedom: the ideal is the end of history. Thus, the ethical moment aims at eliminating itself on behalf of a calm plenitude. The contradiction of ethics is that it requires its own disappearance: ultimately, the prescriptions of the ethical will become social reflexes; the identity of Being and Good, which existed at the starting point and which one finds again at the finish, will entail the disappearance of values. Virtue is the death of conscience because it is the habit of Good, and yet the ethic of the honest man infinitely prefers virtue to the noblest agonies of conscience. Thus, being poses nonbeing and eliminates it. There is only being.

On the other hand, however, for the artist value is primary. It is value that inspires him in his work. And that, I think, is the essential difference between the Good and the Beautiful: in the first case, activity submits to being; in the second, to value. But this difference does not trouble the Good man, since the artist works on appearances. The Just man leaves it to the painter, the writer, the musician to discipline images; he reserves for himself the *serious,* that is, the original relationship to being. The theory of art for art's sake is much more a demand of the Good man than a conception of the artist: "For you the images, for me the reality."* This sharp delimitation of the two empires is indispensable to the efficient functioning of an authoritarian society.

But at certain moments, in the presence of what is called the beauties of "nature," we sometimes perceive in the manner that one imagines: we apprehend the real as unreality, being disappears in the presence of its own appearance. Everything is present, the trees, the spring, the peasants, the wheat, and yet, like Genet at the Polish border, we feel that we have entered an image. Do we not say that we "think we're dreaming"? It is because the landscape appears to us to bear witness to an evident finality, and we thought it had been created to manifest that finality. In short, we have read in phenomena that value is prior to being and engenders it. But if being proceeds from value, if it is the means that value chooses in order to manifest itself, it has no end other than to bear witness to value; and if its sole end lies in this testimony, one might as well say that being is pure appearance, for it *is* only insofar as it bears witness; thus, the being of being is its appearing. Things gleam with an unwonted brilliance, but at the same time they appear to us to be floating; all of reality is in suspense in nonbeing: in subordinating being to value, this illumination makes of that-which-is the symbol of that-which-is-not, it presents the universe to us as a vast process of involution which resorbs being into nothingness. In the Beauty of "nature" being is revealed in vanishing perspective.

The just man rarely has these visions: he is afraid of them and quickly returns to his antlike labor. If a person endeavors to prolong this illumination, to maintain this derealizing attitude all his life, we say that he is an aesthete. His aim is to reduce the universe and man himself to the simple play of an imagination. To be sure, he hides his designs, he declares that he is a pure lover of Beauty: it takes a thief to catch a thief; but aestheticism does not derive from an unconditional love of·the Beautiful: it is born of resentment. Those whom Society has placed in the background, the adolescent, the woman, the homosexual, subtly attempt to reject a world which rejects them and to perpetrate symbolically the murder of mankind. If they affirm the primacy of values, it is because value exercises a corrosive action on being.

When Wilde writes: "I admit that I think it better to be beauti-

---

* At the present time, it is the conservatives who demand it. M. Thierry Maulnier offers the comic spectacle of a political writer who makes his living by anti-Communism and who, in *political* articles and plays, calls for, on *political* grounds, a "noncommitted" art.

ful than good, but, on the other hand, no one is readier than I to admit that it is better to be good than ugly,"* the aesthete shows the cloven hoof: his "Beautiful" is an engine of war with which he intends to destroy the Good: and his sole aim is to infect others with a very subtle defeatism. Wilde also says: "Nature imitates art," and this phrase which can be taken and has been taken in so many different senses means first and foremost that the real tends toward appearance and the fact toward value, hence that being aims at being engulfed in nothingness. In view of this, it is not surprising that the evildoer becomes an aesthete: for him, Beauty destroys being, therefore it is identified with Evil. When the initial vow to prefer appearance to reality in everything seems to be a dizziness, a disturbing diversion, it is called a choice of Evil; but as soon as the play of appearances is organized, the evildoer finds it more amusing to charge a value with effecting this systematic destruction; that makes for an additional mystification. The aesthete's Beauty is Evil disguised as value.

This brings us back to Genet. His aim is to transform the good citizen into an aesthete: is there any finer revenge against the spirit of seriousness? In the movement of the closed fist which swings, opens and throws seeds, he will force the just man and the peasant himself to see only the stately gesture of the sower; he will reveal that land and fields, peasants and seasons, were created only to furnish a pretext for this grand gesture. And he will make of the gesture itself the embodiment of an eternal gesture: the entire world will be condensed into a gesture devoured by a haughty absence. He will end by convincing the peasant himself that his hard labor is justified only by the painting he inspires. In the universe which he wants to reveal to the decent folk, a universe which is no other than *this one,* houses exist only for their roofs and the roofs for spotting the blue of the sky or the green of the foliage with a drop of blood, and that drop of blood for manifesting harmony in difference, unity in diversity. The just man will realize with astonishment that he is being judged by a higher tribunal whose existence he did not even suspect. He thought he was upright and virtuous, and now it is revealed to him that he is ugly and that this ugliness, in the new system of weights and measures which is being used to appraise it, far outweighs his finest action: "Ugliness is one of the seven deadly virtues."† At best, he will learn that he was unwittingly serving secret purposes, that he ran

---

* Retranslated.—Translator's note.   † Oscar Wilde.

out of his house, last July 6, not, as he thought, to rush generously to the help of the widow of his childhood friend, but so that his suit would be a dark spot amidst the light spots of Rue Mouffetard.

For Genet, Beauty will be the offensive weapon that will enable him to beat the just on their own ground: that of value. Until then, he lacked aggressiveness, he was playing a losing game: of course, he prided himself on his failings, he confessed to them in lofty terms; but in so doing he was accepting the values of the decent folk; in judging human actions, he referred, as they did, solely to the system of Good and Evil. That is all the good citizen asks: *tenemus confidentem reum;* to the magistrate, the forms of the confession matter little. In boasting of the most heinous crimes, Genet confirmed the Others in their opinion. Everything changes if the culprit appeals to Beauty as his authority: one value is being set up against another; the Good man is disconcerted, for he pushes hatred of Evil to the point of wanting the evildoer to hate himself and to recognize his error with loathing; nothing mystifies him more completely than happiness in crime. In demanding to be judged according to the norms of the Beautiful, the culprit escapes and flits off into a fourth dimension. It should be noted, however, that Genet does not entirely adhere to aestheticism: the aesthete challenges common morality and demands to be judged according to his own laws. Genet, however, retains the ethical system in its entirety; he is willing to be condemned, he *requires* that he be condemned. Ever since the original crisis he has aspired to define himself by the sentence that was laid on him: it is too late to change. No: the belated recourse to Beauty, as he says in one of his poems, "makes emergency exits open in his darkness." That is all, but it is enough: he will escape if he wants to; sure of escaping, he will let himself be condemned if he likes. *In the universe of the just* he is a villain; he is lucky if there still remains the dubious resort of Saintliness. But should he go to the trouble of entering the universe of the aesthete, the world of honesty becomes an object in turn and it is the just man who has to account for himself. Genet blithely plays a double game: the greatest crime in the first system will be the most beautiful gesture in the second; the abominable act of the murderer is at the same time the tragic gesture of the sacrificer. Genet does not choose: he adds a whirligig to his collection. Beauty is first of all the dirty trick that a hoodlum plays on virtue.

Mystification is merely the quite external aspect of his attitude. Beauty is not only trickiness: it is a terrifying reality that manifests itself to Genet by *revelations.* We are familiar with the old dream of vanishing which he keeps brooding over: he wants to turn round on himself fast enough to disappear by annihilating the Universe; at other times, "bursting with emotion, I wanted to swallow myself by opening my mouth inordinately and turning it around over my head so that it would take in my whole body, and then the Universe, until all that would remain of me would be a ball of eaten thing which little by little would be annihilated." To kill himself discreetly: never! It would horrify him to slip out of the world and leave it just as full. But if he could drag *everything* along in his gradual disappearance, suicide would tempt him. For the time being, he finds partial satisfaction in the practice of the dream: in the dream he derealizes himself in derealizing things. Always ready to be transformed into an appearance, on the lookout for the slightest opportunity to metamorphose what is about him, he sensitizes himself to the imaginary; he lives in a state of waiting, like a mystic; a trifle will suffice to make him capsize. The flick that causes these sudden upsets is the encountering of Beauty. It does not appear to him in paintings or books: what does he care about the imagination of others. Nor in precious objects or landscapes. But at times, in prison, in some Court of Miracles, anywhere, he is struck all of a heap by the arrangement of the most common objects; Genet sinks, he drowns, appearance closes over him: he has *experienced* Beauty. Let us recall his encounter in Antwerp: "My heart awoke, and at once my body thawed. With wild speed and precision the boy registered on me: his gestures, his hair, the jerk of his hips, the curve of his back, the merry-go-round on which he was working, the movement of the horses, the music, the fairground, the city of Antwerp containing them, the Earth cautiously turning, the Universe protecting so precious a burden, and I standing there, frightened at possessing the world and at knowing I possessed it."

This possession is imaginary: how could this pariah possess the universe if the latter had not changed into an appearance in order to elicit an appearance of possession? What has happened? Nothing. Nothing, except that a utilitarian act, by its precision and rhythm, and also by the memories it evokes, suddenly seems to suffice unto itself. That kind of thing does not surprise us: with respect to human activities, Genet has only too great a tendency to adopt an attitude of pure, quietistic contemplation. But, as a result, the practical purpose of this action is now only its pretext. Time is inverted: the blow of the hammer is not given in-order-to-put-up-the-merry-go-round, but the fair, the future earnings on which the owner is counting, the merry-go-round, all exist only in order to bring about the blow of the hammer; the future and the past are given at the same time in order to produce the present. This regressive time and the progressive time which Genet continues to live suddenly interfere, Genet lives in eternity. Meanwhile, the booths, the houses, the ground, everything becomes a setting: in an outdoor theater, as soon as the actors appear the trees are cardboard, the sky changes into painted canvas. In being transformed into a gesture, the act all at once drags the enormous mass of being along with itself into the unreal. Reality, possessed by its strange finality, crowds round the gesture, proclaims that it is there only to serve as its background. Everything organizes in a twinkling, everything contracts, the gesture is astringent, its unity is imposed upon the whole and governs it. In the same way, it is the Pimp's *movement* that subjects Genet to his charms. A motionless Pimp, Genet himself tells us, is seldom handsome. But "beauty is movement." Yes, because the tough guy's movement is a gesture. The Pimp starts walking: he rolls his shoulders *like Sebastopol Pete,* he sways as he walks *like Divers the Crook,* in short he calls down upon himself another's gesture; the useful is the pretext for a dance, he walks *in order to make a gesture.* Immediately the gesture swallows him up; the walls of the prison, the mud floor and the sky make an unreal frame for him; Genet capsizes: he no longer sees the objects which surround him, he does not know them: no doubt they still exist and dazzle him, but without his being able to observe or come to know them: the fathomless richness of being has vanished, Genet perceives *as one imagines:* something makes its appearance within the world, and this simple happening has been enough to transform this world into an infinite iridescence at the surface of nothingness. What is the strange power that makes the gesture gather things about it as does a shepherd his flock? It lies in the fact that the gesture is itself an absence, the simple manifestation of an archetypal gesture. And how can the archetype itself corrode a whole universe? It can do so because it *is not at all:* it is a simple, empty signification which is lost in an abstract heaven. The world exists only to permit a gesture, the gesture only to manifest an archetype, and the archetype is only a nothingness. Genet receives this painful illumination like the stab of a knife. Nothingness is the absolute end of being. This illumination is Beauty. Let me make the point clear: Beauty does not *first* appear in order *then* to bring about the derealization of being: it *is* the very process of the derealization. Usually it is Genet who plays, with more or less felicity, at changing things into images. But now suddenly "the matter becomes serious": something has been set off outside, something about which he can do nothing. When the derealization of the world imposes itself on him despite himself as an external event, Genet gives the name Beauty to the objective necessity of this transformation. Thus, Beauty is neither an appearance nor a being, but a relationship: the transformation of being into appearance. It is a fixed disappearance, it is there before him, within him, and yet he cannot touch it: if he puts out his hand, it fades away, the world immediately regains its thick and commonplace density; there is even no question of seeing Beauty, for it is the impossibility of seeing what one sees, the necessity of imagining what one sees, the necessity of imagining what one perceives. It is a dazzling blindness, a tremendous nightmare that gives the key to the universe, a terrible revelation that teaches nothing. Yet it is there, in his eyes, on the world, within him and beyond reach, being only this fixed vanishing; if he makes a gesture to touch it, it disappears, the world regains its density, its vulgarity. Nothing can be done about it; to try to see it would be pointless because it is invisible: it is neither a being nor an appearance, it is the transformation of being into appearance. In its presence, one can only prostrate oneself, fall down; it is a tremendous nightmare in which the world is swallowed up, and it is a revelation that gives the key to the world: being is meant for nothingness. Intuition of the beautiful is a fainting while fully conscious.

One would like to think of that other visitation: Poetry. We have seen that it, too, puts Genet in contact with nonbeing. And it is true that poetry and beauty can be given together. When he hears the word *envergué* (yarded)* in a prison corridor, the poetic intuition envelops an experience of beauty: the word that is uttered and its real meaning seem suddenly to be only an appearance; they and the universe of discourse are derealized, and the truth of language is the absent signification which eludes Genet himself and is accessible only to God. But there are moments of beauty without poetry: when Genet, speaking of Java who has been knocked down by a tough and is trembling with fear, says that his cowardice made him handsome, we are to understand that he is sensitive only to the abstract mechanism of derealization: Java's hard muscles, his obvious strength, his pugnacious air, all change into pure appearance since he is incapable of defending himself; his muscularity is a full-dress cloak, it is not meant for use. Java can

---

* See p. 298.—Translator's note.

be transformed into a statue: not for a moment will he become *poetic*. Nor will Darling nor Paulo nor Armand. Vice versa, the purest poetry is not always accompanied by an intuition of Beauty: one has only to recall the chairs in the meadow. The reason is that poetry and beauty are almost contradictory: poetic nonbeing is revealed in failure, when being triumphs with all its bulk; it is not so much given as sensed, as hoped for. Beauty, on the other hand, manifests the triumph of nothingness. In the first case, being crushes; in the second, being grows lighter, rings hollow, its pressure diminishes; the reason is that Genet the poet zealously wills the real to the point of his own ruin and, like Mallarmé, proclaims that he has been wrecked and that "nothing has taken place except the place"; whereas Genet the aesthete witnesses the destruction of the world. Poetry is Evil that has been knocked down and is even more evil in its impotence; Beauty is Evil victorious. The one is willful, it coincides with the most extreme tension; the other is a swoon—the swoon so longed for—Genet collapses, his heart fails him, he is going to die. "I kept moving forward among the same flowers, among the same faces, but I sensed, from a kind of uneasiness that was coming over me, that something was happening to me. The scents and colors were not transformed, yet it seemed to me that they were becoming more essentially themselves. I mean that they were beginning to exist for me with their own existence, with less and less the aid of a support: the flowers. Beauty too was becoming detached from the faces. Every child who passed tried to hold it back, but it ran off. Finally it remained alone, the faces and flowers had disappeared. . . . Strange hell of Beauty."

Strange hell, indeed: Beauty does not fill, it hollows; it is the frightening face of Negativity. It is painful because it shrouds a rejection, yet it brings help: it is Genet's ally since it fulfills—at times in spite of him—the wishes of his resentment. And if, when we are in front of a painting, the finality of the colors and forms refers us to the artist's freedom, how could Genet, perceiving the secret finality of being, *which is only in order to be annihilated in value*,* not feel himself designated by an anonymous freedom? These collapses of being are signs which are made to him, the gluttonous nothingness which devours being is the reverse of a liberating intention. But a freedom has only one way of addressing another freedom: *to demand*. If Genet feels in his heart that Beauty

---

* At least, that is the meaning of his aesthestic intuition. *Natural* beauty and *chance* beauty seem to indicate the pre-eminence of value over being. Artistic beauty, on the other hand, bears witness to the priority of being and to the human effort to manifest it in terms of value.

concerns him, the reason is that, like evil, it demands of him the most difficult conduct. It requires that he live according to its law, the law that Wilde, prince of aesthetes, calls style and Genet elegance. "In matters of great importance," says the former, "the vital element is not sincerity, but style."* And the latter: "The only criterion of an act is its elegance." Elegance: the quality of conduct which transforms the greatest quantity of being into *appearing*. An act is the less elegant as it leaves a larger quantity of waste, of unassimilable residues, as it involves a greater degree of utilitarian conduct. Gratuitous and destructive, the act is all the more elegant as it transforms reality into appearance for a larger number of spectators. Beauty calls Genet back to his project: he must disturb the good citizen, must whisk away the ground from under his feet, must make him have doubts about morality and Good; he must enchant criminals and destroy them; he himself must change into an infernal machine. Beauty is this project itself become exigency and returning to Genet, through being, from the depths of nothingness. He will therefore construct act-traps which have only the external appearance of praxis and conceal a corrosive nothingness; when they conflict with the acts of others, they will explode and disintegrate them. Their aim is to disconcert the just man by provoking aesthetic illuminations in him artificially. As soon as circumstances warrant, Genet will invent the gesture that derealizes: "Divine is always being presented with odd-shaped pieces of marble that make her achieve masterpieces." He "will make of his life a work of art"; he "will publicly make himself a work of art": he will constantly make use of his acts and needs and feelings to manufacture beautiful, disconcerting appearances, as the painter uses brush, paint and canvas to produce a beautiful image.

The Beautiful is not only an objective property of gestures; it requires that it be a virtue of thoughts. An aesthete should have beautiful desires only; his inner elegance should make of his very needs a pretext for gratuitous acts of will. A young aristocrat manages, by a noble abstraction of his sense of smell, no longer to smell bad odors. In like manner, the aesthete must derealize the vulgar requirements of his body, hunger, thirst, fear. Beauty is both an objective necessity and an ethic of sensibility. It, too, has its categorical imperative: the aesthete's will must be not only a will to Beauty but a *beautiful* will; needs, life, death itself must be consumed in beautiful, blazing gestures which all at once transform their authors into actors, the spectators into extras and the place

---

* Retranslated.—Translator's note.

into a stage set. Divine is a hole through which the world empties into nothingness; that is why she is called Divine: when she appears, she causes a hemorrhage of being: "At about two A.M. she entered Graff's Café in Montmartre. The customers were muddy and still shapeless clay. Divine was limpid water. In the big café with the closed windows and the curtains drawn on their hollow rods, overcrowded and foundering in smoke, she wafted the coolness of scandal, which is the coolness of a morning breeze, the astonishing sweetness of a breath of scandal on the stone of the temple, and just as the wind turns leaves, so she turned heads, which all at once became light. . . . From a tiny black satin slide-purse she took a few coins which she laid noiselessly on the marble table top. The café disappeared, and Divine was metamorphosed into one of those monsters that are painted on walls—chimeras or griffons—for a customer, despite himself, murmured a magic word as he thought of her: 'Homoseckshual.' " She dances: "All her acts were served by gestures that were necessitated not by the act but by a choreography that transformed her life into a perpetual ballet: she quickly succeeded in dancing on her toes, she did it everywhere." Her gestures redeem the basest matter by consuming it in the fire of the unreal: Divine has placed on her hair a crown of fake pearls; the crown falls, the pearls scatter over the floor: "Then Divine lets out a burst of strident laughter. Everyone pricks up his ears: it's her signal. She tears the bridge out of her open mouth, puts it on her skull and, with her heart in her throat, but victorious, she cries out in a changed voice and with her lips drawn back into her mouth, 'Damn it all, ladies, I'll be queen anyhow!' " Her acts escape from her and go off to take possession of others, they *possess* others, they are incubi, succubi; Darling, an aesthete despite himself, copies Divine's gestures: "He was at the mercy of another's will, another who stuffed his pockets with objects which, when he laid them on the table in his room, he did not recognize." And when a soul falls a prey to these poisoned gestures, they lead it to death. It is they that will expose Our Lady: for they suddenly set fire to the web of our utilitarian undertakings and turn our batteries against us. Our Lady has killed out of need, out of fatality; under Divine's influence he convinces himself that he has killed out of love of the beautiful; he sets up in his room a strange mortuary chapel in which a wicker dummy represents his victim. He should have concealed his crime, he proclaims it: this aesthete's gesture, voluminous, absurd, obscene, leads to his being caught. Evil projects the destruction of being; if it wishes to carry out this destruction without resorting to the powers of being, if it wishes to become efficacious and yet not compromise with order and reason, it will have to change into beauty. Beauty is the law of organization of the imaginary world, the only one that establishes an order and subdues the part to the whole *without being good*. Evil is Beauty glimpsed by Hatred; the Beauty of the aesthete is Evil as power of order.

If we wish to get a closer view of the relationship between these two notions, we must watch Genet at work: let us observe him while he is in the process of transforming an "odd-shaped piece of marble into a masterpiece." And, since Divine is Genet himself, since she enacts the horrible homosexual decline which he feels and the signs of which he tries, with the anguish of an aging woman, to detect in every mirror, let us return to Divine as she places her denture on her head and cries: "I'll be queen anyhow."

Genet-Divine is sitting at a bar, with a "little coronet of false pearls" on her head; she is queen. She is sitting in state, she is drinking, she is chattering away amidst the fairies, of whom she is one, quietly engrossed in everyday banality. The imaginary, however, is already chilling this peaceful abandon to the immediate: by virtue of each of her gestures, each of her thoughts, Divine invents for herself her femininity, her royalty. The very notions she uses in picturing herself are ambiguous: a queen, in slang, is a passive homosexual, which definition *really* applies to Divine. But the word exceeds its slang meaning and, by virtue of its usual signification, opens out into the unreal: when she is *named* Queen, this pansy, who is docile to the call of her name, escapes to a phantasy court, becomes the absent spouse of a monarch. We shall say, nevertheless, that she has not yet left reality: Divine has been established so long in this overhanging attitude wherein words are skylights that look out on Nothingness, wherein every truth has a dimension of falsehood, that this constant play-acting has become second nature: she is Divine because she plays indolently at being so; she thinks she is what she makes others believe she is; she sustains effortlessly, almost without thinking, a role that seems to require exhausting tension. What she sees in the immediate is a reality more than half corroded by phantasmagoria; what she calls her repose is a small minor exertion of which she is no longer even aware. Moreover, we are not so different from her, each in his own way: *are* you a magistrate, a member of Parliament, a doctor, or are you playing at being one? The thickest doughs contain a leaven of phantasy.

The crown falls and breaks; it is the *stage episode:* Polonius flops on his behind, Stilitano erroneously takes a tough for a *"maricon."* The peaceful, modest illusion of everyday banality is in danger of bursting and disclosing the monster. *Reality* lies in wait for Divine. Reality or Nature: "hateful, antipoetic ogress swallowing up all spirituality." In point of fact, as Divine is the embodiment of a symbol, as all her gestures aim at being symbolic, as the fairies around her, morning glories, polyanthus, tea roses, are themselves graceful metaphors, the fall of the crown appears to the audience to be a symbol: that of the destruction of all symbols. "Condolences, to which malicious joy gives rich tonalities: 'The Divine is uncrowned! . . . She's the great Fallen One! . . . The poor Exile!' " An ambiguous joy: for homosexuality is only a fairy tale. If the magic ceases, what remains? Divine reflects to the girl queens, whose "bad smell" she is, the image of a mean-eyed little old man, *their* own image.

Grace then intervenes: invention of a desperate will, last sally of a garrison that will not surrender. This sudden break in her dream and the ominous appearing of Nature drive Divine into genius. The pearls rolling in the sawdust, the kneeling fairies, the upright, impassive Pimps, her own uncrowned head: these constitute the "odd-shaped piece of marble" that makes her achieve a masterpiece. Experience always and everywhere ends by rejecting the indolent play acting to which Divine would like to abandon herself: there always comes a moment when she must harden, must master herself if she wants "to be Divine *anyhow.*" And it is at the crucial moment that the two contradictory components of her person are revealed. The invention will be born of their transcended conflict.

To begin with, realistic will: out of pride, Divine decides to live her Destiny to the bitter end. As the uncrowning reveals her in her nakedness, she will make of this downfall an adornment, she will carry her misfortune to an extreme, will take possession of this trivial incident and will treat it according to her methods; she will draw herself up, outraged, in the midst of the frightened fairies and will scream at them: "Yes, I'm old, tottering, decrepit, yes, my flabby flesh holds together only by force of habit. And look, I even have a denture." She is divine because of the ease with which she denies the real, and she will remain divine by virtue of her will to assume it. Of course, this will overshoots its mark and is derealized at the moment of its birth: one cannot will that which is. But though it is not in her power to produce the poison and waste matter that have been clogging her organism for a long time, at least she will produce the *appearance* of them, that is, she will *manifest publicly* the attrition of Genet. To will to be fallen is to will to appear so in the eyes of her triumphant rivals. Divine will yank out her denture in order to reveal her *true* face, her toothless jaws, her drawn lips, in order to make heard her *true* voice. But this, too, is to play what she is, for this proclaimed truth is not *the* truth. Or rather Divine is playing a double game: she would like her natural, physiological truth to be taken for her human truth, for the *true* Divine is neither the Queen of the fairies nor this old eunuch, but rather a man who is resisting old age inch by inch, who laces himself in a corset, who, in the morning, out of a sense of decency in relation to himself, places his denture in his mouth even before looking in the mirror. We are not natural beings, our modest and tenacious defenses against death define us as much as does the progress of death in our organs. This obscene and terrible decrepitude is an invention of despair. Divine's gesture, which reveals to all what she conceals from herself even in her solitude, launches a challenge to the real and to the Other: in out-doing catastrophe, she makes herself mistress of her audience; she was bound to feel the dropping of her coronet as a mortal accident, but she becomes active again when she transforms the wicked joy of the spectators into discomfort and scandal.

And here is the other term of the conflict: it is not a simple denture that Divine places on her head: it is a denture-diadem. Her gesture, though making a show of realism, expresses the fierce will to maintain the fairy tale *against everything*. If Nature is "voracious," Beauty is "greedy": it is Beauty which will ultimately swallow Nature. Divine will remain queen; and since the emblem of royalty betrays her, she will choose another: the most abject. At the very moment that she shows her denture, she derealizes it. The metamorphosis is effected by both the magnificence of the gesture and the inexhaustible resources of language. An unnoticed, unformulated and, be it added, slightly wrong locution directs the whole operation: a dentist "places a crown." But, in addition, teeth, when they are beautiful, are commonly compared to pearls. It is by means of this banal and familiar image that the trick is brought off. The profoundly homosexual idea of *falseness* will serve as a link: the pearls were false; the false teeth become the false pearls of the false diadem of a false queen. The teeth—false—are forgotten, they become the *analogon* of *real* false pearls. Divine's gesture has two contradictory and simultaneous purposes: it carries her wretchedness to an extreme and transfigures it. She makes of the denture that humiliates her the instrument of her torture: everyone will know that Divine is toothless. But at the same time she justifies it: her gesture, by a retroactive effect, goes to seek the bridge in the very depths of the past in order to confer an aesthetic meaning upon it: so long as Divine thought she had acquired it for practical reasons, the appliance seemed to her vile; but she has just learned that it was obscurely destined to serve a handsome gesture, to be changed into a jewel in her ingenious fingers: Beauty required that it be in her mouth just as it requires a red spot, hence a roof, then a whole house, on the painter's canvas. Thereupon everything is rehabilitated, including the painful sessions in the dental chair.

There thus appears an iridescent, mystifying object which is rather similar to the object-poems of the surrealists but which nevertheless defines Genet's "manner." From one point of view, he discloses the world's horror and the truth which we do our best to gloss over: that human beings grow old, decompose and are always in the process of dying; and, from another point of view, tormented by the most royal absence, he transports the gathering and the bar, with all its lights, to the imaginary world. The starting point is a horror which is real but which is immediately derealized by the will to assume it, to face it squarely and to communicate it to everyone by means of a scandalous exhibition. This diligent horror will choose its props in accordance with the perspectives of a quietism of resentment which "establishes relationships among objects that seem to have conflicting purposes." On the basis of this, gestures which are invented on the spot in response to the stresses of the moment will treat this matter according to the principles of aestheticism and will force it, by violent means, to symbolize luxury, order and power. This "treatment," moreover, aims not at eliminating the horror, but at making the admiration aroused by beauty shimmer at the surface. Thus, the mystified horror is derealized into its opposite.

This whole phantasmagoria vanishes in an instant: in placing her denture on her head, Divine had performed a fake act that changed into a gesture all by itself: she had done so in order not to perform the ignoble and degrading action of getting down on all fours and looking for the props of her play-acting under the tables. This was tantamount to stepping back in order to take a longer leap: but now, by an inverse movement, the handsome gesture changes into a squalid act; the comedy is over: "Her gesture was a slight thing compared to the grandeur of soul required for the other: taking the bridge from her head and putting it back into her mouth." A utilitarian act, humble and realistic: the queen-for-an-instant must return to the world of men; the diadem is again a denture, the movement that puts it back into a mouth is no longer the haughty display of human wretchedness but the acceptance of it; we are back in the baleful world of the just, where values are subordinate to being. Divine willed the real unto the imaginary; she now wills the imaginary unto the failure of all aestheticism, unto the triumph of reality. And for once she must display real will: for the act is *to be done,* it is required by the circumstances, although that does not dispense the will from deciding to do it nor the arm from executing it nor consciousness from living it. Genet presents it to us as the climax of the whole phantasmagoria, so that we wonder whether the latter was not invented for the express purpose of leading to this "moment of truth" in which it suddenly vanishes and in which an old man, with "grandeur of soul," sticks his denture back into his mouth before the ironic eyes of the onlookers. We see the various phases of this little drama: at first the play-acting is not differentiated from daily reality; then an accident endangers it; and then are born both the will to espouse the real to the very limit and the will to save the illusion by absorbing the real into it: from this tension springs the brief blaze of the gesture. When it dies out, one returns to action, that is, to stoical acceptance of reality: one sweeps up after the party. And the system is so well organized that it can be interpreted either way: we shall never know whether the magic was conceived and executed for only the final moment which dispels it or whether the moment of truth is only an unpleasant consequence that must be accepted out of love of magic.

For the time being, it is Beauty alone that concerns us. We have been considering it in its pure form as a simple relationship of being to appearance. But we must not forget that this relationship is particularized in each case: at one time it is a denture which changes into a crown, at another it is a young maid who plays the role of her mistress or a young burglar who borrows the cold brilliance of the jewels he has stolen. Let us examine these examples more closely: perhaps we shall find that they have common structures; perhaps Genet will let us catch a glimpse of the particular structure of *his* Beauty, that is, the law of his imagination. One can suppose that the subordinate fairies* enjoyed limited

---

* The word "fairies" is to be taken here in its literal sense.—Translator's note.

powers: the one whose job was to change pumpkins into carriages was not qualified to make court dresses out of thistles. The same for men: there is no comparison, however preposterous it may seem, of which one can say with certainty that it will never be made, but this does not mean that anyone can change any reality into any image. Wilde and Genet are both aesthetes and yet Wilde would have shuddered with horror at the spectacle of an old queer placing a denture on his skull. The beauties of both men are equally venomous, but Wilde's wants to insinuate itself into men's souls and Genet's wants to do violence: the former is as easy and pleasant as the latter is difficult and repellent; Wilde's beauty exercises its derealizing action only on objects whose matter gratifies the senses, Genet's is less concerned with pleasing than with manifesting its magical power. Since it is Genet's beauty which is involved here, let us try to discover the law underlying the episode of the denture.

What strikes us first in this case is the extraordinary discrepancy between the imaginary and the real. Dorian Gray *resembles* his portrait; but between a denture and a coronet there is only one relationship: contradiction, mutual contestation. The crown inspires respect, admiration; the sheen of pearls pleases the eye; whereas teeth, which are wet, which are yellowed by tobacco, which contain bits of food, arouse feelings of disgust and repulsion. For both Wilde and Genet the final term of the metamorphosis seems the same: one must enter the enchanted world where handsome young men wearing precious cloths play with gems. But what a difference at the starting point! The ignoble reality which Wilde made a point of not seeing and which, at Reading, unexpectedly pounced upon him and broke his back is that which Genet takes as the matter of his art. Once again he has chosen what is most difficult, if not impossible. This does not surprise us. As a child, he dreamt of luxury, of beauty, of nobility, and as he has had no experience of the good things he longs for, he asks cheap novels and songs to furnish his covetous desires with objects: rose gardens, marble gardens, gilded drawing rooms, jewels, flowers, oriflammes, garlands, necklaces: a shopgirl's dreams, stock images with which songwriters casually stud their verses for the sake of the rhyme. Nevertheless, it is these old gilded trappings, which have been relegated by the bourgeois to the proproom, these trinkets, this frippery, that provide Genet's reveries with their lusterless light. But, as we have seen, even the imaginary needs matter, and our wretched alchemist has only lice, crabs, spit and excrement to work with. Though these props are *real*, though they are part of his *real* unhappiness, they are no less conventional than the shoddy that enchants him: tatters and stink, filth and decrepitude, you will find all these hackneyed devices in the pages of the apprentice writer who wants to "get at reality." Genet thus finds himself confronted with two contradictory systems of stock images. His originality lies in his making one the matter of the other. Perhaps he might have escaped and lost himself in dulcet dreams were it not for the pride and resentment that constantly brought him back to the sordid reality of his situation. Perhaps he would have ended with a grotesque and cynical epic of ugliness were it not for the conventional sweetness of his early desires. In short, his job is laid out for him: he must transform sordidness into imaginary luxury, rubbish into wreaths, his rags must be made to look like princely finery. His tireless diligence will be expended in this undertaking: he must set up a vast system of equivalences that will enable him at any moment to metamorphose waste matter into a luxury product.

The quietistic attitude that fixes utensility on the utensil makes it possible to bring the useful and the gratuitous together. For the angel and the outlaw, both of whom are nonhuman and consequently view our activity as we view that of ants, a denture on a head is certainly a subject of astonishment, but no more than is a denture in a mouth. Let us bear in mind that Genet, who at that time was wandering among the fixed gazes of houses, among declassed minerals, had reached the point of wondering whether it is true "that one drinks from a glass." He is on the right track: the object, alienated from its use, can take on whatever meanings he wishes to give it. Other connections become apparent: waste is the unusable, luxury is uselessness; the beggar's rags are no longer even good for protecting him against cold and dampness: his wearing them seems capricious; they will be comparable to a dress sword, the hilt of which sparkles but which does not protect. But these formal similitudes constitute only a springboard: for each individual object he will have to invent, in each particular case, methods of transfiguration; he will have to establish, term by term, relationships between the "luxury" system and the "destitution" system, will have to seize upon the concrete analogies between physical aspects and functions, at times simply between names. We have seen the metamorphosis of the denture into a diadem take place on two levels corresponding to the double relationship: teeth-pearls (physical analogy, conventional and literary parallel) and false teeth—false pearls (identity in both cases of artificialism) . In the mouth of Solange the maid, spit is transformed into a spray

of diamonds. Here, too, each of the terms is a stock image: the
spray of diamonds is the most commonplace sign of wealth; spit, the
most vulgar expression of contempt. But: "If I have to stop spitting
on someone who calls me Claire, I'll simply choke! My spurt of
saliva is my spray of diamonds!" The *real* spray spurts from a head
like a jet of water and falls as spit on the poor, whom it humiliates;
inversely, the contempt of the poor man for the rich man, which is
all the more sumptuous, all the more gratuitous, in that it knows
it is more impotent, represents his pride and luxury; the mouth
of a poor wretch is an excavation in a diamond mine, a diamond
of the finest water is extracted from it and glitters. The jet of saliva
and the spray, which are similarly useless, tremble with the same
liquidity, with the same disdain, each can serve as a symbol of the
other. There is a passage in *Our Lady of the Flowers* in which
Genet, like a conjurer who repeats his trick in slow motion, oblig-
ingly describes for us in detail the work of his imagination: "If he
says, 'I'm dropping a pearl' or 'A pearl slipped,' he means that he
has farted in a certain way, very softly so that the fart has flowed
out very quietly. Let us wonder at the fact that it does suggest a
pearl of warm orient: the flowing, the muted leak, seems to be as
milky as the paleness of a pearl, that is, slightly cloudy. It makes
Darling seem to us a kind of precious gigolo, a Hindu, a princess
who drinks pearls. The odor he has silently spread in the prison
has the dullness of a pearl, coils about him, haloes him from head to
foot, isolates him."

When these correspondences are firmly established, Genet will
have to invent the gesture that will bring them out in strong relief,
that will condense into a single movement all the analogies, all the
sophisms, all the metaphors; and this gesture is often painful, as
we have seen: in order to change poverty into wealth, one must
start by displaying it. It is not enough for Divine to compare a
bridge to a coronet: Beauty requires that she impose this comparison by transferring her denture to her head; the aesthete is an
oblate, he invents sublime and grotesque sacrifices so that Beauty
may be; he strips himself naked and shows his wounds in order to
change them into jewels.

But when the conjurer puts a handkerchief into his hat and takes
out a rabbit, it is not the rabbit that is interesting: it is the hand-
kerchief-become-rabbit. The appearance that Genet is going to
produce will be neither spit nor diamonds, neither fart nor pearl,
but spit-in-the-process-of-becoming-diamond, fart-in-the-process-of-
changing-into-pearl. At times, Genet's undertaking arouses indig-

nation: he wants to degrade the Beautiful, to caricature it; at times, it transports: if we are to admire the artist who is able to work with the most sumptuous matters, how much more admirable is the one who uses only waste matter.* Occasionally Beauty remains abstract, unable to rest on a support which does not resemble her sufficiently: that ogress, greedy though she be, does not want to eat the garbage that is offered her. At times, this very dissimilarity discloses her inaccessible purity; one would think that Genet wanted to indicate that Beauty is the transcendence of being and that nothing can quite express it. Yet it would be nothing without the gesture, without the body that incarnates it; if we tried to look at it in itself without the intermediary of those disgusting materials, it would fade away, there would remain only a gaudy luxury; one must see it, willy-nilly, via excrement. "The art," says Genet, "of making you eat shit." This beauty is not easy: it requires constant tension, a sustained effort to make the two terms which repel each other—trash and jewel—hold together; it is exhausting. Moreover, for the spectator the metamorphosis rarely comes off: the discrepancy between the matter and the form is too great for the form to be able to mask the matter completely. At times, Beauty is contaminated by the filth, and its putrid opalescence only increases our disgust; at times, we do not succeed in leaving the real; we are always on the point of *seeing* the diamond, but it always steals away and the gesture which attempts to derealize it indicates to us an ascetic path that our weakness prevents us from following. Even if we did attain the intuition that is offered to us, we would be no further ahead: this Beauty does not gratify.

Unlike artists, who usually heighten beauty of form by pleasantness of sensation and who carve even their monsters in marble, Genet denies us all delight: the diamond he offers has to be sought in a gob of spit; the more its gleams attract us, the more the saliva repels us; although the jewel may fascinate us, we cannot forget that our hand is going to touch an ignoble substance. In order to find the dullness of pearls in the visceral odors of Darling, one has to fill one's nostrils with them, and the moment in which we are closest to perceiving their orient will be that of our greatest nausea.

Genet delights in these half-failures. Why should he gratify us? —he doesn't care for us. In order for the hoax to be complete—for he wants only to hoax us—his stratagem must first shake Being to

---

* Alexander Calder, for example, who is convinced that beauty lies in form, prefers to work with poor materials, tin, sheet iron. He feels that the height of luxury is to transform zinc into a luxury object.

its foundation; we must feel that we are about to leave reality. Luxury suddenly challenges poverty: the poor man does not even retain his pride of poverty; he disguises himself before our eyes as a rich man. At the same time, poverty challenges luxury: if spit can become a spray of diamonds, who cares about the spray? There is a luxury above luxury which destroys by its magnificence anything that money can buy. But as soon as our heavy terrestrial mass takes off, it turns turtle and falls: the derealization is impossible. It suffices for Genet that we retain an uneasy memory of this abortive attempt: is it that too much was asked of us? Or are we overloaded, too sunk in matter to be able to get clear of it? Was it legitimate to reject a Beauty which is embodied in foul substances? After all, Parmenides taught the young Socrates that there is an Idea of Filth: may it not rather be that we do not have the sense of the Beautiful? Is Beauty only a lure or is it a secret of being that escapes us and that others have perceived?* That is precisely the state of indecision into which Genet wanted to put us: it was for that purpose that he constructed this new whirligig in which nonbeing first challenges being—since the gesture invites us to see in spit the absence of diamonds—and in which being immediately challenges nonbeing. As if he were saying to us at the same time: "Beauty is everywhere, in mud, in pus, as much as it is in gold and marble," and "Beauty is not of this world." But isn't this the very thing he says about Evil? We recognize this incipient destruction which ends in an avowal of impotence: it is this destruction alone that the evildoer allows himself to wish for. Yes: Evil is the other name of *this* Beauty. Both names designate an *antiphysis* which is achieved for an instant only at the cost of unbearable tension; under both names a cruel imperative postulates the human realm, addresses itself to man alone, elects him and assigns to him, as ultimate end, the destruction of man. Whether she be called Evil or Beauty, a greedy ogress devours Being and Good, rebuffs her austere lovers, demands hatred and love at the same time, forces them to want what they do not want and not to want what they do want, allows herself to be glimpsed through pain, pretends to be abandoning herself and finally refuses to give herself; Evil and

---

* The answer is obvious: if, in some circumstances, even the foul can have beauty, this unexpected beauty is born of the object itself and of its concrete relationships with what surrounds it. It must be observed and learned; it reveals a *new aspect* of being. Whereas in Genet it is a matter of constantly finding new mediations between two a priori systems, that of the foul and that of luxury. These mediational relationships are abstract and reveal nothing. But he performs his tricks of sleight-of-hand so skillfully that one does not realize it immediately.

Beauty, two names for the same vermin, for the same parasite, a Nothingness that borrows its being from Being in order to annihilate it; two names for the same impossibility.

And yet, in another sense, Genet is sincere: he actually experiences horrible raptures: he really wants to retain them, to bear witness to them. When he attempts to reproduce them in public by means of a gesture, do not think that his sole intention is to mystify: he would like, through the intermediary of the spectators, to be changed into a miracle worker; since he is unable to possess this Beauty which manifests itself to him like a sudden disconnecting, like a fall, and which he cannot touch, he would like to create it.

He hates Matter. Excluded, he contemplates the goods of this world through a pane of glass as poor children look at cakes through the window of a bakery. The force of his desire, the acuteness of his intelligence, the richness of his sensibility enable him to imagine better than anyone their unctuous sweetness, their taste: through the eyes of the mind he possesses them; their significations stamp his soul with their seal. Only a series of chances, of material contingencies, prevent him from possessing them *in his body* too: material resistance of the pane, material presence of a cop, material force of the shopkeeper. Matter is the unintelligible, the insurmountable outrage; it represents his impotence and the reality of his exile. Genet's poetry is thus a powerful labor of erosion, a kind of Platonic ascesis which aims at eliminating the outrage, at destroying the repellent forces through poetic possession. But, inversely, in the muck into which he has been cast the reality of his torment comes from the materiality of the filth, the pus, the cold, the blows. Pretending to glorify mud in a transport of love, he derealizes and dematerializes it by magnification. If he chooses for his "masterpieces" the vilest of marbles, he likewise does so out of love of form and in order that form not be absorbed by matter. If he could make a form appear by itself, without content, a form that emerged "like a proud, looming emptiness," then something of which he could say that he was the sole creator would be born in the universe. Since man cannot create being and since being supports the work of man, Genet's vainglorious aim is progressively to eliminate all matter from his creation. At times he builds up a pyramid of appearances, each of which is lighter than the preceding one since its matter is itself appearance, and at times he maintains such a gap between content and form that the latter seems to be floating in the air all by itself. Thus, Genet's Beauty will be glaringly false: it is a fictive creation and a false destruction. A false creation since its aim is to eliminate being by pretending to create a "masterpiece"; a false destruction since it so intensifies the conflict between form and matter that the destructive "masterpiece" cannot take shape. That is precisely what we should have expected, since Genet wants to live *simultaneously* creation, destruction, the impossibility of destroying and the impossibility of creating, since he wants both to show his rejection of the divine creation and to manifest, in the absolute, human impotence as man's eternal reproval of God and as the testimony of his grandeur.

3. The Word

This labor of distillation must lead to the Word; it is by being inscribed in language that Beauty will transcend its contradictions. Genet attempted to derealize things by gestures. In doing so he was going to needless trouble; it was sufficient to speak, for speech is a gesture and the word is a thing.

Speech is a gesture: when Divine cries out: "I'm the Quite Mad," she designates herself and bedecks herself as much as if she were placing a denture on her skull. These words make her a woman and a queen, as does her coronet; they show her, shape her and transform her; in solitude she names herself in order to change herself. Words are elves; since childhood Genet has been in the habit of metamorphosing himself with a sharp stroke of their black wands: "Generally, when he was alone, he felt no need to utter his thoughts aloud, but today an inner sense of the tragic bade him observe an extraordinary protocol and so he declared, 'My despair is immense.' He sniffed, but he did not cry. . . . He fell asleep like a harlequin on the stage." He uses denominative power to change into what he wants to be; he can say: I'm a grasshopper or I'm a king. Was it not a "dizzying word" that turned him into the Thief? And besides, if language is gesture, gesture is already language: it is meant to *appear;* it is consumed in signifying.

The word is a thing: it is within language that the verbal Gesture will find its dentures and diadems. We have just seen that Genet hates matter: he prefers the tin knife to the steel one and the hazel wand to both of them; the ideal thing would be to carve a knife in the wind. Now, there exists an even more pliable, more fleeting and more invisible matter which lends itself to all transformations: the breath of the voice. The hazel wand and the word "knife" are inhabited substances: but the materiality of the first is manifest; that of the second is masked. I am aware there is another difference; the wand is a symbol, the word is a sign; the former *represents* the object, the latter indicates it; with a stick one can strike, can hurt, but one cannot brandish a word. But this distinction is valid *for us.* For us, the just, who possess language as a patrimony. Genet, who was excluded from language, sees words from the outside: in the word that marked him forever the thief's *being* was hidden. For him, as for primitives, the name is the being of the object named. In his solitude, words stand him in stead of the goods which he will never acquire; their meanings, instead of escaping toward the thing, will remain in them like souls. If he murmurs the name *"Brésil"* [Brazil] it is in order to have Brazil in his mouth. *Braise, îles, îles grésillantes de braise, grands bœufs braisés par le soleil:** assonances, vague associations, bottomless depths. The name is a face: "From the look of the word Nijinsky (the rise of the *N,* the drop of the loop of the *j,* the leap of the hook of the *k* and the fall of the *y,* graphic form of a name that seems to be drawing the artist's élan, with its bounds and rebounds on the boards, of the jumper who doesn't know which leg to come down on) he sensed the dancer's lightness, just as he would one day know that Verlaine can only be the name of a poet-musician." The word "knife" *is* a knife; the word "flower" *is* a flower. Genet once told me that he loathed flowers: it is not the rose that he likes, but its name. He rarely uses language for communicating, it is therefore not a system of signs. Nor a discourse on the world: it is the world with Genet inside. Later, he will be very careful about the choice of his heroes' names. One muses on the name *Querelle,*† which makes discord prevail, reveals the natural aggressiveness of the criminal sailor and nevertheless has the somewhat playful quality of a nickname. Querelle is a thug; he ought to be called Crime or Murder; one has the impression that a naïve, hesitant voice has graciously chosen this euphemistic name for him. The flexional ending imparts to this hairy athlete a secret femininity; this masculine name is haunted by the feminine article,‡ just as its bearer is haunted by a desire to give himself to males. This word is an emblem even more than a proper noun: he makes of this sailor-killer a character in the *Roman de la Rose.* Added to this is the taste for playing on words: *Querelle de*

---

* Literally: "embers, islands, islands crackling with embers, big oxen braised by the sun" (i.e., beef braised by the sun).—Translator's note.

† *Querelle de Brest* (Querelle of Brest): Querelle is the name of the chief character, but as a common noun the word *querelle* means "quarrel."—Translator's note.

‡ *Querelle* and *la,* respectively.—Translator's note.

Brest evokes *tonnerre de Brest.** And what is to be said about
Harcamone, Bulkaen, Divers? Each of them *is* his name, *is only* his
name: "I shall transmit their names far far down the ages. The
name alone will remain in the future, *rid of its object.* 'Who were
Bulkaen, Harcamone? Who was Divers?' it will be asked. And their
names will be disquieting, as the light from a star dead a thousand
years disquiets us." The name is the glorious body of the thing
named.

Genet will then fall into the habit of economizing on the gesture
and replacing it by its verbal equivalent: the statement. And since
the function of the aesthetic gesture was to convert a sordid reality
into a luxurious appearance, the verbal gesture will be a categorical
judgment of the *"x is y"* type in which the subject will be regularly chosen from among the terms of the "destitution" system and
the predicate from among those of the "luxury" systems. In each of
these judgments, which affirm of a Nay that it is a Yea, of a privation that it is a plenitude, the verb "to be" will assume the derealizing function of homosexual aestheticism. One has only to read
the following lines from *The Thief's Journal:* "When Java cringed
with fright, he *was* stunning. Thanks to him, fear *was* noble. It *was*
restored to the dignity of natural movement, with no other meaning than that of organic fright, panic of the viscera before the image
of death or pain. Java trembled. I saw a yellow diarrhea flow down
his monumental thighs. Terror stalked and ravished the features
of his splendid face that had been so tenderly and greedily kissed.
It *was* mad of this cataclysm to dare disturb such noble proportions,
such inspiring, such harmonious relationships, and these proportions and relationships *were* the origin of the crisis, they *were* responsible for it. So lovely *were* they that they *were* even its
expression, since what I call Java *was* both master of his body and
responsible for his fear. His fear *was* beautiful to see. Everything
became a sign of it. . . ." Or the following, at the end of a splendid
page which develops by numerous comparisons the implicit judgment "Prison is a palace": "I pitched myself headlong into a
miserable life which *was* the real appearance of destroyed palaces,
of pillaged gardens, of dead splendors. It *was* their ruins . . ." etc.
And this: "I am writing this book in an elegant hotel in one of the
most luxurious cities in the world, where I am rich, though I cannot pity the poor: I *am* the poor." "With Stilitano I *was* hopeless
poverty." One immediately feels that Genet restores to the verb an

---

* *Tonnerre de Brest,* an old oath, literally "thunder of Brest," euphemism for "thunder
of God."—Translator's note.

ontological power. The verb usually has two quite distinct functions: when, with respect to a reality whose existence is questioned, I forcefully assert that it *is,* the verb possesses a revelatory, manifestative, almost creative value; it draws being from the shadow, envelops it in light, imparts to it a kind of absolute proximity: it *is.* But if I say of Socrates that he is mortal, the copula acquires an affirmative power and the sense of disclosure. The reason is that the copula usually unites not a substantive and an adjective but a substantive and another substantive: the denture *is* a crown, the night *is* a light. And as, in general, the substantives conflict, since one is the negation of the other, the verb seems to indicate both an identity and a developing. Indeed, we cannot prevent ourselves from reading that the night *becomes* a light (that is, disappears with the breaking of day) , but at the same time we know that, for Genet, the night is a light without ceasing to be a night. Thus, the word maintains, over and above the absolute diversity of the terms, an unrealizable identity: there is and there is not movement, there is and there is not development; the incipient movement freezes, the activity becomes a passive synthesis, the disclosure discloses nothing at all, the metamorphosis is an appearance of metamorphosis. But the art here is to prepare it, to excite the listener's mind, to lead it by sure paths to the categorical judgment into which it rushes so ardently that, in the last analysis, it no longer knows whether it has *effected* the unrealizable signification or whether it has had the *illusion* of understanding. The verb thus leaves a strange taste of passive action, of motionless movement, of frozen expansion.

Of course, in Genet's literary works the categorical judgment is more often than not screened by the artifices, but it does not take much searching to find the nakedness of the inner language, its stereotypes. Here is Darling, "luminous with extinguished pride"; let us translate this: pride *is* light; pride debased, humiliated and, finally, destroyed, is therefore night; but Darling's somber pride *is* a will to go to the very limit of abjection; this night *is* therefore the most brilliant brightness, the absence of pride *is* pride.

Here is Pilorge: "His face, cut out of *True Detective Magazine,* darkens the wall with its icy radiance, which is composed of his will to death, his dead youth, his death. It spatters the walls with beauty. . . . Your face is dark, as if a shadow had fallen over your soul in broad daylight." One could quote any number of passages. The most beautiful moments of this lyricism always amount to variations on the two basic motifs: night is light, light is darkness. "In these handsome hoodlums I shall always strive to express as best I can that which, charming me, is both light and darkness. I shall do what I can, but I cannot say anything other than that 'they are a dark brilliance or a dazzling darkness.' This is nothing compared to what I feel, a feeling, moreover, that the most worthy novelists express when they write: 'the dark light . . . the fiery shade . . .' trying to achieve in a short poem the vivid, apparent antithesis of Evil and the Beautiful." In Pilorge's soul the sun begets a shadow: there is a shadow of light. But this shadow which is murder and death, that is, negation of life, becomes in turn light, icy radiance.

Genet is going to "pay the honors of the name" to his wretched heroes, to the hideous props of his beggar's life. He will constantly name them silently, in his head. But one must understand that this *naming* has all the features of an official act: Genet names his Pimps murderers and his traitors saints as a government names one of its officials to a higher post. I shall call this magnification.

It is a veritable transubstantiation: when Genet repeats to himself in a whisper: "Harcamone is a rose," he transforms this criminal into a flower before his own eyes. This is self-evident, since Harcamone, a pure appearance, is nothing other than his name. The analogies which facilitated the *gesture* of aesthetic unification are often replaced on the verbal level by recurrences of sound: the *o* of Harcamone becomes that of rose and, in entering the predicate, draws the whole subject along with it. Without wanting to yield to "verbal automatism," Genet does not mind the predicate's presenting itself as an oral distortion of the subject: *"Son postérieur était un reposoir"* [His posterior was an altar]. In *reposoir* you still hear *postérieur*. Indeed, *"reposoir"* is *"postérieur"* itself, but slightly dented. The words are clay which is constantly being modeled. A few pressures of the fingers change the verbal physiognomy, give it another expression.

But, on the other hand, each transubstantiation results in progress on the path of dematerialization. The noble word refines the matter of the ignoble word, it rarefies it, it acts as a unifying and astringent principle. "Should I have to portray a convict—or a criminal—I shall so bedeck him with flowers that, as he disappears beneath them, he will himself become a flower, a gigantic and new one." The flower is the profound unity of the convict, it reduces the diversity of his characteristics, tightens his being: "Convicts' clothes are striped pink and white . . . the material evokes . . . certain flowers whose petals are slightly fuzzy." As a result of the action of this synthetic principle, the convict's clothing enters his flesh, becomes his skin, the pink merges with the white; finally the entire convict is nothing but a passing mode of the floral substance. A Chinese philosopher who may well be no other than Jean Paulhan used to ask why, instead of "the fish are swimming," one should not write, "the swim is fishing."* I suppose that this formula had, as he saw it, the advantage of doing away with the multiplicity of fish by making each of them a figure of the eternal swim. Similarly, in Genet, "jailbird florality." In circulating through so many criminals, hoodlums, gangsters, the flower is stylized, loses its individuality as a flower and becomes a pneumatic principle; while emptying the ignoble word of its substance, the noble word loses its matter: "My words invoke the carnal sumptuousness, the pomp, of the ceremonies of the here-below, not, alas, the would-be rational order of ours, but the beauty of dead and dying ages. I thought, in expressing it, to rid it of the power exercised by the objects, organs, substances, metals and humors which were long worshiped, diamonds, purple, etc., and to rid myself of the world they signify." The convict thus disappears behind the flower, and the flower becomes the convict's emblem. Genet's verbal aestheticism is, strictly speaking, emblematic, and one can apply to him what he says of armorial bearings: "It is not for me to know the origin of the emblems, animals, plants, objects, but I feel that the lords, who at first were military leaders, disappeared beneath the escutcheon, which was at first a sign, a symbol. The elite which they formed was suddenly projected into an abstract region, against an abstract sky on which it was written." And he adds: "Thus, the tattooing makes the toughs. When a sign, even a simple one, was engraved on their arms, at the same time they were hoisted onto a pedestal and plunged into a remote, inaccessible darkness."

By means of magnification, Genet "writes his heroes on an abstract sky." But the "animals, plants, objects" to which he likens them are thereby impoverished and take on the stiffness of heraldic figures.

Thus, this *magnifying* aestheticism is not an idealization of the real, a transition to the myth, to the legend, to the epic, nor even a very innocent and very generous way of giving names, like jewels or necklaces, to unnamed heroes: it kills what it speaks of as Genet kills the handsome pimps who think they are subduing him. He proceeds to an Assumption by emptying, he drains matter, plucks from it its contingency, its density, its infinite divisibility. The

---

* To avoid confusion with the normal meaning of "fishing" in English, one might substitute "the eels are swimming" and "the swim is eeling" for the two quotations in the text.—Translator's note.

abstract space in which his words are inscribed is Spinoza's space without parts. Ultimately there would remain only a simple signification which would vanish in the void. From the steel knife to the emblem, a patient labor of erosion has worn away the substance, has thinned it down until it is transparent. Genet's creation is the reverse of the divine creation: he starts from being, as does God from Nothingness, and constitutes regions of existence, each of which symbolizes the preceding one; but whereas the divine creation is a procession which goes from nonbeing to the infinite multiplicity of being, that of Genet is a recession which draws indefinitely nearer and nearer to nothingness without ever quite reaching it. It may be that his poetry is the art of making us eat shit, but it is also the art of dematerializing it. Excrement, vomit, stink: all this hardly shocks us in his work; read Zola's *La Terre* or *Pot Bouille* and you will see the difference between thick, warm, odorous dung and the distinguished, icy turds which Genet strews in his books and which resemble glazed fruit. The magnifications to which he proceeds in thought give him the impression that he is relieving the world of its matter as a pickpocket relieves a victim of his wallet. If he later decides to write, it will be in order to re-experience this feeling of lightness which is precisely the effect of his ascensional movement, of his flight to the abstract sky of emblems and glorified bodies: "To write and before writing to enter into possession of that state of grace which is a kind of lightness, of inadhesion to the ground, to the solid, to what is usually called the real."

In this ceremonious naming, each object that loses its contingency assumes the rank of appurtenance of the cult; the thieves' den is transformed into a mystic abode; the foul realities are the manifestations of a having-to-be secret: "I sought the secret meaning of the unctuousness and whiteness of his spit." The gaze pierces the matter and aims, through it, at the value of which it is the symbol. The categorical judgment has disclosed to us its deepest structure: the substance-subject is the fact and the predicate represents potentiality. The world vanishes, or rather we catch a glimpse of it in the process of evanescence. Relationships among beings are transformed: these accidental relationships, thickened by the opaque matter of the objects which they unite, always deflected, refracted, by the inertia of being, will become, as the matter grows thinner and thinner, sacred relationships, half ritualistic, half dramatic. By the power of words Genet will change his pariah's life into an "original adventure." One cannot keep from thinking of Mallarmé: Mallarmé, too, wants to *lighten* being: "An imperceptible transfiguration is taking place within me and the sensation of lightness is melting little by little into one of perception."* He, too, wants to wrest himself from anecdotes, from "contemporary incarnations," in order to become "an imaginary hero half-mingled with abstraction," sole character of an original drama which is found in the Greek tragedies and in the Mass as well as in the revels of nature and which is the dream of man, "latent lord who cannot become," and of "the antagonism between the dream and the mischances dispensed to his existence by misfortune." In Mallarmé, as in Genet, "transfiguration" aims not at attaining a stable universe of Platonic essences, but at reproducing what might be called a sacred Platonic drama. Genet's "original adventure" and Mallarmé's "solitary drama" have one and the same subject, which is the crushing of man by the course of the world, but with a final reversal: the failure becoming a token of victory. There is an *eidos* of this drama, an elementary, eternal and sacred form, and the *interpretation,* as Genet says, consists in rising dialectically from the anecdote to this *eidos,* from real characters to imaginary heroes half-mingled with abstraction, Harcamone, Divine, Bulkaen, emblematic like "the emblematic Hamlet," from these to what Genet calls *constellations:* "The constellation of the sailor, that of the boxer, that of the cyclist, that of the violin, that of the spahi, that of the dagger," and finally from the constellations to the metaphysical protagonists of the drama, being, nothingness, existence, Evil and Good, the Yea and the Nay. The aesthete is a mediation between being and nonbeing; his Passion is to lose himself so that being may change into nothingness; he stands between the emblematic heroes and the constellations; he is the movement from the former to the latter.

From these examples the reader will have grasped the true function of the verb *to be:* since it must derealize the Nay into the Yea, must transform the fact into a value and the real into an appearance, its frozen movement reproduces the dizzying and annihilating apparition of Beauty. In fact, it *is* this apparition itself in the realm of language. The magnifying phrase in itself engenders the aesthetic experience. But it does so *for others.* It does not matter that these listeners are absent or abstracted or that they "receive it with laughter." Genet speaks for an audience, in order to procure for others an impression which he does not feel. It stands to reason that

---

* *Œuvres complètes,* Pléiade, p. 262.

the intuition of Beauty can be procured only by means of a phrase that is *heard*. The one who invents and utters it remains at the shore of the promised land. We seem to be approaching rhetoric and literature. But no, Genet is a long way from thinking of writing. These magnifying phrases are still gestures. No doubt he undertakes to achieve, in speech and for others, aesthetic derealization. But he has not thereby become an artist: let us say rather that he has taken the place of the Ogress who eats being and makes us eat it too. Yes, it is with Beauty itself rather than with the artist that Genet, for want of being able to touch or see it, identifies himself. The process is always the same; first stage: in the presence of Stilitano, in the presence of Beauty, Genet collapses; second stage: he robs them of their Being and installs it in himself. "I am Stilitano. I am Beauty. The freedom that corrodes the world is mine." Beauty is Evil and Evil is Genet.

His original willing is realistic. He wills what is. But the object itself of this willing soon changes into a dream. Without ceasing to will the real, Genet launches out into the imaginary. Faithful to his first plan, he refuses to abandon himself to fiction: he will not be one of those who turn their backs to the universe and bewitch themselves with their images. Since he wills the real and since he is compelled to dream, it is the real that he will transform into a dream; he will be able to say of himself proudly, as of Ernestine the dreamer, that he never leaves reality. One would find few or no images if one could look into his mind: nothing other than intentions which are directed at "things that are" with the aim of changing them into appearances. As we have already noted, this strange visionary is the most well-adjusted of men, except for his falling occasionally into states of deep astonishment. He sees everything, he observes everything, and yet, in a certain way, he is so absorbed in derealizing what he sees that he perceives nothing. The most precious auxiliary in this undertaking is the word; his head buzzes with magnifying words; he has devised a whole sophistry and a whole rhetoric which enable him to decompose being. He moves, depending on the exigencies of the moment, from poetry to prose and from prose to poetry. In the one, it is language that murmurs by itself, like a nocturnal forest; in the other, it is Genet who is speaking for imaginary listeners.* But in any case words succeed

---

* Example of passive poetry: "Harvester of cut breath." Example of aestheticizing prose: "The night is a light." In the period that we are examining—Genet is twenty-four years old—his head is full of verbal gestures and poetic nuggets.

words. This mind refused to let itself be invaded by dreams in order to be invaded by words. And these words themselves are images of words rather than real vocables: images because they are uttered in the throat by an imaginary speaker, images because they are addressed to absent listeners. Everything is set up for him to write: the apparatus is ready; the technique, the vocabulary, even the style are already there. But he has to emerge from the dream: writing is an act, not a gesture—and an act that is performed with real words. For the time being, tossing back and forth between his moments of poetic despair and the terrifying visitations of Beauty, Genet sleeps with his eyes open: "If I have a bad break, for example if the cops arrest me, as soon as I have a moment's respite, as soon as there is the slightest pause between questions, my mind busies itself with masking the too frightful reality. It quickly weaves for me a world in which I am a courtesan, or prince, or king, or cabin boy. . . . It is as if someone had sprung open a trapdoor through which I fall into an imaginary avenging world. I do not quite know what I am going to seek there. Perhaps I use a procedure of self-defense. . . . It may also be because my true function is to dream and that, since my restless life does not permit me to exercise it, as soon as this life is sharply cut off, without any apparent break of continuity, and my attention is no longer required, the dream returns to its prey." He knows that he is drowning but it seems to him natural to sink to the bottom of his phantasmagoria. And yet, on the other hand, his dreams are growing poorer, are becoming stereotyped, they bore him, at times frighten him: it is impossible for him to deliver himself without the help of an external event, but it is equally impossible for this event not to occur. Human reality oddly resembles the atoms of undulatory mechanics and seems to be likewise composed of a corpuscle that is linked to a train of waves: when it has sunk down into its inveterate habits, into its anxieties, into its stereotyped ruminations, it is already outside, far far ahead of itself.

I WENT TO THEFT AS TO A LIBERATION,
AS TO THE LIGHT

Around 1936, when he was twenty-six years old, Genet returned
to France after a long period of wandering, met a professional burglar and accompanied him on his expeditions. "I had the revelation of theft." According to him, this revelation was decisive: "I
went to theft as to a liberation." That is how he views his life: a
long period of absence between two interventions from without.
The first of these contacts caused the original crisis, set him on the
path of Evil and finally put him to sleep: he became a strange
dreamer, turned in on himself, impermeable to experience, dragged
along in his inner whirlwinds. The second woke him up, freed
him from his fate, made a man of him. From then on, he opens
himself to the world, to life. Are we to adopt this reconstruction
unreservedly? We cannot decide without having heard him.

When he makes the acquaintance of the burglar, Genet is no
longer a mere beginner: he has already broken locks and cut wires,
but only now and then and without relish. "Begging," he tells us,
"was better suited to my indolence." Prostitution, too. He stole,
for the most part, what happened to be at hand, disposed of counterfeit money, smuggled dope, robbed old queens. During these
operations he relied on a tutelary divinity, Armand or Stilitano,
who backed him up. His encounter with Guy is a *revelation*. What
is new about it? In the first place, he takes risks which are, if not
graver, at least more immediately apparent: "All of this light moment is under the threat of the one black, pitiless eye of the revolver." In addition, he runs these risks on his own. He had prostituted
himself *for* Armand; he had smuggled *for* Stilitano: now, he is stealing for himself. Rid of his lord, the vassal becomes "his own

heaven." But, above all, he is performing *acts* and even, in a certain sense, he is *working*. Begging is all politeness: one must move to pity or must please; but in burglary one deals primarily with things; one must become a carpenter, a locksmith, must learn the laws which govern matter. "I had trained myself to break open other doors, in safe places, the door of my own room and those of my friends. I carried out the operation in a very brief time, perhaps three minutes, the time it took to force the bottom of the door with my foot, insert a wedge, force at the top with the jimmy and insert the second wedge between the door and the frame, raise the first wedge, lower the second, wedge the jimmy near the lock, push . . ." Apprenticeship, work: burglary is an outlaw profession, but it is a profession. Genet's social status changes: he was a faggot, a fake sharp, a beggar, a slave; in the underworld he belonged to the "un-skilled" proletariat; as a housebreaker, he becomes a specialist, he enters a corporation which has its rules and its professional honor; for the first time, he is entitled to say *we*. Actually, he does not have the experience of professional solidarity: burglars are solitaries. But they are united by the same pride and the same privileges. "A burglar," he says proudly, "cannot have base sentiments, for he lives a physically dangerous life. . . . Burglars are a scornful aristocracy." This aristocracy has nothing in common with the romantic chivalry of the great criminals and the glamorous Pimps: it is rather a tech-nical elite; one is not a member of it by birth. For that very reason, Genet, who is a commoner of Evil, feels at ease in it. He does not have birth, but he will be able to shine by his talent. Surrounded by well-built hoodlums, he suffered for a long time because of what he called the "softness" of his muscles. But burglary does not re-quire physical strength: it calls for adroitness, patience, know-how, courage. "I shall be so coy as to say that I was a clever thief," he will write later. "Never was I caught in the act." Then he realizes that he had exaggerated his physical weakness. It was only his reli-gious respect for the "toughs" that prevented him from resisting them. He dares to fight. In short, between the wretched plebs from which he sprang and the barbaric nobility which spurns him he discovers a proud, positivistic bourgeoisie: at Fontevrault Prison, the housebreakers feel for the Pimps some of the contempt that hard-working engineers have for idlers; they "remain among them-selves." Thanks to burglary, Genet's passive obedience is replaced by the spirit of initiative, mystical thinking by rationalism, the romantic and anachronistic taste for feudal relationships and mili-tary hierarchies by the more modern consciousness of professional worth: he carries out by and for himself the Revolution of 1789. The immediate result of this transformation is to make a man of him, to change him into himself and to dispel his dreams.

"The exact vision which made a man of me, that is, a being who lives solely on earth, corresponded with what seemed to be the end of my femininity or of the ambiguity and vagueness of my male desires. As a matter of fact, although wonderment, that gladness which suspended me from scrolls of pure air, was born in prison chiefly of my identifying myself with the handsome hoodlums who haunted it, as soon as I acquired total virility, or, to be more exact, as soon as I became a male, the hoodlums lost their glamour. . . . I no longer yearned to resemble them. I felt that I had achieved self-fulfillment. Glamorous models no longer presented themselves to me. I made my way jauntily, with a weightiness, a sureness, a steadiness of gaze which are themselves a proof of strength. Hoodlums no longer charmed me: they were my peers. . . . I wanted to be myself and I was myself when I proved to be a burglar. All housebreakers will understand the dignity with which I was adorned when I held in my hand the jimmy, the 'pen.' From its weight, its matter, its caliber, in a word from its function, there emanated a man's authority. I had always needed that steel penis to free myself completely from my muddy states of mind, from my humble attitudes, and to attain the clear simplicity of manliness."

He feels himself becoming "an accurate, disenchanted visionary." And he adds: "Great was the difficulty of reimmersing myself in my dream stories, which had been fabricated for that disheartening game of solitude. . . . Everything was without mystery for me, and yet this destitution is not without beauty because I establish the difference between my former vision and my present one, and this discrepancy charms me. Here is a quite simple image: I had the impression of emerging from a cave peopled with wonderful beings that one only senses (angels, for example, with multicolored faces) and of entering a luminous space in which each thing is only what it is, without extension, without aura. What it is: useful. This world, which is new to me, is dreary, without hope, without exhilaration. . . . Convicts are only poor wretches whose teeth have been rotted by scurvy, who are bent with sickness, spitting, sputtering, coughing. . . . They stink. They are cowardly in the presence of the guards, who are as cowardly as they. They are now merely scurrilous caricatures of the handsome criminals I used to see in them when I was twenty years old, and I shall never expose sufficiently the blemishes and ugliness of what they have become, in order to avenge myself for the harm they did me, for the boredom caused me by the proximity of their matchless stupidity."

Have his new activities changed him as profoundly as he says? I don't think so: this whole story seems to me to have been reconstructed subsequently; its effect is to give his life a slightly too edifying turn, the aspect of a *Bildungsroman*. There is a tendency to caricature in all of Genet's work: he takes pleasure in grimly parodying our commonplaces. The story of this fag who regains human dignity by becoming a burglar has been told dozens of times in high-minded books: it is the classical adventure of the black sheep of distinguished family who saves himself from abjection by adopting a dangerous profession. We sense in the background the ironic use that Genet makes of our holy maxims: "Work is a form of culture, work is freedom." In short, let us beware of his smile.

Moreover, it is *Miracle of the Rose* that dwells on the pedagogic and cultural role of burglary. *The Thief's Journal* merely mentions the "revelation of burglary," without giving it this decisive importance. Besides, if Genet had really saved himself by practicing this profession, we would not even know his name, *Our Lady of the Flowers* would never have come into being. Then why does this bourgeois of crime write? What will he have to say? At the time of his love for Stilitano, all objects seemed to him strange; the reason was that he had not learned to use them. His present professional activity has rescued him from quietism: "Objects are dead. All their purposes being practical ones. I know what they were and I cannot draw from them the sparks of life that our contact strikes from new objects." What will this honest housebreaker who is absorbed by his professional achievements say about a clothespin? That it is a clothespin and that it holds wash on a line. In fact, he will not say anything at all about it; one does not talk about tools: one uses them. If Genet has really returned to the utensil world from which he was excluded by a curse, he has only to work and be silent. For he has nothing to say about his own case either: the master of tools, as we know, is *anybody*. "I became myself," says Genet. That may be, but then this "himself" is likewise Divers or Bulkaen or any burglar; in short, everybody and nobody. He was a slave, to be sure, and now he is free. But, like the Stoic who becomes free by posing the universal and empty form of thought, Genet merges the concrete person with the most abstract determinations of activity. Furthermore, the difficult will to Evil must have disappeared at the same time as the muddy mirages of his fancy:

was not Evil the imaginary? We recall the moral skepticism flaunted by the Greek in his replies to the questions of the Tzedek Test: if Genet has "become free," as he claims, he is liberated from Evil and Good alike, and it is to this cynical and positive amoralism that he must adhere. What remains of him? A diligent, resourceful and realistic burglar: if *that* is what he calls his deliverance, it is manifested in so radical a liberation that this "readjusted," "normalized," "redeemed" dreamer must not even be able to understand that there are people who fling themselves into the mad enterprise of writing.

Most fortunately the change is not so radical. We find not a trace in his work of this vulgar and traditional amoralism—it is, at bottom, that of Callicles, of Thrasymachus and of any contemporary go-getter: every man for himself, a cynical variation of Victorian utilitarianism. The obsession with Evil has never left him. The enchantment, he says, has faded away. I doubt that very much, for the moment he says it he makes an apology for Evil; and evil *is* enchantment. In addition, why does he claim *to be discovering* the defects and physiological wretchedness of hoodlums? He *always knew* that they were dirty, cowardly, sick. One of the dominant features of the homosexual is, as we have seen, his wanting to dupe himself and to take revenge for being a dupe by sudden recurrences of cynicism. Genet knew that Stilitano was a contemptible creature. In fact, had he not been, he would never have been able to enslave Genet. I mistrust illuminations: what we take for a discovery is very often only a familiar thought that we have not recognized.

Moreover, can burglary really liberate? Evil, in both its principle and its end, develops in accordance with the norms of Evil; this means both that it retains an imaginary or, if one prefers, a poetic dimension and that it cannot reintegrate the one who practices it into the only really industrious community, that of the Just. Burglary is a technique, I grant that, but in reverse: I have shown that it destroys instead of producing, and besides, though it may be true that it utilizes objects, it does so for such singular purposes, purposes so far removed from their primary end, that the burglar drifts from Scylla to Charybdis: if he turns away from quietism, it is in order to enter the realm of magic. Burglary does not stand opposed to begging as the act does to the word: we have observed, on the contrary, that Genet's thefts are transformed into gestures, regardless of what he does. He himself says: "Theft . . . had become a disinterested undertaking, a kind of active and pondered work of art that could be achieved only with the help of language." And in the same book, in which he dwells upon the liberating value of burglary, a curious passage shows us the struggle, within the theft itself, between the act and the gesture, the real and the imaginary, utilitarianism and enchantment. I quote it in full: "I always carried out my burglaries alone,* from the first day until the one that was to lead me to Fontevrault,† and during this succession I was purifying myself increasingly. I did my jobs in accordance with rites which I had learned from conversations with the men. I respected superstitions, I displayed a wonderful sentimentality—the very sentimentality of the hardhearted—and I would have been afraid, as they were, of drawing down lightning from heaven by emptying into my pockets the kid's piggy bank lying on the mantelpiece. But this aspiration to purity was constantly being hindered by my, alas, too wily intelligence. Even on the boldest jobs—and among them the robbery of the P—— Museum—I was unable, while involving my physical person to a maximum, to keep from adding my individual ruses to classical courage, and this time I invented the device of locking myself into a historic piece of furniture, a kind of cabinet, of spending the night in it, and of tossing through the windows the tapestries which I had taken down, after having walked about on my heels (one walks more silently on one's heels than on tiptoe, beneath gilded ceilings, among illustrious memories), and I realized at last that every Saint-Just can vote for the death of the tyrant and bedizen himself, in the secrecy of the night or of solitude, or of reverie, with the crown and lilied cloak of a beheaded king. My mind still obstructed me, but my body lived supply and strongly, like the body of any burglar. That life saved me. For I feared lest oversubtle devices depend, by virtue of sublety, more on magic than on intelligible intelligence, and put me in contact again, despite myself, with the spells of which I am afraid, with the invisible and evil world of elves. That was why I preferred, to all the sinuous combinations of my mind, the direct means of burglars, whose brutality is frank, earthly, accessible and reassuring." In short, the ideal thing would be to be a supple, brutal body animated by a utilitarian intelligence; but the practice of burglary is not sufficient to achieve this all by itself. On the contrary, Genet spontaneously impregnates his thefts with poetry: he walks *on his heels* and "spins round" among illustrious memories in order to change into a high-heeled lord; he hides himself for no reason in historic pieces of furniture: in short he displays his homosexual prankishness: we

---

* Incorrect. Cf. *The Thief's Journal.*
† A state prison.—Translator's note.

are reminded of Divine's poisonous gestures. Burglary does not liberate: all depends on how it is carried out. And the "direct means
of burglars" are so foreign to Genet that he cannot resort to them
without playing at being brutal. In short, he can escape from his
operas only by changing roles: he abandons the character of Divine
in order to slip into that of a man of action without imagination.
But one does not thereby escape from the infernal circle of play
acting. The fact is, he says things that are disturbing: "I made my
way jauntily, with a weightiness, a sureness, a steadiness of gaze
which are themselves a proof of strength." Some time earlier, when
the handsome Serb still possessed him: "Stilitano," he said, "would
subtly insinuate himself into me; he would fill out my muscles,
loosen my gait, thicken my gestures, almost color me. He was in
action. I felt in my footsteps . . . the weight of the ponderous body
of that monarch of the slums. . . . My transformation adorned me
with manly graces." The same words are applied to the same attitudes. He describes himself as he was supposed to appear *to the
others*. The eminent presence of his flesh-and-blood lord and the
abstract memory of his new burglar's dignity produce in him
the same gestures, the same play-acting. We see what Genet's words
"to be oneself" mean at this time. He is himself when he plays the
Tough without an intercessor.

Actually, he is delivered from neither Evil nor dreaming nor
homosexuality. His first "actions" have simply put him into an
unstable and contradictory state in which fantastic play-acting and
realistic play-acting are perpetually in conflict, in which fake femininity and fake masculinity constantly clash and thwart each other.
When examined closely, this pretended "virility" which he claims
to have acquired looks extremely fishy: I grant that burglary developed in him a taste for risk and action, a spirit of enterprise,
courage. But a homosexual can aspire to anything except virility:
in order to be virile one must sleep with women.

There is no doubt that Genet's sexuality underwent a veritable
metamorphosis about this time. He has described it in *Our Lady
of the Flowers:* "Until then [Divine] had loved only men who were
stronger and just a little, a tiny bit older, and more muscular, than
herself. But then came Our Lady of the Flowers, who had the moral
and physical character of a flower; she was smitten with him. Something different, a kind of power, sprang up (in the vegetal, germi-
native sense) in Divine. She thought she had been virilified. A
wild hope made her strong and husky and vigorous. She felt muscles growing, and felt herself emerging from a rock carved by

Michelangelo in the form of a slave." Similarly, in *Miracle of the Rose* Genet desires Bulkaen, who is seven years younger than he. And Bulkaen has neither the royal glamour of Stilitano nor the bestial toughness of Armand: he is a little woman, "Roxy's kid," who is nicknamed Jewel, and Genet loves him as one loves a woman. He plies him with gifts, tries to dominate him. For the first time, he dreams of a brilliant feat that would win the admiration of the beloved. For the first time, he makes the following melancholy comment: "The feeling of a handsome kid for the one who he knows adores him is rarely tender." Doesn't this sound like the regret of an aging ladies' man? To what is this transformation due? Genet gives a complex explanation of it in *Miracle of the Rose:* on the one hand, the practice of burglary has, in making him virile, given him the possibility of loving like a male; on the other, it has dissipated his reveries; as a result, he has looked back to his childhood and, in particular, to his years at Mettray. Now, Bulkaen also comes from Mettray: it may therefore be a reflection of himself and of his past that Genet loves in Bulkaen; it may be that we are back at the play of mirrors that characterizes Genet's loves; it may be that he is loving himself as Another in the beloved. The explanation in *Our Lady of the Flowers* is simpler and more bitter: if Divine loves Our Lady, it is not because "she" has become virile; she has become virile because she loves him. And why does she love him? Quite simply because she is growing older. I for one consider all these explanations to be true simultaneously. The aging Genet tempts the toughs less and realizes it; at the same time, burglary gives him assurance: he dares love a child.

But let us recall Darling's discovery: a male who fucks another male is not a double male; he is a fairy. Genet's transformation is not so radical as he would like to make us believe. In the first place, Bulkaen, despite his "whore's mug," is not of the breed of girl queens: he resembles Our Lady and Maurice. He belongs to the elite of burglars: "Bulkaen had known the jimmy, I saw that right away. These kids are burglars, therefore men." He is a little roughneck and Genet is at times afraid of him, as he formerly was of Armand: "[His] gaze frightened me with its toughness. I guessed what my fate would be if such a gaze transfixed me, and what followed frightened me far more, for Bulkaen's eyes softened when they turned to me." Moreover, he is marked by the stamp of death, the glamorous sign of all the great male corpses that Genet has loved; and when Genet dreams about him, it is to adorn him with the stately end that he reserves for criminals: "To that life which a dozen times was rebegun and transformed I gave, despite myself, through the play of invented events, a violent end: murder, hanging or beheading." Thus, Genet's mythological power operates fully, is exercised on the "pale hoodlum," transforms him, consecrates him and confers upon him the powers and destiny of a Pilorge: Bulkaen has all the terrible virtues which, a few years earlier, would have enabled him to possess Genet, to subject him to his whims and finally to inhabit him. The very coldness, the rejections, the capricious indifference of this good-looking kid who is in love with himself are a kind of subdued replica of the icy indifference of the handsome males and the criminals. Bulkaen, who is more complex than Our Lady, is a man and a woman at the same time: it is the virility of this young male that Genet desires, but the femininity that shimmers gently on his soft skin makes it possible to disguise this desire, to make of it a will to possession.

Moreover, we find in this love all the characteristics of Genet's former passions: they are simply disguised by new elements. Bulkaen's beauty *staggers* Genet, knocks him to his knees like the raging fist of an archangel. Now, if the male is overwhelmed, he can be so only by a mad desire to crush, to bite and to take. In the presence of Bulkaen, Genet does not first appear as a hunter; he is first a prey. It is his age, his new state, the demands of the elite to which he belongs that oblige him to conceal his excitement. Accustomed to tempting the toughs by a show of agitation and submissiveness, Genet must deeply repress his desire to offer himself; it is now *he* who must subdue. His virility, a sacred characteristic that a society has conferred upon him by initiation, manifests itself to him as a categorical imperative: "My virility," he confesses, "is an attitude of mind rather than a physical courage or appearance." And this imperative comes into conflict with a female sensibility. This conflict between the psychic and the sacred is embodied in Lieutenant Seblon (*Querelle of Brest*) more clearly than in any of Genet's other characters. Male by virtue of force, because Society has delegated its powers to him and given him authority to command, he is Querelle's superior; his virility is his rank. The entire navy within him requires that he impose his authority: that is his duty. But he dreams of abandoning himself like a woman. This perpetual conflict gives rise to his ambiguous attitude, which is too stern and too weak. He punishes Querelle for a trifle, persecutes him, and then, suddenly, humiliates himself in the boy's presence. The imperious remarks which he utters reluctantly are a cover for the words of adoration which he does not speak: "In a curt tone:

" 'Don't you know it's forbidden to twist your hat out of shape?'

"At the same time, he grabbed the red tassel and removed the sailor's beret. As a result of having caused so fine a head of hair to appear in the sun, the officer almost betrayed himself. His arm, his gesture, were suddenly leaden. And, in a changed tone, he added as he handed the cap to the astonished sailor:

" 'You like to look like a hoodlum, don't you. You deserve (he hesitated, not knowing whether he would say: ". . . everyone's kneeling, all the caresses of the wings of seraphim, all the fragrance of lilies . . .") . . . you deserve to be punished.' "

Querelle is not taken in. He "discerns a painful slackening of the officer's rigidity." And such, henceforth, is Genet's sexual attitude: within a heightened tension, a secret desire to swoon. To be sure, he strikes, staggers and subdues Bulkaen, but what an effort it takes! We feel how strained and nervous he is. We sense that what is happening is a sudden and violent contraction that may end in a fit of hysteria. The little male always perceives the weakness underlying his lover's violence: Genet knows this and grows more irritated at being unmasked. But neither Lieutenant Seblon's haughtiness nor his enormous social power will prevent Querelle from despising him; nothing will prevent Erik from despising the executioner, neither the man's terrible profession nor his physical strength. The movements of the fake male betray him: the executioner wants to kill Erik; he draws his knife; then, "as if he were escaping the lust for blood into which everything—his nature and his function—were drawing him," he "looks at his weapon with terror" and throws it out of the window. He thinks that in doing so he has been violent, that he has proved equal to a "tragic situation." He is wrong; Erik is not taken in: "The executioner had lost. Although his entire attitude, when he drew his knife from his pocket, had frightened Erik, the youngster was quickly reassured when he saw the gesture with which the man threw it: instead of taking the blade by the point, which would have made the weapon turn in the air and describe a parabola, the executioner threw it by the handle, with his hand down. The extent of his weakness was betrayed by the gesture. His nature was without brilliance. It was crumbling. Erik realized that he had just witnessed a bit of play-acting."

Play-acting: it could not be stated better. In virilifying himself Genet thought he was escaping from it; and now he is being forced to engage in additional play-acting: he must *play* the male, while knowing that he plays it badly, that "he's not right for the role, that he's out of character." The sexual imperative extends its exigencies as far as coitus: Genet must now *take,* when his deepest desire is to be taken. He has shown Divine deciding to enter Our Lady—a young hoodlum who offers no resistance, "in play"—and, at the last moment, seized "with the dizziness she knew so well, the abandonment to the male," sliding under the handsome criminal and becoming a woman again: "In short, she resumed possession of her soul." And he adds: "To love a young boy for a long time, dearly, and then, unable to bear the heroic act any longer, I give in. My muscles and mind relax. I literally stagger. And I finally adore, in a frenzy, the muscles that torture me, that bow me under them, and this domination is as soothing as a sob after too long a time on the crest of a drama high as death." But Divine, who has chosen forever to be a girl queen and a "saint," has no reason to resist her giddiness, whereas Genet, even if he gives in to his, is obliged by his new dignity to be tricky about it. No doubt he will be able, in solitude, to indulge freely in his female dreams. But, in real life, he must "take." If he wants to reverse the roles without incurring his partner's contempt or losing his sacred prestige as a burglar, he will present this reversal as a freak of fancy, a whim, a passing amusement. The condition of an aging fairy is a strange one. Though physiologically male, that is, possessing male sex organs, he is forced to *play at being a male,* that is, to play what he is, as Solange the maid plays at being a servant.* And if, tiring of the game, he "resumes possession of his soul," if he becomes a fairy again, he is forced to present his truth as play-acting. The executioner, who is older, stronger and richer than his young lover, "grants Erik the role of male." One feels the full hypocrisy of this "grants": one would really think it was the kindness that a lord grants to his liegeman or the favor an adult grants a child when he allows it to hold the steering wheel of a car for a moment. Actually, this lofty kindliness conceals a supplication. But the hypocrisy will continue to the very end: the executioner will pretend that he is being tractable, whereas he is giving himself. This little game spoils everything. When Genet was taken by Armand, he was really raped; he could swoon with joy while thinking that he was procuring real pleasure for the male or while murmuring, like Divine: "The God, it's the God." But now it is he who must dominate the other: when he is taken, he is in a situation comparable to that of the masochist who pays a prostitute to whip him and is aware of the girl's mercenary servility through the insults and blows. It is out of submis-

---

* Cf. Appendix III.

siveness that this indifferent and amused young boy subdues Genet. He does not really desire him: he is too young to take Genet and too old to be taken. Therefore, the imagination must operate here too; the girl queen must derealize the scene at one remove: she must dream, through this languid possession, of a real, savage rape. But at the same time Genet must pretend to will the youngster's diligent obedience: it is by prestige that he maintains his hold on the beloved; he must retain his prestige at all costs. He will therefore order the other to play the male or will grant him permission to do so, and this authoritarian attitude makes the reverie more difficult, more clandestine: once again, Genet wills what he does not want, that is, the real, and does not will what he wants, that is, the imaginary. Moreover, if he goes back to his playing at virility, it is even worse: he dreams that the violence which he is doing to that docile flesh is being practiced on himself; he imagines that he himself is receiving the caresses which he gives. And, by a strange reversal, as a result of the fact that formerly his pleasure was due to his being unsatisfied, it is his present pleasure which becomes a lack of satisfaction. What used to gratify Genet was "the sweetness of being the cause of the male's satisfaction," of being "the pious witness of his collapsing into joy." He has said time and again that "happiness is greater when the partner performs artfully (which he cannot do if he is attentive to his own pleasure). When the mind is straining for pleasure, one cannot profit from the happiness of seeing or feeling that the other has come." He used to take his own pleasure afterward, listlessly, clandestinely: but now others are eager to give it to him. *He* is the one who is going to come. This unimportant coming becomes the sacred purpose of the ceremony, and the young male whom he holds beneath him, who has been entered and is suffering, experiences in his stead the intoxication of forgetting his own interests. Genet, the new Tantalus, is envious of the sacrifice of which he is the unworthy beneficiary and of the voluptuous suffering which he causes: his fingers, his mouth, his penis raise up in the other an inaccessible Genet; through the coming which gratifies him he senses in the other the absence of pleasure; he attempts to utilize his fullness as an analogue of a painful emptiness; formerly, he experienced the other's pleasure as his own; at present, he vainly strives to become another in order to experience his own pleasure as the other's. His sexual life was formerly a play of appearances, a shimmering of significations without matter: unlike Gide, who attempts in *Corydon* to outline a naturalism of homosexuality, he cherished his inversion because it was against nature. He made it a point of pride to sustain, at the cost of tremendous tension, a false pleasure, to come fictively; this priority of the Other over the Same and of the imaginary over the real was the triumph of *antiphysis* and of Evil within the sexual act itself.* Genet's artificialism and aestheticism have, in a curious way, given him a most Christian horror of the flesh, a most Platonic horror of all matter. The flesh now takes its revenge; pleasure invades him; by a sudden reflex, nature swamps him; matter flows into him and clogs him. Is not the partner who "plays the man" in a homosexual couple performing a natural function within the antinatural framework? Does he not enjoy his companion the way a male enjoys a female? Confronted with this pleasure which he has so often mimed and which is becoming a reality, Genet feels as disgusted as Divine would feel if she were metamorphosed for good into a "titty female." Besides, that is not the worst: coitus was for Genet a form of mystical possession; the Pimp descended into him like the voodoo loa into the body of an initiate; he felt that he was inhabited, protected against his solitude. But now it is he who enters, who possesses. When Paulo, who abandons himself to Hitler —a Hitler of the imagination who is Genet himself—realizes that his lover has decided not to enter him, "he suffers in the presence of his free and lonely personality whose solitude was revealed to him by the detachment of God himself." Genet's virilification is precisely the detachment of God. He becomes "his own heaven"; he loses the liegeman's courage and tranquillity of mind and comes to know, despite himself, the suzerain's anxiety and solitude. God is dead. And the moment in which one feels this death with the greatest despair is the same in which Divine cried: "Behold the God," the moment of orgasm. Furthermore, there is a kind of panic in Genet's love for young males: he does not know *what to do with them*. Coitus, whether heterosexual or homosexual, is never more than a factitious solution to the couple's problems; it condenses in the moment the long, patient duration of conjugal life. In coitus, the energy that is usually consumed in domestic concerns is consumed in war and revelry. Coitus substitutes the tragic for the

---

* In *Funeral Rites*, Hitler, who abandons himself to a French prisoner, suddenly moves away: "It is rather difficult to indicate precisely the sudden impulse of modesty that ripped the veils of the dream and of pleasure. He feared lest a Frenchman experience the selfish and evil pleasure of possessing him." This passage reveals to us a new twist of pride: Genet wants to dream that he is being raped, but if his young lover dropped his indifference, if Genet could think that the child is excited and enjoys possessing an adult, the desire and the emotion would vanish immediately. Genet is masochistic. He is willing to be really and truly humiliated by the Pimp because he denies God consciousness. But the fairy, who is on the side of the saint, *must not* really and truly humiliate him.

comic and the nontemporal for repetition: that is precisely why it reflects only what one puts into it. Although orgasm is an irreducible fact, it is never a *raw* fact: it gathers into itself and condenses in its particular *quality* the entire drama of the two lovers. Now, when Genet "played the woman," the sexual act had a precise function: it symbolized this girl queen's constant effort to install within herself the power and fatality of the criminal; to desire Stilitano was to desire to *be* the cruel, handsome pimp. But Genet can no longer desire to *be* Bulkaen: "I no longer wished to resemble hoodlums. I felt that I had achieved self-fulfillment." In other words: the girl queen wanted to be possessed in order to acquire, through the intermediary of her lover, the abstract qualities of courage and heroism which composed the Pimp's essence; the burglar acquired them by another means and without intermediary; he therefore can no longer desire them in the others: he *finds* and *recognizes* himself in Bulkaen, and this recognition is prior to any amorous relationship. In a sense, he is no longer poor enough to envy the riches of the young burglar; he can only contemplate them. They gleam from afar, refracted by another substance, but how is he to get them? He already has them; they are right in front of him, yet out of reach; he caresses them on his companion's young body, but without being able to take them away from him. Similarly, Erik wants to embrace his image in the mirror and is able only to run his fingertips over it. If Genet sleeps with his lover, he is quite aware that he does so in desperation and because there is nothing better to do; and he also knows that he has nothing to gain, except a pleasure of which his harsh spirituality is contemptuous. He seems never to have quite made up his mind about the change in his sexuality. Only a few years ago, he said to me: "The so-called active homosexual remains unsatisfied at the height of pleasure and longs for passivity." Torn between the demands of his virility and his feminine tastes, he manages as best he can; he combines certain practices which are reputed to be masculine with others that, according to the rules of his milieu, are only for girl queens. He enters his lovers, but does so only rarely, and he never speaks of these acts of intercourse with the pomp and lyricism that he reserves for celebrating those in which he played the passive role. On the other hand, he practices fellatio readily and, with casual partners, often practices only that. The reason is that it is regarded by inverts as the function of the female: one gives pleasure to the indolent male. But, at the same time, the one who sucks is not entirely passive: he *caresses,* he acts.* He can thus present his passivity as a masculine caprice although he experiences it as feminine submission.

Thus, in acquiring virility Genet has not drawn closer to the real; quite the contrary, his sexuality has been completely perverted. Far from leaving the imaginary, he has sunk into it more deeply: his fantasies grow complicated, come into conflict and get in each other's way; while performing his burglaries he no doubt felt that he was a male, that he had been liberated, but between "those light moments" his virility was only just another role to play.

Evidently the experience of burglary has proved to be a half-failure. It is not true that praxis has destroyed the imaginary by establishing a new contact with the world: no sooner does the act touch the world than it fades into a gesture and joins the fictions which it was supposed to destroy: Genet formerly played at being Stilitano, he now plays at being a burglar. It is not true that "masculinity" is an awakening: it is a new dream which, entering his imaginary world, causes telescopings, collisions and a breaking down of images. He is merely dreaming that he has awakened. How could it be otherwise? The original situation has not changed appreciably; the roots of his imaginary life remain: a few robberies are not sufficient to unprime an infernal machine that was so carefully devised and that has been ticking away for such a long time. At every moment Genet is in danger of drowning in his dreams; at the slightest provocation he lets himself sink down, and his long stays in prison, which are direct consequences of his burglaries, incline him, what with inaction and solitude, to pick up the thread of his dreams and deprive him of the benefits of his male activity.

Yet something has changed. Despite everything, the resort to praxis has not been entirely in vain. The collisions of images which it has caused, the struggle between the female principle and the male imperative which it has determined, Genet's new tastes, new habits, his more complex and more disappointing roles, have all forced him to become aware of his state. He still dreams, but in dreaming that he is awakening he takes a reflective view of his dreams; he no longer believes in them entirely, he no longer quite enters them. Not that he is seeking the *truth;* but each illusion finds itself thwarted by the opposite illusion: though he may want to resume his female dreams, the male *character* in him no longer

---

* A few proud creatures, far from considering fellatio a sign of subjection to the male, regard it as a means of being his equal. It seems to them that they possess him, and they would rather practice it than be entered.

believes in them. "I have now only to start day dreaming and my throat gets dry. Despair burns my eyes. Shame makes me lower my head. My day dream breaks up." But if he tries his hand at male dreams, his profound femininity disperses them: he makes an effort to see himself in a virile role, and then suddenly his attention flags, his excitement fades: "I suffer at never having possessed Bulkaen. And death prevents all hope. He refused on the stairs, but I invent him more docile. His eyes, his eyelids, tremble. His whole face surrenders, he consents. But what prohibition weighs upon him? While a stern act of will thrusts from my thoughts the images which are not his, I eagerly strain my mind toward a vision of the most beautiful details of his body. I am obliged to invent the amorous positions he would assume. This requires great courage on my part, for I know that he is dead and that I am violating a corpse. I need all my virility, which is for the most part an attitude of mind rather than physical courage and bearing. But the moment I am about to enter him in thought, when I feel the sperm rising in my penis, my penis grows soft, my body relaxes, my mind drifts." In any case, the image remains in the air and presents itself as what it is: a lure. With regard to Darling, who naïvely allows himself to be occupied by his familiar divinities, he writes: "He is thus like me, when I re-create these men, Weidmann, Pilorge, Soclay, in my desire to be them, but he is quite unlike me by virtue of his faithfulness to his characters, for I have long since resigned myself to being myself." He continues to play with his characters but is no longer quite able to take an interest in them; when he wants to slip into them, part of himself remains behind. Thus, the conflict wrests him from the immediate. He sees himself dreaming, he tosses about and becomes frightened, he knows that he is afraid, he would like to wake up but is not quite able to, like a sleeper who a dozen times is about to escape from a nightmare and a dozen times falls back into it. He is afraid of everything: of leaving the imaginary and of sinking into it entirely; of returning to the real with its train of misfortunes and of abandoning it forever. "I fell . . . last night. No outstretched, merciful arm tries to catch me. A few rocks might perhaps offer me a stony hand, but just far enough away for me to be unable to grab it. I was falling. And in order to delay the final shock—for the feeling of falling caused me that intoxication of absolute despair which is akin to happiness during the fall, but it was also an intoxication that was fearful of awakening, of the return to things that are—in order to delay the shock at the bottom of the gulf and the awakening in prison with my anguish at the thought of suicide or jail, I accumulated catastrophes, I provoked accidents along the verticality of the precipice, I summoned up frightful obstacles at the point of arrival." In like manner, the convicts at Fontevrault were afraid both "of falling to the bottom of the imaginary until they themselves became imaginary beings" and of "colliding with the real." Genet, unstable and unsatisfied, wants and does not want to continue his dreams, wants and does not want to awaken.

Thus, this half-failure is a half-victory: once again Genet finds himself confronted with a desperate situation and faced with a new choice: the unforeseen consequence of his original unshakable will to realism has been the derealization of reality; he can no longer renounce either the real or the imaginary, but each is an obstacle to the other, and Genet, who is incapable of really returning to action, has lost the means of continuing frankly with his dreams. These contradictions oblige him to move to the reflective level, to re-examine himself, to seek once again a way out. The solution lies, as always, in the statement of the problem: in order not to escape into delirium, into the poor, vague images of madness, he attempted to turn "the corrosive power of the imaginary" upon *things-which-are,* in short, the derealization of the real was an attempt at synthesis, he wanted to unify his realism and his power to dream. This synthesis has failed: why not attempt the inverse operation, why not *realize the imaginary?* To be sure, it is not a matter of "realizing one's dream" as one buys a house after a lifetime of saving; in that way Genet's dreams are unrealizable: he neither can nor wants to become a *real* male, and even less a "titty female." Besides, that would amount to betraying: the dream would be realized only by ceasing to be a dream; he would have to give up the sumptuous dreams of the beggar, the quietism of the exile, the massive destruction effected by the aesthete's gestures; Genet would have to choose among his possibilities, would have to reject some of them, would have to stick to a single project and, in order to carry it out, would have to involve himself completely in the world of utilitarian objects. And even if he wanted to, does anyone think that the Just would let him? Whether or not he wants to dream, let us not forget that his lot is and remains the impossibility of living. Did he not say in the passage quoted above that he was going to be confronted, upon awakening, with "suicide or jail"? No: to realize the imaginary means to include the imaginary in reality *while preserving its imaginary nature;* it means unifying, within the same project, his realistic intention and his derealizing intention. Can he find an act which, taking the derealization of the real as a starting point, would strive to realize this derealization as such, that is, to communicate to it the independent, permanent objectivity which characterizes the real? What if Genet, who is confined to the imaginary by a pitiless order, decided not to scandalize by acts of theft and aesthetic gestures? What if he established, by means of acts that create gestures, the imaginary as a permanent source of scandal? What if he so contrived matters that his impotent reveries derived from their impotence an infinite power and challenged, despite all the police in the world, society in its entirety? Would he not have found a meeting point for the imaginary and the real, for the inefficacious and the efficacious, for the false and the true, for the rule and the fact? It is true that images exist only through one's consciousness of them. But for that very reason an image will achieve its entire development and full independence if one obliges others, all others, to form it. When a fantasy depends only on my subjectivity, it remains relative to me, to my own sweet will, and if I turn my attention away from it, it vanishes, but if I succeed in imposing it on everyone, it then can and must be conceived by anyone. It still requires a constituting subjectivity, but the latter becomes anyone's: it can be yours as well as mine, we are interchangeable, I no longer have special power over my images, and people's minds appear as the *means* it chooses for realizing itself. Don Juan and Don Quixote never existed historically, yet I know very well that these characters do not depend on me; if I stop thinking about them, they continue their existence because others are thinking about them or could think about them, just as the table in front of me continues to exist if I look away from it. There are sacred images which appear to the one who forms them as collective representations: since an entire society has made itself guardian of them, the individual who once invokes them feels inessential with respect to them; they are almost more real than he himself: he will die before Don Quixote disappears. Genet must therefore get society to adopt the images which he invents and to endow them with objectivity. To will his dreams to the very end, until they escape and carry on their existence elsewhere, is to want to impose them on others: he will attempt to integrate them into the *objective mind* and to have them consecrated as *cultural facts*. If I persuade my neighbor to take one decision rather than another, I am said to have acted upon him: I shall therefore have acted in like manner if I predispose him to form an image-making consciousness rather than a perceptive consciousness. Up to this point, the others had the initiative; Genet flitted about as they watched him. He now attacks and reduces these absolute ends, these pure and severe gazes, to the rank of means. He will make use of the others to objectify his images. This exile who vainly attempted to derealize the world by his own powers now decides to dream through intermediaries. The ideal thing would be to transform all of society into a vast conspiracy against being: how glorious if Genet had only to begin a dream for all minds to be affected by it, for all mankind to lose its bearings, let go of the helm and drift into the impossible! He would then suddenly interrupt his dream and proudly contemplate those billions of slaves whose sole function and reason for being would be *to dream for him*.

However, there is no means of acting on others directly, except physical coercion, which Genet cannot practice. I act upon the person with whom I am speaking only by constructing a trap in which his freedom can be caught. A line of argument which I present to him is a snare. If he wants simply to understand it, be it only in order to refute it, he must warm it up and quicken it: his freedom holds the words together, links the statements to each other. Taken up and supported by a mind, this congealed snake grows warm, and only then does it distill its venom: it convinces. Or rather freedom has convinced itself. All that we can do is to devise *evidence for the prosecution:* if these exhibits are properly contrived, the other will tie himself up. The only way that Genet has of disposing the minds of others to form images is to catch them in the trap. I leave it to the reader to imagine whether Genet enjoys this job: it is a piece of trickery. Did he not say about Divine: "She, the Giddy One, leaves in her wake traps, cunning pitfalls, deep dungeons, and because of her the minds of Darling, Our Lady and their pals bristle with incredible gestures: with their heads high they take falls that doom them to the worst of destinies." But Divine, who is an aesthete, is herself a snare and a delusion; in order to draw the others into the imaginary, she derealizes herself and falls asleep. She does not act, she transforms herself into a gesture; this volatile gesture sparkles for a moment, then explodes; all that remains is an old fairy. Moreover, Genet is not concerned with contaminating a few pimps and queens: it is the Objective Mind that he wants to make "bristle with incredible gestures"; it is in Culture that he wants to make holes and contrive dizzying falls. Divine becomes Genet when she gives up *being* a human trap and decides to *manufacture* material traps. The material trap is again, of course, the Thief himself: himself carrying out his own derealization; but it is himself outside of himself, in front of himself, in the dimension of objectivity. Divine, the girl queen, called herself the Giddy One because unreality visited her in the form of brief fits of madness; she filled the world with extravagant *gestures*. Genet, the fake male, constructs giddy objects. These objects are, at first, *things;* they belong to the physical universe, they maintain relationships with the other objects, occupy space; they can be carried from one place to another; they thus offer themselves *first* to our perception, as does a tree or a stone. But as soon as we turn our gaze on them, they derealize themselves and draw us along with them into the unreal. Thus, the girl queens turned to look at Divine, who was one of them, a creature of flesh and blood, and suddenly saw a crowned queen. Genet decides to people the world with these effigies. He who looks them full in the face will be stricken with a brief spell of madness: he will become Divine, it is he who will experience the plunge into the imaginary and the sickening return to reality. Genet's *act* is the insertion of a gesture into being; he will use the inertia of matter to support his dreams, and the minds of others to restore them to life. By his *gesture-creating act* he re-enters the world and installs himself in it. For the ambiguity of the material traps results in the insertion of the imaginary as such into the web of the real. When Genet formed the subjective image for himself, it was only an epiphenomenon, an individual superstructure, an effect which could not be transformed into a cause; it manifested its author's absolute impotence, his belonging "to the obscene, which is outside the scene of the world." The paradox of a work of art is that its meaning remains unreal, that is, outside the world and that nevertheless it can be the cause and the end of real activities. A painting involves economic interests; it is bought and sold. In wartime it is "evacuated" as if it were a person. When the peace treaty is signed, it can be the subject of a special clause which the victor imposes upon the vanquished. And no doubt this is due to its *value,* to the traditions associated with it, etc., but individual interests, national pride, aesthetic appreciation, in fact everything, relate, in the last analysis, to a primary signification which is imaginary. In other words, the *reality* of a society involves the socialization of certain *unrealities*. "Accepted" works, which are imaginary insofar as they relate to events that never took place or to characters who never existed, at times even to laws that are not those of our world, are *real* in that they cause real actions, real sentiments, and define the historical development of a society. In fact, collectivities defend themselves as long as they can against images: specialists, who are called "critics," have the function of delaying their admission. Genet knows this, but he also knows that if he wins he will return with the honors of war to the community of the Just which exiled him. And I am not speaking here of the membership cards that the bourgeoisie will issue to him later: Genet dares not wish for this, and I am not even sure that in the heyday of his revolt and despair this wretched man would have accepted being appointed honorary bourgeois as a great foreign writer is given an honorary doctor's degree by a university. When he starts to write, it is something quite different that he desires: he wants to infect the Just with his images, and since he is nothing other than his dreams, this social ghost decides to come back in person to haunt the community of honest folk.

Burglary, age and weariness have slowly and slyly acted upon Genet: without awakening him, their patient action has disgusted him with dreaming; without virilifying him, it has forbidden him to play at femininity. In one respect, his aestheticism was formerly a product of his evil dreams and, in another, an extension of his sexual play-acting: the denuded Queen Divine, exhibiting her denture, prostitutes herself to all, draws everyone along with her into her ghastly dream. But now Genet finds himself forced to play at being a male: in extending to all domains, this sexual transformation is going to lead Genet from aestheticism to art. As an aesthete, he was a prey to derealizing gestures; as an artist, he invents acts which realize gestures. The new choice that is offered him will enable him to transcend *all* his contradictions. Activism and faith are going to unite in the project of creating: in the work of art the mystic will give himself being, he will draw his portrait on the canvas and will remain its captive for eternity. But since it is a matter of objectifying his dreams, the sleeper will take action. Genet, the sole hero of his books, has fallen entirely into the imaginary and he becomes imaginary *in person*. But, at the same moment, an austere, lucid, calculating consciousness comes into being, freed from all dreams, freed from even the dreamer who dwelt in it. This pure freedom of the artist no longer knows either Good or Evil, or rather it now makes of them only the object of its art: Genet has liberated himself.

As one can readily imagine, these reflections do not occur to him all at once. Nor in that order. One can also assume that he did not reach his decision overnight. Writing: what could be stranger, more ridiculous, and more intimidating too, for this vagabond? Can one conceive the insolence and madness of the project of imposing himself upon the Just who condemn him or are unaware of him? And besides, to write is to communicate: if he wishes to infect right-thinking people with his dreams, he will have to be concerned with what goes on in their heads. Thus far, they have been only sacred appearances, congealed in an attitude of reproval; they are going to become men: it is perhaps this transformation of his relations with others that will cost him the greatest effort. We have seen him go from the act to the gesture and from the gesture to the word; but in order to go from the word to the work of art he must travel a long road, a road full of pitfalls. It is along this road that we are going to follow him.

4. THIRD METAMORPHOSIS: THE WRITER

A MECHANISM HAVING THE EXACT RIGOR OF VERSE

I shall explain later why Genet's works are false novels written in false prose. But prose, whether false or not, springs from the intention to communicate. Now, at the age of twenty-eight Genet does not have a single thought, a single desire that he can share, or wishes to share, with others. Except for his monotonous string of magnifying judgments—which, moreover, are intended for an imaginary public—he uses language like a drug, in order to immerse himself in his secret delights; if he does *speak,* it is in order to deceive or betray; in short, he is a prisoner of a stolen, a sham speech. In order for him to reach the point of planning *to make himself understood,* a radical conversion of his attitude toward others is required; and even that is not enough: he must relearn to speak. The fact is that these two changes condition each other: the onanist resumes contact with others when the "poetized" poet who *experienced* his poems becomes a versifier who *makes* them. One can expect that his first writings will be monsters and that they will reflect all of his conflicts: we shall find in them quietistic mysticism and voluntarism, alienation and freedom, an autistic egocentrism and a first effort to communicate: but above all he is going to attempt to link up the "sound units" (which take shape in his mind spontaneously) by means of a web of meanings, a conjunctive tissue that makes it possible to move smoothly from one to the other. In short, by means of *prosaisms*. And it is by virtue of these prosaisms—hence, through the waste matter of his poetry—that he will discover prose.

He made his major decision when he wrote his first poem and read it in public: all the rest will flow from this little by little. But where does the decision itself come from? We know that there was no reason at the time for Genet to make it. What impelled him to take the leap? The answer is simple: if Genet performs this first creative *act* at a time when he is concerned only with *gestures,* it is because this act proposed itself to him as a gesture.

Let us first note the fact that he knew how to "make" verses. He says to us: "The first line of verse which to my amazement I found myself composing. . . ." But this statement, like everything that he chooses to tell us about himself, is both true and false. Yes, it was the first which he composed to his *amazement;* but he had twice before made others, *without being amazed*. When he was sixteen years old, he was taken in hand by a well-known song writer. An unimportant episode in this restless life which ended with a theft and with the thief's return to the reformatory. But meanwhile he had amused himself writing songs. It was only a kind of game: elsewhere he would have learned to do crossword puzzles or play bridge. However, he thereby had occasion to familiarize himself with prosody and the laws of rhyme. Four years later, he wrote his first poem, which he has not preserved. "I was twenty years old; a little girl whom I loved had died ten years before, and it was the anniversary of her death. I wrote the verses in order to be moved."

In order to be moved: all Genet is in these words. I suppose that he was sincerely grieved when the child died, but he subsequently made of her death a symbol: it represents the child that he was, "dead in me long before the ax chops off my head"; this will later be a minor theme of his work: it inspires the burial in *Our Lady of the Flowers* and in *Funeral Rites;* he has even thought of making it the subject of a film. And we can be sure that he celebrated this anniversary for a long time with funeral ceremonies. The poem is connected with one of them: that year, he no doubt felt that he was not sufficiently moved, or perhaps he felt within him a muted emotion which would manifest itself fully if only it were helped. The fact remains that he employed the methods which the songwriter had taught him. Poetry serves his spiritual exercises: he hopes to read his own verses as if they were someone else's. "If you want to read a book," says M. Lepic to Poil de Carotte, "start by writing it."* And such, at first, is Genet's aim: if he speaks, it is in order to hear himself *as Another;* when he writes, it is in order to read himself. Did he succeed in making contact with himself? I do not know. The fact is that ten years went by without his repeating the exercise. It is during this period that his language becomes poetized and that the sound units suddenly fill his mouth, solely with the aim of *moving* him. The great poetic disintegration of the Word and the use he makes of it remain hidden from all, like a shameful secret. If at times he does reveal something of it, Stilitano or Armand promptly discourages him: "Are you nuts or something?" The fact remains that he is able to make verses, that he knows he can and that this knowledge enters into his pride of being a clerk in the black feudal society.

It is his feeling of intellectual superiority that will dictate his decision. Prisoners are adolescents: they fill their endless days with bragging, challenges, competitions. One day, Genet thought he was being challenged, or rather he challenged himself: but he did so precisely because he judged himself *capable* of winning. He composed verses the way a bully beats up the one who has provoked him: to establish his superiority. But the bully wants to prove his superiority *to the others,* and Genet wanted to use the others in order to prove his to *himself.* Here is how he related to me the circumstances that led him to write:

"I was pushed into a cell where there were already several prisoners in 'city' clothes. You're allowed to wear your jacket while you're still awaiting trial. But though I had filed an appeal, I was made, by mistake, to wear the prisoner's outfit. That weird getup seemed to be a jinx. They despised me. I later had the greatest difficulty in overcoming their attitude. Among them was a prisoner who composed poems to his sister, idiotic, sniveling poems that they all admired. Finally, in irritation, I said that I could do just as well. They challenged me and I wrote *The Condemned Man.* I read it to them and they despised me even more. I finished reading it amidst insults and jeers. A prisoner said to me, 'I write poems like that every morning.' When I got out of jail, I made a particular point of finishing the poem, which was all the more precious to me for having been despised."

I, for my part, do not conceive an act as having causes, and I

---

* In Jules Renard's *Poil de Carotte.*—Translator's note.

consider myself satisfied when I have found in it not its "factors," but the general themes which it organizes: for our decisions gather into new syntheses and on new occasions the leitmotiv that governs our life. In this behavior—the last of Genet's gestures, the first of his poetic acts—the reader will easily perceive the themes which overlap and correspond.

The backdrop is exile. With his prisoner's outfit Genet creates a scandal: once again he is the Other, the black sheep, the Undesirable. Among these men in jackets who protest their innocence and still have hope of being acquitted, he is the Condemned Man whom they do not want to be. We know the old story: amidst the prisoners he is once again the child who has been abandoned to the disdain of the rightful sons, he is the seedy-looking wretch who walks through a park beneath the gaze of the bourgeois, the tramp who defiles with his presence a French Consulate, the thief who faints in a Yugoslav prison. In short, once again he embodies *the Guilty One,* the troublemaker. It may be objected that this is a matter of pure chance. Of course: the prison authorities made a mistake, that is all. But in what would have been, for someone else, a passing humiliation, Genet manages to recognize the signs of his original guilt. Indeed, a second theme is immediately sounded: that of Fatality. For Genet knows that he is innocent: he has filed an appeal. His conviction is not yet an actual sentence, he had a right to wear his own clothes, it was the anonymous order of an official body that—out of error or cruelty—forced him to don the "livery of crime." This order symbolizes for him the abandonment by the mother and the providential rigor which overwhelms him with its "miracles of horror." But it suffices to be accused in order to become guilty. Hence, once again destiny and the fault interpenetrate: Genet's destiny is to be at fault. The God who is testing him placed him, at the very beginning, in a state of guilt with respect to the little community which was to receive him. This introduces the third theme, which is only the inversion of the first: the guilt of the Other. Genet appalls his fellow prisoners because he presents them with the image of their destiny. The outfit awaits them in the future, reflects their greatest fear and terror: five years, ten years of imprisonment. They try hard not to think about it. Genet enters the cell like an ominous dream; he announces the fatality which they reject; in short, he is once again forced to embody *the negative.*

These prisoners immediately behave like honest folk: plucking from their minds the obsessive thought of their future conviction, they fling it far away. It falls to earth and becomes Evil, that is,

Genet. And, as always, all is reflection, play of mirrors, appearance: for the sentence which Genet reflects to them like a threat has not yet been inflicted upon them and, after all, perhaps never will be. Dreams and lies, superstitions: poetry.

"I later had the greatest difficulty in overcoming their attitude." These words set off a new leitmotiv, that of the quest for love. It is sufficient for this community to reject him for Genet to want to be adopted by it, at all costs. In the past, the child tried to love his judges. This theme is immediately inverted to become that of resentment: Genet withdraws and draws pride from his isolation; he both seeks and rejects reciprocity; whatever he does in the attempt to be reintegrated into the black society will be a deliberate courting of failure. Does he want the group to assimilate him or is he trying to prove that assimilation is impossible? He himself does not know. In any case, these attempts to draw closer to it are meant to be less efficacious than demonstrative: he makes, he can make, *only gestures*.

Suddenly, above this thematic ensemble, appears the event: a prisoner reads poetic rubbish to his admiring cellmates. This fathead will be the clerk of the little secular society. He is Abel. And Genet, who listens to him, is Cain. Cain is delighted and irritated at the same time: "That poem is idiotic. How can the prisoners be such jerks as to be taken in?" He *knows,* he already knows, that he can do better without even trying. But this weird test, which he ridicules, seems to him, nevertheless, to be a sacred ordeal. And it is all the more sacred because of its puerility. It mingles the grotesque and the "numinous," like the customs of the village into which K. the surveyor vainly attempts to be admitted. For it is true that the test is easy and that anyone can write bad verses. But it is also true that it is not meant for Genet and that he is forbidden to submit to it. The poetic act per se is scandalous because it misuses language; in order for a collectivity to tolerate it, it must present itself as a song of innocence and above all must emanate from a *white* personality. Genet knows this; he knows that this poetry pleases because of its vapidity and not in spite of it: every prisoner finds in it his own image. In a small, very puritanical town in the south of France there lived a man who, to everyone's knowledge, was a transvestite. The lyricism of his dress ought to have shocked people; I have seen people stoned for far less. Nevertheless, people were very nice to "Madame." "How is it," Cocteau asked Radiguet, "that they accept him?" "It's because he's common," replied Radiguet. There you have the heart of the matter: if you are *common,* you can dress up as a woman, show your behind or write poems: there's nothing offensive about a naked behind if it's everybody's; each person will be mirrored in it. Genet is uncommon: he enters the cell like a bird of ill omen; therefore, let him keep his mouth shut! A bird of ill omen writing poems—that would be intolerable. He knows this, he is not unaware that he has lost in advance. Besides, what do his rival's verses deal with? With the family, with a sister, with life out-side the walls, with virtue; these poems are religious services: they titillate the prisoners' spirituality. Since this society debases itself and reveals its bad taste, Genet can only rejoice: to be adopted by it becomes all the less desirable. The matter seems closed: it would be the worst possible blunder to enter into competition with the official bard: what would be the point of seeking the favor of these vulgar souls? The excluded man has only to remain silent, scornful of their contempt.

It is then that there occurs the slight click which, in certain circumstances, transforms the unlucky little thief into Jean Genet: what might be called the martyr's reflex. In the Yugoslav prison, his cellmates wanted him to practice robbing a sleeping prisoner, like everyone else: he managed to faint so as not to do what was ex-pected of him. Here, however, he is asked only to remain silent, and the same dizziness comes over him: in order to make himself *thor-oughly* undesirable, he will speak. And besides, this bad taste fascinates him; he must be a victim of it, must suffer from it to the point of passion: he likes bad taste; he likes it because it is Evil. He wishes to ensure its triumph: it is not enough that the prisoners, who represent the universal public, applaud bad poetry, they must also jeer at good poetry. If Genet sacrifices himself, it is in order to bring about once again the crushing of Good by Evil: in that way the Saint was superior to her master, the Criminal; and the Crimi-nal is superior to the female squealer who betrays him: the pattern is always the same. And, of course, the whirligig whisks us from sacrifice to the proudest self-affirmation: he who loses wins; the others' contempt will weave a wreath for him; their laughter will consecrate him as a poet. Self-punishment, resentment, pride and masochism, the whole machine is set in motion, the wheels start racing and Genet launches his challenge: "I can do just as well." He offers to undergo the test because he is sure of failing.

In order to have the odds with him, he accumulates provocation: these mediocre spirits did not have the courage to renounce Good; they wanted to be moved to pity at their own lot and to be made to feel that they were better than their lives. Well and good, he

will therefore hail Evil: crime, homosexuality. Does his outfit displease the inmates because it evokes their future conviction? Never
mind that, his subject will be the hopelessness and loves of a man
condemned to death. Can't you see him sitting in a corner, a little
off to the side, composing a poem each word of which will, as he
knows, arouse laughter, adopting as rule the displeasure of his
future listeners? In order to contrive an intolerable torture for
himself, he has decided to read his verses aloud. There are cases of
writers who resigned themselves to displeasing, but how many of
them drew their inspiration from boos and jeers? Yet such is the
case of Genet. Does this mean that he is going to write *bad* verse?
Quite the contrary: since it is bad verse that gives pleasure, he will
try to write the most beautiful poem he can, and, since singularity
shocks, the most original. But this beauty will be for him alone: the
only testimony he wants is the gibes of the others. We find him here
as he has always been: ceremoniously preparing the theatrical performance of a sacrifice. Indeed, let us note the fact that his audience's judgment is beyond appeal. Nowhere does there exist a
higher court. To whom can he be expected to turn? To the guards?
To the bourgeois? He can be heard only by these poor wretches
surrounding him. The judgment they are going to deliver will
signify to him both that his poems are execrable in men's eyes and
that, in his own kingdom, which is the realm of the unclean, they
are the best that have ever been written. So he reads: a reading is
a repetition of the creative act; he wants to be caught in the process
of creating as he was caught stealing in the faraway days of his
childhood; each word emerges from his mouth as it emerged from
his heart:

> This rose which is cut and which noiselessly rises
> To the white page where your laughter receives it.

He reads impassively amidst the laughter: he is Divine crowning
herself with a denture. These jeers and insults are "the reverse of a
perpetual Adoration." Once again his asceticism seeks to attain the
Positive beyond the Negative, Being beyond Nothingness. He reads:
these sarcasms, this hooting, all this din, have been provoked by the
imaginary alone; these cries of hatred are addressed to dreams;
Divine, she of the venomous gestures, once again draws the whole
world into her dream.

Shall we call this painful reading a "communication"? On the
contrary, this first work seems to be the desperate negation of any
audience. The listeners are there in order to despise and in order
that this contempt may make them despicable. It is through con-

tempt for contempt that Genet will feel the value of his verses. He began by rejecting reciprocity; he *does not* submit, despite appearances, to the others' judgment: he disarms it in advance and solicits it only in order to impugn it. Similarly, St. Theresa wished to be slandered in order to raise herself above men and to remain alone in the presence of God. Genet's God is himself, himself as Other. His supers stand aside when they have played their role: they were only the instruments of the Consecration; Genet asked their insults to consecrate once again his singularity. The despised poem, sparkling with the others' disdain, reveals to him—*to him alone*—its beauty. The audience of this incomparable work of the most irreplaceable of beings is reduced to its author. No, Genet does not write for the others. If later on, when he gets out of prison, he takes up his poem again, if he works on it passionately, it is precisely because they found it bad: not in order to correct it, but because it has become dear to him, that is, because he alone loves it. Thus, the poetic act is still only a gesture. It is not the poem which is the end, but the poet's martyrdom.

However, he wants to displease, and in order to displease he must move his audience. Since his aim was to force the Others to recognize his singularity, he is going to pour into his verses the sound units, the hermetic phrases, which an anonymous voice utters through his mouth and which he repeats to himself in solitude: for that is the most singular thing about him. But his intention to *compose a poem* with them will oblige him to link them together. If he wants to rouse the others to indignation by the *subject* which he has chosen, he must abandon passivity, must impose governing themes and unity upon his spontaneous creations. In order for the praise of Evil to shock, it must also be understood. Thus, the profound will to reject communication obliges him to communicate, at least in appearance. He will have to embroider, to festoon, to invent limpid verses whose prosaic function will be to explain and unite these erratic units. Most of our transformations are effected by two-sided acts, which, though they may seem to us to be stereotyped repetitions, are nonetheless original inventions *as well*. The fact is that an act can no more be reduced to what it is than can a man: it transcends itself. Viewed subjectively, it escapes by virtue of its objectivity, and sooner or later its objective signification returns in the most unexpected way to strike it directly even in its subjective depths: sooner or later, "objective" betrayal becomes subjective and taints our innocence. Viewed objectively, the act escapes by virtue of its subjective reality. Genet thought that he was only making a gesture; he wanted only to display the blurred, vomited units of words, as Divine wanted to display her dreadful, aging nudity. This public reading was, in a sense, only an act of *exhibitionism:* in like manner Rousseau displayed the "ridiculous object" to the washerwoman. But precisely in order for the gesture to achieve its purpose, it must be supported and realized by acts: the denture must be taken from the mouth, the trousers must be lowered. An "exhibition" is only a *gesture;* no doubt it is prepared for by *acts,* but these rarely attract our attention: nobody thinks of the fingers that part the cloak, that quickly unbutton the fly: nobody, neither the exhibitionist nor his victim. But in the particular case of poetic exhibition, acts assume a fundamental importance: for they cannot be likened to the simple repetition of an ordinary mechanism; they classify, unify, arrange, explain, in short, they are present for their own sake and end by affecting the substance of the gesture itself, by corroding the gesture and substituting for it.

Let us examine the first two stanzas of *The Condemned Man:*

> *Le vent qui roule un cœur sur le pavé des cours*
> *Un ange qui sanglote accroché dans un arbre*
> *La colonne d'azur qu'entortille le marbre*
> *Font ouvrir dans ma nuit des portes de secours.**

[The wind that rolls a heart on the pavestones of courtyards
An angel that sobs caught in a tree
The column of azure round which twines the marble
Unlock in my darkness emergency exits.]

A mad, dead voice whispers the first line; its beauty isolates it. Most certainly Genet heard it in his throat months before, perhaps years; he draws it from his memory to set it in his poem. The verb is lacking, as in "harvester. . . ." But though the verse asserts nothing, it stands up by virtue of its own strength and the amazing cohesion of its monosyllables† which is cemented by the rhythm.‡ It ends by itself: the last word draws the voice and stops it, the voice rests there; the "meaning" draws into it the mind which stops there and finds no reason to leave it: the poem is ended. If you attach a verb or complement to this sound unit, it will be from the outside. Had Genet written: *"Et le vent roule un cœur . . ."* etc. ["And the

---

* Here and elsewhere in the present chapter it may help the reader to have the French verses before him. In each case, the original lines will be followed by a literal translation—Translator's note.

† Ten monosyllabic words out of eleven, since the mute *e* of *"roule"* is elided.

‡ ∪—∪——∪∪∪——.

wind rolls a heart . . ." etc.], he would have been composing prose: as subject of the clause, the wind would become a substance indifferent to the accident it supports and defined by its abstract nature, an atmospheric phenomenon; the sentence would relate a precise, dated event, a *fact* which, though curious, is nevertheless possible. Imagine the following headline in *Samedi-Soir:* "Storm in Brest: the wind rolls a calf's heart over the pavestones of the slaughterhouse yard": all poetry disappears. It is the use of the relative pronoun that gives the verse its mystery: an anonymous voice particularizes a blast of air by conferring upon it an absurdly human function; only a man can make a heart roll, by pushing it with his toes or with the tip of a cane. This wind is mad, it takes itself for a man.

The third line too, I think, came all at once, one day when Genet, for the thousandth time, looked at the sky through the narrow rectangular opening of his cell. It has the resistance of elementary organisms and I recognize in it, poetically undifferentiated, several of his favorite themes: the transfiguration of a prison into a palace, the twining of the girl queens around the Pimps, that is, ultimately, of fullness around "looming emptiness, sensitive and proud, like a tall foxglove," in short, of being around nothingness. The first and third lines are the archaic foundation of the quatrain and perhaps of the whole poem: they had existed for a long time, pure *things,* hard and encysted, before Genet dreamed of uniting them.

The second is already of another kind. Called forth by the rhyme and by that alone, although it resembles the first outwardly (The wind that . . . An angel that . . .) , it is only a synthetic pearl; it has been chemically restored so that the reader can merge it with the other two, but it is sham: *accroché* [caught, hooked] belongs to Genet's vocabulary;* but neither angels nor archangels are part of his props. He plays around a bit, in the poems and a few times in *Our Lady of the Flowers,* with these winged creatures which he has borrowed from Baudelaire and Cocteau.† In this inhabitant of

---

* And I for one prefer the following more precious but more authentic version: *"Les arbres du silence accrochent des soupirs."* ["The trees of silence catch hold of sighs."]

† In *Our Lady of the Flowers* he affects, for a moment, a false, wonderstruck nonchalance. He writes, with his pinky in the air, piously amused, very much the campy virgin: "Will my books ever be anything other than a pretext for showing a soldier dressed in azure, a fraternal angel and Negro playing dice or knucklebones in a dark or light prison?" But in the same book he admits that he loathes angels: "Do they have teeth, genitals, etc.?" As a matter of fact, the angel is the miracle. But there is no miracle for Genet, or rather the miracle is that there is none. No room for cherubim in his mythology; his homosexuality itself, which calls for monsters and demons, is not favorable to them. Heurtebise belongs strictly to Cocteau.

heaven who has been parachuted to earth and who is encumbered by his equipment, whose giant wings prevent him from flying, in this fallen creature who is endowed with mysterious powers but whose white magic is clearly insufficient for fighting against the wickedness of men we recognize a Cocteau character who has entered the wrong poem and will presently withdraw, apologizing for his error.

What is new is that Genet has deliberately imitated the voice that produced the sound units within him. He wanted to attempt a synthetic reconstitution of one of those spontaneous products of his passivity. In short, he is becoming a falsifier. Formerly, he merely witnessed the birth of verses; he now *makes* them, after the same pattern. "An angel that sobs . . ." etc., is a bad line, facile, mawkish, insincere. But through it the poet discovers his creative activity and learns that poetry is perhaps not a destiny.

This will appear even more clearly if we examine the fourth line, which is frankly explanatory. Each of the first three maintains only relationships of juxtaposition, of pure contiguity, with the other two; the function of the fourth is to inform us why these rocky units are united. The sole reason is that the objects of which they speak resemble each other through the action which each of them exercises on the poet. In short, this fourth verse is the explanation which is invented *afterward*. No doubt the theme of the "emergency exits," unlike that of the "angels," is authentic: it is a matter of the outlets which, according to Genet, are to be found even in the most hopeless situations. In the same way, the word *"nuit"* [night, darkness] can be regarded as a key word of his vocabulary; we know what he puts into it: the darkness of the cell, of death, of Evil, the sparkling darkness of crime, etc. Nevertheless, the line is fabricated: only an *act* of the mind, analogous to numeration, can bring to this set of irreducibles a kind of formal unity which holds them together from without. In like manner, the poet of *The Arabian Nights* invented Scheherazade as a link for the tales which he had collected. The verb "unlock" is emptied of its meaning because it has three radically distinct subjects: a natural force, a person, a passive bulk. Yes, the wind sometimes does open a door and we have all been startled by the dull-witted mischievousness of two folding doors springing away from emptiness. But if the angel wants to enter, he turns the latch. As for the column, unless it collapses, knocking down the walls and tearing the door from its hinges, what is it doing there? "Unlock" conceals three different relationships, three operations which interfere with and cancel each other. "The wind opens the window," "The archangel opens the door": these statements are poetic because they *make us see* while they annihilate; the angel's big hands are a key, they exist and do not exist; the waggish will of the wings exists and does not exist; an action passes like an electric current from the subject to the complement. But in Genet's quatrain the current does not pass: the verb seems to be set down beside the subject; isolated, relegated to the end of the quatrain, it is a superadded determination which remains suspended in the air and expresses no real action. It can be suitable to these very different subjects, which, be it added, are locked up in themselves, only if it expresses an abstract relationship. The wind, the column and the angel "are for the door an occasion for opening"—that is what we read despite ourselves.* The influence which the subjects exercise upon the verb from a distance very soon corrodes its soul; the physical and kinesthetic images contained in the word "unlock" go up in smoke. But thereupon the abstract spreads like a drop of oil: the darkness is not a real darkness nor is the door a real door. Darkness "means" unhappiness, captivity; door "means" escape into the imagination, a way out. "No," Breton once roared, "Saint-Pol Roux did not *mean* . . . If he had meant it, he would have said it!" That is true: poetry cannot be translated into prose. And, as a matter of fact, the first and third lines, if viewed alone, are untranslatable: they *signify* nothing, they have a sense. But if one joins them by means of the fourth, then they too signify. We *understand* that the howling of the wind, the songs of the prisoners, the sky seen through a skylight, are consolations for Genet, occasions for his reverie. The reason is that the fourth line is disguised prose and that it draws the entire quatrain along with it into prosaism. It is through his attempt to *make* poems by linking discontinuous poetic intuitions that Genet, having become a versifier, learns the use of prose.

The second quatrain is even worse: it is entirely *fabricated* in the image of the first:

> *Un pauvre oiseau qui meurt et le goût de la cendre*
> *Le souvenir d'un œil endormi sur le mur*
> *Et ce poing douloureux qui menace l'azur*
> *Font au creux de ma main ton visage descendre.*

---

* Note, on the other hand, how Cocteau emphasizes the *hands* of the wind which are required by the verb "to open":

The hands of the sky opened, slammed the doors,
Hands shook the curtains to frighten us.

(*Opéra: Prière mutilée.*)

[A poor bird that is dying and the taste of ash
The memory of an eye asleep on the wall
And this aching fist that threatens the azure
Make your face descend to the palm of my hand.]

The author is here introducing into the poem the child with
whom the condemned man is in love. He therefore explains that
certain facts dispose the soul of Pilorge to dream about him, and
these facts are presented in the same way as the preceding ones; the
first three lines contain four *subjects,* two of them in the form
adopted earlier: *the wind that, the angel that,* become: *a poor bird
that, this aching fist that.* Besides, are they not the *same facts:* is not
the poor bird an angel that is dying? And is not the fist that
threatens the sky made of marble? Genet transcribes, translates.
The verb appears in the last line; it is similar to the one of the first
quatrain: "make your face descend" corresponds, term for term, to
"unlock exits." There is only one difference: in the first quatrain
the verb was invented afterward, in order to unite the first three
lines; in the second, the first three lines were fabricated in order to
give the verb a subject. But Genet, who is already a falsifier, counts
on the genuineness of the first quatrain to make us believe in that
of the second.

Nobody is taken in: these lines are flat, they reek of fraud. That
poor bird flew straight out of the poems of François Coppée: "Do
birds hide when they die?" No, they do not hide; but when Coppée's
birds feel sick, they go off to die in Genet. As for the fist that
threatens, you may say it is "aching" and may call the sky "azure,"
but it will never be anything but a fist raised against the sky. "He
shakes his fist at the sky," there you have a stock image, a hackneyed
expression, but it is good prose: not a single unnecessary word. "An
aching fist threatens the azure": that too is prose since it means
exactly the same thing, but it is bad prose.

In the second version of *The Condemned Man* and in the poems
that Genet wrote immediately afterward (spurred on by his success,
that is, by his having provoked laughter) , the prosaism is accentuated and at the same time the efforts to mask it are intensified. At
the beginning, Genet had allowed his own voice to recite verse only
in order to link up the words uttered by the anonymous voice. But
now it is his own voice that recites the entire poem, it is his voice
that he wants to hear and to feel in his throat. In *The Condemned
Man,* I was Another: it was Pilorge who was speaking; Genet, reading amidst jeers, was guided, possessed, by the dead Pilorge, as he
had formerly been by Stilitano; the voice which they are mocking
is his and is not his, the reading is a wedding of the kind he dreams

about: the faltering bride leaves the church holding the arm of her
husband, the guillotined man; the hatred of the witnesses unites
them: these poor wretches do not know what they are doing; they
are committing the sacrilege of jeering at the message of a dead
hero: one thinks of Cocteau's Orpheus writing from dictation the
verses of the deceased Ségeste. But in the following poems the "I"
is that of Genet himself. He amuses himself in detecting his own
thoughts in the sound units which he fishes up and brings to light.
All his favorite themes are present in these *disjecta membra* of a
poem which will never be written, but they are too compressed, too
concentrated: they have to be developed, decompressed, classified.
Little by little, syllogisms and hypothetical, disjunctive judgments
invade his poems. Note how logical significations now prevail over
poetic meaning; note how they form the metallic framework of the
following stanzas:

Too often from my pen did chance draw forth
The greatest of chances in the heart of my poems
The rose with the word Death which the black warriors I loved
Wear on their arm badge embroidered in white.

What garden can flower in the depths of my darkness
And what painful games are played there that they pluck the
    petals
Of this rose which is cut and noiselessly rises
To the white page where your laughter receives it?

But though I know nothing precise about death
So often have I spoken of it in a tone of gravity
That it must live within me to spring forth effortlessly
To flow from my slaver at my slightest word.

I have said that *true* poetry is untranslatable. But note how close
these lines are to prose; they must be translated since they ask to be
understood:

"When I wrote poems, the words 'rose' and 'death' flowed together from my pen *too often* for me to persist in attributing these
encounters to chance: there *must* have been certain forces in my
unconscious (complexes, childhood memories, desires, etc.) which
produced this association so regularly. There must have been,
otherwise the fact *would not be intelligible. You will object* that I
know nothing precise about death, but *since* I have spoken about it
so often in a tone of gravity, *it is* because death must live within
me. The proof is that it springs forth at my slightest word," etc.

I am quite aware that Genet's verses are more eloquent than this pedantic demonstration. But all the same it is the didactic labor of the prose writer that is hidden beneath the ellipses, condensations and allusions.

But Genet, who is a prose writer in spite of himself, clings to poetic language. He is right: prose is communication, a joint quest of truth; it is recognition and reciprocity. What would he do with it? In order to mask the prosaisms of his writings, he borrows the devices of contemporary poets. Note how he attempts, in the preceding stanzas, to veil the rigor of his argumentation, how he substitutes noble or poetic words for precise terms: "in my poems" is replaced, in the second line, by "in the heart of my poems," because "heart" belongs to the sacred language. The unconscious is called the darkness; the S.S. are "black warriors"; what psychoanalysis calls "complexes" is given the name of "flowering garden." He piously conceals the positive, scientific ugliness of "automatisms arising from complexes" by presenting them as "games." He makes the word "rose" the rose itself; he shows it as "noiselessly rising to the white page." Noiselessly: that goes without saying. But he makes an effort to introduce from without a touch of discretion and elegance. In vain: a choice must be made between signification and sense. These words are no longer *things:* they signify, they express; the use of images saves nothing: no sooner are they expressed than they change into metaphors; the terms "darkness," "garden," "rose," which will soon, in his prose, regain their virulence, droop and fade; they are as dead as the "fires," "chains" and "blood" of Racine.

Before long he calls to his aid the whole arsenal of modern poetry. This writer who is so singular, so utterly unique that one can barely mention, in connection with *Our Lady of the Flowers,* an almost imperceptible influence of Jouhandeau,* this thief who has reinvented literature draws inspiration from one and all when he writes in regular verse:

> When you sleep horses break in the night
> Over your flat chest and their galloping
> Thrusts aside the darkness into which sleep leads
> Its powerful machine torn from my head
> > Without the slightest noise.
>
> Sleep makes so many branches flower from your feet
> That I am afraid of dying choked by their cries

---

* And of *encounters* with Jean Cocteau.

> For want of your fragile hip I discern
> Before it fades a pure face written
>   In blue on your white skin.

> But should a guard awaken, O my tender thief
> When you wash your hands, those birds which flit
> About your grove laden with my pains
> You gently break the stems of stars
>   On his flowering face.

These lines recall Cocteau's *Plain-Chant:*

> I do not like to sleep when your face inhabits
>   The darkness against my neck
> For I think of death which comes too quickly
>   To put us too fast asleep....

> Bed of love, halt . . . let us leave there at the edge
> Our docile feet, horses sleeping side by side. . . .

> The horse of sleep which with rapid hoof
> Sets you down at the brink which I fear. . . .

> You awake, then the dream is forgotten
> Again I find myself bound to your tree [etc.]

The superiority of Cocteau's lines is that they *make us see.*
Genet's art does not aim, will never aim, at making us see: as we
have observed, the avowed aim of his magnifying attempts is to
annihilate the real, to disintegrate vision. And later, in his false
prose, having become conscious of his end and of the means which
enable him to attain it, he will produce an inimitable tone, the
most beautiful and most mournful poetry, an extraordinary Dance
of Death. But for the time being he does not know whether he
ought to hide or show. The result is an accumulation of images
which destroy one another and, far from reducing the world to
appearance, are effaced by *logical* signification. Here are branches
which sleep causes to flower and whose cries choke: they die because
cries destroys *branches* and because *choke* cancels *cries.*

At other times, one thinks of Valéry:

>   . . . roses
> Lovely effect of Death . . .

> But this pure movement . . .

> I am amazed and go astray in following your course
> Amazing river of water of the veins of speech. . . .

Scaling . . . the eternal night
Which fixed the galley to the pure sky of boredom . . .

Your soul will have cut across by secret ways

> To escape from the Gods
> Withering in accordance with my wishes
> I make fast the silence
> When the firebirds
> Of my tree spring forward.

Or of Mallarmé:

> This aching fist that threatens the azure.
> A pink avalanche died between our sheets . . .
> A dizzying word
> From the depths of the world abolishes the lovely order.

At other times of Verlaine:

> Forgive me my God because I have sinned
> The tears of my voice, my fever, my sufferings
> The hurt of flying away from the fair land of France
> Stumbling with hope.

And also of Hugo, of Baudelaire,* of everyone.

The fact is that Genet is beginning to see the devices and techniques that will enable him to achieve his goal; he already realizes that in order to reproduce the whirligigs of his thinking he must argue, must construct shams and chains of reasoning which are traps, he must be ruthlessly logical, must overwhelm with false demonstrations. He is the opposite of an intuitive writer: his art will be a scheming, a set piece, a machine; he is served less by terrorism than by rhetoric; he is not meant for producing brief formulas "translated from silence" but for grappling with language and all the resources of syntax; he is a *discursive* writer. But at the same time he cannot give up overhearing himself, enchanting himself with the "sound units" that are born within him spontaneously, he cannot bring himself to abandon *sense*, which is vague and enchanting, for *signification*. Besides, he has not found his audience nor decided upon his attitude toward his readers. No doubt the *other* has intervened, but as a mediation between Genet and himself and only to efface itself immediately. Can Genet rea-

---

* The second hemistich of the first line of *The Condemned Man* is borrowed from Baudelaire: "*Sur le pavé des cours . . . .*"

sonably hope to convince himself or burden himself with sophisms that he knows by heart? Even while writing them he veils them over. He hopes that they will regain a certain power in his eyes if they present themselves masked. In short, he plays hide-and-seek with himself.

Let there be no misunderstanding: I am not reproaching Genet for this abstract language, for the systematic destruction of the anecdote and of the real that we admire in Mallarmé. I mean simply that what serves Mallarmé's purpose (to reveal Nothingness as the immediate meaning of poetry) is not suitable to Genet's, which is to commit a *murder,* that is, to show us the real, its derealization and finally the unreal as the gulf in which the real is swallowed up. Many of his lines, when read individually, are beautiful, but they are caught in a kind of poetic jelly, in the quivering inconsistency of superimposed imaginary layers. This fault affects even the words: Mallarmé used half-extinguished words that illuminated each other with their reciprocal gleams; Genet chooses dazzling words whose lights extinguish each other reciprocally; everything is swallowed up in semidarkness. Caught in the mold of versification, the strictly poetic words clash with other words that were formerly figurative and are now only empty abstractions; the latter impart to the former an abstract generality. To write in verse that the beloved's hands are "birds that flit" is to play a game which is lost in advance, for as soon as the reader opens the book, he expects hands to be birds, butterflies, spiders, claws, and for that very reason he regards these different words as simple synonyms for the word "hands." In vain does Genet torture his imagination; the reader will see hands and only hands, like the character in the play who was always recognizing the amateur detective beneath his disguises. Finally, we are dealing with a conventional language that corresponds, term for term, with ordinary language. Poetry becomes sacred prose. At times, dimly conscious of this danger, Genet tries to localize the poetic explosions; he prepares long in advance and highlights by versified reasoning, by choice bits of eloquence, the alien words that are intended suddenly to explode and to challenge language; in vain: he gives us the feeling that a bourgeois prose is disguising itself in order to play at being a gentleman,* and we are so annoyed

---

* One could quote by the dozen the flat lines that recall Coppée, Sully Prudhomme and even M. Prudhomme:

It seems that next door lives an epileptic . . .

I am not going to be guillotined this morning
I can sleep in peace. . . .

by this discovery that the poetic firecrackers fizzle out. At times Genet lavishly strews jewels and angels; their excessive number devaluates the pure moments of poetry; at times he argues and reasons with precise words, but the rhythm and rhyme spoil this budding prose and mask the beauty it contains. He has two opposing conceptions of poetry which correspond to the two terms of the perpetual conflict by which he is torn: one, which is fatalistic, expresses his quietism, his belief in destiny and his quest of the Other that he is for the Others; the other, which is voluntaristic, symbolizes his will to assume his condition. In him as in Baudelaire we find the conflict between Destiny and Freedom; both these poets pursue the impossible dream of poetry's being both the result of the most lucid labor and the raw product of inspiration.*

Are his first two poems therefore so bad? No. Quite the contrary. They fascinate us by a kind of rough, primitive richness. The fact is that they contain, in their perpetual lack of balance, all of Genet's future prose and all of his past poetry. Yet it suffices that he write a dedication at the end of *The Condemned Man* for the poetry suddenly to explode and volatilize the prose, as in the following lines, for which I would give the entire poem which was its pretext:

"Every morning when, thanks to the guard's complicity, I went from my cell to his to bring him a few cigarettes, he would smilingly hum and greet me: '*Salut, Jeannot-du-Matin* [Greetings, Morning Johnny].'"

One may wonder why the courts condemn
A murderer so handsome that he makes the sun pale....

Each revel of the blood delegates a handsome lad
To support the child in his first ordeal....

It may be that one escapes by going through the roof...

The solemn morning, the rum, the cigarette...

Prison is a dull school for dying....

You bow very low and say to her: "Madame!..."

Pluck from who-knows-where the maddest gestures
Steal from children, invent tortures
Mutilate beauty, work at faces
And arrange with the boys to meet in Guiana...
Etc., etc.

[M. Prudhomme is a "character invented by Henri Monnier (1852) given to the utterance of sententious platitudes; he is the personification of the pompous and empty-headed bourgeois" (*Harrap's Dictionary*).—Translator's note.]

* This is the whole problem of modern poetry. Mallarmé and Rimbaud, Valéry and Breton, give solutions which oppose each other like the thesis and the antithesis.

Between *Funeral Dirge* and *The Galley,* a major event took place: Genet began to write *Our Lady of the Flowers.* He is going to discover little by little that he must prefer the reader to himself, if only so as the better to destroy him, and that earnest hatred has the same concerns as love. From the very beginning of *Our Lady,* the words have a new ring: "I shall speak to you about Divine, mixing masculine and feminine as my mood dictates, and if, in the course of the tale, I shall have to refer to a woman, I shall manage, I shall find an expedient, a good device, *so that there may be no confusion.*" Everything has changed: he now addresses the reader and makes a courteous effort to help him avoid certain errors. But though he provides him with the necessary information, he does not hide from us the fact that he does so in order to trick him. To explain so as the better to mislead: that's Genet all over. In short, he is in the process of discovering his art and his public; all the quibbling and trickery that encumbered his first poems are going to be transferred to his prose. Poetry is thus liberated: to explain, to signify, to fool, are the functions of prose. Genet returns to poetry even before finishing *Our Lady:* he re-enters himself, he writes *The Galley* "for relaxation." We can take this to mean that he wishes, for a moment, to go back to the state of dreaming and the happy passivity in which he could indulge when writing his early poems, before the taste for martyrdom transformed him into a Creator. In short, he wants to abandon the activism of prose in order to be able to listen to himself in his verse as if he were another. Thus far he has refused to choose between poetry-fatality and deliberate poetry. But the choice has now been made: he will put fatality into his poems and his deliberate art into prose.

It is too late. The voice that said "Harvester of cut breath" has been silent for a long time. Genet will later recover that anxious, ventriloquous voice, at the highest pitch of willful tension; but for the time being he can no longer doubt that he is the author of his verse; it is he and he alone who says "I"; there is no turning back.

Nevertheless, he will try. He will spread confusion in an effort to fool himself, will break up the natural architecture, will violate syntax, will try to mislead by jumbling the words. What a far cry from the polite statement in *Our Lady of the Flowers:* "I shall find an expedient, a good device, so that there may be no confusion." Confusion is what he is looking for. Read the following lines:

> In the shadow on the wall of what navigator
> His fingernails worn away by the salt but on a level with
>   my eyes

Among the bleeding hearts jumbled by thoughts
Profiles, alases, the arms we have laid down
Undecipherable to those who do not fight in the darkness
Where wolves are the words will have a shining nail
Let by my wild eyes the devouring roar
Tear to the very bone the name Andovorante.

What was the reason for this careful disjointing? Only the wish to rob the author himself of the meaning of his own lines. No relationship with the obscurity of Mallarmé, which is not desired for its own sake but is a necessary consequence of the poet's subtlety. Here one has only to re-establish the order of the words to find a perfectly clear and prosaic *meaning:* "The fingernail of what navigator (a fingernail that shines, a fingernail worn away by the salt) has, in the shadow—on the wall, on a level with my eyes, among the bleeding hearts that are jumbled by thoughts, profiles, alases, which are the arms that we have laid down—has let the devouring roar of my wild eyes tear to the very bone the name Andovorante, (a name) which cannot be deciphered by those who do not fight in the darkness where words are wolves."

Genet muses in his cell; he looks at the graffiti on the walls which are, in a way, the prisoners' coats-of-arms; at times it is a maxim (he quotes some of them in *Miracle of the Rose*) , at times a simple "alas," at times a profile drawing (of a naked woman) ; often the inscriptions overlap, some of them cover up hearts that have been pierced with arrows. Genet's eyes, which are accustomed to the semidarkness, discover the name Andovorante, which is difficult to decipher if one has not grown accustomed to the darkness, difficult to understand if one is not a poet; day after day he looks at this name which a fingernail has traced on a level with his eyes; he "devours it with his eyes," he muses on it so often, so long, that he finally wears it down to the bone. He likes to fancy that the signer was a navigator whose hands had been eaten by the salt.

I have "translated" in order to show that what Genet wrote was a prose sentence which he wanted to make incomprehensible. Is not this an avowal of failure? The "sound units" are a thing of the past; whatever he tries to write is *meaningful.*

Yet the poem is obscure. But the reason is that in order to deceive himself Genet resorted to an utterly childish and demoniacal ruse: "At about that time I wrote two poems which have no relationship to each other. I mixed them up, thinking that I was thereby making my verses more obscure, giving them greater density." Unable to recapture his impressions of an earlier time, he hopes that chance will restore them. Juxtaposing verses from different sources, he uses the appearance of unity which results from the rhymes and rhythm to suggest a nonexistent unity of meaning. He fights against the logical and deliberate thought which emanates from him despite himself and which makes his poems transparent. Thus, the Saint wants to imagine that she perceives Being beyond nothingness. But one cannot fool oneself very long: although he heaps up traps and mystifications, he will never again read his poems as if they had been written by someone else. A door has closed behind him, his retreat is cut off: he must walk in the broad daylight of prose. After this abortive attempt, he stops writing regular verse.* It has been only a transition, only the necessary bridge between the aesthete and the writer.

---

* Most of his other poems are contemporary with *The Galley*, that is, prior to *Miracle of the Rose* and all his great works. Only *The Fisherman of Suquet* is relatively recent (1945). But if Genet went back to regular verse in this love poem, it was quite simply because he was in love: lovers speak in verse.

AND I, GENTLER THAN A WICKED ANGEL,

LEAD HER BY THE HAND . . .

Our Lady of the Flowers, which is often considered to be Genet's masterpiece, was written entirely in prison, but, this time, in the solitude of the cell. The exceptional value of the work lies in its ambiguity. It appears at first to have only one subject, Fatality; the characters are puppets of destiny. But we quickly discover that this pitiless Providence is really the counterpart of a sovereign, indeed divine freedom, that of the author. *Our Lady of the Flowers* is the most pessimistic of books. With fiendish application it leads human creatures to downfall and death. And yet, in its strange language it presents this downfall as a triumph. The rogues and wretches of whom it speaks all seem to be heroes, to be of the elect. But what is far more astonishing is that the book itself is an act of the rashest optimism.

French prison authorities, convinced that work is freedom, give the inmates paper with which they are required to make bags. It was on this brown paper that Genet wrote, in pencil, *Our Lady of the Flowers.* One day, while the prisoners were marching in the yard, a turnkey entered the cell, noticed the manuscript, took it away and burned it. Genet began again. Why? For whom? There was small chance of his keeping the work until his release, and even less of getting it printed. If, against all likelihood, he succeeded, the book was bound to be burned; it would be confiscated and scrapped. Yet he wrote on, he persisted in writing. Nothing in the world mattered to him except those sheets of brown paper which a match could reduce to ashes.

In a sense, *Our Lady* is the height of aloofness. We do not even find in it—or at least not at first—the attempt at communication (a hesitant and contradictory attempt, to be sure) that resulted in *The Condemned Man*. A convict lets himself sink like a rock to the depths of reverie. If the world of human beings, in its terrible absence, is still in some way present, it is solely because this solitude is a defiance of that world: "The whole world is dying of panicky fright. Five million young men of all tongues will die by the cannon that erects and discharges. But where I am I can muse in comfort on the lovely dead of yesterday, today and tomorrow."

The world has isolated him as if he were pestiferous, it has cooped him in. Very well, he will intensify the quarantine. He will sink to depths where no one will be able to reach him or understand him; amidst the turmoil of Europe, he will enjoy a ghastly tranquillity. He rejects reality and, in order to be even more certain that he will not be recaptured, logic itself. He is going to find his way back to the great laws of the participationist and autistic thinking of children and schizophrenics. In short, we are confronted with a regression toward infantilism, toward the childish narcissism of the onanist.

One is bored in a cell; boredom makes for amorousness. Genet masturbates: this is an act of defiance, a willful perversion of the sexual act; it is also, quite simply, an idiosyncrasy. The operation condenses the drifting reveries, which now congeal and disintegrate in the release of pleasure. No wonder *Our Lady* horrifies people: it is the epic of masturbation. The words which compose this book are those that a prisoner said to himself while panting with excitement, those with which he loaded himself, as with stones, in order to sink to the bottom of his reveries, those which were born of the dream itself and which are dream words, dreams of words. The reader will open *Our Lady of the Flowers,* as one might open the cabinet of a fetishist, and find there, laid out on the shelves, like shoes that have been sniffed at and kissed and bitten hundreds of times, the damp and evil words that gleam with the excitement they arouse in another person and which we cannot feel. In Gide's *The Counterfeiters,* little Boris inscribes on a piece of parchment the words: "Gas. Telephone. One hundred thousand rubles." "These six words were the open sesame of the shameful paradise into which sensual pleasure plunged him. Boris called this parchment his *talisman.*" In a certain sense, *Our Lady* is Genet's collection of erotic talismans, the thesaurus of all the "Gas. Telephone. One hundred thousand rubles" that have the power to excite him. There is only one subject: the pollutions of a prisoner in the darkness of his cell; only one hero: the masturbator; only one place: his "evil-smelling hole, beneath the coarse wool covers." From beginning to end we remain with him who "buries himself under the covers and gathers in his cupped hands his crushed farts which he carries to his nose." No events other than his vile metamorphoses. At times, a secret gangrene detaches his head from his body: "With my head still under the covers, my fingers digging into my eyes and my mind off somewhere, there remains only the lower part of my body, detached, by my digging fingers, from my rotting head." At others, an abyss opens at the bottom of the hole, and Genet falls into the fathomless pit. But we always come back in the end to the gesture of solitude, to the flying fingers: "A kind of unclean and supernatural transposition displaces the truth. Everything within me turns worshiper."

This work of the mind is an organic product. It smells of bowels and sperm and milk. If it emits at times an odor of violets, it does so in the manner of decaying meat that turns into a preserve; when we poke it, the blood runs and we find ourselves in a belly, amidst gas bubbles and lumps of entrails. No other book, not even *Ulysses,* brings us into such close contact with an author. Through the prisoner's nostrils we inhale his own odor. The "double sensation" of flesh touching itself, of two fingers of the same hand pressing against each other, gives us a phantom otherness-in-unity. This self-intimacy is traversed by an ideal separating surface, the page on which Genet writes *Our Lady of the Flowers.*

But, at the same time, this work is, without the author's suspecting it, the journal of a detoxication, of a conversion. In it Genet detoxicates himself of himself and turns to the outside world. In fact, this book *is* the detoxication itself. It is not content with bearing witness to the cure, but concretizes it. Born of a nightmare, it effects—line by line, page by page, from death to life, from the state of dream to that of waking, from madness to sanity—a passageway that is marked with relapses. *Before Our Lady,* Genet was an aesthete; *after* it, an artist. But at no moment was a decision *made* to achieve this conversion. The decision *is Our Lady.* Throughout *Our Lady* it both makes and rejects itself, observes and knows itself, is unaware of itself, plays tricks on itself and encumbers itself everywhere, even in the relapses. On every page it is born of its opposite, and at the very moment it leads Genet to the borderline of awakening, it leaves on the paper the sticky traces of the most monstrous dream. At times the art of the tale aims only at bringing the narrator's excitement to its climax, and at times the artist makes the excitement he feels the pretext of his art. In any case, it is the artist who will win. Seeking excitement and pleasure, Genet starts by enveloping himself in his images, as the polecat envelops itself in its odor. These images call forth by themselves words that reinforce them; often they even remain incomplete; words are needed to finish the job; these words require that they be uttered and, finally, written down; writing calls forth and creates its audience; the onanistic narcissism ends by being stanched in words. Genet writes in a state of dream and, in order to consolidate his dreams, dreams that he writes, then writes that he dreams, and the act of writing awakens him. The consciousness of the word is a local awakening within the fantasy; he awakes without ceasing to dream. Let us follow him in these various phases of his new metamorphosis.

1. The Creatures

Under his lice-ridden coverings, this recumbent figure ejects, like a starfish, a visceral and glandular world, then draws it back and dissolves it within itself. In this world, creatures wriggle about for a moment, are resorbed, reappear and disappear again: Darling, Our Lady, Gorgui, Gabriel, Divine. Genet relates their story, describes their features, shows their gestures. He is guided by only one factor, his state of excitement. These figures of fantasy must provoke erection and orgasm; if they do not, he rejects them. Their truth, their density, are measured solely by the effect they produce upon him.

Here is Divine. Divine is Genet himself, is "a thousand shapes, charming in their grace, [that] emerge from my eyes, mouth, elbows, knees, from all parts of me. They say to me: 'Jean, how glad I am to be living as Divine and to be living with Darling.'" Genet objectifies himself, as we all do in our dreams. As a sovereign creator, he cannot *believe* in the real existence of Darling; he believes in him through Divine. As Divine, he has the disturbing and voluptuous experience of aging; he "realizes" his dreadful fear of growing old. She is the only one of his creatures whom he does not desire; he makes her be desired by the others. She excites him through Darling or Gorgui. Divine is an ambiguous character who serves both to bring his entire life into focus in the lucidity of his gaze and to let him plunge more deeply into sleep, to sink to the depths of a cozy horror, to drown in his opera.

The others—all the others, except the girl queens—are the creatures and objects of his feminine desires. The whole graceful procession of Pimps, those lovely vacant-eyed does, are the means he chooses for being petted, pawed, tumbled and entered.

Here is how Darling was born: "Very little of Roger the Corsi-can remains in my memory: a hand with too massive a thumb . . . and the dim image of a blond boy. . . . The memory of his memory made way for other men. The last two days I have again, in my daydreams, been mingling his [invented] life with mine. . . . For two successive days I have fed with his image a dream which is usually sated after four or five hours. . . . I am worn out with the in-vented trips, thefts, rapes, burglaries . . . in which we were involved. . . . I am exhausted; my wrist has cramps. The pleasure of the last drops is dry. . . . I have abandoned the daydream . . . I have quit, the way a contestant in a six-day bicycle race quits; yet the memory of [him] refuses to disappear as the memory of my dream friends usu-ally does. It floats about. It has less sharpness than it had when the adventures were taking place, but it lives within me nevertheless. Certain details persist more obstinately in remaining. . . . If I con-tinue, he will rise up, become erect. . . . I can bear it no longer. I am turning him into a character whom I shall be able to torment in my own way, namely, Darling Daintyfoot."

Our Lady "was born of my love for Pilorge."

Here is Gorgui: "Clément Village filled the cell with an odor stronger than death. . . . I have tried to recapture in the cell where I am now writing the odor of carrion spread by the proud-scented Negro, and thanks to him I am better able to give life to Seck Gor-gui. . . . You know from *Paris-Soir* that he was killed during the jailbreak at Cayenne. But he was handsome. He was perhaps the handsomest Negro I have ever seen. How lovingly I shall caress, with the memory of him, the image I shall compose, thanks to it, of Seck Gorgui. I want him to be handsome, nervous and vulgar."

Sometimes a gesture alone remains, or an odor, or a simple relic whose erotic potency, which has been experienced over and over, is inexhaustible. A few schematic features can be sufficient: what remains of Roger the Corsican? A nebulous, "dim image of a blond boy," and a few solid elements: a hand, a gait, a chain, a key. Around these sacred remains Genet drapes another flesh. He "fits" them with other memories richer and less sacred: the color of a skin or a look which excited him elsewhere, on another occasion. Dar-ling's eyes will be weary after lovemaking; Genet will "cull" this fatigue and the rings under the eyes from the face of another youngster whom he saw leaving a brothel. This mask of flesh is becoming to the archaic skeleton. Whereupon Genet gets an erec-tion. This erection is not merely the index of his achievement, but its goal—as if Flaubert had described the poisoning of Emma Bo-vary only to fill his own mouth with ink. The character has no need to be judged according to other criteria. There is no concern with his mental or even physical verisimilitude: Darling remains the same age all his life. To us who are not sexually excited, these creatures should be insipid. And yet they are not. Genet's desire gives them heat and light. If they were conceived in accordance with verisimilitude, they would perhaps have a more general truth, but they would lose that absurd and singular "presence" that comes from their being born of a desire. Precisely because *we* do not desire them, because they do not cease, in our eyes, to belong to another person's dream, they take on a strange and fleeting charm, like homely girls who we know are passionately loved and whom we look at hesitantly, vaguely tempted, while wondering: "But what does he see in her?" Darling and Divine will always baffle the "normal" reader, and the more they elude us, the more true we think them. In short, we are fascinated by someone else's loves.

As soon as the character is modeled, baked and trimmed, Genet launches him in situations which he evaluates according to the same rules. He is telling *himself* stories in order to please *himself*. Do the situation and the character harmonize? Yes and no. The author is the only one to decide whether or not they do. Or rather, it is not he who decides, but the capricious and blasé little fellow he carries between his thighs. Depending on Genet's mood of the moment, Darling will be victim or tyrant. The same male who cleaves the queens like a knife will stand naked and dirty before the guards who manhandle him. Does he lack coherence? Not at all. Amidst his metamorphoses he retains, without effort, a vital, ingrained identity that is more convincing than the studied unity of many fictional characters because it simply reflects the permanence of the desire it arouses. At times Genet submits to the Pimps, at times he betrays them in secret, dreaming that they are being whipped. But in order for his pleasure to have style and taste, those whom he adores and those who are whipped must be the *same*. The truth about Darling is that he is both the glamorous pimp and the humiliated little faggot. That is his coherence. Although his other features are only dream images, they have, nevertheless, the gratuitousness, mystery and stubbornness of life. Each time Darling is arrested, he is proud of dazzling the jailbirds by the elegance of his attire. The prospect delights him in advance. This is the "kind of detail one doesn't invent." And indeed, Genet did not invent it. But he did not observe it either. He simply has his hero experience in glory what he himself experienced in shame. Humiliated at having to appear for questioning in a prisoner's outfit, he takes his revenge in fantasy, in the guise of Darling.

We can be sure that our "dreamer" never leaves reality; he *arranges* it. That is why this introvert, who is incapable of true relations with others, can create such vivid figures as Darling, Divine and Mimosa. He weaves a dream around his experiences, and that means, most of the time, that he simply changes their sign. Out of his hatred of women, his resentment against his guilty mother, his desire for femininity, his realism, his taste for ceremonies, he will create Ernestine. She will try to murder her son because Genet's mother abandoned him and because the author dreams of killing a young man. She will shoot wide of the mark because Genet knows that he is not of the "elect," that he will never be a murderer. She will march in Divine's funeral procession as the servant girl will march in that of her child* because Genet, when he was a child, followed (or dreamed of following) that of a little girl with whom he was in love. All these traits will finally compose a fleeting and inimitable figure that will have the contingency and truth of life and that will be the obverse of the fake coin of which Genet himself is the reverse. He plays, he alters a situation, a character, sure of never making an error since he is obeying his desires, since he checks on his invention by his state of excitement. At times he stops and consults himself; he hesitates playfully: "So Divine is alone in the world. Whom shall I give her as lover? The gypsy I am seeking? . . . He accompanies her for a while in the passing crowd . . . lifts her from the ground, carries her in front of him without touching her with his hands, then, upon reaching a big melodious house, he puts her down . . . picks up from the mud of the gutter a violin . . . [and] disappears." The scenery is put up as he goes along, as in dreams: Genet brings out the props when they are needed, for example, the gypsy, a leitmotiv of his solitary pleasures. We are told he plays the guitar. The reason is that Genet was once in love with a guitarist. Besides, for this fetishist the guitar is an erotic object because it has a round, low-slung rump. We read in his poem *The Galley:* "Their guitarlike rumps burst into melody"; the low-pitched sounds of the plucked strings are the farts that "stream from downy behinds." Later, in *Funeral Rites,* Jean Decarnin will be metamorphosed into a guitar. In this autistic thinking, the guitarist *is* his own guitar. When Genet brings Divine and the gypsy together, immediately "he lifts her from the ground without touching her with his hands." On his penis, of course. Our lonely prisoner dreams of straddling a huge, powerful member that rises slowly and lifts him from the ground.

---

* In *Funeral Rites*, cf. below.

Later, it will be the mast that Genet climbs in *Miracle of the Rose* and the cannon in *Funeral Rites*. But this pattern is linked more particularly—I do not know why—with his desire for gypsies. In *The Thief's Journal,* he will spring into the air on a gypsy's prick. The scene is merely outlined in *Our Lady,** for the reason that other forces and desires prevented it from being filled in. This triumphal cavalcade was not meant for poor Divine. It does not succeed in exciting Genet; he immediately loses interest in it. From the gypsy is born a melody, which floats for a moment, then suddenly condenses and becomes a "melodious house," just a bare detail, the minimum required for the gypsy to be able to push open a door and disappear, dissolved in his own music.

Genet shows everything. Since his only aim is to please himself, he sets down everything. He informs us of his erections that come to nothing just as he does of those that come off successfully. Thus, his characters have, like *real* men, a life *in action,* a life involving a range of possibilities. Life in action may be defined as the succession of images that have led Genet to orgasm. He will be able to repeat the "effective" scenes indefinitely, at will, without modifying them, or to vary them around a few fixed elements. (Here too a selection takes place. There are some whose erotic power is quickly exhausted: the "dreams are usually sated after four or five hours." Others, which have deeper roots, remain at times in a state of virulence, at times inert and floating, awaiting a new embodiment.) The possibilities, on the other hand, are all the images that he has caressed without attaining orgasm. Thus, unlike *our* possibilities, which are the acts that we can and, quite often, do perform, these fictional possibilities represent simply the missed opportunities, the permission that Genet pitilessly refuses his creatures. He once said to me: "My books are not novels, because none of my characters make decisions on their own." This is particularly true of *Our Lady* and accounts for the book's desolate, desertlike aspect. Hope can cling only to free and active characters. Genet, however, is concerned only with satisfying his cruelty. All his characters are inert, are knocked about by fate. The author is a barbaric god who revels in human sacrifice. This is what Genet himself calls the "Cruelty of the Creator." He kicks Divine toward saintliness. The unhappy girl queen undergoes her ascesis in an agony. Genet diverts himself by imposing upon her the progressive austerity he wishes to achieve freely himself. It is the breath of Genet that blights the soft

---

* In fact, Genet dropped the entire passage from the revised edition.—Translator's note.

flesh of Divine; it is the hand of Genet that pulls out her teeth; it is the will of Genet that makes her hair fall out; it is the whim of Genet that takes her lovers from her. And it is Genet who amuses himself by driving Our Lady to crime and then drawing from him the confession that condemns him to death. But cannot the same be said of every novelist? Who, if not Stendhal, caused Julien Sorel to die on the scaffold? The difference is that the novelist kills his hero or reduces him to despair in the name of truth, of experience, so that the book may be more beautiful or because he cannot work out his story otherwise. If Julien Sorel is executed, it is because the young tutor on whom he was modeled lost his head. The psycho-analyst has, of course, the right to seek a deeper, a criminal inten-tion behind the author's conscious motives, but, except for the Marquis de Sade and two or three others, very few novelists take out their passions on their characters out of sheer cussedness. But listen to Genet: "Marchetti will remain between four white walls to the end of ends . . . it will be the death of hope. . . . I am very glad of it. Let this arrogant and handsome pimp in turn know the torments reserved for the weakly." Moreover, the author himself, that owl who says "I" in the heart of his darkness, hardly comes off any better. We shall see him strike and dominate Bulkaen, or slowly get over the death of Jean Decarnin. Later, Jean Genet will become "the wiliest hoodlum," Ulysses. For the time being, he is lying on his back, paralyzed. He is passively waiting for a judge to decide his fate. He too is in danger of being sent to a penal colony for life. Yes, *Our Lady of the Flowers* is a dream. Only in dreams do we find this dreadful passivity. In dreams the characters wait for their night to end. In dreams, stranglers pass through walls, the fugitive has leaden soles and his revolver is loaded with blanks.

2. The Words

Yet, by the same movement that chains him, in his work, to these drifting, rudderless creatures, he frees himself, shakes off his reverie and transforms himself into a creator. *Our Lady* is a dream that con-tains its own awakening.

The reason is that the imagination depends on words. Words complete our fantasies, fill in their gaps, support their inconsist-ency, prolong them, enrich them with what cannot be seen or touched. It was long ago pointed out that no image can render so simple a sentence as "I'm going to the country tomorrow." This is perhaps not entirely so, but it is true that abstract connections are

expressed more frequently by our inner monologues than by the
play of our imagination. "Marchetti will remain between four
white walls to the end of ends." We can be fairly sure that this sentence occurred to Genet spontaneously and that it replaced images
which were too vague or schematic. The reason is that there are
abstract relationships which can be erotic. The *idea* that Marchetti
will remain a prisoner *forever* is certainly even more exciting to
this resentful sadist than the *image* of his being humiliated by the
guards. There is something final and inexorable about it that only
words can render. Images are fleeting, blurred, individual; they
reflect our particularity. But words are social, they universalize.
No doubt Genet's language suffers from deep lesions; it is stolen,
faked, poeticized. Be this as it may: with words, the Other reappears.

   We observed earlier that Genet's two contradictory components
(quietism-passivity-masochism; activism-ferocity-existence) united
for a moment in masturbation only to disunite after pleasure. Genet
the onanist attempted to make himself an object for a subject which,
disguised as Darling or Gorgui, was no other than himself, or, as
subject, he hounded Divine, an imaginary object and also himself.
But the Word expresses the relationship of Narcissus to himself;
he is *with* the subject *and* with the object. It is no accident that the
Word frequently accompanies the act of masturbation, that Gide
shows Boris uttering his incantatory formula as an "open sesame."
The onanist wants to take hold of the word *as an object*. When it is
repeated aloud or in a whisper, it immediately acquires an objectivity and presence that is lacking in the object. The image remains
something absent; I do not really *see* it, nor do I hear it. It is I who
exhaust myself trying to hold it up. But if I utter the word, I can
hear it. And if I succeed in taking my mind off myself when the
word comes out of my mouth, if I succeed in forgetting that it is I
who say it, I can listen to it as if it *emanated from someone else,*
and indeed even as if it were sounding all by itself. Here is a phrase
that still vibrates in Genet's ears. What does he say? "To the end of
ends." To the end of ends Marchetti will remain in jail. It seems
that an absolute sentence has been delivered in the cell and that the
images have taken on flesh. To the end of ends: is it therefore true?
But this *object* which has surged up in the real world, as the sound
units used to surge up in the solitude of the fields, has a shape, a
face. Genet can pluck from its visual physiognomy or sound structure the erotic object which he lacks. When he speaks of Darling's
"downy behind" we can be sure that he does not couple these
words for the truth or beauty of the assemblage, but for its power

of suggestion. He is enchanted with the feminine ending of the masculine noun *derrière* [behind]. Fake femininity? Fake masculinity? The rump is the secret femininity of males, their passivity. And what about *douillet* [downy]? Where does its *meaning* begin? Where does its signification end? The fleshy blossoming of the diphthong suggests a kind of big, heavy, wet, silky flower; the trim, dainty flexional ending evokes the coy grace of a fop. Darling drapes himself in his behind as in a quilted wrap [*douillette*]. The word conveys the thing; it is the thing itself. Are we so far from poetry? May it be that poetry is only the reverse side of masturbation?

Genet would not be true to himself if he were not fascinated by the sacrilege to be committed. We saw a while ago that he *listened* to words. He is now going to direct his attention to the verbal act, to perceive himself in the process of talking. The naming of forbidden pleasures is blasphemous. The man who masturbates humbly, without saying a word or being too preoccupied with what his hand is doing, is half forgiven; his gesture fades out in the darkness. If it is named, it becomes *the* Gesture of the masturbator, a threat to everyone's memory. In order to increase his pleasure, Genet names it. To whom? To nobody and to God. For him, as for primitives, the Word has metaphysical virtues. It is evil, it is delightful that an obscene word resounds in the semidarkness of his cell, that it emerges from the dark hole of his covers. The order of the universe is thereby upset. A word uttered is word as *subject;* heard, it is *object*. If you read *Our Lady of the Flowers,* you will see the sentence manifest one or the other of these verbal functions, depending on the poet's mood. Read the description of the lovemaking of Darling and Divine, or of the first night that Divine spent with Gabriel, or of Gorgui's sexual play with Divine and Our Lady. Read them, for I dare not transcribe them or comment upon them too closely. You will be struck, in most cases, by the incantatory use of the present tense, which is intended to draw the scene into the cell, onto Genet's body, to make it contemporary with the caresses he lavishes on himself. It is also a finical, slightly breathless precision, expressing an eagerness to find the detail that excites. Here the word is a quasi-object. But this hoarse, hasty, scrupulously careful voice that is panting with incipient pleasure suddenly breaks. Genet's hand puts down the pen; one of the scenes is hastily finished off with "and so on"; another ends with a series of dots. The next moment, Genet, still in a swoon, moans with gratitude: "Oh, it's so sweet to talk about them. . . . The whole world is dying of panicky fright. Five million young men . . . will die. . . . But where I am I can muse in comfort on the lovely dead of yesterday, today and tomorrow. I dream of the lovers' garret." This time the word is subject; Genet wants to be heard, to create a scandal. This abandoned "where I am I can muse in comfort" is the giggle of a woman who is being tickled. It is a challenge.

At the beginning, Genet *utters* the words or dreams them; he does not write them down. But before long these murmurs cease to satisfy him. When he listens to himself, he cannot ignore the fact that it is he who is speaking, for his utterance no longer resounds in a vacant soul as did the sound units of his vagabond days. It is in the eagerness for pleasure that he speaks, and he does so in order to excite himself further. And as soon as he surprises himself in the act of speaking, his sacrilegious joy vanishes. He is aware that he alone hears himself, that he alone "offers himself the ideal fault of roses" and that a moan of pleasure will not keep the earth from turning. Therein lies the trap: he will write. *Scripta manent:* tomorrow, in three days, when he finds the inert little sketch that confronts him with all its inertia, he will regard the phrase as an erotic and scandalous object. A drifting, authorless sentence will float toward him. He will read it for the first time. A sentence? Why not a whole story? Why not perpetuate the memory of his latest pleasures? Tomorrow a dead voice will relate them to him. He writes obscene and passionate words as he wrote his poems, in order to reread himself.

This is only an expedient. Even when he reads the sentence, Genet still knows who set it down. He is therefore going to turn, once again, to the Other, for it is the other who confers upon the word a veritable objectivity—*by listening to it.* Thus do toilet-poets engrave their dreams upon walls; others will read them, for example that gentleman with a mustache who is hurrying to the street-urinal. Whereupon the words become huge, they scream out, swollen up with the other's indignation. Unable to *read* what he writes, Genet empowers the Others to carry on for him. How could it be otherwise? They were already present in the heart of the word, hearers and speakers, awaiting their turn. It was Another who spoke those words which were uttered in the absolute; it was to Others that Genet dedicated these blasphemies which were addressed to the absolute. What Others? Certainly not the prisoners in the neighboring cells who are singing and dreaming and fondling themselves in their melancholy solitude? How could he hope for a moment to scandalize these brothers-in-misery? But, long before, he had been taken by surprise and singled out by men. Later, when he became a thief, he danced before invisible eyes in empty apartments. Is it not to this same omnipresent and fictive public that he is going to dedicate his solitary pleasures? The Just —*they* are his public. It is they whom he is taunting and by whom he wants to be condemned. He provokes outraged voyeurs in order to take his pleasure in a state of shame and defiance.

Thus far, there is no art. Writing is an erotic device. The imaginary gaze of the gentle reader has no function other than to give the word a new and strange consistency. The reader is not an end; he is a means, an instrument that doubles the pleasure, in short a voyeur despite himself. Genet is not yet speaking *to us;* he is talking to himself, though wanting to be heard. Intent on his pleasure, he does not so much as glance at us, and though his monologue is secretly meant for us, it is for us as witnesses, not as participants. We shall have the strange feeling that we are intruders and that nevertheless our *expected* gaze will, in running over the words on the page, be caressing Genet physically. He has just discovered his public, and we shall see that he will be faithful to it. A real public? An imaginary public? Does Genet write without expecting to be read? Is he already thinking of publishing? I imagine that he himself does not know. As a thief, he streamed with light, wanted to be caught, to end in a blaze of glory, and at the same time, frightened to death, did all he could to elude the cops. It is in the same state of mind that he starts to write.

A dream public, dream orgies, dream speeches. But when the dream word is written down, it becomes a true word. "Divine," writes Genet, "sat down . . . and asked for tea." This is all that is needed to generate an event in the world. And this event is not the materialization of Divine, who remains where she is, in Genet's head or around his body, but quite simply the appearance of letters on paper, a general and objective result of an activity. Genet wanted to give his dream characters a kind of presence. He failed, but the dream itself, as signification, is present on the sheet "in person"; the sentence is impregnated with an event of the mind and reflects it. Whereupon Genet ceases to feel; he knows that he *did* feel. Let us recall little Culafroy's reverie that was condensed into the single word "suns," which he uttered in the presence of a real listener. Genet immediately observes: "It was the word-poem that fell from the vision and began to petrify it." He has also said of Divine that "it was necessary that [she] never formulate her thoughts aloud, for herself. Doubtless there had been times when she had said to herself aloud 'I'm just a foolish girl,' but having felt this, she felt it no longer, and, in saying it, she no longer thought it." When confronted with the words that were uttered, she thinks that she thought it. She reflects upon herself, and she who reflects is no longer she who experienced; a pure Divine gazes at herself in the mirror of language. Similarly with Genet: while writing, he has eyes only for Divine, but as soon as the ink is dry he ceases to see her, he sees his own thought. He wanted to *see* Divine sitting down and asking for tea. A metamorphosis takes place beneath his pen and he sees himself thinking that Divine is sitting down. This mystifying transformation is the exact counterpart of that which led him to his semimadness. Formerly, he wanted to act, and all his acts changed into gestures. Now, he wants to make a gesture, to brave an imaginary public, and an act is reflected in the signs he has traced: "I wrote that." Has he thus awakened at last? In one sense, he has, but in another, he is still dreaming, steeped in his excitement, tangled up in his images. A curious kind of thinking indeed, a thinking that becomes hallucinated, reflects upon its hallucinations, recognizes them as such and frees itself from them only to fall again into the trap of a delirium that extends to its reflection. It envelops its madness in a lucid gaze that disarms it, and its lucidity is in turn enveloped and disarmed by madness. The dream is at the core of the awakening, and the awakening is snugly embedded in the dream. Let us read a passage taken at random from *Our.Lady:* "Darling loves Divine more and more deeply, that is, more and more without realizing it. Word by word, he grows attached. But more and more neglects her. She stays in the garret alone. . . . Divine is consumed with fire. I might, just as she herself did to me, confide that if I take contempt with a smile or a burst of laughter, it is not yet—and will it be some day?—out of scorn for contempt, but rather it is in order not to be ridiculous, not to be reviled by anything or anyone, that I have abased myself lower than dirt. I could not do otherwise. If I declare that I am an old whore, no one can better that, I discourage insult. No one can even spit in my face any more. And Darling Daintyfoot is like the rest of you; all he can do is despise me. . . . To be sure, a great earthly love would destroy this wretchedness, but Darling is not yet the Chosen One. Later on there will come a soldier, so that Divine may have some respite in the course of that calamity which is her life. Darling is merely a fraud ('an adorable fraud,' as Divine calls him) , and he must remain one in order to preserve *that appearance of a rock walking blindly through* my tale (*I left out the "d" in blindly, I wrote* '*blinly*').* It is only on this condition that I can like him. I say of

---

* The words in italics do not appear in the revised edition.—Translator's note.

him, as of all my lovers, against whom I butt and crumble: 'May he be steeped in indifference, may he be petrified with blind indifference.' Divine will take up this phrase to apply it to Our Lady of the Flowers." A story at first, up to "Divine is consumed with fire." Genet lets himself be taken in by it, grows excited; this is the dream. Suddenly, the awakening: jealous of the emotion that Divine's misfortunes have aroused in him and that they may arouse in an imaginary reader, he cries out in annoyance: "I too could make myself interesting if I wanted to." Implying: "But I have too much pride." This time, he speaks about *himself*, not about an invented hero. Is this a *true* awakening? No, since he continues to affirm the real existence of Divine: "I might, just as she herself did to me. . . ." But the very next moment Divine is herself: "All [Darling] can do is despise me." An awakening this time? Yes and no. Genet has resorbed Divine into himself, but Darling continues to live his independent life. Here and there we come upon sentences which seem to have been written without a pause and which give the impression that Genet, completely taken up with lulling his dream, has not reread what he has set down. Certain sentences limp because they have not been looked after; they are children that have been made to walk too soon: "I might, just as she herself did to me, confide that if I take contempt with a smile or a burst of laughter, it is not yet—and will it be some day?—out of scorn for contempt, but rather it is in order not to be ridiculous, not to be reviled by anything or anyone, that I have abased myself lower than dirt." Two propositions have collided: "this contempt that I take with a smile or a burst of laughter is not out of scorn of contempt, but rather it is in order not to be ridiculous (infer: that I like it) " and "it is not out of scorn for contempt but rather in order not to be ridiculous that I have abased myself lower than dirt." In short, at this level the words are inductors with relation to each other; they attract and engender one another, in accordance with grammatical habits, within an unheeding consciousness that wants only to weep tears over itself. The sentence takes shape all by itself; it is the dream. But immediately afterward, Genet writes, parenthetically: "I left out the *d* in blindly, I wrote 'blinly.' " This time he reflects *on the sentence,* hence on his activity as a writer. It is no longer the love of Divine and Darling that is the object of his reflection, but the slip of his sentence and of his hand. This error in spelling draws his attention to the meaning of the sentence. He contemplates it, discovers it and decides: "Divine will take up this phrase to apply it to Our Lady of the Flowers." This time we feel we are reading a passage from *The Journal of Crime and Punishment* or *The Journal of The Counterfeiters*. A perfectly lucid writer is informing us of his projects, goes into detail about his creative activities. Genet awakens; Darling in turn becomes a pure and imaginary object. Will Darling be the Chosen One? No, "Darling is merely a fraud ... and he must remain one," etc. But *who is it* who has just awakened? The writer or the onanist? Both. For we are given two reasons explaining why Darling must not change: "in order to preserve my tale," and "it is only on this condition that I can like him." Now, the former is that of the creator who wants his work to keep its severity of line, but the latter is that of the masturbator who wants to prolong his excitement. In the end he seems to merge with himself as the pure will that keeps the fantasies well in hand, for he writes, with sudden tranquillity: "It is Darling whom I cherish the most, for you realize that, in the last analysis, it is my own destiny, whether true or false, that I am laying (at times a rag, at times a court robe) on Divine's shoulders. Slowly but surely I want to strip her of every kind of happiness so as to make a saint of her. ... A morality is being born, which is certainly not the usual morality. ... And I, gentler than a wicked angel, lead her by the hand." But this very detachment seems suspect. Why plume oneself on it, why bring it to our attention? Is it that he wants to shock us? Where does the truth lie? Nowhere. This lucid dreamer, this "wicked angel," retains within himself, in a kind of undifferentiated state, the masturbator, the creator, the masochist who tortures himself by proxy, the serene and pitiless god who plots the fate of his creatures and the sadist who has turned writer in order to be able to torture them more and whose detachment is merely a sham. *Our Lady* is what certain psychiatrists call a "controlled waking dream," one which is in constant danger of breaking up or diverging under the pressure of emotional needs and which an artist's reflective intelligence constantly pulls back into line, governing and directing it in accordance with principles of logic and standards of beauty. By itself, the story becomes plodding, tends toward stereotypes, breaks up as soon as it ceases to excite its author, contradicts itself time and again, is enriched with odd details, meanders off, drifts, bogs down, suddenly reappears, lingers over trivial scenes, skips essential ones, drops back to the past, rushes years ahead, spreads an hour over a hundred pages, condenses a month into ten lines, and then suddenly there is a burst of activity that pulls things together, brings them into line and explains the symbols. Just when we think we are under the covers, pressed against the warm body of the masturbator, we find ourselves outside again, participating in the stony power of the demiurge. This development of onanistic themes gradually becomes an introspective exploration. The emotional pattern begets the image, and in the image Genet, like an analyst, discovers the emotional pattern. His thought crystallizes before his eyes; he reads it, then completes and clarifies it. Whereupon reflection is achieved, in its translucent purity, as *knowledge* and as *activity*.

A rapid study of the "free play" of his imagination will enable us to understand this better. We are going to see Genet inflate his dream to the breaking point, to the point of his becoming God, and then, when the bubble bursts, to discover he is an author.

3. The Images

He amuses himself. His comparisons and metaphors seem to obey only his fancy. The sole rule of this sinister playfulness is that he be pleased. But this is the sternest of rules. Nothing is so constraining as to have to flatter the quirks and fancies of a single master. The master requires of his fictions that they show him things as they are—that is his realism—but with the slight displacement that will enable him to see them as he would like them to be. Behind each image is, to use the words of Kant, a pattern "in unison with the principle and the phenomenon, which makes possible the application of the former to the latter." In the case of Genet the poet, the principles are his basic desires, the rules of his sensibility, which govern a very particular approach to the world. The patterns come afterward. They organize the images in such a way that the latter reflect back to him, through the real, his own plan of being. Their structure and "style," their very matter, express Genet and Genet only. The stones, plants and men of which he speaks are his masks. His imagination has a certain homosexual and criminal twist.*

There are two types of unification in modern poetry, one expansive, the other retractile. The aim of both is to enable us to perceive an aesthetic order behind the freaks of chance. But the first tendency—which is that of Rimbaud—forcibly compels natural diversity to symbolize an *explosive unity*. We are gradually made

---

* It must be understood that to *prove* is also a function of the imagination. The imagination *represents* objects to us in such a way as to incline our judgment in the direction we wish. The drawings of a madman do not simply *express* his terrors; they aim at maintaining them and confining him within them.

to see in a miscellaneous collection the breaking up of a prior totality whose elements, set in motion by a centrifugal force, break away from each other and fly off into space, colonizing it and there reconstituting a new unity. To see the dawn as a "people of doves" is to blow up the morning as if it were a powder keg. Far from denying plurality, one discovers it everywhere, one exaggerates it, but only to present it as a moment in a progression; it is the abstract instant that congeals it into an exploding but static beauty. Impenetrability, which is an inert resistance of space, the sagging of a dead weight, is transformed into a conquering force, and infinite divisibility into a glorious burst of continuity; persons are refulgent sprays whose dynamic unity is combustion. If this violence congeals, the flare falls in a rain of ashes. We shall *then* have discontinuity and number, those two names of death. But as long as the explosion lasts, juxtaposition signifies progress. *Beside* means *beyond*. For each object, scattered everywhere, in all directions, launched with all the others upon an infinite course, to *be* is to participate in the raging tide whereby the universe at every moment wins new areas of being from nothingness. This Dionysian imagery gladdens our hearts, fills us with a sense of power. It derives its force from an imperial pride, from a generosity that gushes forth and spends itself utterly. Its aim is to force the externality of Nature to reflect back to man his own transcendence. For those who want "to change life," "to reinvent love," God is nothing but a hindrance. If the unity is not dynamic, if it manifests itself in the form of restrictive contours, it reflects the image of their chains. Revolutionaries break the shells of being; the yolk flows everywhere.

Compared to them, how *miserly* Genet seems (as does Mallarmé). His patient will-to-unify is constricting, confining; it is always marking out limits and grouping things together. His aim is not to present externality as an expansive power, but to make of it a nothingness, a shadow, the pure, perceptible appearance of secret unities.* In order to do so, he reverses the natural movement of things; he transforms centrifugal into centripetal forces. "A cherry branch, borne up by the full flight of the pink flowers, surges all stiff and black from a vase." As we read this sentence from *Our*

---

* If I were not afraid of opening the way to excessive simplification and of being misunderstood, I would say that there is a "leftist" turn of imagination and a "rightist" one. The former aims at representing the unity that human labor forcibly imposes upon the disparate; the latter, at depicting the entire world in accordance with the type of a hierarchical society.

Lady, we actually feel a transformation taking place in our very
vision. The image does, to be sure, begin with a movement; in
Genet's pansexualism, the erection of the penis plays a very special
role. But the erectile movement—stiffening, hardening, swelling
—is not at all explosive. It accords very well with the poet's essentialism. The penis proceeds from potentiality to the act, *regains*
its favored form, that is, its natural limits, from which it will depart
only to collapse. The cherry branch is thus a penis. But in the very
same sentence its expansive force disappears. It *surged* stiff and
black from a vase; it is now borne up by flowers. It is passive, indolently supported by angels. A flowering branch normally suggests
the image of a blossoming, of an expansion, in short, of a centrifugal
explosion. The poetic movement parallels the natural movement
and goes from the tree to the bud, from the bud to the flower. But
Genet's image, instead of bringing the flowers *out* of the branch,
brings them *back* to it, glues them to the wood. The movement of
the image is from without inward, from the wings to the axis.* In
general, his poetic patterns present closed and stable units. When
Divine enters Graff's Café at about 2 A.M., "the customers were
muddy and still shapeless clay." The creator's power agglutinates
the customers, presses the discrete particles against each other and
gives them the unity of a paste. The next moment, "as the wind
turns leaves, so she turned heads, heads which all at once became
light." The allusion to the wind creates circularity. The whirl of
faces that are turned inward reflects Divine, at the center. The
movement closes in on itself; a form has just been born, a form
which has the calm cohesion of geometric figures. In the same way,
a few astringent words are enough to transform the courtroom audience into a single being: "The courtroom crowd . . . is sparkling
with a thousand poetic gestures. . . . It is as shuddering as taffeta. . . .
The crowd is not gay; its soul is sad unto death. It huddled together
on the benches, drew its knees and buttocks together, wiped its
collective nose and attended to the hundred needs of a courtroom
crowd." And further on: "The judge was twisting his beautiful
hands. The crowd was twisting its faces." The moments of a succession are united by a dynamic form: "A clerk called the witnesses.
. . . They were waiting in a little side room. . . . The door opened,
each time, just enough to let them edge through sideways, and one
by one, drop by drop, they were infused into the trial." The words

---

* See also, at the end of the book: "The swan, borne up by its mass of white feathers,
cannot go to the bottom of the water," etc.

"drop by drop," though stressing the fact that each witness is a *singular object,* refer to a unity without parts, to the undifferentiated continuity of a liquid mass filling the "little side room" and pressing against the door as against the inner surface of a vase. Divine is sitting in a bar. Customers enter, men who have perhaps never seen each other. They come from diverse places and have diverse destinies. In order to unify them, Genet makes use of the revolving door: "When the revolving door turned, at each turn, like the mechanism of a Venetian belfry, it presented a sturdy archer, a supple page, an exemplar of High Banditry." The word "presented" agglutinates these individuals, changes them, by analogy, into fashion models *presenting* gowns, subjects their comings and goings to a providential design, makes of each angle of the revolving door a niche, a little cell, a loggia. This time the privileged witness—Divine, Genet's substitute—is external to the system, and the painted wooden figures turn their faces outward. But the word "mechanism" recaptures them, assembles them about their axis of rotation and sets the merry-go-round in motion, thus re-establishing the reign of circularity.

This passage and others in the same vein warrant our comparing this kind of arch fancy to the humor of Proust. Proust, too, has a tendency to tighten the bonds of the real world, which are always a little loose, to give an additional turn of the screw, to assume that there is an order among objects that actually have none. The author of *Cities of the Plains,* also a homosexual and a recluse, likewise practiced "a selection among things which rids [him] of their usual appearance and enables [him] to perceive analogies." One need only recall the description of the restaurant at Rivebelle. "I looked at the round tables whose innumerable assemblage filled the restaurant like so many planets as planets are represented in old allegorical pictures. Moreover, there seemed to be some irresistible attractive force at work among these diverse stars, and at each table the diners had eyes only for the tables at which they were not sitting. . . . The harmony of these astral tables did not prevent the incessant revolution of the countless servants who, because, instead of being seated like the diners, they were on their feet, performed their evolutions in a more exalted sphere. No doubt they were running, one to fetch the hors d'oeuvres, another to change the wine or with clean glasses. But despite these special reasons, their perpetual course among the round tables yielded, after a time, to the observer the law of its dizzy but ordered circulation. . . . People began to rise from table; and if each party while their dinner lasted . . . had been held in perfect cohesion about their own, the attractive force that had kept them gravitating round their host of the evening lost its power at the moment when, for coffee, they repaired to the same corridor that had been used for the tea-parties; it often happened that in its passage from place to place some party on the march dropped one or more of its human corpuscles who, having come under the irresistible attraction of the rival party, detached themselves for a moment from their own."* The same circular, planetary units; the same homosexual archness, which, in the case of one, metamorphoses men into wooden effigies and, in that of the other, into stellar masses; the same fundamental resentment; the same contemplative quietism; the same Platonism. But in the case of Proust, who is more positive, the whimsical humor is counteracted by the will to give his comparisons a scientific basis. Genet, who rejects modern culture, bases his on magic, on craftsmanship. He pushes the "organization" of his universe to the point of identifying persons with their symbolic properties and attributes.† Here is Divine's fan: ". . . she would pull the fan from her sleeve . . . and unfurl it, and suddenly one would see the fluttering wing in which the lower part of her face was hidden. Divine's fan will beat lightly about her face all her life." At times, an entire human body, an entire person, extends through others and serves as their link, their entelechy, their unity. "He awaited Alberto, who did not come. Yet each country lad or lass who entered had something of the snake fisher about him or her. They were like his harbingers, his ambassadors, his precursors, bearing before him some of his gifts, preparing his coming as they smoothed the way for him. . . . One had his walk, another his gestures, or the color of his trousers, or his corduroy, or Alberto's voice; and Culafroy, as one who waits, did not doubt that all these scattered elements would eventually come together and enable a reconstructed Alberto to make [a] solemn, appointed and surprising entry." Of course, this is merely a way of saying that, while waiting for Alberto, Culafroy thinks he recognizes him in every passer-by. But Genet takes this pretext for kneading the matter of the world and pursuing his act of unification. Here, too, the movement is retractile. It is not a matter of Alberto's exploding in all directions and spattering on all the figures, but rather of a condensation of scattered elements which sud-

---

* *Within a Budding Grove,* translated by C. K. M. Scott-Moncrieff.

† For Mallarmé, the element of chance and the externality of the Real are expressed by the word "outspread" [*éployé*]: "all the futile abyss outspread." And the unifying act of the poet is expressed by its opposite: "to fold its division." It is thus a matter of compressing multiplicity until the elements interpenetrate and form an indivisible totality.

denly spring together to effect the synthetic reconstitution of the snake fisher. Even when Genet says of Our Lady that he *is* a wedding feast, his aim is not to disseminate *Our Lady* over all the wedding guests, but to bring them all together in Our Lady,* just as he brought all the country people together in Alberto. He effects a recomposition.

In short, one might contrast the humanistic universe of Rimbaud or Nietzsche,† in which the powers of the negative shatter the limits of things, with the stable and theological universe of Baudelaire or Mallarmé, in which a divine crosier shepherds things together in a flock, imposing unity upon discontinuity itself. That Genet chose the latter is only to be expected. In order to do evil, this outcast needs to affirm the pre-existence of good, that is, of order. At the very source of his images is a will to compel reality to manifest the great social hierarchy from which he is excluded. There is a manly generosity in the explosive images of Rimbaud. They are ejaculations; they manifest the unity of the *undertaking*. An entire man plunges forward. It is his freedom in action which will unite the diverse elements. He *maps out* the lines, and they exist through the movement that maps them out. The quite feminine passivity of Genet thrusts him into a ready-made world in which the lines and curves struggle against the dispersion and splintering ad infinitum by means of an objective power of cohesion (intermediary between activity and passivity) analogous to the fixed exigencies that the outlaw observed in tools.‡ When the prisoner *wants to please himself,* he does not imagine that he is acting, that he himself is imposing unity upon diversity, but he pleases himself in being, *as creator,* at the source of the magical cohesion that produces the objective unity of things. In short, incapable of *carving out* a place for himself in the universe, he *imagines* in order to convince himself that he has created the world which excludes him.§

---

* The fact is that the content suggests an incipient outburst, for the image is meant to signify the joyous blossoming of the murderer. But this burst is immediately checked and organized, just as the stiff, black surging is checked and fixed forever by its contours.

† Nietzsche used to call himself an explosion, an infernal machine.

‡ This perhaps parallels a distinction between the "feminine" imagination (which reinforces in the woman—when she is her master's accomplice—the illusion of being at the center of a beautiful order) and the "manly," explosive imagination (which contains and transcends anguish by means of the images it forms).

§ In Mallarmé, the act is not the unification of the diverse by a progressive operation, but a *form in action* which, if it exists, appears all at once and which is dispersed by the diversity of the real: "The place a lapping below, sufficient for dispersing the empty act." It goes without saying that between Mallarmé and Rimbaud, the two pure and opposite types of imagination, there exists a series of mixed, transitional types.

When he was free, we saw him roaming over Europe, convinced that the events of his life had been planned by Providence, of which he was the sole concern. Rejecting even the idea of chance, his mind acted upon his perception so that it could discern everywhere the signs of an external and providential order. When he thought he had discovered beneath the disordered multiplicity of human beings an aesthetic form that ensured their cohesion, he allowed his intense satisfaction to substitute for actual fact: ". . . populous streets on whose throng my gaze happens to fall: a sweetness, a tenderness, situates them outside the moment; I am charmed and—I can't tell why—that mob of people is balm to my eyes. I turn away; then I look again, but I no longer find either sweetness or tenderness. The street becomes dismal, like a morning of insomnia." The reason is that he had succeeded in discovering an order in this concourse of chance elements. And if he found it there, it was because he had put it there. His questing eyes roamed over nature as if it were a picture puzzle in which he had to discover the hunter's rifle between the branches or in the grass. Later, during his period of imprisonment, he again made use of these patterns, but instead of using them to decipher, he transformed them into rules for building. In reconstructing the universe in his book, he satisfies his desire since he makes himself both the Providence that governs things and the man who discovers the designs of Providence. As we have already seen, in most of his descriptions a circular movement is organized and the objects, which are drawn into this round, turn their faces to the motionless center. In general, this motionless mover is Genet himself or one of his substitutes. But even when the center is merely a figurehead, this planetary attraction which makes things gravitate about a central mass is to him a symbol of Providence. He reconstructs the real on every page of his books in such a way as to produce for himself proof of the existence of God, that is, of his own existence.

This hierarchical conception of a world in which forms dovetail has a name: essentialism. Genet's imagination is essentialist, as is his homosexuality. In real life, he seeks the Seaman in every sailor, the Eternal in every pimp. In his reverie he bends his mind to justifying his quest. He generates each of his characters out of a higher Essence; he reduces the episode to being merely the manifest illustration of an eternal truth.

The chief characters in *Our Lady,* those whose function is to embody Genet's destiny, can be viewed as examples of Platonic idealism: "To Divine, Darling is only . . . the physical expression,

in short, the symbol of a being (perhaps God) , of an idea that remains in heaven." Most of the time, however, his essentialism takes
on the features of Aristotelian alchemy, because he forces his fictions
to furnish him with proof of the powers of language. He wants to
convince himself by means of his own tale that naming changes
being. When he was named a *thief* he was transformed; since then,
as we have seen, the verb *to be* has been enchanted. "His head *is* a
singing copse. He himself *is* a beribboned wedding feast skipping
. . . down a sunken April road." "The policemen held me up. . . .
They *were* the Holy Women wiping my face." The verb in these
sentences expresses an inert and instantaneous metamorphosis intermediary between the state and the flux, as the cohesion of forms,
which we mentioned above, is intermediary between activity and
passivity. Genet says "Gabriel is a soldier." This sentence does not
have the same taste in his mouth as in ours. He immediately adds:
"The army is the red blood that flows from the artilleryman's ears;
it is the little lightfoot soldier of the snows crucified on skis, a spahi
on his horse of cloud that has pulled up at the edge of Eternity, the
masked princes and brotherly murderers in the Foreign Legion,"
etc. To us, "to be a soldier" means to exercise a function for a
limited time, to become a subject who has been given abstract
rights and duties. To Genet it means to share suddenly and magically in the virtues, mysteries and legendary history of a huge,
multicolored beast; to be a soldier is to be the entire army, just as
the latest bearer of a noble name is both his entire family and his
entire House. This is so because Genet, an exile from our bourgeois,
industrial democracy, was cast into an artificial medieval world.
He was thrust into a grim feudal system; he belongs to the military
society of "strong" and "weak." For him, *to be* is to be identified
with a group that confers the honors of the name. The progression
from one caste to another is a new birth which occurs by formal
naming, and the new member of the caste possesses, within himself,
the entire caste: a Sailor is the entire fleet, a murderer is all of crime.
Names are titles, and "titles are sacred." In the twelfth century this
conception of society was justified by an essentialism that extended
to all of nature. In order for a knight to be defined by his membership in the order of knighthood, God had to have created the
world in such a way that the rose was defined by its belonging to
the order of florality. The social hierarchy is legitimate if God
willed it, and the manifest proof of this will is to be found in the
hierarchy of things. Inversely, the thinking of an agricultural
community is naturally essentialist; wheat, cattle, all the goods of

this world, reproduce by birth, and these births, which are sacred, symbolically manifest initiation, just as initiation symbolizes birth.

This philosophy of concept was destroyed by science and industrial practice which substituted for it a philosophy of judgment. Inactive, parasite of an industrious society, convinced of his predestination, Genet must liken his thinking to the idle and parasitic thinking of the medieval clerk. The logical framework of the social world which he invents for his ethical needs is the military hierarchy of concepts. Does he *believe* in it? Of course not. He is far too intelligent. He cannot entirely overlook the discoveries of science nor the working world that terrifies and disgusts but also fascinates him. But *precisely because he does not believe in it,* he must convince himself. One of the major demands he imposes upon his imagination is that it present to him the everyday world—our world—in such a light as to *verify* his *conceptualism.* From the universe that he re-creates with the purpose of offering it to himself as an object of imaginary experience one could derive the principles of a scholastic philosophy: *the concept is the form that is imposed upon all matter* (in other words, it is initiation or birth that creates the person); *in changing form, the same matter changes being* (in other words, one moves from one caste to another as a result of naming); *any reality that, in any aspect of its nature, pertains to a concept immediately becomes the singular expression of the entire concept*—thus, every object can *simultane~~sly* or *successively* express immutable and conflicting Ideas, and these Ideas are concrete totalities, actual principles of individuation. (In other words, since the group is eminently present in each of its members and confers upon each his sacred reality, an individual who belongs to several groups at the same time is simultaneously and entirely each of these groups.) Is this a kind of Aristotelianism? One would think so at times, for it seems—this is the theory of gesture which we set forth above—that men and things are visited by essences that settle upon them for a moment and disappear: if they make a movement or strike another attitude or if there is simply a change in the surrounding environment, they immediately receive a new name, a new being. Policemen have only to be attentive to Divine and they immediately become Holy Women. And in order for Divine to be an infanta all that is needed is a four-wheeled carriage and an iron gate. The animating force of all these metamorphoses is, as for the medieval clerk, *analogy;* every apparent analogy is a sign of deep identity. Resting against the cushions of a carriage, Divine is in a position analogous to that of an infanta; therefore she *is* an infanta. The weight of the word "infanta" crushes the details of the image that might check the metamorphosis and does away with Divine's masculinity and poverty. In the realm of the imaginary, the operation succeeds every time: "the royal idea is of this world." Take the word "royal" as in the old expression "royal art": this is conceptualism. The aim of this masturbator is very like that of the alchemist. He wants to change lead into gold. For Genet this means to place, in imagination, a piece of lead in a system of relations that ordinarily refer to gold, and then imperceptibly to speak of lead as if it were gold.

Time—opaque, irrational, nullifying time, the time of chance and of ignorance, the time through which we grope our way—disappears in this perspective. An event is nothing other than a transubstantiation, in short—like the one that determines his life —a naming. A being receives a new essence and a new name. When Genet describes a scene minutely, he does so because it excites him. Moreover, these favored—and, in general, erotic—scenes are *frequentative*. That is, he gathers together in a single narration a hundred events that recurred in the course of time in an identical way. And, in that case, the tale is not, as one might think, a later "digest" of a hundred experiences whose fundamental identity is gradually isolated. On the contrary, the identity is posited at the very beginning; it is the concept that is temporalized, the sacred essence that is projected into and developed in duration. Thereupon, the event becomes a ceremony, and the tale changes into a ritual. At times the characters exchange words, but these words reach us in the flow of the sacred discourse that announces the rites. Most often the words are the rites themselves: "She meets him in the evening on the middle lane of the boulevard, where he tells her very sweetly the story of his life, for he knows nothing else. And Divine says, 'It's not your life story you're telling me, Archangel, but an underground passage of my own, which I was unaware of.' Divine also says, 'I love you as if you were in my belly,' and also, 'You're not my sweetheart, you're myself. My heart or my sex. A branch of me.' And Gabriel, thrilled, though smiling with pride, replies, 'Oh, you little hussy!' His smile whipped up at the corner of his mouth a few delicate balls of white foam." Note the sudden change to the past tense; the *words* are in the present because they are *carmina sacra*.

As for the events which he reports, they are of only secondary interest to him. We know that he loathes history and historicity. In the case of a unique and dated fact that cannot be passed over in silence, Genet limits himself to a summary account of the experience. He describes a petty agitation which has no interest other than that of preparing for the formal appearance of the *essence*. For example, Divine *meets* Gabriel. The onanist hesitates for a long time: in what form will this event give him the most pleasure? Will Gabriel appear in a bar, "presented" by the revolving door? Will he be walking down a steep street? Or will he emerge from a grocery shop? Genet finally does not choose. The circumstances matter little to him, provided they comply with requirements whose origin is his own choice of himself. All that is necessary is that they magnify the meeting without failing to satisfy Genet's deep resentment toward all handsome men. In short, it is a matter of inventing the overwhelming advent of an archangel with the soul of a doll. The revolving door will *present* the handsome soldier in the magnificence of a crystal setting. Immediately Genet compares its incessant rotation to the "mechanism of a Venetian belfry," the effect of which is to transform all who enter, and Gabriel himself, into painted wooden figures. If the soldier goes down "an almost vertical street," he is changed by his movement into an angel who swoops down upon Divine from the sky. Genet immediately re-establishes equilibrium by comparing him, in parentheses, to a bewitched dog. The ringing of the grocery bell preludes the meeting majestically, like a theater orchestra announcing the coming of the emperor. But the soldier who comes out of the shop is holding in his hand a very childish object: a surprise package. Wooden beauty, dog-archangel, emperor with the soul of a doll: slyly and discreetly the tale is composed in such a way as to suggest in the order of the succession the major qualities that constitute the essence of the "boy queens," a staggering beauty, a soul that is a "looming emptiness, sensitive and proud." The story is a projection of the concept into the temporal flow. But time itself is suddenly effaced. All these details have been given only to prepare for a meeting. Now, the meeting is intemporal: "I should have liked to talk to you about encounters. I have a notion that the moment that provoked—or provokes—them is located outside of time, that the shock spatters the surrounding time and space." This is so because the meeting is not to be confused with the clash of two atoms that happen to be projected against each other and that cling to each other. It is the appearance of a celestial form which "of two make but one," a conceptual and intemporal unit that is imposed upon the soldier and the old queen. From that moment on, the characters themselves are transformed. Gabriel becomes *the soldier;*

Divine is no longer Divine, the vicious "camp" who will kill a child and destroy Our Lady: "Aging Divine sweats with anxiety. She *is* a poor woman who wonders, 'Will he love me?' " And the transition from duration to timelessness is marked by the substitution of the present for the past tense. "The revolving door presen*ted* . . . Gabriel appear*ed* . . . he had just *bought* a surprise package . . . he *was* a soldier." And then suddenly: "Divine, of course, *calls* him Archangel. . . . He *lets* himself be worshiped without batting an eyelash. He *doesn't* mind . . ." etc. We are on the inner side of the meeting, in the eternal present of love.

Genet has systematically neglected the particulars. We shall never know what Divine and Gabriel said to each other, which of the two took the initiative of approaching the other, etc. Nevertheless, Genet, like all great writers, is a storyteller, and we shall find in *Our Lady* several accounts of specific and dated events, for example the murder of old Ragon or the trial of Our Lady of the Flowers. But even then the fictional or pseudo-fictional episodes offer a surprising mixture of the temporal and the eternal. Genet, who is both a realist and an idealist, shows himself in his accounts to be both an empiricist and a Platonist. These accounts offer at first the resistance and irrational opacity of the event only to be metamorphosed all at once into classifications and descriptions of essence. In Plato, the hierarchy of ideas represents the immutable truth; the myth introduces time, space and movement into this calm sphere. In Genet, the relations are reversed, but in any case it is art, art alone which, in both writers, links truth to the myth. Art alone enables *Our Lady of the Flowers* to be both the "golden legend" and the botany of the "underworld." It is art that gives this tear- and sperm-soaked manuscript the air of being a "Mirror of the World." G. K. Chesterton said that the modern world is full of Christian ideas run wild. *Our Lady of the Flowers* would surely have confirmed him in his view. It is an "Itinerary of the soul toward God," the author of which, run wild, takes himself for the Creator of the universe. Every object in it speaks to us of Genet as every being in the cosmos of St. Bonaventura speaks to us of God. Sabunde, following Lully, declares that the Creation "is a book," that God "has given us two books," that of Holy Scriptures and that of Nature. Genet reverses the terms. For him, the Book is the Creation of the World; Nature and the Holy Scriptures are one and the same. This is not surprising since, in his view, words contain within themselves the substantial reality of things. The being of the thief is contained in the name "thief." Hence, the being of trees and

flowers, of animals and men, is contained in the words that designate them. For the medieval philosophers, "life is only a pilgrimage
to God: the physical world is the road that leads us to Him. The
beings along the way are signs, signs that may at first seem puzzling
to us, but if we examine them carefully, faith, with the aid of
reason, will decipher, behind characters that are always different, a
single word, a call that is always the same: God."* Replace God by
Genet and you have the universe of *Our Lady of the Flowers,* whose
only reason for being is to express Genet—who has written only in
order to be read by Genet—and to recall him constantly to love of
Genet.†

Each creature is the word incarnate. As in Bonaventura, none
of them is in itself the sufficient reason for its existence; each of
them opens out in order to reveal, in its depths, its creator. In each
of them, multiple forms are graded hierarchically so as to constitute
a unit. Each is a microcosm that symbolizes the whole universe and,
through it, God the creator of the universe. Note how the following few lines recall medieval poetry, the attraction of like by like,
the participations, the magical action of analogy: ". . . children ran
about in the glades and pressed their naked bellies, though sheltered from the moon, against the trunks of beeches and oaks that
were as sturdy as adult mountaineers whose short thighs bulged
beneath their buckskin breeches, at a spot stripped of its bark, in
such a way as to receive on the tender skin of their little white
bellies the discharge of sap in the spring." Whiteness of the little
bellies, whiteness of the moon. At the contact of the children's
flesh, the trees become flesh and their sap sperm. The tree symbolizes the man. In the following passage, the man symbolizes an
entire forest: "Under his rough blue bark he wore a white silk
shirt, which blends with the oriflamme of Joan of Arc that floats
very blandly at the end of a banner, sole pillar of a basilica."‡ And
finally he symbolizes everything, he is a little world that concen-
trates the great world within itself: "What is a malefactor? A tie
dancing in the moonlight, an epileptic rug, a stairway going up flat
on its belly, a dagger on the march since the beginning of the
world, a panicky phial of poison, gloved hands in the darkness, a
sailor's blue collar, an open succession, a series of benign and
simple gestures, a silent hasp." And: "Swallows nest under his arms.
They have masoned a nest there of dry earth. Snuff-colored velvet

---

* Gilson, *La Philosophie au Moyen Age.*
† *"Creatura mundi est quasi quidam liber in quo legitur Trinitas fabricatix."*
‡ This passage was dropped from the revised edition.—Translator's note.

caterpillars mingle with the curls of his hair. Beneath his feet, a
hive of bees, and broods of asps behind his eyes."* Genet's reveries
about words ("the poetry . . . contained in the word *esclave* [slave],
in which are found . . . the word *clé* [key] and the word *genou*
[knee]"† recall those of Vincent de Beauvais and Honorius of
Autun (*mulier = mollis aer; cadaver = caro data vermibus*) ; his
bestiary evokes that of Alexander Neckham. When he writes, for
example: "Certain animals, by their gaze, make us possess at one
swoop their absolute being: snakes, dogs," he brings to mind the
definitions in *The Book of the Treasure:* "The cock is a domestic
bird that dwells among men and by its voice tells the hours of the
day and night and the changes of the weather . . . when the crocodile conquers men, it weeps as it eats them." Our industrial twen-
tieth century has witnessed the birth of three medieval edifices, of
unequal value: the work of Giraudoux, *Ulysses* and *Our Lady of
the Flowers*.

Thus, Genet is God. When he was free, he wished to be only the
object of providential solicitude, and if he identified himself with
Providence, he did so chiefly to be sure of being well treated. In
short, he was still *of the world*. In prison, he lets go, he drifts out of
the universe. In the isolation of the cell, the captive's imagination
takes a cosmic turn. He gives his characters the All for setting.
"Darling is a giant whose curved feet cover half the globe as he
stands with his legs apart in baggy, sky-blue silk underpants."
"Your face, like a lone nocturnal garden in Worlds where Suns spin
about." And again: "Snow was falling. About the courtroom, all
was silent. The Criminal Court was abandoned in infinite space,
all alone. It had already ceased to obey the laws of the earth.
Swiftly it flew across stars and planets." In a later work too, Genet
will revert to this strange longing of a soul that wants to be all
because it is nothing: "A blazing or casual meditation on the
planetary systems, the suns, the nebulae, the galaxies will never
console me for not containing the world. When confronted with
the Universe, I feel lost." In fact, even when the Universe is not
mentioned, it is present; it slips into Divine's garret, into the
dormitories of the reform school. The silence of the young inmates
is "the silence of the jungle, full of its pestilence, of its stone
monsters . . ."; "the hand of the man condemned to death . . .

---

* Cf. *Elucidarium:* "The flesh of man is the earth, his breath is the air, his blood the
water, the fire is his vital heat, his eyes are the sun and the moon, his bosom receives the
humours of the body as the sea the waves," etc.

† Or his verbal prankishness: "Wagram, battle won by boxers!"

which I see when he puts it through the grating of his cell . . . is the Space-Time amalgam of the anteroom of death." Time and again Genet says of his heroes that they are "alone in the world." And when he refuses Divine the happiness of loving and being loved so as to doom her more surely to the heaven of his black mystique, he apologizes for not saving her by "a great *earthly* love." The adjective stresses Divine's relationship with the entire globe. In short, his characters are not first defined by the relations they maintain with their fellows but by the place they occupy in Creation. Before being human and social, the persons and events have a religious dimension: they have dealings with the All. If Divine and Darling suddenly become conscious of themselves and their solitude, they could say, with the mystics, "God, the world and I." And God, of course, is the great barbaric goddess, Genet, the Mother, Genemesis, who probes them with her fingertip. And as if that were still not enough, this savage demiurge takes pleasure in the universalizations, the morbid generalizations that are found particularly in schizophrenics. Every event refers to the entire world because it makes the individual think of all the events of the same type that are taking place on earth at the same moment: "The corpse of the old man, of *one of those thousands of old men whose lot is to die that way,* is lying on the blue rug." In the outhouse, the child Genet finds "a reassuring and soothing peace . . . [feels] mysteriously moved, because it was there that *the most secret part of human beings* came to reveal itself." At other times, he starts from the universal, then, on a sudden impulse, stops short at a particular exemplar, just as Napoleon would suddenly swoop down on one of the soldiers of his Old Guard and pinch his ear: "Recently [the guards] have been wearing a dark blue uniform. . . . They are aviators fallen from the sky. . . . They are guardians of tombs." And so on for two pages. Then, suddenly, laterally, at the turn of a sentence, Genet introduces *a* guard, who seems the embodiment of all jailers. "Not a flower bespatters their uniform, not a crease of dubious elegance, and if I could say of one of them that he walked on velvet feet, it was because a few days later he was to betray, to go over to the opposite camp, which is the thieving camp. . . . I had noticed him at Mass, in the chapel. At the moment of communion, the chaplain left the altar. . . ." It is as if a movie camera, as in King Vidor's *The Street,* were first trained on the city, ranged slowly over the panorama, stopped at *a* house, approached a window, slid along ideal rails, entered *a* room and there, from among a thousand characters, all more or less alike, suddenly focused upon *an* individual who thereupon woke up and started living. This is the sport of a god.

Apart from the very particular case of philosophical intuition, one is rarely able to perceive creatures against the background of the universe, for the reason that they are all involved in the world and are equally part of it. If a given clerk, a given magistrate, wanted to view the earth in perspective, he would have to cut himself off from his function, his family, would have to break the bonds of his social relationships and, from his self-enclosed solitude, consider men as if they were painted objects. The novelist himself often has difficulty in establishing this distance between himself and his creation. No sooner are his characters conceived than they enter into various relationships with other characters, and the latter with others, and so on. The author exhausts himself in the effort to follow these relations in detail; he sees things and people through the eyes of his heroes, who are threatened by specific dangers and thrust into particular situations; he never has the leisure to raise his head and take a commanding view of the whole. In fact, if he has any fellow feeling for the human beings about whom he is writing, he will plant his feet on the ground with them. Only a god can take a lofty view of his work and of the living creatures that people it, and he can do so because he has never been in the world and has no relation with it other than that of having created it. A god, or a pariah whom the world has rejected. Society excluded Genet and locked him out; it drove him from nature. He was forced from the very beginning into the solitude that the mystic and the metaphysician have such difficulty in attaining: "The whole world that mounts guard around the Santé Prison knows nothing, wishes to know nothing of the distress of a little cell, lost amidst others." For this captive, the universe is everything that is denied him, everything from which the walls of his prison separate him. He, in turn, rejects what is denied him; his resentment finishes the job: "The world of the living is never too remote from me. I remove it as far as I can with all the means at my disposal. The world withdraws until it is only a golden point in [a] somber . . . sky." When he creates an imaginary universe on paper, he produces it at a respectful distance. It is the same universe from which he was excluded, as far away and inaccessible as the other, and it discloses totality because of its remoteness. This absence of connection with external reality is transfigured and becomes the sign of the demi-urge's independence of his creation. He works at arm's length, he stands clear of the object he is sculpting. In the realm of the imaginary, absolute impotence changes sign and becomes omnipotence. Genet plays at inventing the world in order to stand before it in a state of supreme indifference. The "golden point in a somber sky" ends by becoming the sole object of the creator's efforts, just as it is the object of all the captive's thoughts. He molds his characters— even those who have no function other than that of exciting him —out of common clay, at a distance, and they appear to him at once in their relation to the All. Divine and Darling are inhabitants of Montmartre and Montmartre is a province of the Universe. They meet on the street to which Genet will perhaps never go back; they frequent bars to which he cannot return. They are *beings of the outside* and their *involvement in all Being* is not meant to manifest to Genet *his* own presence but to let him see his absence from All in the most favorable light, to convince him that this absence is deliberate. If he is not in the midst of men, it is because he has drawn them from clay and fashioned them in his own way, it is because he governs their destinies. Since the pariah and God are alike external to nature, it will suffice for the pariah, in his cell, to dare invent being: he will be God. Genet creates in order to enjoy his infinite power. However, his too-human finiteness makes it impossible for him to conjure up the celestial sphere and the globe in the detailed distinctness of their parts; he sees the world as a big, dark mass, as a dim jumble of stars, *as a background*. Genet fakes; unable to follow the royal progression of Creation, he creates his heroes *first* so as to introduce *afterward* into each of them a primordial and constituent relation to the universe. No matter—it suffices to look at Divine or Darling in order for this unseen, unnamed universe which they imply to spread its dark velvet about them.

To us, this overweening pride and reckless unhappiness often seem exquisitely naïve. The just man, immersed in his community, determines each individual's importance, including his own, by means of an infinite system of reference in which each man serves as a measure for all and each. Whatever the object he considers, he knows that its dimensions vary with the perspective, distance or unit of comparison, that what appears to him to be a mountain will be a molehill to someone else and that the other's point of view is neither more nor less true than his. But Genet, who is shut in, has no point of comparison. If he serves a two-year sentence, he is equidistant from Brazil and the Place Pigalle, that is, two years away. He does not touch the earth; he soars above it. Since he is equally absent from everything, his imagination is omnipresent;

he is not in space. Every object therefore takes on for him the dimensions his fancy confers upon it, and these dimensions are *absolute,* that is, they are not given as a relationship of the object with other objects but as the immediate relationship of the thing to its creator. They can increase or diminish without those of the other varying, and since Genet wishes to ignore the severe and disagreeable laws of perspective—which are all right for the free citizens of French society—a hoodlum in Montmartre and a star in the sky seem to him equally close. Often he amuses himself by enlarging or shrinking a victim (all things remaining equal, moreover), in order to punish or test or glorify him. This ghastly book has at times the naïve poetry of the early astrolabes and maps of the world. Against a background of oceans, mountains or fields of stars appear animals and persons—the Scorpion, the Ram, Gemini—all of the same size, all equally alone. But this strange freshness is only an appearance. We sense behind it the maniacal will—which has become exacerbated in prison—to regard the Nay as the symbol of the Yea and the Nought as the symbol of the All. Precisely because he feels lost "when confronted with the universe," he wants to delude himself into thinking that he is creating the universe. If his characters are cosmic, it is because he is confined in "the obscene (which is the off-scene, not of this world)." The God of the Middle Ages wrote "the book of creatures" to reveal his existence to man, his only reader. Similarly with Genet: his "book of creatures" is *Our Lady of the Flowers,* and he intends it for only one reader, only one man, himself. By their suffering and purity, Our Lady and Darling, saints and martyrs, bear witness before this wonder-struck man to his Divine existence.

So Genet has become God in reverie. He creates the world and man in his image; he manipulates the elements, space, light-years; he has gone quite mad. But the awakening is contained in the dream, for in the depths of his delirium this imaginary creator of Reality connects with himself as a real creator of an imaginary world. His feeling of omnipotence leaves him with a taste of bitterness and ashes. His characters are too docile; the objects he describes are both blinding and too pallid. Everything collapses, everything ends; only the words remain. To be frightened, at the height of one's powers, by silence and the void, to elect to be God, to produce beings by decree and to find oneself a man and a captive, to feel a sudden need of others in the lofty pride of solitude, to count on others to confer upon one's creatures the flesh, density and rebelliousness that one is incapable of giving them—such is the lot of the creator of images. The artist is a god who has need of human beings. It is not through their self-sufficiency that the creatures escape their creator, but through their nullity. Genet and Jouhandeau, ambushed in Nothingness, hoped to avoid the gaze of God, who sees only Being. Their fictions play the same trick on them. Owing to the modicum of reality that Genet communicates to her, Divine *is Genet.* She merges with him; she dissolves into a kind of turbidity, into moistness and swoons. She can *be Divine* only insofar as she is not Genet, that is, insofar as she is *absolutely nothing.*

Thus, the characters in *Our Lady of the Flowers,* born, for the most part, of Genet's fancy, change into quiet exigencies; they will live only if he believes in them. Genet the creator therefore calls Genet the reader to the rescue, wants him to read and be taken in by the phantasmagoria. But Genet cannot read his work; he is too aware that he has put into it what he wanted to find in it, and he can find nothing in it precisely because he cannot forget what he has put into it. So long as he fondled them in reverie, the figures seemed domesticated and familiar; when they are set down on paper, they are reproaches, shadows that can neither take on flesh and blood nor vanish, and that beg *to be:* "Forget what you know, forget yourself, prefer us, imagine that you're meeting us, believe in us." And since Genet is powerless to animate them, to confer *objectivity* upon them, they beg to exist for all, through all. If the "book of creatures" was composed in order to tell men about God, there had to be a God to write it and men to read it, and Genet cannot be God and man at the same time. Now that his dreams are written down, he is no longer either God or man, and he has no other way of regaining his lost divinity than to manifest himself to men. These fictions will assume a new objectivity for him if he obliges others to believe in them. And at the core of all his characters is the same categorical imperative: "Since you don't have faith enough to believe in us, you must at least make others adopt us and must convince them that we exist." In writing out, for his pleasure, the incommunicable dreams of his particularity, Genet has transformed them into exigencies of communication. There was no invocation, no call. Nor was there that aching need for self-expression that writers have invented for the needs of personal publicity. You will not find in Genet the "fateful gift" and "imperiousness of talent" about which the high-minded are in the habit of sounding off. To cultivated young men who go in for literature, the craft of writing appears first as a means of communication. But

Genet began to write in order to affirm his solitude, to be self-sufficient, and it was the writing itself that, by its problems, gradually led him to seek readers. As a result of the virtues—and the inadequacies—of words, this onanist transformed himself into a writer. But his art will always smack of its origins, and the "communication" at which he aims will be of a very singular kind.

ON THE FINE ARTS CONSIDERED AS MURDER

> *Allow a poet who is also an enemy to speak to you as a poet and as an enemy.*
>
> —The Child Criminal

It is within the framework of Evil that Genet makes his major decision. Moreover, he has not at all given up stealing: why should he? It is hard to imagine him renouncing burglary for belles-lettres the way a repentant embezzler gives up swindling and opens a shop. "The idea of a literary career would make me shrug." When he writes these words, he has already had two plays performed and has published a volume of poems and four of his great books; he is completing the fifth and is preparing a film scenario; in short, it is the moment when people are beginning to talk about his work. All the more reason for affirming his loathing of the idea of having a literary career. Each of his works, like each of his thefts, is an isolated offense which may be followed by other offenses but which does not require them and which is self-sufficient. In each of them he bids farewell to literature: "If I finish this book, I finish with what can be related," he says in *Miracle of the Rose.* "The rest is beyond words. I must say no more. I say no more and walk barefoot." And in *Funeral Rites:* "If I submit to the gestures [of thieves], to their precision of language, I shall write nothing more. I shall lose the grace that enabled me to report news of heaven. I must choose or alternate. Or be silent." And in *The Thief's Journal:* "This book is the last . . . for five years I have been writing books. I can say that I have done so with pleasure, but I have finished."

This mania for taking leave may make us smile: one would think he were Mayol bidding farewell to the stage. But it is true that Genet's creative act is a summing-up. *All* the basic themes of his thought and life are to be found in each of his works; one recognizes the same motifs from book to book: would anyone dream of reproaching him for this? If so, one would have to condemn Dostoievsky for having written the same novel over and over and Kafka for having written the same story a hundred times. Nothing is more foreign to Genet than the prudence of men of letters who are careful to reveal themselves gradually—a little bit of oneself in each work—so as to remain new for a longer time.

And, in another respect, he is even further removed from Zola and the famous *nulla dies sine linea*. He would find it intolerable to force himself, day after day, to work away patiently, like a craftsman: literature would become an honest trade, a livelihood. When, after long months of idleness, he is seized by a desire to write a book, he sets to work immediately and keeps going day and night until the job is done. Or rather he considers it to be done when the desire ceases. Often he slackens before the end and quickly knocks off the last few pages. In *Our Lady of the Flowers,* he suddenly declares that "Divine is beginning to bore him"; in *Querelle of Brest,* he writes: "A sudden weariness made us drop *Querelle,* which was already beginning to peter out." He scamps the conclusion of *The Thief's Journal.* He has no particular desire to produce a "well-made work"; he is unconcerned with *finish,* with formal perfection: for him, beauty lies elsewhere, in the ceremonious splendor of sacrilege and murder. When the criminal impulse is satisfied, he lets go, finishes off as quickly as possible, shuts up shop and returns to everyday life. The creative tension, like the orgasm, is followed by a period of relaxation and dejection in which the very thought of writing is repulsive to him. And it is not the least strange or least charming feature of these severe and classical structures, these ceremonious and complicated works of architecture, that suddenly they soften, "peter out" and come to a stop, as if the artist, who is so contemptuous, so haughty, were finally turning his contempt upon himself, as if the "wily hoodlum" were saying to the poet: "I'm sick and tired of your nonsense."

But what chiefly repels Genet in the man of letters is that he remains, regardless of what he does, on the right side of the barricade. The literary man is, to be sure, a liar: literature is a tissue of lies and hoaxes, it hides everything, it hushes up scandals, and if a writer does speak out, his work is expurgated or burned; but that is precisely why the window dressing of the man of letters gets an official stamp; he is honest, he does not misrepresent his merchandise: he writes to meet the demand and sells his products at the official price; often he specializes and builds up a clientele which he does his best to please. Genet does not deign to be a shopkeeper, particularly an honest shopkeeper: he is unconcerned about the demand, he offers nothing; above all, he does not want to please his readers. He wants to make money from his writings, but on condition that the money be obtained by fraud: the purchaser will derive no advantage from his acquisition, it is unusable; Genet lies no more than does an academician, but he lies otherwise and his lies are not edifying. The fact is that if he prefers the work of art to theft, it is because theft is a criminal act which is derealized into a dream, whereas a work of art is a dream of murder which is realized by an act.

"I remained forever haunted by the idea of a murder that would detach me from your world irremediably." What tempts him in crime is not blood, and even less the suffering and cries of the victim or the soft sound of the knife entering the flesh, but rather the glory it procures. In this "irremediable detachment" we recognize "the infamous glory" of the condemned man. As we have seen, a "beautiful" murder breaks through the police barrier, installs itself in the consciousness of honest folk, violates it, fills it with horror and giddiness; the great criminals are more famous than honorable writers who are their contemporaries; there are people who remember the name of Landru but who never knew or have forgotten that of M. René Doumic. No doubt, Genet knows perfectly well that he will not kill anyone. But since murderers achieve glory by forcing good citizens to dream about Crime, why should he not enjoy similar glory by forcing them to dream about it without becoming a criminal? The criminal kills; he *is* a poem; the poet *writes* the crime; he constructs a wild object that infects all minds with criminality; since it is the specter of the murder, even more than the murder itself, that horrifies people and unlooses base instincts, Genet will call forth this specter within society. Crime is the major theme of his works;* all the other motifs twine round this black marble, like the queens round the pimps. Genet's work resembles the symbolic sacrifices that replace human sacrifice in religions which become humanized. Everything is pres-

---

* Except *The Thief's Journal*, which closes a period of his agitated life and which is more a commentary by the poet on his writings than a poem.

ent: the officiant, a corpse in effigy, everything but the blood. A
fake murderer who has really been sentenced to death haughtily
confesses, from the top of the scaffold, to his crime. All of Genet's
books ought to be called *"Exécution capitale"*—in every sense of
the term.*

The fact that society considers these imaginary confessions to be
felonious is sufficient proof that they are mitigated crimes. The
poem of the evil action is itself an evil action. Moreover, it is fitting
that the fate of the work reflect that of its author. The book, which
is a corpus delicti, must be hounded, forbidden, like Genet himself; our author writes so that they will prevent him from writing;
if they do not succeed, so that they will prevent him from publishing; if they fail again, so that they seize his writing and try to
suppress it. Unlike our "great minds" who proclaim the non-
responsibility of the writer, he means to pay for his work, and the
greatest tribute one could pay him would be to imprison him for
inciting to murder. It would thus be manifest to everyone that his
literary creation is indeed an act and that it undermines the foundations of our society. The wild object, which is an apology for
evil, a felonious work of a delinquent, must exercise, by a return
shock, a magical action on Genet's life and provide him with the
blackest of destinies. Creation will then really be a *Passion:* a passion because the author suffers, in the realm of the imaginary, with
the sufferings of his heroes and because his characters' crimes will
entail further persecutions in real life. He writes proudly: "If I am
worthy of it, [my book] will reserve for me the infamous glory of
which it is the grand master, for to what can I refer if not to it? . . .
Is it not logical that this book draw my body along and lure me to
prison?"

Before writing, what is he? An insignificant little worm, a bug
that scurries, unnoticed, between the slats of the floor. He has a
feeling that he is horrifying all of Society, but he also knows that
this horror is purely virtual and that, moreover, it relates to the
thief *in general,* to *any* delinquent and not to Jean Genet. Society
condemns theft: but it does so without thinking about it, by means
of a specialized organ whose function is precisely to substitute
systematic and general repression for diffuse repression, in short
to hush up scandal. The culprit's crimes *never* come to the knowledge of the just man; the just man *never* thinks about the culprit;
as a citizen of a democracy, he alone is qualified to punish, and the

---

* The term *exécution capitale* means "capital punishment." But the author is suggesting
that it can mean "major work" as well.—Translator's note.

judiciary power emanates from him, as do all powers: but he has delegated his functions to the police, magistrates and prison guards and no longer thinks about the matter. The contempt which these civil servants display for Genet in the name of the just man is not true contempt: it is impersonal, professional, like the smile of a salesclerk; they are paid to display it. As an anonymous object of an impersonal and, in general, virtual loathing, Genet is, in point of fact, ignored, forgotten: he squirms about in a shaft of light, blinded by the gaze that Society has been fixing upon him since his childhood; this gaze penetrates him to the soul and sears all his thoughts; he is public, never alone with himself. But *at the same time* he knows that *nobody* is looking at him, that nobody, except a few cops, is aware of his existence. He would like to cry out to them: "Look at me, I'm a criminal, it's you who have condemned me." No one hears him, people come and go, he calls out to them. Wasted effort. He will end by believing that he is invisible. If he has been dreaming since childhood of horrifying them *for good,* it is in order to be able to feel that he exists for someone and to transform these phantom witnesses into a real audience. He wants the dead gaze which enveloped him to sparkle, and, since the relationship which constitutes him in his very core is a relationship to all, he wants to actualize his dimension-for-the-Others. Whoever sees him despises him, but nobody sees him: how restful it must be to be seen: "The newspaper photo shows Nadine and her husband leaving the church where the priest has just married them. She is stepping across the swastika. The people of Charleville are looking at her hostilely. 'Give me your arm and close your eyes,' her husband must have murmured to her. She walks smilingly toward the French flags which are bedecked with crepe. I envy this young woman's bitter and haughty happiness." Genet steals so that people will think about him, so that he, too, can become a taboo object: *an object of loathing.* Loathing is closer to love than indifference. The perfidious solicitude that an examining magistrate shows for him in order to trip him up is, as we know, enough to make him confess to his crime: "a trifle would suffice" for that solicitude to become tenderness. When he was a child, other children spat in his face: "Yet, a trifle would have sufficed for that ghastly game to be transformed into a courtly game and for me to be covered with roses instead of spit. For as the gestures were the same, it would not have been hard for destiny to change everything: the game is being organized . . . the youngsters make the gesture of tossing . . . it would cost no more for it to be happiness. . . . I awaited the roses. I prayed

God to alter his intention ever so little, to make a wrong movement so that the children, ceasing to hate me, would love me. . . . I was then invested with a higher gravity. I was no longer the adulterous woman being stoned. I was an object in the service of an amorous rite." When love is absent, blame and sanction are sacralizing rites. No sooner has Querelle killed than he belongs to all; he thus becomes a sacred object. What Genet wants is to become an accessory of the cult, a ritual object. But the more he steals, the less they are concerned with him. And furthermore, although he feels, in the scene related above, that he is being metamorphosed into an object, he has no perspective that would enable him to enjoy his objectivity: the latter is only a flight of all his being into the fathomless freedom of his tormentors. A later experience suggests another ruse to him: instead of becoming an object for the others, why not identify himself with a particular, material object that would be the butt of their hatred? He would then be able to see himself: he would see *the object that he is,* shining with their gobs of spit, shimmering in the light of their gazes. That is what happened once in Barcelona: the police arrest him; before jailing him, they search him and confiscate a tube of vaseline that he used when making love. The ignominious accessory is taken from him and put on a table; it becomes Genet himself: firstly because it is his property, and secondly because it reveals and symbolizes his homosexuality. "I was in a cell. I knew that all night long my tube of vaseline would be exposed to the scorn—the contrary of a Perpetual Adoration—of a group of strong, handsome, husky policemen. So strong that if the weakest of them barely squeezed two fingers together, there would shoot forth, first with a slight fart, brief and dirty, a ribbon of gum which would continue to emerge in a ridiculous silence. Nevertheless, I was sure that this puny and most humble object would hold its own against them; by its mere presence it would be able to exasperate all the police in the world; it would draw upon itself contempt, hatred, white and dumb rages. It would be slightly bantering—like a tragic hero amused at stirring up the wrath of the gods—indestructible, like him, faithful to my happiness, and proud." The tube of vaseline, which is an effigy of Genet, flouts the cops *by its inertia.* Genet "in person" would be less able to resist them: he is sensitive, he can suffer. The inertia of the matter represents an invincible haughtiness, and yet this matter is haunted by a soul. Sheltered from blows and insults, Genet can peacefully dream in his cell about that obstinate little brute which he has delegated to receive them, in short he can take pleasure in himself.* Although he remained passive during the operation: it was purely by chance that the policemen found the tube in his pocket.

But what if he gave himself, *by an act,* the power of existing elsewhere, in all his virulence, for horrified minds? What if he conferred ubiquity upon himself with his own hands? What if he deliberately invented a way of embodying himself in strange substances and forced the others to discover him there? Then the contempt of "all the police in the world" would no longer be undergone but demanded, and the bantering pride of the inanimate object would rightly express Genet's irony. Hidden behind a wall, this crafty hoodlum could enjoy at will the astonishment of decent people. He would *see* them *seeing* his image, and they would become objects for him precisely insofar as his reflection was an object for them. We have just defined the work of art according to Genet: it is an object of horror, or rather *it is Genet himself engendering himself by a criminal act as an object of universal horror and turning this horror into his glory because he has created himself in order to provoke it.* In *Our Lady of the Flowers* he says of a poem: "I have shat it out." Such is his aesthetic purpose: to shit *himself* so as to appear as excrement on the table of the just. "Without disappointing the enthusiasm of the peasants" Sarah Bernhardt could have appeared in the shape of a little box of matches. Box of matches, tube of vaseline, poem, they are all one. There are wild objects which embody persons. When one produces one of these objects, one is an artist, and when this object arouses horror, one is a criminal to boot. Haunted by the problem of the Other, which is *his* problem, Genet has spent his life meditating on the phenomenon of embodiment. He had to *make himself become* the Other that he already was for the Others. He had tried everything, he had attempted to make himself be reflected by a mirror, by the eyes of a lover, by those of the beloved, to have himself be possessed by the Other, by himself as Other: each undertaking ended in

---

* The sticky tube of vaseline reminds Genet of a beggar woman over whom he had wanted to "slobber." It is apparent that we are dealing here with a "constellation" of images: the child who was dripping with spit compared himself to a penis wet with sperm; and the tube which he uses to smear his penis with vaseline makes him think of a face sticky with slaver. Finally he dreams of smearing the entire body of his lovers with vaseline, and "their muscles bathe in that delicate transparence." We turn to a new theme: that of the transparent veil, of the gauze that puts objects into a kind of aesthetic perspective. One can see the gradual transition from one term to the other. Spit, sperm, vaseline: vitreous transparency which protects bodies and makes them shimmer. The basic image is sperm. Furthermore: the insult appears as a protection of pride. Lastly, tulle: "voracious" beauty derealizes, inserts itself between the gaze and things, like a transparent veil.

failure. Recourse to art is his final attempt: thus far he has been unable to be his own cause except in imagination, since it was the Others who had first, and spontaneously, affected him with this otherness. He now *realizes* this imagination in an object-trap which forces the Others to see him as he wants to be seen. He will be his own creature since his book is himself creating himself as Another and making the others breathe life into his creation. They made a thief of him; he now turns their formidable objectifying power against them and forces them to make him a fish, a flower, a shepherd, whatever he wishes. At last he sees himself, he touches himself: this big banned book that is harried by the police* is he; if you open it, you are suddenly surrounded by characters, who are also he. He is everywhere, he is everything, men and things, society and nature, the living and the dead. Imagine his joy: he lives alone, secretly; he hides from the police; he signs hotel registers with a false name; he effaces his footprints, all traces of his presence; he barely exists: yet he is everywhere; he occupies all minds, he is an object of veritable horror. About his books one could say, without changing a word, what he said about his tube of vaseline: "I was sure that this puny and most humble object would hold its own against them; by its mere presence it would be able to exasperate all the police in the world; it would draw upon itself contempt, hatred, white and dumb rages. It would be slightly bantering . . . indestructible . . . faithful to my happiness and . . . exposed to scorn —the contrary of a Perpetual Adoration."

Will he succeed? Will his clandestine works be able to shock, whereas his thefts, which were more serious offenses, and more severely punished, went unnoticed?

Yes, because Society puts up more easily with an evil action than with an evil word. For specialists, magistrates, criminologists, sociologists, there are no *evil* acts: there are only punishable acts. For the man in the street, there *are* evil acts, but it is always the Others who commit them. Genet wants to reveal to the former that Evil exists and to the latter that its roots are to be found in themselves.

No sooner is the offense committed than it is apprehended, generalized, integrated into statistics, turned over to criminologists, psychiatrists and sociologists whose function is to eliminate the delinquent. When Genet went to Nazi Germany in 1934, he had "the feeling that he was walking about in a camp organized by

---

* All of Genet's books (that is, his nondramatic works) were at first privately printed in limited de luxe editions and sold by subscription. It was not until several years later that they were issued in trade editions.—Translator's note.

bandits"; convinced that the mind of the most scrupulous German "contained treasures of wickedness," he makes the following curious remark: "It is a nation of thieves. If I steal here, I perform no singular action which fulfills me: I obey the usual order. I am not destroying. I am not doing evil, I disturb nothing. Scandal isn't possible. I am stealing in the void." And he longs to "return to a country where the laws of ordinary morality are worshiped." But no sooner has he set foot in France than he discovers that the situation of the thief there is the same as in Germany, though for other reasons: in a moral society, just as in a community of brigands, to steal is "to obey the usual order": is not the rate of criminality as constant as the birth rate or marriage rate? If Genet were to "destroy" this order, he would, by his own force, have to transform the annual crime rate to the point of making it the symptom of a pathological state: only then would it appear to statisticians as a virus, in short as a social disease. But this is an absurd dream: far from modifying the *normal* rate of criminality by his thefts, the thief, who is a *normal* product of social disassimilation, contributes to maintaining it; one does not steal against statistics. In France, as in Nazi Germany, he "disturbs nothing," he is not doing evil, he "steals in the void." In France, as in Nazi Germany, "scandal is impossible," or rather if, by chance, a murder creates a small local disturbance, the collectivity immediately pulls itself together; by means of its machinery of repression, it proceeds to get rid of the culprit physically and leaves to experts the job of disposing of him socially. Society becomes conscious of itself and of its members through scientific knowledge: it sees itself, it describes itself, it sees the thief as one of its innumerable products; it explains him by general factors. When it has finished its work, nothing is left of him. The collective mind is reassured, and the delinquent, doubly bamboozled, physically and mentally vanquished, is swallowed up in the ocean of averages. Genet then realizes that there is no escaping the calculations of statisticians. Since they reflect upon society, one must place oneself on a higher level of reflection and sift from the crimes which they have analyzed the residue that escapes them. Even if, in his dying moment, the criminal should go so far as to repudiate his crime, he remains, in his ignorance and fear, haunted by a supernatural negativity. In like manner, the armchairs that were left in the field were haunted by the human order. The delinquent is a poetic object. "Wretched perhaps when seen from within, [a man's grandeur] is then poetic if you are willing to recognize that poetry is the breaking apart (or rather the meeting at the breaking point) of the visible and the invisible. Culafroy had a wretched destiny, and it is because of this that his life was composed of those secret acts, each of which is a potential poem." Lawyers, judges and psychiatrists see all that is visible and only what is visible: they comprehend the crime in its objectivity, but its poetry escapes them. Genet begins his work where they leave off. Without rejecting their explanations, he discovers and reveals, over and above the facts, the poetic reality. He tells us at times that he is going to rehabilitate criminals and hoodlums. Does that mean he wants to celebrate their virtues, to emphasize the coolness, courage and lucidity that murder requires? Not at all; it is their cowardice that he stresses, their stupidity. To rehabilitate means, for Genet, to attribute poetically to a gratuitous and luxurious will to do evil what sociologists and psychiatrists present as the result of a determinism.

A group of counterfeiters have surrendered without putting up a fight. Everyone who is with Armand condemns them. "They didn't have guts. They got cold feet." Whereupon they seem less exceptional: "If they did all they claimed . . ." One step further and they would enter statistics. Armand *rehabilitates* them: he transforms their failings, their shortcomings, into a will to nothingness: "The moment they saw it was all up, they wanted to give themselves a treat that they never in their lives had time for: getting cold feet." And Genet adds: "His kindness consisted in his transforming into a revel, into a solemn and ridiculous display, a contemptible desertion of duty." Imitating Armand's generosity, Genet will everywhere transform his characters' weaknesses and inadequacies into destructive forces, into corrosive voids. "Darling was cowardly in a magnificent way. I maintain that cowardice is an active quality that, as soon as it takes on this intensity, spreads, like a white dawn, a phantasm about handsome cowardly youngsters." The poet's generosity lies in ascribing consciousness in Evil to the vanquished. As a sexual object, the criminal was a corpse haunted by an inverted consciousness; as a poetic object, he is a dead man haunted by an invisible freedom-to-do-evil. And as this freedom is only an absence, it haunts the experience of criminologists but does not fall within their jurisdiction. It is perhaps sufficient to seek the *explanation* for a crime in the social situation and the criminal's psychopathic makeup, but only a poet can elucidate its *human meaning*. "If your soul is base, call the impulse that drives a fifteen-year-old child to an offense or to crime 'unconsciousness.' But I call it by another name. For it takes real guts, fine courage, to oppose so strong a society." Genet begins by granting to the scientists and the educators that the young criminal does not know what he is doing; but when society triumphs and finds a maladjusted person in this supposed evildoer, when doctors and criminologists start speaking of substituting re-education for repressive sanction, the poet then reverses the terms and redeems the victim by revealing the irreducibility of Evil. When the experts establish the fact that the culprit's responsibility is limited, Genet, without rejecting their conclusions, gives his poetic conclusions: full responsibility; the culprit *deserves* death; and if the criminal admits that he yielded to temptation, to the impulse of the moment, Genet reveals the poetic premeditation over and above this admission; he takes away from Society even the initiative to punish: "The child criminal wants rigor. He demands it . . . they demand that the ordeal be terrible. As for the reformatories, they are indeed the projection on the physical level of the desire for severity buried in the hearts of young criminals." In demanding that jails be ferocious, he disarms Society; all its defenses merely serve evil. And if, on the contrary, it tries to reclaim offenders rather than punish them, he shows the vanity of these "efforts to castrate": "If the inmates at Saint Hilaire or Belle île lead a life that is similar in appearance to that of a trade school, they cannot fail to know what it is that gathers them here, in this particular place: namely evil. And as a result of being kept secret, not exhibited, this reason inflates each intention of each child." If the actual derives from the potential, if the possible is only a particular case of the impossible, if knowledge is in abeyance within the darkness of unknowing, then the world turns upside down; everything is retained, but in an inverted way: in the beginning is Evil, which is a will to discord, an enemy to itself, and which produces being in order *to have something to destroy* and poses the universal so as to be able to achieve, by the violation of every rule, particularity. The Just are the playthings of this evil will; everything they do is turned against them: the only purpose of their science is to mask the urgency of the inexplicable, the only effect of their precautions against crime is to make it more difficult, hence more beautiful; they live in a state of constraint and consume their energy in respecting the law so that the elect may treat themselves to the luxury of breaking it; they think they are a supreme end and a measure of the human whereas they are only the means of the crime and the corpus delicti; their vile existence is justified by only one reason: the murderers need victims. As a thief, Genet served the established order; as a poet of theft, he destroys it. His offenses were unable to ruffle the mind of the just man; but the representation of the offense affects us to our very marrow: if he is right, everything is false; we are big fowl waiting to be eaten, we shall die fooled. Our police and our experts are effective protection against crime; we have no defense against the poetic truth of crime since it lies beyond causes and beyond being, since it is the elusive triumph of those whom our watchdogs have already reduced to impotence; no victory is conceivable against Evil, since it is the fixed gaze of the vanquished who die unreconciled and the secret defeat of the victors. What is to be done about these phantoms? Must we deny poetry? But poetry is an undeniable fact: we may be able to blind ourselves, but we know that this blinding is willful. Shall we declare that Genet is mistaken, that criminals "are not as he sees them"? But it is a delinquent who is speaking—and who is speaking about himself. He will readily grant that the order of Evil is valid for him alone: but that is enough for us to have lost the game. The inexpiable act consists not in doing Evil but in manifesting it.*

Moreover, Genet addresses not the criminologist or sociologist but the "average Frenchman" who adorns himself with the name of good citizen; for it is he who preserves the idea of Evil, while science and law are tending to break away from it; it is he who, burning with desires that his morality condemns, has delivered himself from his negative freedom by throwing it like a flaming cloak on the members of a minority group whose acts he interprets on the basis of his own temptations. What a prey! The Just man is so good at playing innocent that he gets caught up in his own game: evil thoughts remain foreign to him since, by definition, they are the other's thoughts; he encounters them with sad astonish-

---

* But, it may be argued, there are graphs and averages for banned books just as there are for crime: they represent a normal and relatively constant percentage of the literary output. Could we not catch Genet again by showing that his books merely help to maintain this annual percentage? No, for if his thefts are *classifiable*, his books are not. The pornographic novel, like the edifying novel, meets a social demand, satisfies the needs of a particular public. All licentious writings follow the same pattern and are based on well-tested recipes; there is no difference among them except for the names of the places and characters. If the plot remains the same, the reason is that the purchaser does not want it to change; he wants to dream, each time, that he is having the same pleasures in the same order. None of this is very disturbing: these productions satisfy the quirks of a few eccentrics and their stereotyped poverty bores the well-adjusted citizen. Genet's works are not boring, and yet, far from aiming to please a specialized clientele, they are addressed to everyone and aim to displease everyone. Composed with all the resources of art, their value destines them for the objective Mind, while their obscenity forces them to remain clandestine. Beautiful and unpleasant, pursued by the police and extolled by the critics, they belong neither to "special literature" nor to official literature. Clandestine in broad daylight, these paradoxes are unclassifiable and it is by virtue of their singularity that they are disturbing.

ment in the course of his experience and recognizes them precisely by *the fact that they are Other,* by the fact that *he* would not have had the indecency to conceive them. As for the thoughts that spring up in his own mind, they are self-evidently good: they have a transparency, a familiar and simple goodheartedness that inspires confidence at once. In short, he does not know what Evil is. He must learn about it from life, and even then he contemplates it with surprise, without ever quite understanding it. In order to have a thorough knowledge of it, he would have to be, at the same time and in his own eyes, himself and the Other.

Genet, who has been a victim and instrument of the good citizen since childhood, is now able to avenge himself at last: he is going to apply to him the *lex talionis.* He will make that innocent discover the Other in himself; he will make him recognize the Other's most improper thoughts as his own; in short, he will make him experience with loathing his own wickedness. Poetic traps will captivate his freedom and will reflect it to him as being half his own and half alien. He will be forced to see himself and will be able neither to *recognize* himself nor reject himself. It is with words that Genet will lay his traps. Words are the matter and weight of the soul; if they assemble within it to form evil thoughts, the soul is lost. It served as a refuge against threats and suffering: what will be its refuge against itself? The trap is a book, an object as stubborn and inert as a tube of vaseline: black strokes on sheets of paper sewn together. Nothing more. And the object will remain that dead thing which is waiting for nothing, which fears nothing, which continues to grow until its owner himself decides to attend to it, to link up the signs, to project their meanings through the words, to organize the meanings among themselves. No sooner is it opened than an idea emerges, or a feeling, or a vague figure, and the reader knows that these furtive beings were already there in some way, but he also knows that they would not have appeared in that place and on that day without the complicity of his mind. He had only *not* to read, and moreover he can always stop. If he settles down and tries to understand, he constructs a complicated object which exists only through him and which will be dispersed in a multitude of black pothooks as soon as he diverts his attention from it: it is he who draws these phantasms from nothingness and maintains them in being; to read is to perform an act of directed invention. No doubt he does not adhere completely to what he reads; no doubt he waits until he has understood before giving or refusing his assent. But he has already circumvented himself: to understand is to accept; if later he wants to reject this foreign sensibility, he will have to take himself in hand, will have to make a sharp break, will have to tear himself away from the increasing giddiness. His freedom, which keeps the phrase suspended in its light, seeks thoughts everywhere, seeks memories which will facilitate an understanding of the text. If he reads that "beauty is Evil," the sentence has no meaning for him at first: if he wants to understand it, to breathe life into it, to adapt it for his personal use, he must recall the most beautiful faces, most beautiful paintings, that he has seen, those which he has been particularly fond of. No doubt he evokes them only as examples, but that is sufficient: he sees the Other's voracious thinking with his own most inward being, with his beautiful regrets, with his beautiful cares. The words are already hemming him in, giving him, despite himself, a past, a future which he does not recognize: if he wants to understand what he is reading, he must refer to what he has just read; thus, all the paradoxes which he condemns form, despite himself, his immediate past; he senses the existence of others which are on the horizon and which are making a new future for him. Invisible walls surround him; he is in a world which he would not have wanted to create and which would not have been if not for him. He spontaneously shapes his present thoughts and feels himself shaping them: they are indeed his own; and yet, despite their transparency, they have the disquieting depth of the thoughts of others since he does not hear them at first and has to decipher them. You may point out that that is what happens whenever we read a scholarly or philosophical work. But that is not so, for Genet demonstrates nothing. He is far too clever to attack the good citizen head-on, to arouse suspicion by offering theories. No, he relates as simply as can be things that have happened to him. He has a simple way of referring to his own principles as if they were accepted by everyone or of deriving some unacceptable consequence from those of the just man: the bamboozled reader starts by following Genet and then finds himself in the process of affirming the opposite of what he thinks, of denying what he has always affirmed.

Genet is careful not to propose: he *demands*—therein lies his diabolical cleverness. In order for him to fight against the restive attention of his readers, in order to force them to have thoughts which are distasteful to them, there must be a categorical imperative—constantly lurking behind the words—that requires unconditional adherence. In short, the work must be beautiful. I have shown elsewhere that beauty presents itself as an absolute end: it is the free appeal that creative freedom addresses to all other freedoms. And as nothing can be created once and for all, except bridges and dams, since, as Mallarmé says, being has taken place, artistic creation is imaginary: through the work of art it presents the entire world as if it were produced and assumed for human freedom. Formerly the beautiful was an integral part of theodicy: the artist "showed" God his work as the enfeoffed vassal showed his lord the fief which the latter had just given him; he used his freedom to create appearances in order to reflect the supreme freedom which had devoted itself to creating being. Today God is dead, even in the heart of the believer, and art becomes an anthropodicy: it makes man believe that man created the world; it presents his work to him and justifies his having made it. There is an ethic of Beauty; it requires of us a kind of demiurgic stoicism: optimism without hope, acceptance of Evil as a condition of total unity, affirmation of human, creative reality over and above its failures, of a universe that crushes it, assumption by freedom of suffering, faults and death; we must will being as if we had made it.

Genet is quite aware of all this, and there is a certain amount of trickery involved, for, after all, we have not made the world, and, besides, when we yield to the artist's demands, it is *his* universe that we are approving. Genet prepares to make diabolical use of this inconsequential mystification. By the beauty of his style, of his images, by the aesthetic depth of his inventions, by the rigorous, classical unity of his works, he will make us reperform spontaneously the free act that makes it possible to reassume the world: but the world which is assumed will be that of crime. It has been said that beauty in itself is a proof. Precisely: it will prove itself. Now, as we have seen, for Genet the other face of the Beautiful is Evil. Thus, Beauty will be a proof of Evil. Genet tempts us by the best of ourselves; he addresses our generosity, our free will; he demands, as does any artist, that we be a party to his undertaking, at least sufficiently to discover its beauty. We obey this order, as we do whenever we approach a new work: and we find ourselves in the process of accepting for its formal beauty a universe whose moral ugliness repels us. As I have said, there is a stoical and foul optimism of beauty: it asks us to accept pain and death for love of order, of harmony, of unity. Genet plays on this optimism: but it is not *a* particular suffering, *a* fault that he makes us accept in the name of general order, but rather Evil in its entirety. Isn't that the best trick one can play on decent folk? There would be no point in remaining on guard and taking the Beautiful while leaving Evil,

for the Beautiful and Evil are one and the same thing. Indeed, one
is entitled to think that the Beauty of the works will be the verbal
representation of the terrible Beauty of the aesthetic gesture, of that
devouring Ogress who changed Being into appearance. As a woman
reader of Genet has written to me: "When you shake off his prose,
it's too late: you've been hooked by Evil." Too late, yes, for to
read is to reperform the writer's operation of synthetic unification;
it is to will each sentence and to organize it with the others. We
must affirm if we want to understand and must give if we want to
feel. Is the author guilty? If so, the reader too will be guilty. In
short, in openly and frankly asking us to will with him that the
Beautiful be, he has forced us to make Evil exist. We catch ourselves
willing what we do not want, affirming what we have always denied.
Since to read is to re-create, we re-create, for the sake of its beauty,
the homosexual intercourse that is sumptuously bedecked with the
rarest of words. But the words vanish, leaving us face to face with
the residue, a mixture of sweat, dirt, cheap perfumes, blood and
excrement. Is *that* what we willed? Behind us Genet snickers:
"Poetry is the art of using shit and making you eat it." Genet's art
is a mirage, a confidence trick, a pitfall. In order to make us eat shit,
he has to show it to us, from afar, as rose jam. That is the purpose
of the "magnifying judgments" of which we have spoken. In any
case, the purpose is achieved: Genet has got even with us; he makes
us experience the original divorce which transformed the religious
child that he was into a hoodlum. Without ceasing to be himself,
the Just man is already the Other.

But Genet does not yet feel satisfied: the good citizens had endowed him with a fictive and monstrous Ego which he was unable
either to assume or reject; he wants to return it to them and install
it within them. In order to make sure that he is substituting his own
self for that of the reader, he talks about himself in the first person.
Now, regardless of who the writer is, when the sentence starts with
"I," a confusion arises in my mind between this "I" and my own.
No doubt if I saw the other person, if I saw the words come out of
his mouth, I would relate his speech to his person. But I am alone
in my room, and if a voice somewhere utters the words that I read,
it is mine; in reading, I speak in the bottom of my throat and I feel
myself speaking. At the present moment, in this room, there is only
one man who says "I," to wit, myself. Caught in the trap: since, in
order to understand the sentence, I must relate the "I" to a subjectivity, it is to my own that I refer. That is the way in which a reader
of novels spontaneously identifies himself with the character who is

telling the story. "I was afraid; I ran down the stairs": that is all that is needed to endow us with an imaginary past; we have the feeling of gradually recalling the events of a bad dream; little by little someone familiar yet unexpected emerges from the mist: a person suffering from amnesia starts remembering things, the members of his family relate to him his past actions, and, as they begin each story, he wonders anxiously: "What else did I do?"

Note how artfully Genet introduces himself in *Miracle of the Rose:* he is a disenchanted thief who is being carried off to prison. We let ourselves be caught up immediately: we are used to that kind of beginning, we do not disdain to read the books in the *Série Noire** and to identify ourselves with the delinquents. This man can't be really guilty. Besides, what has he done? Stolen. He must have been driven to it by poverty or perhaps a bad environment. Furthermore, he will repent toward the end; that is a law of this type of book; he will find Wisdom in prison, like so many others. The decent man very gingerly sticks his toe into this still water, then makes up his mind and dives in: there he is, filled with pity, in the office of the court clerk; he has become a petty crook who is going to serve his sentence. He has only to turn ten pages to discover himself: *I* am bad, repentant, a homosexual, *I* am a monster. Meanwhile, the story goes on, innocently, as if Genet were sure of our agreement in advance. At times he even apologizes for not having been bad enough: "I could have put his eyes out, torn out his tongue, but after all, one has one's weaknesses." Or else: "I had to rely on a little physical beauty in order to attain Evil." And it is *in us, to us,* that he makes these surprising apologies. It is we who are sorry that we were not bad enough. But there is even more trouble in store for us, for Genet now tells us about his loves. If Restif de la Bretonne informs us of his sexual exploits, we are delighted; we are eager to be that Hercules who is so flattering to our sex; our arms will gallantly carry swooning beauties to a sofa and we shall not refuse to prove our ardor a dozen times an hour. Now, the "I" of *Miracle of the Rose* starts by bewitching us in the same way: it draws us into itself and endows us with its desires. When Genet tells us of his love for Bulkaen, of his vain efforts not to betray his excitement in the presence of the beloved, of the latter's coyness, we cannot refrain from slipping our personal memories into his account: have we not tried to conceal our feeling for a coquette who would have shamelessly taken advantage of them?

---

* A widely read French series of detective stories and thrillers.—Translator's note.

Have we not had the feeling of being detected and played upon?
It is we who are being talked about; or rather *it is we who are talking.* It is we who say: "Two beds away from me is his little face,
which is contorted by some mysterious drama . . . his perfect set of
imperfect teeth, his mean, shifty, look, his stubborn, never satisfied
expression and, under the white, starched shirt, that splendid
body which neither fasting nor blows have been able to impair, as
noble and imperious as I saw it when we went swimming in the
summer—with its heavy torso, the chest like that tool which is
called a maul, at the end of a flexible handle. His waist; his chest
which I also dare compare to a rose whose head is too heavy, on a
stem that bends." Through Genet's eyes I see this young creature,
a new and eternal object of my love; in comparing the person's
chest to a heavy rose, *I* occasion the swelling of two rich and delicate
breasts. But at the same time I know that Bulkaen is a man; and
this knowledge arouses strange feelings in me. Yves Mirande relates
in his memoirs how he met a charming woman at the Opera Ball,
took her home in a carriage, and how, when caressing her, suddenly realized that his conquest was a man in disguise. What he
felt at the moment of this discovery gives a good idea of the state
of mind of the reader of Genet: the horror-stricken desire which
nevertheless remains, unable to fade away, and which persists in
seeking the woman in the unmasked male. That anguished desire
is *our* imaginary desire in the presence of Bulkaen, who is a little
woman, Divers' kid, and at the same time a formidable hoodlum.
Captive of this *I* which I have animated with my own consciousness, I struggle in vain; *it is I* who desire the boy. If I have the
slightest inclination for men, even if it is repressed to my very
depths, I am caught, constrained, in the shame of avowing my tastes
to myself. If I really have no partiality for boys, then *I* become, in
myself, the Other. Another uses me to desire what I cannot desire;
my freedom lends itself, I am possessed by a homosexual zar and,
what is more, voluntarily possessed. If I want to free myself, to
return to myself, then the young hoodlum takes on—without ceasing to be a male—all the secondary characteristics of womanhood:
his skin becomes smoother, his curves rounder, he molts and becomes the most boyish girl I can desire or, more accurately, the
matter grows, as it were, lighter; I find myself in the presence of a
half-abstract, asexual but living and desirable flesh, or, better still,
confronted with the anonymous desirability of all flesh, as an ultimate signification of the words. The very next moment the face of
the androgynous creature has hardened; an adjective has covered

that soft blond skin with a fuzzy fleece; I again become that Other who is an enemy to myself. The right-thinking man, caught up in a whirlwind, oscillates continually from one extreme to the other: either he desires the flesh of a boy who is secretly a girl or he desires the boy insofar as his *I* is a secretly homosexual Other. In *Our Lady of the Flowers,* the web is even better woven, since Genet calls his hero "Divine" and speaks of him in the feminine. Let us listen to him: "Divine was limpid water . . . and just as the wind turns leaves, so she turns heads. . . . From a tiny black satin purse she took a few coins which she laid noiselessly on the marble table top." Who would not desire this charming adventuress? The trouble is that this woman is a man. Homosexual because of the power of words, we taste for a moment, in the realm of the imaginary, the forbidden pleasure of taking a man and being taken, and we cannot taste it without horrifying ourself. "But," you may object, "what if I *really am* homosexual?" Wait! Genet reserves his hardest blows for homosexuals: women do not particularly like each other. He will lead them a little further than us, perhaps to the point of embrace and then, all of a sudden, he will show his cards: filth, shit, organic smells, farts; all of a sudden, that is what you must like if you want to follow him. Will you, like his Hitler, lick your befouled mustache? As you can see, you *must* abandon him sooner or later: but he holds you, and you will follow him with horror to the very end, and the longer you are his accomplice, the more horrified you will be: Genet's worst enemies are to be found among homosexuals.

What does he care about homosexuals? He has played his best trick on decent folk. Fair revenge: formerly it was they who thought inside him; now it is he who thinks inside them. The word *thief* was a bottomless abyss: if they open his books, it is now they who topple over the precipice. His procedure has not varied since the time when he was a young hoodlum who let himself be taken by the Pimps in order to steal their ego. He lets himself be taken by readers: there he is on the shelf of a bookcase, someone takes him down, carries him away, opens him. "I'm going to see," says the right-thinking man, "what this chap is all about." But the one who thought he was taking is suddenly taken. How could Genet dream of a fuller restoration of civil rights, since the Just man who reads him, with veritable and singular passion, loses himself so that Genet may be.

I know: there is a defense. One can pull oneself together, can stop reading, can thrust the book aside with disgust. But, in the first place, Genet expects this disgust, he hopes for it: is it not the inverse of a Perpetual Adoration? He is delighted that, more or less everywhere in the world, his books are the impassive objects of impotent fury. And besides, what is disgust? Quite simply an incipient vomiting. And what you vomit must in some way have been inside you. How Genet laughed at M. Mauriac's painful efforts to vomit him out: he would have liked, I think, to speak to him somewhat as follows: "The disgust which you manifest when confronted with my books is a magical effort to reject that Other who is no other than yourself. But when, in desperation, you make such a fuss, it is already too late. One does not vomit up one's soul, and it is your soul that is rotten. Is there any way of my knowing, when confronted with your wild frenzy, what loathsome instincts have awakened in it? After all, you were considered a specialist in Evil before I appeared on the scene. We are confreres. You, however, had got into the habit of stopping in time, out of respect for your public, or else, after describing lost, ignoble souls, you wrote a preface to praise the divine creation and to recommend that we practice Christian charity. I, on the other hand, do not write a preface. I have led you further than you wanted to go. In unmasking myself, I unmask you. You are an evildoer, like me, but a shamefaced evildoer. Your fury sheds a very singular light on your own works. Wasn't Thérèse Desqueyroux a poisoner? How glad I am to write openly and how the wickedness that dares not speak its name must suffer." He would be greatly disappointed if it occurred to anyone to say to him that M. Mauriac's clownish indignation simply expressed a mediocre author's hatred of a great writer.*

There remains the simple possibility of *not reading* him. That is the only risk he runs, and it is a big one. But, in the last analysis, whether he is read depends *on him,* on him alone. Let his works be beautiful: that is the necessary and sufficient condition for his having readers. And if his reputation is established, the Just man who wants to object to him will force himself to ignore a social and cultural fact. It is this restive gentleman who will make himself conspicuous, who, on at least one score, will dissociate himself from the society in which he lives. If Genet's fictions have sufficient power, they will compel recognition; the community will socialize them in spite of itself, as it has done with Julien Sorel, that murderer, and Baron de Charlus, that homosexual.

---

* The preceding passage refers to a violent attack on Genet by François Mauriac, who, though recognizing Genet's genius, denounced him as an instrument of the devil.— Translator's note.

But the stake is even more complex than we have said: it is not simply a matter of ruining the others, they must save him by ruining themselves. It is *by them* that his Saintliness must be recognized, by them that the term Saint must be applied to him, like a balm on the very spot where the word "thief" had wounded him. He must lead *the others* to declare that "the thief is a Saint."

One can well imagine that they will not make this declaration willingly. And, what is worse, they cannot even understand such a statement, for they will recognize at most that a certain man could have been a thief and have become a Saint or even that a thief can, in other circumstances, and in other respects, behave like a Saint. But the words "the thief (as thief, that is, as culprit) is a Saint" (that is, a man who delivers himself little by little from human guilt) are meaningless to them. We, however, who have been following Genet since childhood have recognized in that sentence a magnifying judgment. Genet must therefore lead the Just man to juggle, in spite of himself, with magnifying judgments. Do these judgments violate common sense, logic, prose? Never mind that: he will start by undertaking a general challenging of prose. If Genet can wrest words from their usual purpose, if he can pervert them, subject them forcibly to monstrous unions, his bewildered, mystified reader will have to declare, despite himself, in favor of final rehabilitation: "Being a thief in my country who had used, in order to become one and to justify myself for having become one, the language of the robbed—who are myself, because of the importance of language—was to give this status of thief the opportunity to be unique." The thief expresses himself in the language of the robbed which has neither words nor concepts to approve of him in his acts or to justify him in his being. Indeed, everything in the language accuses him. He will therefore endeavor to bend to his own glorification an entire language that has been conceived against him. He is willing to express himself as a robbed person, to become such a person. He speaks to his new confreres; he evokes, with their words, objects and acts; he pretends to utilize speech so as to communicate with them. What is the language of the robbed if not quite simply prose? And what does Genet become when he writes in this language if not a prose writer? As a matter of fact, if you open his books, it is the prose that will strike you. He writes like everyone: the Marquise went out at five o'clock. "She had gone to the hospital very early, and when she passed the gate, which a sleepy porter opened for her, the maid found herself in the most flowery of gardens blazoned with dawn. . . . The maid entered. The lecture-hall attendant greeted her very quietly. He was chatting with the coach-man and the undertaker's assistant." This is, of course, lofty, ner-vous prose, prose eager to get it over with, crammed with images, but prose all the same. His broad, cursive writing is ceremonious: it is a speech, a funeral oration, the haughty confession of a man condemned to death. The thought takes shortcuts, uses ellipses, but is expressed in long, noble phrases, often abstract, the architec-ture of which is complicated; whence the curious impression of calm, ample periods consumed by a wild inner speed. Writing is a religious act, a rite suggestive of a Black Mass, and Genet does not dislike pomp: his sentences are difficult and rich, loaded, shimmer-ing, full of old, resuscitated constructions (inversion, ablative abso-lute, subject infinitive) ; he likes to stretch out a sentence until it breaks, to suspend its course by parentheses: deferred and awaited, the movement better reveals its urgency; at the same time, he uses syntax and words like a great lord, that is, like someone who has nothing more to lose; he does violence to them, he invents con-structions, he decides insolently how they are to be used, as in the following admirable sentence: *"Je nomme violence une audace au repos amoureux des périls"* ["I give the name violence to a boldness lying idle and hankering for danger"]. At times precious to the point of oddity, at times incorrect, he never lets his prose be over-shadowed by the object; it pushes itself forward, makes itself con-spicuous and does not allow the reader to overlook it; it wants to leave in the mouth of the one who utters it a violent *flavor of prose* which at times is even slightly sickening. At times he is a stylist who, as Gide says, "prefers himself" and at other times he is quite simply a great writer.

This prose is false. It is so highly adorned only in order to serve all the better as a prey to poetry. Genet has submitted to the lan-guage of the robbed in order the better to betray. In this magnifi-cent instrument which is just a bit too showy, a word opens up from time to time, revealing a gulf; others explode like grenades, which are "dangers for the practical understanding of the discourse." Let us follow the young servant girl who was referred to above in a prosaic language that would have repelled Valéry: she is now walk-ing behind a hearse: "On the balcony of a very simple house ap-peared Hitler. . . . 'Hitler must have recognized me,' thought the maid." And further on: "The maid raised her eyes. She first saw the police station, which is always at the entrance of a village. The policemen were sleeping. . . . The fight against pilfering in the countryside is fatiguing. But had one of them been standing at the window in his untidy uniform and half-open shirt and seen the maid go by, he would not have recognized the wiliest of hoodlums beneath that grief, beneath that extravagant mourning."

That was the point of the patient description of the burial: to make the ground open suddenly beneath our feet, to reveal to us suddenly that the maid whose grief we had finally taken seriously as a result of *seeing* the wretched little thing was only—in whose eyes?—the disguise of the wiliest hoodlum. The hoodlum lifts for a moment the veil of grief and shows us the laughing face of Genet; then the veil falls again and the story continues as if nothing had happened: "She was so weary that she felt smaller than a stone," etc. Have we been dreaming? No: the fact is that Genet's prose is the *medium* of his poetry. It is Being, it is Good: it is therefore created only for Evil; Genet's poetry is a parasite of prose as Evil is a parasite of Good. One never sees it; it appears only *at the expense* of a prose sentence: it is a leprosy of prose. The *order* of his periods, their number, their density, existed only in order to be corroded: for if poetry is murder, it must be given something to murder; and if crime is a systematic destruction of order, there must first have been the most rigorous order. A rebellious young bourgeois will create a reign of terror in language; he will shake words up in a hat and throw them into the air; he will *realize* disorder. As for Genet, he makes of poetic disorder an invisible rot. He is against terror and for rhetoric because it is beautiful to sacrifice the most beautiful prose to poetry. By means of language the Just man has made Genet *a thief:* with the *naming,* this sudden debasement of his being had appeared in the daily web of his acts. Genet thereby experienced the hemorrhage of words: none of them quite belonged to him; each of them had its true meaning *out there,* in the minds of the Just. In short, the Just had installed in Genet's heart an unrealizable signification and a permanent reference to the other; they had forbidden him to use prose. Genet takes his revenge: he lulls the reader's distrust with a prose discourse and then suddenly intervenes, exactly as the Just intervened in his life at the moment of his original crisis; he steals a word, only one, and the reader realizes that it *is spoken,* that his discourses change, in a denominative world, into strange events, the meaning of which escapes him. But poetry cannot be confined; if you walk about at night in a forest where you feel there is a thief, all the trees are thieves, the forest is haunted; the same holds for prose, which is haunted by the poetic catastrophe that one expects at the end of each sentence. By the word "thief" alone you had stolen language from him: he steals it from you in turn.

The basic element, the fundamental poetic unit, is, as one surmises, the magnifying judgment. In every way and by every possible means Genet must be able, at any moment, suddenly to reveal to the reader that he is no longer safe in language; he must be able to upset the balance, to cause a small verbal breakdown by asserting that a no is a yes, that an evil is a good, that $-1 = +1$. These judgments dig holes in discourse: they transform being into appearance and dissolve the appearance in nothingness. It goes without saying that Genet does not introduce them without preparation: he must put the reader into the right state of mind. But he contrives at the same time to preserve their shock effect. He will little by little incite the reader to make a point of effecting this unrealizable signification: if the just man is convinced, he will make vain efforts, and when he leaves the word or sentence he will remain convinced that *someone* must be able to grasp it. He will then have the impression that the words are turning away from him and are going off to be understood elsewhere, by someone else, and that the simplest language has a double meaning. I shall give three examples of these "preparations."

Thus, the preparation for a magnifying judgment: "To vomit on his mother's hands is to pay her the finest tribute." Here is how Genet will go about it: "A little old woman . . . approached me, told me she was very poor, and asked for a little money. The gentleness of this moonfish face revealed to me at once that the old woman had just come out of jail.

" 'She's a thief,' I said to myself. As I walked away from her, a kind of intense reverie . . . led me to think that it was perhaps my mother. . . . I know nothing of her who abandoned me in the cradle, but I hoped it was that old thief. . . .

" 'What if it were she?' I thought. . . . Ah, if it were, I would cover her with flowers, with gladiolus and roses, and with kisses! I would weep with tenderness over those moonfish eyes, over that round and foolish face! 'And why,' I went on, 'why weep over it?' It did not take my mind long to replace the customary marks of tenderness by some other gesture, even the vilest and most contemptible, which I empowered to mean as much as the kisses, or the tears, or the flowers.

" 'I'd be glad to dribble all over her,' I thought, overflowing with love. [Does the word *glaïeul* (gladiolus) mentioned above bring into play the word *glaviaux* (gobs of spit)?] To dribble on her hair or vomit into her hands. But I would adore that thief who is my mother."

Diabolical cleverness: everything is brought into play to lead us to justify the final proposition. First trap: the abandoned child will love his mother, whatever her occupation, *even* if she is a thief. This is calculated to satisfy our morality, which requires that one respect one's parents, whatever they are. In the sentence: "I know nothing of her who abandoned me in the cradle, but I hoped that it was that old thief" there is a discreet appeal to pity. Genet feels so alone that he wants to find his mother, even if it be in the person of a stupid old thief. Of course, this pious twaddle conceals his resentment: it is partly out of vengeance on his mother that he takes pleasure in imagining her on the lowest level of abjection, and partly to deride the filial respect which the Just require. But none of this is said, and he plays on a misunderstanding: what can he expect, says the just man to himself, what can this bastard, this thief, expect if not a mother who is a beggar? And he is grateful to Genet for the humility of his wishes: Genet might have wished that his mother were a duchess, since he knows nothing about her. But no, he will be content with that little old woman. That proves he is conscious of his unworthiness. The just man will thus be moved to pity when Genet confides to him his dream of covering the old woman with kisses and flowers. He is caught: he trustingly embodies himself in Genet; it is he who weeps with tenderness "over that round and foolish face." The terms "round and foolish face" do not shock him; they refer to the first impression that Genet felt in the presence of a woman who, after all, is not his mother; they show, thinks the just man, that filial love is not to be measured according to the merits of the object to which it is addressed. Isn't that what is required of mother love; mustn't one love *in advance,* whatever he or she may be, the child or the mother that fate has given? It is at that moment that Genet starts the conversion: since he is in the depths of humility, since he, a thief, has found a mother who is a thief, since he deliberately refuses to dream of a brilliant birth, why not go to the very limit of modesty? Those flowers and tears bear witness to excessive pride. Are they really proper among these pariahs, these untouchables? The deeper the love, the more discreet it should appear. Isn't he ridiculing that poor old woman by covering her with flowers? Isn't that tantamount to wanting to make of her a noble mother, a duchess? And does the thief have a right to give flowers? Any gesture will be preferable, provided it *signify* tenderness. Here, too, Genet knows how to win his reader's approval: he is backed by proverbs: *"How* one gives is more important than *what* one gives. It's the intention that counts," etc. Deeply moved, the reader imagines a furtive contact, a slight clenching of the hand: the thief is giving *all* that he can give. He charges the most humble gift with his tremendous love. It is the widow's mite. But in that case, why, between these vile, reprehensible beings, who nevertheless love each other, would not the best language be the most reprehensible, the vilest? The reader grows a bit uneasy but sees no reason for stopping. Furthermore, before he has time to catch his breath he reads: "I'd be glad to dribble all over her." And there we have the decent man in the act of puking on his old mother. Even if he then pulls himself together, he does not quite realize what has happened: the reasoning seemed to him to be correct and to proceed from lofty ideas: even now he feels that this whole reverie has a meaning: he cannot shake off the impression that there is another world where, for other minds, the mark of the deepest contempt is identical with a show of the deepest respect. Genet requires no more: he has captured the just man's freedom and has forced it to give a semblance of existence to the false as a parasite of the true, to the impossible as a transcendence of all possibles. We have seen that saintliness represents for him the instant in which the destructive changes back into the constructive, in which zero is identified with plenitude, in which the mystery of the impossible nothingness reveals that of the ineluctable substance. Thus, the structure of the poetic sentence very accurately reflects the ontological structure of saintliness. And the reader, who is drawn by the thief's art into the pursuit of the impossible adequation of nothingness with Being, of privation with abundance, realizes, in Genet's stead, the asceticism of the Black Saint. To be a poet means, for Genet, to become a Saint in the realm of the imaginary through intermediaries.

" 'The gardener is the loveliest rose in his garden' ": this sentence, which is casually slipped in among twenty others, like a counterfeit coin among genuine ones, is protected only by its air of innocence and its comfortable banality. A hasty reader sees that a young man is a rose: he does not quite approve, perhaps, of one's comparing a male to a flower, but does Genet mean a flower? The image is a trite one, it has lost its bloom. He continues reading; he installs within him this seeming commonplace without having noticed that Genet was unable to keep from setting it off by quotation marks. Of course, no sooner has the gilding entered than it melts. We have been tricked. Why is it that we no longer understand this hackneyed locution? The cleverest reader will realize—too late—that the gardener, his roses and the banal comparison were chosen only in order to mask the aberrant form of the proposition. However, imagine a gallant saying to a flower girl: "Madam, you are the loveliest rose in your bouquet." The *meaninglessness* would be more manifest. The loveliest rose *in the* bouquet, yes, if need be: one can imagine her being a girl flower among flowers. But, after all, she is carrying the bouquet, perhaps she gathered it, it is *her* bouquet. While the verb slips the woman among the roses, the possessive opposes the bouquet to its owner, sets it off and closes it; one must choose: to *have* the roses or to *be* one of them. Genet's sentence is more cunning, for I can easily see the gardener *in* his garden. While walking along the road, Genet caught sight of that half-naked man bending over a flower bed; but if he meant to mention only what he saw, if he wrote: "I saw among the flowers a man who appeared to be a rose," he would not be departing from prose; he would be presenting something to be seen. But his purpose is *to remove from sight.* He will stress the actual relationship between the gardener and *his* garden: the gardener is growing the flowers; how could he be, at the same time, this creature who is external to his work and *a* creature among all those which he has made? Genet himself stresses the logical reason which forever prevents the image from taking and the gardener from being likened to a plant. He establishes within the phrase itself a short-circuit between a trivial physical image (a naked back, buried in the flowers, a man *in the middle* of a flower bed) and an unrealizable meaning. Thus, the proposition offers and rejects itself at the same time, as Genet the traitor offers and denies himself to the desire of the handsome gangsters. A homosexual sentence if ever there was one, and more so in its form than in its content. Does this mean that it is a pure destruction, a pure derealization of the material content of a perception? To be sure, it represents, all by itself, a transition from Being to Nonbeing; a parasitic meaningless sentence that lives in a state of symbiosis with a real organism. But at the same time it allows us to glimpse beneath the "vibratory disappearance" of the signification an elusive and deeper meaning. Nature takes back this worker the moment he bends her to the human order: he perishes beneath the clustering of the flowers that he has brought into being. Is not this the poetic object par excellence? A drawing room in a lake, two armchairs in the middle of a field, a man buried beneath roses: the intention is the same. These images are the poetic representation of our condition, since we are entirely in the world and entirely out of it. In an even more profound way, this whirligig, which by turns crushes man in nature and exiles him, refers us even more profoundly to Genet and to the choice of writing: if the gardener can become a rose in his garden, it is because one produces a work in order to re-create oneself in it. The poet is the most poetic phrase in his poem, Genet is the most moving character in his books. Thus, the sentence is absurd only in appearance: it *alludes* to Genet's entire history, to all his hopes. We sense this as soon as we start to read. Yet it is impossible to *realize* this signification; every precaution is taken to prevent us from doing so: a good, round prose sentence, a "cliché," suddenly challenges itself, is swallowed up, and the wreckage seems to point vaguely to an inaccessible constellation: therein lies all the poetry of Genet.

In this example, the unrealizable meaning corrodes the material content of the sentence. In the end, nothing remains of the first impression (the barebacked man weeding or digging in the middle of his garden) . But, inversely, Genet likes to set before us manifest contradictions, glaring illogicalities which suddenly disappear, masked by a sudden condensation of sensory images. That is what happens, in particular, whenever he unites light and darkness: "gloomy brightness," "dark light," "dazzling night," "blazing shadow." The logical signification is unrealizable, since darkness is defined by the absence of light; but, on the other hand, as it is the light of *day* that is wanting, the words "dazzling night" evoke, in spite of us, the memory of great nocturnal glares, torches, arc lamps, beacons, lightning. It is *true* that there are dazzling nights. But we have shifted from a certain acceptation of the word *night* (darkness, total absence of light) to another (night: *social* division of the day) . The image indicates the meaning by destroying itself. One first evokes a night *lit up from within,* like a grotto, and then moves on to the image of darkness engendering its own light—that is, one retains the preceding image, but by replacing the human and technical aspect of the light by natural halos, stars, will-o'-the-wisps, glowworms, northern lights, midnight suns. Finally, one dims these lights until the sensory image has the transparency of the idea. It seems to us that *ultimately* night, instead of containing or even producing lights, would be itself a light, but an invisible light. In effacing itself, in derealizing itself, the image indicates an infinite progression at the end of which the sentence would be understood. Mingled with this is a third acceptation of the word *night:* for us it is not only a social division of time or an absence of daylight, but also an undifferentiated mass of being, a vital medium, a substance. The use of Night as a symbol of Nothingness is valid only insofar as Night is a negativity, a nothingness of light, but Genet slyly awakens within us the idea of *thick* darkness and in-duces us to give a massive density to nonbeing. Hardened, condensed, impenetrable, this darkness can gleam by itself, like the black carapace of an insect, like jade, like the polished, glossy surface of a slab of black marble: while we are still racking our brains to understand how the negative can be positivity, our imagination, which is being worked on from below, has already convinced us: a black, hard substance such as steel is already gleaming with a thousand fires. The image is proof; we are thus convinced of what we cannot believe and we believe that we think what we do not think.

One could go on endlessly listing these fakings and exposing their workings. There are times, of course, when the author shoots wide of the mark. He is at times irritating. Sometimes he imitates himself. As a matter of fact, it would not be difficult to write "in the manner of" Genet. "Rich with all his poverty," "laborious with all his laziness," or the following: "I never wearied of wondering at his horrible eyes, one of which had been put out and was blinding with all its blindness. I sometimes had to lower my head, unable to sustain the piercing gaze of that gazeless eye. I would then contemplate his mouth and the milky sheen of those rare pearls: the five front teeth which he was missing."* If one wanted to be spiteful, one could compare his less happy efforts to Maurice Chevalier's song: "It Was in the Month of August Beneath the Snow One July Fourteenth." But if we sometimes think of parodying him, it is because he nods: when malice keeps him on the alert, he is inimitable. To appreciate the originality of his undertaking, one need only compare it to that of the surrealists.

For Breton, the powers of language are fundamentally poetic and magical: "The practical utilization of speech is a degradation of the verbal universe, since language was given to man to be used surrealistically." The reason is that the young bourgeois of surrealism were born within the language of "decent people"; they have no prior question to ask themselves: the Word is theirs, they have received it as a heritage, they can squander it since they have the *jus utendi* and *abutendi;* they can also claim that the co-owners are misusing it, are not taking advantage of all its resources, and they can plow it up the way a farmer plows up his land to find a treasure

---

* Are we not used to similar literary endeavors in our civilization of the Nay? Here is a passage from Blanchot: "He bent over the void in which he saw his image in the total absence of images. He was overcome with the most violent giddiness, a giddiness that did not make him fall but prevented him from falling and made impossible the fall that it made inevitable" (*Thomas l'Obscur*, new version, p. 50).

in it: the soil and the subsoil of "their mother tongue" belong to them equally; it is a *given* reality that these great lords share with the commoners. Genet, on the other hand, starts with the feeling that language belongs to the others and that they exploit it to the utmost; thus, the spoken and written language is at every moment all that it can be, it has no secret bottom. The meaning which he gives to words wrests them from nature and from truth instead of bringing them closer to a primary and divine purpose. For Breton, the practical use is a perversion of the Word; for Genet, it is its original purpose. Surrealist poetry claims to rediscover the original use of poetic *realism*.* Genet stands opposed to all realism and all naturalism. Poetic language is a burglary; he steals words and subjects them to wrong uses; this language is artificial and false and has no real basis. Poetry uses vocables to constitute an apparent world instead of designating real objects. For that reason Genet is in the line of Baudelaire and Mallarmé; the surrealists, who are heirs of Rimbaud and Lautréamont, make of poetry the instrument of their revelations; behind the burning of words one perceives Being: they are terrorists. For Genet, poetry reveals nothing; when the words burn and turn to ashes, there remains only nothingness; he is a rhetorician. Thus, surrealist poetry can be written by everybody: language can recompose itself in everyone in accordance with its authentic laws, provided simply that it not be prevented from doing so; but Genet's poetry is strictly individual; it is born with him and will die with him, as will its secret; by means of it he goes to the limit of the human and to the outermost point of the inhuman. He is inhuman when he sings of his wretched heroes—since everything in his song is theft, distortion, perversion, fakery and trap—he is *most human* by virtue of this rejection of all *natural* use of speech, for the human is also, and above all, *antiphysis*, and Genet invents for his personal needs a radical artificialism of language. Although the surrealists are mistrustful of what bourgeois science calls truth, the adequation to the superreal presupposes a certain submissiveness to being even in automatic writing: Genet, on the other hand, warns us: "I am lying," he says in *Our Lady of the Flowers;* and in *Funeral Rites:* "It's a hoax." He attempts once

---

* There is ambiguity in the term "surrealism," which signifies both an activity superior to realism (it might be an idealism of the imagination) and a behavior having to do with the superreal. In the latter acceptation, surrealism becomes a superior realism, for the superreal is assimilable to total reality. In this sense, there is a *realism* of speech, insofar as its original function is to reveal the superreal. And the practical use that is made of it by Christian bourgeois civilization can be regarded, on the other hand, as *idealistic* since one discovers significations in accordance with certain abstract principles.

again—but this time by taking language for subject—to set before us what has existence only for and through man: the false.

As a consequence of his principles, Breton allows language to organize itself freely within him: that is what he calls automatic writing. Genet rejects the control of reason as much as the surrealists do, but he does not want to abandon himself to the spontaneity of the mind. Having written about Stilitano: "Here I must have recourse to a religious image: his posterior was an altar," he immediately apologizes: "I refuse to be prisoner of a verbal automatism." His poetry is entirely directed, though its regulating principles are themselves poetic. In the first place, because Genet is contemptuous of all forms of abandon: they are not in keeping with his asceticism of Evil, with his thief's puritanism; there is a fecundity, an exuberance, in automatic writing that repels him. But, in addition, abandon frightens him: he guards his self-control. To rely, however little, on intoxication, inspiration or automatism is to run the risk of seeing strange monsters appear, monsters which would lead him to suicide. Gorgui worked with blinders so as not to see the gulf opening at his feet; the beggars "avoid any crack by which grief might enter." "Put yourself," writes Breton, "into the most passive or receptive state that you can." But Genet, who is forced to master the daily horror, *cannot* abandon himself. Quite the contrary, he always keeps in reserve the word that magnifies, ready to transfigure the sordid event, the miracle of horror that is going to loom up. The surrealists lie on their backs and float; Genet remains standing, stiff, bristling, determined to keep his head above water. The surrealist poet's irresponsibility follows immediately from his passivity: the accused agrees at once with the prosecution to "stigmatize most of the ideas. He limits his defense to asserting that he does not regard himself as the author of his book, which can be considered only a surrealist production that excludes all question as to the merit or demerit of the one who signs it." Genet attempts to save himself by means of language; indeed, he considers himself eminently responsible for his poems. It is not enough to say that he is the author of them: he *is* himself the poem. "How can anyone like me personally," he often asks, "if he doesn't like my writings?"

For both Breton and Genet, "I is Another." But this Other does not occupy the same position for the former that it does for the latter. The surrealists place the Other *behind* consciousness: "So one evening, before falling asleep, I discerned, clearly articulated . . . a rather odd phrase . . . a phrase that seemed to me insistent, a phrase, if I may say so, that *knocked on the windowpane.*" The phrases that follow surprise him no less and leave him "with an impression of such gratuitousness that the self-control which he had had until then seemed to him illusory." All of surrealist poetry aims at "reproducing artificially the ideal moment in which man, possessed by a particular emotion, is suddenly seized by the 'stronger than he' that hurls him, against his will, into the immortal." Projected by these subterranean forces, the poet becomes an object, a "document that one copies." The poet would have to decipher the meaning of his own words. "Soluble fish: am not *I* the soluble fish?" Breton asks himself. "I was born under the sign of the Fish and man is soluble in his thoughts." Thus, the Other sends the message and consciousness deciphers it. The meaning does not flee. Consciousness extracts it, touches it on the words; new and visible beings surrender to its intuition. Breton can, for a moment, imagine this water creature that melts in water, can behold, through the words, its evanescence. Surrealist poetry comes from fullness and remains a fullness. For Genet, the Other is both behind consciousness and in front of it, both the secret being of all thought and its witness. It is not the one who speaks but the one spoken to. Consciousness assembles words in accordance with poetic connections which it senses without seeing them and presents them to the I-Other which is to decipher them. Genet has no poetic *intuition*. The surrealist is filled with his images. He "little by little grows convinced of their supreme reality." They are present, dense and consistent, dazzling: these flashes are the Other's gifts. Genet's poems flee from him into the consciousness of the Other, he writes them blindly, in the darkness. They deserve, much more than do those of Henri Thomas, to be called "Blind Man's Work."

For therein, perhaps, lies the worst hoax that he contrives for the just man: when the latter makes a vain effort to view convicts as hollyhock roses, he remains convinced that this intuitive signification is manifest to the poet who vouches for it. And as a matter of fact when the others guaranteed his being a *thief,* Genet did not doubt that they knew what they were talking about. And rightly: the Others read theft on his face. But the reciprocal is not true: Genet would be quite unable to effect the significations which he offers us. He sees language in reverse; its sound-matter hides the meaning from him; and as he cannot "realize" what it is to *be* a thief or what it is to *be* a saint, he has no scruples about linking these terms that elude him and creating new, unrealizable significations, as, for example, "the thief is a saint," even if he has to charge the Other with realizing them for him. This sudden halt at the edge of the Promised Land characterizes him in all his activities. He offers his body to the Other and it is the Other who ejaculates inside him. Pleasure, in his case, is this absence of coming; poetic emotion is this absence of emotion. But let there be no misunderstanding: in both cases he is overwhelmed. When he speaks of his sexual excitement, he calls it "vertigo"; the "stormy night buries him"; and, in like manner, words are "vertiginous," the poem "sucks him into the depths of a wonderful night." But it is the night of unknowing, the night of nonpleasure. The thief does not ejaculate, because he owns nothing. Everything is the other's: the money he has in his pocket is the other's, the orgasm in his body is the other's, the word in his mouth is the other's. He feels the budding of a singular emotion, and hardly has he uttered the word that expresses it than the emotion disappears into it; the word absorbs it and offers it to the other. He says of Divine—whose " 'woman' judgments" are "poetical conclusions"—that "in order to think with precision she must never formulate her thoughts for herself aloud. No doubt she did at times say to herself aloud: 'I'm a poor thing,' but having felt it she no longer felt it and, in saying it, no longer thought it." And when the crippled child who is vaguely dreaming about the word "Brazil" utters the word "suns," we learn that "the one-word poem that fell from this vision . . . began to petrify it." In like manner, the declaration of love absorbs the love more than it expresses it:

"I love him mad—

"Even in his mind he did not manage to finish the word 'madly.' Born of the words 'I love him,' the passion continued—growing at wild speed and leaving him breathless, halfway through the dizzying word that ended with the very shudder that animated the beginning—through Riton's body."

And in *The Thief's Journal:* "I murmured inwardly, 'I love you . . . I love you . . . I love you . . .' My love will perhaps end by emerging, I said to myself, carried off by these words as a poison is by milk or a purge."

Genet's poetry is *unrealizable.* Born of words, the emotion is carried off by them "as a poison is by a purge"; it continues its movement with them and in them at wild speed and leaves the poet behind, emptied. What he was going to feel was exhausted in the ceremonious act of *naming;* it is now for the Others to feel it instead of him: Genet can no more *see* a convict as a rose than we can. He has a feeling that he is *going* to see him, that he *might* see him, and his vision crystallizes in the word. I have often heard him find fault with writers for allowing their works to be adapted for the stage or screen. "The words of a literary work, that is, a work written for readers, do not," he says, "admit of visual transcription." He has pointed out to me that the splendid passage in *Miracle of the Rose* in which Harcamone's chains burst into bloom would change into a succession of grotesque images if it were "visualized" on the screen. He did not *see* the miracle, even in his mind's eye: he *spoke* it immediately. And it is *for the Others* that he spoke it. He recognizes this implicitly in *The Thief's Journal:* "Far from achieving poetry here—that is, *communicating to the reader an emotion of which I was then unaware—of which I am still unaware*—my words appeal to carnal sumptuousness."*

But the fact is that the reader, in reading, becomes Genet himself, that is, he is unable to effect the significations that are offered him. He vaguely perceives a convict and a rose, but these approximations do not stand up; they collapse and the signification remains like a task which it is impossible to carry out. Nevertheless, it is there, it exists: it seems that others, elsewhere, understand it, that it turns its shining face to thieves. Thus, both the author and the reader leave to the other the task of *realizing* the poetic meaning of the sentence. Each in turn falls into "the vertiginous darkness." The author charges the words with an emotion he has not felt, and the reader, mystified and uneasy, is convinced that there is a secret dimension of language and that the discourse, which is innocent *as prose,* is guilty *as poetry*. Genet's poetry is the dizzying flight from significations to nothingness. Everyone is fooled, but each guarantees for the others—and all for each—the *objectivity* of the significations that are presented. Let us bear in mind that for Genet the *poetic object* was that which symbolized triumph beyond failure by causing to appear behind the world of significations and facts that of unknowing, of the non-fact, of the inexplicable. When Genet wearies of being the passive revealer of poetic situations and decides to become a creator of object-poems, he leaves to prose the realm of facts, the irrefutable explanations of the criminologist and the merciless determinism which manifests to all the impossibility of evil. But his own prose, like the real that supports the poetic accident, is superdetermined: in addition to a discourse which seems to be self-sufficient, his reader introduces unrealizable significations, the mere shimmer of which is sufficient to achieve the destruction of the prose. Without ceasing to be itself, the latter is transformed

---

* My italics.

before our eyes into the pure matter of poetic Nonbeing. Let us
bear in mind that, before his decision to write, Genet saw all his
acts change into gestures. He charged his work with the function of
symbolizing this metamorphosis: prose is the denominative act that
changes into gesture in the reader's mind. Beauty *devours*, as he
used to say. Hence, poetry devours prose, it is its perpetual derealization. To read Genet is to let poetic beauty feed on prose. And it is
also, for the reader, a new way of being a criminal. As we saw above,
the poetic phrase is similar to crime: just as the latter reduces its
utilitarian motives to mere pretext, so the former manifests to the
poet an unknown *self* that must be learned: the dead Monsieur
Ragon reveals to "Our Lady" his Being-Other; the pair of words
"flowers, death" reveals to Genet his Being-Other. But this Being-
Other is not, as for Breton, the manifestation of an unconscious
that lurks behind consciousness; for Genet, the Being-Other is the
Being-for-Another. Querelle, after committing his murder, feels
himself *becoming an object:* and so for the poet. And for the reader
of poems: the Devil's share exists, it is the meaning of our acts for
the Devil. When reading Genet, the Just man becomes Jean Genet,
not *in his own eyes,* but for Another who effects, instead of him, the
unrealizable significations. To read Genet is to become an object
for the Other as the criminal becomes an object for his crime. *Who*
is the Other? The only one who can effect the accursed signification: the spirit of Evil. To read Genet is *to be thought by the spirit
of Evil,* in complicity with it. One can see why the critics, who have
been affected by twenty-five years of surrealism, find fault with
Genet for his shams and optical illusions, why they accuse him of
being a conjurer: Breton, like Genet, holds that poetry discloses
a being beyond the being of daily reality. But he thinks that this
being can be seen and touched in certain exceptional circumstances;
he plunges to the depths of himself and brings back monsters which
he lets us see. And as he becomes an absolute passivity in order to
capture the poetic event, as the phrases that flow from his pen are
dictated to him by forces over which he has no control, we are
entitled to speak of his utter good faith, his complete sincerity.
Genet, on the other hand, deceives us consciously. He constantly
allows us to catch a glimpse of a poetic event which does not take
place: he is a trickster. That is true. But the terms could be reversed: in the first place, it is an established fact that Breton *corrects*
his poems. But above all, he claims that the object which he shows
us is *superreal* or a message of the superreal in the real; he presents
it to us as a realization of the superreality. Now, although its matter

is real (like that of all works of art), the object itself obviously belongs to the imaginary; it, too, arises out of the self-destruction of the real. There is thus an element of cheating in surrealist sincerity.* And, inversely, in Genet's cheating there is the equivalent of profound good faith: that imperious necessity of being, that irresistible need to re-enter the framework of a society that expelled him, his real resentment against those who set themselves up as judges. Moreover, did he not torture himself during his ethical period, and did not his asceticism aim at attaining, through renunciation of everything, a wealth that would be beyond being? Was not his Saintliness an attempt to make positive use of privation? Was it not, like Beauty, a possession without enjoyment? The murderer who feels himself becoming an object for the police, the aesthete who transforms his acts into gestures, the Saint who transforms negation into an ideal affirmation, the passive homosexual, that imaginary woman, who derives pleasure from the absence of pleasure, the vanquished man who sees in his failure the sign of a mysterious triumph, all the characters that Genet was in succession or at the same time merge into a single one, *the poet,* who loses himself in order to bear witness to an unattainable reverse side of things. Genet could very well not have written; if he wrote, he could write only what he did write. His poetry could be only a tampering with prose: prose is Good, Nature, the Real, the Useful, the symbol of the Society of the Just; poetry is Evil, and it must, like Evil, be a relative absolute: relative to prose as Evil is relative to Good, it must at the same time *make prose pass* as a chosen victim of the poetic attack, just as the evildoer *makes Good pass* as a simple means of achieving Evil.

"Pretexts for my iridescence, then for my transparence, and finally for my absence, the boys I speak of evaporate. All that remains of them is what remains of me: I exist only through them, who are nothing, existing only through me." This curious passage, which is itself a whirligig, a thing unrealizable, defines Genet's poetry: two nothingnesses which prop each other up disappear together. In the magnifying judgments Genet has so contrived matters that the two terms are negative: the concrete positive embodies moral privation (cowardice, ugliness and poverty); the moral positive (beauty, nobility, elegance) is only an absence. Thus far, there is nothing new: to magnify gangsters is to murder them. What is new is his making the reader do the work. To read Genet is to make

---

* As there is in all writers. The law of rhetoric (and we know that terror, too, is a rhetoric) is that one must lie in order to speak the truth.

a pact with the Devil. What does Satan give in return for a soul? *Nothing*, that is, an appearance which vanishes, drawing being into nothingness along with itself; the Devil purchases souls with dead leaves, and his future victim draws other creatures along with him in his fall, for with these dead leaves he in turn buys the honor of men and the virtue of women. As Klossowski says, after the Church Fathers, the demon "must borrow a being other than his. As he himself is only a negation, he needs another existence to exercise his negation." So we are now demoniacal: we lend to the Demon our body, our eyes which give birth to the words on the pages of the book, our throat and tongue which utter them. In exchange for what? For dead leaves. Genet gives us *nothing:* when we shut the book, we shall know no more than we did before about prison or ruffians or the human heart. Everything is false. Let us recall the dilemma that blocked him for so long a time: to destroy being is to resort to force, to organization, to order, therefore to being, therefore to Good. But to preserve the original purity of evil will is to condemn oneself to a dream world. At present, Genet can rejoice: in writing out his dreams, he does Evil without resorting to Being. By his action as an artist and poet who finally realizes the unrealizable, he forces the others to support, in his stead, the false against the true, Evil against Good, Nothingness against Being. The inexpiable Evil is the act that forces Others to do Evil. Genet's poetry, which is a premeditated murder of prose, a deliberate damning of the reader, is a crime without extenuating circumstances.

Each crime is a work: the unrealizable significations organize into a whole, a rigorous unity of that contradictory multiplicity: *the* subject of *the* book. And the single subject of the single book that Genet has written and rewritten five times is Genet himself. But not the flesh-and-blood Genet, the anecdotic little martyr who drowns in the muddy flood of a wasted life: that Genet is nothing, nothing but a crazy tale told by an idiot, nothing but a raw, unjustifiable existence, nothing but a *pretext*. "I refuse to live for any end other than the one which I found to contain the first misfortune: that my life must be a legend, that is, legible; and that the reading of it must give birth to a new emotion which I call poetry. I am no longer anything but a pretext." Let there be no misunderstanding: it is not a matter of saving his life by making it the occasion for a beautiful book, the object of a beautiful song, but of dissolving it entirely in the magnifying song. "Pretexts for my iridescence, then for my transparence, and finally for my absence, the boys I speak of evaporate." Thus, Genet evaporates; he believed seriously, profoundly, in a transubstantiation that would wrest him from his actual life and embody him in words, those glorious bodies. Poetic language is the soul objectified. It emerges from the body carried by the "physical breath," which can be compared to the "string of a ball" that he draws from his mouth and rewinds on another spool, the work. With the string, the entire body unwinds little by little, grows thinner, dwindles, the organs are transformed into *phrases designating the organs:* "This wonderful language reduces the body, wears it down until it is transparent, until it is a speck of light." Unwound, then rewound on the other spool, Genet exists —at last!—facing himself. He has literally emptied himself: his truth is outside of him; in the realm of the real nothing remains but a pure consciousness that contemplates its appearance. Isn't that what he formerly wanted? To go to himself as another, in the legendary guise of a criminal, as Erik went to himself from the depths of the mirror, to see himself. As a matter of fact, he still eludes himself, but this time he is resigned. No, he will not see himself, but he is going to put himself into circulation in the form of a diabolical Host, he will force men's minds to see him as Another, he will create himself *in the others* as a spellbinding object. He will be, really and truly, his *creator;* in the consciousness of the other he will become both subject and object: the reader will have no Ego other than that of Genet, and this Ego will learn its own legend by means of Genet's words.

But the fundamental derealization is consequently that of Genet: it is he first, it is he alone that he transforms into an appearance and that he *realizes,* for and by the other, as a pure unrealizable appearance. The being who has no other end than to lend his being to appearance is himself. Just as the noble disappeared behind his coat of arms and the hoodlum behind his tattooing, so Genet is finally going to disappear behind his epitaph, that is, his work. "To swallow myself by opening my mouth inordinately wide over my head, then putting my whole body into it, then the universe, until I am nothing but a ball of eaten thing which is gradually annihilated—that is my way of seeing the end of the world." It is also the aim of his poetry: to dissolve his history in his legend, his nature in its magnification, to wear down his body by the words that express it, to do away with himself as a living creature in order to find himself in the eyes of the others as a legendary hero half mingled with abstraction, absent from all life. Thus far, he has been derealizing himself in a dream world; his art fixes the derealization, local-izes and objectifies it, it is the adumbration of a suicide: behind the handsome, impassive Pimps, behind the Sailors, the criminal S.S. men, are their Ideas, their constellations. But the latter are none other than Genet himself, the pole of this star-spangled sky. Stilitano is he; Bulkaen and Divine are he; Harcamone, Erik and Querelle are likewise he. Whatever the relief of his characters, there always comes a moment when he resorbs them into himself. He is the most beautiful rose in his garden, but he is also all the roses and the whole garden. For a moment he makes a creature shine and sparkle in the reader's eyes, he alienates himself in it and the following moment it vanishes, there remains only Jean Genet, Jean Genet, the impossible nonexistence, the sham, parasite of a wily hoodlum, the verbal appearance whose translucency finally reveals nothingness.

Each of Genet's poems presents itself first as a novel. Since each creature, in passing close to him, awakens a constellation, that is, actualizes an aspect of Genet himself, it is necessary that *all* creatures be present in his work. Everything is in it: men and even women, wars, crimes, love affairs, and also skies, trees, rocks. Complex and improbable relationships develop among the characters: Querelle, the sailor and murderer, has a brother who is the very image of him and who has become the lover of Norbert the hotelkeeper; Querelle sleeps with Norbert, then with a detective. Now, this detective happens to be the one who is investigating the crime that Querelle committed. The book is unfinished, but one can guess how Genet intended to use such carefully contrived relationships. Erik, a Nazi soldier, sleeps with Madame D., mother of the Jean D. whom Genet loved and who was killed by Riton the militiaman. Riton and Erik meet and become lovers. After a hundred ups and downs the two boys meet again on the roofs and shoot at the F.F.I. When they are about to be captured, Riton kills Erik out of love. Our Lady, the handsome murderer, meets by chance the father who abandoned him twenty years earlier, and this father happens to be Divine's lover, Darling Daintyfoot, etc. The origins of these plots are the stories which Genet read in prison: as we have seen, he draws his original inspiration from the most popular sources; he has assimilated the poetry of the adventure story as well as that of music-hall songs. Darling and Our Lady are the homosexual replica of Prince Rodolphe and his daughter;* the couple Hitler-Erik is the counterpart of the couple Sir Williams–Rocambole;* *Querelle of*

---

* Characters in Eugene Sue's *The Mysteries of Paris.*—Translator's note.

Brest was originally going to be called "The Mysteries of Brest."
The wax dummy that was found by the detective in Our Lady's
room recalls the blood-stained dolls of Fantomas.* Genet borrows
the paraphernalia of the adventure stories partly out of fidelity to
the prisoner that he was, partly to pull the leg of the bourgeois intellectual by making him swallow the kind of cock-and-bull story that
he claims to despise, but mainly because he wants his works to have
a "taste of fiction" as violent and sickening as the "taste of prose"
of his false prose. He needs to fill his books with imbroglios, vicissi-
tudes, conspiracies, traitors, victims, heroes, detectives: he needs
these devices *because his novels are false novels*. All these fictional
props are present in order to be suddenly sacrificed to Genet himself, as prose is to poetry. If he has gone to the trouble of telling us
the full history of the maid in *Funeral Rites*, he has done so for the
sake of the baffling moment when we realize that she is none other
than Genet. Men, women, trees: yes; but when the reader puts out
his hand it is Jean Genet that he touches. The adventures of Querelle
and Erik are the false subject of these false novels: the true subject
is the gradual dissolution of the external world in the poet's mind.
He makes a serious effort to interest us in his characters, but only
so as the better to delude us: hardly have we begun to believe in
Divine, in Paulo, than the author breaks in: Peekaboo, here I am!
There's no one but me, there's never been anyone but me. . . . He
dreams in our presence: What am I going to do with Divine? He
suddenly gets annoyed: Divine bores me, I'm fed up with Darling.
Or, quite simply, quite undisturbedly, he puts himself in the place
of Erik or Hitler or Paulo and continues the account of their adventures in the first person. We shall, each time, feel the poetic
shock that he felt innumerable times in the days of "the state of
dream," and we shall witness, with a kind of terror, a strange phenomenon: the entire world ripping apart like a piece of cloth to
reveal the ironic face of *a single man;* the universe existed only for
Genet. And we who read, who are we? Jean Genet himself or figments of the imagination who will fade away, who will be resorbed
into Jean Genet? And what is Jean Genet, since he "is nothing but
his characters" and since his characters are nothingness? We finally
discover a new type of magnifying judgment: Paulo *is* Genet, the
maid *is* the wily hoodlum, just as the convict is a rose. And just as
the flower and the prisoner disappear in the darkness, so Paulo,
Hitler, Erik, the executioner, the maid and Jean Genet vanish

---

* Heroes of a famous French serial.—Translator's note.

together into the abstract. Once again we are confronted with the play of Nothingness and Being: the work is both the Universe as a hypostasis of Jean Genet and *nothing*. It is an exalting of the author and a suicide. Genet captivates a consciousness to the point of being one with it, then suddenly annihilates himself; the reader experiences a strange, sickening awakening. Let us consider the matter more closely: let us take an example and examine the play of this imaginary solipsism; let us see by what interlacing of fugues the characters appear, assert themselves, change into Genet and suddenly become themselves again.

Jean Decarnin, Genet's lover, was killed on the barricades in August 1944. Genet suffers. Now, to suffer is to refuse to suffer: he must free himself from suffering, must forget the dead. But, on the other hand, to forget is to become Another. The widower is in agony because he wants to stop suffering without ceasing to be himself. Genet seeks and finds the poetic resolution of this conflict: that is the entire subject of the book. He is going to resorb the death into himself. The absence will become a presence; better than a presence: an identity. Not quite, however: Decarnin will remain the Other, the Other whom Genet has not ceased to be for himself; thus, the bond of love will remain; since he continues to love, Genet will remain himself; since Jean Decarnin becomes Jean Genet, it is, once again, *himself* that Genet will love. *Funeral Rites* is the account of Genet's efforts to transform his dead lover into his own substance, or, as he says, to *eat* him. In like manner, Lieutenant Seblon transform his sailors into an Idea, then discovers that this idea is only himself.

The book is thus the account of a liquidation and the liquidation itself; the author delivers himself in relating his deliverance, or, if one prefers, the labor of mourning is carried out in writing.* However, Genet has done things the hard way: if he masters his pain, it will be as a result of running his hands over all his wounds; he will explore all the sensitive spots and will systematically develop all the possibilities of despair, of suffering. He will stop *when there is nothing more to suffer*, as a candle stops burning when the flame has nothing more to consume. "I am aware that this book is only literature, but may it enable me to exalt my pain to the point of expelling the pain from itself and of no longer being, as fireworks cease

---

* Cf. Cocteau:
   Your cries, even under torture,
   Are written cries, pride helping.
   (*Opéra:* The Oracle.)

to be after the explosion." A realistic will: Genet heightens the horror, cultivates it and abandons himself to it so as to eliminate at least the horror of the horror. But the realism is immediately derealized, developing his horror in all directions to the point of making a plenitude of it. Genet will suffer *in the realm of the imaginary:* strained, diligent, tense, evil, he seizes upon the slightest sensation, inspects it, inflates it, forces it, like the character La Fanfarlo who burst out laughing when she felt like smiling.

More than one reader is already irritated: nothing shocks us so much as insincere grief, although every sorrow contains elements of insincerity. Transforming his suffering into an instrument of exploration, Genet pushes his pain far beyond what he feels; he seems to us to be playing, in every sense of the word: playing his sorrow, playing *on* his sorrow, playing *with* it. And, as a matter of fact, he *is* playing; he readily admits it: "This book is true and it's hokum." But that is precisely his way of being sincere: the characteristic feature of his feelings is that they are active. He pushes them to an extreme so as to be their master and because he does not want to submit to anything; therefore, as we have seen, he only half-feels things. His sorrow is precisely the zeal with which he plays it in order to get rid of it; it is his book. The completed book will be the grief itself, finished, settled and done with; in order that this printed grief detach itself from him completely, he will attach a stone to it, that is, the following dedication: "To Jean Decarnin." The grief is an offering to the dead man; locked up in the book as in a coffin, it joins the dead.

But that is not all: since the anecdote does not count, since the story is a pretext for legend, the wretched moments of this actual suffering can be justified only by serving as matter for an unreal and legendary sorrow; it is therefore less important to feel this sorrow than to make it, by means of rigorous exercise, the archetype of sorrow. The event will be pushed to the point of perfection, if not in truth at least by means of words. This concern for art already involves a truly moral preoccupation that Genet will later express in *The Thief's Journal:* "Acts must be carried through to completion. Whatever their starting point, their end will be beautiful. It is because an action has not been completed that it is vile." *Funeral Rites* continues the "labor of mourning" to the point of transforming the actual sorrow into an Eidos of sensibility and to the point of the fullest and clearest consciousness of it: "Since they were at the edge of the world, at the summit of the rock set at the outermost point of *Finis Terrae,* they were able to look without anxiety, to

devote themselves entirely to the perfect execution of the act. . . .
It had to be made as intense as possible, that is, each of them had to
be at the height of consciousness in order to concentrate in that
act the maximum of life. Let their moments be brief, but charged
with consciousness." And, in the same vein, he writes in a later
work: "What I have sought above all is to be the consciousness of
the theft whose poem I am writing." Genet could have written
that he wanted to be the consciousness of the mourning. I mean by
this that he endeavors to transform the grief which is experienced
in the immediate moment into a reflective consciousness of grief,
that is, to dissolve it into its Idea by his consciousness of it. The
digesting of a dead man and the resorbing of a grief into a consciousness of the grief are the two tasks that define his poems: at the starting point there was a fresh grave, an absent person; at the finish
there will be only Genet, the one and only. This process of involution characterizes all his books: at the end of *Our Lady of the
Flowers,* Divine is dead, Our Lady decapitated, Darling in prison;
freed from his fantasies, Genet remains alone; he remains alone in
Miracle of the Rose after the deaths of Bulkaen and Harcamone;
he continues on his way alone on the last page of *The Thief's Journal* while Armand, Stilitano, Guy and all his vague companions
sink into oblivion. "To go into mourning is first to bow to a sorrow
from which I shall escape, for I shall transform it into the strength
needed in order to depart from customary morality."*

Funeral Rites is thus the story of a grief, or rather of a burial,
as is indicated not only by its title but even more so by the odd
hearse that winds its way all through the book. We are familiar with
the book's basic motif, which is that of the void. The chief character *no longer is;* the book describes a living man's relations with a
dead one. Love, desire, friendship: but a term is missing; and as
reciprocity is lacking, the feelings empty into the imaginary. But

---

* If the reader is annoyed by these "written cries," if he regards them as a sign of
inauthenticity, I remind him that sorrow is not *first* a silent fullness that relishes itself
excruciatingly. It is first a *lack.* A dear being—or some other good—is gone. And one lives
one's relationship with this being *by default.* Sorrow is abstract, as Camus says; it is an
obsessive void that one lives in a state of nerves, a void that would like to be a fullness,
that is vainly *played* as a fullness. The *word* is the indispensable accessory of suffering:
it not only expresses suffering, but attempts to give it body. "It is when one suffers that
one reasons," says Pirandello. Suffering is an endless soliloquy. That being so, the verbal
mode matters little: it varies with individuals. One speaks aloud or in a whisper, one
writes. In any case, one tries either to fill the void with words or to make of it, by means
of words, an object that one can *look at* and consequently thrust aside. A sorrow *is* a cry,
but it *is* also a letter full of explanations, a fragment of a personal diary or a sonnet. In
this sense, Genet's "labor of mourning" is simply the faithful representation of the behavior characteristic of all suffering.

does Genet distinguish clearly between those aroused in him by a dead man, the absent object of a lonely love, and those he showered on phantoms, on nonexistent objects of onanistic desire? In both cases, the transcendence is false; the object is merely an intermediary between Narcissus and himself; Genet flees from the void in a state of almost unbearable tension and enjoys feeling empty within his flight itself. In both onanism and mourning, it is *nothingness, his* own nothingness, that attracts him, just as he is attracted by the effort to maintain in being an object which no longer is and which was never anything but an appearance. In mourning he discerns Evil. Not only because he suffers, but because of that indefinably suspect element in one's feelings for a dead person. Just as he earlier manipulated Darling, he now manipulates Jean Decarnin; he models him, transforms him, places him in imaginary situations, links up, by fictitious episodes, his real memories, which are few and which have already congealed—and which are probably spurious. Jean becomes the pretext for his irisation, provides him with the motifs of his arabesques. Genet can communicate with others only if they display the docility and inertia that characterize objects of phantasy and the dead. Jean hampered him when he was alive; he was an absolute center of references whose consciousness stole his being, a center of indetermination with unpredictable reactions. Genet has always detested the consciousness of his lovers. Now that Jean is dead, Genet is once again the master of his character.

The fact is that he uses his dead friend in the same way that he used Stilitano after their break: we know how he installed Stilitano inside himself and how the one-armed hoodlum became a *persona,* then an *archetype,* then an *idea,* then a mystic quality of the universe, then nothingness. Unlike Stilitano, Jean ventured to *love* Genet. Fortunately, death rearranges matters: it endows the too tender young man with a hardness he was far from having; it performs the same function as the indifference of the handsome Pimps. Genet is grateful to Jean for freeing him, for enabling him at last to despair. The impassiveness of the Pimps transformed them into corpses; inversely, the death of Jean is merely an element of impassiveness. Genet is going to be able to start loving him. Does that mean he did not love him? Exactly, he did not love him. He was fond of Jean, he desired him and was even on friendly terms with him, but since love is, for Genet, synonymous with despair, how could he have loved that handsome, considerate and submissive youngster. "All these wounds informed me of my love." And further on: "If my feelings are real only by virtue of my consciousness of them, ought I to say that I would have loved Jean less if he had died in China? And what was perhaps the strongest and most painful emotion I ever felt, Jean alive, and charming and handsome in my memory, would not have succeeded in revealing it to me, whereas Jean seemed to me to be the sole pretext for it. In short, all my grief—hence the consciousness of that beautiful love, hence that love—would not have been if I had not seen Jean with horror."* And: ". . . the terms of the sentence: 'My grief in the presence of Jean revealed to me the strength of my love of him' can be replaced by these: 'My grief in the presence of my dead virtue revealed to me the strength of my love of it.' "

Love desires reciprocity. Such reciprocity was possible when Jean was alive: Jean loved Genet; the birth of a reciprocal love between them depended on Genet alone; he was no doubt very bored by such a love. Now that Jean is dead, Genet's will to the impossible awakens: it is the moment for desiring, with tears in his eyes, a reciprocity of tenderness, of caresses. What he is cultivating in this quite new and deliberate love is not faithfulness to his earlier feelings—since he felt only a rather mild affection for Jean—but rather Evil, suffering, the impossible. Let us go further: ever since Genet virilified himself we have been hearing him complain about being unable to love sufficiently, and he has been nostalgic for the violence of his past love, for passive homosexuality. This death which enables Jean to play the tough, to resist, like Stilitano, adds spice to Genet's languishing desires; it rejuvenates him.

The reader senses that this funeral rite pertains not only to a particular, episodic death; he has the impression that the present mourning is only the passing form of a permanent mourning: the widower is eager to let us know that his present grief symbolizes the one he felt when confronted with "the death of his virtue." We are again referred to the terrible moment of the original crisis. Genet is so constituted that his feelings have a double and triple bottom. The keenest and newest passion is also a pretext for reliving the decisive moments of his childhood. He himself is surprised at this: "Although it is true that the avowed aim of this book is to sing the glory of Jean D., it has perhaps more unexpected secondary aims. . . . Why am I going to describe presently the third burial in each of my three books? Even before I knew Jean, I had chosen the burial of the bastard of the unmarried mother which you will read about further on." The burial of the illegitimate child represents the perpetual funeral of the child Genet "dead in him long before

---

* He has just seen Jean's corpse again.

the ax chopped off his head." The dead Jean Decarnin is immediately identified with the dead childhood of his lover and thereby
joins the fictive dead that Genet has escorted to the grave. He is
already more than half assimilated to Genet himself and consequently more than half imaginary. He *is* Divine, Stilitano, Darling,
little Culafroy; one would think that he died in order to gratify
Genet, to satisfy his necrophilia: was Genet not awaiting this violent death from the very start? When he begins his poetic tales,
most of his heroes are dead or doomed to die: *Our Lady of the
Flowers* opens with the burial of Divine; the gory end of Bulkaen
is announced in the opening pages of *Miracle of the Rose;* as for
Harcamone, we know that the guillotine is in store for him. What
is more curious is the fact that the *real* death of Pilorge seems to
have been the dress rehearsal for that of Jean. Genet no more loved
the living Pilorge than the living Jean: he does not hide the fact
that the young murderer was a sneak, a coward (*The Thief's Journal*) and a bore (*Miracle of the Rose*) . Yet as soon as Pilorge is sentenced, one feels that Genet discovers him with amazement: "His
body and radiant face haunt my sleepless nights"; he begins to love
him, he dedicates his poems to him just as he later dedicates *Funeral
Rites* to Decarnin. In connection with the execution of Pilorge, as
with the death of Jean, he questions himself about the deeper purposes of his work. He is surprised at his uniting roses and death in
his poems just as he will be surprised at his putting funerals into
his books. He ends by descending into himself, guided by this
Ariadne thread, and discovers "the touching meadow of his open
childhood." All these similarities might make us think that Jean
Decarnin never existed. Yet the fact is that Jean Decarnin did live,
that he loved Genet, that he died during the uprising of Paris. We
are simply seeing our author's voracious and solvent mind at work:
he does not stop until he has reduced the external events to repeating his sacred drama. Around the death of Jean are sounded all the
themes of Death according to Genet.

Love is death. (Diabolical pastiche of the Platonic twaddle of
Sparkenbroke.)

To love a living person is to love him dead. (Darling sees himself
dead in Divine's eyes.)

To love is to want to kill. (As early as *Our Lady of the Flowers,*
Genet dreams of murdering a handsome boy. Erik kills a child;
Riton ends by killing Erik.) This theme is given a new form in
Funeral Rites: we know that Genet can free himself from a misfor-
tune only by imagining that he has willed it. His labor of mourning

will therefore consist in taking upon himself the death of Jean as if he were responsible for it, in short, in killing the dead boy in his imagination: he will symbolically hand him over to Riton, will worship the supposed murderer of his lover, will profane the dead boy in a thousand ways. Three years before his mourning he explained that the murderer is possessed, in the strict sense of the word, by the person he murdered: "Your dead man* is within you, mingled with your blood; he flows in your veins, oozes from your pores, and your body lives on him as cemetery flowers sprout from corpses." In order to install his dead man within himself, he must make of him his victim; in order to derive moral benefit from his mourning, he himself must have caused it.

To love is to be alone. (He loves Riton because the crowd hates him; he loves the dead Jean because those who honor him did not really know him; he loves the boy for his secret homosexuality when the good citizens respect in him the member of the Resistance who died for his country. He steals Jean from society.)

To live is to survive a dead child.

To live is to be at the point of death and to prepare a lavish funeral for oneself. (In ensuring Decarnin's glory by means of a book, he is, in actual fact, ensuring his own glory, symbolically and in reality. Symbolically because it is he himself that he is burying; in reality because the book will win for him the black celebrity which is that of murderers. "The poet is a dead man.")

This time the reader's indignation is at its height: we have seen him being fooled by a supposed filial love and vomiting on his mother; Genet now wants to make him join in the rifling of a tomb. On the strength of the early pages, the good citizen was expecting to read a poignant and melancholy *lamento*. He was willing to overlook the perversity of the forbidden love because of its sincerity, but he finds himself drawn into the most extraordinary mixture of tragedy and buffoonery, of tenderness and sadism. He thought he was honoring a hero of the Resistance and now finds himself profaning the corpse of a murdered young fairy. That's more than he can take. Yet he is unable to thrust the book aside: the reason is that this monstrous masquerade is *at the same time* a splendid love poem; nowhere has Genet expressed more magnificently the desperate desire of the lover to be one with the beloved. A worthy professor of political economy was quite moved by it: nobody, he said to me, speaks of love like Genet.

But I greatly fear that the good citizen is being fooled once

---

* That is, the man you have killed (he is addressing criminals).

again. It is true that Genet wants to surmount the duality of minds, but *to his profit*. Let us recall Divine's saying to Gabriel: "You're myself." This praying mantis wants to eat her male in order to re-create him inside herself with her own substance and as she sees fit. We return to our starting point: at its highest degree of solitude and despair Genet's love is only the lofty name which he gives to onanism. *Funeral Rites* invites the surprised reader to indulge in the disappointing pleasure of morose delight.

A dead consciousness is the secret void of everything. Jean has gone away from everywhere, not only from the places where he lived but also from those he never saw. His omnipresent absence is the taciturn soul of things. In order to express Nature's and men's hostility toward him, Genet has been saying for a long time that he is a dead man on a visit to the living and that a race of dead men has carried the secret of tools and gardens to the grave. Why not charge *a single dead person* with epitomizing all the hostility of the universe? Objects now reject him doubly: they will never let themselves be seen as they appear to honest people, their rightful owners, nor ever again as they appeared to Jean. When Jean was alive, he could try to *make Genet see* what he saw; now that he is dead, the face that things had for him alone no longer exists, except as a kind of mental restriction which they impose on everyone. If that is the case, with a bit of skill Genet will merge these two rejections. Jean, who has been devoured by Genet, will devour things and persons. In the end, it is Genet who eats everything up. *Funeral Rites* is a tremendous undertaking of transubstantiation. Jean's soul, which is absent from everything, is everywhere. Jean becomes a cipher disk for deciphering the world: objects will be classified—as Genet sees fit—as Jean or Non-Jean, just as they are classified as Bears and Non-Bears for the primitive of the Bear clan. The matchbox that he carries in his pocket will be the coffin in miniature. Moreover, he tells us, in reasonable fashion, that "the pocket has no religious character. As for the sacred character of the box, it will never prevent me from treating this object familiarly." At the same time, he is careful to legitimate his piece of sorcery: "You have cenotaphs, don't you? Masses are said over false coffins." What is one to answer? The reader is caught in his own trap. Moreover, we know the incantatory value that Genet accords the gesture: in order to transform a stick into a knife one has only to treat it as such. These *sacralizing gestures* will transform the box into a funeral urn. "With my hand caressing the box, I performed in my pocket a miniature funeral ceremony." This funeral ceremony is a magical dance; it draws Jean into this new coffin. "It did not contain a particle of Jean's body, it contained all of Jean. His bones were of the size of matches, of pebbles imprisoned in whistles. It was somewhat like the wax dolls swathed in cloth on which enchanters cast their spell."

Meanwhile, the priest is saying Mass in the presence of the crowd: thus, magic is quite naturally opposed to religion as Evil is to Good, as the individual is to the social. The little bones in the matchbox are Jean himself, Jean spirited away from the glory of the public ceremony so that an outcast can secretly worship him in this loathsome way. The matchbox in Genet's pocket evokes their forbidden love: "He was my lover; all of you who are paying homage to him would have paled with disgust had you known of our pleasures." To complete this Black Mass Genet gently caresses the little coffin: the trouser pocket is one of the essential elements of his erotic mythology; through it one caresses, one caresses oneself, one slips one's hand into it to steal. Genet can dream of no greater delight than to slip his hand into the pocket of a Negro with the purpose of stealing a gold piece and to close his fingers about a penis. And the knife in the pocket, near the penis, becomes a phallic symbol. The caresses that Genet lavishes on this simulacrum are quite simply the gestures of masturbation. In making them Genet does not content himself with secretly profaning the public ceremony: he transforms the world into a young corpse and this young corpse into his own penis. The Marquis de Sade dreamt of extinguishing the fires of Etna with his sperm; Genet's arrogant madness goes further: he jerks off the Universe. Moreover, there is an element of black magic in this dwarfing: the dead boy becomes a baby, a plaything. Genet is already beginning the labor of mourning which will little by little reduce the grief, which will shrink it. The reader will recall the poisonous tenderness with which Genet saw the penis melt with pleasure and shrivel: it is the same tenderness that he feels when he fingers this miniature male in his pocket.

In what follows, Jean becomes embodied in a series of the most miscellaneous objects. Genet caught crabs from him. The crabs "sucked his blood." They will first be "tiny, secret hermits . . . whose function is to keep alive in these forests the memory of a dead boy." Later they will become Jean himself, and Genet—let us remember Pierrot and his maggot—will put one of them into his mouth: "I felt in my mouth the presence of the insect that carried Jean's secrets." In this passage, which will make the reader shudder with horror or shrug, depending on his mood, Genet inverts his usual manner: pretending to inveigle his readers into profaning pious traditions, he amuses himself by making them feel, with disgust, an emotion of which they would have approved had he not travestied it. In appearance he is merely ridiculing a rite of mourning. We recognize the procedure: if you touch and caress the objects that belonged to the dear departed, why not put the crabs that he carried into your mouth? Does this particular object shock you? But what does the object matter? From a formal point of view, the rite is strictly observed. And besides, those live little insects, swollen with his young blood, are, after all, closer to the dead man than the shoes he wore.*

Forewarned by his earlier misadventures, the just man is no longer taken in: he will not let himself be fooled by these crude sophisms, by this caricature of a sacred cult. And *for that very reason* he is again duped: behind this offensive trickery Genet has hidden the most admirable exigency, which he obliges the just man to refuse.

Odon of Cluny, whose aim was to disgust Christian souls with human love, wrote, after Chrysostom, that the beauty of the body is only skin-deep: "Indeed, if men were endowed, like the lynxes of Boeotia, with the power of visual penetration and could see what there is beneath the skin, the mere sight of women would nauseate them: that feminine grace is only saburra, blood, humor, bile. Consider what is hidden in the nostrils, in the throat, in the belly: filth everywhere. . . . How can we desire to hold in our arms the bag of excrement itself?"†

Anyone who has ever been in love can *feel* the unpardonable stupidity of this homily. *Answering* it is another matter. The fact is that nobody had ever answered it before Genet.‡ When the Marquis de Sade imagines malodorous lovemaking, it is out of sadism: he shares the monk's views, but draws the opposite conclusions. Now, there is only one answer: that one loves nothing if one does not love everything, for true love is a salvation and safeguarding of all man in the person of *one* man by a human creature. That is precisely what Genet answers: "Language expresses the soul. . . . The soul

---

* One can see the kinship between the two magnifying judgments: the finest gift one can make one's mother is to vomit on her hands—the finest memory one can retain of a dead person is the crab he carried. In both cases, the ceremony (of the gift, of mourning) is noble and sacred, but the *matter* is vile. In each case, the rehabilitation of the matter by the ceremony and the profanation of the ceremony by the matter are Genet's simultaneous goals.

† Odon de Cluny, *Opéra*, Paris, 1735, XII, 523.

‡ Except D. H. Lawrence. Preface to *Lady Chatterley's Lover*. But his answer is smeared with a philosophical jam that makes one gag.

appeared to be only the harmonious unfolding, the extension in fine and tenuous spirals of the secret labor, the movements, of algae and of waves of organs living a strange life in its deep darkness, of these organs themselves, the liver, the spleen, the green coating of the stomach, the humors, the blood, the chyle, the coral canals, a sea of vermeil, the blue intestines. Jean's body was a Venetian flask. I did not doubt that a time would come when this wonderful language which was drawn from him would reduce his body, as un-threading reduces a ball of thread, until it was a speck of light. It taught me the secret of the matter composing the heavenly body which emitted it and that the shit which was accumulated in Jean's intestine, his raw, heavy blood, his sperm, his tears, his mud, were not your shit, your blood, your sperm . . ."

The best reply to the good monk of Cluny is this will to love the base matter which emitted Jean's "wonderful language" and to transfigure it by seeing it as a reflection of the language which it emits, in short, to love the body through the soul and the soul through the body. The decision to go to the limit of Evil leads Genet to the limit of love.

To be sure, the primary intention is evil: resentment, despair and sacrilege incite him to prefer that which symbolizes our finite-ness, the lowliness of our extraction and the clay of which we are made. He, a waste product, an excrement of the earth, claims the right to love the intestines where excrement is formed. His will to the impossible is eager to cherish what, in point of fact, repels him as much as it repels others; in order to become the most irreplace-able of beings, this Nathanaël of the underworld will devote his predilections to that which is loathed by *everybody;* evil by deci-sion, he would like the sexual act to be a Black Mass which, in celebrating the debasement of man, produced this debasement by itself. But love stands its ground: it can and must *also* love "the mud," but if it loves only that, it becomes rage, pure hatred, any-thing but love. In one way or another, it must address itself to the person: physical desire itself is directed to the person through the flesh. Genet knows this; what he loves must also be Jean's love of him, Jean's smile, his voice, the poems he wrote, the tender gen-erosity with which he gave himself, in short Jean himself. Thus, the *evil* will to love the sordid in man changes into a *good* will to love Jean even in the "secret labor, the movement of algae and of waves of organs living a strange life in its deep darkness," in short, to love all of Jean. After that, what does it matter that a childish kind of provocation leads him to symbolize absolute love by placing a crab on his tongue? After all, this repulsive image *also* means that nothing should repel love.

To what extent does this narcissistic ogre, who is busy dragging a corpse into his den, feel the passion of which he speaks? Does it not conflict with his solitude and with the malediction that prevents him from getting out of himself? My answer is that he does feel it, but *in his book:* since, for him, language is the soul, the affections of his soul are moments of speech. I would add that he feels it *for a dead person:* since *all* of Jean has disappeared, it is easy to incorporate into himself and to re-create *all Jean;* and besides, he rises to these heights only intermittently: the very next moment he transforms Jean into a garbage can, into sausage meat, into an old beggar woman. "Jean can have existed momentarily in any form whatever, and I was able, for a period of ten minutes, to contemplate an old beggar woman bent over her stick,* then a garbage can overflowing with rubbish, eggs, decayed flowers, ashes, bones, soiled newspapers. Nothing prevented me from seeing in the old woman and the garbage can the momentary and marvelous form of Jean, and over them, in thought, I spread, along with my tenderness, a veil of white tulle with which I would have loved to cover Jean's adorable head."

Genet is amusing himself: Jean is no longer in the way; he can become anything since he *no longer is anything.* Since he is absent from the world, as the rose was absent from any bouquet, one can enjoy his absence from a garbage can as well as from a crab. Immediately afterward, he becomes, in a splendid passage, the very day which Genet is living, the endless day of his mourning: "I had spent myself within a living day whose life was emitted like a dawn around the manger by the luminous corpse of a twenty-year-old child, having, in its wrappings and swaddling clothes, the form and consistency of a soft almond."

Jean's soul is the light of day, it is the air; finally it becomes *the Other's gaze* which envelops Genet wherever he goes and constantly reminds him that he *is Another.* In this invisible, incompressible, conscious and painful medium, Genet is going to be able to indulge in his favorite sin: dead eyes watch him betray, watch him have sexual relations with those who have murdered his lover: "Jean's soul enveloped the room to which Erik imparted a hard precision." The function of this soul is to add spice to the betrayal. Jean be-

---

* We recognize this beggar woman. She is the old thief in *The Thief's Journal.* The dead lover is identified with his absent and perhaps dead mother. Both of them *abandoned* Genet.

comes a pretext for a poetic game which is under its own spell: "What would his life be like in this form of a crude guitar without string or plectrum, speaking with difficulty through a slit in the board, complaining about his condition? I don't care. He would be living and would be present. He would be in the world and I would put a white cloth on him every day. . . . My grief, which made me rave, invented this flowering, the sight of which is a joy to me. The more Jean is transformed into fertilizer, the more will I be scented by the flowers that grow from his grave."*

Jean's soul, which has drifted out of the world, and Genet's consciousness, which was cast into the mud, are symmetrical: their absences correspond on both sides of the mirror; looking at himself in the glass, Genet, the living corpse, sees Jean who sees Genet, his image. The dead Jean becomes the reflection in eternity, in non-being, of the Death that Genet lives in being from day to day. Genet and Jean are, for each other, *all* by virtue of being *nothing:* Genet is transformed into all by a rejection of all, he is the All-Evil; Jean, *who no longer is,* is in all the Absence of All. After his death, being is as full as it was before; nothing is ever missing from it, it is all that it can be. But even though reality manifests itself to the living in its high and deep fullness, the fact remains that it would have revealed to Jean other aspects of itself; one can think and talk about the charm that a certain street in the Belleville quarter of Paris had for him or the charm that a certain house or garden might have had for him, but one can do so only in the void. In the heart of the busy street, of the blue sky, of the fullness of Being, there appears an imponderable deprivation: there we have the other world, the other aspect of things, the shadowy face that they turn toward death. But was not poetry, for Genet, the meaning that words offered an absent gaze? Jean's death had a purpose: to make of Poetry a *person,* to give an Ego to Nothingness. This death is a triumph of being; but the dead Jean is the secret victory that is hidden in the heart of the failure. And you can be certain that Genet does not believe in survival. If anyone succeeded in convincing him that Jean's soul is immortal, that it continues really to see him and love him, he would be quite embarrassed, just as he would have been ten years earlier if Armand or Stilitano had suddenly declared to him that they adored him. If Jean were immortal, he would no longer depend on Genet; and besides, if the soul remained, even though it were mute one could attempt to establish

---

* Let us bear in mind that in Genet's erotic symbolism the guitar is an image of the masculine backside.

reciprocity of feeling. No, no, none of that! The only existence that Genet allows his dead friend is that of *appearance*. Let us recall that Evil tempts by its inexistence, that appearance gratifies the evildoer's pride because it would be reduced to nothingness without his support. Thus, Genet takes pride in supporting this phantom by a continued creation: he was evil when he toiled and strained so that Darling might live; he remains evil when he lends his body to the shade of Jean. Is it therefore *evil* to remain faithful to a dead person one loves? Of course not, but he would like to convince us that it is. We find here again the faking that we expected above: there is a deep flaw in our devotion to the dead; the absence of the departed ends by engendering in us an absence of the soul; there remains an imaginary feeling. The "normal" man who wants to preserve his faithfulness in defiance of death persists in this feeling *despite* its unreality. Genet, who did not love the living Jean, decides to love him when he is dead *because* this love is unreal. Thus, Jean's death is nothing other than Nature effecting in a particular individual the aesthetic transition from being to appearance. The dead Jean has become the appearance of which Genet has made himself the guardian.

As does the universe, Genet turns his shadowy face to the departed. He was legendary in the boy's heart, Jean loved him. A bothersome love, a legend of bad quality: who cares what goes on in a kid's heart and head! But the child dies. That's perfect: congealed in inertia, Jean's love of him becomes the unappealable sentence of the Beyond of Being, the hidden sense of the real, the underside of the cards. Genet strikes poses for this dead gaze, makes gestures for it, speaks for it. Out there, for the *personal Nothingness* that Jean has become, he feels himself becoming his own legend: sustaining in being this appearance that sees him, he is "within a hair's breadth" of seeing himself; the living Genet foreshadows for the dead Jean who loved him what the dead Genet will be for the living posterity that will love him. What a lucky thing this death is: a deceased child, who is none other than his own childhood, proclaims to him his future glory and saintliness. Genet, in his legendary truth, is an appearance that exists only for and through Jean, and Jean is an appearance that exists only through Genet.* The coupling of these two symmetrical nothingnesses is going to beget the characters of *Funeral Rites:* these

---

* One may maintain that he also exists for other persons: for his mother, his brother, his girl friend, etc. But Genet has taken precautions: he alone knows the *true* Jean (that is, the boy who gave himself to a man).

shadows rise up at the "breaking point" between Being and Non-being; each of them condenses and epitomizes both appearances at the same time; each is entirely Jean and entirely Genet. The broken couple exists again in these phantoms, the two lovers melt each other, and their double appearance takes on a new face, a new name. Paulo, Erik and the executioner must all be interpreted according to two systems of reference. As traitors, criminals and homosexuals they unquestionably belong to Genet's mythology, and they cannot be said to renew it. But, at the same time, they are Jean. They represent his absence, and as this absence is a refusal, a nothingness, their evil souls will be only impotence and refusal. They will kill in order to realize in their own way that absolute Evil, the death of Jean.*

Death is an act of aggression perpetrated by the deceased against his family: there is often an element of rancor in mourning. The rancor of the widower awakens in Genet that of the abandoned child. These two feelings impel Genet to torture the servant girl (who was Jean's girl friend), to kill her child, to hand Jean over to Riton, to deceive him with Erik, etc. But what is more important is that they have engendered the *executioner,* a hideous monster who hides his pansy weakness under a show of tremendous muscularity. If this Hercules is an executioner, it is quite simply because he represents the dead Jean: in this funereal book no one enters unless he has killed or is prepared to kill. But at the same time he has inherited from Genet a liking for capital punishment. Let us watch him being born: "The executioner's face little by little grew harmonious. I know that it was a distortion of Jean's face. With my memory, as from behind a pane of glass, I saw the youngster's face watching me. The more I spoke and wrote about the executioner, the further away, it seems to me, I drew from Jean's face, or the closer I came to it. I was choosing my angle of action. Finally, having found it, I stared at Jean. The concave turn of his nose, the height of his brow, the prominence of his chin, imposed upon me the image of the executioner. I accentuated all these characteristics by mentally willing the flattening of the face, upward. An evil thought, evil like everything creative, made this face even flatter. The root of the nose almost disappeared between the eyes—which themselves grew deeper and deeper. The chin became horizontal. I obtained a stupid, sneaky face in which there remained a certain gentleness and an ineffable sadness."

---

* Several of them, for example, the maid, were "inspired" by real people. But what remains of the models? Practically nothing.

Only one feature of Jean remains: gentleness. The executioner's sadness symbolizes the impotence of the dead: an age-old tradition, which has survived the impact of Christianity, depicts them as sorrowful shades. His weakness is the amorous docility of Jean, who played the passive role in his relations with Genet. And, of course, this monster also represents Genet himself, Genet who is unhappy about not being handsome (he speaks to us elsewhere about the incurably sad look he has in a photograph of himself when he was a boy). As for his secret femininity, it will recall Divine's. The executioner loses his prestige in Erik's eyes (Genet was afraid of losing his in the eyes of Bulkaen). He is a fake male, like Lieutenant Seblon. Erik's contemptuous hatred of him is the hatred Genet encounters or is afraid of encountering in his young lovers. "A handsome kid's feelings for the one who he knows adores him is rarely tender." In short, the executioner represents the uncertain virilification of Genet.

Paulo, Jean's brother, resembles him as Querelle resembles his brother, as Solange resembles Claire, so much so that Genet almost mistakes him for Jean. We find here, in a rudimentary form, the Dioscurism dear to our author. Paulo is Jean as Other. "My despair at the thought of Jean's death is a cruel child, it is Paulo. . . . Abandoned on my bed, he will be a polished instrument of torture, a dagger ready to function and springing, pale and with clenched teeth, from my despair. It is my despair incarnate. It enables me to write this book." Paulo symbolizes Genet's despair and the executioner symbolizes his rancor. Genet as sadist sees his lover in the form of this wretched, sorrowful monster; as masochist he gives him the frightening features of Paulo. This hoodlum is an old acquaintance of ours: he was called Darling when Genet was Divine.

A Saint's love is fulfilled by betrayal: Genet will create the militiaman Riton with the express purpose of handing Jean over to him. Rancor, asceticism, sado-masochism, liking for profanation: one can put into it whatever one wishes. In any case, these are old themes. But there is something else: Genet does not want to submit to anything; since he has been unable either to prevent or cause his lover's death, he invents a murderer for him; so he is now a murderer himself by a curious retroactive effect of his creation. We have already seen him attempt to jump back from himself in order to place himself at the origin of his own nature. This militiaman represents Genet's realistic will; he shows us its necessary derealization: the stoic relentlessness in *willing* Jean's death ends quite simply in imagining Riton. For a long time Genet has been wanting to create an ideal couple. In *Our Lady of the Flowers,* he said: "I had always wondered what would result from the meeting of a handsome young criminal and a handsome young guard. I took pleasure in the following two images: a gory and mortal shock or a sparkling conflagration in a riot of sperm and panting." Jean the Resistance fighter and Riton the Militiaman are given the function of representing, in *Funeral Rites,* this pair of enemies and lovers. "Between them will be a game of murder, a war dance, an orgy that draws blood." But Genet soon grows impatient, takes Riton away from Jean and gives him to Erik: he prefers this hierarchical couple to a pair of equals. The handsome and gentle Riton will love his German as Jean loves Genet. In the end, the old Divine awakens in Genet and lets herself be fascinated by the submission to the male. The author installs himself in his creature in order to abandon himself, through her, to Erik's bidding.

Erik himself is only a meeting point of themes; he is the least engaging of Genet's creatures. Conceived for the pleasure of sacrilege, he was born of Genet's admiration for strength. This character is a rape: the rape of France. Erik the German, who is a prince of Evil, has a melancholy that Genet rarely feels. He is not a dead man, since Genet has endowed him with a narcissistic mind and since he is haunted by his reflection in mirrors, by his name and by his image in the executioner's eyes: I would say rather that he is Death. He has the sadness and inexorable rigor of death.

Germany provides another character: old Divine has the audacity to disguise herself as Hitler. The couple Hitler-Paulo is the counterpart of the couple Erik-Executioner. Like the executioner, Hitler represents the formidable old queen who abandons herself to the young man. But the executioner was only a weak creature; Hitler's wickedness makes him strong. Genet has chosen him to fulfill an old dream. "Five million young men are going to be killed," he said in *Our Lady of the Flowers.* In *Funeral Rites,* he proclaims, in the form of the Führer: "Five milion young men are being sent to death by me." The masochistic girl queen is the executioner; the sadistic girl queen is Hitler. The death of Jean, who was killed by the Germans (then, in the course of the story, by a militiaman who was a friend of the Germans), symbolizes the defeat of France, which was murdered by the German army. Let us not be surprised at this: love is death. Thus, the murderer of the young member of the Resistance represents a symbolic marriage of France and Germany, a marriage symbolized moreover by the "Franco-German" couples (Paulo and Hitler, Riton and Erik) and by the short-lived love of Jean and Riton.

Among the women, too, we find the familiar theme: Madame D., Jean's mother, is the guilty mother; she sleeps with Erik, one of the murderers of her son. The maid is also the mother, but the humiliated mother. She is raped on her child's grave. These two women are one and the same: Genet's resentment invents the former, the hard, triumphant sinner who abandons her child, and it is also his resentment that kills the child of the second for the express purpose of taking revenge on the former.

The rhythm of the story is marked by a simultaneous double movement of expansion and involution. Genet blossoms out into a big bouquet, the flowers of which are "his twilight guard"; but at the same time he waits patiently, like a praying mantis, to capture and eat his young lover. Genet is twice present, that is, he is both the hero who carries out his "labor of mourning" and the author who decides about everything, at times breaking through the painted backdrops and showing his mischievous face instead of the faces of his characters. In this extraordinary crisscross in which everything is Jean, in which everything is Genet, the creator explodes and multiplies in the way that dawn, in Rimbaud, becomes a race of doves. The dead boy contains these blossomings of his austere form, of his absence which binds everything in the manner of Platonic "Ideas." Meanwhile, the author resorbs his characters and the bubble bursts just at the moment when the widower, in assimilating Jean's flesh, absorbs and digests the world. Now, Jean belongs to that twilight guard of which Genet says: "[It] exists only through me who exist only through it." Jean and Genet vanish together on the last page of the book, along with Erik and Riton, who embody them. The result is zero. The work cancels out: there were only dead leaves.

The construction of *Funeral Rites* can be compared to that of a hall of mirrors. The fact is that there are only reflections and reflections of reflections organized about a central reflection. Genet's sacred drama—whether it be called a struggle between Nonbeing and Being or a conflict of Good and Evil—is reflected in this empirical adventure: *a* death followed by *a* mourning. Jean is the Good: he died a hero, the Just honor his memory; Genet regrets the boy's death as he regrets the loss of his virtue. But the Good has a secret flaw: this hero was a homosexual, he had made a compact with the powers of darkness; and besides, he *no longer is;* so the Good is corroded, dissolved by Evil, which itself is a nonbeing. This fantastic widower who is trying to swallow his dead mate represents nonbeing trying to dissolve an absence. In this heartbreaking book, being is absent, has gone by, it *was;* the present is only a nothingness. The original couple is only a nothingness. Throughout the book Genet pretends to be tempted by Good: Jean, symbol of Virtue, of Uprightness, is going to serve as his intercessor. And since this dead person who *belongs* to Genet is being buried ceremoniously in the city of the Just, cannot the Thief regard this funeral ceremony as his secret reintegration into society? In desiring Jean is he not desiring the Good, just as in regretting the loss of Jean he regrets the loss of his Virtue? Not at all: the praying mantis ends by devouring her male, Genet swallows the Good and the glorified body of his lover as if they were a host; he digests them. The reader is fooled once again: Genet incorporating the Good is Evil closing about Being in order to dissolve it. In the final shipwreck of All, it is Evil that triumphs by disappearing. But this primary reflection is encircled by a round of secondary reflections; the intercourse of the old queen and the young hero, who himself represents the rape of Good by Evil, is reproduced a dozen times, two dozen times: as in a ballet, each dancer repeats the star's movements. *All* the pairs of dancers are Jean, are Genet, are Jean and Genet, participate in Good and Evil *through Jean and Genet* and directly. There is a hierarchy of reflections: they are so arranged as to represent a black knighthood. Hitler, though he is at the same time a girl queen, represents the Number One Big Shot whom Green Eyes refers to and who bears the weight of the world. Hitler, who, with a sign, can have Paulo tortured to death and who submits to his sexual whims, is an excellent image of Genet, the weakest and the strongest; and an excellent image too of the "Passion" of the creator who has the power of life and death over his creatures and who, for that very reason, is embodied in them and suffers with their sufferings. Below, the Executioner seems to be a blurred and shapeless caricature of him, the projection of the Archetype in some distorting medium. Thus, the Executioner is a reflection of Hitler who is a reflection of the Author. Opposite are Erik and Paulo, the toughs. Below, Riton and the Maid, two images of Genet the masochist who wants to be subdued and raped; Riton is a reflection of the young Genet, and the maid a reflection of Riton; they are the *women* of this novel. The couples organize: in the middle are Jean Decarnin and Genet; the Executioner and Erik, Hitler and Paulo, are the minor and major reflections of this primary couple. In all three cases, an old queen sleeps with a young hero. Let us simply note that the reflections do not produce *everything;* they are really images without life: the Executioner *possesses* Erik, it is he who makes the gestures of the male, but he has no authority over the other; Hitler crushes Paulo with his sovereignty, but he offers himself. The function of this dichotomy of the reflection is to express the inner contradiction of the desire of the author, a former girl queen who has become, despite herself, a boy queen. At the very bottom, we have an additional couple which symbolizes that of the *living* Genet and the *dead* Jean, namely Erik and his reflection in the mirror, that elusive reflection which he kills because he is unable to attain it. We find here the metaphysical composition of the medieval world: a universe of analogies; images arranged in accordance with the hierarchies of a black society, each of which symbolizes everything and tells everything about all the others. We are no longer accustomed to this kind of composition: in most novels, the characters are *complementary;* each expresses only part of its author's thought or sensibility; they must all be added up to recompose the universe. In Genet, each character is a different modulation of the original theme, like the Leibnizian monads which reflect all of the divine creation, but each from a different point of view. In this feudal society of which the German army and the militia provide the model but which is itself only the reflection of a dream and expresses in a new form Genet's old love of the feudality of the outlaw, each character (and each homosexual couple) is the symbol of his superior and of his inferior. That is the reason why one and the same theme can be taken up and modulated twenty times, through twenty different characters; that is what gives the impression, which is so rare nowadays, of a fugal development. There are *voices* which all sing the same despair and the same blasphemy; each dominates in turn, and the others serve as its bass, or else they all blend or sing in unison. *Point Counter Point* is a more fitting title for *Funeral Rites* than for Aldous Huxley's novel. And there can be no doubt that it is this rigorous unity that gives Genet's work its singular beauty. Life and death are twin sisters. Thus, each reflects the other, and you are likely at every moment to mistake one for the other. Good and Evil, Being and Nonbeing, are twin enemy brothers. Starting with this fundamental Dioscurism, you can conceive the magnificent counterpoint of *Funeral Rites:* symbols, analogies, substitutions, inversions of theme, anacruses. The ballet *'Adame Miroir* that Genet wrote for Roland Petit is the Thief's *ars poetica.* In this work, the games that the hero plays with his reflection and with death multiply to such a degree that we can no longer tell whether he is not quite simply his own reflection or the reflection of the reflection of his own death; we perceive there in its nakedness the *composition* which Genet usually conceals behind the anecdote and the artifices of language. Skillful and deliberate though it appears, this composition is not the consequence of an aesthete's fancy: it *is Genet* himself, Genet present in his work, not only in the various forms of his characters, but also and above all *as the internal structure of the work,* for this counterpoint of the reflection-reflecting and of the reflection-reflected defines the inner workings of the thief in quest of his being. Genet has won: he has put all of himself into his work; his book is himself. Novelists are usually concerned with problems of an aesthetic order or having to do with the effectiveness of their work, and these preoccupations blur their image. Their technique, which has been inherited or perfected or renewed, is *objective;* it was conceived as an answer to objective questions. The only rule underlying Genet's inventions and compositions is Genet himself. For him, to compose is to re-create *himself.*

MY VICTORY IS VERBAL AND I OWE IT
TO THE SUMPTUOUSNESS OF THE TERMS

By infecting us with his evil, Genet delivers himself from it. Each of his books is a cathartic attack of possession, a psychodrama; in appearance, each of them merely repeats the preceding one, as his new love affairs repeat the old: but with each work he masters increasingly the demon that possesses him. His ten years of literature are equivalent to a psychoanalytic cure.

The style of *Our Lady of the Flowers*, which is a dream poem, a poem of futility, is very slightly marred by a kind of onanistic complacency. It does not have the spirited tone of the works that follow. At times it is invaded by a swarm of nightmarish words; at others, it slackens and falls into a melodious softness. We are still close to autism, to the prelogical forms of thought. Genet, who can be so merciless with himself, frequently lets himself be moved by his misfortunes. The dark mass of dreams is only dimly lit up by the dawn of lucidity. With *Miracle of the Rose* there is a sudden break, an awakening: though written in jail, this book is the story of a liberation. In addition, it is the last time that Genet situates his characters in prison. And what a difference there is between the prison of *Our Lady*, which is a well of loneliness, and that of *Miracle*, which is a veritable microcosm, a society in miniature, a horrible boarding school. Furthermore, even before leaving prison forever, Genet has lost his illusions about it: he becomes an "exact visionary." Technician of burglary and of literature, able to handle the pen and the jimmy, he looks at everything from a utilitarian point of view. To measure the distance that has been covered one has only to compare the solitary narrator of *Our Lady*, the frenzied masturbator lying on his bed in a half-mad state, to the nervous, active, self-assertive little man who is forever wandering through the prison, who, when he is in love, wants to have the upper hand, wants to dominate the beloved. At the same time, the element of the marvelous condenses and is localized in two miracles: apart from these two exceptions, the thinking becomes firmer, logical, becomes an exact vision. In *Funeral Rites,* the calamitous aspect of homosexual love completely disappears, at least as regards the story of Jean and Genet. Genet's love of Decarnin is all the more active in that he has to resorb the dead boy into himself. But even in the memories which he evokes there is no fundamental difference between his attitude and that of a "virile" man toward a girl. In particular, when he relates their first night of love he is as moved by Jean's gift of his body as a "normal" lover receiving the favors of a virgin. And for the first time the subject of one of his books is an *enterprise* that is carried out, in short—despite all the exaggerations and caprices—an act: the *labor* of mourning. But as a result, since it is a matter of installing Jean's person in himself and since Jean is on *the side of Good,* the question of his relations with ethical values is put to Genet from a new point of view: Evil seems to weary him; why not experiment with Good? The fact is that the question remains open, he does not make up his mind; and I have shown above that there is an element of hoax in the temptation by Good. But we can appreciate the change that has taken place since the writing of *Our Lady* if we bear in mind that Genet has not considered it impossible a priori to return to common morality. This does not mean that he has really been *tempted* to go back to the society of the Just, but rather that the acuteness of his malediction has been attenuated, that the "original crisis" which is reproduced by each of his books becomes more abstract, more stereotyped, less felt, in short that he is liberating himself from it by dint of repeating it. Moreover, he says at the end of the book that the community of the Just has at last welcomed him back. This "return of the prodigal son" is symbolic: in becoming Jean, whom the good citizens regard as one of themselves, Genet magically incorporates into himself his lover's titles and glory. But it remains significant that he has been able, even poetically, to play with the idea of being reinstated. This shows to what extent he now feels liberated. *The Thief's Journal* appears as a literary testament or at least as a conclusion; the style at last takes on a swiftness, a dry, abstract pomp, an insolent splendor, an irony, a lightness which reveal a Genet who is master of his words and technique. As a result, the element of "poetry" is smaller; we no longer find the extraordinary metamorphoses that plunged us into a poisonous world. Genet attempts for the first time to *understand* himself. His early books were dreams about life; the *Journal* is a meditation on his past and particularly on his works. He formerly related his memories, his inner adventures; he now writes about his writing. He attempts to take his bearings: Who is he? Where does he now stand? Where is he going? The temptation of morality recurs several times. Is there a morality? Can the singularity of a unique undertaking be reconciled with the universal exigencies of ethics? Here too Genet comes to no conclusion. But he is already drawing recipes and maxims from his experience. This book leaves us in a state of uncertainty: it has disconcerted the better critics, for what they admired in Genet was the radicalism of his negations and they are now surprised not to find them in his latest works. But they feel as they do because they have failed to notice the slow and steady advance from one poem to the next and the progressive liquidation of the original crisis. They have not seen that little by little the dream gives way to lucidity, that passivity gives way to action, the immediate to the reflective, the meditation on life to a meditation on ethics and art.

Let us go back to the beginning: tossed from one image to another, Genet did not have time to tell himself that he was dreaming. Eventually his dream flickers and wants to become a written dream; so Genet writes it down and the dream is consolidated. But no sooner are the words penned than they drink the dream; then they dry and demand that they be read: the dreamer, who has been cast into the world of men, learns that the power which is consuming him is for them only an object; yet, for the others his dream belongs, *qua dream,* to the real world; it is a psychic event that took place on a given day in the mind of a given Thief. He, in turn, attempts to see himself from the point of view of the other and thereby half-liberates himself: the others' contempt has disenchanted his dream.

Genet resents their contempt and is going to try to drown them in his dream. He will lay traps, will throw worm-eaten footbridges over the water, will conceal ditches beneath branches, in short, he will work with his hands: he views his task in perspective, his gestures change into acts. Now, the nature of the act is to be conscious of itself and to pose the existence of a Truth. If Genet wants to make us dream his dream, he must be certain that it is *that particular dream* which he is imposing upon us: this suffices to define a certain truth at the core of the lie. The solipsistic dreamer destroys the true; the liar, on the other hand, believes in it increasingly the more he lies: his lies must be understood; since he does not know the truth, he runs the risk of uttering it.

The dreamer, the fake saint and the charmed thief vanish: there appears a "horrible worker." His tool is the Word; his material, the mind of the other; his aim, by means of the Word to drive the other mad. He will collect recipes, will invent techniques for producing offhandedly, elsewhere, intuitions that he will never have again. His own dream loses its colors, goes flat: there remains a model that the poet copies. He who formerly demolished in the twinkling of an eye now needs time to build. He prefers the deferred pleasure that he produces in the other to his own imaginary but immediate pleasure; caprice gives way to calculation, the results of which remain uncertain until the very last moment. In order to want to become, in the eyes of all, the most singular of beings, Genet finds himself forced to reintroduce reciprocity. So as the better to mislead—of course. Nevertheless, if he wants to know the effect that the words have on others, he will have to judge it from the effect they have on himself. He can fool the others as much as he likes, but he is obliged to gauge their reactions on the basis of his own. If he questions himself as an artist, it is in order to know, on the basis of the sensibility of which he is so proud and which he regards as unique, the universal characteristics of all sensibility. It is indeed no longer a matter of derealizing everything and anything at all costs, no matter how: what is needed is an unreality which *lasts,* that is, which installs itself in the other and which cannot be driven out. Genet therefore reintroduces into himself order, truth, reciprocity and the universal, which are, if I am not mistaken, characteristics of Good. Can it be that Claudel is right? Are we to believe that the worst is not sure? No: Genet has not returned to Good. His intention is to harm, and his work aims at being an evil action. If he goes back to certain rules, it is in order the better to do Evil; if he gets rid of his poisons, it is by poisoning others; if he wrests himself from the dream, it is by making his victims dream in his stead. It is true that he builds, and in so doing he adopts certain norms of the builder, but he does so in order to destroy, in order to horrify good souls, to cast them into sin, to set them on the paths of Evil, to undo in each of them the bonds that attach the mind to reality. His prose is a false prose, his novels are false novels, his characters are decoys: but however he may want to use them, Genet has reintroduced virtues into himself; he is *no longer the same.* And besides, these nullifying reveries which incite the reader to destroy all objectivity are organized for Genet into a harmonious object. The reader loses himself so that the work may be: in the moment when the dream swallows him up, a new reality arises out of this abolition for Genet, who watches him dream and knows that he himself is the careful instigator of these reveries: this reality is the reader's dream *as object*. At the beginning, the reverie, which was a dream for Genet, was an object for the other: it is now a dream for the other and an object for Genet. The sentence which he tested before writing by repeating it under his breath was only a murmur in his mouth; when, in turn, it is repeated by a thousand throats, it comes back to him like the roar of a tide. His characters were only absences, the sour derealization of his onanistic gestures; they return to him in the form of *creations of the collective imagination*. Darling Daintyfoot, product of a destructive rage, was only the desperate negation of the real and of all truth, but there is now a truth about Darling. People *talk* about him, they judge him; one can even be wrong about his character, can make mistakes about him, can assert, for example, that he is a character in *Funeral Rites*. He has a moral and aesthetic existence; the infinite number of possible readers endow this poor, schematic* figure with an infinite density: it is enriched by whatever they put into it. Nevertheless, Genet remains faithful to his original purpose, which was to destroy: Darling's being is steeped in nonbeing. In order for this beautiful absence to loom up in the cell, the walls, the blankets and the prisoner himself were required, and everything had to capsize in nothingness. He intensifies the massacre, makes of these nullities the pretext for a tremendous holocaust of words: the destruction suddenly becomes a creation; the poet succeeds where the saint failed: he causes being to rise up beyond nonbeing; at first, all of being moves into nonbeing (radical derealization of the world), then all of nonbeing flows back into being (objectification of the work as a creation of the collective imagination). It will be noted that he has not resorted to the *third term* which is usually required to effect a synthesis. In fact, there has been no synthesis at all. Was it not this identity of opposites *without unity* that he was supposed to attain through ascesis? But what need has he of Saintliness? The poet has proudly created the order of being which the Saint was humbly seeking to disclose beyond annihilation.

What does Genet talk about if not Genet himself? The object that the minds of others reflect to him is thus Jean Genet. To be sure, he had been an object for a long time, ever since the decent

---

* Neither more nor less schematic than the other fictional figures; they are all made up of a few features chosen from reality.

folk had called him a thief, but an immanent object, an object at the back of the soul. He had been unable to make his mind and his objective being coincide and had exhausted himself in vain efforts to make that Ego the goal of his activity, in short, to recreate himself in his own eyes as the others had made him. He has now understood his error: he wanted to make himself what the others saw him to be, whereas he should have made the others see him as he wants to be. He will plunge his hands into their souls, he will knead that white dough and will give it the shape he wants it to have. The consciousness of others is the medium in which man can and must become what he is. In making himself exist as an object *for others,* Genet creates himself *in the per se.* No doubt he will never have an intuition of what he is creating. But though he cannot enjoy himself in the other, at least he knows the joy of producing himself. He plays on a keyboard whose sound he does not hear, but he knows that it is being heard over there, in the next room; the notes follow each other in the order that he has chosen, with the loudness that he has desired. He feels the movement of his fingers, the resistance of the keys, he senses that all his effects are making an impression on the listeners. He has won. Regarded as a thief, he wants to become a thief; but one does not give being to that which is. The stroke of genius, the illumination that finds the way out, is the choice of writing. He will create himself as a thief in another domain by establishing other relationships with the good citizens. He becomes the person who *manifests theft:* reflecting upon his acts of larceny, he transforms them, by a constant "carrying to the limit," into exemplary thefts, as the mathematician transforms the vague outlines of natural things into firm geometric lines. The source of all these perfect thefts will be for the reader an exemplary Genet who is as different from the flesh-and-blood thief as a circle is from a round figure drawn in the dust. Henceforth, the "crepuscular"* existence that he drags out in the universe is, in his own eyes, merely a by-product of the immanent being that he has conferred upon himself in the mind of the other; it is an epiphenomenon, a dream, which, as Plato says of the Place, "can be attained only by a kind of bastard reasoning" and which borrows its weak reality only from its involvement in the Idea of the Thief. Genet's crude, contingent life is now only a thin film that unites and separates two absolute freedoms, one of which *creates its own being* in the other.

Thus, he is now freed from the unbearable obligations of aestheticism. His manner has become very simple, his behavior

---

* Mallarmé uses the same expression to designate himself. He is "sterile and crepuscular."

natural, his movements are few and precise: he no longer has a *role* to play. It is no longer necessary for him to invoke by incantatory attitudes the sacred essence of the criminal or the queen: he puts himself entirely into words and puts the words into his books; he who was an aesthete has become an artist or a naked power to produce images in others.

Nevertheless, he still plays, but in and by the act of writing. He plays at being loved, at *being* the Poet.

His literary adventure is not unlike an amorous adventure: while seeking to arouse horror, Genet writes in order to be loved. I refer here to an infernal love that aims at subjugating a freedom in order to take shelter in it from the world. To win love, to subdue a mind, to make it want to be dependent, inessential, to become for it, with its complicity, the sovereign object: is not this what wicked love and Genet desire? The mind of the reader will oddly resemble that of a lover: it forgets itself, it loses itself so that the Thief may appear. Under the effect of poetic philters, the reader treats himself as an inessential means. He says "I" with Genet and yet he is and is not Genet: aesthetic distance—what Genet sometimes calls "tulle" and sometimes "politeness"—and the concerted use of the perfect and imperfect tenses tend to stop him in the middle of his fall, to perpetuate the fascination and the giddiness, to make of the "I" which rashly offers itself a mixture of itself and another. To become oneself in the Other, to transform the Other into oneself: is not this the goal that the lover pursues as far as orgasm? The beloved, however, becomes an object: he calls attention to himself, he shows himself, he surrenders so as the better to take. Coquetry, finery, masochism: such are the mainsprings of Genet's art, an art feminine in its nature. Was it not by offering himself, by becoming an object, that he formerly aroused the desire of males? Was he not taken by them and did he not suffer? Caught in the act and called a thief, the child is made an object by the other; his reaction is to make himself even more of an object, with the zeal that drives him to will the worst in order to assume his misfortunes; he practices passive homosexuality and abandons himself to pimps. But the underlying contradiction in his attitude is that he plays the perfidious and evasive role of the beloved while demanding the sufferings of the lover. His semivirilification poses the opposite contradiction: he plays the role of the lover, but without loving, while regretting that he cannot become an object. Liberated and pure, his desire to become an object will find its "sublimated" satisfaction in the literary operation. The latter reproduces the original crisis once

again. Genet offers himself, lays himself bare, has himself taken.
But this time he neither likes nor wants to suffer. Glamorous,
legendary, hated, fascinating, he fully assumes the role of the beloved and transforms the reader into a bashful lover; he occupies a
mind that can neither quite get rid of him nor quite identify itself
with him. It is he who now adorns himself with the painful, the
staggering beauty that he worshiped in the pimps. They were
silent, implacable, steeped in indifference: such is his work. Darling
cleft the girl queens in two slices which came together again with
a sigh: this sickle stroke, this path of a cold, gleaming blade which
one thinks one possesses and which slides off without leaving a
trace is the passing of one of Genet's poems through our mind. And
the deep void that is concealed by the impenetrability of the toughs
is the "looming emptiness, sensitive and proud, like a tall foxglove," the secret purpose of his art. Genet wants us to "hate him
lovingly," to love him with horror and even to be damned with
him, but he does not love those whom he wants to charm; they are
the bourgeois, the rich, the just.

Consequently, it is the reader who assumes the contradictions
of Genet, who, as we have just seen, was both the beloved—since
he made himself a thing to be taken—and the lover—since he took
upon himself all the sufferings of love. The reader is going to experience the conflict in reverse: he will become a *lover* by the act
of reading, he will attempt to slip into the thief's subjectivity; he
will become an inessential subject by losing himself so that the
object, Jean Genet, a legendary thief, may be. But no sooner has
he entered this foreign subjectivity than he feels that an ironic gaze
is objectifying him, and he becomes a *thing to be taken,* to be
handled, like a beloved creature. Inversely, Genet, who offered
himself to the readers as an object, suddenly transforms himself,
as soon as they have opened the book, into a subject, for the
imaginary world which closes up about them, and which is *this*
world become nightmare, shows the readers that it has an author.
The readers have identified themselves, despite themselves, with the
character—a thief, a beggar, a homosexual—who said "I." But this
"I" now opens and discloses the "I" of the Creator: "I give the
name violence. . . . I shall speak of Divine as I see fit. . . ." No
identification with him is possible, since we are *reading* the book
which he has *written.* The readers are being tricked: they are
damning themselves and some demiurge is watching them damn
themselves. A cynical and peremptory freedom is imposing itself

upon their freedom, is enveloping it and maneuvering it. If they suddenly find themselves vomiting on their mother or violating a grave, it is because they have been led along trick paths. They thought they were alone and there was someone in the room, someone who arranged for them to fall into crime and awaken with remorse. They struggle and get indignant, but their fury was foreseen, and they know it. The author wanted them to protest in precisely *that* way. This time the roles are reversed: the scapegoat is taking his revenge. He has been the object of their gazes and now they are the object of his. Bending over his paralyzed victims, the wily hoodlum discovers himself through their discomfort: he is the secret bad conscience of the good consciences. As his freedom is, for his readers, only an irritating absence that maneuvers them without letting itself be seen, they reflect it to him as a privation, as an emptiness: the dead Jean Decarnin haunted the world in like manner. Genet haunts these frightened souls, manifests himself by acts of levitation; he is a rapping spirit that drags chains through corridors, lifts up a thought, displaces a feeling. When his freedom comes to him from the depths of a consciousness, it is the fatality that freezes the other's freedom, it is the reverse of his readers' destiny. "An object," says a historian of religions, "becomes sacred insofar as it incorporates (that is, reveals) something other than itself. A sacral stone is a thing, and yet in its depths a thing is revealed."* Appearing through an object, the power preserves a specter of objectivity, but it is itself a subject: the sacred is the subjective manifesting itself in and through the objective by the destruction of objectivity; it is a gaze-object that appears within our universe and in the aspect of a thing, but which robs us of the world and of our own subjectivity by conferring upon us the status of *thing gazed at*. That is precisely what Genet is in his own eyes when he looks at himself in the reader's soul: for the readers, he is a gaze that rises up from the word; and as the Just feel themselves changed into a thing by this gaze, Genet, who is bent over these souls that are thickening and coagulating before his eyes like a mayonnaise, reveals himself as the secret ferment which is causing this solidification. His pure freedom is reflected to him as a power which is other than being and which manifests itself through being, as a negative transcendence of all: he has been crowned king by the reader. In point of fact, the latter is not aware of this consecration: he *recognizes* Genet's freedom and knows that he is not recognized by Genet; that is all. But for Genet there is a consecra-

* Mircéa Eliade, *Traité d'histoire des religions*, p. 25, Payot.

tion because the creature who recognizes him becomes inessential and secondary by virtue of this recognition. The reader differs from a thing only in that he *becomes* a thing, whereas the thing is passively what it is. And this difference itself operates in Genet's favor: his audience humbles itself before him by consenting to recognize a freedom which, as it very well knows, does not recognize its own. He defrauds us: that is the consecration of the Poet. "I will be the Thief," says Genet. And now: "I am *the* Poet." With regard to this privileged case, we shall note one of the essential differences that set the poet off from the writer of prose. The latter, who is *profane* by nature, recognizes his readers' freedom exactly insofar as he asks them to recognize his: prose is based on this reciprocity of recognition. The poet, on the other hand, requires that he be recognized by a public which he does not recognize. The writer of prose *speaks* to the reader, attempts to convince him in order to achieve unanimous agreement on one point or other; the poet speaks to himself through the mediation of the reader. The writer of prose uses language as a middle term between himself and the Other; the poet makes use of the Other as an intermediary between language and himself. Between the writer of prose and the reader, language is canceled so as to further the ideas of which it has been the vehicle;* between language and the poet, it is the reader who tends to be effaced in order to become a pure vehicle of the poem; his role is *to objectify speech* in order to reflect to the poet his creative subjectivity in the form of sacred power.†

In a certain sense, Genet the poet knows himself as being, for the other, identical with what he is to himself. He thus rids himself of his *objectivity*, of his *nature*. Yet, from another point of view, there subsists a slight discrepancy owing to the fact that the recognition is not reciprocal; and though the naming of *Poet* designates a free and conscious activity, it refers to that freedom as Another. Genet thinking himself as Poet thinks himself as Another for the Others and as Another than self. For the readers, the Poet's freedom is a *power* because they cannot prescribe a future for it, because they know that, whatever they do, they will be surprised and will see their forecast confounded. My freedom becomes a power for the Other, even if he views it in its subjective spontaneity, simply by virtue of the fact that it is a transcendence, that it is other. Genet, whose own creative subjectivity is announced to him by the other, tries to test it as if it were that of another. He would like to be for

---

* This is so only at the extreme limit. All language is poetic to a certain extent.

† In the case of Mallarmé, the reader and the author are canceled at the same time; they extinguish each other so that the Word alone may exist in the end.

himself the sacred power that he is for his readers, *the* Poet: not
only the man who has written and plans to write poems, but the
one who *has* the sacred power to write them. Thanks to the Other,
he reinstalls a little of the outside mist into the translucency of the
"inner space," a little inertia into his pure activity, a little mystery
into his self-knowledge; with the Other's expectation, he awaits
himself. But how can Genet be blamed for this very slight discrepancy between the subject for the self and the subject for the
other, between the act and the powers, between the will and
the waiting for self, that small oscillation between the profane and
the sacred? Was it not necessary that, in order to win, this victim
of the sacred become its master? At the moment when "an illustrious poet" places the Thief's hand "on his brow"* the latter can
enjoy his victory. Who could dispute this aching soul's right to the
first pleasure of triumph? Over whom, if not over the Other,
should he have won his victory? And if the Other, in him and
outside him, was the hydra that had to be slain, was it not necessary
that deliverance appear to him also as a play of the Other and of
the Same? If he takes one more step, the Other will dissolve.

He aimed first at making himself the most irreplaceable of
beings, thus at giving himself the particularity of an object; he tried
in vain to be in himself and for himself the goldsmith and the
jewel; then, realizing that he was an object through and for Others,
he decided to engrave his particularity on the freedom of Others.
Thereupon, this particularity as a defined thing falls away from
him; a third Genet springs up, one who is neither the poor tramp
nor the legendary hero of the poems, but the synthetic activity that
turns the former into the latter; this activity, which effects the
regulated transformation of one objective reality into another objective reality, cannot belong to the world of objectivity. Genet's
particularity shifts: it now lies in his will to create *this* particular
work. And this particularity which is no longer an object for anyone, not even for himself, which is not, which is in the making, is
situated beyond being and language: anyone wishing to describe
and name it would always find himself naming the operation or
describing the work. But it is more than that and something else,
since it produces the work and is a consciousness of the operation.
We know what this creative consciousness is: it is *existence*. The
original will to Evil appeared to us as an existential tension, but

---

* The reference is to Jean Cocteau, who did a great deal to get Genet out of the clutches
of the Law.

we immediately saw all the contradictions of the situation oblige it to submit to essence: so long as Genet wanted to be a "Thief-in-itself," he hid his deeper existence behind his essentialist passion. But now, leaving to the minds of others the job of realizing his being, he frees himself from it: he is now only a faceless freedom that sets fascinating traps for other freedoms.

By technical means, this freedom dissolves the darkness that clouded it: it is a pure consciousness of itself and of its objective ends. In fulfilling its ends, it transcends them. Let us bear in mind what Hegel says of the artist and his work in the "Animal Kingdom of the Spirit": the work is the limited reality which consciousness gives itself, but which it immediately overflows. "The work, like the original nature which it expresses, is something determined, but in the presence of the work the consciousness is determined as that which had within itself determinability by virtue of negativity in general. Thus, the consciousness is the universal with respect to this precise determinability of the work. The consciousness withdrawing from its work is in actual fact the universal consciousness because it becomes, in this opposition, absolute negativity . . . whereas its work is the defined consciousness." In determining himself *in his work* as the Thief, Genet escapes this determination; he stands opposed to it as a free creative consciousness which can be defined only in terms of undetermined free activity; in creating himself in the other, he empties himself of himself and becomes the absolute void as an unconditioned power to create. In making himself the Thief for the Other, he makes himself a creator for himself. A moment ago, he found Being at the end of nothingness; at present, in affirming his being to the very end, in endowing it, by means of words, with a new reality, in depositing it as filth in the other, he frees himself from it and finds himself in that pure negativity, that presence of nothingness to itself, that perpetual transcending of the given, namely consciousness. In carrying commitment to an extreme, he again becomes available. He has put himself entirely into his poems, with his heavy past, his murdered childhood, his present life of crime and dreams, and his destiny, already determined, which is to lead him, from prison to prison, lower and lower until he is taken by death. But by the same token he wrests himself from the past by giving himself an entirely new past as a creator, by substituting for his childhood memories the memory of the words that sing it; he frees himself from the present by transforming his gestures into acts and his dreams into literary motifs; while his passive future as a thief, which has been prophesied, settles in his work as a future-which-is-an-object, and thereby changes into a past, the work which is in progress or which is being planned offers the creator a free future of creation. Even his feelings are modified: he "communicates emotions which he does not experience" and all of which enter words. No sooner does he feel an incipient excitement than he makes of it a means of moving others: he feels the upheaval caused by love or hatred, but he feels it *over there,* in the Other, insofar as the other becomes Genet. As for the creator himself, he experiences a kind of ataraxia because he no longer undergoes anything: Genet has finally succeeded in introducing activity even into pure affectivity. "Pretexts for my iridescence, then for my transparence, and finally for my absence." What he said about young boys applies to his books. They are pretexts for his absence, for the absence whereby Valéry defined *the man of mind* and which he reduced to the refusal to be anything whatever: "All phenomena, stricken thereby with a kind of equal repulsion and, as it were, successively rejected by an identical gesture, appear in a kind of equivalence. The feelings and thoughts are enveloped in this uniform condemnation which extends to everything perceptible."* But Valéry, who is intellectualistic, refers to the knowing and observing consciousness: Genet's consciousness, which, like beauty, is voracious, unfeeling and absent, is in active relationship with the universe: it keeps the universe at a distance and covers it with a veil, but its aim is not so much to know the universe as to draw from it the subject of a work whose purpose, like the poems of Mallarmé, is to *make the world useless.*† His consciousness has at last come to terms with itself: the little thief was eager to *will* Being as a whole, whereas it can be accepted only in detail. The cold, solitary consciousness of the rebel now *accepts* large parts of the universe that it hated; with greedy indifference it draws from the universe the materials of its work; everything interests it; it seizes upon raw events and works on them, "interprets" them in order to give them at last a symbolic meaning, to force them to speak of sexuality, murder or poetry. The world was the thorn in his flesh; by *willing* it, Genet was fleeing from it, was producing an imaginary world. When, by a slight shifting of his

---

* *Variety I:* Leonardo da Vinci.

† After the crisis of 1865-1867, Mallarmé, too, discovered, by following a quite different path, the "universal determinability" and "absolute negativity" of consciousness. He, too, was to extend this "uniform condemnation to everything perceptible": "My Mind, that habitual solitary of its own Purity, which is no longer dimmed even by the reflection of Time" (letter to Cazalis, May 14, 1867).

intention, he decides to *realize* this imaginary world, to make of it, with the cooperation of others, a fictive object, a network of signs and figures whose sole purpose is to indicate Genet himself, the real world belongs to him: simply because it becomes *usable*. Starting with *Miracle of the Rose,* the attentive reader finds a shade of optimism in his works. To be sure, the object of his thinking remains despair, but the sentence itself, with its noble vivacity and its boldness, leaves us with a less desperate impression. The man who writes: "I give the name violence to a boldness lying idle and hankering for danger" is certainly not a *"misérabiliste."* For him the ogress Beauty gives meaning to the universe, despite her dreadful rigor: she uses it as a pretext for language. The poet's ambiguous situation lies in his taking God's creation in reverse: he puts the Word at the end. To absorb the universe into language is to destroy the universe, but it is to create the poet. What exactly happens? Is the real annihilated in significations? Does the contingency of being give way to necessity? Both. For language, as Blanchot has observed, is both the flight of being into significations and the evaporation of significations, in short, annihilation—and it is also *being,* whipped air, written, engraved words. Engaged, like the surrealists, in a process of demolition, Genet must, like them, construct a war machine in order to achieve his ends; and this machine has two faces, one of shadow and the other of light: it is the evil sacrifice of being to nothing, but it is also the inclusion of nothingness in being. It attempts to dissolve reality, but it salvages nonbeing. Genet's optimism comes from his presenting Evil, in the imaginary, as being produced in Being by freedom. And in the last analysis it matters little that being means this or that: it is enough that it means something. Optimism is the affirmation not that man is or can be happy but simply that he does not suffer for nothing. Even if the world has been created only to be annihilated in a cone of cold light, ultimate resplendence of an eye whose optic nerve is cut, this annihilation would still have a meaning. In wanting to dissolve being in nonbeing, Genet reconquers nonbeing on behalf of being; he confines it in his books like the devil in a bottle. His works are, in one respect, repeated suicides and, in another, the renewed affirmation of human grandeur. We find here, once again, the game of loser wins. But this time Genet knows the rules: he wins every single time. Masturbation and homosexual intercourse gave him nightmarish joys: ever since he has been *telling* about his masturbation and intercourse Genet has known happiness.

> *Sooner or later it will have to be*
> *recognized that he is a moralist.*
> —COCTEAU

He is much too lucid to be unaware of this aspect of his undertaking; he knows that it is liberating him. Whatever progress he
makes as a result of it, one can be sure that he is the first to know
about it. But as he has been refusing since childhood to submit to
anything, as he wants to get nothing from Providence or fortune,
he cannot accept passively, as if it were a simple return shock, the
moral benefits of his literary activity: pleasure and pain must come
from him. Moreover, his poetry is voluntary: to write is to explore
systematically the situation into which he is thrown; he is a poet
as a result of becoming completely aware of what it means for him
to be a thief; poetry will withdraw into itself if he becomes aware
of what it means for him to be a poet. His books are born of what
I have called cathartic crises; since the poet must become a full
consciousness of himself and of the world, he must provoke these
crises, must direct and observe them; and since the book is nothing
other than this consciousness as expressed in words, it must return
to the latter in order to relate his deliverance. These monstrous and
perfect works want to be *consciousness through and through,* without the slightest zone of darkness, ignorance or inertia. They will
contain both the story and the story of the story, the thoughts and
the history of the thoughts, the spiritual procedure, its method
and the progress report, in short a poem and a journal of a poem
which, unlike that of Gide, will accompany the creation by ethical
comments. Whence the Jansenistic austerity and moral pedantry
which combines so strangely with the shocking portrayals. It is this
will to edify that is least forgiven him; the high-minded reader
would, if need be, overlook his obscenities but does not tolerate his
moralizing about them. We would be less indignant if we first
realized that this display of moralism does not concern us. No doubt
Genet knows that he shocks us; no doubt he secretly enjoys doing
so; but he has never dreamed of making us better and he does not
want us to profit from his instruction; the one he wants to edify is
himself. "It is with good sentiments," said Gide, "that one writes
bad books." Genet wants to write good books with bad sentiments:
he thinks that a gratuitous art would not be worth bothering about,
and this ought not to surprise us since ethical values have always
been his chief concern. No doubt he was chiefly interested in profaning them, but that is a way of recognizing them. And besides, as

one can imagine, his edifying discourses bear little resemblance to those of the average clergyman. They are moral because the comments which they attach to the characters' acts remain in the sphere of the might-be. But this moral art is not a moralizing art: Genet upholds no thesis, does not want to demonstrate anything; though his works are criminal assaults upon his readers, they are, at the same time, presented as systematically conducted ethical experiments which are their own comments upon themselves. Furthermore, he defines his creative activity as follows: "Creation is not a somewhat frivolous game. The creator has committed himself to the fearful adventure of taking upon himself, to the very end, the perils risked by his creatures. . . . But then the creator will charge himself with the weight of his characters' sins. . . . He must take upon himself—the expression seems feeble—must make his own to the point of knowing it to be his own substance, circulating in his arteries, the evil given by him, which his heroes choose freely."

Thus, creation is a passion. Not content with producing characters from his own flesh, the author embodies himself in them and suffers with their suffering: each of them provides him with an opportunity to explore a humiliation, a despair, an anger. Having entered Querelle, he will feel the anguish that follows murder; with Green Eyes he will writhe in an effort to escape the consequences of his crime, then will decide to face them; as Divine he will have the experience of aging; as Erik, that of beauty; with the executioner, that of ugliness; once, lost in the dense darkness of Lysiane, he will be a woman.

What is the purpose of these Passions? Suffering? Yes, of course, and, besides, he tells us so himself. He needs, as he informs us, the rule and sorrows of a penal colony: "I shall wear myself away with slow, minute patience, I shall perform the painful gestures of the punished. . . . I shall become as polished as they, pumiced." But the penal colony no longer exists. That does not matter. Genet will install his penal colony in himself, he will live the colony through the convicts whom he invents: "But I am speaking of a colony that has been abolished. Let me therefore restore it in secret and live there in spirit as in spirit the Christian suffers the Passion." We know about his fake masochism, his sham dolorism, we know that Christianity has left its mark on him and that he was able to bear his wretched lot only by aspiring to be the Iphigenia of a pure sacrifice offered to all and to nothing. But, when all is said and done, we must not lose sight of the fact that these sufferings are imaginary: he does not feel them. We know him well enough not to be taken in by these appearances: the beautiful word Passion is hollow when Genet uses it. Moreover, we have never seen him really seek suffering: when he does experience it, he carries it to an extreme in order to master it; he magnifies it or tries to utilize it. But it offers him nothing in itself. One has only to compare Genet's spiritual exercises with those of Bataille, who is a godless mystic. The latter tells us, in *The Inner Experience*, that he is sometimes entranced by the photograph of an executed criminal, as the Christian is by the Crucifixion. I regard this meditation as a fake. At least the photograph is a real object, at least the person whose picture we see really lived, really suffered: the ghastly ecstasy of his smile and the wounds on his chest inspire real horror; perhaps it is possible to intensify this horror to the point of "execution," to realize for a moment, by means of it, the suffering state of man, his abandonment in Nothingness. But that is not and never has been Genet's purpose. Can one imagine him meditating on the face of the Chinese who has been flayed alive? He doesn't give a damn about the pain of others; as for suffering humanity, he detests it: if everybody suffers, suffering is devaluated. You will not find any mournful suffering or meditation on "agony" in Genet. Far from proclaiming the absurdity of universal suffering, he tries to give meaning to his own. His dolorism is mainly sexual, and we have seen his reveries on Divine's woes end peacefully with masturbation. No: we have discovered the trap, we are not taken in. Let us see whether he has not specified, in other passages, the moral value he attaches to his works.

Such passages are not wanting. I quote the following at random: "I liberate myself by declaiming poems that leave my mind clarified," he says in *Our Lady of the Flowers*. "And with Divine dead, what is left for me to do, to say? . . . I have given up my desires. I too am 'already way beyond that.'" "I can keep dying until my death. . . . Have I said all that ought to have been said about this adventure? If I leave this book, I leave what can be related. The rest is beyond words. The rest is silence. I remain silent and walk barefoot." He does the same at the end of *Funeral Rites*, which was likewise an ascesis; it is now finished: "I belonged to the tribe . . . by the grace of an adoption. . . . In short, I belonged to the France which I cursed and so desired." And in *The Thief's Journal:* "This journal is not a mere literary diversion. The further I progress, reducing to order what my past life suggests, and the more I persist in the rigor of composition—of the chapters, of the sentences, of the book itself—the more do I feel myself hardening in my will to utilize . . . my former hardships."

These passages—and a dozen others—all have the same intention: they make of his work an ascetic experience which is achieved
by the Word and whose fulfillment is to dissolve language into
silence. Let us follow this lead.

In his cell, Genet produced images in order to heighten or maintain his excitement, thus, in order to act upon himself. The function of the story that he told himself was to bring him to orgasm,
after which it dissolved. When the masturbator changes into an
artist, he likewise does so in order to act upon himself; let us recall
that he throws himself into writing as into stealing, as into lovemaking, frenziedly, doped by dexedrine tablets, and that he does
not put down his pen until he has finished. This verbal frenzy ends
with the breaking-up of the word as does the onanistic imagery
with the breaking-up of the images. He hastens toward the moment
when he will write "THE END" at the bottom of the last page and
when he will have *nothing more to say* because he will have *said
everything*. Nothing more to say: the words are there, but there is
no further need to use them; if he tried, he would start, despite
himself, to write sentences he had already written. But how can he
be sure of having said everything? By systematically developing in
the realm of the imaginary all the possibilities contained in the
situation itself, particularly those which have not been realized.

The operation takes place in two stages: his heroes, who are
products of masturbation, were at first only the transparent film
that separated him from himself. He was then "mean, like all creators," and prolonged his excitement by torturing his creatures as
children torture flies. But as his heroes are, in another sense, himself as Other and as he has assigned to each of them the function of
embodying what he wants to become or is afraid of becoming, he
inflicts imaginary tortures upon himself by making them suffer. A
shifting of intention is enough for these sadistic games to become
spiritual exercises. Genet, who is passive, full of hatred, a prisoner
and an onanist, will humiliate Darling in order to take revenge on
the toughs or to satisfy an old sexual dream; when he is free and
active and lives with a handsome boy, his sadistic will fades away.
However, the themes remain, because they are the major motifs of
his sensibility. Every mishap of his heroes then reflects to him an
aspect of his situation, a possibility of suffering that has been denied
him, a conclusion that destiny has not drawn. In developing these
adventures, Genet achieves what logicians call a *mental experience*.
Does he not have that wonderful instrument of investigation, the
gesture? "One has the momentary soul of one's gesture." In order

to know what a particular beggar or princess is thinking, he has only to install his or her gestures in himself. He borrows the fatal movements of one, the gait of the other, copies the bodily movements that he has observed, with the aim of discovering the mental movements that correspond to them. Thus, "he will possess" Erik, Darling and the executioner, as he formerly possessed Stilitano. Before long the word will be a substitute for the gesture; the experience will take place in and through language. What exactly is this "mental experience"? An inquiry by Genet as to his potentialities, nothing else. It is, if need be, a valid method of investigation. You've never committed a crime? Then imagine that you are going to commit one. Choose the victim, ponder the motive, try to feel your fear before and after the murder, ask yourself whether you would experience remorse, etc. At the end of the exercise you will have certainly learned something about yourself. Of course, you will still not know how you would really kill. Besides, you will never kill, or if you have not already done so it is because you do not have the vocation. But you will have explored certain feelings which you tend to hide from yourself, and by reviewing your story in your mind you will be able to discover the real difficulties and desires that it reveals. If you go further, if you carry out the investigation systematically, if you make it your duty to rework the story of your life, to bring forth, in thought, what might have been, if your aim is to group about you all your possibilities in order to escape the niggardly contingency that realizes only a few of them and in order to be able to make contact with yourself as a *totality*, you will begin to understand Jean Genet. But, you may say, all novelists do that. They do not: to begin with, most of them want to know the others as much as and more than they want to know themselves. It is not true that all the characters in *War and Peace are* Tolstoy: we know the models he used; and if he depicts himself, in spite of everything, by his way of describing them, by his choice of their characteristics, he does so unwittingly and in spite of himself.* And, in addition, a novelist invents in order to write; Genet

---

* A feeble fashion perfectly in keeping with present-day complacency. It is claimed that the novelist depicts himself in his characters and the critic in his criticism. If Blanchot writes about Mallarmé, we are told that he reveals much more about himself than about the author he is examining. This is the residue of nineteenth-century bourgeois idealism, that inane subjectivism which is responsible for a great deal of the nonsense written (even by Proust) about love. See what it leads to: Blanchot has seen, in Mallarmé, only Blanchot; very well: then you see, in Blanchot, only yourself. In that case, how can you know whether Blanchot is talking about Mallarmé or about himself? That is the vicious circle of all skepticism. So let us drop this outmoded cleverness. To be sure—I am ashamed to repeat these truisms, but our sophisticates are so shallow and silly that it has to be said—

writes in order to invent. Art, style and composition enable him to impart to the experience its full rigor; they fix it.

The content of these figments of the imagination is *moral,* as are the comments attached to them. In this respect, the most striking passage is the account of the sexual relations between Paulo and Hitler. Nothing is spared us. Genet uses every possible means of shocking us. But at the same time this sexual play is described in terms of ethical voluntarism. Every gesture reveals a moral concern, an intention that relates to value and being more than to pleasure: "This single and shy evidence of graciousness *heightened my gratitude.* . . . Having . . . with *sovereign and self-confident authority* made him turn around, I covered the back of his neck with kisses. . . . His mother's presence, rapid and *sacred,* flashed through his mind. But he felt *the disadvantage of such a posture for meditating on a mother.**. . . His right hand, that big, thick, broad hand, be-

---

to be sure, Blanchot's point of view is personal to him. In like manner, whatever the instruments that the experimenter employs, he perceives the result of the experiment with his own eyes. But although objectivity is, to a certain extent, distorted, it is also *revealed.* Blanchot's passions, sensibility and turn of mind incline him to make one conjecture rather than another, but it is Mallarmé who will verify Blanchot's conjecture. A critic's mental attitude and emotional makeup serve as "revealers," prepare the intuition. The conjecture, whether true or false, helps to reveal. If it is true, it is confirmed by the evidence; if false, it indicates other paths. No doubt the critic can "force" Mallarmé, can use him for his own purposes; that is precisely proof that he can also shed light on his objective reality. But, you may answer, the critic is a historical creature and his judgments are related to the age. That is true, but it would be wrong to confuse the historicism of our sophisticates with their idealistic subjectivism. For, if it is true (I say "if it is true," for I believe in the existence of transhistorical truths. There is nothing sublime about these truths. But if I say, for example: "Descartes wrote the *Discourse on Method,*" that is true for all ages. This truth is not "eternal," since its content is historical and dated. But it is transhistorical, for it does not depend on the economic, social or religious evolution of mankind. It will be as true in a hundred years as it is today.) that the critic, who is a historical creature, reveals only Mallarmé's significance *for our age,* it is also true that this significance is objective. In short, we must return to very simple and very vulgar verities: in a *good* critical work, we will find a good deal of information about the author who is being criticized and some information about the critic. The latter information, moreover, is so obscure and blurred that it has to be interpreted in the light of all that we know about him. Furthermore, not everyone is capable of this kind of insight. One has only to read the nonsense that is written every day. Man is an object for man; the value of objectivity must be restored in order to dispose of the subjectivist banalities that always try to beg the question.

(You can see what they are driving at. I am reminded of the bourgeois salons where the hostess knows how to avoid quarrels because she has the art of reducing objective value judgments [that play is *bad,* that political operation is *blameworthy*] to purely subjective opinions [I *don't like* that play, etc.]. If it is taken for granted that you are merely depicting yourself in condemning police repression of a miners' strike, you will not be disturbing anyone. "I disapprove of the death penalty," said Clemenceau. To which Barrès, who was fond of the guillotine, replied: "Of course. Monsieur Clemenceau can't bear the sight of blood.")

* The sentence is, of course, ironic. Again the theme of the "humiliated mother." But the very irony masks a sacrilegious will, including a recourse to antivalues, far removed from abandonment to sensuality.

came very tiny, docile, quiet, and murmured, 'Thank you.' My hand and I understood this language. . . . He suffered in the presence of his regained *wholeness,* in the presence of his free, lonely personality whose *solitude was suddenly revealed to him by the detachment of a God.* . . . By the grace of an *unequaled generosity* the fabulous emblem of Satan's chosen people went down to live in that simple dwelling. . . . I was about to—I mean that no part of the gesture was revealed overtly, but its intention had already given me greater self-control by describing it from its beginning to its end, inside myself, who thereby felt a lightening capable of making time go backward—I was about, as I was saying, to jump on the bed, but I quickly pulled myself together and very deliberately lay down beside Paulo. By this sharp gesture which remained internal and of which *I had and had not been master, my soul meant to place itself on the level of Paulo's soul* and my gestures to have the gestures of his age. . . . With Paulo I was able to make natural gestures. . . . It was the great disorder—or rather *the systematic labor* —in which *I sought, by every possible means,* to reassume the larval form thanks to which one returns to Limbo," etc.

Were it not for the context—which context I spare you—who the devil would ever think that the passage deals with anal intercourse? You will not find this moral preciosity in *Our Lady of the Flowers.* The reason is that Genet was trying to be excited; his descriptions were meant to be erotic. But I do not think that the relating of this act of intercourse excited him for a single moment. Yet he does more than imagine it: he substitutes for Hitler in order to take part in it and suddenly says "I," although in the preceding line he used the third person singular. But since he does not really and truly feel the crushing weight of another body, since he supports a pure appearance by an effort of will, since he must, while imagining the scene, find the right words and accurate phrase, these fleshless shadows arouse in him only a shadow of excitement: the movement of his hands to caress a naked thigh would have been caused in reality by the insolent blooming of a young body. Even if the moral signification and intention had existed, they would have been drowned in desire. When systematically imagined with the purpose of being written about, the same movement loses its massive inertia; its substance is will and, if it is thus *willed,* it cannot be willed for itself but for its signification. The latter, in turn, instead of being painfully extracted from a memory by means of retrospective analysis, is given to us in the account itself as the goal of the gesture. The gesture is performed because Genet's soul "means to place itself on the level of Paulo's soul." But the ends which are posed by an act of freedom are characterized by the fact that they are *values*. Thus, the sexual act becomes, in the realm of the imaginary, a dramatization of the values: the very slight opacity of being melts; being becomes a dialectic of sexual communication. Hitler the war lord humiliates himself before Paulo, whom he terrorizes, and the latter affirms his superiority during the act without even wanting to do so, by the mere force of the dominating gesture. These shadows disappear; there remains a pure movement. The moral values surrender and humiliate themselves before vital values; transcendence yields to the massiveness of being; communication must take place through the bodies and first by the submission of the weaker to the stronger. But the supremacy of the ethical is reaffirmed immediately thereafter; transcendence aims at new ends beyond being. This dialectical connection between ethical domination and sexual domination, the latter being only a generously accepted reversal of the former and the former disappearing after the orgasm for the benefit of the latter, is the transcription, on a moral level, of the sexual problem of the virilified ex-fairy Genet* and at the same time the effort to find a solution: Divine wanted to take Our Lady and then slid under him in a swoon—that is the fact. How is she to give herself to an adolescent without losing all authority over him?—that is the problem. Let the gift be an act of generosity on the part of the superior, let the latter affirm his superiority even in his momentary submission—that is the solution. Genet carries out the experiment via Hitler and Paulo, then, immediately thereafter, goes beyond it; he classifies it and integrates it into his knowledge.

For Genet has only one purpose in setting up these moral experiments: *to go beyond them*. He makes of these situations, of these problems and their solutions, the skeleton of an event which is invented so that the ethical dramas *have already taken place, in order for him to have already experienced it* and to find himself beyond the conflict as one wakes up one day and finds oneself cured of an illness or an unhappy passion: he wants to establish for himself an imaginary past, with its unfulfilled possibilities, its dramas, its abortive undertakings. All this *has already been,* the story of it *has been written* in a book, there is no point in going back to it. The function of Genet's imaginative conceptions is to enable him to progress in the realm of the imaginary. Each experience is an inventory followed by liquidation. We have seen the example of

---

* And, of course, you will find in the background the dialectic of the Criminal and the Saint.

this in *Funeral Rites:* the entire book is only the exercise of an exaggerated, heightened and thus imaginary suffering. To suffer becomes a *duty:* Genet will become the source of his pain in order to deny the contingent reason for his mourning, the "anecdotic" death of Jean; he will transform his grief into a perfect and absolute essence of pain and will thereby do away with its particularity, its humble reality as a feeling that has been experienced; he will aim at incorporating into himself the actual person of Jean and will thereby destroy at one and the same time both the dead person and the mourning. At the end of the book he is again free, empty, ready for something new. The mechanism of the ethical experience is thus as follows: one carries a real experience to the point of changing it into an *appearance;* one dissolves the appearance in the might-be; one makes of the *contingent accident* a pure movement and of the latter an idea of movement, that is, a word. The moral experience is, at bottom, only a verbal experience. The creator produces his characters in order to live through them, to the very dregs, his own possibilities and thereby to divest himself of the latter; he will deliver himself from his desires, his astonishments, his last illusions, and also of his obsessions. *In the book* he will submit to the Pimps, then will betray them, then will betray betrayal; in the book he will, by a verbal ascesis, experience all the stages of *Saintliness.* And Saintliness becomes "the most beautiful word in the French language." The moral world is *in the words;* one sacrifices the words to each other; the ethical events are events of language. In the end, all the words are sacrificed to the one word Beauty, which in turn disappears. The book is finished: the verbal divesting ends in silence; Genet, delivered from the poem, perceives himself as a pure abstract form of thought. Saintliness was that which was beyond nothingness; but since it becomes a language and *speaks,* Genet makes contact with himself as something beyond Saintliness, as a freedom. The moral experience produces the same result as the artistic experience; it *is* the artistic experience of which Genet becomes conscious and which he translates into another language. He has delivered himself from the Word by the "full employment" of the terms; he has delivered himself from Beauty by making it enter language: being the pure organization of the verbal world, Beauty sinks into silence along with this world. Above all, he has succeeded in what he did not plan to undertake: *he has freed himself from Good and Evil,* both of which have crept into the work and no longer have meaning except through the work: Evil is a certain sophistical order that is imposed upon words and that gives rise to unrealizable significations; Good, which is the logical order of the words that designate Being, exists only to be violated by the magnifying judgments. When the work grows silent, when, dragged down by its own weight, it sinks to the depths of darkness, Good and Evil sink into the same nothingness: Juve and Fantomas, the enemy brothers, perish in the same shipwreck. The deeper meaning of Genet's moralism is finally disclosed: he has put the moral element into words in order to get rid of it.

"My victory is verbal and I owe it to the sumptuousness of the terms." In point of fact, he has won on all the boards: he escapes from poverty, from prison, from horror; the decent folk support him in style, seek him out, admire him; even those who still censure him have to accept him since he has filled their minds with obsessive images. What does he give in return? Nothing. A moment of horror, a suspect beauty that disappears: he has spoken at length about a sinister and iniquitous world and yet has managed to say nothing about it. His extraordinary books are their own rebuttal: they contain both the myth and its dissolution, the appearance and the exposure of the appearance, language and the exposure of language. When we finish them, the reading leaves a taste of ashes since their content cancels itself. The good conscience dreamed of fullness, of being; Genet disturbs it by giving it "the notion of an escaping object that is missing." This happens because he has not called anything into question nor created new values. He has entered the readers' hearts and imparted to them his infernal lightness. He will henceforth be in them this sudden, suspicious lightness, this void; he has restored *negativity* to them.* *Verbal* victory: what Blanchot aptly says about Mallarmé can be applied word for word to Genet: "It is the singularity and wonder of language to give creative value, lightninglike power, to nothing, to pure emptiness, to the nothingness which it approaches—but does not attain —as its limit. . . . Let us note that in this endeavor to detach us from being, poetry is a hoax and a game. It necessarily deceives us; dishonesty and lying are its virtues. Like the hero of Igitur, it says: 'I cannot do this seriously. . . .' One would think that, owing to the fact that man speaks and by means of speech gives new meaning to the world, man is already dead . . . and, by the silence that enables him to speak, he attempts at every moment, to be missing from himself and from everything." Indeed, it was Genet who said:

* Mallarmé, too, wanted "his future poems to be [for people] . . . poisonous phials, frightful drops." We know what the phial of Igitur contains: "The drop of nothingness which is lacking to the sea."

"The poet is a dead man." His victory is his being able "to be missing from himself and from everything": at the end of each poem he
has said everything, and this was nothing. The book has closed upon
itself and upon the universe; it sinks into the reader's mind; a phantom Genet installs himself in the reader's soul; but the real Genet
has delivered himself from this character, that is, from his empirical
self: he remains a pure absence in which creation and negation
coincide; he is both this extraordinarily living emptiness that can
produce fantasies by the thousand, that can distribute them among
us, and the "corrosive," voracious nothing that absorbs and dissolves everything. He has, one by one, in a vacuum, gone through
his experiences of progressive "destitution": he has said nothing
and yet has nothing more to say; he has identified himself with all
the passions, all the creatures, so as the better to escape them;
instead of acquiring a new quality with each embodiment, he abandoned a little of himself. But at the end of the divesting, he retains
eminently the Goods which he rejects, as do St. Theresa and the
real saints, for he carries within himself, in the transparency of his
consciousness, the world which he has, with one and the same movement, created and dissolved. Outside, in the midst of the world, he
triumphs: in people's minds, in newspapers, in books, he is Genet
the Thief; during this time he is, within himself, a quiet and total
absence. He has delivered himself from himself: he can no longer
will Evil or even Good; at the moment when the hoodwinked
society of the Just *accepts* him, he metamorphoses himself, by the
very act that obliges us to install him within us, and places himself
above our subjugated minds. What would the little tramp who was
pushed around by the police not have given for a show of tenderness? Our Lady so needs love that he loves his judges. But the poet
would have to make only a gesture for us to give him our friendship, and he despises it. A word, a smile, would be enough. It would
be enough if he recognized our good will, our efforts, if he were
grateful to us for becoming his accomplices. He does not deign to
make the gesture or utter the word. Rather, it is we who need his
tenderness since we do not want to have damned ourselves for
nothing, and it is he who refuses to let us have it since he despises
us for having let ourselves be taken in.

And now here is a story for an Anthology of Grim Humor: "An
abandoned child manifests evil instincts in his early childhood. He
robs the poor peasants who adopted him. Though reprimanded, he
persists. He escapes from the reformatory into which he had to be

put, steals and plunders more than ever and, in addition, prostitutes himself. He lives in squalor, committing petty thefts and begging. He sleeps with everybody and betrays everyone. Nothing can discourage his zeal. This is the moment he chooses for devoting himself deliberately to evil. He decides that he will do the worst in every circumstance and, as he has come to realize that the greatest crime was not the doing of evil but the manifesting of evil, he writes, in prison, abominable books which stand up for crime and which fall within the provisions of the law. Precisely for that reason he will cease to be abject and squalid and will get out of prison. His books are printed and read. A stage director who has been decorated by the Legion of Honor mounts one of his plays which incites to murder. The President of the Republic nullifies the sentence he was supposed to serve for his latest offenses, precisely because he boasted in his books of having committed them. And when he is introduced to one of his former victims, she says to him: 'Delighted to meet you, sir. Please continue.' "

You will say that this story lacks verisimilitude. And yet that is what happened to Genet. "Rubbish," I was told by a pretentious idiot. "Stop looking for complicated explanations. Genet wasn't saved by his persisting in evil. If he succeeded, it's because he had talent." Very well: and if you're a failure, it's because you haven't any. But Genet's case isn't as clear as yours. *Precisely* because he has talent. What do you think talent is? Mildew of the brain? A supernumerary bone? I have shown that his work is the imaginary aspect of his life and that his genius is one with his unswerving will to live his condition to the very end. It was one and the same for him to will failure and to be a poet. He has never gone back on his pledges, he has never given in, has never abdicated, and if he has won, it is because he has steadily played loser wins.

For he has won. He comes and goes. He is free. It is almost eight years since he was last in prison. He has money, "honorable friends." This common-law criminal lives part of the time in Paris and part in Cannes, leading the life of a well-to-do bourgeois. He is "received." He is taken up by followers of fashion, is admired by others, but as he has not stopped associating with burglars and queers, he goes from drawing rooms to Montmartre bars, plays *The Mysteries of Paris* all by himself and, because he comes from nowhere, feels at home everywhere. The finest proof of his victory: two letters which he has received, one from a cop and the other from a turnkey, both requesting that he use his influence on their behalf.

What then? He has won. No doubt about it. But the game of

loser wins has reversals that are to be expected: he has lost, therefore has won; but if he wins, then he loses. The secret failure of
every triumph is that the winner is changed by his victory and the
loser by his defeat: when Genet put out his hand to sweep the
board, the stake had disappeared. When the enemy is at the height
of his power, it would be sweet to humiliate him; the day after the
victory, when he is in chains, miserable and trembling, he is a mere
man, and, whatever the victor may decide to do, there lurks in his
decision a profound disenchantment: to be eager to punish out of
fidelity to oneself is to want to cling to a dead past, to prefer what
one was to what one has become; magnanimity, on the other hand,
repudiates past sufferings, rises above years of struggle and hope.
Genet's enemies are the Just. When he was an underdog, he
dreamed of a Day of Glory when they would be forced to accept
him while continuing to reject him. This contradiction reflected
his own conflict: society had to welcome him *as he was,* that is, *as
an evildoer.* But is not the evildoer the man whom all society
rejects? It therefore had to glorify him precisely to the extent that
it condemned him. Whence those strange inventions, those fancied
impostures: the son of a fake prince, received with open arms by a
family that would throw him out if it suspected his real origin. But
these fictions cannot fulfill his desire: the noble family welcomes
him because it does not know the truth, whereas the Just would, in
order to satisfy him, have to accept him while condemning him as
unjust and to love him without ceasing to hate him. And as that
is not possible, both Genet and the Just are transformed as they
approach each other. The thief decided to write in order to know
the glory of the criminal; society, in its shrewdness, accords him
that of the poet. In the privacy of our home each of us damns himself in reading Genet; each of us experiences, while reading, a deep
inner conflict. The love we feel for the good writer is thwarted by
the horror aroused by the evildoer. But as soon as the reader is
back among his fellows, he regains his assurance: they decide together to honor Genet *for his talent* and *in spite of* his crimes. They
admire the art while condemning the subject, as if form and content could ever be separated. He keeps screaming at them: My
talent is my crime. But to no avail. They persist in regarding him
as a freakish poet who has devoted his genius to glorifying vice, or
else they see him as an unhappy man whose hostility is forgivable
because he has suffered so much. In a sense, they are not wrong, and
we have said much the same thing: it was the impossibility of living
that made Genet. However, we have shown that he decided to do

Evil, that he willed himself unequivocally and that he defined himself, in his own eyes, by this decision. He does not want readers to pity him or to tolerate him as a singing derelict, but to recognize his dignity, the dignity of a self-made man. There are others who deliberately close their eyes to the obscenities, sophisms and provocations in his books and pretend to see him not as the infernal Saint that he wants to be but as a Saint purely and simply, a *veritable* oblate personifying all human suffering. And, once again, there is an element of truth in this attitude: *in a sense,* any suffering is always all suffering. But that is a bit hasty: for Genet's misfortune has a particular aspect that these high-minded souls fail to recognize. His is the horrible and grating misfortune of the damned. Thus, he has the bitter experience of never being taken *for what he is.*

Moreover, in accepting him the Just change, for one cannot be perfectly just and *at the same time* read his criminal works. The ideal Just Man does not read anything; all literature is suspect to him. If any cultivated man *recognizes* Genet's talent, that means he is "broad-minded" or that his conscience has been troubled. In the former case, he personifies the "tolerance" that Genet particularly detests and that he has denounced in *The Child Criminal.* In the latter, he goes astray; he reveals by his disturbance that he is not all of a piece: he is already less just; his sacred "aura" flickers and goes out. The one who should have recognized Genet has not recognized him. The one who has recognized him should not have recognized him. Besides, are there any Just men? At times, in his youth, Genet had to thrust aside an unbearable doubt: "What if I were not the *only* one who does Evil?" But now he can no longer hide the truth from himself: evil will is the most widespread thing in the world. *People* lie, *people* steal, *people* kill. It is true that they refuse to overstep certain limits, that they have a certain sense of decency and that there are strict rules for both murder and theft: for example, a father has a right to kill his child, but children are forbidden to kill their fathers. Nevertheless, if the just man is not entirely just, the unjust man is not entirely unjust. Good and Evil disappear together.

The satanic bonds that tied him to the Toughs have slackened: he has come to realize that they are "sorry creatures . . . as cowardly as the guards . . . the scurrilous caricature of the handsome criminals he dreamed about when he was twenty" and that he is bored "in the vicinity of their unequalable stupidity." But the new friendships which he has formed do not satisfy him either: at bottom, he would have liked to associate with magistrates and district attorneys, to whom he is as deeply attached as was Baudelaire to his board of guardians, or even with some puritanical family. These bourgeois still have principles of a kind displayed by the moralistic writer who once made the following delightful confession: "I admire Villon, but I would not have invited him to dinner." Genet has not yet dined at the home of the chief magistrate of the Court of Appeals or of the Rev. Mr. Boegner. The new associates of this thief have been chosen in the "marginal" world of intellectuals. Half clown and half wizard, writers and artists remind him too much of his own history: they are white déclassés as he is a black déclassé, not honest enough for him to respect them and not lawless enough for him to like them. In his relations with them he is courteous, faithful, obliging and dependable, but he feels no friendship or love for these professional magicians; their concerns are not his and he cares little for their works. With fashionable sophisticates he is capricious, violent and perfidious in order to measure his power and because he is annoyed with them for not being quite simply honest people. But this anger is feigned. Why get worked up? Such cattle aren't worth it. He remains an exile amidst the fashionable people who make a fuss about him; he is as foreign to them as they to him.

What can he do? Commit a theft? An indelicate act? On occasion and if need be, he will not refrain from swindling or filching. But he will do so for strictly utilitarian reasons. The magic of Crime has vanished; there is only one place in the world where it can now be found: in his books. And, in addition, he runs few risks: it is enough for some sophisticate with "pull" to have the matter hushed up. Even if he is convicted, the sentence is no longer the same; writers will testify for him in court, and even the guards may treat him with respect. Where are the rigors of yesterday? He realizes with disgust that the Fourth Republic is literate; it will avoid sending great poets to prison unless it is forced to. The attacks by M. Mauriac and M. Rousseaux gave him a flash of hope: there was something about their articles that reminded him of the cop and the provocateur. But they were so ridiculous that all they did was to cause an additional disappointment. In a certain sense, his past still sets him apart; he is still the man who stole, who begged; when literary tribute is paid to him, he can still say to himself: "This tribute is being paid to the Barcelona beggar." But it is not the Barcelona beggar who rejoices, but a courteous, disenchanted little man who is amused for a moment by the thought and then forgets

about it. At first, it diverted him to play the thief; as he left a recep-
tion, he could say: "One of the women had a sable coat! I kept
wondering how I could steal it." But before long that kind of thing
seemed to him childish. He no longer thinks of such matters and
"goes out" less and less. He has exchanged the highly colored,
poetic sufferings of his adolescence for a kind of dreary freedom,
for a severe ataraxia that is not far from the sheer boredom of living. What is there that could delight him? Poetry? He found that
in the slums, in prison. He now "communicates to readers an emotion he does not feel." For twenty years he was possessed by it and
now he no longer experiences it: he manufactures it. Will he find
something in luxury, in sensuality, to compensate for what he has
lost? No, we know that he is austere. This puritan of Evil has never
known the abandon needed for gluttony. For a while, luxury
amused him, but neither that nor wealth is what he is seeking: this
pariah's only dream was to be a saint. His needs are modest. And
as for love, his virilification has disenchanted him with it. He has
enough money, intelligence and prestige to attract young men who
are still hesitant about their sex. He lives for a while with one and
then another. They are new Jean Decarnins. He enjoys being with
them, he is fond of them, he likes to sleep with them, but he does
not love them.

What is even worse is that he no longer quite knows why he
writes. When he was working on *Our Lady of the Flowers,* the
poem was the way out, the "emergency exit that was open in his
darkness," the only salvation. Those difficult and painful awakenings still had the magic of the dreams; each word was a dream and
an awakening; the work was a talisman, a conjuration; Genet spoke
to himself even more than to others. A little later, writing became
a methodical and deliberate but criminal activity. Prison was not
far off, the police still threatened him, he was in hiding; a prison
sentence which he had not yet served endowed him with a secret
halo. And, in addition, the Just were not yet beaten. He had to
fight, to construct his books like implements of war. The sources of
his inspiration were hatred, suffering, abjection; he could have
written, like Chénier:

> . . . O my dear treasure
> O my pen! gall, bile, horror, gods of my life
> Through you alone I still breathe.

But he is now awake, he has been pardoned, nothing threatens
him. He has sufficient means. What is there that could shock him,

ruffle him, what is there that could provoke, as a defense reaction, the magnifying reflex that is the source of his poems? As for prison, he forgets about it, despite himself. And how could he persist in onanism when he is rich and free and has an opportunity to satisfy his desires? Now that he is awake, now that he has been rationalized, without anxiety about the future, without horror, *why* should he write? To become a "man of letters"? But that is precisely what he does not want. And *for whom* is he to write? He has attained his goal: he now *knows* the way out that his venture was to have. He can no doubt think about producing *still* finer work, but that is an artist's concern and not a criminal's. As one can imagine, an author whose work issues from so deep a need, whose style is a weapon forged for a precise purpose, whose every image, every thought so manifestly sums up his entire life, cannot suddenly start *to talk about something else,* to describe, for example, as well-intentioned people sometimes suggest to him, "the world of intellectuals as seen by a thief." He who loses wins: in winning the title of writer Genet loses the need, desire and occasion to write.

Is the result entirely negative? Has Genet become M. Teste? That would be hard to believe.

In the first place, he is completing the liquidation of the *former* Genet. It is not by chance that he has authorized the publication of his complete works in a regular trade edition with a biographical and critical preface, like the editions of Pascal and Voltaire in the Great French Writers series. Does that mean he has opened his arms and discarded his hatred? Has this Philoctetes given his bow to some Neoptolemus of the Gallimard publishing house? *Complete* works? Will he publish nothing more? Then that means he is dead. Some people have objected to the length of the present study: "When one writes so much about a living person, it is because one wants to bury him." But why should *I* want to bury him? He doesn't bother me. The fact is that a certain Genet has just died and that Jean Genet has asked me to deliver the funeral oration. I myself have been buried alive so many times that he probably thinks I'm an expert. At the same time, he permitted a few friends to request the President of the Republic to grant him a pardon. Note how he rejects that future as thief and poet which was for so long *his* future: with his literary work still unreprieved and prison still threatening him, he liquidates everything, all mortgages on the future, all debts. The funeral ceremony is a strictly private affair: the *Figaro Littéraire,* the Penitentiary Department, Gallimard and Company and the National Foundling Society are represented. I deliver my speech before an empty grave; the wiliest hoodlum has hidden behind a cypress. At first he wept a little, because he was being talked about; but now he is winking at me and making faces. He goes off whistling: *he must try to live.*

He *will* live. He has reread his books and considers them very bad: he had to. This disgust is the last stage of the ascesis, the last renouncement. The new Genet had to be unjust to the old one. He had wanted to say everything and, saying *everything*, to say *nothing:* he now declares that he spoke *in order to say nothing*. The poet had buried the saint; the man is now burying the poet. It is not the writer who is judging his past writings; rather, it is the man who is judging the enterprise of writing. Will he be silent? He was very earnestly advised to do so and he gave the matter serious thought. He does not seem to have decided to do so, although he has written nothing for four years. But as a result of having been on the verge of literary suicide, he is now like the desperate people who have not been able to kill themselves: he has "dropped out"; he looks at literature the way they look at life. If he returns to it, it will not be by force of habit or as a result of the momentum acquired. He has published *his complete works;* they have closed up; they sink into the past. Anything can come out of his present state of indecision: a Trappist monk or a completely new writer.*

I think that he is beginning to discern the face of this writer. Of course, I am taking into account our latest conversations, and I know what conversations are worth. Have I quite understood what he meant? And was he sincere? Does he talk about his still unshaped projects as he formerly did about the book he was then working on, with the same passion? Or is he trying to get drunk on words, to fool himself, to cover up the waiting and the inner emptiness? The work will decide. In any case, this admirable and cynical mind has thoroughly grasped the situation and knows how to make the most of it. The heart of the matter is that Genet *has liquidated the Sacred;* he no longer believes in Saintliness and Evil, and yet there is nothing else he can write about. If he is to compose new poems, he will therefore have to use *his* themes, but will have to *treat* them differently. Since the inner movement of each of his works was an ascension from the anecdotic and fleshly concrete to the abstract heaven of "Constellations," and since the movement of his life reproduces this ascension, since he has divested himself of his

---

* *The Balcony, The Blacks* and *The Screens* were written after the publication of the present study.—Translator's note.

shame and sufferings, since he has awakened from his night-mares, since the horrible Fatality that dictated his poems and the ineluctable Destiny that revealed itself in blazing illuminations have given way to a virgin, unshaped future in which everything is possible, in short, to the abstract possibility of being everything, why should he not continue that austere renunciation to the very end? Why should not this Consciousness carry to an extreme the Saint's resolution to be nothing? In short, if Genet writes, he will continue the adventure of Igitur; he will endeavor to attain the supreme state, that is, the highest degree of abstraction and reflec-tion. He will see from on high the themes of the Flower, the Con-vict and Crime, but without believing in them: they will shrink beneath his gaze. Purged, condensed, emptied of their anecdotic or physical content, they will finally become absences and will serve as pretexts, as rules for a more closely woven, more self-conscious counterpoint. In like manner, Mallarmé borrowed from Baude-laire the themes of hair, perfumes and bad luck and, after squeez-ing all the juice out of them, used them to express only the play of death and chance. Genet has got under way: as happened to Mal-larmé, what he took as an *end* in his earlier poems—the poetic expression of a certain attitude and a certain situation—will be-come the *means* of his future poems. Mallarmé chose worn, tar-nished, half-faded words which then lit each other up; Genet first used words that were *too* picturesque, *too* odoriferous; he used argot and a whole erotic and scatological vocabulary. But as a result of dwelling upon these words, he *wore them out himself*. To a faith-ful reader of his books, the word "pimp" or "queen" seems as drab in his pages as the word "azure" in Mallarmé. These words are blazons; it is time for him to write heraldic poetry. In the universal equivalence of figures which was noted earlier by Leonardo da Vinci and M. Teste he will see an opportunity to establish a system of universal symbols. He will retain only one component of Evil, namely Beauty. He wishes also to establish a play of falsely varied appearances which enter each other and finally disappear. But what interests him in this gradual disappearance is no longer its demoniacal aspect but the rigor of its dynamic unity. The counter-point which he introduced in *Funeral Rites* was still too weighted with matter. But actually he has been moving away, since child-hood, from materiality, from the flesh. He is thus in harmony with his oldest project when he contemplates writing fugues that will be tighter, more precise, of mathematical purity. I have the impres-sion that he is trying to go as far as possible and that he is dreaming of a work in which each particular element would be the symbol and reflection of each of the others and of the whole, in which the whole would be at the same time the synthetic organization of all the reflections and the symbol of each particular reflection, in which this symbolic whole would be at one and the same time *the* symbol of all the symbols and the symbol of Nothing. What is this if not the dream of Absolute Necessity, that is, of Reduction to the Identical. Parmenides, a philosopher, is troubled by the kaleidoscopic abundance of phenomena; he must account for them. But the Eleatic artist, on the other hand, needs this motley multiplicity, for Beauty, as he sees it, lies in the movement that closes the world like a fan, makes images enter each other and compresses the last of them until it melts between his fingers. The result is Being, the Being that is identical with itself and that dissolves and eats away, within itself, at pain, colors, time, the event and space. But this unqualified Being is identified with Nothingness. Genet will find on this plane, transposed, purified and sublimated, his passion for annihilating the world and himself. One can understand his not yet knowing whether he is going to speak or remain silent: on this level of abstraction speech and silence are one and the same. It is Genet who can write the "Mallarméan novel" of which Blanchot once spoke.

But while the *poet* ponders this pure verbal symphony which is to give an equivalent of silence and in which the only temporality will be that of the "vibratory disappearance" of the universe, at the moment when he is attempting to effect for the totality of being the astringent movement which we have seen him indicate in each of his images, the *man,* rid of the physical and too emotional content of his favorite ruminations, rises to a higher level of reflective consciousness and attempts to appreciate his "case" by seeing it in its historical and social context. This consciousness had been alienated: it pulls itself together. Freed from the phantoms which he called the Just, Genet discovers men, who are neither just nor unjust but, at one and the same time, just in the depths of their injustice and unjust at the very source of their good will. He discovers *himself* among men, not as *the* Thief or *the* Saint, but as a certain man who is like everybody and nobody. Since the sacred has abandoned his universe, he no longer thinks he is an oblate or a culprit. He wants to understand himself as he was, to redo—otherwise, no doubt, and better—the job that I have attempted to do on him, with the following essential difference: his effort to know himself will be, at one and the same time, an act, a way of life and a poet's undertaking. In the past, he substituted, so as the better to destroy, the canons of aesthetics for the rules of morality. At present, now that he is delivered from Evil, the movement is reversed: it is the Word that saved him by its magnificence; since the evil child changed into a man by following his aestheticism to the very end, aesthetic values must, to a certain extent, contain and reveal the values of ethics. It is no longer a matter of denying the latter for the benefit of the former, but of probing the former until he finds in them the latter, in short, of writing, on the basis of an examination of his own history, a treatise on the Beautiful which is a treatise on the Good. Is it a matter of writing *three* books, one on universal symbolism, another about his own case and a third on the ethics of art? A poem, an autobiography and a philosophical treatise? Of course not. Genet dreams of composing *a single work* with these three subjects, a work that will be a poem from one end to the other. Is that possible? In a sense, the undertaking is unparalleled; the work will have to be a mixture of *Un coup de dés, The Seven Pillars of Wisdom* and *Eupalinos.* But, on the other hand, Genet has always mingled the poem, the journal of the poem and a kind of infernal didacticism; if the work is ever written, it will be the completion of his art: not a revolution but a going to the limit.

In his private life, he attains at least the virtue that resembles him, generosity, *his* virtue. I, for one, rate this virtue rather high, because it is in the image of freedom, as Descartes realized. But let us not forget that it is freedom refracted through the feudal world. In a certain sense, it places man above things; in another, it confirms him in the illusion of possessing: one gives only what one has. In a world where man is alienated from things, this ambiguous virtue does not eliminate alienation, but displaces it: in liberating himself from the object which he gives, the donor alienates himself from the thing given; the beneficiary is doubly enslaved: to the thing and, through it, to the man who gave it to him. A saint or benefactor is said to give all he has: that is good. But Simone Weil lived in a shabby hotel in Puy and put whatever money she had on the mantelpiece; the door remained open, and anyone could help himself: that is better. The benefactor swaps a government bond for merit; in his case, property, which is transcended but carefully preserved in this very transcending, changes into merit; everybody agrees: generosity is the cardinal virtue of the owner. Simone Weil was not acquiring virtue, not even merit: she gave nothing, for she did not consider the money to be hers.* I am not claiming, as the

---

* There is no reason to speak of "detachment" or "saintliness" in this connection. Simone Weil quite simply did not think that the money belonged to her because she thought that the present wage system was absurd.

reader can imagine, that her attitude—which sprang from an individualistic idealism—is a solution to the social problem. I am
reporting the fact, as it was reported to me, to indicate the limits of
an ethic of virtue and, particularly, of generosity. This example
indicates, I hope, beyond the various ethics of the alienated man,
the domain proper of morality. But the important thing to point
out is that Genet's ethical attitude cannot yet go beyond the stage
of generosity. The child of a laborer has no difficulty in understanding that he is the victim of a bad social organization: it is clear to
him that he is not inferior *by nature* to the young bourgeois of his
age. But Genet had been considering himself a monster since childhood; even before committing his first theft he felt guilty about
having been abandoned; he was bound to regard his destitution as
a punishment for his original sin. The injustice of his lot was
masked by shame and pride: possession of property is the reward of
honest people; a monster is not entitled to anything; and later he
stole *in order to be* a monster. Where could one find a more explicit
recognition of the principle of property? Does he not proclaim in
all his books that theft is a crime? Mauriac, Rousseaux, you who
condemn him categorically, how can you fail to see that he is on
your side? Aren't you aware that bandits have always been the best
collaborators of the wealthy? So much so that they are still being
used in Sicily to oppose the pressure of small landowners and day
laborers. How could Genet find the delicious taste of sacrilege in
his thefts if he did not, like you, consider property sacred? And
now he has just acquired a "decent" competency. Yes, decent. Although his first works were sold under the counter, he *earned* the
money that this sale brought in. Was that the moment he was going
to choose to proclaim that this money belonged to nobody? You
wouldn't want him to do *that*. Moreover, we know that he sacrifices
reality to right and that he dissolves matter in order to reveal
essences in their abstract purity. We also know that he is in the
habit of rejecting the miracle since he claims to derive only from
himself. He must therefore get rid of these *holdings* that come to
him by a stroke of luck; he must assert his right of possession by
destroying the thing possessed; he must exchange his material
status as a *holder* for the honorific title of *possessor*. Being an ascetic
and having almost no needs, he retains only the *naming* which
symbolizes for him his virtual integration into the society of the
Just. That is precisely what we have called generosity. This virtue,
which is more feudal than bougeois, is also appropriate to him
because he still belongs to the black knighthood of delinquents. As
for the nobility which he so desired, he will have its gestures, that

is, according to his personal conceptions, its soul. He gives. However, one must not expect to see him scattering the manna of his bounty broadside. In the first place, he is not so rich; he will frequently have need of the generosity of others: the thief will become a sponger. And, in addition, this new attitude entails inner conflicts: although the burglar who is now openly squandering the proceeds of his burglary feels a vocation for generosity, the passive homosexual tends rather to be miserly. In Genet these inclinations come to terms between themselves, although generosity prevails by far. But what is most important is that Genet has not yet found a way of universalizing his human relationships. This singular individual has only singular relationships. Instead of dividing his gifts among as many people as possible, he prefers to shower them upon a few chosen ones.

Until he freed himself from his wretched childhood, the childhood of others fascinated him. It was childhood that he sought in Bulkaen, in Jean Decarnin, in Riton. He tried to possess in them the adolescent that he had been; far from helping them escape from wretchedness, he wished them all the rigors of fate *for the beauty of it* and so that they might resemble him more. And when he wrote *The Criminal Child,* he adjured judges to be very severe in order to populate the prisons with little Genets. His work, his success, have detached him from his childhood. He is still seeking it, but not in the same way. When he finds this gentle image of himself in others, it no longer overwhelms him, it moves him to pity. He no longer desires to touch it; he compensates it. Deep within him, the shame and sufferings of the youngster he was have never ceased. As long as Genet suffers, he heightens his bitter, masochistic pleasure by reviewing them in his mind over and over. At present, now that the *man* has freed himself from his sufferings, he wants to efface them in the *child.* But since they are out of reach, *past,* since nothing can allay the pain of that inconsolable child, he will console his youth *in others.* He falls in love with and then ceases to love a very young man, R., who somewhat resembles Jean Decarnin; and when the love dies, he is able for the first time to change his passion into friendship. Did he actually feel passion? At bottom, from the time they met he was seeking this future friendship; he loved R. in order to be able to become his friend, to shake off the feeling of love and in order that his feelings, which were not pure at the beginning, might be purified with use. Their brief love was, I imagine, a test. When the candidate has passed the test—and he passes it brilliantly —Genet adopts him, that is, he adopts himself and completes the

circle by recovering his childhood: I have not said that his generosity was free from narcissism. It is not enough for him that his
maturity should enjoy all the things that his childhood vainly
desired: this retroactive generosity wishes to gratify yesterday
through today. He reckons up exactly what he lacks and that is what
he offers his adopted son—no more, no less. He was a thief and
gives the young man a trade; he was a tramp and gives him a house;
he was a homosexual and gives him a wife. The latter, a calm, quiet
widow, a little severe and certainly kind, a few years older than her
young husband, with three children by a former marriage, no doubt
reminds Genet of "everything that makes a mother a mother: tenderness, slightly nauseating whiffs from the half-open mouth, deep,
swelling bosom." At one and the same time he provides his protégé
with maternal tenderness and normal sexual relations. I have been
told that the young people loved each other before he intervened.
That may be. But he would not have done better if he had chosen
the wife himself. And does anyone think that if this young Rubem-
pré had hankered after a pin-up girl that our Vautrin would have
let him have her?

The unforeseen result of his generosity is that he has acquired
a family.* This eternal wanderer, who possesses nothing except
ready cash and a few articles of clothing, this solitary who lives in a
hotel and changes hotels several times a year, has built a home for
himself. Somewhere between Saint-Raphaël and Nice a house is
awaiting him. I have seen him there, surrounded with children,
playing with the older ones and dressing up the younger, passionately discussing their upbringing. At first, he was interested in the
young woman and her sons only through his protégé. But now he
is concerned with the whole family, and R. is only one member of
it. He once said to me that undertakings must be carried through
to their ultimate consequences, that the only vile or ugly acts are
those that are not completed. I agreed with him as to the principle.
"But," I asked him, "suppose R. said to you one day that he was
fed up with this marriage that you were so eager for him to make?"
"If he did," he replied without a moment's hesitation, "I'd prevent
him from breaking it up." "Yet you wanted R. to be happy." "Of
course." "In that case, you'd have to give up the idea of his being
married or his being happy." "I won't give up anything," he said.
"At a certain time, R.'s happiness depended on this marriage. The
boy was unable to find himself except in a family. I therefore cre-

---

* Homosexuals frequently set up these artificial families for themselves when they reach
their middle years.

ated the family. It now exists, and to want to preserve it is to carry through my act. The object of my will hasn't changed; the object has simply become more complex." This reply gives an indication of the morality that he has derived from his experience and that he will expound in his future work. One must will an act to the very end. But the act is alive, it changes. The goal one sets at the beginning is abstract and consequently false. Little by little it is enriched by the means employed to attain it, and ultimately the concrete goal, the true goal, is what one wants at the *finish*. The interrupted act spoils and depreciates, just as the truth that stops midway changes into error. In willing himself, unreservedly, to be a thief, Genet sinks into the dream; in willing his dream to the point of madness, he becomes a poet; in willing poetry unto the final triumph of the word, he becomes a man; and the man has become the truth of the poet as the poet was the truth of the thief. Similarly, in wanting to provide R., who was a wavering adolescent, with normal practices, he has made of him a husband and head of a family. And the family has become the truth of the couple, just as the heterosexual couple was the truth of the young man who was uncertain about his sexual tendencies.

Genet's generosity broadens out; he grows interested in other causes, he tries to help other men. Nevertheless, this virtue, which has given him a family, tends, in other respects, to confine him in his solitude. However one looks at it, the gesture of giving separates us from men; it does not engender *reciprocity* since it fetters the beneficiary by gratitude exactly to the degree in which it liberates the donor. The source of generosity cannot be a jointly felt need: it is freedom grasping itself in its absolute gratuitousness. "I wasn't asking for anything," says the benefactor frequently, "only for a little gratitude." But what is one to be grateful for? Simply this: that he did not act out of self-interest or out of fear or out of puritanical obedience to some harsh, austere law, or even in order to submit to love, but that he decided in all independence and that his unconditioned freedom placed itself *without a motive* on one of the scales of the balance. Inversely, if the gratitude you feel is a burden, you will try to find reasons for the "disinterested" act: "It was to his interest" or even "It gave him pleasure." One recognizes that one "is under *obligation*" to the donor because one has been the *object* of an imprescriptible freedom; and if there existed a man to whom all others were "obligated," that man would be completely alone. Genet, who is a generous man and a poet, feels doubly solitary, for the creator and the donor are alike in that they challenge the world, one by destroying property and the other by producing appearances, and in that the origin of their challenge is in pure existence, that is, in the incommunicable. In giving, Genet puts himself above those who maintained him below themselves: and, to be sure, generosity has its joys, as does creation, but there are other joys that this taut and lonely spirit, which is brilliant out of necessity, will never know: that of receiving, that of sharing. Though Genet is accepted and made much of, he remains in exile amidst his triumph. So much the better: this new failure and the permanence of his exile safeguard his grandeur.

PLEASE USE GENET PROPERLY

I have tried to do the following: to indicate the limit of psychoanalytical interpretation and Marxist explanation and to demonstrate that freedom alone can account for a person in his totality; to show this freedom at grips with destiny, crushed at first by its mischances, then turning upon them and digesting them little by little; to prove that genius is not a gift but the way out that one invents in desperate cases; to learn the choice that a writer makes of himself, of his life and of the meaning of the universe, including even the formal characteristics of his style and composition, even the structure of his images and of the particularity of his tastes; to review in detail the history of his liberation. It is for the reader to say whether I have succeeded.

As the present work draws to a close, I begin to have a certain scruple: have I been fair enough to Genet? I think I have defended Genet the man against all and sometimes against himself. Have I defended the writer sufficiently? This study was meant to be an introduction to his work. What if it were to turn people away from it? I know what can be said: "Let him write, if he wants to, but we don't have to read him. His poems are premeditated crimes, he tries to base his salvation on our destruction and to trick us by means of words. These are excellent reasons for admiring his works from afar and for not buying them."

I admit that Genet treats his readers as means. He uses them all to talk to *himself* about himself, and this peculiarity may alienate readers. When he asks himself: "Should *I* steal?" why should he expect the answer to interest *us?* "What I write," says Genet, "is valid only for me." To which the public replies: "What I take the trouble to read should be valid for everyone. Let him preach theft!

One could at least discuss the matter, could take a stand for or against his views." But he does not say that one should steal. Quite the contrary, he knows that it is wrong of him to steal and it is in order to be wrong that he steals. But he does not even ask us to be wrong: he asks us nothing at all. If anyone planned to become his disciple, I'm sure he would answer: "How could anyone act like me if he's not me?" This poet "speaks to us as an enemy": is it worth while surmounting the horror he inspires only to discover in the end that he is the sole recipient of his message and that he pretends to communicate with others only in order the better to depict himself for himself in his incommunicable particularity?* I am in an embarrassing situation: if I reveal that one can derive profit from his works, I incite people to read them but I betray him; if, on the other hand, I lay stress on his particularity, I likewise run the risk of betraying him: after all, if he has published his poems, that means he wants to be read. If I must choose between betrayals, I pick the former: I shall at least be faithful to myself. I have no police record and no inclination for boys. Yet Genet's writings have moved me. If they move me, that means they concern me. If they concern me, that means I can profit from them. Let us attempt to point out how Genet can be "used properly."

He plays loser wins with his work and you are his partner: thus, you will win only by being ready to lose. Let him cheat; above all, do not defend yourself by adopting attitudes: you have nothing to gain by putting yourself into a state of Christian charity, by loving him in advance and by accepting the pus of his books with the abnegation of the Saint who kisses the leper's lips. High-minded individuals have brooded over this infected soul: it thanked them with a fart, and they deserved it, for their polite kindness was only a precaution for disarming his wiles. You will deplore the misfortunes he suffers only in order to hide from yourself his free will to do harm. In that case, you are helping a thief by trying to find excuses for him; to find excuses for the poet is to wrong him. Furthermore, do not take refuge in aestheticism; he will drive you from under cover. I know people who can read the coarsest passages without turning a hair: "Those two gentlemen sleep together? And then they eat their excrement? And after that, one goes off to denounce the other? As if that mattered! It's *so* well written." They stop at Genet's vocabulary so as not to enter his delirium; they admire the poem so as not to have to *realize* the content. But form and

---

* Unlike Montaigne who also depicts himself in his particularity, but *for others* and with the intention of communicating.

content are one and the same: it is *that* content which requires *that* form. So long as you play at amoralism you will remain at the threshold of the work. So? So you must not resist, you must let yourself be fooled, must remain yourself, must let yourself be naïvely indignant. Do not be ashamed of being taken for a fool. Since this fanatical challenging of all man and all his loves is expressly meant to shock, then be shocked, do not fight against the horror and uneasiness that the author wants to arouse in you. You will appreciate this sophist's trap only if you fall into it. "But," you may say, "if I become indignant, then what distinguishes me from M. Rousseaux?" I understand what you mean. M. Rousseaux's fulminations are ridiculous; this critic's incompetence is so sustained that one is tempted to maintain the opposite of everything he says. Yet that is the necessary test: if we want to win, we must be humble to the degree of becoming like unto M. Rousseaux.

That is the only way out of hell: you will be delivered by the horror with which Genet inspires you, on condition that you use it properly. What M. Rousseaux cannot see and what M. Mauriac, who is shrewder, sees clearly but hides is that the horror is *recognition*. That monkeys are thieves and dogs homosexuals are facts that merely make you laugh. But Genet repels: therefore, he endangers. And I do not mean merely that he throws light on the mud that one wants to hide: even if you are pure as snow, completely unrepressed, even if you automatically go straight to virtue as the moth goes to the light and M. Rousseaux to error, Genet would still repel you, therefore you would still be endangered.

We ask the writer to communicate to us his reflections on general situations. We "normal" people know delinquents only from the outside, and if we are ever "in a situation" with respect to them, it is as judges or entomologists: we were astounded to learn that one of our bunkmates had stolen from the regimental cashbox or that the local storekeeper had drawn a little boy into the back of the shop. We blamed, condemned and stoutly declared that "we didn't understand." And if we grant the novelist the right to describe such baneful individuals "since they exist, since one runs into them," we do so on condition that he consider them from the outside and as species.* That amounts to forbidding the thief to speak about theft, and the homosexual to speak about his love life. A person who laughs heartily when Charpini appears on the stage might be unable to read a single page of *Funeral Rites:* the reason is that

---

* This does not mean that he may not show us what they are thinking or feeling, provided he artfully suggest that we are separated from them by an abyss.

Charpini is only a *spectacle;* in exaggerating the idiosyncrasies of the invert he makes of the latter an insect: laughter is sufficient to shake it off. One is willing to allow a repentant culprit to confess his sins, but on condition that he rise above them; the *good* homosexual is weaned away from his vice by remorse and disgust; it is no longer part of him. He was a criminal but no longer is. He speaks of what he was as if he were *Another,* and when we read his confession we feel ourselves *absolutely other* than the poor wretch he is speaking about. Proust himself cleverly, and somewhat cowardly, spoke of homosexuals as if they were a natural species: he pretended to be making fun of Charlus or to pity him; he told Gide that he regretted "the indecision that made him—in order to give body to the heterosexual part of his work—transpose all the graciousness, tenderness and charm of his homosexual experience to the 'budding grove' of girls, with the result that there remained for Sodom only the grotesque and discreditable."* What was the use of his subsequently denying that he had "wanted to stigmatize uranism"?† The fact is that he became his readers' accomplice. What matters to us is that he does not let us hear the voice of the guilty man himself, that sensual, disturbing voice which seduces the young men, that breathless voice which murmurs with pleasure, that vulgar voice which describes a night of love. The homosexual must remain an object, a flower, an insect, an inhabitant of ancient Sodom or the planet Uranus, an automaton that hops about in the limelight, anything you like except my fellow man, except my image, except myself. For a choice must be made: if every man is all of man, this black sheep must be only a pebble or must be *me.*

Genet refuses to be a pebble; he never sides with the public prosecutor; he never speaks to us *about* the homosexual, *about* the thief, but always *as* a thief and *as* a homosexual. His voice is one of those that we wanted never to hear; it is not meant for analyzing disturbance but for communicating it. J. Vuillemin once wrote the following about Shakespeare: "He sometimes succeeds in doing away with the divinity of the spectator. . . . In *Hamlet* the actor's point of view becomes true . . . the spectator's point of view is transformed in turn; though the footlights do not disappear, at least they grow dim. *We participate instead of seeing.*" That is precisely what Genet does: he invents the homosexual *subject.* Before him, the homosexual is the plaything of external occurrences; regardless of what he says and thinks, we are prompted to

* *Journal d'André Gide,* Pléiade, p. 694.
† *Ibid.*

believe that his thoughts and words are more the effect than the expression of a psychophysiological mechanism; one has only to show it in order to reassure: since it is by nature an object for man, it falls outside the human. But Genet declares himself to be in the right, he ponders himself and ponders the world. You can try to reduce his vice to a physiological defect, but even if you establish the fact that there is something wrong with his secretions, you would not attain that absolute consciousness which approves of itself and chooses itself. A child who had seen Fernandel on the screen a dozen times once met him in the street. "What," he asked, frightened, "he *exists?*" When reading Genet, we are similarly tempted to ask ourselves: "Does a homosexual *exist?* Does he think? Does he judge, does he judge us, does he *see* us?" If he does exist, everything changes: if homosexuality is the choice of a mind, it becomes a human possibility. *Man* is a homosexual, a thief and a traitor.* If you deny this, then renounce your finest laurels: you were pleased to exceed the speed of sound with the aviator, with him *you* pushed back the limits of human possibilities, and when he appears, it is *you* whom you acclaim. I see no harm in this: every human adventure, however individual it may appear, involves all mankind; that is what Catholics call reversibility of merits. But then accept the reversibility of crime; be willing to moan with all girl queens when they make love, be willing to break into apartments with all burglars. The reader may recall the story of the ward of the National Foundling Society who was beaten and underfed by the brutal peasants who had adopted him. At the age of twenty, he did not know how to read. He did his military service. When he left the army, the only thing he had been taught was how to kill. Therefore, he killed. "I'm a wild animal," he said. "The public prosecutor has asked for my head and he'll probably get it. But if he had lived my life he might be where I am now, and if I had lived his, I might be prosecuting him." Everyone in the courtroom was terrified, they had seen an abyss, they had seen a naked, undifferentiated existence which was capable of being everything and which, depending on circumstances, became a murderer or a public prosecutor; in short, human existence. I am not saying that this *is* completely true: it is not *this particular* public official who would

---

* He is *also*, of course, heterosexual, honest and faithful. Ancient dogmatism concluded that since he can be an honest man or a thief, he is therefore neither one nor the other. The result of this was that man was nothing. Contemporary thought, which seeks the historically concrete, views mankind as the totality of its contradictions. Since there are licit sexual relations, there is a human possibility of rejecting them and of seeking vice. Inversely, since there are vices, licit sexual relations become *normal*.

have become *this particular* criminal. The fact remains that the argument struck home, that it will continue to do so. And besides, the murderer demonstrated the truth of it afterward: he was reprieved, learned to read and changed. What is noteworthy in all this is the vacillation of the self that occurs in us when certain minds open before our eyes like yawning chasms: what we considered to be our innermost being suddenly seems to us to be a fabricated appearance; it seems to us that we have escaped only by an incredible stroke of luck from the vices that repel us most in others; we recognize, with horror, a *subject*. He is our truth as we are his; our virtue and his crimes are interchangeable.

Genet invents for us betrayal and homosexuality; they enter the human world; the reader sees them as his personal way out, the emergency exit that has been made for him. We shall not derive from these poems any *knowledge* about ourselves or others; one can know only objects; as for us who wander in the labyrinth of the homosexual sophisms that we are made to adopt even before we have understood them, we are changed into homosexual subjects. What will remain when the book has been closed? A feeling of emptiness, of darkness and of horrible beauty, an "eccentric" experience that we cannot incorporate into the web of our life and that will forever remain "on the margin," unassimilable, the memory of a night of debauchery when we gave ourselves to a man and came. There are books which address themselves, in each individual, to all, and we feel that we are *the* crowd when we enter them. Those of Genet are brothels into which one slips by a door which is ajar, hoping not to meet anyone; and when one is there, one is all alone. Yet it is from this refusal to universalize that their universality is due: the universal and incommunicable experience which they offer to all as individuals is that of solitude.

This does not seem, at first, to be a very new theme; many writers have complained of being lonely, often in agreeable fashion: people were unable to see their merits, their genius had raised them to such a height that nobody could breathe that rarefied air, etc. But this proud and melancholy loneliness is of no interest, except to students of comparative literature. Spiritual solitude in the great Romantics, the solitude of the mystics, solitude in Europe in the century of the Enlightenment, solitude in the eastern provinces between 1798 and 1832, in the French sonnet, among the predecessors of Malherbe: these are fine subjects for dissertations. Those people were not alone, or else one must believe in the solitude of adolescents "whom nobody loves, whom nobody understands";

invisible cohorts floated above their heads and future hands crowned them with laurel. Stendhal was not alone: he lived in 1880 with "the happy few"; Keats was more alone: "Here lies one whose name was writ on water"; but this despairing epitaph which he wrote for himself was addressed *to the Others*. You are not really alone so long as your thoughts are communicable, even if bad luck prevents you from communicating them, nor if you think you are right, even if against all, nor if you are sure that you are doing Good, nor if you succeed in your undertaking; you will not be really alone so long as you have a secret tribunal to absolve you. For a long time we believed in the social atomism bequeathed to us by the eighteenth century, and it seemed to us that man was by nature a solitary entity who entered into relations with his fellow men *afterward*. Thus, solitude appeared to be our original state; one emerged from it if all went well, but one could return to it if one's luck changed. We now know that this is nonsense. The truth is that "human reality" "is-in-society" as it "is-in-the-world"; it is neither a nature nor a state; it is made. Since a child first knows himself as a son, grandson, nephew, worker, bourgeois, Frenchman, etc., and since he is little by little defined by his behavior, solitude is a certain aspect of our relationship to all, and this aspect is manifested by certain types of behavior which we adopt toward society.*

Man, says Marx, is an object to man. That is true. But it is also true that I am a subject to myself exactly insofar as my fellow man is an object to me. And that is what separates us. He and I are not *homogeneous:* we cannot be part of the same whole except in the eyes of a third person who perceives us both as a single object. If we could all be, simultaneously and reciprocally, both object and subject for each other and by each other, or if we could all sink together into an objective totality, or if, as in the Kantian city of ends, we were never anything but subjects recognizing themselves as subjects, the separations would cease to exist. But we cannot carry matters to an extreme in either direction: we cannot all be objects unless it be for a transcendent subject, nor can we all be subjects unless we first undertake the impossible liquidation of all objectivity. As for absolute reciprocity, it is concealed by the historical conditions of class and race, by nationalities, by the social

---

* Physical isolation is not solitude. A colonial who is lost in the bush may feel homesick for his native land, may miss his family, his friends, his wife. But as he continues to be part of society, as his relatives and friends have not ceased to love and approve of him, he remains identified *with all:* his relationship to all has simply changed from a concrete one to an abstract one without changing nature.

hierarchy. A leader is never a subject to his subordinates; if he is, he loses his authority. He is rarely a subject to his superiors. Thus, we usually live in a state of familiar and unthinking vagueness; we pass unnoticed. In our profession, our family, our party, we are not quite objects and not quite subjects. The Other is that instrument which obeys the voice, which regulates, divides, distributes, and it is, at the same time, that warm, diffused atmosphere which envelops us; and that is what we, too, are for others and consequently for ourselves. However, this immediate vagueness contains the germ of disequilibrium: you are with all, you write for all, you take God to witness, or the human race, or history, or your next-door neighbors; you are the docile instrument of a family, of a social group, of a profession, of a party, of a church; you receive your thoughts from the outside by means of newspapers, the radio, lectures and speeches and immediately redistribute them; not a moment goes by without your speaking and listening, and whatever you say or hear is what anyone would have said or heard in your place; from morning to night you submit to the tyranny of the human visage, you have no secrets, no mystery, nor do you want to have any—and yet, in a certain way, you are alone. And I do not locate this solitude in our private life, which is only a sector of public life, nor in our tastes, which are social and shared: I find it everywhere. Being a negation, it is the negative of our loves, of our actions, of our personal or political life. It is neither subjectivity, in the strict sense of the word, nor objectivity, but the relationship between the two when it is experienced as a failure. It is born within communication itself, as poetry is within all prose, because the most clearly expressed and understood thoughts conceal an incommunicable element: I can make them be conceived as I conceive them but am unable to make them live as I live. This solitude is found within mutual love: when you are unable to make your wife share a taste which you have in common with thousands of other people, when you remain separated from her within pleasure. In these examples, subjectivity does not succeed in dissolving objectivities. But we are *also* alone when we cannot *become objects sufficiently:* surrounded, supported, fed, re-created by your party, you may want to be only a cell of that great organism and yet you feel your solitude for the simple reason that it always remains possible for you to leave the party and that your very loyalty is deliberate, or else out of fear of being led one day to criticize the leaders and to refuse obedience, in short, because of the anxiety you feel when confronted with your freedom and exactly insofar as you are not the stick or corpse which you are making an effort to imitate; the victor is alone because he cannot identify himself completely with the beautiful possession which is being led in triumph: because of his hidden defeat. This vague sense of a want of exact correspondence between the subjective and objective would still be nothing, for we spend our time hiding the fact from ourselves; but our professional mistakes, our thoughtless acts, our blunders and our mishaps suddenly exasperate it: the error, the slip, the foolish act creates a vacuum around us; suddenly the others *see* us, we emerge from the original indistinctness, we have become objects; at the same time, we *feel ourselves being looked at,* we feel ourselves blushing and turning pale: we have become subjects. In short, our solitude is the way we feel our objectivity for others in our subjectivity and on the occasion of a failure. Ultimately, the criminal and the madman are pure objects and solitary subjects; their frantic subjectivity is carried to the point of solipsism at the moment when they are reduced for others to the state of a pure, manipulated thing, of a pure *being-there* without a future, prisoners who are dressed and undressed, who are spoon-fed. On the one hand are dream, autism, absence; on the other, the ant heap; on the one hand, shame and the impotent hatred that turns against itself and vainly defies the heavens, and on the other the opaque being of the pebble, the "human material." The man who becomes aware of this explosive contradiction within himself knows true solitude, that of the monster; botched by Nature and Society, he lives radically, to the point of impossibility, the latent, larval solitude which is ours and which we try to ignore. One is not alone if one is right, for Truth will out; nor if one is wrong, for it will suffice to acknowledge one's mistakes for them to be forgotten. One is alone when one is right and wrong *at the same time:* when one declares oneself right as subject—because one is conscious and lives and because one cannot and will not deny what one has willed —and when one declares oneself wrong as object because one cannot reject the objective condemnation of all of Society. There is only one path leading down to the solitude of the unique, the path that leads, through impotence and despair, to error and failure. You will be alone if you know that you are now only a guilty object in everyone's eyes, while your conscience continues, despite itself, to approve of itself; you will be alone if Society ignores you and if you cannot annihilate yourself: Genet's "impossible nullity" is solitude. But awareness of it is not enough; you must live it, must therefore make it: on this basis, two attitudes are possible.

Bukharin conspires. That does not mean he is opposed *as a subject* to the government's policy. He does what the objective situation requires. Everything takes place among objects: objective deviations require their objective corrective; that is all. If he had seized power in time, the revolution would have continued without a hitch: who in the U.S.S.R. would have dared comment upon a change among the rulers? Had he won, he would have remained a stick and a corpse; as an instrument controlled by history, it would not have been he who changed things, but rather things would have been changed by him; and since, as Merleau-Ponty says, "the paradox of history . . . is that a contingent future looms up before us when it has become the present as something real and even necessary,"* the manifest success of his victory would have finally dissolved him in the historical process. But he fails, and the necessity of his defeat reveals to him that his undertaking was impossible, that it was rejected a priori by objective reality. It had only the consistency of shadows and could have sprung only from a shadow, to wit, the Communist who turns against history.† Bukharin learns what he is not, what he will not do: he *is not* the historical process, he *will not make* the required correction. Since history rejects him, he now defines himself only by *nonbeing:* he is the man who *has not* succeeded, who *could not* succeed; he is error, he is impotence. Does he retain the hope that some day others will succeed? Perhaps: but they will be other men, with other means, in other circumstances. Their victory will demonstrate that his attempt was useless and premature; it will make him even more guilty. Come what may, history can only decide that he was wrong. It had not chosen him; he had chosen himself. Wrong, error, presumption, failure, impotence: these negations designate him, in his own eyes, as a *subject.* He is a subject because of insufficiency and not because of excess: because of everything that he did not understand, everything that he did not do. He is a subject because of the nothingness that is in him. Impossible nullity. Does he therefore think that he was mistaken even in his evaluation of the historical situation? Probably not: but it was not time to correct those deviations; history was taking another path, one that was slower but surer, the only possible and only necessary one. It was not *for him* to reason and reflect: *it was wrong of him to be right.* And since

---

* Merleau-Ponty, *Humanisme et terreur.*

† The Christian who turns away from God is likewise a shadow. For him the worst is not sure. In Marxist terms: a traitor is not sufficient to deflect the course of history. Jouhandeau's abjection, which reveals to him his *person* in and by the radical inadequacy of his being, is the religious equivalent of Bukharin's treason.

his intention was bound to lead to catastrophe, it was vitiated at the very beginning. "Here we encounter a stern idea of responsibility, which is not what men wanted but what they happen to have done in the light of the event." The opposition which seizes power can save a country that is in danger; the opposition which fails can only weaken it. "In the light of the event," Bukharin discovers at the same time, and by means of each other, his subjectivity and his betrayal. To be sure, he did not want to betray; but that was not enough: he ought to have wanted not to betray, therefore to lie low; he is blamed, here again, for a nothingness, an absence, in the intention; in like manner, a reckless driver is condemned for man-slaughter *through negligence,* that is, for *not having thought* of slowing up: he is condemned for what there *was not* in his mind and not for what there was. Thus, Bukharin is a traitor. A traitor for having run the risk, in case of failure, of serving the enemies of the revolution; a traitor for having departed from objectivity, for hav-ing judged as a subject and for having accepted the possibility that his undertaking might remain subjective, that is, might be a failure and endanger the building of socialism; a traitor not for having discarded revolutionary principles, but, quite the contrary, because he still accepted them when he was endangering the revolution. Since he can appeal to neither his former comrades who condemn him nor his enemies whom he continues to hate, nor posterity which may not maintain the charge of betrayal but which will rank him among the blunderers of history, he is alone. He finds in him-self only nothingness and failure. And since he is a nothingness, he attacks this subjectivity which isolates him; his last act, which un-fortunately is also subjective, is to annihilate himself; he refuses to listen to his own testimony and to see himself as anything other than an object; he will now be only the traitor that he appears to be to everyone, still a stick but a broken stick; he pleads guilty. That is the first attitude: the solitary individual escapes from solitude by a moral suicide; rejected by men, he becomes a stone amongst stones.

Here is the second one. For Genet is the Bukharin of bourgeois society. Chosen victim of a compact and militant community, he was tossed into a ditch while it continued on its way; failure and impotence revealed his solitude to him too. He knows that bourgeois history will eternally declare him wrong. He is alone be-cause he continues to affirm the principles which condemn him, just as Bukharin maintained to the very end the revolutionary prin-ciples in the name of which he was executed. "Since the accused

Marxists were . . . in agreement with the prosecution on the principle of historical responsibility, they became self-accusers, and in order to discover their subjective honesty we must examine not only the indictment but also their own statements." This sentence from Merleau-Ponty's book is applicable to Genet word for word: agreeing with the court as to the sacredness of private property, he becomes his own accuser in the name of the fundamental principle of the bourgeoisie which excludes him; in short, like Bukharin he discovers his subjectivity by judging himself according to the objective maxims of society. Both men confess. When the record is signed, one will be a traitor forever and the other a scoundrel in the eyes of eternity.

Bukharin, however, confesses to his betrayal with humility, whereas Genet takes pride in his. To be sure, Bukharin cannot entirely destroy the subjectivity which he discovers in the failure and which he condemns along with his judges: "Although he does not recognize personal honor . . . he defends his revolutionary honor and rejects the imputation of espionage and sabotage." On the eve of death, he is still arranging his defeat; this pure nothingness which cannot annihilate itself attempts, to the very end, to make the impossibility of living livable. But Genet is of another society, one that has other myths and other mores, and since bourgeois society recognizes the right of every individual to exist, it is this right which he demands. Bukharin, who is a black sheep of a revolutionary community, persists in calling himself a revolutionary; Genet, who is an outcast of a "liberal" society, demands, in the name of liberalism, freedom to live for the monster that he has become. This means that he persists in his failure, in his anomalies, that he heightens his exile and, since he is now only a nothingness, he becomes a proud consciousness of not being; impotent, evil, unreasonable and wanting to be unto annihilation, he will be nothing but the narrow limit which separates negativity from nothingness, nonbeing from the consciousness of being nothing. Negation of everything and even of negation, he chooses, in the light of the failure, to be the pure, incommunicable, irretrievable subjectivity oscillating between the Nothingness which cannot annihilate and the Nothing which causes itself to exist solely by the consciousness of not being. The Just spit in his face and list the wrong things he has done. But, unlike Bukharin, he proclaims in defiance of all that he *is right to be wrong*. He *alone* declares himself right; he knows that his testimony is inadequate and he maintains it *because* of its inadequacy. He is proud of being right *in the realm of the impossible* and of testifying to the impossibility of everything. Do you finally realize who Genet is? Bear in mind Merleau-Ponty's comment on Bukharin, a comment which has aroused loud protest: "Every opponent is a traitor, but every traitor is only an opponent." You who do not share the principles of Soviet society call Bukharin a defeated opponent and you are indignant that he can be called a traitor. In that case, allow Genet, who horrifies you, to be, for others who do not share your principles, only a defeated opponent of bourgeois society. I know that he fills you with genuine disgust. But do you think that Bukharin does not fill the faithful Communist and the Stakhanovite with disgust? In any society, the guilty man is solitary and the solitary is guilty; there is no other way of assuming solitude than to claim the fault and consequently to arouse horror. For solitude is the social relationship itself when it is lived in despair; it is the negative relationship of each individual to all. Genet's origin is *a blunder* (there would not have been a Genet if someone had used a contraceptive), then *a rejection* (someone rejected that hated consequence of a blunder), then *a failure* (the child was unable to integrate himself into the milieu that received him). Blunder, rejection, failure: these add up to a *No.* Since the child's objective essence was the No, Genet gave himself a personality by giving himself the subjectivity of the No; he is the absolute opponent, for he opposes Being and all integration. Although he is a taboo object for everyone, he becomes a sacred subject for himself, and the subjectivity which he claims is the proud internalization of the object's pure being-gazed-upon, of the tube of vaseline, for example. Genet is first a pure thing—what Bukharin will be only by virtue of the confession and the death that follows immediately—a thing that cannot be assimilated (*because it is a thing*) to a society of subject-objects, and his subjectivity is only the internalization of his "thingness" as a separatory inertia. The insolence with which the tube of vaseline mocks the indignant cops is quite simply its *inertia,* an inertia that is lived and acted by the culprit as a gesture of bravado, a terribly active and anxious consciousness which *makes itself a passivity:* such is the *person* of Genet as a particularity. But also as a universal: theft, homosexuality and betrayal, as contents of this particular essence, come afterward: "One must first be guilty," that is, *an object for everybody.* In claiming absolute objectivity, Genet seems to be *a* particular opponent of *a* historical society: he achieves, for all, the pure form of opposition reduced to impotence. For all: for you and for me, for every reader. For we are all *at one and the same time* victorious conformists and defeated opponents. We all hide, deep within us, a scandalous breach which, if it were revealed, would instantly change us into an "object of reprobation"; isolated, blamed for our failures, especially in unimportant circumstances, we all know the anguish of being wrong and of being unable to admit we are wrong, of being right and of being unable to accept our being right; we all oscillate between the temptation to prefer our self to everything else because our consciousness is, for us, the center of the world, and that of preferring everything to our consciousness; when beaten in an argument, we have all constructed "whirligigs" and sophisms in order to postpone the moment of "objective" defeat when we already knew in our heart that we were beaten and in order to maintain our error, that nothingness, against the blinding evidence. Thus, we have been kings of shadows and shams; it is indeed difficult for consciousness—which is, on principle, self-approval—to conceive of its errors and its death. In his latest article in *La Table Ronde* Thierry Maulnier discusses one of the strangest and basest inventions of our age, the Chinese accusation meetings at which the assembled population of the town or village enjoys the anguish, repentance, pallor and sweat of the accused persons and condemns them itself, anonymously, by a show of hands; it enjoys seeing the verdict written on the faces of the condemned, follows them to the place of torture and with mockery, insults and cries of joy watches them die."* That is indeed base. But why "Chinese"? Or else we are all Chinese without realizing it, both Chinese victims and Chinese executioners, for I see in these accusation meetings the image of our situation: we are accusers with everyone else and at the same time we are alone and accused by everybody. Since the social relationship is ambiguous and always involves an element of failure, since we are simultaneously the laughing Chinese crowd and the terrified Chinese who is led to torture, since every thought divides as much as it unites, since every word draws one closer by virtue of what it expresses and isolates by virtue of what it does not say, since a fathomless abyss separates the subjective certainty which we have of ourselves from the objective truth which we are for others, since we do not cease to judge ourselves guilty even though we feel innocent, since the event transforms our best intentions into criminal desires not only in history but even in family life, since we are never sure of not becoming traitors retrospectively, since we constantly fail to com-

---

* Thierry Maulnier, "Mort Courageusement," *La Table Ronde*, January 1952.

municate, to love, to be loved, and since every failure makes us feel
our solitude, since we dream at times of effacing our criminal particularity by humbly acknowledging it and at times of affirming it
defiantly in the vain hope of assuming it entirely, since we are
conformists in broad daylight and defeated and evil in our secret
soul, since the one resource of the guilty person and his only
dignity is obstinacy, sulkiness, insincerity and resentment, since we
cannot escape from the objectivity that crushes us nor divest ourself
of the subjectivity that exiles us, since we are not allowed even to
rise to the plane of being or sink into nothingness, since we are,
in any case, *impossible nullities,* we must listen to the voice of
Genet, our fellow man, our brother. He carries to an extreme the
latent, masked solitude which is ours; he inflates our sophisms until
they burst; he magnifies our failures to the point of catastrophe;
he exaggerates our dishonesty to the point of making it intolerable
to us; he makes our guilt appear in broad daylight. Whatever the
society that succeeds ours, his readers will continue to declare him
wrong, since he opposes *all* society. But that is precisely why we are
his brothers; for our age has a guilty conscience with respect to
history. There have been times that were more criminal, but they
cared not a rap for posterity; and others made history with a clear
conscience; men did not feel that they were cut off from the future;
they felt that they were creating it and that their children would
remain in tune with them; the succession of generations was merely
a medium in which they felt at ease. Revolutions are now impossible. We are being threatened by the most idiotic and bloodiest of
wars. The propertied classes are no longer quite sure of their
rights, and the working class is losing ground. We are more aware
of injustice than ever, and we have neither the means nor the will
to rectify it. But the lightning progress of science gives future centuries an obsessive presence; the future is here, more present than
the present: men will go to the moon, perhaps life will be created.
We feel that we are being judged by the masked men who will
succeed us and whose knowledge of all things will be such that we
cannot have the slightest inkling of what it will be; our age will be
an object for those future eyes whose gaze haunts us. And a guilty
object. They will reveal to us our failure and guilt. Our age, which
is already dead, already a *thing,* though we still have to live it, is
alone in history, and this historical solitude determines even our
perceptions: what we see *will no longer be;* people will laugh at our
ignorance, will be indignant at our mistakes. What course is open
to us? There is one which I perceive and which I shall discuss

elsewhere. But the course which one usually takes is to install one-self in the present moment of history and to will it defiantly with the stubbornness of the vanquished; one invents sophisms in order to maintain principles which one realizes are going to disappear and truths which one knows will become error. That is why Genet the sophist is one of the heroes of this age. He is held up to obloquy before our eyes as we are before the gaze of future centuries; the Just will not cease to cast blame on him nor will History cease to cast blame on our age. Genet is we. That is why we must read him. To be sure, he wants to impute to us mistakes that we have not committed, that we have not even dreamed of committing. But what does that matter? Wait a bit until you are accused: the tech-niques have been perfected, you will make a full confession. *There-fore,* you will be guilty. At that point you will have only to choose: you will be Bukharin or Genet. Bukharin or our will *to be together* carried to the point of martyrdom; Genet or our solitude carried to the point of Passion.

If we maintain the hope and firm intention of escaping this alternative, if there is still time to reconcile, with a final effort, the object and the subject, we must, be it only once and in the realm of the imaginary, achieve this latent solitude which corrodes our acts and thoughts. We spent our time fleeing from the objective into the subjective and from the subjective into objectivity. This game of hide-and-seek will end only when we have the courage to go to the limits of ourselves in both directions at once. At the present time, we must bring to light the subject, the guilty one, that mon-strous and wretched bug which we are likely to become at any moment. Genet holds the mirror up to us: we must look at it and see ourselves.

I

SELF-PORTRAIT OF THE GOOD CITIZEN

On July 8, 1908, a famous writer who had just become a member of the French Academy delivered the following speech in the Chamber of Deputies:

MAURICE BARRÈS. I am in favor of maintaining the death penalty, of maintaining and applying it. I shall not bring up the host of arguments raised by this great question. M. Failliot has already discussed some of them. I would like to limit myself to one particular point and to contradict, to refute, if I can, the opinion of those who think that the elimination of the death penalty would make for the moral progress of French society.

This sentiment permeated the speech of M. Joseph Reinach which we have just heard, and it is a very powerful tradition in the political life and political literature of this country. Many persons, very generous persons, to be sure, think that the abolition of the death penalty is a step forward on the way to progress.

Well, I am not going to argue abstractly. I am going to examine the situation in the city of Paris.

If we do away with the death penalty, if we undertake this experiment in disarmament, at whose risk will it be? One cannot deny the fact that it is the poor whom we shall be exposing, it is they who will be the first to suffer. Regardless of what is done, the police will unquestionably always protect the rich better than they will the poor. (*Exclamations at the left and far left.*)

I think that my colleagues quite understand the observation which I am making here. If we stroll through the center of Paris, we see an eternal policeman walking up and down, day and night, in front of the door of a certain famous banker. (*Interruptions.*)

If we simply read from day to day the crime items in the newspapers we see that, apart from a few sensational murders that arrest the public's attention, the great majority of the victims are slum dwellers and people who are weak and unattached. Thus, one cannot but observe that this reform, which you consider a generous one, would increase the dangers to which the lower classes are exposed. (*Applause at the right.*)

Will this elimination of the death penalty at least ennoble our civilization? If any persons are inclined to think so, it is because they desire to harmonize our society with the data provided by science. We listen to doctors who say to us, with respect to criminals: "They're forced to commit crimes. A's crime is due to atavism. B's is due to his environment."

Undoubtedly there are conclusions to be drawn from these statements by doctors. The conclusion to be drawn, it seems to me, is that it is our duty to fight against the conditions which have paved the way for this atavism, to cleanse the environment in which such-and-such a man has been perverted. (*"Quite right, quite right."*)

Science provides us with information which we legislators know we must utilize. Let us fight the causes of degeneracy. But when we are in the presence of the limb which has already rotted, when we are in the presence of the unfortunate individual, unfortunate if we consider the social conditions which molded him, but wretched if we consider the sad crime into which he has fallen—it is the general social interest that should govern us and not sentimentality about the social question. (*Commotion at the far left.*)

Let us get to the heart of the matter.

It seems to me that the traditional inclination on the part of many eminent and generous minds to take into consideration the interests of the murderer, to brood over them with a kind of indulgence, is based on the erroneous belief that we are confronted with a kind of bright new barbarian who lacked some of the social advantages which we more favored individuals possess. That was, if I am not mistaken, the view of Victor Hugo, and it should be examined in a political debate on the death penalty, for Hugo's lucubrations unquestionably had a strong influence on the intellectual formation of republicans during the last years of the Second Empire.

Hugo thought that the murderer was too new a creature, a quite new, unlicked human matter that had not profited from the accumulated advantages of civilization. He summed up his views in saying: "If you had given him the book, you would have destroyed the crime."

Well, that hypothesis is not in line with the information that science gives us. Ah, the elements, that which emerges from the mass and which has not yet assumed civilized form, are precious, are sacred. These new elements are of greater worth than we, are perhaps more precious than the civilized man who has attained a high degree of development. This bright new barbarian still has everything to offer us. But hooligans are not forces overflowing with life, they are not fine barbarians who shatter the framework of common morality; they are degenerates. Far from being oriented toward the future, they are bogged down by vile defects. Usually, when we are in the presence of a criminal, we find a man on the downgrade, a man who has fallen outside of humanity, and not a man who has not yet reached the stage of humanity. (*At the right:* "*Bravo.*")

JEAN JAURÈS. It's Christians who say "Bravo." It's strange to hear the doctrine of the irremediable fall proclaimed by right-wing Christians. (*"Quite right" and laughter at the left.*)

MAURICE BARRÈS. I think that a Christian might reply, M. Jaurès, that the two spheres must not be confused and that we are legislators who are here to do a certain limited, nonreligious, social job. (*Ironic exclamations at the far left.*)

Gentlemen, you will allow me to believe that I am correct in saying that there are indeed great difficulties that can be resolved in another world, but that our job as legislators is performed on a quite other plane. The law itself understands this in assigning a chaplain to the unfortunate creature who is going to the guillotine, and in saying: "There is a secret understanding between these two men which takes place under certain conditions that it is not for me, the civil law, to consider."

As for myself, I continue to ask that society continue to rid us of these debased creatures, of these degenerates, in accordance with present-day legal traditions and in line with the information provided us by competent scientists when they tell us that a given individual should be put into an asylum rather than be punished. I think that it is advisable to resort to exemplary punishment. And by exemplary punishment I do not mean punishment in public. I think that the example can be even more striking, as in England, where capital punishment, carried out quietly behind high walls, seems to me even more terrifying than the kind of unspeakable apotheosis which we offer on public squares. (*Applause.*)

And now, gentlemen, allow me to ask you, and to ask myself, whether we are not all suffering from a certain passing disease of the intelligence (*agitation*), to wit, a difficulty in assuming responsibility. This difficulty is due, I grant, to a scruple that is praiseworthy in itself, a scruple of a cultivated and highly civilized man, but does it not have a great social disadvantage?

I was greatly struck, in reading the many studies that have been made here and there of the question of the death penalty, to see that, in the last analysis, most of the conclusions amounted to the following: "I do not feel capable of judging a man."

A reluctance, indeed an inability of overcultivated people to accept responsibility. Yes, I have seen it more or less clearly stated that it is a weighty obligation for a man—and so it is—to speak out in no uncertain terms and to say: "That man is guilty, that man must be punished, scourged."

But yet, isn't that a necessity of life itself, and does it not seem that if we accepted as praiseworthy delicacy what is actually weakness, a weakening of the will, to call it by its name, we would be yielding to the doctrine that is being expressed and proposed with brilliant but very dangerous force in another country? I am referring to Tolstoy and the doctrine of nonresistance to evil.

Gentlemen, a few years ago, in England, thugs roamed the streets of London, terrifying the population. An appeal was made to the young members of the athletic clubs who killed a few of these hooligans. The surplus returned to occupations less dangerous for the public and for themselves. (*Various reactions.*)

I beg you to view this example in the context of my argument. I am not saying: "That is what we ought to do." I am not even saying: "We should resort to corporal punishment in dealing with hooligans." But in the presence of this powerful current of nonresistance to evil which we seem to be welcoming, I urge you to see in a splendid civilization a singular social manliness.

Gentlemen, I loathe bloodshed as much as any of you. I was once present at an execution—I cannot say that I saw it, for it is indeed an intolerable spectacle. I happened to be standing not far from the Prime Minister. The next day, M. Clemenceau wrote a fine article in which he expressed the disgust he had felt, the moral and physical repulsion that one cannot but feel.

But what does that prove? It proves first that the Prime Minister did the right thing in giving up his medical career, which might have led him to perform surgical operations. (*Exclamations.*)

As for myself, would I not experience that painful emotion if I had to witness those terrible operations which are nevertheless a salvation, a resource of the art of healing? Life is itself a cruel thing, and it is no argument against the death penalty to declare what nobody denies, that the witnessing of an execution is a ghastly thing.

It is out of love of social health that I vote for the maintenance and application of the death penalty.

In any case, allow me to say in conclusion that this measure, which you think is a generous one, is an act of generosity at the expense of others. And you would have provided this vote against the guillotine with much more authority when a man threw a bomb into this Chamber and you allowed him to be executed.

I should like to say to the abolitionists that there was a day when they missed a unique opportunity to affirm their horror of the death penalty, and that was when they themselves were the victims. (*Applause at the center and at the right.*)

On July 13, 1908, a journalist who signed himself *Junius* and who was none other than Paul Bourget approved of Maurice Barrès in the following terms:

July 13, 1908. Junius' Column. What with the schoolteachers, Morocco, the income tax and M. Loisy, I did not have enough space to set down the reflections aroused in me, and, I imagine, in many good Frenchmen and good Catholics by one of the incidents that marked M. Maurice Barrès' courageous speech on the death penalty. M. Jaurès had just interrupted the speaker upon the latter's wise and vivid statement: "Usually, when we are in the presence of a criminal, we find a man on the downgrade." "It's Christians," cried the Socialist orator, "who proclaim the doctrine of the irremediable fall." M. Barrès replied, with the same wisdom: "The two spheres must not be confused. We are here to do a certain limited, nonreligious, social job."

Whereupon Abbé Gayraud, no doubt wishing to give Abbé Lemire—who nevertheless does not need it—a fine example of false thinking, cried out: "We cannot accept that point of view."

It is particularly important for us Catholics to protest against this protest since it has unfortunately been taken up by the newspapers of our party and because, even more unfortunately, it expresses a state of mind frequently encountered at the present time, and from that state of mind has sprung the monster of Christian democracy in which anarchy and the Gospels, the idiotic logomachy of the Declaration of Rights and the sublime Sermon on the Mount, are amalgamated as in that other Piltdown creature of an equally fearful type, namely Tolstoyism. Yes, M. Barrès is right. There are two spheres in human life and to wish to confuse them is to go counter to the very words of the Scriptures: "My kingdom is not of this world. . . . The kingdom of God is within you."

Either these famous passages are meaningless or else they signify that the natural order and the supernatural order are separate in the social world as they are in the physical world. The social world and the physical world each have their own laws. Hierarchy is one of these laws, a law which the Gospel is careful to affirm: "Render to Caesar the things that are Caesar's." Inequality of fortune is another such law: "For ye have the poor always with you." When one wishes to engage in political action, one must seek out these laws from the quite experimental point of view that takes into account only observation.

II

THE TZEDEK TEST

The aim of the Tzedek Test is to explore the "moral judgment."
The experimenters ask fifteen questions about "fifteen situations
requiring a practical decision." In each case, the subject must "tell
what he thinks is right." The following concerns a delinquent,
thirty-four years old, numerous convictions: willful homicide and
theft, housebreaking, etc. "When questioned, he expresses himself
politely and without hostility. He seems to regard us, especially
when we put the questions of the test to him, with slightly ironic
compassion. . . . Alert, sarcastic, his face is drawn by a somewhat
bitter smile. His speech is rapid, voluble and clear. The replies are
given in a passionate tone. . . . He is categorical about his offenses:
'Money should be taken wherever it is,' 'no reason for me to work,'
'it's normal to steal.' About his emotional life, proud and bitter
statements: 'I'm alone, always alone, solitary . . . I have no friends
. . . I don't know what it is to love a woman. . . .' "*
  The following are some of the questions and his answers:

A serious offense has been committed in a government office. A
certain person is vaguely suspected without sufficient proof. Nevertheless, he is seriously punished on the grounds that an example
must be set. What do you think of this decision?
  Answer: That's pretty much the way government agencies usually act. . . . It's all right for them. I personally don't consider it
right.
  A young man eagerly desires a job that is held by someone else.

---

* Henri Baruk and Maurice Bachet, *Le Test Tzedek*, p. 75.

He makes malicious comments about the other person, who is finally dismissed. What do you think of his behavior?

Answer: Everything's a rat race.

Two candidates are up for election. . . . One of them invents slanderous facts about his opponent's personal life. . . . What do you think of this attitude?

Answer: It's a rat race. . . . People are always slandering.

A young man has a good job. . . . His mother, who lives alone, commits a moral offense. . . . She is indicted and condemned. The young man refuses to go to see her and to look after her on the grounds that she is guilty. What do you think of this attitude?

Answer: A lousy thing to do.

There is a food shortage . . . and rationing is introduced: very large rations for able-bodied persons who produce and work, starvation rations for old persons who are no longer able to work. What do you think of this?

Answer: They ought to be killed instead.

A shopkeeper reserves his merchandise for his most powerful and richest customers, etc.

Answer: He's right. He knows on which side his bread is buttered. What he does is normal. It's also normal to steal.

During a period of rationing, it is decided to give the citizens of the country a higher ration than foreign residents. What do you think of this?

Answer: It's perfectly normal. Though I did my military service in France, I kept my foreign nationality. But I don't care either way. I never had a food card during the Occupation, and I assure you I never lost weight."

The delinquent counterattacks. He energetically refuses to play the role that the questioners are trying to impose upon him: he will not be a scapegoat, he will not have a guilty conscience. If he is distinguished from the herd, it is neither by perversity nor any psychic disorder: it is only because he has drawn all the inferences from a state of affairs that everyone recognizes; he obliges the society which is imprisoning him to maintain reciprocal relations with him despite itself. He rejects the ethical notions of Right, Justice and Virtue in the name of which he is condemned and substitutes the ambiguous notion of *normality*, which enables him to approve of himself. What is *normal* is the fact that every individual and social group pursues its own interests exclusively, that relations between persons are based solely on violence and craft, on the notion of might makes right. The words "normal," "natural" and "regular" mask and hide a transition from fact to right. It is normal and natural that the strong crush the weak, that's what has always happened: this is the basic notion. Moreover, anyone who acted otherwise "would be pretty dumb." Everyone has the right to defend himself and it's his duty to do so. "It's natural to steal" because "good citizens" find it natural to slander, starve, hoard and exploit. It is also natural for society to lay hands on the thief and put him into jail: this is a pure and simple application of the law of might makes right. But let it not venture to condemn him morally: by virtue of what right could it do so since it is based on injustice? Between collectivities and persons, between individuals, *there exists a state of war.* My enemy is my fellow creature in that he tries to destroy me just as I try to destroy him. The judge who sentences me is neither better nor worse: to judge a robber and to rob a judge come to the same thing: it's all a rat race. If man is a wolf to man, I find in universal war the reciprocal relationships that society tries to deny me. This thief has exchanged the guilty conscience that they were trying to palm off on him for the good conscience of the warrior. But he does so because his childhood differs from Genet's in every respect: "Thirty-four years old, of Greek descent, he comes from a working-class family in the south of France. There seems to have been no family trouble. He seems not to have gone to school because of a paralysis of the arm of which there are no longer any signs. Nevertheless, he is rather educated. He was taught by his mother, a former schoolteacher, and even knows a foreign language. No psychic disorder or perversion in childhood. Seems to have been a waiter in a café and then a navigator. At the age of eighteen, he enlisted in the army for five years and was very soon condemned for disobedience. His enlistment was annulled at the end of eighteen months." Thus, it seems that he developed normally until puberty. If his solitary education and his foreign status, as well as the suspect disability of which not a trace remains, instilled in him the seeds of revolt, their effect did not manifest itself before he was eighteen. It should be noted that the only *ethical* answer which he gave has to do with filial duties: the son who abandons his guilty mother is a louse. (Indeed, one might have expected him to declare: It's natural, he has a good job and doesn't want to get into trouble, it's a rat race.) This rather manifests the depth of the bonds by which he is still attached to his mother. The decisive crisis seems to have occurred when he was about eighteen. On only one occasion did he emerge from his chronic and bitter indifference, and that was to proclaim that "the army is a school for crime" and to "rattle off in a passionate tone a sixty-line poem on the subject." He seems to have been unable to adapt himself to military discipline. But when the conflict broke out, he was ready to defend himself. Or, to adopt the language of the experimenters, he was already in full possession of the "individualistic and idealistic rationalism of the period of puberty." Hegel would have said that he was already condemning the course of the world in the name of the law of the heart. It was not difficult for him to transform rationalism into cynicism and, like Schiller's *Robbers,* to justify his robberies by the law of the heart. The crisis, which occurred in the course of adolescence, perpetuated in him the moment of puberty. He will remain congealed to the very end in the moment of the liquidation of family values. But this stereotype of negativity constitutes for him the best of defenses.

III

THE MAIDS

The most extraordinary example of the whirligig of being and appearance, of the imaginary and the real, is to be found in one of Genet's plays. It is the element of fake, of sham, of artificiality that attracts Genet in the theater. He has turned dramatist because the falsehood of the stage is the most manifest and fascinating of all. Perhaps nowhere has he lied more brazenly than in *The Maids*.

Two maids both love and hate their mistress. They have denounced her lover to the police by means of anonymous letters. Upon learning that he is to be released for lack of proof, they realize that their betrayal will be discovered, and they try to murder Madame. They fail and want to kill themselves. Finally, one of them takes her life, and the other, left alone and drunk with glory, tries, by the pomp of her posturings and language, to be equal to the magnificent destiny that awaits her.

Let us indicate at once a first whirligig. Genet says in *Our Lady of the Flowers:* "If I were to have a play put on in which women had roles, I would demand that these roles be performed by adolescent boys, and I would bring this to the attention of the spectators by means of a placard which would remain nailed to the right or left of the sets during the entire performance."* One might be tempted to explain this demand by Genet's taste for young boys. Nevertheless, this is not the essential reason. The truth of the matter is that Genet wishes from the very start to *strike at the root of the apparent*. No doubt an actress can play Solange, but the derealizing

---

* *The Maids* was actually performed by women, but this was a concession which Genet made to Louis Jouvet, who produced the play.

would not be radical, since there would be no need for her to play at being a woman. The softness of her flesh, the languid grace of her movements and the silvery tone of her voice are natural endowments. They constitute the substance that she would mold as she saw fit, so as to give it the appearance of Solange. Genet wishes this feminine stuff itself to become an appearance, the result of a make-believe. It is not Solange who is to be a theatrical illusion, but rather *the woman Solange*.

In order to achieve this absolute state of artifice, the first thing to do is to eliminate nature. The roughness of a breaking voice, the dry hardness of male muscles and the bluish luster of a budding beard will make the defeminized and spiritualized female appear as an invention of man, as a pale and wasting shadow which cannot sustain itself unaided, as the evanescent result of an extreme and momentary exertion, as the impossible dream of man in a world without women.

Thus, what appears behind the footlights is not so much a woman as Genet himself living out the impossibility of being a woman. We would see before us the effort, at times admirable and at times grotesque, of a youthful male body struggling against its own nature, and, lest the spectator be caught up in the game, he would be warned throughout—in defiance of all the laws of stage perspective—that the actors are trying to deceive him as to their sex. In short, the illusion is prevented from "taking" by a sustained contradiction between the effort of the actor, who measures his talent by his ability to deceive, and the warning of the placard. Thus, Genet *betrays* his actors. He unmasks them, and the performer, seeing his imposture exposed, finds himself in the position of a culprit who has been found out. Illusion, betrayal, failure; all the major categories that govern Genet's dreams are here present. In the same way, he betrays his characters in *Our Lady of the Flowers* and in *Funeral Rites* by warning the reader whenever the latter is about to yield to the illusion of the story: "Watch out. These are creatures of my imagination. They don't exist." The thing to be avoided above all is the spectator's being caught up in the game, like children at the movies who scream, "Don't drink it, it's poison!" or like the naïve public that waited at the stage door for Frédéric Lemaître in order to beat him up.

To seek being through appearance would be to make *proper use* of the latter. For Genet, theatrical procedure is demoniacal. Appearance, which is constantly on the point of passing itself off as reality, must constantly reveal its profound unreality. Everything must be so false that it sets our teeth on edge. But by virtue of being false, the woman acquires a poetic density. Shorn of its texture and purified, femininity becomes a heraldic sign, a cipher. As long as it was natural, the feminine blazon remained embedded in woman. Spiritualized, it becomes a category of the imagination, a device for generating reveries. Anything can be a woman: a flower, an animal, an inkwell.

In *The Child Criminal* Genet has given us the keys of what might be called his algebra of the imagination. He speaks of the director of a home for children who boasts of giving the children tin knives and who adds, "They can't kill anyone with that." Genet makes the following comment: "Was he unaware that by departing from its practical destination the object is transformed, that it becomes a symbol? Its very form sometimes changes. We say that it becomes stylized. It then acts secretly in children's souls. It does more serious damage. Hidden at night in a straw mattress or concealed in the lining of the jacket or, rather, of the trousers—not for greater convenience, but in order to be close to the organ it symbolizes—it is the very sign of the murder that the child will not actually commit but which will feed his reverie and, I hope, will direct it toward the most criminal manifestation. What good does it do to take it away from him? The child will only choose some more harmless-looking object as a sign of murder, and if this also is taken from him, he will guard within him preciously the sharper image of the weapon." As the material grows poorer—steel knife, tin knife, hazel twig—as the distance increases between itself and what it signifies, the symbolic nature of the sign is heightened. The reveries are directed, fed and organized. His maids are fake women, "women of no gynaeceum," who make men dream not of possessing *a* woman but of being lit up by a woman-sun, queen of a feminine heaven, and finally of being themselves the matter for the heraldic symbol of femininity. Genet is trying to present to us femininity without woman.

Such is the initial direction of his derealization: a falsification of femininity. But the shock boomerangs and the performance affects the actor himself. The young murderer, Our Lady of the Flowers, dresses up as a woman one day just for the fun of it. "Our Lady, in his pale blue faille dress, edged with white Valenciennes lace, was more than himself. He was himself and his complement." We know that Genet values above all the labor of derealization. The thing that attracts him in Our Lady of the Flowers is the spectacle of a man being worked upon by femininity: "Our Lady raised his bare arm and—it's astounding—this murderer made the very same gesture, though a trifle more brutal, that Émilienne d'Alençon would certainly have made to rumple her chignon." This hybrid creature, of the race of centaurs and sirens, begins as a male only to go up in smoke as female fireworks. In order to express his superiority both to young men and to all women, Genet invents a wonderful sign: "The chauffeur opened the door. . . . Gorgui, because of his position in the group, ought to have stepped in first, but he moved aside, leaving the opening free for Our Lady. Bear in mind that never does a pimp efface himself before a woman, still less before a fairy. . . . Gorgui must have placed him quite high." The appearance of the imaginary upsets social conventions. Gorgui the Pimp spontaneously adopts bourgeois courtesy. He effaces himself before a glamorous young male who derealizes himself into a young lady whose grace is heightened by the glamour of the murderer. The grace of women is usually despised by roughnecks because it signifies weakness and submission. But here it shimmers at the surface of the great dark force of killers. Hence, they must bow before it. Crime becomes the secret horror of grace: grace becomes the secret softness of crime. Our Lady is the vestal of a bloodthirsty goddess, a great cruel Mother of a homosexual matriarchy.

Thus far we have seen nothing we did not already know. All this is still the reciprocal derealization of matter by form and of form by matter. But now the first whirligig is set going. Genet's poetic themes are, as we know, profoundly homosexual. We know that neither women nor the psychology of women interests him. And if he has chosen to show us maids and their mistress and feminine hatreds, it is only because the necessities of public performance oblige him to disguise his thought. The proof of this is that his second play, *Deathwatch*, the characters of which are all men, deals with exactly the same subject as *The Maids*.

There is the same hierarchy: in one case, Monsieur, in the other, Snowball; the intermediate divinity, Madame and Green Eyes; and the two youngsters who dream of murder but fail to commit it, who love and hate each other and each of whom is the other's bad smell, Solange and Claire, Maurice and Lefranc. In one case, the play ends with a suicide that the police will take for a murder; in the other, with a fake murder, that is, a real killing which rings false. Lefranc, who is a fake, is a real traitor; Maurice, however, who is too young to kill, is of the race of killers; thus, they too form "the eternal couple of the Criminal and the Saint," as do Divine and Our Lady. This is the same eternal couple that Solange and Claire want to

form. And their ambiguous feeling for Madame is discreetly homosexual, as is that of Lefranc and Maurice for Green Eyes. Moreover,
Genet himself has known the maids' hatred of Madame. He tells us
in *Our Lady of the Flowers* that he himself was once a servant,
and in *Funeral Rites* he tells us of another servant, the suffering
mother who concealed beneath her skirts "the wiliest of hoodlums."
Similarly, it has been said that "Proust's Albertine should have
been called Albert." The young actors in *The Maids* are boys playing at being women, but these women in turn are secretly boys.
However, these imaginary boys who gleam behind the feminine
appearances of Solange and Claire are not to be identified with the
real adolescents who embody the characters. They too are dreams,
since in the other play they are called Maurice and Lefranc. They
are, if you like, on the vanishing line of the appearances, giving
them their appearance of depth. But the spectators dimly sense the
homosexual drift of the plot, and when the actor raises his bare
arm and reveals too much muscle, when he adjusts his bun and
makes a gesture "a trifle more brutal" than that of Émilienne
d'Alençon, the spectator does not know whether this inordinate
muscularity and too evident brutality represent a rebellion of
reality or whether they transcend this story about women and
symbolize homosexuality. Are the dry and angular gesture and
the brusque gait merely the awkwardness of a young male hampered by a woman's dress, or are they not Maurice, who has taken
possession of Solange? Are they a return to Being or are they the
quintessence of the imaginary? Being changes at this point into
appearance and appearance into being. But it may be objected that
the homosexual drama is the *truth* of this ancillary fiction. Well
and good. But it is an appearance which becomes the truth of
another appearance. And then, in another sense, these fake women
were the truth of the adolescent boys who embodied them, for
Genet, like all homosexuals, is able to discern a secret femininity
in the most male of men. As in psychodramas, his actors play what
they are. They resemble, feature for feature, the real hoodlum who
played the fake-prince-who-is-a-real-hoodlum and who, through the
mediation of the prince, was derealized into himself. But if these
fake women are the disguise of imaginary men, the young actors
are swallowed up by a new absence. As they interpret their own
drama, they are the unconscious pawns in a game of chess which
Genet is playing against himself.

But we are still at only the first degree of derealization. These
fake women who are fake men, these women-men who are men-

women, this perpetual challenging of masculinity by a symbolic femininity and of the latter by the secret femininity which is the truth of all masculinity, are only the faked groundwork. Upon this evanescent foundation there appear individual forms: Solange and Claire. We shall see that they too are faked.

The play has four characters, one of whom does not appear, namely, Monsieur, the *man*. Monsieur is Harcamone of *Miracle of the Rose;* he is Snowball of *Deathwatch.* Pilorge is he who *is never there.* His absence represents the eternal abstraction of the handsome Pimps, their indifference. In this bourgeois atmosphere he is the only one who is ennobled by prison. To be sure, he is slanderously accused of a crime which he has not committed, but we know that for Genet guilt comes to the offender from without. It is a collective image, a taboo that settles upon him. Behind this homosexual *Arlésienne* whom everyone talks about and nobody sees is Madame, an ambiguous figure, a mediation, a girl queen in relation to Monsieur and a boy queen in relation to the two maids. To Monsieur she is a faithful dog. Genet ascribes to her his old dream of following a convict to the penal colony. "I wanted to be," he tells us, "the young prostitute who accompanies her lover to Siberia." And Madame says: "I don't think he's guilty either, but if he were, I'd become his accomplice. I'd follow him to Devil's Island, to Siberia." But something warns us—perhaps her volubility or the wild gaiety of her despair—that she is a fraud. Does she love Monsieur? Probably she does. But to what point? There is no way of telling. At all events, she has found, like Ernestine in *Our Lady of the Flowers,* the finest role of her life. It will be noted that Green Eyes, a symmetrical character who is also an intermediary and a "daimon," though he has committed an honest-to-goodness murder, plays, in his state of exaltation, at being a murderer. In Genet's plays every character must play the role of a character who plays a role. In relation to the two maids, Madame represents pitiless indifference. Not that she despises or mistreats them; she is *kind.* She embodies social Good and Good Conscience, and the servants' ambivalent feelings about her express Genet's feelings about Good. Being kind, Madame can desire only the Good. She feels sorry for them: she gives them dresses; she loves them, but with an icy love, "like her bidet." In like manner, wealthy, cultivated and happy men have, from time to time, "felt sorry" for Genet, have tried to oblige him. Too late. He has blamed them for loving him for the love of Good, *in spite* of his badness and not *for* it. Only an evil individual could love another evil individual for the love of Evil. But evildoers do not love.

As a woman in relationship to Monsieur, Madame has only *relative* being. As the maids' mistress, she retains an absolute being. But the maids are relative to everything and everyone; their being is defined by its absolute relativity. They are *others*. Domestics are pure emanations of their masters and, like criminals, belong to the order of the Other, to the order of Evil. They *love* Madame. This means, in Genet's language, that both of them would like to *become* Madame, in other words, to be integrated into the social order instead of being outcasts. They *hate* Madame. Translate: Genet detests the Society that rejects him and he wishes to annihilate it. These specters are born of the dream of a master; murky to themselves, their feelings come to them from outside. They are born in the sleeping imagination of Madame or Monsieur. Low, hypocritical, disagreeable and mean because their employers dream them that way, they belong to the "pale and motley race that flowers in the minds of decent people." When he presents them before the footlights, Genet merely mirrors the fantasies of the right-minded women in the audience. Every evening five hundred Madames can sing out, "Yes, that's what maids are like," without realizing that they have created them, the way Southerners create Negroes. The only rebellion of these flat creatures is that they dream in turn: they dream within a dream; these dream dwellers, pure reflections of a sleeping consciousness, use the little reality which this consciousness has given them to imagine that they are becoming the Master who imagines them. They flounder about at the intersection of two nightmares and form the "twilight guard" of bourgeois families. They are disturbing only in that they are dreams that dream of swallowing up their dreamer.

Thus, the maids, as Genet conceives them, are *already* fake. Pure products of artifice, their minds are inside out, and they are always other than themselves. That there are two of them is a stroke of genius. Two, exactly the number needed to set up a whirligig. To be sure, Genet did not invent these criminal sisters out of whole cloth. The reader has probably recognized Claire and Solange; they are the Papin sisters.* But we already know that Genet has distilled the anecdote, that he has retained only its quintessence and presents it to us as a "cipher." The *maids* are the mysterious cipher of the pure imagination and also of Genet himself. There are two of them because Genet is double: himself and the other. Thus, each of the two maids has no other function than to be the other, to be—for the other—herself-as-other. Whereas the unity of the mind is

---

* The reference is to a famous French murder case.—Translator's note.

constantly haunted by a phantom duality, the dyad of the maids is, on the contrary, haunted by a phantom of unity. Each sees in the other only herself at a distance from herself. Each bears witness to the other of the impossibility of *being* herself, and, as Querelle says: "their double statue is reflected in each of their halves." The mainspring of this new whirligig is the perfect interchangeability of Solange and Claire, which makes Solange always appear to be elsewhere, *on* Claire when we look at Solange, and *on* Solange when we look at Claire. To be sure, this interchangeability does not exclude certain differences. Solange seems harder; perhaps "she tries to dominate" Claire; perhaps Genet has chosen her to embody the glamorous appearance and the secret cowardice of the criminal; perhaps he has elected the gentle and perfidious Claire to symbolize the hidden heroism of the Saint. In actual fact, Solange's attempts at crime fail: she does not succeed in killing either Madame or her own sister. Claire also botches a murder, but, pushing their play-acting to its extreme consequences, she takes her own life. The girl queen has more real courage than the tough. This means that the fake courage of Solange finds its truth in the secret courage of Claire, that the fake pusillanimity of Claire finds its truth in the profound cowardice of Solange.

But Genet does not linger over these familiar themes, which he develops abundantly elsewhere. Solange and Claire are much less differentiated than Maurice and Lefranc; their dissimilarities are dreams which ill conceal a fundamental identity. Both of them are characterized by the imaginary splendor of their projects and the radical failure of their undertakings. In reality, Genet has set before us *a single object,* though a profoundly faked one, neither one nor two, one when we want to see two, two when we want to see one: the ancillary couple as a pure crisscross of appearances. And the bond that unites these two reflections is itself a faked relationship. Do the sisters love each other, do they hate each other? They hate each other with love, like all of Genet's characters. Each finds in the other her "bad smell" and one of them proclaims that "filth doesn't love filth." But at the same time, each inwardly clings to the other by a kind of carnal promiscuity which gives to their caresses the tepid pleasure of masturbation. But where is the truth of the ancillary couple? When we see Solange and Claire in the presence of Madame, they do not seem real. Fake submission, fake tenderness, fake respect, fake gratitude. Their entire behavior is a lie. We are led to believe that this falsifying comes from their false relationships with their mistress. When they resume their joint solitude, they put on their true faces again. But when they are alone, they play. Claire plays at being Madame and Solange at being Claire. And we await, despite ourselves, the return of Madame which will cause their masks to fall and which will restore them to their true situation as servants.

Thus, their truth is always elsewhere; in the presence of the Masters, the truth of a domestic is to be a fake domestic and to mask the *man* he is under a guise of servility; but, in their absence, the *man* does not manifest himself either, for the truth of the domestic in solitude is to play at being master. The fact is that when the Master is away on a trip, the valets smoke his cigars, wear his clothes and ape his manners. How could it be otherwise, since the Master convinces the servant that there is no other way to become a man than to be a master. A whirligig of appearances: a valet is sometimes a man who plays at being a man; in other words, a man who dreams with horror that he is becoming a subman or a subman who dreams with hatred that he is becoming a man.

Thus, each of the two maids plays, in turn, at being Madame. When the curtain rises, Claire is standing in front of the dressing table of her mistress. She is experimenting with Madame's gestures and language. For Genet, this is an actual incantation. We shall see later on that, by imitating the gestures of his superior, the domestic treacherously draws him into himself and becomes saturated with him. There is nothing surprising in this, since Madame herself is a fake Madame who plays at distinction and at her passion for Monsieur and who dreams of drawing into herself the soul of a whore who follows her pimp to jail.

Similarly, Genet could, without difficulty, *make himself* Stilitano, because Stilitano himself played at being Stilitano. Madame is no more true in Claire than in Madame herself; Madame is a gesture.

Solange helps her sister put on one of her mistress's dresses, and Claire, playing her role in a state of exaltation, taut and strained, as is Genet himself, insults Solange, as she does every evening, until the latter, driven to extremities, as she is every evening, slaps her. This is, of course, a ceremony, a sacred game which is repeated with the stereotyped monotony of schizophrenic dreams. In short, Genet, whose reveries are themselves often dry and ceremonious and who repeats them day after day until their charm is exhausted, introduces the spectator into the very privacy of his inner life. He allows himself to be overheard in a spell of incantation; he betrays himself; he gives himself away; he hides nothing of the monotony and childishness which spoil his secret festivities and of which he is perfectly aware. And he even invites us to see what he himself will never see because he is unable to get outside himself: the inside and outside, the *reality* (if there is one) and its disguise. As for the role itself, we recognize quite easily Genet's favorite themes: to begin with, the maids *want,* to the point of despair and horror, the servile condition that is imposed upon them; in like manner, Genet wants to be the bastard, the outcast that society has made of him. And this cruel game provides the rigorous demonstration of what we suggested a while ago: one cannot want to be what one is in the imaginary; in order to live their wretchedness to the point of *passion,* to the very dregs, they must make themselves the cause of it. Thus, Solange plays the role of servant. But she would be sticking too close to reality if she remained Solange; there would be no way of deciding whether she takes upon herself her menial condition or whether she *really,* and out of habit, performs her servile tasks. In order to change herself into a maid by her own will, Solange *plays at being* Solange. She cannot *want to be* Solange the servant, because she *is* Solange. She therefore wants to be an imaginary Claire so as to acquire one of the chief characteristics of this Claire, which is to be a servant. A phantom Claire dresses an imaginary Madame. Here a small local whirl is set up: an actor plays the role of a servant who is playing the role of a servant. The falsest of appearances joins the truest being, for to play at being a maid is the truth of the actor and the phantasy of Solange. The result is— and this does not fail to delight Genet—that in order "to be true" the actor must *play false.* The fact is that Solange, who is not a professional actress, plays her role of maid badly. Thus, the nearer the actor draws to his reality as actor, the further he withdraws from it. Fake jewels, sham pearls, Genet's deceptive loves: an actor plays at being an actor, a maid plays at being a maid; their truth is their lie and their lie is their truth. The same may be said of the actor playing the role of Claire-playing-Madame; Genet confirms it in his stage directions: "Her gestures and tone are exaggeratedly tragic."

The reason for this is that the ceremony has still another meaning: it is a Black Mass. What is played every evening is the murder of Madame, a murder always being interrupted, always uncompleted. It is a case of committing *the worst:* Madame is benevolent, "Madame is kind"; they will kill their benefactress, precisely because she has been Good to them. The act will be imaginary, since Evil is the imagination. But *even in the imaginary* it is faked in advance. The maids know that they will not have time enough to get to the crime.

"SOLANGE: The same thing happens every time. And it's all your fault, you're never ready. I can't finish you off.

"CLAIRE: We waste too much time with the preliminaries."

Thus, the playing of the sacrilege conceals a failure in behavior. It is imaginary to the second degree: Claire and Solange do not even play the fictitious murder; they pretend to play it. They are thereby merely imitating their creator. As I have pointed out elsewhere, Genet prefers imaginary murder to real murder because in the former the will to evil, though remaining entire, pushes the love of nothingness to a point where it reduces itself to impotence. In the last analysis, Solange and Claire are fully satisfied with this *appearance* of crime; what they like about it more than anything else is the taste of nothingness with which it leaves them. But they both pretend, by means of a further lie, that they are disappointed at not having gone through with the thing to the very end. And besides, what would there have been at "the very end"? The true murder of the fake Madame? The fake murder of Claire? Perhaps they don't even know themselves.

The fact remains that in this phantom play-acting, which, even as play-acting, never concludes,* the great role this evening is reserved for Claire: it is for her to personify Madame and so to exasperate Solange that she commits a crime. But Solange personifies Claire. Whence, a new disintegration: the relationships of the fake Madame with the fake Claire have a triple, a quadruple basis. In the first place, Claire makes herself be Madame *because she loves her;* for Genet, to love means to want to be. As Madame, she blossoms out; she escapes from herself. But, in addition, she makes herself be Madame *because she hates her:* resentment derealizes; Madame is merely a passive phantom who is slapped on Claire's cheeks. Besides, the interpretation of Claire is forced; she is not aiming at showing Madame as she is, but at making her hateful. Madame, the sweet and kind Madame, insults her maids, humiliates them, exasperates them. And we do not know whether this distorted caricature tends to reveal the mistress in her true light, to expose the truth of that indifferent good nature which may be concealing a pitiless cruelty, or whether it already wreaks an imaginary vengeance by metamorphosing Madame, by the incantation of the gesture, into a harpy. As psychoanalysis has revealed to us, one of the motives of acts of self-punishment is to force the judge to punish unjustly and thereby to burden him with a guilt which discredits him and makes him unworthy of judging. By means of her performance of Madame's role, Claire transforms her into an

---

* Genet is an old hand at these unfinished ceremonies. He confides to us in *Miracle of the Rose* that he used to caress Bulkaen in thought but would abandon him even before attaining erection.

unjust judge and rids herself of her. But at the same time, in the guise of Madame, she insults and humiliates Solange, whom she hates, Solange, her bad smell: "Avoid pawing me. You smell like an animal. You've brought those odors from some foul attic where the lackeys visit us at night." But Solange is sheltered: she is playing the role of Claire. First, as we have seen, because it is easier for her as the fake Claire to assume her menial condition; then, because Claire can be Madame only if she seems Madame in her own eyes. Solange's becoming Claire represents the astounding effort of a reflective consciousness turning back on itself and wanting to perceive itself as it appears to others. This attempt is doomed to failure; either the reflective consciousness is real and its object melts into the imaginary (Genet can *see himself* as a thief only poetically), or else the object remains real and it is the reflection that slips into the imaginary (Eric, in *Funeral Rites,* imagines seeing himself with the eyes of the executioner). Solange's play-acting belongs to this second category; it is Claire taking upon herself a reflective view in the imaginary. Claire's audience is the phantom of herself-as-other. It is thus *herself* whom she humiliates; it is to *herself* that she says: "Keep your hands off mine! I can't stand your touching me." Solange, Madame, the intermediate appearances, all vanish. Claire stands alone facing her mirror, in the desert. Thus, the love-hatred she feels for Madame conceals her feeling for Solange and finally her feeling about herself. And each of these feelings has an imaginary side; her hatred of Madame takes on a double aspect; insofar as Claire is the source of it, she derealizes herself and exhausts herself in her caricatural interpretation of this character; but, on the other hand, she passes into Solange, who, as fake Claire, directs upon the fake Madame, on behalf of her sister, a fictive hatred. As for Claire's hatred of Solange, it is completely covered and disguised by the play-acting: it is not, to be sure, fictive, but it finds within reach only fictive instruments and modes of expression; in order to hate Solange, Claire has no other resource but to make herself Madame-hating-Claire. Finally, Claire's hatred of herself makes it necessary that at least one of the two terms of this affective relationship be imaginary: in order to hate and to love, there must be two; hence, Claire can hate only a phantom of herself embodied by Solange. But we again fall upon a whirligig: for *at the same time* the feelings are true; it is true that Claire hates Madame, true that she hates Solange and that, through the mediation of Solange, she tries to hate herself. Once again the false is true and the true can be expressed only by means of the false. And

when Claire calls Solange "You slut," when Solange, *in ecstasy,*
cries, "Madame's being carried away!" *who* is insulting *whom?*
And *who* feels the insult with that masochistic pleasure? Inversely,
who tempts *whom* to commit murder? And *who* slaps *whom?* This
slap is a sacred rite which represents the rape of Genet by the Male.
But this whirligig of appearances has made us so dizzy that we do
not know whether it is Claire who slaps Madame, Claire who slaps
Claire, Solange who slaps Claire or Solange who slaps Solange.*
It may be objected that the true Solange has nevertheless performed a real act and that the true Claire has felt true pain. So they
have. But the same holds for this slap as for Genet's thefts. As I have
pointed out elsewhere, though these thefts were *really* committed,
they were lived in the imaginary. This slap is therefore a poetic
act. It melts into a gesture; the very pain that it causes is lived
imaginarily. At the same time, it is slurred over, for this true slap
which is felt imaginarily is a fake slap that an actor pretends to give
another actor.

This extraordinary faking, this mad jumble of appearances, this
superimposing of whirligigs which keep sending us back and forth
from the true to the false and from the false to the true, is an infernal machine whose mechanism Genet is careful not to reveal to
us at the beginning. When the curtain goes up, we see an impatient
and nervous young lady who is rebuking her maid. From time to
time an unusual word or an inappropriate gesture casts a disturbing light upon this familiar scene. But suddenly an alarm clock goes
off: "The two actresses, in a state of agitation, run together. They
huddle and listen." Claire, in a changed voice, mutters: "Let's
hurry! Madame'll be back." She starts to unfasten her dress. "It's so
close this evening"; they are "exhausted and sad"; in order to put
their short black skirts on again they need some of that "greatness
of soul" that Divine displayed when she put her bridge back into
her mouth. However, the spectator, in a dazzling flash, sees through
the heart of the darkness to this astounding mechanism of appearances: everything was fake; the familiar scene was a diabolical
imitation of everyday life. The entire scene was prepared in order
to impose this deception upon us.

The high value of appearance is due, in Genet's eyes, to the fact
that, like Evil, of which it is the pure embodiment, it corrodes and
does away with itself. Cases of volatilization are rare in ordinary
life; the plate breaks and the pieces remain. But appearance offers

---

* For Solange hates herself in Claire as Claire hates herself in Solange.

us a certain being. It gives it to us, hands it over to us, and, if we put out our arm, this being is suddenly reabsorbed. The victim of the three-card trick has not lost sight of the ace of hearts; he *knows* that it is the first card of the third pack; he points to it; the performer turns it up: it's the ace of spades. He then feels a strange and brutal disappointment in his flesh. For a moment he thinks that he has an intuition of nothingness. Yes, the nothing becomes an apparition, nonbeing a richness which fills him; the absence of the ace of hearts is much more virulent, much more immediate, than the presence of the ace of spades. The following instant his perception has regained its fullness, but the instant remains mysterious. The nothingness has disappeared; it allowed itself to be glimpsed and then vanished.

But since nonbeing *is not,* how can it *no longer be?* It is this perverse intuition that Genet prefers to all else: it makes the *nothing* shimmer at the surface of *all.* Where is being? Can it be that something *is?* If the ace of hearts has vanished, why should not the ace of spades disappear as well? And what is nonbeing, if it can suddenly fill me with its emptiness? In *The Maids,* the ambiguous instant of deception, when superimposed illusions collapse like a house of cards, rightly deserves the name of pure instant of the Lie. For when the Saharan mirage vanishes, it reveals true stones. But when the deceptive appearances in the play are dispelled, they reveal in their place *other appearances* (the fake Madame becomes Claire again, the fake maid, the fake woman; the fake Claire becomes Solange again, the fake servant). At this moment the spectator has first the demoniacal intuition of nothingness, that is, being is revealed to be nothing, but, as appearance is usually effaced in the presence of being, the illusions which vanish leave him with the illusion that *it is being* which replaces them. Suddenly the pantomime of a young male who pretends to be a woman *seems to him to be the truth.* It is as if he suddenly understood that the only true thing is play-acting, that the only real women are men, and so on. Being has been revealed as nonbeing and thereupon nonbeing becomes being. This moment in which the lights flicker, when the volatile unity of the being of nonbeing and the nonbeing of being is achieved in semidarkness, this perfect and perverse instant, makes us realize from within the mental attitude of Genet when he dreams: it is the moment of evil. For in order to be sure of never making *proper use* of appearance, Genet wants his fancies, at two or three stages of derealization, to reveal themselves in their nothingness. In this pyramid of fantasies, the ultimate appearance dereal-

izes all the others. Thus, the youngster who plays the role of Claire
is derealized into a young man so that the latter may be derealized
into a mistress. But, as I have shown, an appearance borrows its
being from being: thus, "Claire" borrows her being from the boy
who interprets her. But the "fake Madame" is supported in being
by *Claire,* who does not exist. And since she thus derives her being
from a fantasy, the being of this appearance is only an appearance
of being. Whereupon Genet considers himself satisfied; on the one
hand, he has achieved pure appearance, the one whose very being is
appearance, that is, the one which appears to be appearance through
and through, to borrow nothing from being and finally to produce
itself, which, as we know, is one of the two contradictory demands
of Evil; but, on the other hand, this pyramid of appearances masks
the being which supports them all (the true movement, the true
words uttered by the young actor in the play, the movement and
words which, in actual life, help Genet dream), and as, nevertheless, they *are* in some way, it seems that each borrows its being from
the one that immediately precedes it. Thus, as being fades into
appearance at all degrees, it seems that the real is something melting, that it is reabsorbed when touched. In these patient fakings,
appearance is revealed at the same time as pure nothingness and as
cause of itself. And being, without ceasing to set itself up as absolute reality, becomes evanescent. Translated into the language of
Evil: Good is only an illusion; Evil is a Nothingness which arises
upon the ruins of Good.

Jean-Paul Sartre was born in Paris in 1905. Educated at the Ecole Normale, he then taught philosophy in provincial *lycées*, and in 1938 published his first novel, *Nausea*. During the war, he participated in the Resistance and completed the major work which eventually established his reputation as an existential philosopher—*Being and Nothingness* (1943). After the Liberation, he founded the socialist journal *Les Temps Modernes*. He has been a prolific playwright, producing, among other works, *No Exit* (1947), *The Devil and the Good Lord* (1951), and *The Condemned of Altona* (1959). In 1960, he published his second basic philosophical work, *Critique of Dialectical Reason*. In 1964, his account of his childhood, *Words*, received worldwide acclaim. That same year he was awarded the Nobel Prize for Literature, which he refused. In 1971–1972, the first three volumes of his ambitious study of Flaubert's life and work appeared. He died in 1980.

Other Pantheon Paperbacks by or about Jean-Paul Sartre

BETWEEN EXISTENTIALISM AND MARXISM
Sartre on Philosophy, Politics, Psychology, and the Arts
by Jean-Paul Sartre, translated by John Mathews

In this collection of his most important essays from the 1960s, Sartre takes stock of his work and his world, offering fresh insight into his most characteristic subjects.

"Strenuously . . . touchingly . . . powerfully part of the history of a mind."
—*The New York Times Book Review*

0-394-71584-5

REASON AND VIOLENCE
A Decade of Sartre's Philosophy, 1950–1960
by R. D. Laing and D. G. Cooper

A concise guide to the three great works of Sartre's later years, *Saint Genet, Search for a Method*, and *Critique of Dialectical Reason*.

"A very clear, very faithful account of my thought."—Jean-Paul Sartre

0-394-71582-9

SARTRE ON THEATER
by Jean-Paul Sartre, edited by Michel Contat and Michel Rybalka, translated by Frank Jellinek

A collection of Sartre's lectures, writings, and interviews on the theater and on his own plays, including *No Exit, Dirty Hands*, and *The Condemned of Altona*.

"Will no doubt become a classic."—*The New Republic*

0-3-49-73312-6

LIFE/SITUATIONS
Essays Written and Spoken
by Jean-Paul Sartre, translated by Paul Auster and Lydia Davis

A collection of Sartre's last essays and interviews.

"We should salute such resilience. . . . There is iron in [Sartre's] soul yet."—*The New York Times Book Review*

0-394-72460-2

Forthcoming in Hardcover
ADIEUX
by Simone de Beauvoir, translated by Patrick O'Brien

Simone de Beauvoir's farewell to Jean-Paul Sartre: Part I is an extraordinarily moving account of the last ten years of his life, Part II an interview she conducted with Sartre a few years before his death.

0-394-53035-7